THE AMERICAN BIKING ATLAS & TOURING GUIDE

THE AMERICAN BIKING ATLAS
& TOURING GUIDE

by Sue Browder

Illustrated by Robert Smith

WP

Workman Publishing Company New York

Special thanks to the League of American Wheelmen and avid cyclists Wayne Alfred, Nick Arkontaky, Cheryl Ball, Tom Carroll, Cecilia C. Combs, Bill Currey, Denise de la Rosa, Russ Devey, Judi and Ross Faris, Tyler Folsom, Javie Granados, Barbara Gunn, Beatrice Hill, Harry House, Masaru Kawamoto, Alan Korslien, Ricky Krahn, Jerry Kruse, Little Miami Inc., Horace G. Marshall, Don Mason, Christine Morris, Dave Mroczek, the Naturalist Scouts, Ed Pittman, Jock Purinton, George M. Rapier, Charles Siple, Ken Vos, Ray Willis, Bob Wilson, Bob Woodke, and Kathy and Lee Zaborowski.

Workman Publishing Company, Inc.
231 East 51st Street
New York, New York 10022

Design by Norma Erler Rahn
Illustrations by Robert Smith
Maps by Peter A. Crab and Norma Erler Rahn
Photographs by Ann Endres, Norma Erler Rahn, and
    Ewing Galloway
Typeset by Vermont Photo-Tape
Printed and bound by the George Banta Company

ISBN:
    Hardbound—0-911104-35-6
    Paperback—0-911104-36-4

Second printing, January 1975

This book is dedicated to Don Burrell,
Jud and Betty Clifton,
Keith M. Cottam,
Clifford L. Franz,
William N. Hoffman,
Leonard Kantziper,
Lynn Kessler,
Charlotte LaRoy
T. Robert Mayer,
Joe Reed,
and Dorothy Urban,
enthusiastic,
expert cyclists all.

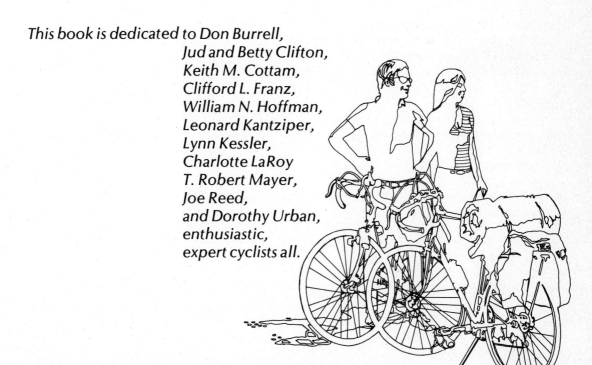

CONTENTS

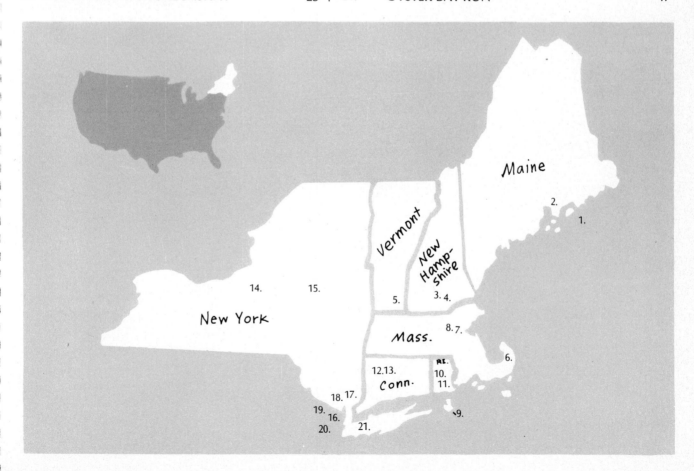

CONTENTS

MID-ATLANTIC STATES

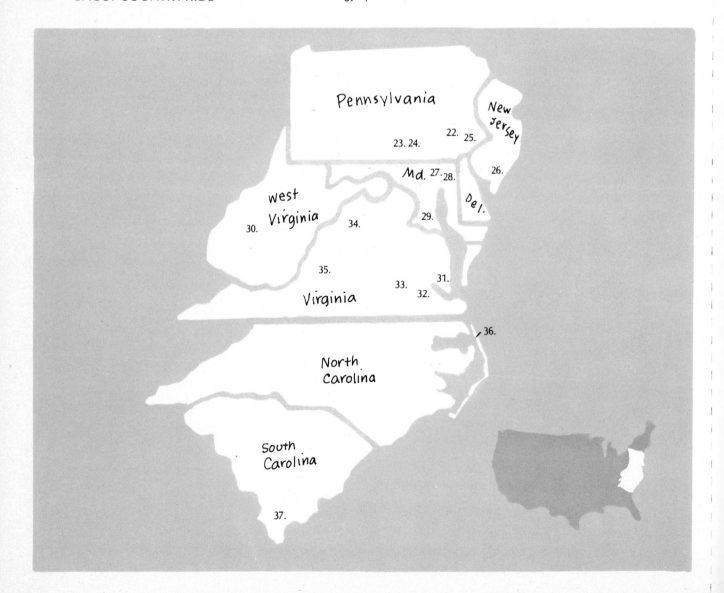

CONTENTS

THE SOUTH

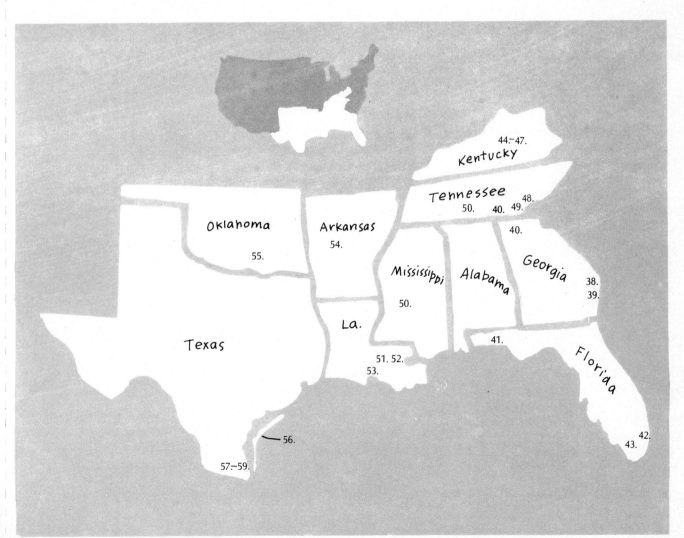

CONTENTS

THE MIDWEST

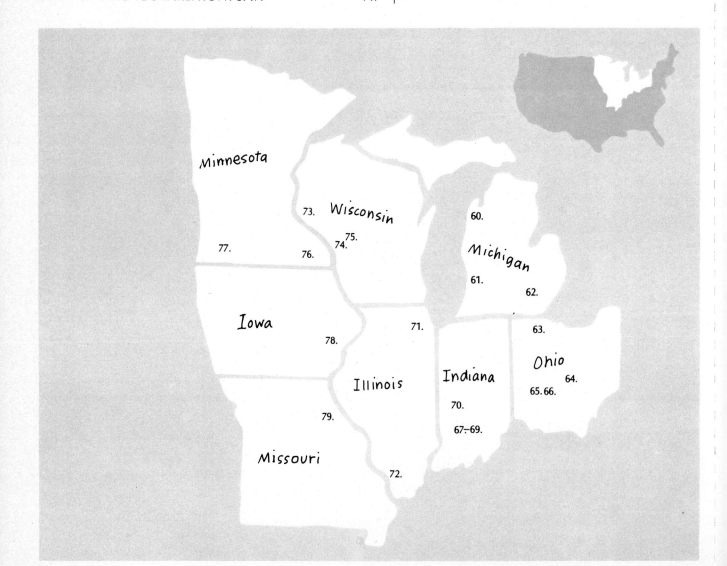

CONTENTS

THE GREAT PLAINS

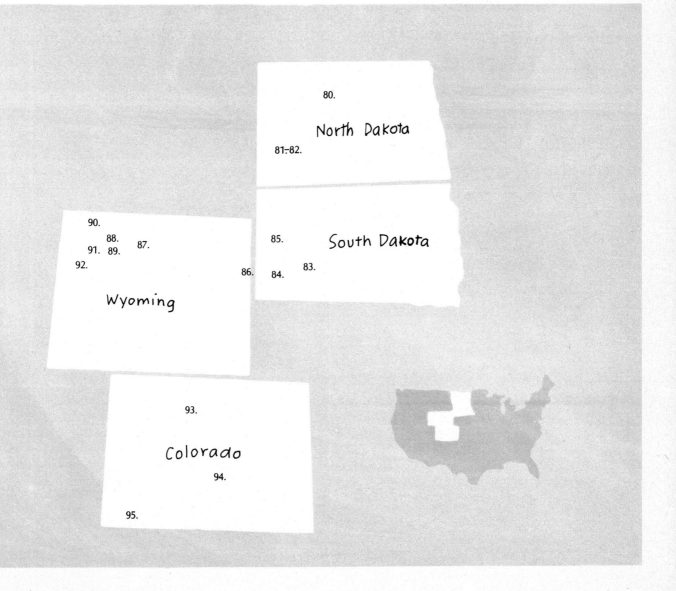

CONTENTS

THE NORTHWEST

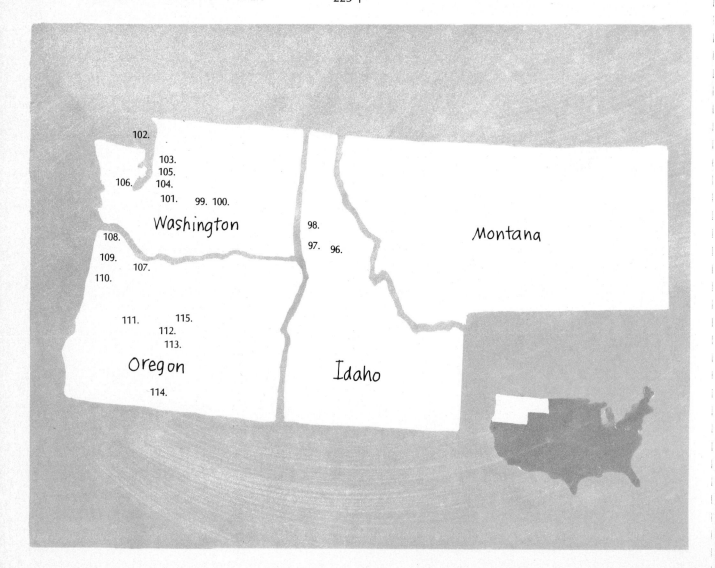

CONTENTS

CALIFORNIA AND THE GREAT SOUTHWEST

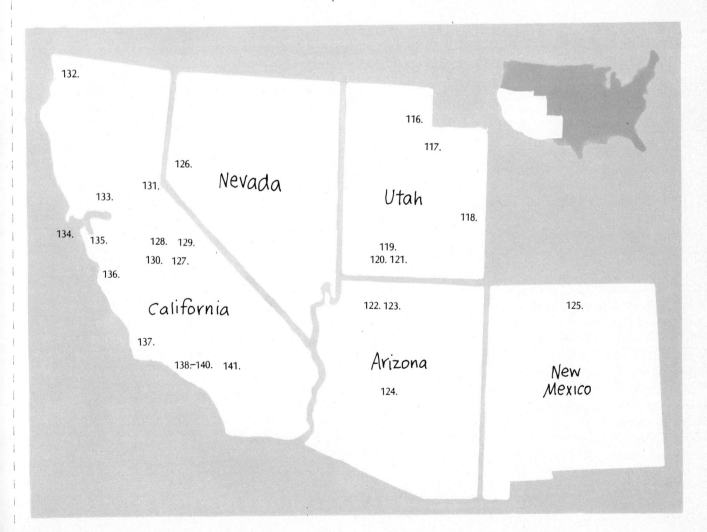

CONTENTS

HAWAII, ALASKA, AND CANADA

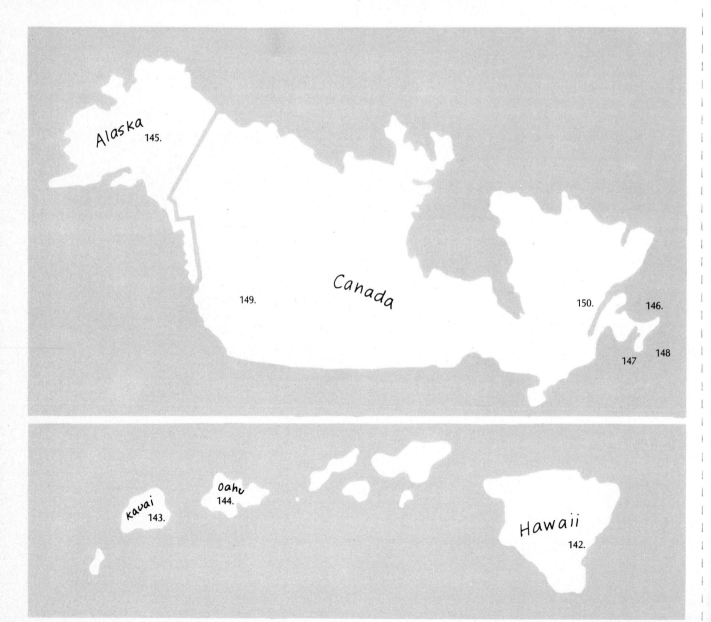

INTRODUCTION

Take your next vacation with a bike. You're missing too much if you travel only by car, bus, train or plane. There's a world you can see by bike and no other way. Fresh air, country inns, ripened blackberries, forests, wood-smoke campfires, hidden pools and myriad experiences new and special. Try maple sugaring with the Vermont Yankees, discover tea herbs in a Wisconsin wildflower meadow, sit down to a homemade dinner with a Mennonite family in Pennsylvania Dutch country or stalk elk on the Wyoming prairies. You see life magnified from a bicycle and you get to know a place—not just how it looks, but how it feels.

Biking is freedom—freedom from the city, from your cares, from the humdrum. It invigorates and brings muscles to your legs. It brings you in touch with what's happening around you and in tune with nature. Experience the romantic changes of the day—a crisp dawn, a sunny noon, a starry night. Feel the breezes, taste the salt sprays off the ocean, touch a redwood. Enjoy the best things about being alive.

Cycling solves the "If only I had a car" problem. You can take short local jaunts to discover your own backyard or more extensive excursions by arriving at a new spot with your bike in tow. You can go anywhere. The logistics of getting where you want to be are simpler than you thought and suggestions on how to get there are given here.

The economy of biking is an obvious virtue. There are free campsites in the woods and parks where you can pitch a tent or put down a sleeping bag. Youth hostels are available for the budget-minded traveler. Inexpensive and charming country inns and cottages dot the byways and backroads and are

welcome retreats at the end of an exhilarating day.

Leave your daily routine and schedule at home. Plan to travel at your own speed. Pull off along the road side to watch a bluebird in flight, nap in a meadow, picnic by a pond. Breathe the fresh air. Don't just promise yourself these pleasures. Don't wait for tomorrow. All you need is a bike. Dust off the two-wheeler in the attic, borrow, rent or buy a bicycle and go—now.

WHAT YOU NEED TO GET STARTED

Bikes vary from 1-speed (the kind kids used to have with the balloon tires) to 15-speeds or higher. The best bike for you depends on where you plan to ride. If tackling Mount McKinley is your ambition, you'll need at least 10-speeds and preferably alpine gears. But if you're pedaling through Kansas wheat fields or over Indiana's grassy, rolling hills, 3- or 5-speeds will be enough. The best all-purpose bike for touring is a 10-speed. It is lightweight and has enough gears to allow you to climb a steep incline without exhausting yourself.

If you are in the market for a bike, you can buy a new or used model. Great sources for second-hand bikes are newspaper want-ads, laundromat and supermarket bulletin boards, college or university swap boards and police auctions.

Plan to spend anywhere from $100 to $150 for a new bike: a 3-speed bike is about $100, a 5-speed around $120 and the 10-speed model close to $150. These prices are for a basic bike without accessories. Cheaper bikes (the $59.95 specials, for instance) will cost you money in repairs and take hours away from precious exploring. You can always rent a bike (all major cities have rental shops listed in the yellow pages) or borrow one from a friend. You might want to try several rented or borrowed bikes before you decide exactly what model to purchase.

Buying a bike can be as complex as you wish to make it, and you can find volumes on the subject at your bookstore or bike shop. Gadgets—and there are many on the biking market—create extra weight and may not be worth their touted advantage. Buy the least amount of equipment you can and add items as you discover you need them—especially if you are just starting to ride.

The basics to check when buying a bike are included below.

CORRECT SIZE. Check any bike for fit. Straddle the bike with your feet flat on the floor. If the bike is the right size for you, you should clear the top bar by an inch or less. (Note: The old open-framed girls' bike is still available, but many women today are buying the stronger men's bicycles.) Then sit on the bike and place your foot on the pedal. With the pedal in the down position, your leg should be almost straight if the seat is the correct height for you.

PRECISION-WELDED JOINTS. Some bikes are constructed so poorly that the joints are already ragged, with paint chipping near the corners. Make certain the joints of your bike are smooth and solid.

A COMFORTABLE SEAT. This item can be tricky if you haven't ridden much. Experts who have pedaled thousands of miles seem to prefer a quality leather saddle and advise against plastic saddles, which become hot and hard after about 30 miles. The wide, padded seats which come with many tourist bikes may look plush, but by about midafternoon their fanned shape makes it impossible to find a new, more comfortable position.

GOOD BRAKES. Choose any style brakes you prefer, but be certain both wheels are equipped. Otherwise on steep gravel or slippery roads—which are hazardous anyway—you can hardly stop without flipping.

SAFE LIGHTS. Most state laws require a front light and rear reflector, but one other light is indispensable —the French armband (about $3), a small bright bulb between plastic that shines white in front and red in back. As the name implies, the armband is made to be strapped to your arm, but put it on your left leg instead, just below your knee. Motorists can see the moving light from far away. Do anything to make your bike and yourself more visible. Tape Scotchlite on the pedal edges, frame, and back fender, add extra lights, wear iridescent clothing.

ACCESSORIES. You can buy loads of equipment, some expensive, some cheap and much that you may never use. However, the important accessories are a loud horn and a repair manual (usually free with a new bike). Handy, but not essential, items are a special touring bag which attaches to the handlebars for carrying lunch, purchases and odds and ends; toe clips which strap your foot to the pedal and allow you to pull up as well as push down when you climb a hill; a dog repellent (you'll see why later), and a water bottle (some types can be used for either hot or cold drinks) which attaches to the bike frame.

THE LOCK

Unfortunately, bikes are being stolen today in great numbers. You can never be too careful. One Seattle woman chained her expensive new custom 10-speed bike inside her car, covered it with old rags so that it looked like a pile of dirty laundry, locked her car, locked the garage with the locked car inside, and still had her bike pilfered before sunrise.

If you prize your bike, buy a heavy chain (about $15). Though all locks can be cut, the big chain deters thieves because it looks tougher. Another good protective devise, especially for biking in the city, is a small alarm with an ear-piercing screech called the Tyco Howler ($18). It attaches permanently to your bike and reacts only when the cable is sliced.

No lock or alarm is completely thief-proof. The best protection of all is leaving your bike unattended as seldom as possible. Pick restaurants with wide front windows through which you can watch your bike while you eat and take your bike with you (even inside) whenever you can. If you must leave your bike, chain it to something imposing like a tall pine or telephone pole.

THE EMERGENCY KIT

Biking's simplicity is one of its greatest appeals and preparing for possible mishaps is relatively simple. Carry a few tools, spare parts, and a repair manual, which usually comes with your bike. You can buy a small tool kit at any bike shop or assemble your own. Basically all you need are a tire pump, a small screwdriver, and a small, six-inch crescent wrench or double-ended bike wrench. On long trips—especially when you are cycling in no-man's land without a bike shop for miles—carry spare tires (for sew ups), patch kit or tube (for clinchers), spokes, a brake block, chain links and brake and derailleur cables.

Also, for headaches or scratches, assemble a light "first-aid kit." Band-Aids, adhesive tape, a few sterile gauze pads, antiseptic cream, aspirin, salt tablets, an ammonia inhalant, scissors or a covered razor and a needle.

CLOTHING

The clothing you pack for bike touring should be suitable for anything. The time of year and destination of your trip will determine what to take. Always try to wear comfy, old clothes and the brighter the better. Fluorescent jacket and pants (found in many large bike shops) are safest, especially after dark.

For the mountains you need rain gear, mittens, and many light warm layers, while Arizona deserts require a white shirt, sunglasses and a broad-brimmed hat. Whenever special clothing is required on a tour, this information is listed with the tour description. Use the following list as a guide, keeping in mind it is totally flexible and should be adapted to your needs.

HAT. Canvas or water-proofed, short-brimmed preferred. Generally you should avoid vision-blocking floppy brims. Deserts are exceptions.

SUNGLASSES. They prevent glare no matter where you ride, and also keep tiny bits of dust or bugs from temporarily blinding you.

HEADGEAR. Though few cyclists seem to use them, safety helmets are highly recommended. Unfortunately, few biking helmets on the market today even approach being safe. One expert who has experimented with headgear has found the kyak helmet to be the best so far, but as he says, these are hard to find.

SHIRTS. Light, cool, brightly-colored, with a small collar. Wide or stiff collars catch bugs and bees and should be avoided.

PANTS OR SHORTS. Avoid jeans or other pants with ridged inner seams that can cause blisters. You can buy special riding pants lined with chamois, comfortable but expensive.

SOCKS. Light cotton, nylon is too hot.

SHOES. Tennis shoes are best except in scorching deserts where the rubber absorbs heat and you need leather instead. Rubber soles also grip the pedals best.

NIGHT RIDING. Wear fluorescent clothing. Jackets, vests and gloves are all available at bike shops.

FOOD

Before you take off, pack food for picnics and snacks. Experienced biking adventurers usually fill a plastic bag with a quick-energy concoction called "gorp" (good-old-raisins-and-peanuts). Create your own gorp according to taste. Any combination of dried fruits, nuts (including coconut), and small candies like chocolate chips works great.

HOW TO GET STARTED

To reach the starting point of your tour with a bike is simple. You can 1) bike from your front door; 2) carry your bike with you on a bus, train, plane or car; or 3) rent a bike on arrival.

BIKE FROM YOUR FRONT DOOR

If a tour you want to take is near your home, bike to its starting point. Obtain county maps (usually available from the county clerk) and plot a route on back roads. Or ask a local cycling club the best way to get there. Local clubs are listed in the yellow pages under "Clubs." However, you can write for the free pamphlet "Bicycle Clubs Directory and Other Stuff," available from the Bicycle Institute of America, Inc., 122 East 42nd Street, New York, New York 10017. Other information on touring and clubs is available from the League of American Wheelmen (LAW), a national touring society, with headquarters at 5118 Foster Avenue, Chicago, Illinois 60630.

You can reach faraway places on a bike, too. Link several tours in this book together (notes under the "Nearby" sections at the end of each tour often suggest how). Or plan your own route. If your impulse is to pedal across several states or even cross-country, you might check on the status of the proposed national trail, a fantastic 3,000-mile transamerica bike trail which, at this writing, would stretch from Oregon through Virginia. For the most current information on the trail, write Bikecentennial 76, 317 Beverly Avenue, Missoula, Montana 59801.

CARRY YOUR BIKE WITH YOU ON THE TRAIN, BUS OR PLANE

You can also reach the region you want to tour by bus, train or plane if you have no car. Many trains and some buses and planes will permit you to take a bike aboard. Do check ahead, though. Regulations vary considerably from town to town and one carrier to another. Trains usually allow you to carry a fold-up bike (like the Raleigh Twenty) with you and will store a larger bike in the baggage car for a small fee.

Some friendly bus drivers allow fold-up bikes, but often buses and airlines require that you pack your bike in a carton. To do this, obtain a carton from a bike shop and, while there, ask if you can see how a new bike fits into the box so that you can pack your bike in the same way. Usually you will have to remove the front wheel, seat, handlebars, stem, and pedals. Be certain to pack your bike carefully, wrap the package with tape and rope, and stamp "fragile" on the outside. When traveling by air, the best bargains seem to be local or regional airlines which often transport cartoned bikes free as extra luggage.

CARRY YOUR BIKE WITH YOU ON THE CAR

Although you can use trains, buses and planes to reach faraway places, the easiest way to get your bike from here to there (short of pedaling 1,000 miles) is by car. Bike carriers keep you from having to disassemble your bike each time you start out. Carriers come in all sizes and varieties. There are bicycle racks especially designed to fit onto automobile tops or bumpers or trunks and cost about $12 to $15. Which type you buy depends on your car and how many bikes you need to carry—one to six. You might even build your own rack. Visit your bike shop and see what types are available. Here's a brief rundown on what to look for.

CAR-TOP CARRIER.   You can carry as many as six bikes in an upright position with the car-top carrier. Though your bike may look as if it will topple any second, it is perfectly safe if you really tighten all nuts and bolts, bolt the handlebars securely to the rack, wedge the bike seat into a V-shaped bracket, and make certain the rack is securely fastened to the car. Disadvantages: Low tunnels or low-hanging limbs can hit your bike; getting the bike on and off the car requires two people and is still tough, earning this carrier the nickname "the hernia bicycle carrier;" this type is the most expensive.

BUMPER CARRIER.   The best-made bumper carriers have teflon or rubber-covered hanger hooks with two dips into which you can fit two bikes, and are covered with a soft plastic coating to prevent chipping or scratching your bike. Cheaper racks often look chromed, will rust quickly, scratch your bike, and may be unsturdy. Advantages: inexpensive, easy to use. Disadvantage: Transports only two bikes.

Remember when installing any model bumper carrier not to block rear vision or tail or brake lights. Also when you put your bike on the rack, don't rest the rims or tires near the hot ruinous exhaust pipes.

RENT A BIKE

Another way to handle the bike transport problem is to rent a bike. Hop a plane, bus or train, journey to your destination, take a taxi or bus to the nearest bike rental shop and pick up a bike for exploring. Rentals are now available in all cities and near many tourist centers. Rates usually run about $1.50 per hour or $6 to $8 per day. Currently you should have no trouble getting a bike if you go to the shop early enough in the morning; someday, however, you may have to reserve bikes in advance.

WHAT TO WATCH OUT FOR

ROAD CONDITIONS

As with every new adventure you may encounter a few problems. The most upsetting are rotten road, weather or traffic conditions—gravel, sand, pot holes, gratings, high winds, rain, fog or heavy traffic. The best way to cope with such pains is to avoid them, which isn't always possible. If you run into trouble, here are a few tips from the experts to help you recover or manage with at least a shred of poise.

GRAVEL. Try to avoid flats or falls by riding loose, lifting your weight from the saddle and leaning forward. Turn only if you must.

POT HOLES. Steer around these if you can. Otherwise, try to jump the hole by pulling up suddenly on your handlebars, leaning forward off your saddle and keeping your heel flat against the pedal. If you are trapped in a hole before you see it, pedal straight across.

RAIN AND SLIPPERY STREETS. If you are caught in anything more than a mild drizzle, try to stop under a tree, pitch your tent or take cover in a nearby country store until the storm subsides. Your big problem in rain is the brake, which when wet becomes nearly useless. To stop or slow down in rain, brake gently a few seconds to dry your brakes. Then apply harder pressure.

Short slippery stretches require you to grip the handlebars firmly and steer straight without wobbling. Slow down and ride loose or steer around puddles which may conceal all kinds of booby traps—rocks, wires and other tire enemies.

RAILROAD TRACKS. Also gratings and cattle guards. Cross tracks and cattle guards at right angles to the bars. Cattle guards are best tackled at normal speed, but slow down for railroad tracks. Gratings are especially bothersome to narrow tires which can slip through.

TUNNELS. When pedaling through a tunnel, try to see and be seen. Short tunnels ar easiest; just use lights, wear reflective clothing and stay as far right as you can. Long tunnels, however, are impossible to ride without help. A bike light, no matter how bright, will seldom illuminate total blackness. One good tactic is to wait at the tunnel entrance, flag down a passing motorist and request permission to ride through the tunnel in his headlights.

HIGH WINDS. Ride like a jockey, with your weight low, body forward and grip tight. Though strong tail winds are pure delight, avoid the temptation to venture too far on windy days. Returning home against a stiff breeze can require hours longer than you planned.

FOG. This is perhaps the most hazardous of all conditions because you are literally invisible on the road. If you must bike through fog, League of American Wheelmen experts advise you to ride against traffic (the only time you ever do this), stay on lightly traveled routes and move onto the shoulder the minute you hear an approaching car.

DARKNESS. You have lingered too long around the lake and now find yourself pedaling under starry skies. Relax. Though you won't want to make it a regular practice, night cycling on a country road by moonlight is actually quite romantic. Do go slowly and even walk occasionally so if you encounter rocks or ruts, you will still be able to keep bike control.

Mandatory night equipment includes good front and rear lights and reflectors plus a handy item called the French armband light, which you should actually attach to your left leg, just below your knee. As you pedal, this bobbing beam is highly visible to approaching motorists.

FEISTY DOGS. *And other beasts.* For some reason, many lovable furry dogs become obnoxious when they spot you high and free on a bike. Though it is against the law for dogs to bite passing strangers, unfortunately the dogs don't know this. To combat dogs, use either your wits or a weapon.

Using your wits when you are riding downhill anyway is easy. Simply pedal faster and outrun your foe. Going uphill, you must be more courageous, especially if you're not a racer. Talk gently, toss the mutt a doggy biscuit as a peace offering, and move slowly by. Some intrepid souls actually dismount, lie beside their bikes, and play dead. This ploy requires solid nerves, but can change a fierce German shepherd into a meek, confused puppy. A slight variation is to crouch behind your bike and command "no" as firmly and calmly as you can.

If you feel your wits or nerve may vanish in the crucial moment, arm yourself instead. Tire pumps, a weak ammonia-and-water solution in a plastic squirt bottle, or a commercial preparation called Halt are all effective.

Other animals to watch out for include horses, which may become skitterish around spinning wheels, and cows, which are so dumb they may plod right into your path. Give wild animals like deer a wide berth or they may dart before you out of confusion or fright.

- Be alert for the right-turning car. When a motorist turns right, he's usually looking left for cars and doesn't see you even if you are right beside him.
- Always signal when turning and wiggle your hand as you do so; the motion attracts more attention.
- In a traffic jam as you pedal blissfully past blocked cars, watch out for that impatient motorist who may suddenly swerve from the line in front of you.
- Be as visible as possible. A gaudy floral biking shirt, fluorescent cap, or giant vivid flower attached behind your seat work well. Tall fluorescent safety flags and fluorescent jackets and vests can be purchased at some bike shops.
- Be courteous. Tension can mount in city traffic, so don't try to push around a motorist in a two-ton car. He could squash you.

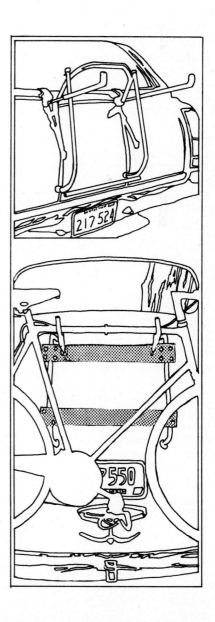

CITY TRAFFIC

City conditions coupled with heavy traffic create many new biking considerations. Use your lock always, even when you plan to be gone only a minute. To deter thieves, either hide your bike completely or leave it where lots of people will see it. Here are a few guidelines for tackling hectic city streets.

- Stay in the right lane where motorists expect you to be and never do anything unexpected to rattle a driver. Exception: On one-way streets it's often' safer to ride in the left (non-bus) lane to avoid breathing bus fumes and being blocked by buses continually.
- To make a left turn through traffic, try to pick up a car going in your direction; then stay close and follow it through the intersection. (Watch ahead to make certain your blocker doesn't stop suddenly.) If you must tackle a left turn alone, either wait for the red light and cautiously ride into cross-street traffic or walk across the intersection.
- Watch at all times for opening car doors. Look into the cars as you ride, and as an added precaution watch under the cars for people's feet so you won't be surprised by someone suddenly stepping in front of you. When on back streets with little traffic, try pedaling several feet from the parked cars to avoid quickly opened doors. Just listen for traffic behind you and pull over when a car approaches.

GENERAL SAFETY

No matter where you ride, a few general rules always apply. The League of American Wheelmen stress these 12 rules in their cycling safety and proficiency course.

- Observe all traffic regulations, one-way streets, stop signs, and traffic signals.
- Keep far right on the road and ride single file in a group.
- Pedal in an arrow-straight line. Do not swerve from side to side, weave through traffic, race, or try stunts.
- Constantly watch traffic movements. Look for cars which may pull into your path or turn in front of you from parking spots, driveways, or side streets. Watch far ahead so you won't be surprised.
- Listen constantly for traffic approaching out of your line of vision.
- Give pedestrians the right of way. Avoid the sidewalks unless permitted and then use extra care, particularly when approaching a pedestrian from behind. Watch out for people who may suddenly stop in front of you.
- Slow down at all street crossings. Look both right and left.
- Have and use an audible signal to warn of your approach. Use hand signals to warn those behind when you intend to turn or stop.
- Never hitch onto other vehicles.
- Be in full control. Never carry other riders or packages that obstruct your vision or interfere with full, firm bicycle control.
- Maintain mechanical perfection. Keep brakes, wheels, tires, pedals, and all bicycle parts adjusted and in top condition.
- See and be seen. For dusk or night riding, have a white light in front and a state-approved reflector at the rear. Wear light clothing.

The LAW also offers additional suggestions for greater enjoyment of your bike.

- Raise your saddle so your leg almost straightens when the pedal is in the lowest position.
- Pedal with the ball of your foot.
- Keep your handlebars lower than the saddle.
- Keep the tires inflated to at least the recommended pressure.
- Do not ride continuously in high gear; your bike should pump easily.
- Keep the nose of the saddle behind the center of the sprocket wheel.
- Ride in a straight line.
- Pedal at a moderate speed.

HOW TO USE THIS BOO

Your *American Biking Atlas and Touring Guide* is designed to be flexible and used. The pages are perforated so you won't have to lug a huge book in your pack. When you're ready to bicycle, just tear out the tour you want, tuck it into your pocket and take off. Also, each tour is described pedal-by-pedal as you see it when you ride. Familiarize yourself with the tour before you start off. This way when you stop for a rest, you can refresh your memory by checking the tour guide for biking conditions ahead before you move on.

Though the tours have been planned by top cyclists and can be run exactly as described, try to tailor each ride to your biking style. Suggested overnight stops are only that: suggestions. If you linger a bit longer than planned along the beach, check the altas for the closest camps or motels in late-afternoon. The routes, too, can be quickly changed. Many optional side trips are listed so you can extend or cut your distance at whim. Often several tours have been planned in the same region so you can link these together for a giant biking holiday.

The maps accompanying the tour descriptions have been rendered to show as many of the points of interest and road names as possible. In some cases the main tour line would become unreadable if it were overloaded with material. Sometimes a spot will be mentioned in the text but not indicated on the map. Rest easy. The museum will be there whether starred on the map or not.

One last note: all the tours have been ridden by expert cyclists and every fact has been triple-checked, but conditions do change. A campground moves up its closing date, pranksters turn a sign 90°, prices change or a bridge washes out. In case of confusion or doubt, always ask local directions.

But enough of this. It's time to hit the backroads. Happy biking!

the North-east

1. ACADIA NORTH ATLANTIC LOOP

Acadia beckons you to stop, listen, and explore. Hear the surf crash and watch it spray on sharp rocks, swim in frigid ocean coves, pause in quaint fishing harbors and see hearty lobster boatmen unload their catch. Back in the soft spruce forests, discover gentler scenes: quiet ponds enveloped in grass clearings and wildflower glades. Though this tour can be completed in a day, try to stay at least three days to explore trails, climb mountains, and perhaps ferry to Nova Scotia.

Many spots make fine starting points: Visitor Center Headquarters, Bar Harbor (with bike rentals), Seal Harbor, or Black Woods Campground. Another good start is from Salisbury Cove, where you can stop at Dunton's Store for snacks before leaving. Pedaling east from the cove on Maine 3, take a side trip left to Sand Point's rugged coast. The side-trip road eventually leads back to Maine 3 again, where you coast to Hulls Cove and then on to Acadia National Park's Visitor Center. Acadia's roads, except for the rolled gravel carriage paths, are "hot top," which Maine cyclists describe as "like blacktop but better." As you pedal along Frenchman Bay, watch for whales: a gray whale and a white one spent the summer of 1973 here.

A bit farther, consider taking the Yarmouth Ferry to Nova Scotia, 720 miles from Acadia by land, but only 100 miles by water. The six-hour cruise costs $30 for a car, but a mere $2 for a bike. Other less extensive boat trips are available from villages throughout the tour.

Turn left at the three-way intersection, then right into Bar Harbor, with its little stores, delicatessens with picnic counters, deep-sea fishing trips, boat rentals, and the island's only bike shop. As you ride back into park boundaries, stay left at the fork to pedal along the ocean. For good, rugged coastal views, lock your bike at Schooner Head and take the footpath down to the ocean, where gulls and cormorants gossip on the rocky shoals. Back on the road, you soon reach a dead end where you go right, then left onto the one-way loop road. Traffic can be heavier here, but should be no problem in spring or autumn.

DISTANCE:	25 miles for the loop.
TERRAIN:	Hilly.
TRAFFIC:	Light in spring and autumn; heavy in summer.
DIFFICULTY:	Good for anyone. Wherever possible, beginners and families with small children should stay on the carriage paths, rolled gravel trails with no cars.
BEST TIME:	Spring and autumn because of light traffic. May, September, and October have delightfully brisk cycling weather. Snows usually close park roads from December through April.
LOCATION:	Acadia National Park, Maine, on Mount Desert Island, reached via Maine 3.

Past a hill called the Beehive, you reach powdery Sand Beach, popular for swimming if you like your water icy. From Sand Beach you coast gradually between mountains and sea to Thunder Hole. Lock your bike once more and climb to this water-beaten grotto. When tides and winds are right, the ground shakes beneath you and the surf lashing at the cavern walls booms like thunder. Now coast on to Otter Cliffs, sixty feet above the waves, then glide down to Otter Cove, filled with small boats.

Beyond Hunters Head you wind inland and coast to an intersection. Here you can continue on the loop road or turn left on State 3 and then right into Seal Harbor, a small fishing village, arriving just in time for lunch.   Just north of town, you can pedal along gravel carriage paths which you see meandering to your right and left. These paths twist through the woods, sometimes dipping beside a pond, other times winding through cool green glades. You will encounter roughness and loosened gravel, but just go slowly and walk a bit.

Back on the main loop, you reach a teahouse to your left where you can try charcoal-broiled Maine lobster or sip tea on the lawn. Afterward ride the carriage path here along Jordan Pond. Soon you climb sharply up Bubble Mountain to Balanced Rock, a house-sized boulder teetering on a precipice. Coast now on carriage paths to spring-fed Eagle Lake and pedal along the shores. About three quarters of a mile after you come off the mountain, at Eagle Lake's north tip, turn right onto State 233. At the main intersection, you reach the park loop. Here you can go straight up Strawberry Hill or go right for a side trip to Cadillac Mountain.

Cadillac Mountain Side Trip

Go south on the park road and turn left in less than a mile for an arduous but rewarding trek on paved road up Cadillac Mountain. From Cadillac's windswept summit, you look across pine, fir, and spruce forests far inland to Mount Katahdin and out to sea. Be sure your brakes work well before trying this, and be careful not to gain too much speed coming back down the slope. Now return on the park loop to Strawberry Hill.

Completing the loop, you climb over Strawberry Hill, where at night you can see the Blue Nose ferry twinkling across Frenchman Bay into Bar Harbor. You coast down the hill, turn left on State 3, and return to Salisbury Cove.

WHERE TO STAY

The only park campground near this loop is Black Woods, 5 miles south of Bar Harbor on Maine 3, operated on a first-come first-served basis and usually filled by noon during July and August. If you plan to overnight here, start your ride from the campground.

Outside the park, numerous private camps are available, including the following: Hadley Point Campground, on Maine 3 northwest of Salisbury Cove; open May 15th to

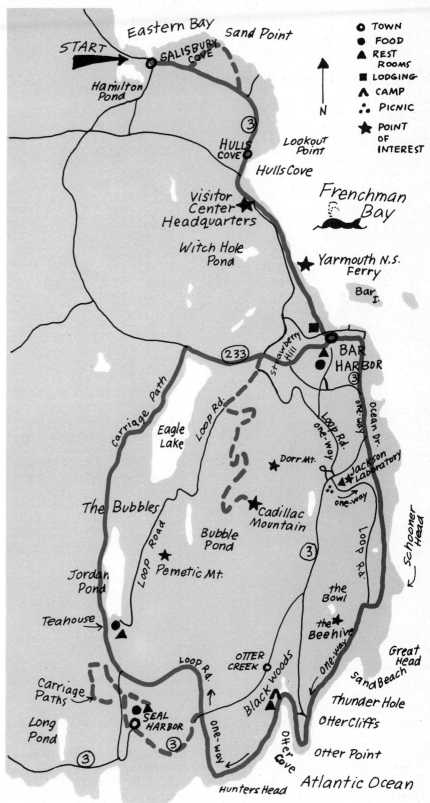

Salisbury Cove is on the central Maine coast on Maine 3; 40 miles southeast of Bangor, Maine, via U.S. 1-A and Maine 3; 150 miles northeast of Portland, Maine, via I-95, U.S. 1, and Maine 3; and 188 miles southwest of Calais, Maine, on the Maine-New Brunswick border, via Maine 9, U.S. 1-A, and Maine 3.

October 15th; $4 for four. For reservations, write Hadley Point Campground, R.F.D. 1, Bar Harbor, Maine 04609. Deposit required. Spruce Valley Campground, one and a half miles south of Maine 3 on Maine 102 and 198; open May 25th to September 10th; $4 for four. For reservations, write Spruce Valley Campground, P.O. Box 577J, Bar Harbor, Maine 04609. Deposit required.

Many motels and guest houses are also available throughout the ride.

FOR SPARE PARTS, REPAIRS, FURTHER INFORMATION

Bar Harbor Bicycle Shop, Cottage Street, Bar Harbor, Maine 04609; (207) 288-3886. Debbie and Greg Grant ride the park roads and will gladly provide information on other routes you would like to explore. Bikes are available for rent here.

NEARBY

Spend several days really seeing

Acadia. Take a ranger-guided ferry to Islesford Historical Museum or through Frenchman Bay. Inquire at the Visitor Center for details. Or pedal along Sargent Sound. Then either pedal or drive to the park's western peninsula to explore. Another full day can be planned for Acadia's most remote, untraveled section—Isle Au Haut, reached only by mail boat from Stonington. Here you pedal through true wilderness; bring spare tires, tools, food, and water, and plan to return by nightfall.

SPRUCE OF THE NORTH WOODS

Red, white, and black spruces grow in Acadia's North Woods. Try the pitch or resin of black and red spruces as a natural chewing gum or experiment with the black spruce needles and young twigs to create spruce beer.

All three species have bluntly pointed, four-sided needles which spiral about the branches, and egg-shaped cones which hang down from the branches. Here's how you can tell Acadia's spruces apart.

Black spruce needles are blue-green, about a half inch long, and slightly more rounded than those of the red or white spruces. Look for this tree near bogs, swamps, and streams. Black spruce grows only thirty to forty feet high, making it the smallest of the three species. The cone scales feel rough along the edges.

Red spruce needles are more yellowish green, a bit longer than those of the black spruce, and lustrous. The cones grow light reddish brown, contrasting with the grayish tint to the black spruce cones, and feel smooth along the edges. Red spruce grows sixty to seventy feet tall and usually prefers the upper mountain slopes.

White spruce grows the longest needles, about one inch long, and these needles twist from beneath the branch to crowd on the branch's upper side. This species resembles the red spruce in that the cone scales feel smooth and the tree grows about sixty to seventy-five feet tall. A certain test for the white spruce is to crush a few needles in your hand; white spruce needles have an unpleasant odor.

2. MAINE ACCURSED TOMBSTONE TOUR

An eerie tale haunts Bucksport, Maine. It seems that in the 1700's a woman was murdered and her body dismembered. When the poor creature was found, only her left leg was missing. Old Judge Buck quickly sentenced an odd hermit to hang for the crime, basing his decision on the man's "strange ways." The doomed man cursed the judge, vowing a "sign" would appear to exonerate him. Years later there appeared on the judge's tombstone an apparition of a woman's leg that cannot be sanded or rubbed away. If such spooky stories appeal to you, bring your pumice stone on this ride. For those with less gruesome tastes, Bucksport and the surrounding region offer the blue Penobscot River, back roads lined with spruce and pine, and rich, clear air.

DISTANCE:	42 miles, excluding side trips.
TERRAIN:	Hilly.
TRAFFIC:	Heavy from Bangor to East Holden in summer; lighter the rest of the year. Usually light on other roads.
DIFFICULTY:	A 10-speed bike recommended for hills.
BEST TIME:	Spring or autumn, when traffic is light and temperatures brisk.
LOCATION:	Starts in Bucksport, southeast of Bangor, Maine, on U.S. 1 and State 15.

Start in Bucksport, where Jonathan Buck's tombstone stands in the center of town. Bring spare parts and tools and pick up snacks before you leave. Pedal awhile around town to absorb the seaside atmosphere, browse through tiny antique shops, and view old sea captains' homes.

Pedal north now on Maine 15 along the winding Penobscot River beneath thick pines and spruce all the way to Bangor. Outside Bucksport there is a steep climb around a cove, beyond which you cross rugged railroad tracks. Several beaches, coves, and inlets offer delightful stops on the riverbanks, but don't swim in these treacherous tidewaters.

Beyond the railroad tracks after you cross into Penobscot County, the road flattens with only gradual hills through forests to Brewer. Follow the main tour right onto U.S. 1-A or go left to explore Bangor.

Bangor Side Trip

Spin along Bangor's streets and stop for free visits to the Bangor Historical Society, 159 Union at High Street, and the Penobscot Heritage Museum, 73 Harlow Street in City Hall. Bargain hunters may want to hunt up the Dexter Shoe Factory Outlet at 419 Main Street which always sells shoes at thirty to fifty percent discounts. Maine lobster is renowned. If you stay overnight, sample the seafood at The Red Lion, 427 Main Street, or at the locally popular Baldacci's, 193 Broad.

Back on the main tour, you cross another railroad track and climb a tough half-mile hill. Summer traffic can be horrendous along this stretch, so always try to avoid rush hours. Shoulders are wide and the surface well paved. Another steep climb leads you out of Holden

Center. Then you coast easily to East Holden and wind south on smooth, untraveled State 46.

As you coast along Mill Stream beneath spruce, aspen, maple, oak, and pine trees, pause to sit along the brook, listen to the birds, and watch trout flash through the water. In summer you might discover the fragrant tiny pink blossoms of the trailing arbutus. Look, too, for rare jack-in-the-pulpits and feathery princess pines.

A gradual climb leads past a hill to your right known locally as Blood Mountain. Then a gradual coast leads to U.S. 1 and State 3, where a right turn takes you into Bucksport. If you turn left, a pleasant side trip leads you past Alamoosook Lake to Toddy Pond for a brisk swim. You can camp along the shore at Balsam Cove, one and a half miles south of U.S. 1 on Back Ridge Road.

Back in Bucksport, another jaunt can be taken on U.S. 1 across Waldo Hancock Bridge to Fort Knox State Park to see the massive fort built during the Aroostook War. You could also pedal over Verona Bridge near the judge's accursed tombstone to ride the loop around Verona Island. End your day by sampling Maine seafood. Famed Jed Prouty Tavern, 52-54 Main Street, was an inn and stagecoach stop in the 1800's. Its registration book boasts the signatures of Presidents John Tyler, William Henry Harrison, Andrew Jackson, and Martin Van Buren.

WHERE TO STAY

Some of the many motels in Bucksport, Bangor, and Brewer are listed below: Jed Prouty Tavern, 52-54 Main Street, Bucksport; (207) 469-3113. Elmac, Main Street, Bucksport; (207) 469-3111. Wedgwood Arms Motor Inn, 480 Main Street, Bangor, Maine 04401; (207) 942-5281. Brewer Motor Inn, 359 Wilson Street, Brewer, Maine 04412; (207) 989-4476. Stable Inn, 448 Wilson Street, Brewer, Maine 04412; (207) 989-3200.

Campgrounds: Masthead Campground, 6 miles north of Bucksport on State 46, on a lake; open June 29th to September 3rd; $3 per family. For reservations, write Masthead Campground, Box 418, Bucksport, Maine 04416, or phone (207) 469-3482. Deposit of $5 required. Balsam Cove Campground, near East Orland, one and a half miles south of U.S. 1 on Back Ridge Road; open May 25th to October 1st; $3.50 for six. For reservations, write Balsam Cove Campground, East Orland, Maine 04431, or phone (207) 469-7771. Fee for one day required as deposit.

FOR SPARE PARTS AND REPAIRS

J.E. Chandler, Ltd., Airport Mall, Bangor, Maine 04401.

NEARBY

Maine's back roads offer superb cycling, and you could easily spend a week exploring in this vicinity if you check locally on road conditions before you start out. The Deer Isle region just south of Bucksport is undiscovered by tourists and contains some of the most impressive seacoast in Maine. While in this area, don't miss Acadia National Park, less than an hour by car from Bucksport. Here you can bicycle on rolled gravel carriage paths shared only with hikers or spin along the main park road with its unmatched forest-and-sea vistas. For details on Acadia, see page 2.

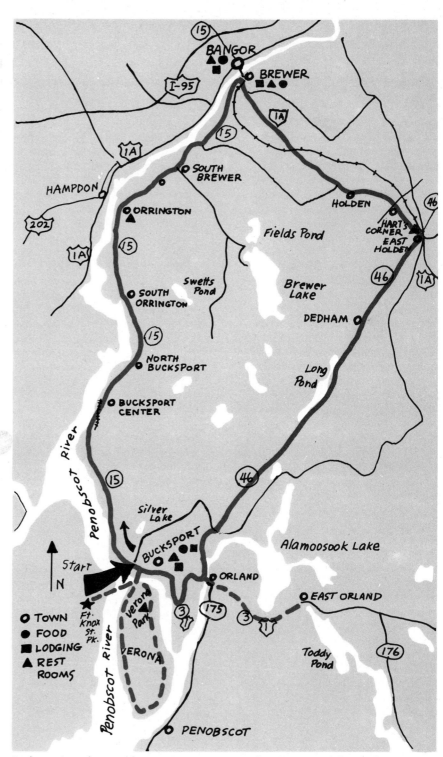

Bucksport is on the central Maine coast on U.S. 1 and Maine 15; 20 miles south of Bangor, Maine, via Maine 15; 118 miles northeast of Portland, Maine, via I-95 and U.S. 1; 140 miles southwest of Houlton, Maine, on the Maine-New Brunswick border, via I-95 and Maine 15.

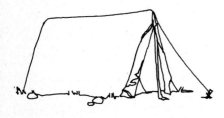

3. NEW HAMPSHIRE ANTIQUE PUTTER

This four-day spin on southwest New Hampshire's wooded lanes allows you to sample all of New England's charms: tranquil ponds tucked among oaks, maples, and willows, villages resembling Currier and Ives lithographs, antique shops, local crafts, maple sugarhouses, superb autumn foliage, and quiet hiking trails through meadows and along wildflower-sprinkled bogs.

Start in Milford, a serene hamlet with several restaurants, a grocery store, and a leather shop. Pedal west on Route 101, where you climb along Souhegan River through Wilton. Beyond West Wilton you tackle a steep grade toward Peterborough. About 6 miles farther, if you feel you can manage an even sharper slope, climb another 1,000 feet up Pack Monadnock Mountain for spectacular autumn foliage scenes. In July and August try blueberry picking here. After a solitary picnic in the woods, lock your bike and climb the mountaintop tower; on a clear day you can see for 100 miles.

Back on the main tour, you glide down into Peterborough, just north of which lies the famed Mac-Dowell Colony, where writers Thornton Wilder, Willa Cather, Edwin Arlington Robinson, and Stephen Vincent Benét once worked. Antique hunters may want to browse through Strawberry Hill Antiques at 2 Elm Street, while art enthusiasts can pedal 5 miles south on State 123 to the Sharon Arts Center, a hub for local artists (free admission).

Proceeding, you pedal up a long slope through woods and crest near Dublin Lake, a good rest spot. Then you coast all the way through Marlborough and into Keene. No matter what your interest, you will find delights here. Venture 2 miles north of Keene on New Hampshire

DISTANCE:	135 miles, excluding side trips.	
TERRAIN:	Hilly.	
TRAFFIC:	Often light but fast-moving; heavy during rush hours and autumn weekends.	
DIFFICULTY:	Requires experience and a 10-speed bike.	
BEST TIME:	Any season but winter; avoid autumn weekends.	
LOCATION:	Southwestern New Hampshire. Starts in Milford, northwest of Nashua, New Hampshire, on Route 101A.	

10 to picnic or swim at Otter Brook State Párk. Or if you're a bargain hunter, scour the town's factory outlets. In early spring for a typically New England experience, take Summit Road to Old Brick Sugarhouse, where Peter and David Barret will show you how the Yankees go sugaring. The sap usually flows from March 1st to April 20th, but you can sample maple-sugar candy and syrup anytime. Around mid-October antique lovers may be lucky enough to arrive for the Yankee Bottle Club's annual show and sale, where you can swap, sell, or buy bottles of every description.

Since Keene lies about 30 miles from Milford, this village makes a convenient overnight stop. Local rooming houses are your best bargain and give you a chance to chat with the residents.

Your second day, either continue on the main tour north on New Hampshire 10 or take an easy day and pedal 10 miles west on New Hampshire 9 to Spofford Lake, a serene wooded spot where you can bask on public beaches all day for 25¢. This jaunt from Keene to Spofford Lake is an excellent one-day bike tour for beginners and families.

Proceeding north on the main tour, you climb gradually for about 16 miles to Village Pond. Then you roll over hills with many flat stretches and coast finally into Newport. The small village of Marlow, about midway between Keene and Newport, has a country store with groceries. There is also a town pond where you can stop for a swim.

At a campground about 3 miles north of Marlow, turn right for a side trip onto blacktopped Sand Pond Road. About a mile along this bumpy lane lies Sand Pond Antique Shop, open every day but Tuesday, with many inexpensive old items—bottles, books, and tins, to name a few. James and Gaye Tillinghast run the shop and can tell you where to find some good local swimming holes.

Newport makes a convenient second-day stop. From here you pedal uphill on Route 103 to Lake Sunapee, a fine spot to picnic, hike, or swim. In autumn take the gondola ride to the 2,700-foot summit of Mount Sunapee to see yellow, burnt orange, ruby, and rose colored trees in every direction. The road levels as you skirt the lake. Then except for one short climb beyond South Newbury, you coast all the way through Bradford.

Beyond Bradford walk your bike through the rough-planked covered bridge. For a side trip, take the next hard-surfaced road right and pedal through Bradford Center to East Washington. Lock your bike near the pond in the center of this village and hike through Bradford Bog, with a stand of Atlantic white cedar and about ninety species of spring wildflowers. Pick up the first trail signs on the maple tree east of the pond and follow the yellow-and-orange markers through the bog. Be sure to wear boots or sloshing shoes.

Back on the main tour (Route 114), you glide with just one uphill spurt beyond Lake Massasecum and into Henniker, a good snack or overnight stop. Outside Henniker the road flattens for several miles, then climbs gradually through woodlands. It levels once more along the Piscataquog River, then gently slopes into Weare. From here in to Milford, you climb and glide over easy knolls with a few tough grades. All along the way, ponds and swift streams provide cool rest spots. You have a breezy downhill into Milford, where you can end your tour with a feast at one of Milford's fine country inns.

WHERE TO STAY

Rooming houses are found in most of the small villages throughout this tour. Motels are more limited and include the following: Valley Green, 1 mile west of Keene on New Hampshire 12 (603) 352-7350. Winding Brook Lodge, 3 miles northwest of Keene on New Hampshire 12; (603) 352-3111. Newport, 2 miles east of Newport on State 11 and 103; (603) 863-1440.

Campgrounds: Swanzey Lake Camping Area, seven and a half miles south of Keene on State 10, then three and a half miles east on Westport-Swanzey Lake Road and follow the signs half a mile north. Open April 15th to October 15th; $3.50 to $5 for a family of four. Mile Away Travel Trailer Park, almost 3 miles east of Henniker on U.S. 202 and State 9, then 1 mile north on Old West Hopkinton Road. Open May 25th to October 14th; $3 for four. For reservations, write Mile Away Travel Trailer Park, Box 493,

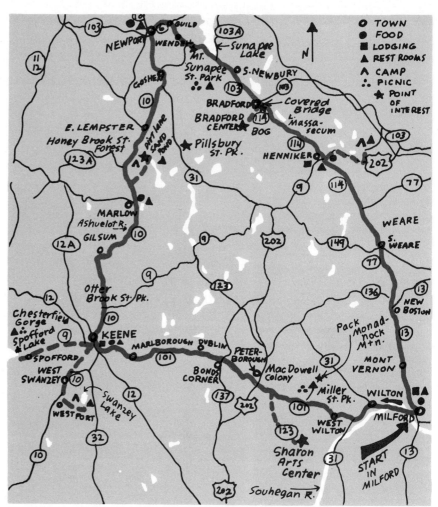

Milford is in southern New Hampshire on New Hampshire 101 and 13; 13 miles west of Nashua via New Hampshire 101-A.

Henniker, New Hampshire 03242, or phone (603) 428-7616. Wildwood Campground, three and a half miles southwest of New Boston on Old Coach Road and on an unmarked dirt road. Open May 1st through November 30th; $2.50 for a family of five. For reservations, write Wildwood Campground, New Boston, New Hampshire 03070, or phone (603) 487-2425.

FOR SPARE PARTS AND REPAIRS

Bike shops are located in Keene and in Hillsboro, the latter near the center of this loop. Plan to bring spare parts, tools, and dog repellent with you.

NEARBY

New Hampshire's wooded back roads offer days of delightful cycling. A good short ride in this vicinity can be taken from Milford north to Manchester or south through Nashua. See the Merrimack Foliage Tour on page 9 for details. Several huge rides through New Hampshiire have been planned by expert cyclists and combined into a package by the state's tourism department. For maps and routing details, write the Department of Resources and Economic Development, State of New Hampshire, Box 856, Concord, New Hampshire 03301, and ask for their free kit "Bicycling in New Hampshire."

4. MERRIMACK FOLIAGE TOUR

New England's wooded country-side offers serene biking in spring and summer. But the time to truly experience New England tradition is in autumn, when oaks, maples, and birches snap with color, pumpkins and squash lie piled on front lawns, and the sparkling air reminds one of fresh-pressed apple cider.

Start in Milford, where you can ask a shopkeeper if you may park your car in his lot. In town you may want to browse through Hayward's Trading Post, specializing in leather goods but filled with many country specialties, too. North of Milford you pedal on well-paved, wide-shouldered State 101. Traffic can be heavy, with a 55-m.p.h. speed limit.

In Amherst you can proceed along State 101, but to get off the beaten path turn right and take the road southeast of town. Then take the first left to pedal through woods to serene Baboosic Lake, a nice spot for a rest, picnic, or swim. Continuing north past the lake, you reach State 101 again, where you climb two hills—the first gradual and the second more steep—and finally coast into Manchester.

Take time in Manchester for a free visit to the Currier Gallery of Art at 192 Orange Street, with excellent sculpture and paintings from the fifteenth to twentieth centuries and fine collections of New England silver, pewter, and furniture. For bargains, don't miss Canal Street, lined with discount factory outlets, where you can pick up sweaters, shoes, and sportswear at discounts of twenty to sixty percent. Indian Head Factory Outlet at 175 Canal Street has bicycling equipment—including touring bags, bike shoes, and various accessories—at twenty to twenty-five percent off.

DISTANCE:	35 miles.
TERRAIN:	Rolling.
TRAFFIC:	Heavy on 101A, especially during weekday rush hours; usually lightest on Sundays. However, to see foliage, try to avoid weekends.
DIFFICULTY:	Some experience needed because of possible traffic.
BEST TIME:	Spring – autumn.
LOCATION:	Loop from Milford, New Hampshire, located on State 101 and State 13 in south-central New Hampshire.

After a snack in Manchester, leave town by going south on Route 3A, which rolls along the Merrimack River. After an initial coast, you climb gradually to the Merrimack Fish Hatchery. Then you coast toward Hillcrest Road, and soon begin a gradual climb. A final long coast leads you to Nashua. Many wooded rest spots are found along this jaunt.

In Nashua you can visit the Craft Shops at 62 East Pearl Street, wander through the National Fish Hatchery at 151 Broad Street, or take a side trip 3 miles east over more rolling terrain on State 111 to Benson Wild Animal Farm, with a zoo, amusement park, and picnic area (admission: adults, $1.20; children, 60¢).

Pedaling on through Nashua, go northwest on 101A (try to avoid rush hours on this road) or take a longer loop on less traveled State 130 to Hollis, then right onto State 122 to Silver Lake State Park. Here you can picnic or take a cool swim. A snack stand along the lake is open mid-June through Labor Day. After a stop at the park, continue north on State 122 to rejoin 101A at Ponemah. This Silver Lake loop adds 8 miles to your tour.

Arriving in Milford, you can stop for dinner in one of several pleasant restaurants. Exclusive and expensive Le Gourmet in a 150-year-old home on State 101 offers six-course dinners which include shrimp hors d'oeuvres, strawberry soup, Caesar salad, trout with shrimp and mushroom stuffing, cheesecake, and coffee.

WHERE TO STAY

Many motels are available in both Nashua and Manchester, and include the following: Howard Johnson's, Main Dunstable Road, on State 111, Nashua; (603) 889-0173. Susse Chalet, on State 111A at Everett Turnpike, Nashua; (603) 889-4151. Hill Brook, Bedford, New Hampshire 03102; on State 101, four and a half miles before you reach Manchester; (603) 472-9788.

No nearby camping facilities are available.

FOR SPARE PARTS, REPAIRS, FURTHER INFORMATION

Goodale's Bike Shop, 31 Main Street, Nashua, New Hampshire; (603) 882-2111. Mrs. Beatrice Hill, proprietor, has lived in Nashua many years and will gladly try to answer any further questions you may have. The shop carries parts for all English bikes and handles repairs.

NEARBY

About 40 miles east of Nashua lies the Atlantic Ocean, with a scenic ride along the coast. State parks with camping facilities, beaches, and quaint sea towns line the coast all the way from Cushing to Portsmouth. This seacoast ride is best taken in spring or autumn; avoid summer weekends, when traffic is impossibly heavy.

NEW HAMPSHIRE PUMPKIN CASSEROLE

Maple sugar, apple cider, brilliant foliage, and heaps of pumpkins signal autumn in New Hampshire. As you spin along the back roads, you will see mounds of pumpkins for sale piled near doorsteps and tumbling onto front yards. Though a pumpkin may be a bit much to tuck into your pack, you may want to recall your travels at home by baking an old New England specialty—pumpkin casserole.

3 cups pumpkin pulp
2 eggs, slightly beaten
½ cup light brown sugar
¼ cup maple syrup (true New England maple syrup is best)
2 tablespoons melted butter
3 tablespoons dark brown sugar
1 teaspoon ground ginger
1 teaspoon ground cloves
¾ teaspoon cinnamon

Combine all ingredients but the maple syrup and the light brown sugar and pour into a buttered quart-sized casserole. Then cook the light brown sugar and maple syrup in a small saucepan over low heat. Stir constantly until the sugar dissolves. Then bring to a boil. Remove from the heat and pour this syrup over the casserole. Bake for forty minutes at 375 degrees. Serve piping hot.

Milford is in southern New Hampshire on New Hampshire 101 and 13; 13 miles west of Nashua via New Hampshire 101-A.

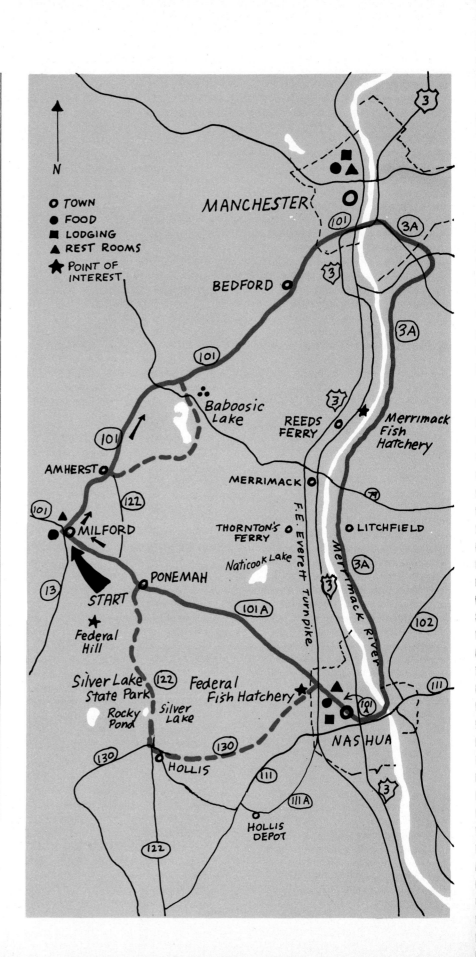

5. VERMONT MAPLE SUGAR TOUR

Putter through maple sugarhouses, bid at antique auctions, and see picturesque covered bridges on this typically New England spin through Vermont. Little streams crisscross woods of sugar, red, and silver maple, birch, and red oak, while from hilltops the splendid Green Mountains are visible.

Start in Brattleboro, where it is best to ask a shopkeeper if you may leave your car in his lot. Antique collectors may wish to phone Thomas Hannon (802-254-2627) before leaving town. His shop, in a restored eighteenth-century schoolhouse, is open by appointment only and specializes in primitive and formal furniture.

Pedal from Brattleboro on Route 9 (Molly Stark Trail) along Whetstone Brook, which trickles beneath Melrose Bridge. After a few minutes on well-paved, rather narrow road, you pass Creamery Bridge, one of Vermont's most well-preserved covered bridges. In autumn you can take a side trip to the right onto Meadowbrook Road and climb uphill to Meadowbrook Orchards, with crisp McIntosh, Delicious, Wealthy, and Northern Spy apples, apple butter, and honey.

A bit farther on State 9 stop at Hamilton Farm on your left, across a small bridge. Here during maple-sugaring season, you can watch sap being hand-gathered from buckets and taken aboard a tractor-drawn trailer to the wood-fired sugarhouse. About three quarters of a mile farther, just beyond the Vermont Maple Museum, you begin a long, steep climb through woods up Hogback Mountain. When the hill finally crests at Hogback Mountain Ski Area, you have views of four states—Vermont, New Hampshire, Massachusetts, and

DISTANCE:	40 miles.
TERRAIN:	Rolling hills, with one long, steep climb.
TRAFFIC:	Usually moderate, but heavy during autumn weekends and rush hours (8 to 9 A.M. and 4 to 5 P.M.).
DIFFICULTY:	For experienced cyclists or strong beginners; not recommended for families with young riders because of traffic on narrow roads.
BEST TIME:	Spring for maple sugar (March 1st to April 15th) or summer; avoid autumn weekends.
LOCATION:	Back roads west of Brattleboro, Vermont.

New York. Coasting now, you reach Molly Stark State Park, a lovely rest, picnic, or camping spot. About midway down the slope at Coombs Beaver Brook Sugar House (specialties: Vermont cheese, maple sugar, syrup, candy, and honey), you can either turn right onto Route 100 and coast into Wilmington or go straight ahead about a mile to picnic along Lake Whitingham.

Arriving eventually in Wilmington, you can browse through the 1836 Country Store, which sells groceries, a candle house, a knitting store, and an old-fashioned

ice-cream shop. Turn right in Wilmington, staying on Route 100, which usually has less traffic than the Molly Stark Trail, and pedal near the outer fringes of Green Mountain National Forest along the north branch of the Deerfield River. When route 100 veers left you stay right to remain on the main tour. But, in autumn continue on 100 for a side trip into West Dover to ride a ski lift.

On the main tour, you soon climb a steep hill, then plunge into Dover. The road continues winding through mountains and toppling into deep valleys past old Vermont country homes. Anytime you see a red auction sign posted, you may want to pause for the antique sale. The most common items include cherry chests, old tools, pine cupboards, ironware, sap buckets, and Hitchcock chairs. Plunging downhill, you can rest beside the river. From here you coast with only gentle rises all the way back to Brattleboro.

Tiny communities dot the valleys, and you can stop anytime to dawdle through an old country store or chat with the Yankees. Folks are friendly here, and should you have a breakdown, you will inevitably be offered a ride back to Brattleboro. Past Williamsville and another covered bridge, continue straight on Route 30. Soon you follow a river around a wide right curve to West Dummerston, then wind back into Brattleboro.

Stop for a New England meal at a Brattleboro restaurant. The unique Common Ground at 22 Elliot Street (upstairs) serves all natural foods, featuring whole wheat vegetarian pizza for lunch and moussaka, paella, Berber Holy Dish, and pan-fried striped bass for dinner. After dinner you can ride to Fort Dummer State Park, about 1 mile south

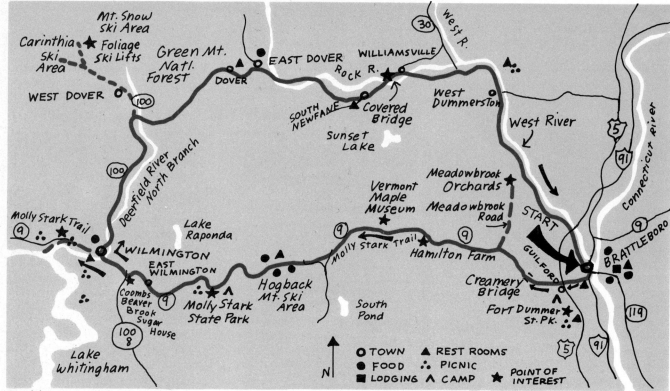

Brattleboro is in southeastern Vermont, on I-91, U.S. 5, and Vermont 9; 86 miles north of Hartford, Connecticut, via I-91; 79 miles east of Albany, New York, via U.S. 4 north, New York 7, and Vermont 9; and 121 miles south of Montpelier, Vermont, via I-89 and 91.

of Brattleboro and a pleasant over-night camping spot. The road is easy, with a slight quarter-mile uphill grade toward the park.

WHERE TO STAY

Motels are available in Brattle-boro and Wilmington.

The best camp spots include Molly Stark State Park, on Route 9, mentioned above, and Fort Dum-mer State Park, south of Brattle-boro, also mentioned above. Fees for both are $1.50 per adult, with a $3 minimum, and both are open May 26th to October 12th.

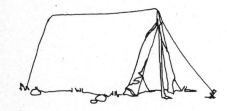

FOR SPARE PARTS, REPAIRS, FURTHER INFORMATION

Red Circle, Inc., 60 Elliot Street, Brattleboro, Vermont; (802) 254-4933. Dave Mroczek operates this full-line bike shop and cycles ex-tensively himself. He will gladly give you any tips on this or other fine cycling spots in the area.

NEARBY

Days of cycling are possible through Green Mountain National Forest if you don't mind hills. Shorter jaunts can be taken north of Brattleboro to Putney, with its cider mills, antique shops, and ma-ple sugarhouses, or west to Ben-nington along the twisty, steeply rolling Molly Stark Trail.

CREATING YOUR OWN MAPLE SYRUP AND SUGAR

Sugaring, as you will soon dis-cover in Vermont, is time-consum-ing but actually quite simple. All you really need to gather your own sap and produce homemade ma-ple sugar and syrup is a maple tree and basic equipment.

Sap usually flows from February to early April, and earlier during thaws. Vermont countryside con-tains red, silver, and sugar maples, but the latter are best for sugar-ing. Here's how to tell the maples apart.

Red or swamp maple is easy to spot in autumn, when it turns vivid crimson, orange, or yellow. The leaves have three to five lobes and the V-shaped winged fruit grows in pairs and ripens in late spring or early summer. Both fruit and twigs are tinged reddish. In early spring

you may spot many gray squirrels foraging in the red maple's branches.

Silver maple, on the other hand, has short-stemmed chartreuse flowers which appear in spring, long before the leaves. In summer the bright green leaf's silvery-white underside and its five deeply separated lobes make the silver maple easily distinguished from the other species. Other characteristics include a dull autumn color and a possible ragged look to the older reddish-brown trunks.

Sugar or *rock maple* has yellow flowers which appear in spring with the leaves. In crowded stands, the sugar maple often grows with a narrow crown and tall, straight trunk, while in open areas the tree becomes more squatty and round. The leaves have five lobes, with rounded, shallow separations, and the fruit is more U-shaped than V-shaped, as in the other two maples. The bark of older trees is thick, light gray or brown, and furrowed.

To "tap" a maple, bore a half-inch hole slanted a bit upward into the trunk. You can buy a commercial spigot or spile in a hardware store to fit into the hole, but for true wilderness foraging create your own spiles by removing the pith from elder twigs about four inches long. An average-sized tree can support two spigots. Now simply catch the sap in a bucket as it drips. You will need three to four gallons of sap to yield a pound of sugar, but a large maple will drip several times this amount, especially on a warm day after a frosty night. Boil the sap in a shallow pan over a wood fire until you have syrup; continue boiling to create sugar.

6. CAPE COD PILGRIMAGE

In historic Provincetown's backyard, there is a place where dense black oak, red maple, and pitch pine woods are sprinkled with fresh-water ponds. Beneath the trees flourish thickets of bearberry, huckleberry and delicate bracken, while cranberry, swamp azalea, blueberry, and sweet pepper bush cluster about the pond edges. Nearby lie huge sand dunes stretching to the Atlantic. Despite the five million tourists who visit Cape Cod annually, you can explore here on a paved bike path without a car in sight.

The Seashore's Province Lands bike trail has access points at Herring Cove and Race Point swimming beaches, the Beech Forest parking lot off Race Point Road, and the Province Lands Visitor Center at Ocean View. Though this ride is short, plan to spend all day. For more vigorous Cape tours, see the suggestions at the end of this tour description. Carry a picnic lunch and snacks with you.

Starting from the Beech Forest lot, you wind through woods beside small ponds and marshes fringed with inkberry, maleberry, and blueberry. Fruit can be picked in the Seashore, but be certain you identify berries properly: some growing here are poisonous. Soon you wind left through stands of pitch pine, black oak, and sassafras, with the forest floor carpeted with broom crowberry, huckleberry, and bearberry. Occasionally you see a lady's slipper peeping through the underbrush or brilliant patches of goldenrod.

The first path to your left leads to Bennett Pond, a good picnic spot overhung with ancient pines. Back on the main trail, you churn through more cool, deeply shaded woodlands, then break suddenly onto the warm, sunny Province Land dunes, sparsely dotted with clumps of beach heather (poverty grass), with slender strands of beach grass waving in the salt breeze. Atop a short hill, stop for wide views of the dunes, Hatches Harbor's tidal flats, the lighthouse on Race Point, and the Atlantic Ocean.

Coasting to the bottom of the hill, you can follow the main trail right or go left to Herring Cove, with a lifeguarded beach open 10 A.M. to 6 P.M. On the way to Herring Cove, you pass sand dunes and stunted pitch pine, while at the Cove seaside goldenrod and wild roses grow to meet the salt spray. Back on the main trail, you soon reach a Y. Here you can take a second side trip left past cranberry bogs and Province Lands Visitor Center to Race Point Beach, a nice spot to swim and sunbathe.

Proceeding on the main trail from the Race Point turnoff, you climb a hill, cross Race Point Road, spin through beech forests, and wind over rolling hills. A few curves around marshes and ponds return you to the parking lot.

DISTANCE:	8 miles.
TERRAIN:	Rolling, with a few easy hills.
TRAFFIC:	None. This is a paved bikeway.
DIFFICULTY:	Excellent ride for beginners and families.
BEST TIME:	All seasons but winter.
LOCATION:	Cape Cod National Seashore, Massachusetts.

MORE EXPLORING

Cape Cod has two shorter bike trails, each 4 miles round trip. Eastham (Nauset) bike trail begins from a parking lot near the amphitheater east of Salt Pond Visitor Center. You wind up a low hill among cedars, past ponds, and through Nauset Marsh to Coast Guard Beach, with more swimming.

The second path, Pilgrim Heights bike trail, begins at the lot just off High Head Road near Pilgrim Lake and follows the first route taken by the Pilgrims in November, 1620, from Provincetown through the Cape. You pass near Pilgrim Spring, where Captain Miles Standish and William Bradford perhaps first tasted New England water. The path ends at Head of the Meadow Beach, which also has guarded swimming.

Heavy traffic often prohibits cycling the Seashore's main road during summer. If you should manage to hit a low-traffic day or come in early spring or late autumn, venture southeast on park roads to Provincetown, where you can meander through the art colony and dine on chowder and blueberry pie.

Farther south on U.S. 6, you can spin into Truro past gray-shuttered saltbox cottages brightened with flower boxes of geraniums and petunias. On busy days you can reach Truro mostly on back roads: from Provincetown take 6A, a bayside residential street; turn left at the southeast end of Pilgrim Lake onto High Head Road; follow Pilgrim Heights bike trail to Head of the Meadow Beach; take the paved road southwest to U.S. 6; turn left on trafficked U.S. 6, and left again onto Castle Road, which leads to Depot Road and Truro.

Proceeding still farther, you reach Wellfleet, with sailboat ren-

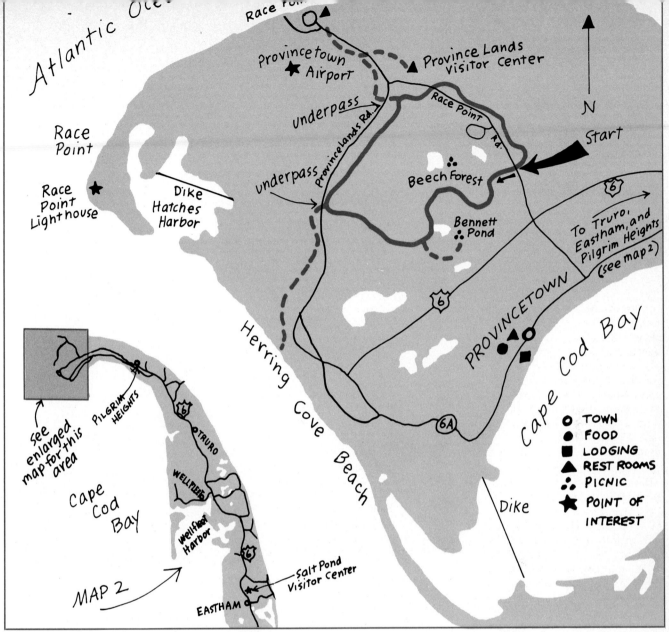

Atlantic Ocean · Race Point · Provincetown Airport · Province Lands Visitor Center · underpass · Provincelands Rd. · Race Point Rd. · Start · Race Point · Race Point Lighthouse · Dike Hatches Harbor · underpass · Beech Forest · Bennett Pond · To Truro, Eastham, and Pilgrim Heights (see map 2) · N · PROVINCETOWN · Cape Cod Bay · Herring Cove Beach · Dike · 6 · 6A · see enlarged map for this area · PILGRIM HEIGHTS · TRURO · WELLFLEET · Cape Cod Bay · Wellfleet Harbor · Salt Pond Visitor Center · MAP 2 · EASTHAM

○ TOWN
● FOOD
■ LODGING
▲ REST ROOMS
⋮ PICNIC
★ POINT OF INTEREST

Cape Cod National Seashore is on the southeastern Massachusetts coast on U.S. 6; 122 miles southeast of Boston, Massachusetts, via Massachusetts 3 and U.S. 6; 198 miles east of Hartford, Connecticut, via I-84, U.S. 6, I-195, and U.S. 6.

tals at Town Wharf. Go through South Wellfleet and pedal to Marconi Station on your left, where you can see a model of Guglielmo Marconi's wireless and enjoy excellent views of Brand Beach. A bit farther south on U.S. 6, a little spur to your right leads to Wellfleet Bay Wildlife Sanctuary, which welcomes visitors daily from 8 A.M. to 8 P.M. and offers beach-buggy wildlife tours to Nauset Beach in summer, a September camping excursion, and a Christmas bird count. Various fees apply. While here, lock your bike and walk an hour along Goose Pond Trail, where you may glimpse the greater yellowlegs, the least sandpiper, or in autumn the myrtle warbler.

WHERE TO STAY

Resort accommodations in nearby villages vary from quaint seaside cottages to luxury hotels.

Camping is available at three private campgrounds within Seashore boundaries and advance reservations are advised from July 1st through Labor Day. Horton's Park, North Truro, Massachusetts 02652; three quarters of a mile northeast off U.S. 6 on South Highland Road; (617) 487-1220. North of Highland Camp, North Truro, Massachusetts 02652; three quarters of a mile east of U.S. 6 on Head of the Meadow Road; (617) 487-1191. North Truro Camping Area, North Truro, Massachusetts 02652; half a mile east of U.S. 6 on Highland ; (617) 487- 1847.

Nickerson State Forest, south of the Seashore, has camping on a first-come first-served basis. At least twenty other campgrounds are found near the Seashore. A complete list is available from the Cape Cod Chamber of Commerce, Hyannis, Massachusetts 02601.

Truro also has an American Youth Hostel (AYH) on North Pamet Road.

CAPE COD BERRY BUSHES

As you bike from the Beech Forest parking lot to Bennett Pond, you pass many fresh-water ponds lined with bushes which bear fruits in summer. Though picking wildflowers or damaging plants is pro-

Ewing Galloway

hibited in the National Seashore, you can pick ripened berries. So gather a few juicy varieties for lunch or a quick refresher as you spin along. Some Cape Cod berries are edible; others are not. Here's how to identify a few species.

Bearberry creeps along the ground, forming thick mats on the forest floor. Its oblong or lance-shaped evergreen leaves are deep green and feel leathery. In summer you will see urn-shaped white, pink, or pink-tipped white flowers, which produce mealy, unpalatable red berries in autumn. Though the berries are inedible, the plant, also called the kinnikinnick, has another use as a tobacco. (See page 151) Look for bearberries in the pitch pine woods after you leave the Great Pond complex at your tour's start.

Inkberry bears dry, hard, inedible black berries which stay on the bush even in winter. You can tell this plant by its scallop-edged evergreen, holly leaves, which feel leathery and are shiny dark green on top and pale light green under-

neath. When the inkberry blooms, small white flowers cluster on long stems. Though you won't want to eat the berries, pluck a few leaves to dry before your campfire and brew fragrant inkberry tea, which unlike most natural teas has a hint of caffeine.

Highbush blueberry bears juicy, sweet wine-red or purple berries in late summer and is well worth looking for. Delicate greenish-white or pink globe-shaped flowers bloom in summer. Look for the highbush blueberry near fresh-water ponds and in the beech forests after you cross Race Point Road.

FOR FURTHER INFORMATION

Write Superintendent, Cape Cod National Seashore, South Wellfleet, Massachusetts 02663.

7. BOSTON GREEN BELT BIKEWAY

DISTANCE:	14 miles round trip.
TERRAIN:	Flat.
TRAFFIC:	Light to none on the bike path.
DIFFICULTY:	Fine for beginners and families.
BEST TIME:	Any season but winter.
LOCATION:	Boston, Massachusetts.

If Boston brings to mind afternoon teas, prim-lace doilies, and vested men in bowler hats, try this breezy ride along the Green Belt Bikeway for a delightful look at contemporary Boston. Though you can ride from the Boston Common past Back Bay Fens to Franklin Park in an hour, plan on an entire Sunday afternoon or pack a picnic and start at 10 A.M. for a really leisurely day.

Begin at the Common, once set aside for use as a cow pasture and still legally available for such, but now used as a free-speech forum. You may see people doing anything from shooting marbles to practicing yoga. Here stands the Boston Massacre Monument, commemorating the Boston Massacre of 1770.

The signed bikeway leads you first along city streets, then across a pedestrian bridge (walk your bike here), and onto an old dirt bridle path. This path is bumpy, with some gravel, sticks, and rocks, so you may want to walk awhile or even stay on city streets if traffic is light. Leave the bikeway to spin through Back Bay Fens, a rich green park with a brook and foot-bridge.

You continue along Boston's Emerald Necklace, so called because the many parks in this vicinity cut a wavy green swath through the city. At Huntington Avenue you can leave the bikeway by pedaling left a short distance to visit the excellent Museum of Fine Arts, 479 Huntington Avenue, with fine American, European, Near and Far Eastern, and ancient art collections (open daily, 10 A.M. to 6 P.M., adults, $1.50).

Back on the bikeway, past Jamaica Pond, you reach the Children's Museum on your left, with cultural displays and various children's activities (adults, $1.50; children 3 to 15, 75¢). Bike racks are provided all along this jaunt; always lock your bike.

Past the museum is Arnold Arboretum, with its six thousand varieties of trees and shrubs and a bonsai display from May through October (free admission). Whether you are permitted to cycle through the arboretum seems to depend on the attendant in charge.

Following the bikeway signs farther, you pedal along a sidewalk, then onto Forest Hills and Circuit drives to Franklin Park, a cool, wooded spot to rest or picnic. Before retracing your ride along the bikeway to the Common, visit the free zoo, with an elephant house, antelope range, aviary, and rose garden.

Freedom Trail Side Trip

Back at the Common, you can take a side trip by either biking or walking along Freedom Trail, a brick path leading past many Boston landmarks, including the Boston Massacre site and Paul Revere's home. You can pick up a self-guiding trail booklet at the information booth located on Tremont Street at the Boston Common. Start at the State House on Beacon Street, bordering the Common, and go southeast on Park Street to the Park Street Church (1809), where gunpowder was stored during the War of 1812. Go left along Tremont Street to the Granary Burying Ground, where Paul Revere, John Hancock, Samuel Adams, and many other patriots of the Revolution are buried.

A bit farther north on Tremont Street is King's Chapel (1748), where you go right on School Street to pass the site of the first free public school, the city hall, and the Old Corner Book Store Building, where Ralph Waldo Emerson, Nathaniel Hawthorne, Henry Wadsworth Longfellow, and Harriet Beecher Stowe held literary meetings. Then go right on Washington Street, left on Milk Street past the Old South Meeting House, left on Devonshire Street, right on State Street past the Old State House, site of the reading of the Declaration of Independence in 1776, and on past the Boston Massacre site.

More turns take you left onto Congress Street, right onto South Market Street, left onto Merchants Row past Faneuil Hall (often called the Cradle of Liberty because the colonists held many meetings here before the Revolutionary War), right onto Union Street, right again onto Marshall Street, right onto Hanover Street, and right onto Richmond Street. Then you proceed left on North Street past the old Paul Revere House, left on Prince Street, right on Hanover Street, through the Paul Revere Mall to Old North Church. From here you can retrace your path back to the Common.

Other Bostonian Rides

Not part of the bikeway, but excellent biking nonetheless, is the Charles River Esplanade, accessible from several pedestrian bridges which span Storrow Drive. Another good ride is Southie, a beach tour to Castle Island. Cambridge Bikepath, on the other side of the Charles River, will soon be paved and will offer fine cycling.

WHERE TO STAY

Numerous motels and hotels are available. You find no convenient camping facilities.

FOR SPARE PARTS AND REPAIRS

Boston has several full-line bike shops. Just check the yellow pages for the shop closest to your hotel.

NEARBY

An excellent historic tour in the Boston area is through Minute Man National Historic Park, past the homes of Ralph Waldo Emerson and Louisa May Alcott. Here you can also visit Thoreau's Walden Pond. See page 19 for details.

Boston is in eastern Massachusetts on I-93 and 95, U.S. 1, State 9 and 2, and several other routes; 209 miles northeast of New York City via I-95; 109 miles south of Portland, Maine, via I-95 and U.S. 1.

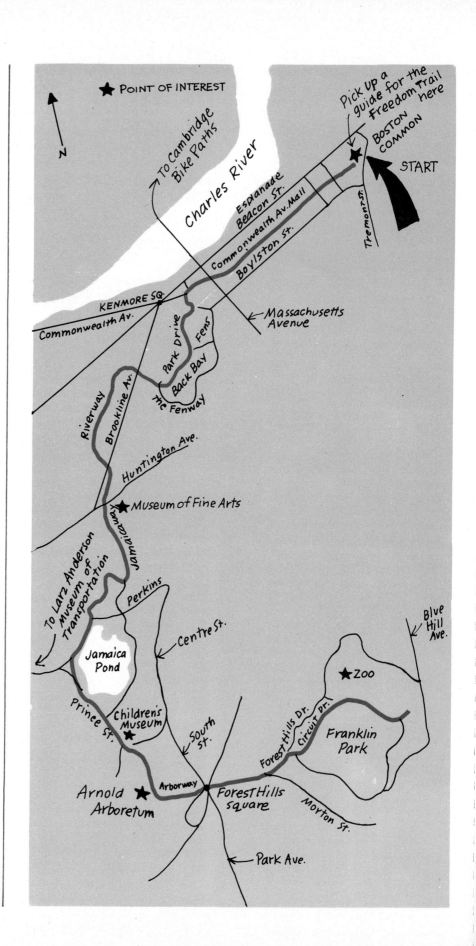

8. MASSACHUSETTS LIBERTY TRAIL

Satisfy a Thoreau-like passion for nature and a minuteman's call to freedom on this liberty trail through the "birthplace of the republic." You pedal past the "rude bridge" where farmers "fired the shot heard round the world," loiter along the banks of Thoreau's Walden Pond, and skim down the lane where redcoats fled before the muskets of the colonists.

Start at the Lexington green in central Lexington. On the green, visit Buckman Tavern (1719), where the minutemen met before battle, and pick up brochures or ask questions at the adjacent Visitor Center.

Pedal west on Massachusetts Avenue to Minute Man National Historic Park Visitor Center. Here you can lock your bike and explore the 1-mile self-guided trail up and around the hill through woods and meadows to Fiske Farm, looted by the redcoats as they fled.

From the Visitor Center, retrace your ride east a short distance to Massachusetts 128 and turn left to follow Old Fiske Road, a 4-mile stretch of the original Colonial highway. Though this road is rough, you can really feel the past here.

Back on the main tour (Highway 2A), a gradual incline begins past tiny Folley Pond. Then you pass Minute Man Park headquarters, old Hartwell Tavern, and the historic Job and Samuel Brooks houses. More wooded countryside brings you coasting into Concord.

Stop on your right in Concord at The Wayside, where Nathaniel Hawthorne, the Alcotts, and Margaret Sidney, author of *Five Little Peppers,* lived (open April through October; admission, 75¢). In adjacent Orchard House, Louisa May Alcott wrote *Little Women* (open Monday through Saturday, 10 A.M. to 5 P.M., and Sunday, 2 to 6 P.M.; admission, 75¢). On Cambridge Turnpike at Lexington Road stands Ralph Waldo Emerson's home (open Tuesday through Saturday plus Sunday afternoons, 10 to 11:30 A.M. and 1:30 to 5:30 P.M.; adults, $1.00).

Take some time to explore Concord's streets lined with Colonial homes, and possibly stop for tea. You can also gather picnic basics and pedal on State 2A, then turn onto Walden Street and ride to Walden Pond. Picnic in Thoreau's wilderness retreat or rent a boat for 50¢.

Returning to Concord, go right on 2A, then left on Monument Street. A right turn on Bedford Street leads to Sleepy Hollow Cemetery, where Thoreau, Emerson, the Alcotts, and Hawthorne are buried. If you continue up Bedford Street, you reach Monsen Road on your left, which leads to the free Great Meadows National Wildlife Refuge. Climb the observation tower in spring or autumn to search the marshes for egrets, herons, ducks, and Canadian geese. You can also view birds from the dirt and gravel trails that wind through the grasslands.

Back on the main tour on Monument Street, pedal past the Old Manse (1770), where Ralph Waldo Emerson's grandfather lived, to Old North Bridge, where the colonists "fired the shot heard round the world." Cross the Concord River and climb the hill to Buttrick Mansion.

Continuing through wooded countryside, you climb past a rise called Punkatasset Hill, then dip down to Sawmill Brook. More rolling hills lead to State 225 (locally called Bedford Road and later Carlisle Road), where you turn right to coast gradually across the river and through Great Swamp. As you spin through the flat marshes, watch for vivid purple loosestrife and American lotus.

At last you climb slightly to an intersection where you bear left to stay on State 225 (now called the Great Road). More flat terrain with a few easy rises leads you to Bedford's motels, restaurants, and grocery stores. Continue through Bedford on State 225, which becomes Bedford Street. The road climbs easily with only a few dips back to Lexington.

WHERE TO STAY

Some of the motels available in Lexington, Concord, and Bedford,

DISTANCE:	17 miles.
TERRAIN:	Hilly, with some steep climbs.
TRAFFIC:	Usually light, but heavy during rush hours (7:30 to 9:30 A.M. and 3:30 to 6:30 P.M.); lightest on Sundays.
DIFFICULTY:	Good ride for anyone. A 10-speed bike recommended for hills.
BEST TIME:	All seasons but winter. Idyllic in spring and autumn.
LOCATION:	From Lexington, Massachusetts, through Minute Man National Historic Park to Concord.

are listed below: Susse Chalet, 440 Bedford Street, Bedford, Massachusetts; at the junction of Massachusetts 225 and 4; (617) 861-0850. Colonial Inn, 48 Monument Square, Concord, Massachusetts 01742; on Massachusetts 2A at Route 62; (617) 369-9200. Arrowhead Motor Inn, 340 Great Road, Bedford, Massachusetts 01730; just southeast of Bedford; (617) 275-6700. Bedford Travelodge, 285 Great Road, Bedford, Massachusetts 01730; located on the bike tour southeast of Bedford; (617) 275-6120.

FOR FURTHER INFORMATION

Write Minute Man National Historic Park, Box 160, Concord, Massachusetts 01742.

NEARBY

Back roads in this region usually are lightly traveled and well surfaced, though you will run into bumpy pavements. Nearby Boston offers chances for excellent city cycling, sometimes on car-free bike paths. As a start, ride the Boston Green Belt Bikeway, described on page 17.

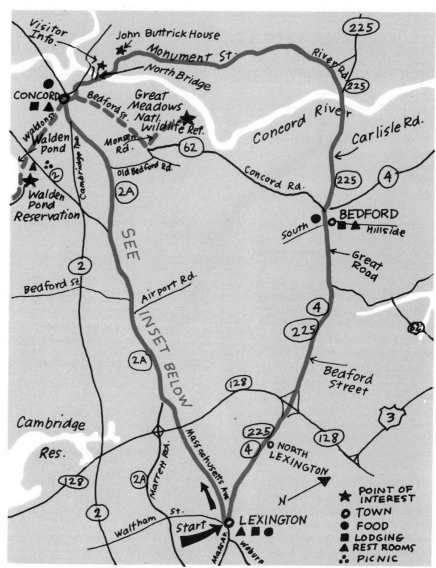

Lexington is in eastern Massachusetts on Massachusetts 225 and 2-A. From midtown Boston take Massachusetts Avenue northwest to Lexington. Top: General map of tour. Bottom: Detail between Concord and Lexington.

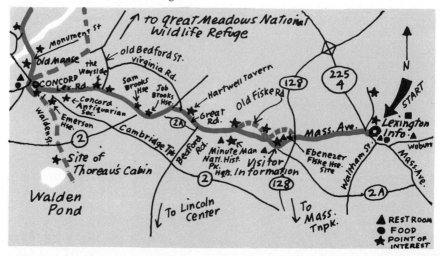

9. BLOCK ISLAND BREEZE

On a sweltering New England day, escape by ferry to Block Island, a gentle green land 12 miles out to sea. Here summer temperatures usually range ten to fifteen degrees cooler than on the mainland, and you pedal past old ships swaying in the harbors, powdery sands, and cliffs towering over the Atlantic. Clamming, crabbing, bird watching, beachcombing for driftwood and garnets, and hiking are only a few of the pleasures the island offers, with the whole mood of the islanders being "do your own thing." Come early and stay overnight to experience the land the Narragansets called "the isle of the little god."

The ferry fee from Point Judith, Rhode Island, is $7.50 for you and your bike if you stay overnight and slightly less if you return the same day. As you float into Old Harbor, head toward the front of the ferry and be ready to ride. From the dock, go right (north) on Water Street, as left offers some tough climbs. Soon you lean around a left curve onto Dodge Street, then go right onto Corn Neck Road between a pond and Crescent Beach. In spring and autumn the island's three hundred ponds are dotted with great flocks of migrating geese, ducks, cormorants, and gulls.

As you wind inland along Great Salt Pond, you start up a long, gradual hill. Near a narrow road to your left called Andy's Way, you tackle a sharp slope for about half a mile. From the crest you plummet downhill through salt air, your coast gradually leveling as you approach Sachem (Chagum) Pond. Here and throughout the tour you encounter bumpy roads, and often sand or dirt will be blown onto the highway. These obstacles, however, are so slight that bicycles on the isle are almost as common as cars.

DISTANCE:	Up to 27 miles of paved roads.
TERRAIN:	Hilly.
TRAFFIC:	Light, but usually heavy on summer weekends.
DIFFICULTY:	Okay for anyone. A 3-speed bike recommended for hills.
BEST TIME:	June through September, when ferry schedules are most convenient and all motels and restaurants on the island are open.
LOCATION:	Block Island, off Rhode Island's south shore.

As you coast to the ocean, wind left to slice between Sachem Pond and the sea and pass Settlers' Rock, a roster of the first settlers. The ocean surrounds you as you reach Sandy Point, littered with lighthouses crushed by storms.

Retrace your ride south past Crescent Beach, the island's best swimming spot. You may want to picnic or buy a snack at the concession. Plan to swim or sunbathe on this side of the island because the west side beaches are rocky.

At Beach Avenue turn right to cut across a fingerlet of Harbor Pond. Then go right onto Ocean Avenue and left on West Side Road. New Harbor has several seafood restaurants, while Veterans' Park offers a shady rest stop. If you want to catch your own lunch, fish for perch, bass, and pickerel in the ponds or for striped bass in the surf. Clams, including the giant quahogs, can be dug, too. Fishing licenses are available at the town hall.

Pedaling west on West Side Road, you begin a long, easy climb up Beacon Hill. Then the road flattens past Franklin Swamp. A left on Cooneymus Road takes you over hills and through pastoral countryside lined with stone fences. At a small cemetery, turn right onto Lakeside Drive. As you pedal, watch for several small dirt paths along which you can hike into wooded Rodman's Hollow to explore on your own.

You ride uphill toward Mohegan Trail, where you turn left and soon climb a short, steep slope along Mohegan Bluffs. Far below waves splash against rocky coves and you view miles of icy water. At Southeast Light Road, go right to old Southeast Light (1874) where visitors are welcome Saturday and Sunday afternoons.

From the lighthouse road, you pedal downhill all the way back to Old Harbor. Take time now to visit the quaint antique and craft shops or to pause for refreshments at an inn overlooking the harbor. For a pleasant summer afternoon, return to Crescent Beach to loll on the sand or search for driftwood. Stay overnight in a resort hotel or rooming house or return to the mainland on the 6 P.M. ferry to Point Judith.

Ferry Schedule

Ferries run between Block Island and Point Judith year round, but operate daily only from mid-June to early September. The ferry leaves Point Judith in summer at 9:30 A.M., 11 A.M., 3:30 P.M. and 6 P.M., and leaves Block Isnd at 8:30 A.M., 12:45 P.M., 3:45 P.M., and 6

P.M., and leaves Block Island at 8:30 winter schedules, inquire locally or phone the Interstate Navigation Company at (203) 442-7891. Ferries also run to Block Island from New London, Connecticut, and Providence and Newport, Rhode Island.

WHERE TO STAY

Motels, hotels, resort cottages, and rooming houses are found throughout the tour. Reservations are mandatory on weekends and holidays and highly recommended at other times. Many facilities close from October through May, making advance planning a must. For a listing of accommodations and restaurants, with opening and closing dates, write the Block Island Chamber of Commerce, Block Island, Rhode Island 02807, or phone (401) 466-2436.

Camping is prohibited on the island by town ordinance.

FOR SPARE PARTS AND REPAIRS

Carry parts and tools, as you find no shops on the island. Many hotels and inns, however, do rent bikes, and in a pinch you might be able to persuade a rental concession to sell you a part. Rentals are available at Ballard's Inn, Cyr's Cycles (in the Surf Hotel), the Royal Hotel, and the 1661 Inn, all in Old Harbor, and at Champlin's Marina and Dick's Last Stand in New Harbor.

FOR FURTHER INFORMATION

Write the Block Island Chamber of Commerce, Block Island, Rhode Island 02807.

BLOCK ISLAND BIRD WATCHING

The best time for bird watching on Block Island is October. Then the trees flame with autumn color, goldenrod and asters pour over the fields, the tourists have gone home, and the birds have begun to migrate. As many as 160 species have been spotted during migration. In early morning when there is a northwest wind, head for the island's north end where birds literally cover the bushes. Species you will see include warblers, sparrows, grosbeaks, mourning doves, vireos, and woodpeckers, to name only a few. As the wind changes to a more southerly direction, follow the birds toward the island's south end.

KEY:
- ○ TOWN
- ● FOOD
- ▲ REST ROOMS
- ■ LODGING
- ★ POINT OF INTEREST

Block Island is off Rhode Island's southern shore in Block Island Sound and can be reached only by ferry from New London, Connecticut; Providence, Rhode Island; and Point Judith, Rhode Island.

10. RHODE ISLAND SHORE SASHAY

Face into fresh salt wind and spin free on this easy, breezy ride beside Rhode Island's rolling surf. Browse through antique shops and art galleries, sample crab cakes, or attend an oldstyle Indian clambake on this Atlantic adventure.

To avoid most city traffic, start at Westerly State Airport southeast of town. Park your car in the airport lot and head south on Airport Road. When Airport Road dead-ends into Watch Hill Road, go left and spin into Avondale. In Avondale continue west on Watch Hill Road, where you coast along Little Narragansett Bay. Soon a paved road off to your right leads you around a loop even closer to the bay for superb views of the water and the opposite Connecticut shore.

Climbing a slight slope, you pass many elegant summer homes dating from the 1870's, then reach Watch Hill Road again and proceed into Watch Hill. Pause in this village to explore the antique shops, see the old Watch Hill Lighthouse on the north side of the entrance to Fisher's Sound (visitors are welcome daily from 1 to 5 P.M. except during storms), and try a whirl on the country's oldest carrousel at Watch Hill Beach.

Breeze east now along the ocean toward Misquamicut. Prevailing winds blow from the southwest, and often you seem to almost float along with the wind nudging your back. At the Y, go right. Then when you reach a dead end, turn right toward Misquamicut. Watch out for sand on the road as you pedal only ten feet above sea level.

Beyond Misquamicut stop at Misquamicut State Beach, lock your bike, and walk onto the beach for a snack above the surf. Food is available at the beach concession. If you would like to spend your afternoon on the beach, you may want to start the bike tour from here. Parking in the large lot is usually free, but costs $1 on weekends and $2 on holidays.

Proceeding east on the flat road, you reach Weekapaug, with more beaches. Turn left in Weekapaug onto Langworthy Road to climb along the eastern tip of Winnapaug Pond. At Route 1-A, go left onto Shore Road, right onto Winnapaug Road, then right onto Airport Road, which leads you back to your starting point.

Westerly and Pawcatuck Side Trip

If city cycling appeals to you, try extending this tour on Post Road (U.S. 1) into Westerly and Pawcatuck. Pedal along the streets of these twin cities past antique shops and art galleries.

If you lunch in a restaurant in Pawcatuck or Westerly, try a unique Rhode Island specialty—crab or clam cakes.

WHERE TO STAY

Motels are numerous throughout this tour and you should have no problem finding a room in April, May, or October, though some spots do close after the tourist season ends. Reservations are advised in summer. Here are several motels along the tour: Blue Star, two and a half miles east of Westerly on Post Road (U.S. 1); (401) 596-2891. The Pony Barn, 5 miles east of Westerly on Shore Road; (401) 348-8216. Pine Lodge Motel, three and a quarter miles east of Westerly on U.S. 1; (401) 322-0333.

There are no campgrounds on the tour described. You can, however, go farther east to Burlingame State Park, where camping is available from April 1st to October 31st at $2 per night. To reach the park on back roads from the airport, take Post Road east to Dunn Corner, then go left on Old Shore road to Bradford, right on Ross Hill Road, bear left on Cookestown Road, and go left before you reach U.S. 1 into Burlingame State Park.

FOR SPARE PARTS, REPAIRS, FURTHER INFORMATION

Ray Willis Toys & Bikes, 53 Railroad Avenue, Westerly, Rhode Island. Ray Willis rents 3-speed bikes by the hour or day and carries spare parts and does repairs on 10-speeds. He knows the back roads around Westerly well and will be glad to suggest other rides.

DISTANCE:	15 miles.
TERRAIN:	Flat.
TRAFFIC:	Light in spring and autumn; sometimes heavy in summer and always heavy on summer Sunday afternoons.
DIFFICULTY:	Good ride for anyone, especially families.
BEST TIME:	Spring through autumn, but avoid summer Sundays because of heavy traffic.
LOCATION:	From Westerly, Rhode Island, near Block Island Sound on the southern shore.

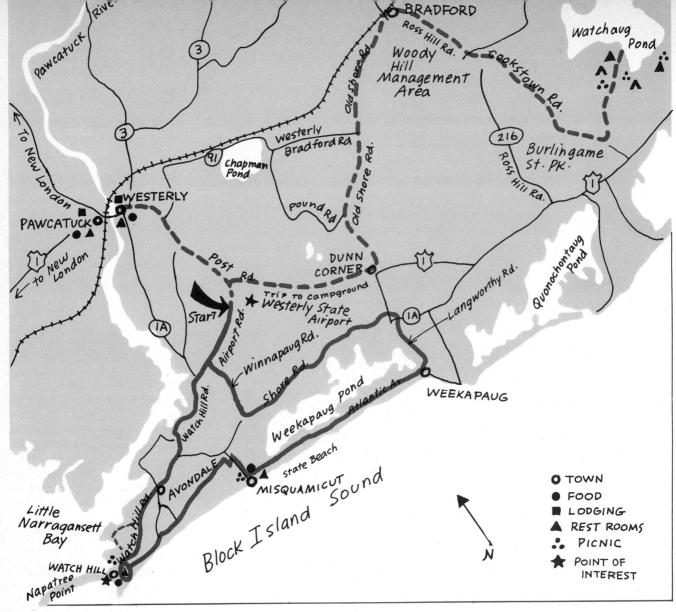

Westerly is in the southwestern corner of Rhode Island on U.S. 1, Rhode Island 3, and Rhode Island 91; 142 miles northeast of New York City via I-95 to New London, Connecticut, and U.S. 1; 50 miles southwest of Providence, Rhode Island, via I-95 and Rhode Island 3; 57 miles southeast of Hartford, Connecticut, via Connecticut 2 and U.S. 1.

NEARBY

Though a tiny state, Rhode Island has unending back roads which can occupy you for hours, days, or even a week. Just a few miles east of this tour lies Charlestown (see the tour on page 25). An excellent free map of Rhode Island is available from the Rhode Island Development Council, Roger Williams Building, Hayes Street, Providence, Rhode Island 02908. When following the map, just stay on the solid black or the narrower solid red roads. It's best to stay off the roads near the beaches in summer because of heavy traffic.

RHODE ISLAND CRAB CAKES

Rhode Island's seafood dishes make fine snacks at the end of a ride through the salt air. Here's one specialty you may want to try.

1 pound well-picked crab meat
½ cup bread crumbs
1 well-beaten egg
1 tablespoon finely
chopped parsley
1 tablespoon Worcestershire sauce
2 tablespoons mayonnaise
¾ teaspoon mustard
¼ teaspoon pepper
1 teaspoon seafood seasoning
sprinkling of salt

Combine all of the ingredients except for the crab meat and mix thoroughly. Then fold the mixture into the crab meat and stir lightly until completely mixed. Form into six round cakes and deep fry at 350 degrees until golden brown.

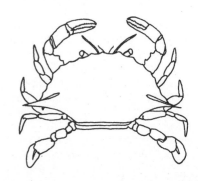

11. CHARLESTOWN HILLS GYPSY

DISTANCE:	20 miles, excluding side trips.
TERRAIN:	Continously hilly, with only one short, flat stretch.
TRAFFIC:	Light on back roads, but often heavy near Charlestown.
DIFFICULTY:	A 3-speed bike recommended.
BEST TIME:	Spring and autumn; summer is too hot and traffic too heavy.
LOCATION:	Countryside north of Charlestown, Rhode Island, on Rhode Island's south shore.

The countryside around Charlestown offers a sampling of New England traditions. Here you can hunt for antiques, comb for driftwood, try clamming, watch hundreds of migrating birds, pedal through rolling farmland, and loiter along a wooded path beside a wildflower-fringed pond—all within in an easy day's bike ride.

Start in Charlestown and buy snacks and picnic basics; two grocery stores are located east of midtown on Post Road. Also in the same vicinity is the Butternut Shoppe, a local antique spot. Bring spare parts and tools with you, as Charlestown has no bike shop.

Pedaling north on South County Trail (State 2 and 112), you climb a hill. As you pedal down the other side, turn right onto Narrow Lane for a side trip to an ancient Indian burial ground.

On State 2 and 112 you tackle two more hills as you ride toward Carolina. Near the crest of the first knoll where State 2 and 112 split, stay left on State 112 (Carolina Back Road) and watch out for the rugged railroad tracks over the next hill as you coast into Carolina.

You go left in Carolina onto State 91 (Alton Carolina Road), climb a short rise, then coast across trickling Meadow Brook and through Wood River Junction and Alton. Beyond the second bridge outside Alton, turn left onto Alton Bradford Road, where you pedal uphill through farmland into Burdickville. In this small village, go left onto smooth blacktopped Burdickville Road, which winds through forests and past a small waterfall. Watch out for the railroad tracks at the bottom of the first hill outside town.

As you climb another hill, go right onto Shumankanuc Hill Road and plunge to Kings Factory Road, where you curve right and meander beside Burlingame State Park's deep woods. Turn right on Prosser Trail leading into the picnic area on the grassy shores of Watchaug Pond. You can swim in the pond and buy snacks at the concession. Then explore Kimball Bird Sanctuary, which you can reach by going through the parking area and turning left. Here along 2 miles of footpaths you see Rhode Island foliage, wildflowers, and wildlife. In spring and autumn you should spot many migrating shore birds.

Back on the road, you have two alternate routes. Either return to Kings Factory Road and go left farther south on Post Road to return to Charlestown, or go right as you leave the picnic area to continue south on blacktopped Prosser Trail, which soon dead-ends into U.S. 1. At this corner, pause at Windswept Farm on your right to buy stick candy at the country store, browse through a fabric outlet mill, or watch pottery being hand spun. A right turn on U.S. 1 will take you on a side trip to the Artists Guild and Gallery (open Thursday through Sunday; free admission), while a left turn leads you downhill back into Charlestown.

Pedal on through Charlestown and go right at the small pond onto Matunuck School Road. Another right on Charlestown Beach Road takes you along Ninigret Pond and across an inlet to Charlestown Beach, where you can swim, picnic, or bask in the sun. At the end of your day, return to Charlestown to feast on local seafood or sample New England clam chowder.

WHERE TO STAY

There are many motels in this area; two are listed below. Willows Resort Motel, on Post Road as you turn right from Prosser Trail or Kings Factory Road, on the way to the Artists Guild and Gallery; (401) 364-7727. Buena Vista Motel, on Post Road farther west of the Willows Resort Motel. Write Buena Vista Motel, Route 1, Charlestown, R.F.D., Bradford, Rhode Island 02808, or phone (401) 364-6798.

Camping is available at Burlingame State Park Campground, which can be reached by taking a shortcut through the Kimball Bird Sanctuary and along the pond. Another way to reach the camping area is to pedal west on Post Road, go right on Cookestown Road, then make a right into the park. A camping fee of $2 per site is charged from April 1st to October 31st; there is no fee the rest of the year.

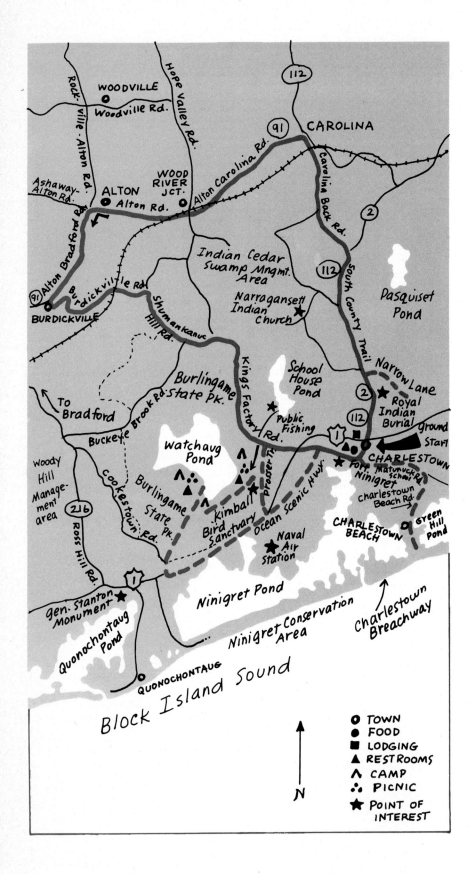

Charlestown is near Rhode Island's southern shore on Rhode Island 2/112 and U.S. 1; 40 miles south of Providence, Rhode Island, via U.S. 1; 73 miles southeast of Hartford, Connecticut, via State 2, State 85, and U.S. 1.

12. 13. HILLY CONNECTICUT TOURS

Connecticut's winding wooded back roads lined with gray stone or wood fences and Colonial saltbox houses remind one of Robert Frost's poetry. Here independent Yankees till the soil, well-to-do old gentlemen live sparsely and proudly plant their tomato gardens each year, and good neighborliness is still a virtue. Linger beside fresh-water ponds, roam the birch, beech, oak, and maple forests, chat with the friendly shopkeepers, and discover New England tradition on these two rural adventures.

NAUGATUCK VALLEY VENTURE

Torrington nestles in the quiet Naugatuck Valley deep in pine-clad hills. Before you start from Coe Park in the middle of town, explore on your own. Pedal along the streets, browse through tidy shops, then fill your pack with snacks. Country-fresh fruits and vegetables are available at Gabriella's, an open-air market at 634 Migeon. In mid-June take a side trip to Indian Lookout Wildlife Preserve, which has a splendid mountain laurel display. To reach the preserve, go east of Torrington on State 4 and turn onto Mountain Road.

Starting the main tour, you go north on Main Street and right onto Winsted Road. Four miles outside Torrington, a road to your left leads to Burr Pond, a wooded spot where you can rest, swim, or hike. You may decide to return later to camp overnight for $2.

Proceeding on the main tour, you climb and coast north on Winsted Road, which becomes Torrington Road before you climb into Winsted. In town go left on U.S. 44. Outside Winsted you tackle a tough hill and then skirt

Highland Lake by following the shore roads—Lake Street, Perch Rock Trail, Wakefield Boulevard, and Sucker Brook Road. Go left on Winchester Road (Route 263) and bear left soon at the Y. Then as the road dead-ends, go right onto Route 272, which leads you over several steep hills before you coast into Norfolk.

For a good place to rest and picnic, continue through Norfolk on Route 272 and follow the sign left into Haystack Mountain State Park. If you pedal up the steep, curvy park road, you overlook the entire Naugatuck Valley. This trek is especially enjoyable in autumn, when the hills and valley flame with color. The Appalachian Trail crosses the park, too, and offers quiet nature walks.

In afternoon retrace your ride through Norfolk past the U.S. 44 junction. At this corner in the E. B. Stoeckel Estate, Yale concerts are held in July and August (admission, $2 to $5). After buying more snacks, proceed south on Route 272. You climb a long, gradual hill which crests near Dennis Hill State Park on your left. Stop at the park to hike through the woods, snack, or rest beneath a sprawling red oak. From here you plummet downhill into the valley and back to Torrington.

CONNECTICUT LAKES LOOP

More wooded back roads, serene ponds, and New England villages are found south of Torrington. Start from Coe Park and ride south on Route 25, which climbs gradually out of the valley and onto a plateau.

Soon you reach Litchfield, which has many eighteenth-century homes, including the Tapping

Reeve House on South Street (admission, 50¢) and the Harriet Beecher Stowe childhood home site at North and Prospect streets. On the green in the center of town, visit the Litchfield Historical Museum to see fine early American art (free admission). Antique devotees may wish to look up Harry W. Strouse on Maple Street; his

DISTANCE:	Naugatuck Valley Venture, 32 miles. Connecticut Lakes Loop, 31 miles.
TERRAIN:	Rolling, with a few steep grades. The Naugatuck Valley ride is the more difficult.
TRAFFIC:	Moderate. It will seem heavy if you are used to Wisconsin's untraveled back roads and light if you tour mostly in the city.
DIFFICULTY:	Not for families with young children because of traffic and tough climbs. A 10-speed bike recommended for hills.
BEST TIME:	Spring through autumn; excellent foliage rides.
LOCATION:	Northwestern Connecticut. Both rides start in Torrington, on State 8 and Route 25.

27

shop is open by appointment or chance.

Buy snacks in Litchfield and pedal south on Route 25. Picnic or rest spots in this vicinity include the Litchfield Nature Center, two and a half miles outside town, and Mount Tom Pond, several hills farther south. At the latter you can also swim, hike, and buy food at the concession.

A sudden coast leads you into Woodville, beyond which there is a steep climb on Route 341. The road levels past a marshy area, then climbs to meet Route 45. Here you go left and soon coast to Lake Waramaug State Park, where you can walk beneath the trees, rest on the green grass, or swim in the icy water. Show Boat Inn here has refreshments. In autumn you might try a foliage tour from the inn aboard an old Mississippi riverboat which floats around the lake. Camping is available, too.

Proceeding on the tour, you pedal on level road with only a few mild dips into New Preston. If you are an antique enthusiast, pause at Grampa Snazzy's Log Cabin to chat with Elisabeth Graves, who sells New Milford pottery, china, glass, and other collectibles.

The road from New Preston leads you past Meeker Swamp on your left to Route 25, where you go right toward Litchfield. This time as you pass through Bantam, detour right on Bantam Lake Road to Bantam Lake, where you can swim, rest, or even rent a canoe.

Return to Litchfield by riding east on Lakeside Road, then going left (north) on East Shore Road, left on White Woods Road, right on Webster Road, left on South Lake Street (Route 63), and on into Litchfield. Follow Route 25 north for a thrilling plunge back to Torrington.

WHERE TO STAY

Motels are available in Torrington, Norfolk, Litchfield, and New Preston. They include the following: Yankee Pedlar, 93 Main Street, Torrington; (203) 489-9226. Black-

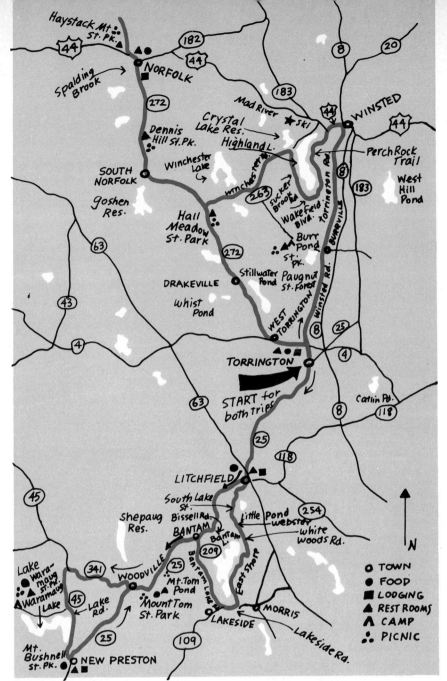

Torrington is in northwestern Connecticut on Connecticut 8, 4 and 25; 20 miles west of Hartford via U.S. 44 and Connecticut 25.

berry River Inn, two and a half miles west of Norfolk on Route 44; (203) 542-5100. Kilravock, 2 miles west of Litchfield on State 25, then half a mile off the highway on Brush Hill Road; (203) 567-9371. Boulders, one and a half miles north of New Preston on State 45; (203) 868-7918. Hopkins, 2 miles north of New Preston on State 45, then off the highway on Hopkins Road; (203) 868-7295.

Camping: Burr Pond State Park, Taylor Brook, 7 miles north of Torrington off Route 8; open April 15th to September 30th; $2. Lake Waramaug State Park, described in the tour above; open April 15th to September 30th; $2.

FOR SPARE PARTS AND REPAIRS

Tommy's, 40 East Main, Torrington, Connecticut; (203) 482-3571.

NEARBY

Connecticut's back roads offer much hilly rural cycling. One possibility is to follow Route 25 from New Preston all the way to Danbury. This jaunt leads you past Candlewood Lake, with Pootatuck State Forest and Squantz Pond State Park on its west shore. You may want to visit Danbury in late September or early October for the famed Great Danbury State Fair, held every year since 1869.

14. ERIE CANAL RIDE

Pedal along the historic Erie Canal, sometimes taking to the towpath and other times spinning along lightly traveled back roads on this serene farmland ride in upper New York State. Eventually the entire towpath will be a paved bike trail, but even now this region offers excellent cycling.

Start in Syracuse, where you could spend a day visiting Onondaga Lake Park, with a salt spring and French Fort; the zoo in Burnet Park; and the Canal Museum in the Weighlock Building on Erie Boulevard East and Oswego Boulevard. Start east of Syracuse at the intersections of Erie Boulevard, Bridge Street, and Towpath Road. Near here you can park your car at Uncle Sam's, a tavern with a large parking lot.

Following the green-and-white bike route signs, you wind east on Towpath Road, turn left at a stop sign onto Kinne Road on which you cross two bridges, turn left on Cedar Bay Road, and left again at a stop sign onto Burdick Road. You encounter some bad bumps here, so take it easy. Soon you cross another bridge and continue over a rugged railroad track to Route 290, where you go right. In this vicinity Green Lake State Park makes a pleasant rest stop.

Following the bike signs and map, you soon spin along New Boston Street into Canastota. Turn right at the stop sign onto North Main Street. Then go left onto Canal Road just before you reach the bridge. Here you can stop for a free visit to the Canal Museum. Before leaving town, you may also want to hunt for bargains in Canastota's flea market.

Outside Canastota on Canal Road, continue going straight at the stop sign. You soon cross a bridge and pedal over the New York State Thruway. When you dead-end into Route 316, turn right across a bridge spanning the canal. Then wind left to another stop sign. At this corner you can continue straight on the main tour or go right for a side trip to the small village of Oneida.

Oneida Side Trip

Oneida (oh-NYE-dah) began as a nineteenth-century "utopia" of Christian communists, or Perfectionists. Group marriages and common property were among the experiments of the colony. Eventually irate citizens drove leader John Noyes to Canada, and Oneida became a stock corporation. You can still visit the original silver factory, now making community plate and William A. Rogers silver. A small restaurant here makes a good lunch stop before you return to the main tour.

Proceeding on the main tour, you go straight at the stop sign (right at this junction if you are returning from Oneida) onto Gala Street, then left onto Oneida Street. Veer right across Center Street past a church on your right and a firehouse on your left, then veer right at the Y onto Foster Street. Across Broad Street and past another church, you pedal along flat farm roads, often without a car in sight. More turns follow: Foster Street ends at Foster Corners Road, where you veer left onto Irish Ridge Road (take care as you cross trafficked Route 31), go right at a stop sign onto Germany Road, and quickly left onto Happy Valley Road, which eventually becomes Verona Mills Road and then Stoney Creek Road. After the signs change to Stoney Creek Road, watch out for the metal-grate bridge over the canal.

Beyond the bridge, you wind right, then left onto Seifert Road,

DISTANCE:	45.6 miles one way.
TERRAIN:	Level to gently rolling hills.
TRAFFIC:	Light on back roads; none on the Erie Canal Towpath.
DIFFICULTY:	Good ride for anyone, including beginners and families.
BEST TIME:	May through October.
LOCATION:	Syracuse to Rome, New York, along the Erie Canal Towpath.

turn right at the dead end onto Heel Path, left across a bridge, and right onto Route 49. Here you can continue on the main tour or take a barge ride the rest of the way into Rome.

If you continue on Route 49, use a lower gear as you climb the tour's only hill into Rome. Winding into Rome, you cross a bridge, turn right at the stop sign onto Erie Boulevard (Route 69), left at the first traffic light onto James Street, and right at the next light onto Dominick Street. Beyond still another bridge, go left onto 6th Street and pedal to Pinti Field, where you can picnic or swim before finding a motel for the night. Return to Syracuse by the same route.

WHERE TO STAY

Syracuse has four Holiday Inns and two Howard Johnson's plus numerous other motels. Rome has a Holiday Inn as well as the following: Adirondack 13 Pines, two and a half miles east of town on State 365; (315) 337-4930. Green Lantern, 3 miles north on State 26, at 8181 Turin Road; (315) 336-5200.

Camping is available at Delta State Park, 6 miles northeast of Rome on Route 46; open May 1st to October 15th; $2.50 for six. Syracuse also has an American Youth Hostel at 635 South Beech Street.

FOR SPARE PARTS AND REPAIRS

Advance Cyclery, 2103 West Genesee Street, Syracuse, New York 13219; (315) 488-0800. This shop handles spare parts for most 10-speed bikes and does emergency repairs.

FOR FURTHER INFORMATION

The above tour is an annual Syracuse-to-Rome ride sponsored by the Onondaga Cycling Club in Syracuse. For details, write the Onondaga Cycling Club, c/o Konski Engineers, McCarthy Building, Syracuse, New York.

Syracuse is in central New York State on I-81 and 90, U.S. 11, New York 57, and 5; 138 miles north of Scranton, Pennsylvania, via I-81; 344 miles northeast of Cleveland, Ohio, via I-90; 313 miles west of Boston, Massachusetts, via I-90; 252 miles southwest of Montreal, Quebec, Canada, via Route 4, U.S. 11, and I-81.

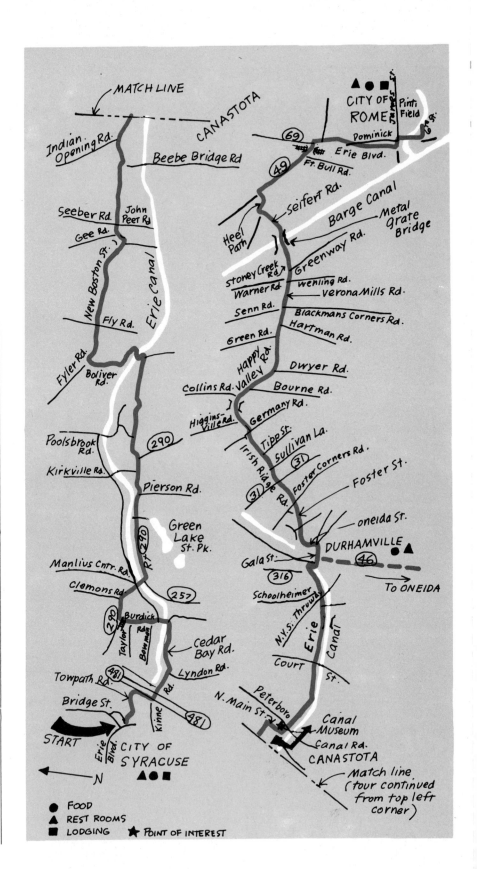

15. LEATHERSTOCKING COUNTRY SOJOURN

DISTANCE:	25 miles, including a 10-mile round-trip ride to Busch Woodlands.
TERRAIN:	Rolling hills.
TRAFFIC:	Light except on State 80; traffic throughout lighter on Saturday than Sunday.
DIFFICULTY:	Good ride for anyone, but a bit strenuous for families with young riders.
BEST TIME:	All seasons but winter.
LOCATION:	Glimmerglass State Park to Cooperstown, New York, about one hour southwest of Schenectady via U.S. 20 and County 31.

Discover the past of James Fenimore Cooper, Babe Ruth, and Wee Willie Keeler on this one-day jaunt along Otsego Lake to Cooperstown, New York. Legend entwines Cooperstown's narrow streets and alleys. Here you can visit six museums, including Cooper's boyhood home, and reminisce on days of gas lanterns, quilting bees, and trolley cars.

Start at Glimmerglass State Park, north of Cooperstown on County 31. Facilities are nonexistent from the park to Cooperstown, so carry snacks, spare parts, and tools. Wooded County 31 (East Lake Road) meanders along Otsego Lake, though you catch only glimpses of the water between trees. The road is two-lane blacktop and a bit rough on the edges, but traffic is nil except on Sundays. You roll over hills handled easily by experts, but a bit arduous for families with young riders. About 6 miles from the park you coast into Cooperstown, where you can browse for hours. Reminders of Cooper's *Leatherstocking Tales* abound even in unexpected spots: a "bump" in the road sign has been revised by a graffiti artist to read "Bumpo." Other landmarks are here, too, just where Cooper describes them: Council Rock, where the Indians held peace talks at the spot where the Susquehanna River meets the lake; the marshes in the lake where woodsman Natty Bumppo met trapper Tom Hatter and the Indian Chingachgook. Signs clearly point the way to most attractions.

One stop should be the Baseball Hall of Fame and Museum, where you can see Babe Ruth's and Lou Gehrig's lockers, Ty Cobb's bats, and Luke Apling's gloves. Also here is the Cooperstown Indian Museum at 1 Pioneer Street, the Cooperstown and Charlotte Valley Railway at 1 Railroad Street, where you can ride an old steam locomotive, and the National Railroad Museum, filled with railroad lore. On a warm summer day you may want to rent a boat at 10 Fair Street and drift on Otsego Lake, then picnic along the banks.

In the afternoon pedal north on State 80 (Sunday traffic can be heavy and the shoulders are bad in spots) about 1 mile to the Farmers' Museum. Here in the farm home, print shop, smithy, tavern, and church you see recreated rural village and farm life from about 1785 to 1860. One of Cooperstown's most fascinating oddities is found here: the ten-foot Cardiff Giant, a statue passed off in an 1869 hoax as a petrified prehistoric man. Across the road from the Farmers' Museum is the Fenimore House, with a good early-American art collection. If traffic is light enough, pedal 1 mile farther north to the Carriage House and Harness Museum. Then 3 miles farther north, stop at Busch Woodlands and Museum, lock your bike, and take a leisurely quarter-mile stroll along a nature trail with labeled trees and wildflowers and walk through the aviary. Museum dioramas depict scenes from Cooper's *Deerslayer*.

Return now to Glimmerglass State Park the same way you came. At the park you can take a cool swim and have a snack at the refreshment stand before the sun sets.

WHERE TO STAY

Cooperstown, with its 2,403 inhabitants, is still definitely a tourist village and motels are numerous and expensive.

The only campground nearby is Cooperstown Tent and Trailer Camp, 3 miles south of Cooperstown on U.S. 28, then 4 miles on County 11, also called Hartwick-Index Road (follow the signs). Open May 15th to October 20th; $3 for four. For reservations, write Cooperstown Tent and Trailer Camp, R.F.D. 3, Cooperstown, New York 13326, or phone (607) 293-7766.

FOR FURTHER INFORMATION

Other facts about Cooperstown can be obtained by writing the Chamber of Commerce, Cooperstown, New York 13326.

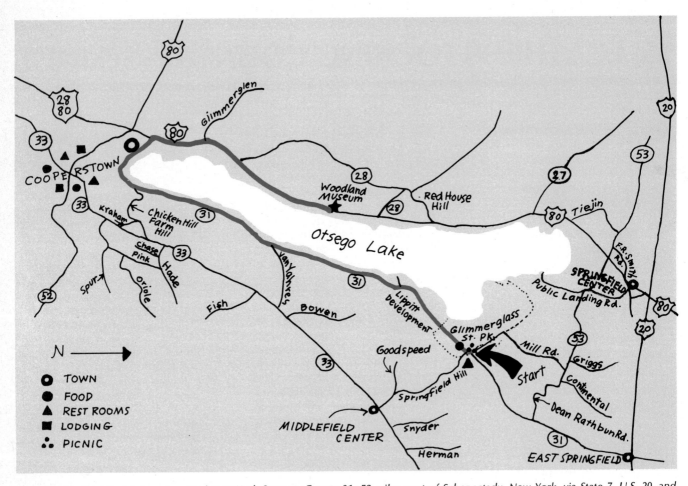

Glimmerglass State Park is in east-central New York State on County 31; 52 miles west of Schenectady, New York, via State 7, U.S. 20, and County 31 south; 80 miles northeast of Binghamton, New York, via State 7 to Colliersville, Route 205 to Cooperstown, and County 31; 33 miles southeast of Utica, New York, via I-90, State 28, U.S. 20, and County 31.

WILD LEATHERSTOCKING BEVERAGES

As you pedal along Otsego Lake's wooded shores, stop often to forage along the banks searching for highbush cranberry or yellow and sweet birch trees. All may be found in this country and produce refreshing beverages for weary woodsmen. Natty Bumppo, Tom Hatter, and Chingachgook no doubt sampled them all.

Woodsman cranberry-ade is made from the highbush cranberry's acidic fruits, which ripen in autumn. Squeeze the juice from several cups of berries, then boil about three cups of berries with a bit of orange or lemon peel, water, and the cranberry juice. Strain and dilute with water for a refreshing punch high in vitamin C. You can also add commercial pectin to the juice to create an excellent clear-red jelly, or you can allow the juice to ferment to make wild cranberry wine.

The highbush cranberry has orange berries which turn scarlet when ripe and contain one smooth pit shaped like a disk. The leaves have three lobes and grow opposite each other and rather resemble maple leaves. Two types of white flowers bloom simultaneously in a cluster of large blossoms, with four white petals around many tiny lacy flowers. Warning: The European snowball bush so closely resembles the highbush cranberry that only a trained botanist can tell them apart. The only way you can tell the difference is to taste a berry: snowball berries are unpleasantly bitter.

Black or *yellow birch teas* can be made by steeping in water the birch bark, twigs, leaves, and buds, or any one of these. Sweet birch contains oil of wintergreen, which produces a fragrant tea. Yellow birch is similar but less aromatic. You can also tap birches, particularly the black birch, to obtain sap from which to make a delightful syrup, quite different from maple syrup but delicious nonetheless.

The black birch has oval or oblong leaves with hairy stems. This tree is easily identified by its reddish-brown wintergreen-scented bark. Yellow birch bark is also distinctive, being bronze or yellow and peeling in long ragged strips. In autumn the birches turn a vivid yellow-gold.

16. BEAR MOUNTAIN MEANDER

When New York City subways become hot and sticky in summer or the crowds push too closely anytime, escape by bike through Sleepy Hollow country and Peekskill to cool, forested Bear Mountain State Park. As you read this, by tomorrow night you could be lounging in elegant Bear Mountain Inn or camping on pine needles beneath the stars.

Be cautious throughout this jaunt because some roads are quite narrow, especially Bear Mountain Highway and parts of U.S. 9, 9W, and New York 17. All routes are paved, but city streets are often bumpy, with some broken glass and debris. Clincher tires are recommended. Though you find many grocery stores and restaurants along the route, carry some snacks so you can relax and picnic in quiet grassy parks or small off-the-road clearings beside a creek or pond. Theft is a big problem, so try to eat in small towns where you can watch your bike through a window, and avoid leaving your bike unattended in the cities.

NOTE: Because this tour has so many turns, complete, numbered directions are listed at the end of the tour description.

Start at Columbus Circle, or if you wish to avoid midtown traffic, in Yonkers, where you can take off from Philipse Manor Hall at Warburton Avenue and Dock Street. This tour, by the way, can be conveniently combined with the Hudson Mansions Tour from Yonkers on page 43.

Pedaling north from Yonkers, pause at the Hudson River Museum and Planetarium at 511 Warburton Avenue (weekdays, free; weekends, 50¢). You pick up U.S. 9 in Hastings-on-Hudson and ride on through Dobbs Ferry, then past Sunnyside, the home of Washington Irving (adults, $1.75), and Lynd-

hurst, former palace of railroad tycoon Jay Gould (adults, $1.50).

In Tarrytown a good rest spot is wooded Kingsland Point Park. Here you can browse through the old trading center surrounding Philipsburg Manor, built in 1683, with an operating grist mill where you can buy flour. Across the road lie Old Dutch Church and Sleepy Hollow Cemetery, where Andrew Carnegie, William Rockefeller, and Washington Irving are buried.

North of Ossining, turn right at Quaker Ridge Road to avoid the freeway across the Croton River. In about one and a half miles, you go right onto New York 129, then left in 2 miles onto Croton Avenue. On this stretch you spin past New Croton Reservoir, with rest spots along the lake. Another left onto Baptist Church Road leads you into Croton, where you turn left on Maple Avenue, then continue straight onto Division Street and into Peekskill. For 25¢ you can take a quick dip in Lounsbury Pond at Blue Mountain Reservation on Welcher Avenue.

From Peekskill it's only a short jaunt on city streets to Bear Mountain Highway, which you follow over the bridge (no toll collected this direction) and ride .7 mile farther to famed Bear Mountain Inn, just south of the traffic circle in Bear Mountain State Park. Nearby you can swim in a large spring-fed lake, hike on wooded trails, and browse through trailside museums. Expert cyclists can take the winding George W. Perkins Memorial Drive (25¢ for cars, free for bicycles) up to the Bear Mountain summit, with superb views of the whole area, an especially scenic trek in autumn. Stay overnight at the inn or in a camp at Harriman State Park, adjacent to Bear Mountain. You may want to stay longer to explore or pedal north along the banks of the

DISTANCE:	96 miles.
TERRAIN:	Hilly.
TRAFFIC:	Heavy traffic may be encountered anywhere.
DIFFICULTY:	For cyclists with good bike control in traffic; the terrain is easy enough for moderately strong cyclists.
BEST TIME:	Spring through autumn. Best on weekdays, when traffic is lightest.
LOCATION:	New York City to Bear Mountain.

Hudson.

Sometime before riding back south through Stony Point and New City, pedal 5 miles north on New York 218 and turn left onto Highland Road to bike through West Point. Cadet barracks and academic buildings are closed to visitors, but you can enjoy many other spots here: West Point Museum, Old Cadet Chapel, Battle Monument, and Trophy Point, all with Civil War relics and memorials. Don't miss the uphill climb to Cadet Chapel, containing a huge organ and elegant stained-glass windows; from the hilltop you view the entire campus.

Returning toward New York City, you pass Stony Point Battlefield Reservation, where General "Mad Anthony" Wayne won a battle against the British, and spin on through Stony Point and New City. You can rest, snack, or swim near New City at Rockland State Park. Caution: On your return, walk your bike the half-mile stretch of

Palisades Parkway at 7 Lakes Parkway merge point; cycling is illegal here. Also, watch out for the railroad tracks on Hardenburgh Avenue just before you turn onto Piermont Road, and be prepared for a long (1.2-miles), steep hill along Englewood's Palisades Avenue.

Refreshing wooded spots en route include Tallman Mountain State Park near Tappan and Palisades State Park, through which you pedal in New Jersey. More turns eventually lead you back to Columbus Circle.

Note: The return to New York City from Bear Mountain is highly flexible. You can go on to Suffern and follow the routing in the tour on page 40 to New York City, or you can proceed back across the Hudson at Bear Mountain and follow the Hudson Mansions Tour on page 43 in reverse, from Tarrytown through White Plains to Yonkers.

Directions

From Columbus Circle, at 59th Street and Broadway, New York City:

1. North on Broadway or on Central Park West (continuation of Eighth Avenue);

2. left (west) on 72nd Street;

3. right (north) on Riverside Drive;

4. right (east) on 165th Street, just before the merge with Henry Hudson Parkway, and uphill two blocks;

5. left (north) on Broadway;

6. follow U.S. 9 through the Bronx into Yonkers;

7. left on Main Street in Yonkers for one block;

8. right on Warburton Avenue;

9. rejoin U.S. 9 in Hastings-on-Hudson, then continue north on U.S. 9 through Dobbs Ferry and Tarrytown to Ossining;

10. continue north on U.S. 9 in Ossining for 1.4 miles;

11 right on Quaker Bridge Road for 2.7 miles;

12. left at the New York water

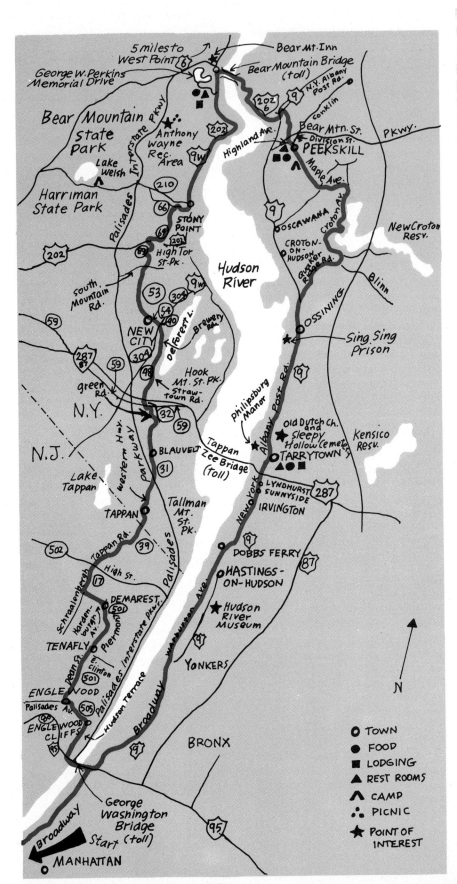

Ride starts at Columbus Circle in New York City.

supply for 1.8 miles;

13. right on Yorktown Road (Route 129);

14. left on Croton Avenue;

15. left on Maple Avenue, which runs into Division Street and leads you into Peekskill;

16. north on Division at Main Street intersection for three more blocks;

17. bear left on Highland Avenue, located .8 mile north of Main;

18. stay left just north of Bear Mountain Parkway to continue on Highland;

19. left (south) on U.S. 9 for .8 mile to a traffic circle;

20. west at the traffic circle onto U.S. 6 and U.S. 202 (Bear Mountain Highway) and pedal 3.5 miles to Bear Mountain Bridge;

21. left over the bridge (eastbound toll only) for .7 mile;

22. south at the traffic circle onto U.S. 9W and U.S. 202 for half a mile to Bear Mountain Inn.

Total mileage from New York City: 49.3 miles.

From Bear Mountain Inn, return to New York by riding this route:

1. South on U.S. 9W and U.S. 202 for 8.1 miles to Stony Point;

2. right just south of State 210 onto County 66 for .3 mile;

3. left on Central Highway for 2 miles;

4. right (west) on U.S. 202 for .2 mile;

5. left (south) on County 89 (Little Tor Road) for 3.7 miles;

6. left (east) on New Hempstead Road to Main Street in New City;

7. right on Main;

8. immediate left on Congers Road for .6 mile;

9. right (south) on Brewery Road, which becomes Strawtown Road, for 4.2 miles;

10. left just south of New York 59 onto Green Road;

11. Green Road turns south, then east before reaching Western Highway in .7 mile;

12. right (south) on Western Highway for 4.4 miles;

13. bear left on Greenbush Road for .5 mile;

14. south on Tappan (*not* Old Tappan) for about .2 mile to New Jersey state line, where you continue south on Tappan;

15. right *before you reach* New Jersey 505 onto Schraalenburgh Road for 2.1 miles;

16. left on Hardenburgh Avenue for 1.1 miles;

17. right on Piermont Road, just after the railroad tracks, and pedal along the tracks for 2.4 miles to Tenafly;

18. the street curves left in Tenafly and becomes Clinton Avenue;

19. take first right onto Dean Drive and follow the railroad tracks again for 2.3 miles;

20. left (east) onto Palisade Avenue (Route 66) in Englewood and up a long, steep hill;

21. right (south) on Hudson Terrace, located one block east of U.S. 9W, for 1.9 miles to George Washington Bridge;

22. use sidewalk on south side of George Washington Bridge and exit east on 178th Street;

23. south on Broadway;

24. right (west) on 165th Street and downhill;

25. left (south) on Riverside Drive;

26. left (east) on 72nd Street;

27. right (south) on Central Park West to Columbus Circle.

WHERE TO STAY

Motels are available in Tarrytown, Peekskill, the Bear Mountain area, and West Point.

Campgrounds include the following: Sprout Lake Park, 1 mile north of Peekskill on U.S. 9, then a quarter of a mile east on New York-Albany Road, and 1 mile north on Sprout Brook Road. Open May 1st to September 30th; $5 for four. Harriman State Park, Lake Welch Tent and Trailer Camp, 5 miles west of Stony Point on State 210. Open April 15th to October

15th; $2.50 to $3 per site.

FOR FURTHER INFORMATION

William N. Hoffman, New York area director of the League of American Wheelmen, planned this tour. If you have questions, write Bill at 220 Pelham Road, New Rochelle, New York 10805.

NEARBY

This tour has been planned to hook up with several other Hudson River rides, and there are many possibilities for further travel. From Bear Mountain you can pedal on to Suffern and take off through the Catskills (see page 39) or continue north past New Paltz's old Huguenot Street and other historic spots to Kingston. You can further extend the ride toward Kingston with a loop through Woodstock's artist colony.

17. COLONIAL HUDSON SPIN

Washington Irving territory on both banks of the broad blue Hudson contains rolling hills, stately old mansions, and lots of history. Here you can visit Franklin Roosevelt's home, George Washington's headquarters, the Marquis de Lafayette's home during the Revolution, historic Huguenot Street, and Woodstock's artist colony.

This tour is as flexible as Rip van Winkle's wanderings through the hills. You can start at Peekskill, Bear Mountain Inn, Columbus Circle in New York City, or somewhere in between or beyond. Though the tour is long, beginners can pick any interesting segment of 20 miles or so or try the 30-mile loop to Woodstock. Many small towns offer food and refreshments, but for a picnic along the Hudson River banks bring your own. Also bring along tools and spare parts. Caution is necessary throughout this tour because of some narrow roads and possible traffic. Clincher tires are recommended, especially on New York City's bumpy streets.

A good starting point is Bear Mountain Inn, on the Hudson's west bank in Bear Mountain State Park. To reach the inn by bike from New York City, see the Bear Mountain Meander on page 33. If you come by car, you will find the inn located near the intersection of U.S. 6, U.S. 9W, State 218, and State 9D.

Pedal east across the river on Bear Mountain Bridge and north on State 9D to Boscobel, a restored home. Farther on at Mount Beacon, you can take a leg-aching side trip to your right up the "mountain" for a spectacular view of the Hudson Valley.

Proceeding north on 9D, you soon pedal into Beacon, where you can either continue on 9D to shorten this ride about eight and a

DISTANCE:	130.7 miles from Bear Mountain; 227.1 miles from Columbus Circle in New York City.
TERRAIN:	Moderately hilly.
TRAFFIC:	Heavy in spots; lightest on weekdays.
DIFFICULTY:	Good bike control required because of some narrow roads and possible heavy traffic, especially if riding from Columbus Circle.
BEST TIME:	Spring through autumn. Summer temperatures are most pleasant, but humidity can be high.
LOCATION:	Hudson River shores north of New York City.

half miles or take the main tour past several historic mansions. The long main route leaves Beacon on Fishkill Avenue, which becomes New York 52 at I-84. Soon you pass Fishkill's Trinity Church and Reformed Dutch Church. Farther east on State 82, you can rest and visit Brinckerhoff Mansion, the Marquis de Lafayette's home during the Revolution. About one and a half miles east on State 82, stop at the John Brinckerhoff House, George Washington's Revolutionary headquarters.

Follow the detailed instructions at the end of this tour description into Poughkeepsie, where you soon pass Franklin Delano Roosevelt's simple home, a national his-

torical site in Hyde Park. This makes a good rest or picnic stop if crowds are light. Other good rest or picnic stops in this vicinity include the Vanderbilt Mansion and museum 2 miles farther north, and Ogden Livingston Mills State Park 3 miles beyond that. If you plan to break this tour into two days, Margaret Lewis Norrie State Park, 2 miles north of the Vanderbilt Mansion, offers camping and cabins.

Beyond Rhinebeck, which has a museum of old planes, you bear left on Old Post Road, then left on Mt. Reston Road to New York 199, which takes you over the Kingston-Rhinecliff Bridge (no westbound toll) into Ulster County. A few city streets bring you to Kingston, with the old Senate House (1676), Old Dutch Church, and many early Colonial homes. From Kingston you can either follow the main tour south about three and a half miles to Hurley, with many seventeenth-century homes, or take a side trip to Woodstock's artist colony, cradled in the southern Catskills.

Woodstock Side Loop

Woodstock is located 12 miles from Kingston. Take the suggested routing at the end of this tour description, then return either the same way or via a longer loop (40 miles) past the Ashokan Reservoir. While in Woodstock, visit the Woodstock Artists Association at Village Green, where nationally recognized artists show their work (weekdays, free; weekends and holiday, 25¢).

Continuing on the main route past Hurley, more turns lead you left on State 213 past the D & H Canal Museum and finally into New Paltz. Here you can follow the signs to pedal along Huguenot

Street, the nation's oldest road, with stone homes built from 1692 to 1712. South of New Paltz, you take State 32 for 17.6 miles to U.S. 9W, just north of Newburgh.

Many stops are possible in New-burgh, and after a snack, you may want to see them all. From Wash-ington's Headquarters on Wash-ington Street, you can go right on Liberty Street to Clinton, then right one more block to the Crawford House, another Colonial mansion. South of town, Knox Headquarters on State 94 provides a good rest spot, as does the Friends Meeting House a bit farther on Quaker Avenue.

Past the Museum of Hudson Highlands, a natural history mu-seum, you ride through Cornwall, where you can buy food. South of Cornwall, turn onto Storm King Highway, a narrow road high above the Hudson with splendid views. Continue south on State 218. You can soon proceed past West Point, but for a pleasant side trip veer right on Highland Falls, which leads you through the acad-emy. Eventually you reach 218 again and then take 9W back to Bear Mountain, the tour's end.

Directions

From Bear Mountain Inn:

1. East over Bear Mountain Bridge;
2. left (north) on New York 9D for 4.5 miles;
3. continue north at New York 403 junction on 9D to Boscobel and Mount Beacon;
4. right on Teller Street to Main Street in Beacon.

Bear Mountain Inn is in Southeastern New York State near the intersection of U.S. 6, 9-D, 9-W, and New York 218; north of New York City via Route 9-A and U.S. 9-W; if riding your bike from New York City, follow the directions under Bear Mountain Meander on page 33.

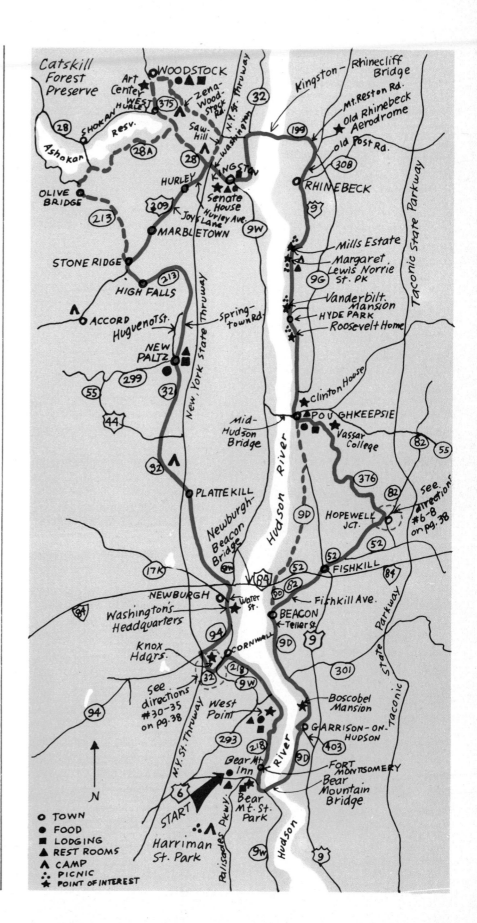

From Teller and Main two routes are possible. Short route (not included in the total mileage): Continue north on 9D for 11.1 miles through Wappingers Falls to U.S. 9 and end of 9D; cross U.S. 9 and go east on Vassar Road for 4.5 miles; rejoin the long tour at State 376 by going left.

Long route:

5. Leave Beacon on Fishkill Avenue, which becomes New York 52 at I-84;

6. right (east) on New York 82 at the Brinckerhoff Mansion;

7. left in .4 mile onto All Angels Road past John Brinckerhoff House and on to New Hackensack;

8. right (north) on Route 376 into Poughkeepsie;

9. right onto Hamilton Street in Poughkeepsie;

10. one block farther at Church Street (U.S. 44 and New York 55 junction), continue north on Hamilton;

11. left at the T onto Fulton Street;

12. right (north) onto U.S. 9 past the Roosevelt Home, Vanderbilt Mansion, Norrie State Park, and Ogden Livingston Mills State Park through Rhinebeck;

13. bear left on Old Post Road, located .4 mile north of Rhinebeck;

14. left on Mt. Reston Road;

15. left (west) on New York 199 over Kingston-Rhinecliff Bridge;

16. left (south) on New York 32 for 1 mile;

17. cross U.S. 9W and follow Flatbush Avenue to its end;

18. left on Albany Avenue for .6 mile across New York 28, then .3 mile on to downtown Kingston;

19. leave Kingston west on Washington Street;

20. left on Hurley Avenue to Hurley;

21. leave Hurley on Joy's Lane;

22. south on Lucas Turnpike for 7.3 miles;

23. left on New York 213 for 3.2 miles, past the D & H Canal

Museum;

24. right on Springtown Road for 8 miles;

25. east on New York 299 for .3 mile to New Paltz;

26. pick up New York 32 from New Paltz and take this road south for 17.6 miles;

27. south on U.S. 9W into Newburgh;

28. leave Newburgh by going south on Water Street, which becomes River Road;

29. right onto State 94 past Knox Headquarters;

30. left onto New York 32;

31. left onto Quaker Avenue past Friends Meeting House;

32. right on Creek Road;

33. left on Hasbroock Road;

34. left on Payson Avenue past Museum of Hudson Highlands through Cornwall;

35. right on Storm King Highway

36. south on New York 218 to West Point;

37. right on Highland Falls through West Point;

38. meet up again with New York 218 and continue south;

39. left on U.S. 9W for 2.7 miles to traffic circle;

40. continue south on 9W past traffic circle for .5 mile to Bear Mountain Inn.

Directions for Woodstock Side Trip

From Kingston:

1. West on Washington Street for 1.5 miles;

2. right (north) on Sawhill Road for 2.6 miles;

3. left (west) on Zena-Woodstock Road for 6.3 miles;

4. continue west on New York 212 for 1.6 miles to Woodstock.

Return to Kingston the same way or take this longer loop past Ashokan Reservoir:

1. South on New York 375 for 3 miles;

2. east on Route 28 for 2.5 miles;

3. west on New York 28A for 12 miles;

4. south on New York for 213 for 10.5 miles to High Falls, where you rejoin main route.

WHERE TO STAY

Motels are located in Peekskill, Poughkeepsie, Kingston, New Paltz, Newburgh, West Point, and the Bear Mountain ski areas.

Campgrounds: Margaret Lewis Norrie State Park, on U.S. 9, 2 miles past the Vanderbilt Mansion in Staatsburg. Open April 15th through October; $2.50 to $3 per site. For reservations, write the park at Staatsburg, New York 12580, or phone (914) 889-4646. Onteora Lake State Park, 4 miles west of Kingston on State 28, a convenient stop for the Woodstock side trip. Open year round; $4 for four. For reservations, write Onteora Lake State Park, Box 183, West Hurley, New York 12491, or phone (914) 331-9312.

FOR FURTHER INFORMATION

William N. Hoffman, New York area director of the League of American Wheelmen, planned this tour and will gladly supply any further details. You can write him at 220 Pelham Road, New Rochelle, New York 10805.

Also, for further travel information on the area, including a map detailing many sights throughout the valley, write the Hudson River Valley Association, 105 Ferris Lane, Poughkeepsie, New York 12603.

NEARBY

Tours through the Hudson River Valley and surrounding region are numerous. Try the Hudson Mansions Tour on page 43 through Washington Irving's Tarrytown, or the Catskills tour through Rip van Winkle country on page 39.

18. CATSKILLS RUNAWAY

When Rip van Winkle roamed the Catskills seeking solitude, he met dwarves playing ninepins, drank from their enchanted keg, and slept for twenty years. Though your adventures in this magic land will no doubt be less bizarre, you may still come away feeling as refreshed as you would after a twenty-year nap.

Getting off the beaten path in the Catskills requires ingenuity, and you will always encounter some cars. But the back roads reward you with rolling wooded hills, slate-blue shadows, and at least a taste of that legendary solitude. Carry spare parts, tools, and warm clothing for cool nights on this delightful ride. Detailed directions appear at the end of the tour description.

Start in Suffern and pedal north over gentle hills on New York 59 and then on New York 17 through Sloatsburg and Tuxedo Park. In Southfields veer left onto Old Orange Turnpike and head toward Monroe. You can continue on through town, but a pleasant side trip can be taken west of Monroe to the restored historic Old Museum Village of Smiths Cove. Then cycle on New York 17M and turn west on Old Chester Road into Goshen, where you can browse through the old Orange County Courthouse and the Trotter Hall of Fame. From Goshen pick up U.S. 6 and New York 17M west of town at the New York 17 intersection and pedal on to Middletown, where you can stay overnight. While here, you may want to visit the Railway Museum.

Continue north on 17M (the *old* 17) through Fair Oaks and Bloomingburg and tackle the steep climb over the Shawangunk Mountain Ridge. From the crest you see Wurtsboro snuggled deep in a Catskill valley, then you plunge down-

hill into the tiny town. You may want to stay overnight here in the old Wurtsboro Hotel, across the street from the firehouse; the owner, Joe, allows you to take your bike upstairs with you to your room.

Beyond Wurtsboro old 17 is often unmarked, but is easily recognized by the many roadhouses vacated when new 17 was built. You pedal over rolling hills and around many turns (follow the directions at the end of this tour description) through Thompsonville and into Monticello, the Catskills' resort center sometimes called the "borscht belt." Opposite the courthouse at Bank and North streets stands the County Historical Museum (free admission).

From Monticello you can go one of two ways: south on State 42 for 20 miles, then east on Route 97 along the Delaware River to Port Jervis for the shorter main tour; or to Route 17B for the extended tour below.

Extended Tour

In Monticello continue straight where State 42 goes left and proceed .8 mile west to Route 17B, opposite the Monticello Raceway. Harness races are held here from May to late September. You go left on 17B for 7 miles, passing through White Lake, and left again onto State 55. The road now winds through rising hills along a clear brook. Stop anytime to linger in this romantic land.

At Eldred you can pick up picnic basics at the grocery store on the corner where State 55 and County 47 meet. Then pedal another 4.3 miles to Barryville and go right onto Route 97 along the Delaware River. A serene, out-of-the-way picnic or rest spot lies about 4 miles outside Barryville—Minisink

Battlefield Memorial Park, half a mile down a little road to your right.

Soon you spin over the Roebling Suspension Bridge (toll, 5¢), built by John Roebling in 1848, thirty-five years before he built the Brooklyn Bridge. Across the bridge, go left (*don't* take Pennsylvania 590) and follow the detailed directions at the end of this tour description. Near the Orange

DISTANCE:	134.4 miles, plus a 31-mile optional loop; 205.2 miles if started in New York City.
TERRAIN:	Hilly, with some steep slopes.
TRAFFIC:	Heavy on summer weekends; lighter during the week and in spring and autumn.
DIFFICULTY:	Requires experience because of the strenuous terrain and distance.
BEST TIME:	Spring, autumn, or weekdays in summer, when traffic is lightest. Nights can be cool, so bring warm clothing.
LOCATION:	Catskill Mountains, New York. Starts in Suffern, on the New York-New Jersey border at the junction of U.S. 287 and New York 15.

County line, the road rises above the river, providing superb views of the Catskills and the Delaware River. Caution: You encounter narrow road and many curves on this stretch. Soon you reach Port Jervis and link up again with the main tour.

Port Jervis has several motels and makes a fine overnight stop. Adventurous bikers can take a strenuous uphill trek south of town to High Point Tower, from which you view three states. Take care as you round the bends on the thrilling ride back down.

From Port Jervis you ride east on U.S. 6 up a mountain. After turning onto Orange County 1, you pedal 17.5 miles to Warwick through level farm country. Watch out for unleashed dogs here. In Warwick pick up New York 17A and ride east up still another mountain for 6.4 miles to New York 17. Here you go right for 7 miles to Seven Lakes Parkway, then pedal 3.9 miles farther to Suffern, the loop's end.

Directions

Starting from Suffern:
1. Pedal north on New York 59;
2. at the end of New York 59, continue north on New York 17 through Sloatsburg and Tuxedo Park;
3. go left at Southfields onto Old Orange Turnpike (County 15) to Monroe;
4. west just before you reach Monroe onto Old Chester Road, which leads to Goshen;
5. left (west) from Goshen on U.S. 6 and New York 17M (pick up this road at the New York 17 intersection just west of Goshen) through Middletown and Fair Oaks to Bloomingburg;
6. left onto 17K into Bloomingburg;
7. continue west on old 17 into Wurtsboro;
8. bear left on the unmarked road located .1 mile past Adams Road;
9. go right in 1.5 miles at the T onto Glen Wild Road;

10. left at the fork in 1 mile and ride 2.2 miles farther to the bottom of a hill;
11. left at the bridge for 1.7 miles to Thompsonville;
12. left on Thompsonville Road for .1 mile;
13. right on unmarked road for 2.8 miles;
14. left just before you reach New York 17, then follow this road across 17 and pedal .1 mile;
15. right at the T on Thompsonville Road for .6 mile (Rocky Ridge Road, which you *don't* take, goes left here);
16. left on State 42 (Pleasant Street) for .4 mile to Broadway in Monticello;
17. from Monticello go south on State 42 for 20 miles;
18. east on Route 97 along the Delaware River to Port Jervis.

Extended tour from Monticello:
A. Go straight where State 42 turns left and pedal .8 mile;
B. left on Route 17B (opposite Monticello Raceway) for 7 miles;
C. left on State 55 as 17B and 55 split, and ride 12 miles to Eldred;
D. straight in Eldred on State 55 for another 4.3 miles;
E. right on Route 97 in Barryville for 4.4 miles to Roebling Suspension Bridge;
F. cross the bridge to Pennsylvania 590;
G. go east on road paralleling the river (*don't* take Pennsylvania 590) and ride 4.3 miles to Pennsylvania 434;
H. left on Pennsylvania 434 for 1.4 miles across the river back to Barryville;
I. right on Route 97 in Barryville for 12.6 miles to the Orange County line;
J. straight (south) for 7 miles to Port Jervis.

Continuing on the main tour:
19. Go left (east) from Port Jervis on U.S. 6 up the mountain for 7.5 miles;

20. right on Orange County 1 for 17.5 miles through level farm country;
21. right at the end of Orange County 1 (Pine Island Turnpike) onto New York 17A, then follow the signs to Warwick;
22. left on New York 17A in Warwick and go east up the mountain for 6.5 miles;
23. straight at the junction of 17A and State 210 for 6.4 miles;
24. right on New York 17 for 7 miles to Seven Lakes Parkway at Sloatsburg;
25. straight through Sloatsburg on New York 17 for 3.9 miles back to Suffern.

Directions from New York City to Suffern (35.4 miles one way)

Starting from Columbus Circle, at 59th Street and Eighth Avenue:
1. Go north on Central Park West (Eighth Avenue);
2. left on 72nd Street;
3. right on Riverside Drive;
4. right on 165th Street and uphill for two blocks;
5. left on Broadway;
6. left on 179th Street for one block, then continue under the bus terminal;
7. *walk* two short blocks west on the south side of 178th Street (which is one-way east) to George Washington Bridge;
8. cross the bridge on the south side sidewalk (the path is wide, but be careful going around the towers);
9. right beyond the underpass on U.S. 9W (Hudson Terrace);
10. left onto Palisades Avenue and down a long, steep hill;
11. right at the traffic light on Engle Street;
12. left in Tenafly on East Clinton Avenue;
13. curve right at the traffic light onto Piermont Road (County 501);
14. follow Piermont Road as it goes 90 degrees left at Andersen

Avenue, then right after several blocks;

15. left across the railroad tracks onto Hardenburgh Road;

16. right on Schraalenburgh Road (County 17 and 39);

17. left on Tappan Road for 1 mile;

18. left on Blanche Avenue;

19. bear right onto Phyllis Drive at Cripple Bush Road;

20. left one block farther onto Charles Place;

21. left on Old Tappan Road for one long block;

22. turn right to ride around Lake Tappan on Washington Avenue (County 132);

23. right on Riverdale Road (County 53) for 1.5 miles;

24. left on Grand Avenue (County 94) through Montvale across Route 503 and the railroad tracks;

25. straight through Garden State Parkway interchange;

26. after the interchange County 94 becomes County 2 (Lake Street);

27. right on West Saddle River Road (County 77) for 1 mile;

28. left on Sparrowbush Road (Route S83);

29. jog right at Carlough Road;

30. straight on East Crescent Avenue (County 81) for a short distance;

31. straight on Masonicus Road (Route S83);

32. left at the T onto Airmont Road;

33. right on Hilltop Road;

34. right at the T onto Franklin Turnpike (Route 507) through Mahwah;

35. cross the New Jersey state line and continue north on U.S. 202 to Suffern.

WHERE TO STAY

Motels are located in and around Suffern, Middletown, Wurtsboro, Monticello, Port Jervis, and Warwick, and along New York 17M and roads parallel to the New York 17 Expressway. Reservations

are advised during the peak tourist season from June through August. Here is a partial listing of accommodations: Motel-on-the-Mountain, Box 569, Suffern, New York 10901; 2 miles north of Suffern on New York 17; (914) 357-2500. Chadwick, Box 332, Middletown, New York 10940; 2 miles south of Middletown on the bike tour route (U.S. 6 and 17M); (914) 374-2411. Wurtsboro Hotel, in Wurtsboro across from the firehouse; (914) 888-2122. Patio, 190 Broadway, Monticello, New York 12701; (914) 794-8800. Warwick, Galloway Road, Warwick, New York 10990; 1 mile east of Warwick on New York 17A; (914) 986-4822. You also find many resorts, cabins, and cottages throughout the tour.

Camping is available only in Bloomingburg at Ponderosa Campsite, on Roosa Gap Road (ask locally for directions). Open June 29th to September 3rd; $4 for a family of six. For reservations, write Ponderosa Campsite, Box 157, Bloomingburg, New York 12721, or phone (914) 733-1388.

FOR FURTHER INFORMATION

William N. Hoffman, New York area director of the League of American Wheelmen, told us about this ride and will gladly try to answer any further questions you may have. You can write him at 220 Pelham Road, New Rochelle, New York 10805.

Suffern is in southeastern New York State on the New York-New Jersey border at the junction of U.S. 287, New York 15 and 59; 29 miles north of New York City via I-95, U.S. 9-W, and I-287; 127 miles south of Albany, New York, via I-87; 117 miles east of Scranton, Pennsylvania, via I-84, U.S. 6, and I-87. This map covers Suffern to Monroe.

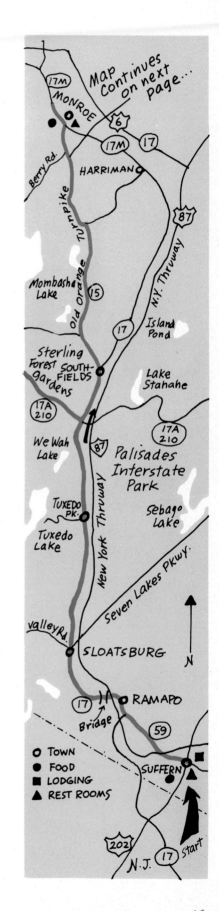

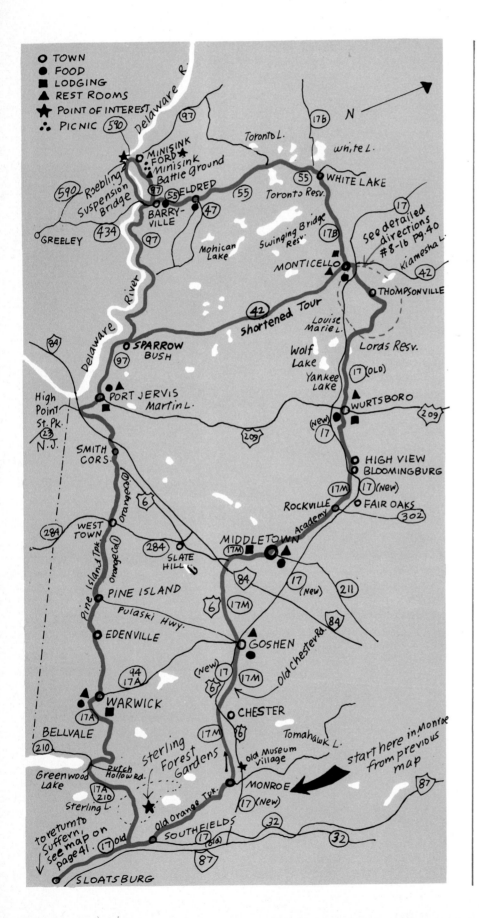

TOWN
FOOD
LODGING
REST ROOMS
POINT of INTEREST
PICNIC

NEARBY

This tour has been planned to hook up with several other rides nearby. See the Bear Mountain Meander (page 33), the Colonial Hudson Spin (page 36), and the Hudson Mansions Tour (page 43) for details.

19. HUDSON MANSIONS TOUR

Though the lands north of New York City have been much populated since the days of Washington Irving, James Fenimore Cooper, and Thomas Paine, you can discover the past in old mansions along the Hudson which date back to the seventeenth century. Certain hazards on this tour are inevitable: watch for traffic, a rugged railroad crossing, and glass and other roadside debris. Clincher tires are strongly recommended.

Start at Philipse Manor Hall in Yonkers' Larkin Plaza, at Warburton Avenue and Dock Street, and browse through this choice old Dutch mansion. Pedal south from here on Warburton Avenue and follow the detailed directions at the end of this tour description. The roads are fairly level, wide, and well paved, with maximum 30-m.p.h. speed limits. You encounter your first steep hill on Nepperhan Avenue, then wind through more city into New Rochelle. At the fourth light in New Rochelle, go left onto North Avenue for a free visit to the Thomas Paine Cottage at the corner of North and Paine avenues, former home of the famous pamphleteer. From here you climb east up Paine Avenue and after more turns coast along Overhill Road.

On Mamaroneck Road you climb a slope past a school on your left to the James Fenimore Cooper House, on your right at the hilltop. You pedal on through Scarsdale and White Plains. About half a mile after you cross I-287, bear left at the light onto Virginia Road, where you can visit Washington's Headquarters in 1776 and 1777. Admission is free. As you proceed on Virginia Road, watch out for the rugged railroad tracks just west of Washington's Headquarters. Soon you cross the Bronx River Parkway,

DISTANCE:	39 miles.
TERRAIN:	Rolling, with a few steep grades.
TRAFFIC:	Heavy during the week; lightest on Sundays.
DIFFICULTY:	Good historic tour for anyone experienced in traffic; not for families with young riders.
BEST TIME:	Spring through autumn. Excellent Sunday ride.
LOCATION:	Loop from Yonkers, New York, on the Hudson north of the Bronx.

turn right onto State 100, and climb a steep, half-mile-long hill, the most difficult slope on this ride.

More turns lead you around Tarrytown Reservoir, past Marymount College on your left, and down a steep slope to Broadway (U.S. 9) where you go right for a .9-mile side trip into Tarrytown to Philipsburg Manor, an eighteenth-century manor house with an operating grist mill in Kingsland Point Park. Across Broadway are Old Dutch Church and Sleepy Hollow Cemetery, where Washington Irving, Andrew Carnegie, and William Rockefeller are buried. Returning south now on U.S. 9 through Tarrytown and across the New York State Thruway, you soon reach Lyndhurst, a Gothic Revival castle on the Hudson once owned by railroad tycoon Jay Gould.

Continue south on U.S. 9 and

turn right at a traffic light onto Sunnyside Lane, on which you coast to Sunnyside, Washington Irving's home and a nice picnic spot. Climb the hill back to U.S. 9 and go right to Hastings-on-Hudson. In the center of this village, U.S. 9 bears left up a hill, but you continue straight on Warburton Avenue, past the Hudson River Museum and Planetarium, located at 511 Warburton Avenue in a grandiose Hudson River chateau. Admission: Free on weekdays, 50¢ on weekends. Past the museum, you pedal south to Philipse Manor, your tour's end.

Directions

From Philipse Manor Hall in Yonkers' Larkin Plaza, at Warburton Avenue and Dock Street:

1. South on Warburton for one block;
2. left on Hudson Street for one block;
3. left on Broadway for one block, past a park on your left;
4. right on New Main Street;
5. follow the one-way street pattern to Nepperhan Avenue;
6. left uphill on Nepperhan;
7. right on Yonkers Avenue through Yonkers;
8. at Bronx River Parkway, enter Mount Vernon on Mount Vernon Avenue;
9. left at the third light onto Lincoln Avenue;
10. left at the fourth light in New Rochelle onto North Avenue;
11. east from Thomas Paine Cottage uphill on Paine Avenue;
12. left at the dead end onto Lyncroft Road;
13. right onto Croft Road;
14. right and downhill onto Overhill Road;

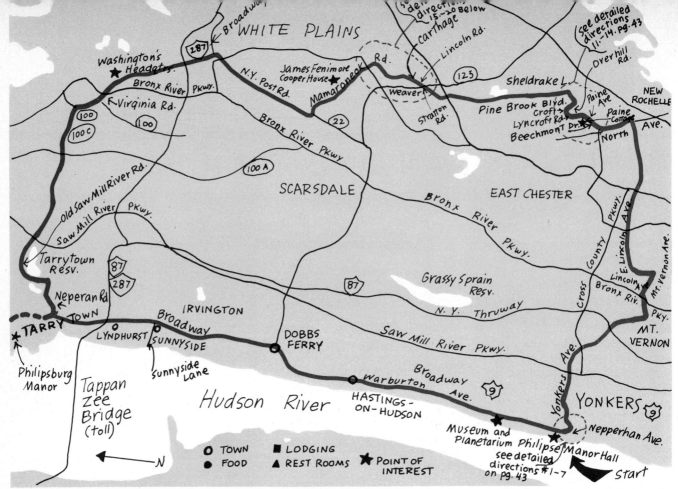

Philpse Manor is in Yonkers, just north of New York City, off Broadway (U.S. 9) at Warburton Avenue and Dock Street; from Manhattan take Broadway to Yonkers.

15. left on Pine Brook Boulevard;
16. right at the stop sign across from the firehouse onto Stratton Road;
17. cross State 125;
18. left at a dead end onto Rural Road, which becomes Lincoln Road;
19. right on Carthage Road;
20. left at a T onto Mamaroneck Road to James Fenimore Cooper House;
21. north from Cooper House on Mamaroneck Road;
22. right at dead end onto Post Road (State 22) north through Scarsdale and White Plains;
23. cross I-287, then .6 mile farther bear left at the light onto Virginia Road, past Washington's Headquarters;
24. proceed northwest on Virginia Road (watch for rugged railroad tracks just beyond Washington's Headquarters);
25. cross Bronx River Parkway;
26. right onto State 100, where you climb a steep hill;
27. straight on 100C;

28. right at the T at the bottom of a hill onto Old Saw Mill River Road (100C, which you leave, goes left here);
29. past Saw Mill River Parkway, the road name changes to Neperan Road;
30. right on Broadway (U.S. 9) for .9-mile side trip into Tarrytown to Philipsburg Manor in Kingsland Point Park;
31. return south on Broadway (U.S. 9) past Lyndhurst;
32. right at the light for side trip onto Sunnyside Lane and downhill to Sunnyside, Washington Irving's home;
33. return to U.S. 9 and go right to Hastings-on-Hudson;
34. straight in Hastings-on-Hudson onto Warburton Avenue (U.S. 9, which you leave, bears left up a hill);
35. past Hudson River Museum and Planetarium to Philipse Manor, tour's end.

WHERE TO STAY

Motels are available throughout this ride, including inns at Yonkers, White Plains, and Tarrytown. No convenient camping facilities are located along the route.

FOR FURTHER INFORMATION

William N. Hoffman, New York area director of the League of American Wheelmen, told us about this ride and will be glad to try to answer any questions you have. Write Bill at 220 Pelham Road, New Rochelle, New York 10805.

NEARBY

South, of course, is fabulous New York City, with attractions unlimited if you can tolerate lots of traffic. Continuing north, you can explore more of the historic Hudson River Valley, including the Bear Mountain area, while northwest lie the steep-hilled Catskills of Rip van Winkle legend. See pages 33 and 39 for further details cycling these spots.

20. SUNDAY IN NEW YORK

DISTANCE:	19 miles.
TERRAIN:	City streets. Mostly flat, with a few hills in Central Park.
TRAFFIC:	Heavy city traffic. Avoid rush hours.
DIFFICULTY:	Requires some experience to handle city traffic.
BEST TIME:	Spring or autumn for the most pleasant temperatures. A good Sunday ride any time.
LOCATION:	Manhattan, New York City.

Tour Manhattan by bike. You can stop at all the great museums, breeze through shady Central Park, and pause where you please without having to locate a parking spot. Though the traffic may at first seem imposing, most New York cyclists wouldn't exchange their city streets for all the little country roads in America. Try this ride on Manhattan's bikeways and find out why.

Bike shops are numerous, so you can ride with nothing to carry. Cycling in city traffic requires special skills; see the helpful tips on city riding included in the Introduction. Lock your bike whenever you leave it and watch ahead for rough spots or holes in the street. Clincher tires are recommended.

You can start this tour from any point on the map. We have arbitrarily chosen to begin uptown, at 120th Street and Riverside Drive,

near Columbia University and Grant's Tomb. Pedal south on Riverside Drive through Riverside Park on the Hudson River. As the park ends, exit left onto West 72nd Street and pedal toward Central Park. Then follow the one-way roads to the right into the park.

Though Central Park is wooded and grassy, with a reservoir, ponds, and a lake, you will never feel as if you were alone in the country. The park is filled with people—ice cream and pretzel vendors, children, strolling minstrels, artists, old people, and young couples. Pedal slowly or walk for a while to enjoy the sights and happenings here.

Proceed south and then north on the loop road to East 72nd Street, where you go right to leave the park. Turn left on Park Avenue, then left on Central Park North (110th Street), and left again on Fifth Avenue, which skirts Central Park. Soon you pass the Conservatory Gardens at 106th Street, the Museum of the City of New York between 104th and 103rd Streets, and the Guggenheim Museum between 88th and 89th Streets.

Lock your bike to the rack in front of the Metropolitan Museum of Art at 82nd Street. The museum is open Wednesday through Saturday, 10 A.M. to 5 P.M.; Tuesday, 10 A.M. to 9 P.M.; and Sundays and holidays, 11 A.M. to 5 P.M. A donation is required. The museum has a snack bar and restaurant.

Pedaling south, you pass the Frick Collection at 70th Street and the Central Park Zoo at 64th Street (open daily, 11 A.M. to 5 P.M.; free admission). At East 60th Street turn right into Central Park and proceed north on the one-way park loop. You ride beneath shady trees and past ponds, and can pause anywhere to rest on a grassy hillside.

Soon you pass Harlem Meer and

wind south. Beyond the reservoir, you can take a side trip to the Hayden Planetarium (admission, $1.75) by turning right onto 81st Street. Two blocks south is the American Museum of Natural History (donation required). The latter has a bike rack.

Re-enter Central Park at 77th Street, spin by the lake, and go right on West 72nd Street's bikeway back to Riverside Park. Follow Riverside Drive north (right) to the tour's end.

WHERE TO STAY

Hotels are located throughout the city. To be certain of getting into the hotel you choose, try to reserve a room ten days to two weeks in advance and ask for a confirmation.

FOR SPARE PARTS, REPAIRS, RENTALS

The city has numerous bike shops, with several located just minutes from the above tour. Their

opening and closing hours vary, so phone ahead to make sure the shop is open or has the part you need. Here is a partial listing of the bike stores near this ride. Bicycles in the Park, Inc., 72nd Street Boathouse in Central Park; 861-6800. Has rentals, but does no repairs. Lincoln Square Bicycles, 29 Columbus Avenue between 60th and 61st Streets; 757-5521. Sally's Cycle Toy Company, 1291 Madison Avenue at 92nd Street; 289-1083. Has rentals and does repairs. West Side Bicycle Discount House, 96th Street and Broadway; 663-7531. Has rentals and does repairs. Park Cycle Bicycle Shop, 457 Columbus Avenue at 82nd Street; 874-4890.

FOR FURTHER INFORMATION

Write the Parks Council, 80 Central Park West, New York, New York 10023.

NEARBY

New York City, of course, offers days of exploring. In addition, several delightful tours along the Hudson River lie just north of the city. You can take the Bear Mountain Meander on page 33 or the Catskills Runaway on page 39, leaving directly from Columbus Circle.

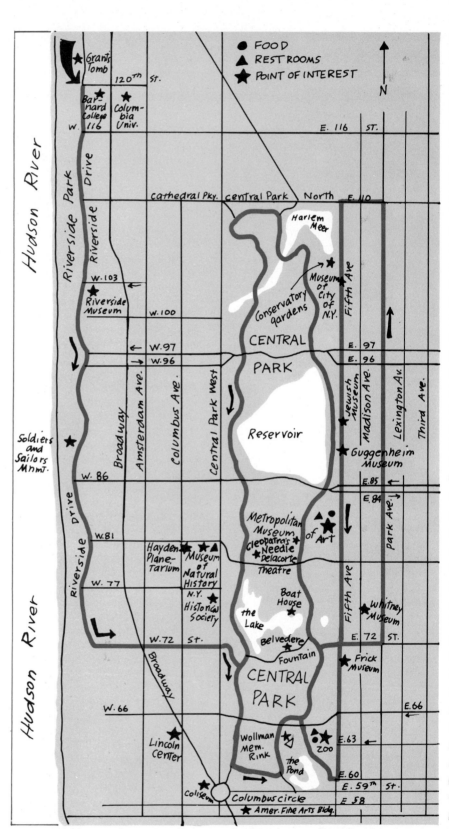

Start at 120th Street and Riverside Drive in New York City.

21. OYSTER BAY RUN

Revolutionary War history, Teddy Roosevelt's home, oyster bars, cider mills, a bird sanctuary, and vivid rhododendron and azalea gardens are found along this delightfully varied tour on Long Island. Try this ride in early spring or in autumn when brilliant foliage swirls about you and leaves crackle beneath your tires.

Start at the Great Eastern parking lot on State 106 and pedal beneath the bridge south on Jericho Oyster Bay Road (106). You will pass a cider mill on your right (open in the fall for cider and honey). Turn left off this heavily trafficked, wide-shouldered highway onto Brookville Road. This narrow, untraveled lane leads you past Christie South County Park, part of an old estate. Then watch for heavy traffic as you cross North Hempstead Turnpike (25A) to Wolver Hollow Road.

Beyond Upper Brookville you go right onto Chicken Valley Road (County 18) and start uphill. Here you can take a side trip right onto Planting Fields Road to visit Planting Fields Arboretum, where you can browse through an amazon greenhouse with orchids and stroll through fragrant azalea and rhododendron gardens. The road to the arboretum is one and a half miles uphill, and you have a thrilling coast back to County 18.

Continuing on County 18, go right on Beaverbrook Road, left at the fork, then right onto Frost Mill Road. Past a little pond, you can go straight for a side trip to Mill Neck Preserve and Bird Sanctuary, where you watch for birds as you walk along wooded paths and over wooden bridges. In autumn continue beneath the railroad bridge to follow the "apple" signs to Mill Neck Manor, which holds a September apple festival offering honey, cheese, cider, and Rome, Cortland, and McIntosh apples.

After the side trip, return to the intersection with one pond (not with two ponds) and go left to a stop sign, then go left again onto Glen Cove Mill Hill Road. You climb a steep hill, then coast past a duck pond to Oyster Bay's Main Street. At 20 West Main Street, stop to explore Raynham Hall, British headquarters during the Revolution. Hours: Monday, Wednesday, and Saturday, 10 A.M. to noon and 1 to 5 P.M.; Sunday, 1 to 5 P.M. Admission: Adults, 50¢; children under 12, free. Oyster Bay has a delicatessen and small restaurant where you can pick up lunch or a snack. Then follow the signs through town for Sagamore Hill.

At Young's Cemetery, where Theodore Roosevelt is buried, you can take a side trip left onto Cove Neck Road, then right onto Sagamore Hill Road and climb a short, steep slope to Theodore Roosevelt's summer White House and home until his death in 1919. Here you see Roosevelt's treasures: rugs given to him by the Turkish sultan, elephant tusks from Ethiopia's emperor, and the pistol he held when charging up San Juan Hill.

Continuing back on Oyster Bay Road, go left onto Moores Hill Road. You climb steeply here, then coast to Route 25A, where you turn left and continue downhill. Near the hill's bottom, you pass New York State Fish Hatchery (tours offered daily), with Cold Spring Harbor to your left.

For a side trip to an old whaling museum, bear left at the traffic light, following the signs for 25A, and follow along the harbor through a small fishing village and past clam and oyster bars. Soon on your left is the old Whaling Museum, open May through October, with old sea relics.

Return to the 25A-108 intersection and continue straight. Go right on Woodbury Road and right again at the fork onto Syosset-Woodbury Road, where you climb a steep hill. Then follow the signs toward Syosset and watch out for the railroad tracks just before town. Before the light in Syosset (not at the light), bear right across Jackson Avenue and go straight. Then turn left onto Jericho Oyster Bay Road (State 106). Watch for heavy traffic as 106 merges with 107. Then go beneath the bridge and turn left into the Great Eastern parking lot, the end of your ride.

WHERE TO STAY

You find no overnight facilities along this ride, but nearby motels include Hicksville Motor Lodge,

DISTANCE:	30 miles.
TERRAIN:	Flat, with a few hills.
TRAFFIC:	Moderate to light.
DIFFICULTY:	Some experience needed because of several trafficked spots.
BEST TIME:	Spring through autumn; exceptionally good when foliage turns, usually the first two weeks in October.
LOCATION:	Long Island, New York, starting from Jericho, north of the Long Island Expressway on Jericho Turnpike.

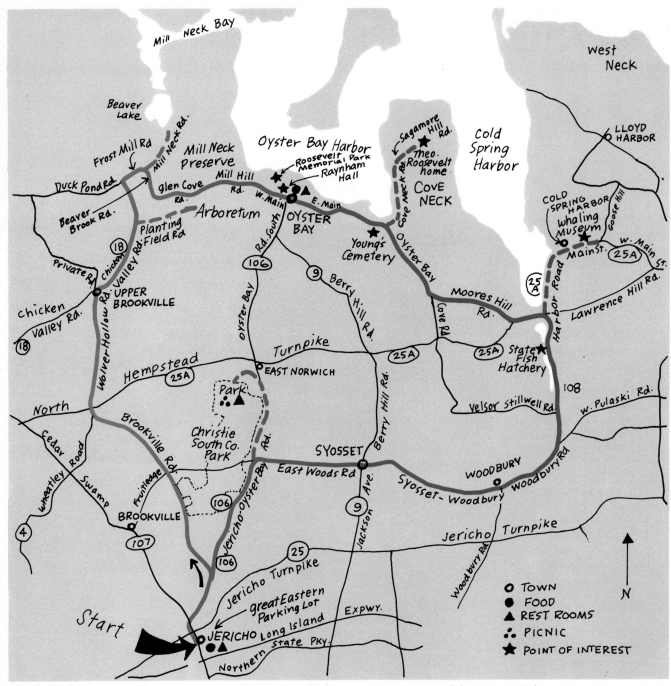

Jericho is on western Long Island at exit 41 on I-495 (Long Island Expressway); 26 miles east of the Queens Midtown Tunnel (west end) via I-495; 24 miles east of Queensboro Bridge (west end) via New York 25.

Old Country Road and Duffy Avenue, Hicksville; Holiday Inn, Sunnyside Boulevard at Fairchild Avenue, Long Island Expressway exit 46 if you go by car; and Howard Johnson's, 270 West Jericho Turnpike, a quarter of a mile west of 110, Huntington Station.

FOR SPARE PARTS, REPAIRS, FURTHER INFORMATION

Brands Cycle Center, 1966 Wantagh Avenue, Wantagh, Long Island, New York; (516) 781-6100. This shop is the nearest to the tour,

so you will want to be certain your bike is in top shape before you start. For further information on this ride, ask Ricky Krahn at the Cycle Center or write cyclist Christine Morris, 83 Duffy Avenue, Hicksville, New York.

Mid-Atlantic States

22. PENNSYLVANIA DUTCH TOUR

Pennsylvania-Dutch country is golden harvests, warm, freshly baked bread, an old wagon bumping down a quiet lane, a farmer pushing a horse-drawn plow in his field. Most of all, Pennsylvania-Dutch country is people—the warm, hearty Mennonites, the shy, gentle Amish. On this back-roads ride through Lancaster County, you bypass the more commercial routes (most lanes on this tour are not even shown on the official Pennsylvania-Dutch map) as you pedal over pastoral hills, past gray stone fences and lovely water-wheels. At the end of your day, try dinner in a Pennsylvania-Dutch farm home.

Park your car in the Terre Hill Restaurant lot (please ask permission first) on Main Street. Make two left turns—from the lot and at the Terre Hill Hotel—and coast gradually on a narrow country lane where you may not see a car for miles. Occasionally a black or gray buggy or rattly wagon passes you. Sometimes the people wave, nod, or smile.

In Martindale turn left at the general store onto Grist Mill Road. Several sharp curves present wide views of the farmland. In spring the aroma of wet black loam seasons the air as mule-drawn plows clang in the fields. Past Conestoga Road, turn left at the white church onto Shirk Road. Just over Route 23, watch out for the rugged railroad tracks—they can flip you. Then bear right to stay on Shirk Road and turn left at the barn and silo onto Zeltenreich Road. Noticeably absent throughout the tour are overhead wires and telephone poles. Here in the brook on your left, a small water wheel supplies power for the house.

To visit a Swiss cheese factory, go immediately right at the brook onto Centerville Road. Back on Zel-tenreich, watch for loose gravel. Go left onto Musser School Road, pass Groffdale Road on your left, and take the second Groffdale Road on your right. In about a minute, a left on Eby Road leads you up a short, easy rise to the white pillars of Stoltzfus Farm, which sells creamy homemade ice cream and beautifully executed hand-made quilts.

Just past the Amish Cemetery, turn left onto Stumptown Road, where you can tour the eighteenth-century Mascot Roller Grist Mill and buy a bag of freshly ground flour. Now you have several turns: left on Newport Road, right on Route 772, right at the fork to stay on Route 772, right at Scenic and North Newport roads, and left at another fork. Beyond Pond Road pause at Ebersole's Chair Shop to watch chairs being made.

Passing many antique shops, you arrive at Intercourse, where you can stop for a snack at the Kitchen Kettle or browse through small craft shops. Pedal east on Route 340 (Old Philadelphia Pike), a macadam road where you may encounter heavy traffic for a quarter of a mile until you turn left at Travelers Rest Motel onto Ridge Road.

A gradual glide leads you to Hex Barn's restaurant, with an old buggy museum upstairs. Then go left on Hollander Road, over easy rolling hills past green-gold corn and alfalfa fields. When you reach a Y, stay on Hollander Road by bearing left and pedal across railroad tracks into New Holland where hitching posts are still used instead of parking meters. Go right onto West Main Street (Route 23), left at the traffic light onto Custer, right in 3 blocks onto Conestoga, left on North Railroad, and right in 2 miles onto Linden Grove Road. This rolling lane leads you into Martindale. Buy a cool soda at the country store. Then follow Lancaster up the long, gradual slope back to Terre Hill.

End your day with dinner in a Mennonite farm home. Bartram M. Leaman and Phares Hurst both welcome guests at no charge. You are served great platters of meat, home-grown vegetables, home-made butter and apple butter on warm bread, applesauce, banana cream pudding, and shoofly pie. Bartram Leaman can accommodate up to one hundred persons at a time and often is booked up for months ahead. Phares Hurst follows his family-style meals with a hayride for the children and lets them milk cows and gather eggs. Though the meals are free, you will want to make a freewill offering. These meals should be paid for and cyclists in the past have found $4 per person to be about right.

SHOOFLY PIE

Shoofly pie and Pennsylvania-Dutch country are practically syn-

DISTANCE:	30.4 miles.
TRAFFIC:	Light.
DIFFICULTY:	Good ride for anyone, including beginners and families.
BEST TIME:	All seasons except winter. Especially pleasant in October at harvesttime.
LOCATION:	Lancaster County's Pennsylvania Dutch country. Start at Terre Hill, north of U.S. 322 and south of U.S. 222.

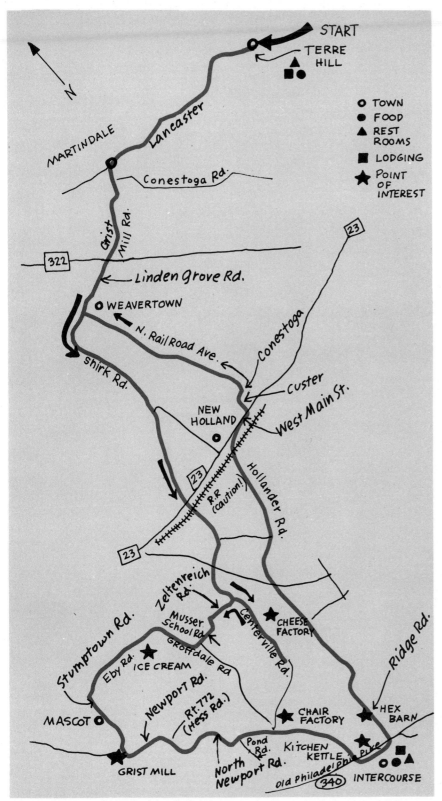

Terre Hill is in southeastern Pennsylvania south of I-76 (the Pennsylvania Turnpike) and north of U.S. 322; 50 miles west of Philadelphia city limits via U.S. 30, U.S. 322, then follow the signs on the county road; 38 miles east of Harrisburg, Pennsylvania via I-76, U.S. 222, then follow the signs on the county road.

onymous. Once you try this treat in a Mennonite farmhome, you may want to duplicate the recipe at home.

Shoofly pie, by the way, is really a molasses-flavored cake baked in a pastry shell. This dessert has a variety of types, varying from wet to dry. The following moist type is often called Wet Bottom Shoofly.

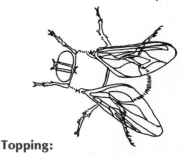

Topping:

¾ cup flour
½ cup brown sugar
2 tablespoons shortening
½ teaspoon salt
½ teaspoon cinnamon
⅛ teaspoon ground ginger
⅛ teaspoon ground nutmeg
⅛ teaspoon ground cloves

Filling:

¾ cup boiling water
½ cup molasses
1 egg yolk, well beaten
½ tablespoon baking soda

Dissolve the baking soda in the boiling water, then add the molasses and the beaten egg yolk. Set aside. Now combine all the dry ingredients with the shortening. Use your hands to work this mixture into crumbs. Line a nine-inch pan with regular pie pastry, pour in the filling, and sprinkle the crumbs on top. Bake at 400 degrees for 10 minutes, until the crust begins to brown. Then turn the oven to 325 degrees and bake until firm.

How to Reach the Farm Homes from the Terre Hill Restaurant

The Leaman Farm: From the parking lot, turn left on Main Street, right on Center Avenue, and right at Linden Street. Then in about 200 feet, go left to the Leaman Farm, the white house on

Ewing Galloway

your right. To reserve space, phone (717) 445-6162.

The Hurst Farm: From the parking lot, turn right on Main Street, left on Route 625N, and go into Bowmansville. In Bowmansville, turn right at the American Youth Hostel. Soon you cross over the Pennsylvania Turnpike. The Hurst Farm is the first farm on your left after crossing the turnpike. To reserve space, phone (717) 445-6186.

WHERE TO STAY

The Bowmansville American Youth Hostel or the hotel across the street from the hostel make convenient overnight stops. A quaint stopover about 9 miles from Terre Hill is the old stone Washington Motor Inn in Churchtown. From here you can look out your window onto rolling rural countryside. To reach Church town from Terre Hill, take 897 south, then 23

east.

FOR FURTHER INFORMATION

You find no bike shops in this rural area, but for further information, write T. Robert Mayer, 545 Woodlynn Terrace, Baltimore, Maryland 21221. Once a year Bob plans a group Pennsylvania-Dutch ride along this route for several hundred cyclists.

23. GETTYSBURG BATTLEFIELD TOUR

Gettysburg is truly best seen by cycling. The 35-mile loop is too far to walk unless you are a sturdy hiker, while traffic often keeps motorists from stopping at all the spots they would like to see. You could take a guided auto tour for $7 or a group bus tour for $15, but the least expensive and most rewarding way to experience Gettysburg's historic battlefield is to take a bike tour. The hills are gently rolling, the distance can be easily handled in a day, and you can stop anywhere to explore. Many cyclists like to combine this tour with the Pennsylvania Apple Blossom Tour on page 55 for a delightful biking weekend.

Start at the Visitor Center and pick up a self-guiding brochure. Roads are excellently marked, so you can't get lost. From the Visitor Center, you coast gradually past High Water Mark, where General Pickett's charge was halted on July 3, 1863, the battle's climax, and on past Pennsylvania Memorial, commemorating 35,000 Pennsylvania soldiers. You pedal easily for a few minutes, then tackle the short, steep slope up Little Round Top, covered in spring with magenta redbud and dogwood.

Soon the main road coasts right, toward Devils Den, but for a pleasant side trip go straight on South Confederate Avenue for about an eighth of a mile to Round Top parking area. Lock your bike, and hike up Round Top hill. From the hilltop you see sweeping views of the battlefield and the entire valley, and in autumn you have superb views of the foliage. A wooded picnic area lies about one mile farther west on the same road.

Back on the main battlefield road, a gradual climb begins near Devils Den and continues past the wheat field and the peach orchard to Longstreet Tower, where the main tour leads right at the intersection. For a rewarding stop, lock your bike and climb the seventy-five-foot tower, from which you survey the park and the neat, clipped Eisenhower farm. Straight ahead at this intersection, Gettysburg Battlefield Park joins with Dwight Eisenhower's Gettysburg farm, now a national historic site but not yet open to the public.

You climb between the Virginia and North Carolina memorials, then coast easily past McMillan Woods, where youth cycling groups can reserve camping sites. Turn left on Route 116 and go a quarter of a mile. Then after turning right onto Reynolds Avenue, you climb easily all the way to Eternal Light Peace Memorial. Plunge on past Oak Ridge and continue the ride on Mummasburg Road to Howard Avenue. Go left on Howard, cross Route 34, and climb easily to Barlow's Knoll. Soon the tour route intersects Business Route 15, where a right turn leads you into Gettysburg. Pause here for a rest stop and a snack.

To continue on the main tour, turn left onto Stratton Street just after U.S. 15 curves right. On East Middle Street make a left turn, pedal one block and turn right on East Confederate Avenue. The road stays level past Culp's Hill and Spangler's Spring. Then you climb about a mile up Cemetery Hill to Gettysburg National Cemetery, where Lincoln delivered his immortal 296-word Gettysburg Address.

Spend the rest of the day browsing through touristy Gettysburg. Country stores and craft, candle, and candy shops line the streets and eleven museums depict and study every detail of the battle. Civil War relics, dioramas of the battle, a Lincoln museum, and General Lee's headquarters are just a few of the attractions here. For a complete listing, write the Gettysburg Travel Council, Inc., 35 Carlisle Street, Gettysburg, Pennsylvania 17325, or stop at the Visitor Information Center when you reach Gettysburg.

WHERE TO STAY

Motels in Gettysburg are numerous, and reservations are a must between Memorial Day and Labor Day. Here is a partial list: Gettysburg Travelodge, 10 East Lincoln Avenue; (717) 334-6235. Peace Light Inn, 1 mile west of town on Route 30, then half a mile north on Reynolds Avenue; (717) 334-1416. Three Crowns, 205 Steinwehr Avenue; (717) 334-3168. Holiday Inn, 516 Baltimore Street; (717) 334-6211. Howard Johnson's, 301 Steinwehr Avenue; (717) 334-1189.

DISTANCE:	35 miles.
TERRAIN:	Easy rolling hills.
TRAFFIC:	Heavy during the summer; lightest on spring and autumn weekdays.
DIFFICULTY:	Easily managed by anyone with a 10-speed bike.
BEST TIME:	Spring, when wildflowers and trees bloom, or autumn, with cool, brisk days.
LOCATION:	Gettysburg National Military Park, Pennsylvania.

There are many campgrounds in the area, including the following. Drummer Boy Camping, 2 miles east of town on State 116. Open April 6th to October 21st; $4 for four. For reservations, write Drummer Boy Camping, Route 5, Box 544, Gettysburg, Pennsylvania 17325, or phone (717) 334-3277. Gettysburg KOA Kampgrounds, 3 miles west of Gettysburg on U.S. 30, then follow the signs toward Knoxlyn south for 2 miles. Open March 30th to October 1st; $3 for a family of eight. For reservations, write Gettysburg KOA Kampgrounds, Route 3, Gettysburg, Pennsylvania 17325, or phone (717) 642-5713.

FOR FURTHER INFORMATION

Write Superintendent, Gettysburg National Military Park, Box 70, Gettysburg, Pennsylvania 17325.

NEARBY

Just 8 miles north of Gettysburg lies apple country, where you can pedal on lightly traveled back roads through peaceful countryside, and in spring through hills carpeted with apple blossoms. See the Pennsylvania Apple Blossom Tour which follows for details on one popular route.

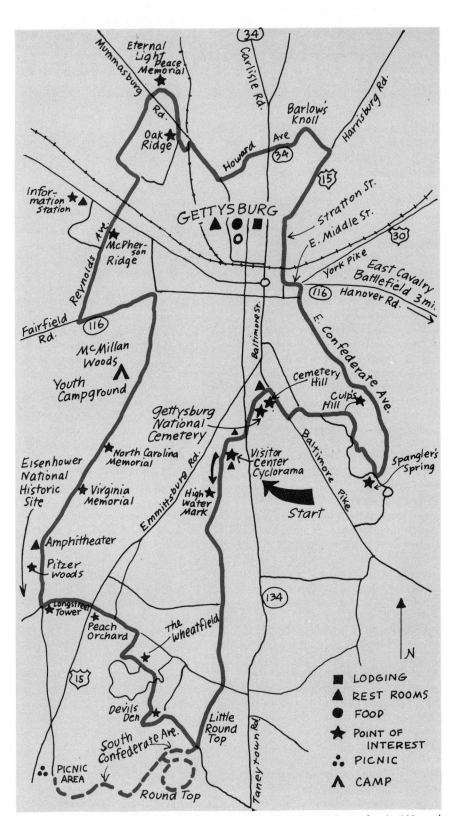

Gettysburg is in south-central Pennsylvania on U.S. 30, U.S. 140, Pennsylvania 116, and Pennsylvania 34; 40 miles south of Harrisburg, Pennsylvania, via U.S. 15 and 30; 43 miles northwest of Baltimore, Maryland, via U.S. 140

24. PENNSYLVANIA APPLE BLOSSOM TOUR

After long winter months, celebrate spring with a joyous ride through hills of cream-colored apple blossoms and pink cherry blossoms. In May these knolls come alive as millions of flowers mingle in the spring-warmed earth. Spend a day cycling, picnicking, and loitering along a quiet lake during this springtime festival.

Park your car at South Mountain Fair Grounds near Arendtsville, turn left out of the lot, and ride to the signs reading "Fruit Growers" and "Brysonia—2 miles," where you go left onto East County 01001. At a red barn and the sign "Camp Newaka," bear right at the Y. Watch for loose gravel as you turn left onto P & Q Road. Then beyond a left-curve sign, bear right at another Y.

You ride now over big rolling hills through apple and cherry country. In spring from every hilltop you view oceans of cottony, fragrant blossoms, while in late summer the green trees are laden with sleek red fruit. As you pass Bear Mountain Road, the shoulder disappears: watch for loose gravel.

In tiny Bendersville you can buy a snack. Prices in these small towns delight city cyclists: $1 buys ham, eggs, toast, and coffee. At Bendersville intersection, bear right at the Y and follow the sign reading "Aspers—2 miles." In Aspers turn left at Hollands General Store. Outside town you roll over moderate hills with a small stream trickling along your left. Stop anytime to relax along the banks and dip your fingers or toes in ice water just thawed by spring.

You climb and coast through orchards and woods to Goodyear, where you go left at Mount Zion Lutheran Church onto Route 34N. There's no shoulder here, but traffic is light. In another half mile, go left onto the road paralleling Route 34 and take care on the rugged railroad tracks. At the dead-end intersection, turn left and pedal to Mount Creek Country Store, a good spot to gather picnic basics. One mile farther lies Pine Grove State Park, where you can rest beneath a budding tree beside clear blue Laurel Lake.

Beyond the park, you turn left on Route 233 and tackle a long hill. You pedal up, level off, then climb; experienced cyclists will breeze over this hill, but beginners will feel the strain. Exactly 8 miles up the hill, turn left onto County

01041 at the sign "Big Flat, Shippensburg, Laurel Lake." This is a hard-to-see turn, so watch carefully.

Now you have an exhilarating downhill coast, the wind nudging your back, the apple and cherry valleys below. Be careful not to lose control. Turn right at the sign "Arendtsville—5 miles" and left at the sign "Biglerville—6 miles." This last turn puts you on County LR 342B and State 234, where you soon reach Hemlock Inn, a picturesque country inn beside a stream. Have a snack, then continue on State 234 to the fairgrounds and your tour's end.

WHERE TO STAY

Campgrounds are located near Mount Creek Country Store, which you pass about 18 miles from the start of your ride.

FOR FURTHER INFORMATION

T. Robert Mayer, Maryland area director of the League of American Wheelmen, planned this tour and even conducts group rides the first Saturday in May. He welcomes inquiries, and you can write him at 545 Woodlynn Terrace, Baltimore, Maryland 21221 or phone (301) 687-3210.

WILD APPLES IN APPLE COUNTRY

In May apple blossoms in apple country burst into bloom everywhere. Two less obvious "apples" grow here, too, but only while hiking or biking can a traveler spot these species.

May apples stand about one or two feet high and sometimes cover

DISTANCE:	34 miles.
TERRAIN:	Rolling hills, with one steep grade.
TRAFFIC:	Light.
DIFFICULTY:	Some experience preferable, but okay for strong beginners.
BEST TIME:	May, when orchards bloom. Avoid the first Sunday in May when tourist hordes attend the Apple Blossom Festival. The first Saturday in May is idyllic. Also delightful in summer and autumn.
LOCATION:	Adams County, Pennsylvania. Start at South Mountain Fair Grounds in Arendtsville, 8 miles north of Gettysburg.

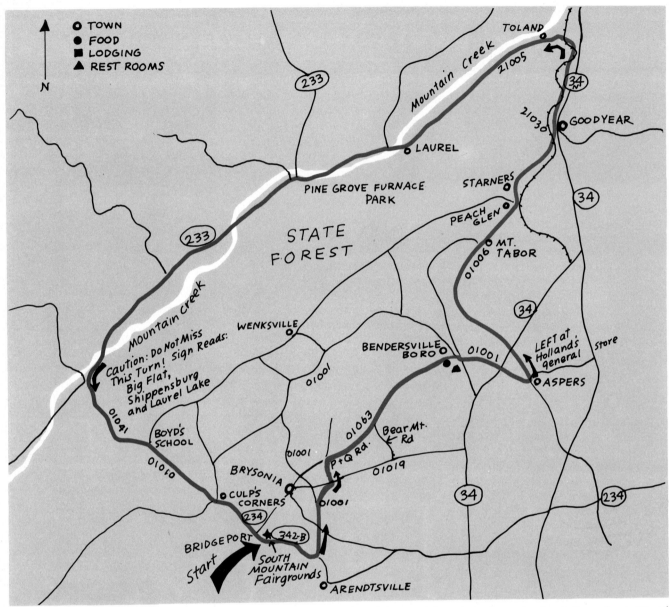

Legend:
- ○ TOWN
- ● FOOD
- ■ LODGING
- ▲ REST ROOMS

N

TOLAND

Mountain Creek

21005

34 N

21030

GOODYEAR

LAUREL

34

PINE GROVE FURNACE PARK

STARNERS

PEACH GLEN

STATE FOREST

MT. TABOR
01006

34

WENKSVILLE

BENDERSVILLE BORO

01001

LEFT at Hollands general Store

Mountain Creek

Caution: Do Not Miss This Turn! Sign Reads: Big Flat, Shippensburg and Laurel Lake

01041

01001

01001

ASPERS

BOYD'S SCHOOL

01063

Bear Mt. Rd

01010

BRYSONIA

P+Q Rd.

01019

34

234

CULP'S CORNERS

01001

234

342-B

BRIDGEPORT

Start

SOUTH MOUNTAIN Fairgrounds

ARENDTSVILLE

233

Arendtsville is in south-central Pennsylvania on Routes 234 and 394; 8 miles northwest of Gettysburg, Pennsylvania, via Pennsylvania 34 and Route 394; 52 miles northwest of Baltimore, Maryland, via U.S. 10, Pennsylvania 34, and Route 394; 40 miles south of Harrisburg via U.S. 15 and Route 394.

vast forest floors with their large, umbrella-shaped leaves. When the greenish-yellow fruit ripens in late summer, it falls into your hand at a touch and tastes juicy and sweet. You can use may apples to create an excellent amber jelly or add the juice to punches, apple juice, or lemonade, lending these a woodsy flavor. The may apple actually belongs not to the apple but to the barberry family.

Pawpaws, members of the

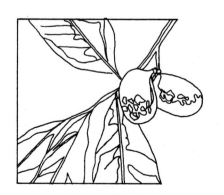

custard apple family, grow on small trees along creek banks. During spring and summer you will observe purplish flowers or immature green fruits, but in autumn, especially after the first frost, the fruits ripen brown outside and creamy yellow and sweet inside. Some people consider the pawpaw's texture unpleasant, but others find it delectable. At home you can bake fresh pawpaw pie or concoct your own recipe for pawpaw jelly.

25. PHILADELPHIA'S LIBERTY TRAIL

When you visit "the cradle of liberty," the Colonial days are literally just around the corner. You pass famed Independence Hall, where the Declaration of Independence and the Constitution were signed; Carpenters' Hall, where the First Continental Congress debated taxation without representation; and numerous old homes, museums, and churches.

Start in Fairmount Park on the Schuylkill River and leave your car in the free lot near the Zoological Gardens. From the parking lot, pedal on Girard Avenue toward the river and go right on West River Drive along the Schuylkill. After you cross the river, follow the map to 22nd Street. Traffic can be heavy at this intersection as you leave Fairmount Park and it's really safer to walk your bike south on 22nd Street to Race Street. Then pedal one block east (left) on Race Street and go right on 21st Street.

However, you can take a slightly different route as you leave Fairmount Park and stay on your bike all the way. Simply go left on 22nd Street to the corner, right on Benjamin Franklin Parkway, and right in one block on 21st Street, where you rejoin the first route.

After you cross beneath John F. Kennedy Boulevard, go left on Market Street to City Hall. Lock your bike here and climb the 548-foot observation tower, which has splendid views of Philadelphia and the Delaware Valley. Leave the City Hall square, going south on Broad Street about half a block. Then turn left on Chestnut Street and ride to Independence National Historic Park.

Soon you pass Independence Square's State House Row, which includes Congress Hall (open daily, 9 A.M. to 5 P.M.; free admission), Independence Hall and the Liberty

DISTANCE:	8 miles.
TERRAIN:	City streets, mostly flat.
TRAFFIC:	Typical city traffic—a bit lighter on Sundays, but impossibly heavy during rush hours.
DIFFICULTY:	Requires experience in city traffic.
BEST TIME:	Spring or autumn for the most pleasant temperatures.
LOCATION:	Philadelphia, Pennsylvania.

Bell (open daily, July through Labor Day, 8 A.M. to 8 P.M.; the rest of the year, 9 A.M. to 5 P.M.; free admission), and Old City Hall, closed for restoration.

At Old City Hall, go left on 5th Street past the Independence Mall Visitors Center to Christ Church Burial Ground on your right, where Benjamin Franklin is buried. Next go right on Arch Street and

walk one block along tree-lined Independence Mall, where you can rest on the grass or beside a fountain.

Go right on 4th Street and left at the Philadelphia Maritime Museum onto Chestnut Street. Here you pass the Marine Corps Museum and Carpenters' Hall. Reaching the New Customs House turn right onto 2nd Street and right in one block onto Walnut Street, past the Bishop White House and Todd House. Stay on Walnut Street through the city to 22nd Street, where you turn right.

Then after you cross Vine Street, go left, back into Fairmount Park, where you can spend the rest of your day pedaling on wooded bike paths.

Instead of crossing the river the way you came, return north on East River Drive past the Philadelphia

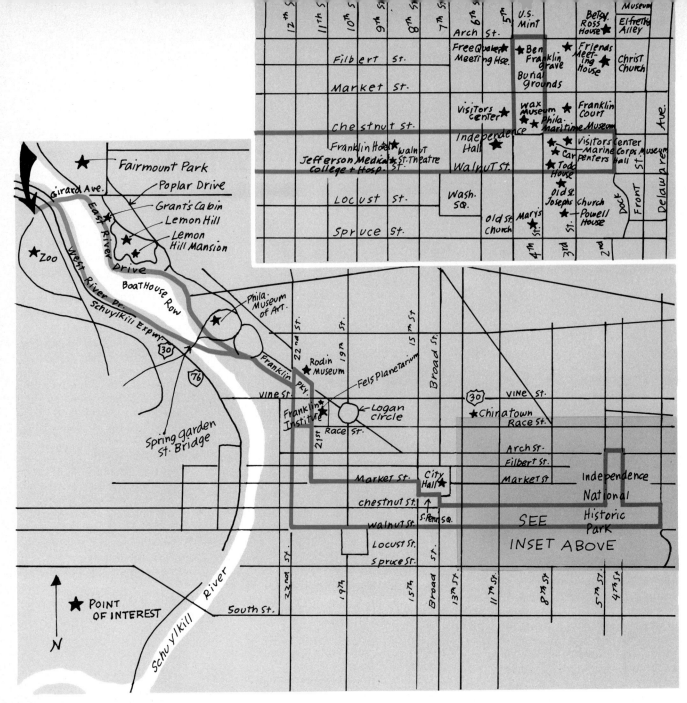

Philadelphia, Pennsylvania. Insert: Historic area.

Museum of Art and several eighteenth-century mansions. After you pedal through the underpass beneath Girard Avenue, go right up the ramp to Girard Avenue which leads you over the Schuylkill and back to the zoo.

WHERE TO STAY

Philadelphia's hotels, motels, and inns cater to every taste. Reservations are advised. Hotels on this tour include: Holiday Inn—Independence Mall, 4th and Arch Streets, Philadelphia, Pennsylvania 19105; (215) 923-8660. Holiday Inn — Midtown, 1305 Walnut Street, Philadelphia, Pennsylvania 19107; (215) PE5-9300. Latham Hotel, 17th and Walnut Streets, Philadelphia, Pennsylvania 19103; (215) LO3-7474. Benjamin Franklin Hotel, 9th and Chestnut Streets, Philadelphia, Pennsylvania 19105; (215) 922-8600.

FOR SPARE PARTS AND REPAIRS

Philadelphia has numerous bike shops. If you need spare parts or repairs, just check the phone directory or ask at one of the information centers on this tour.

FOR FURTHER INFORMATION

Write the Philadelphia Convention and Tourist Bureau, 1525 John F. Kennedy Boulevard, Philadelphia, Pennsylvania 19102; (215) 561-1200. Their brochures include a hotel and motor inn folder, a calendar of events, a restaurant guide, an historic-sites pamphlet, a pamphlet on attractions, and a map of the city.

26. CAPE MAY MEANDER

It's great to loiter in Cape May's briny air beside beaches and sail-bright harbors. That's why people crowd this seaside resort area in summer. But many local cyclists say it's even better to ride through the fertile green fields that back on the oceanfront. Though summer is the traditional season to cycle on boardwalks, Cape May's natives prefer spring, when the first warm breezes make the earth spongy beneath your wheels. Sample both country and seaside on this ride, and decide for yourself which one you like better.

Begin in Ocean City, where you may park your car on almost any side street. It's best to start at about 7 A.M., when the tourists are not out yet and you can pedal alone on the hollow-sounding boardwalk past the shop windows and wide beaches. Maneuver your wheels around sharp shells on the boardwalk, or you may have a flat.

Stuff your knapsack with clams and spin south on Route 585 into the fresh salt air. Summer morning breezes blow gently from the southeast and gain velocity during the day, whereas winter winds come from the northwest.

Four toll bridges between Ocean City and Cape May charge 10¢ each for crossing, but if you steer around the tripper, smile at the guard, you should be able to cross free. The Atlantic stretches to your left as you spin past beaches. Road shoulders are wide, well paved, and clean.

About midmorning pick a spot to stop for a snack or a swim in the surf. In summer pause to watch birds at the wildlife preserve in Stone Harbor.

Then pedal on to the seaside resort of Cape May, where you can dine at a sidewalk café or picnic on the excellent beach. Here rock hounds may find "Cape May dia-monds," chunks of pure quartz rounded by the sea.

As the tourists begin to arrive at the beaches, start north on U.S. 9. Though this is a U.S. highway, the road parallels the Garden State Parkway and is lightly traveled. Pedaling through fertile fields, you pass many small villages where you can hunt for antiques. One pleasant town is Cape May Court House, with its many elegant Colonial homes.

Back on U.S. 9, you continue on excellent road through flat terrain. From Clermont you may wish to take a side trip to Belleplain State Forest and picnic, swim, or camp overnight. To reach the forest, go left on State 83 to State 47 and turn right. You cross Dennis Creek and head toward Dennisville, where you wind north on Route 550, then go left near Belleplain to the state forest. Some of the forest roads are gravel.

Retrace your ride back to U.S. 9 and roll smoothly through meadows and fields to Route 585, which you take right to cross under the Garden State Parkway. Follow Route 585 left along Peck Beach back to Ocean City.

In the evening, try a seafood dinner. Then if you happen to be touring during late June through August, take your bike to the Music Pier, where free concerts are held under the stars.

WHERE TO STAY

Motels are located throughout this ride, with reservations recommended from mid-May through September. Some of the area's many motels are listed below:

Impala, 10th Street at Ocean Avenue, Ocean City, New Jersey 08226; (609) 399-7500. Pavilion, Beach Block at 8th Street, Ocean City, New Jersey 08226; (609) 399-8812. Port-O-Call, 1510 Boardwalk, Ocean City, New Jersey 08226; (609) 399-8812. Sea Spray, 34th Street at Bay Avenue, Ocean City, New Jersey 08226; (609) 399-4670. Sting Ray Motor Inn, 1280 Boardwalk at 13th Street, Ocean City, New Jersey 08226; (609) 399-8555. Coachman's, 205 Beach Drive, Cape May, New Jersey 08204; (609) 884-8463. Golden Eagle, Beach and Philadelphia Avenues, Cape May, New Jersey 08204; (609) 884-8831. Montreal, Beach and Madison Avenues, Cape May, New Jersey 08204; (609) 465-7583. Hy-Land, Hereford Avenue (Box 97), Cape May Courthouse, New Jersey 08210; (609) 465-7305.

Cape May also has a guesthouse, run by avid cyclist Tom Carroll, which caters to cyclists. Tom plans

DISTANCE:	64 miles.
TERRAIN:	Flat.
TRAFFIC:	Heavy along the ocean in summer; light everywhere in spring and autumn.
DIFFICULTY:	Easily handled by anyone during off-season, but beginners should stay away from Ocean Drive Highway in summer.
BEST TIME:	Spring through autumn. The Climate is actually mild year round, but there are high winds in March.
LOCATION:	Beaches and back roads Cape May County, New Jersey.

cycling weekends for his guests during spring and autumn, when traffic is light. He can accommodate sixteen to twenty-five cyclists, and up to thirty-seven cyclists by using a neighboring guesthouse. For information and rates, write Tom at the Mainstay, 24 Jackson Street, Cape May, New Jersey 08204, or phone (609) 884-8690.

Campgrounds include the following: Belleplain State Forest, discussed above; open year round; $2.50. Big Oak Campground, two and a half miles west of Cape May Court House on Hand Avenue; open April 15th to October 15th; $4 for four. For reservations, write Big Oak Campground, Box 123, Cape May Court House, New Jersey 08210, or phone (609) 465-5460.

FOR SPARE PARTS AND REPAIRS

Annarelli's Bike Shop, 1014 Asbury Avenue, Ocean City, New Jersey; (609) 399-2238. This shop handles parts and repairs for 10-speed bikes. It is open Monday through Saturday from 9 A.M. to 5 P.M. Another shop is Hale Bicycle Company, Main and Mechanic Streets, Cape May Courthouse, New Jersey; (609) 465-3126.

FOR FURTHER INFORMATION

Tom Carroll told us about this ride and will be glad to answer any questions you may have. You can write him at 24 Jackson Street, Cape May, New Jersey 08204.

NEARBY

Cape May County's many back roads with wide, well-paved shoulders provide superb cycling. If you plan to spend several days here, write the County Office of Public Information, Cape May Court House, New Jersey 08210, for a free Cape May County map of self-conducted bicycle tours.

CAPE MAY SEASHELLS

As you stroll along Cape May's wide beaches, you will see dozens of seashells. Here is a guide to a few

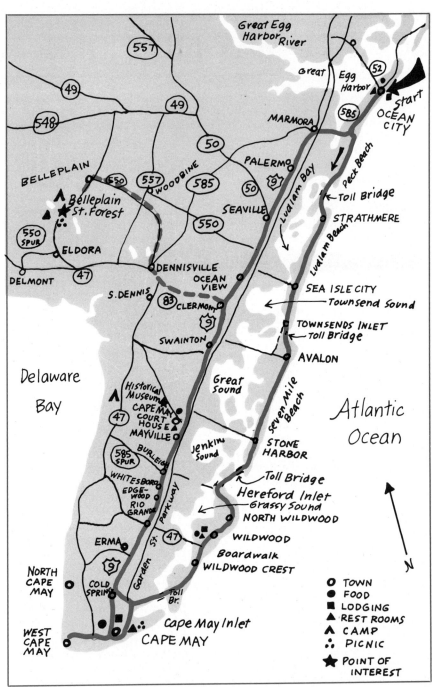

Ocean City is in the southern tip of New Jersey at Routes 52 and 585; 10 miles south of Atlantic City, New Jersey, via Route 585.

of the varieties you might notice.

Turkey wing shells are two to three inches long, brownish and have irregular white stripes. When unbroken, they are hinged like an oyster shell and resemble a bird's wings.

Angel wing shells are large, white, and also resemble wings. Be-cause the shells are so delicate, they are often broken on the beach, and you will have to look hard to find a good specimen.

Florida cerith is one to one and a half inches long, rough and spirals to a point. On some days you can collect these common shells by the handful.

27. 28. MARYLAND-DELAWARE SHORE RIDES

DISTANCE:	Colonial Villages Ride, 47.4 miles. Woodland Beach Tour, 75.3 miles.
TERRAIN:	Flat.
TRAFFIC:	Light.
DIFFICULTY:	Both rides can be managed by beginners and families, though inexperienced riders may want to take two days on the Woodland Beach Tour.
BEST TIME:	Spring through autumn.
LOCATION:	Maryland and Delaware on the Delmarva Peninsula. Both rides start at Bohemia Manor High School, 1 mile south of Chesapeake City, Maryland, off the Augustine Herman Highway (Route 213).

Quaint Colonial villages, well-kept farmlands, bay harbors, thoroughbred horse farms, and eighteenth-century churches fill the flat, serene Maryland-Delaware countryside. Here honeysuckle sweetens the breeze, corn sprouts eight feet high in summer, and the country lanes are decked with blossoming wildflowers from spring through autumn. Salt marshes, tidal rivers, and freshwater ponds filigree the fertile land, too, providing excellent shore bird watching and crabbing.

Bring spare parts, basic tools, and lots of snacks because you find only small farming communities along the route. Everywhere the roads are so smooth you feel as if you were floating; they are straight, untraveled, and flat as ironing boards. The flatness, however, can be deceptive because you must pedal constantly, without relaxing coasts. Also, if you happen to have a head wind on these flat coastal plains, you sometimes feel as if you were climbing a mountain.

Both these tours start at Bohemia Manor High School. Across the street you can eat breakfast at the Chesapeake City Restaurant or use the air pumps at the Texaco station. Pick the tour most suited to your interests or spend several days here and try them both. If you enjoy flat rural back roads, you won't be disappointed.

COLONIAL VILLAGES RIDE

Christmas-card villages dot this tour through farmlands and marshes to Augustine Beach for lunch, then back through more countryside.

You begin with a jaunt through white-steepled Chesapeake City along the Chesapeake and Delaware Canal. The canal's 1851 Pump house and Waterwheel is a national historic landmark. Through town the joints on cement Route 286 can make you bounce a bit, but after a few turns the road smooths. Quiet farmlands and trim country homes take you near the C & D Canal and the marshes. Route 417 (Dutch Neck Road) and Delaware 9, a narrow macadam, continue through swamps. In autumn what appear to be distant flocks of sheep are actually bevies of swans dining on field grain. Here you may also spot thousands of Canadian geese. Buy picnic basics at John's Delicatessen then continue to Augustine Beach, where you can lounge on sand, swim, picnic, and watch the boats in the harbor.

Afternoon takes you through more farmland to little Odessa, a quaint village resembling Colonial Williamsburg without the tourists. Pedal along the streets and note the historic signs posted before many occupied homes. Snacks are available at Odessa's Auto Stop Ice Cream Drive-In, where local cyclists often order a Bicyclist's Special, a concoction of orange drink and two heaping scoops of orange sherbet, topped with a dollop of vanilla ice cream. Across from the ice-cream stand, turn right into Corbett's Alley. Soon you ride through pretty Bohemia Mills and pass Windfield Horse Farms, which welcomes guests for stable tours. More peaceful countryside returns you to Bohemia Manor High School.

Directions

Starting at Bohemia Manor High School:

1. Head north on road paralleling Route 213;
2. go under Chesapeake City Bridge;
3. left just after the bridge onto Route 286;
4. right at the U.S. Army Corps of Engineers sign and go one city block;
5. left on Bohemia Avenue;
6. right at the post office onto 286;
7. right onto 286 at the T and another Army Corps of Engineers sign;

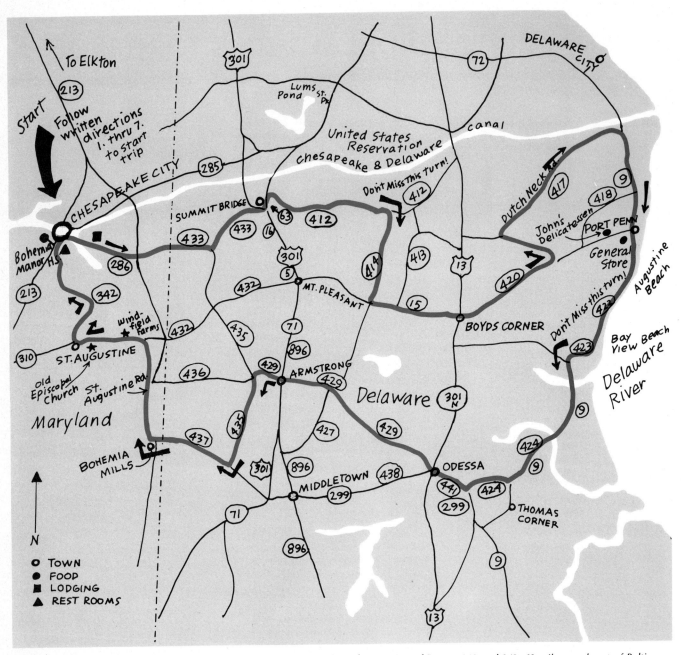

Chesapeake City is on the northwestern tip of the Delmarva Peninsula at the junction of Routes 213 and 342; 63 miles northeast of Baltimore, Maryland, via U.S. 40 and Route 213; 26 miles southwest of Wilmington, Delaware, via U.S. 40 and Route 213. This map is of the Colonial Villages Ride.

8. left beyond Delaware state line at the stop sign onto unmarked road;

9. cross Route 16 (also called State 71 and 301S) at the blinking signal light and ride on 433 through Summit;

10. left onto 63 at the stop sign (red brick house on the corner) and go two city blocks;

11. right onto Route 412 (watch out for railroad tracks and one-lane bridge);

12. right onto Route 414 for 1 mile past the tracks;

13. left on Delaware 15 (also called Maryland 310 and Mt. Pleasant Road), and ride single file here because of 50-m.p.h. speed limit;

14. walk your bike over busy 301N;

15. Delaware 15 changes to Route 420 beyond 301N;

16. sharply left onto Route 2 for 2 miles past 301N intersection;

17. right onto Dutch Neck Road (Route 417);

18. right at the bridge along canal;

19. follow Delaware 9 beyond the bridge, and ride single file on this narrow road;

20. Route 9 becomes County 2, but stay on this route to Port Penn and follow arrows for Route 9 through town;

21. right at the Ballantine Beer sign to Port Penn Market for picnic supplies;

22. straight to Augustine Beach;

23. proceed south on Route 9;

24. right at the T onto Route 423;

25. left in a few minutes at the arrow for Route 9 (County 424), and if you miss this turn, you eventually dead-end into 301N (whatever you do, don't cycle 301N—traffic is fast and heavy);

26. follow the Route 9 arrow right;

27. beyond a metal bridge, you reach a rough wooden bridge (walk your bike);

28. follow Route 424 sharply right about 3 miles beyond the wooden bridge;

29. right onto Route 441 at the stop sign, then cross the bridge into Odessa;

30. straight through Odessa to the ice-cream stand, snack stop;

31. right at the alley across the street from the ice-cream stand

32. left at the alley's end onto Mechanic Street (Route 429);

33. left onto Route 435;

34. right onto Route 437 into Bohemia Mills;

35. right at the Y onto St. Augustine Road;

36. left at the Y with an Episcopal Church sign (Windfield Farms soon on your left);

37. left onto Mt. Pleasant Road (Route 310);

38. right at the Episcopal Church onto Route 342, which leads back to Chesapeake City Bridge;

39. follow Route 213 back to Bohemia Manor High School.

MARYLAND STEAMED CRABS

Maryland has many fine shores for crabbing. Whether you catch your own (see page 217 for crabbing techniques) or buy crabs fresh at a market, here's how to prepare them once you get home.

For one dozen crabs, you need the following:

1 cup water
1 cup vinegar
2½ teaspoons seafood seasoning
3 tablespoons salt

Crabs must be steamed live. Though refrigeration is not necessary, chilling extends a crab's lifespan out of water. To prevent contamination, don't let your cooked crabs touch the baskets or containers which held uncooked crabs.

To steam, pour the water and vinegar into a large pot with a false bottom until you have about two inches of liquid. Boil the water, then pop the live crabs into the pot, sprinkling each crab layer with salt and seasoning. Steam at least a half hour and serve.

WOODLAND BEACH TOUR

A jaunt to sandy Woodland Beach, a spin through Blackbird State Forest, and a visit to the eighteenth-century mission Old Bohemia, plus more bird watching are added to the Colonial Villages Ride on this extended journey through Delmarva Peninsula.

Beyond picturesque Chesapeake City, you ride into countryside past Marydel Horse Farm's tidy green pastures and proud thoroughbreds. The gradual slopes beyond Bohemia Mills are the tour's only hills. On Sunday morning you soon hear the sound of voices filtering from the tiny church in Warwick. At this little church, you can take a side trip right, then right again at the next intersection to pedal a mile to Old Bohemia, a Jesuit mission built in 1704 and the site of the

first Roman Catholic school in the British colonies.

Back on the main tour, you ride through Blackbird State Forest, a pleasant rest spot with a secluded picnic grove. Then you spin into Smyrna, where you can lunch at Smyrna Diner or Gino's or pick up picnic basics and proceed to Woodland Beach. The road to Woodland Beach leads you through swamps with ten-foot reeds. At the beach you can picnic, lunch at the Crab Shack, or take a cool plunge in the Delaware River.

In the afternoon, heading north on Route 9 beyond Woodland Beach, you can spot ducks, cranes, and other waterfowl in the marshes. An observation tower along the route offers excellent bird watching, especially if you bring binoculars. Serene country lanes eventually lead to Odessa (see the Colonial Village Ride for the snack stop here). Going farther, you pass Windfield Farms, home of Northern Dancer, where guests are invited to tour the stables. More countryside returns you to Chesapeake City Bridge and Bohemia Manor High School.

Hazards on this tour include the rough wooden bridge beyond Bohemia Mills (walk your bike here); busy 301 intersections (walk again); Route 486, with a 50-m.p.h. speed limit just before you reach Smyrna; the rough one-lane bridge spanning Smyrna River near Fleming Landing; and numerous railroad crossings (see the directions below for precise locations).

Directions

Starting at Bohemia Manor High School, follow steps **1** through **7** of the Colonial Villages Ride, then:

8. Right in Delaware at the stop sign onto Route 435 (large brick house here);

9. right onto Route 437 past Marydel Horse Farm;

10. left in Bohemia Mills at the Y (rough wooden bridge in 1 mile— walk your bike);

11. left at the little Warwick church (right if you take side trip to Old Bohemia);

12. walk across busy U.S. 301;

13. stop if you like at the Texaco station on your left, last facilities for 14 miles;

14. right onto Route 10;

15. left in .1 mile onto Route 459;

16. straight ahead at the stop sign on Route 459 (rough railroad tracks in .7 mile);

17. left onto Route 463 (another railroad crossing);

18. right onto Route 463A;

19. right onto Route 471 (another railroad track here);

20. left past Blackbird State Forest onto Route 47;

21. right onto Route 486 (50-m.p.h. speed limit) into Smyrna;

22. stay on Main Street to Commerce Street (Route 39);

23. left on Commerce Street;

24. cross Route 13 (DuPont Highway) to Delaware 6 (turn left here for diners);

25. stay on State 6 (County 9) to Woodland Beach;

26. return to County 9 and go right;

27. right at the Y to stay on Delaware 9 (County 449);

28. right at another Y;

29. stay on Route 299 at the junction of routes 299 and 9 to Odessa.

Follow steps 31 through 39 of the Colonial Villages Ride back to Bohemia Manor High School.

FOR FURTHER INFORMATION

T. Robert Mayer contributed these rides and will be glad to answer any further questions. Write him at 545 Woodlynn Terrace, Baltimore, Maryland 21221 or phone (301) 687-3210.

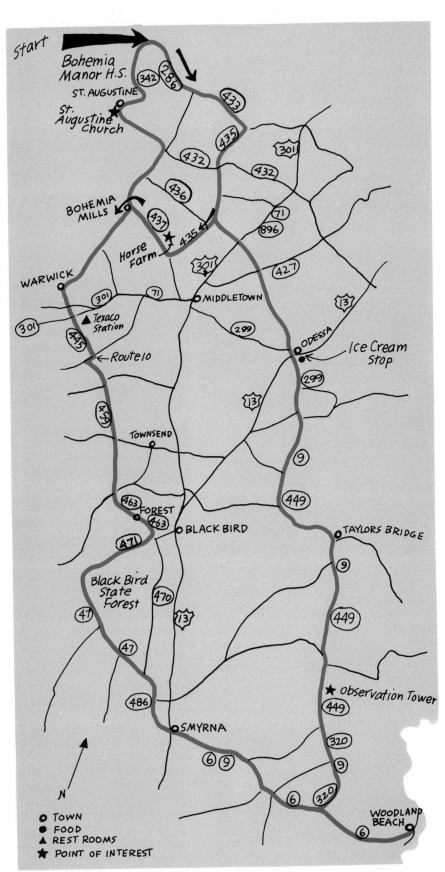

Woodland Beach Tour.

29. D.C. BIKE PATHS

Within metropolitan Washington, D.C., you can pedal along the shaded C & O Canal without a car in sight; spot vivid wildflowers and budding Japanese cherry blossoms; glimpse kingfishers, woodpeckers, and thrushes; and observe muskrats or raccoons on an island in the Potomac. The city's bike paths lead you to cultural attractions, too—Lincoln Memorial, Washington Monument, the National Gallery of Art, Arlington Cemetery, and of course the White House.

Washington, D.C.'s 47 miles of bike trails offer excellent cycling. Because many points of interest lie just a short block off the tour, the following is only a suggested route. Check the tour map and plan your own ride to explore the spots you most want to see.

A good starting point is the parking lot off the George Washington Memorial Parkway on the Potomac's southwest bank near Theodore Roosevelt Island. You can get the kinks out of your legs by pedaling over the footbridge to the island and riding its short paved loop through woods and wild foliage. Raccoons, muskrats, and other small animals dwell here, and you should see a variety of land and water birds.

As you leave the island, go right from the parking lot onto the George Washington Parkway, with its heavy, fast traffic and wide, paved shoulders, to cross the Potomac at Key Bridge. This turnoff angles to your left about one-fifth of a mile before you reach the bridge, so watch closely and don't miss it. A bike trail leads you across the bridge to the C & O Canal Towpath, a wooded jaunt without cars along the old canal. Bikes, canoes, and rowboats may be rented near the canal at Fletchers Boat House, north (left) as you

DISTANCE:	47 miles of bike paths in the city; 15.7 miles to Mount Vernon.
TERRAIN:	Hilly.
TRAFFIC:	Heavy on city streets; none on bike paths.
DIFFICULTY:	Experience necessary for city traffic. Mount Vernon Trail is good for beginners.
BEST TIME:	Late April to mid-May when the Japanese cherry trees are in bloom, or autumn. Summer days are often hot and humid.
LOCATION:	Washington, D.C.

come off Key Bridge.

Following the main tour right from Key Bridge you soon connect with the Rock Creek Park commuter bike trail. Go right to circle the Lincoln Memorial, overlooking a reflecting pool and the Washington Monument. Parking is available if you prefer to start your tour from the Lincoln Memorial. Follow the path along the north side of the Reflecting Pool to 17th Street, where you wind left. Then go right along Constitution Avenue, where you soon pedal right across the green to loop around the Washington Monument. Lock your bike here and hike up the 898 steps (special permit required in summer) or take the elevator for 10¢; the windows at the top offer a bird's-eye view of the capital.

Pedal north across Constitution Avenue to circle the Ellipse. Then

leave the bike path for a short cruise on West Executive, Pennsylvania, and East Executive avenues which circle the White House. Leave the Ellipse loop via 15th Street and ride one block east on Constitution Avenue. Then go right on 14th Street one block to the Mall, on which you pass the Museum of History and Technology, the Museum of Natural History, and the National Gallery of Art. Soon you reach Union Square's reflecting pool, beyond which stands the Capitol.

Return to the Lincoln Memorial and choose your next direction.

South leads through West Potomac Park past the cherry tree-fringed Tidal Basin and across a bridge onto Ohio Drive. An idyllic picnic grove near Hains Point allows you to lunch beneath cherry trees on the Potomac River banks. From Hains Point you curve north along Washington Channel, skirt the Tidal Basin's north shore, and return to the Lincoln Memorial.

North takes you onto the Rock Creek bike path. Pass by the C & O Canal Towpath and continue on the paved path to Rock Creek Park, a natural woodland with nature trails, bike paths, and a meandering brook. Pause on the creek banks to rest or picnic. Another pleasant stop in this vicinity is the National Zoological Park.

West leads over Arlington Memorial Bridge to Arlington Cemetery. Ride the righthand sidewalk over the bridge and pedal on sidewalks all the way to the grounds. Whether you are allowed to take your bike through the cemetery gates seems to depend on the guard in charge.

Mount Vernon Bike Trail

For more exploring, try the excellent 15.7-mile bike trail paralleling the west bank of the Potomac

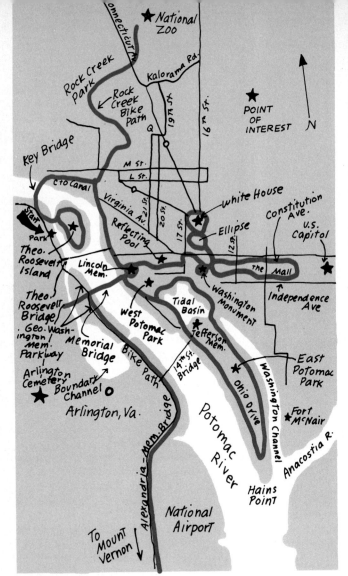

From Washington, D.C., into northeastern Virginia.

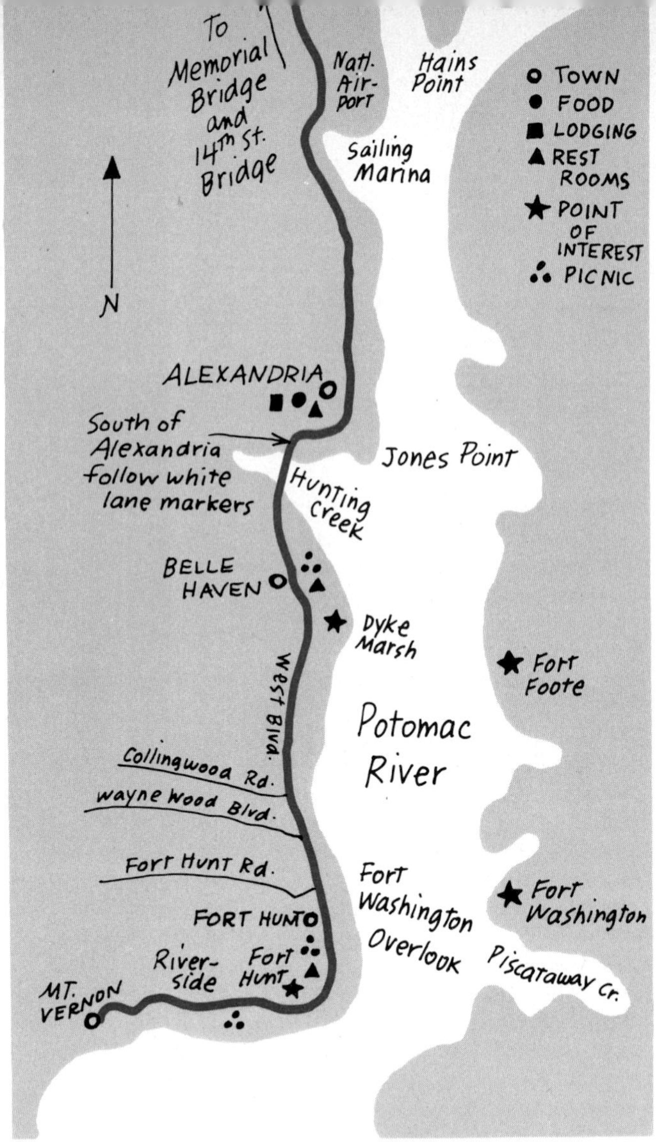

Northeastern Virginia to Mount Vernon.

Map labels (left map):
National Zoo
Rock Creek Park
Rock Creek Bike Path
Connecticut Av.
Kalorama Rd.
19th St.
18th St.
Q
POINT OF INTEREST
N
Key Bridge
M St.
L St.
C & O Canal
White House
Constitution Ave.
Virginia Av.
20 St.
17 St.
Ellipse
12 St.
U.S. Capitol
Start Park
Theo. Roosevelt Island
Reflecting Pool
Lincoln Mem.
the Mall
Theo. Roosevelt Bridge
Washington Monument
Independence Ave
Geo. Washington Mem. Parkway
West Potomac Park
Tidal Basin
Jefferson Mem.
East Potomac Park
Memorial Bridge
Memorial Bike Path
14th St. Bridge
Arlington Cemetery
Boundary Channel
Ohio Drive
Washington Channel
Arlington, Va.
Fort McNair
Potomac River
Alexandria-Mem. Bridge
Hains Point
Anacostia R.
To Mount Vernon
National Airport

Map labels (right map):
To Memorial Bridge and 14th St. Bridge
Natl. Airport
Hains Point
Sailing Marina
N
TOWN
FOOD
LODGING
REST ROOMS
POINT OF INTEREST
PICNIC
ALEXANDRIA
South of Alexandria follow white lane markers
Jones Point
Hunting Creek
BELLE HAVEN
Dyke Marsh
Fort Foote
West Blvd.
Collingwood Rd.
Wayne Wood Blvd.
Potomac River
Fort Hunt Rd.
FORT HUNT
Fort Washington Overlook
Fort Washington
River-side
Fort Hunt
Piscataway Cr.
MT. VERNON

---

and the George Washington Memorial Parkway to Mount Vernon. From Memorial Bridge, this trail is composed of fine, compacted bluestone gravel as far as Alexandria, Virginia (maps and a self-guided tour of the city are available at the Tourist Council, 221 King Street at Fairfax).

South of Alexandria, the path is incomplete in spots; follow the white lane markers which lead you to Mount Vernon. Three picnic areas en route provide good rest or snack stops.

End your tour back in Washington, D.C. by sitting quietly along a stream in Rock Creek Park or by watching the sunset over the Potomac.

WHERE TO STAY

Motels and hotels are numerous. There are no campgrounds on the tour.

FOR SPARE PARTS, REPAIRS, RENTALS

The city has numerous bike shops; just consult the yellow pages or a passerby for the nearest shop. Bicycle rentals are available at the Mall, 12th and Jefferson; Hains Point in East Potomac Park; Thompson Boat Center, Virginia Avenue and Rock Creek Parkway N.W.; Rock Creek Park, 16th and Kennedy N.W.; Fletcher's Boat House, 4940 Canal Road N.W., on the C & O Canal; and Swain's Lock, on the C & O Canal 4 miles north of Great Falls Park, Maryland. Rates usually vary from $1 or $1.50 an hour to $1.50 for two hours.

FOR FURTHER INFORMATION

Write National Capital Parks, National Park Service, Washington, D.C. 20240, and ask for their free brochures "Bike Guide—Washington Area National Parks" and "Mount Vernon Bike Trail." When you arrive, you can obtain maps and ask questions at visitor information centers near the Ellipse, the Lincoln Memorial, and the Washington Monument. Under its "Parks for All Seasons" program, the National Capital Parks sponsors a one-day autumnfest tour on the George Washington Memorial Parkway, bike races on the Ellipse, "bike-ins" down Rock Creek Parkway, and a bike-hike day ending with a rally near the Washington Monument. For information on current bicycling activities, write the above address for the monthly calendar "Washington Area Events of the National Park Service," or phone Dial-a-Park at (202) 426-6975.

30. 'BACCY COUNTRY RIDE

The Hatfields and McCoys may no longer be feuding, and tractors may have retired mules in the west forty, but a you-betcha-by-golly air lingers in the West Virginia tobacco hills. Tobacco leaves dry in the curing sheds. People wave as you pedal by. And the hills are niched with "hollers." Despite the picturesque countryside, the real delight here is chatting with the hospitable residents, who more than likely will offer you iced lemonade or lunch. If you have lived in the city long, it may be pleasant to rediscover a land where folks leave their doors unlatched nights and fear only the good Lord.

On this back-country ride, you find few hazards. The winding ridgetop road has slow, light traffic, and even the dogs don't bite. You may park your car just about anywhere in tiny Red House and then climb the half mile to the ridge, or you can drive to the ridgetop, leave your car off the road, and ride from there.

You glide around sloping bends, looking down upon farmed valleys. In fall the dingles turn vivid with sassafras, maple, and oak foliage. Grocery stores and filling stations appear every few miles. Though the road is narrow, without a "berm" (West Virginian for "shoulder"), the countryside is so quiet you can hear motors coming from several bends ahead. Occasionally you may encounter spots where the road has literally slipped down the hill. This sounds frightening, but really is no problem for bikes. Staying alert for cars, you simply steer around the bad spots.

In Paradise you can pick up fresh fruit at the country store, then wind on toward Liberty past small tobacco fields and cornfields and an occasional tomato patch or vegetable garden. About midway between Paradise and Liberty, you see an old abandoned logging track in the holler. A bit farther, stop at the fire lookout tower and climb to the top for wide views and good photos. Then a quarter of a mile later, you dip down into Liberty. Ranson's General Store here has everything from old kerosene lanterns to chicken feed and overalls, and the stop is fascinating even if you don't buy anything.

Beyond Liberty you soon pass Emma Chapel, a quiet white-frame United Methodist church and cemetery with a pleasant shady lawn for picnicking. On Sunday mornings choirs of voices echo through the dales. You meander through more country, with patches of cedar, maple, oak, sycamore, and sassafras. West Virginians chew the sweet sassafras twigs like toothpicks or use the roots to make tea (see West Virginia Sassafras Tea, at the end of this tour). Soon you coast one winding mile to Kenna. Though the basic ridge ride ends here, you can explore the surrounding hills on your own; any back road makes pleasant, smooth cycling. The return ride is especially fun at dusk when the sun creates red, orange, and golden patterns on the hillsides, giving you more photographic opportunities.

WHERE TO STAY

This ride has no overnight facilities along the route. Fairplain, 8 miles north, has motels and two restaurants. Or pedal 12 miles south of Kenna to Romance, where you can camp, fish, and swim at Rippling Waters Campground, located on Middle Fork Road. Ask for local directions.

FOR FURTHER INFORMATION

Bill Currey's Bicycle Store, 1105 West Washington Street, Charleston, West Virginia 25302; (304) 346-1133. Bill told us about this ride and will be glad to give you any additional information or recommend other West Virginia rides.

WEST VIRGINIA SASSAFRAS TEA

On this jaunt you pedal past many sassafras trees. The natives here dig the roots of the sassafras to brew a heady amber-red tea.

To try this yourself, dig a few roots, take them home or to your evening campfire, and wash and boil them in water. Purists prefer to use only the outer root bark, which is steeped in boiling water until the tea becomes rich red. You can also dry, powder, and bottle the outer bark; use about half a teaspoon of powder per cup. Other enthusiasts

DISTANCE:	44 miles round trip.
TERRAIN:	Winding and rolling.
TRAFFIC:	Light.
DIFFICULTY:	Easy for anyone.
BEST TIME:	Good any season but winter. Particularly pleasant in October.
LOCATION:	On State 34 from Red House to Kenna, West Virginia. About a half hour from Charleston, West Virginia, and four hours from Cincinnati or Pittsburgh.

enjoy making this tea by the gallon by dicing a whole root and boiling it in a huge pot. You can chill and store this tea for many days without sacrificing flavor.

Dried, powdered sassafras leaves have another use: they make authentic Southern gumbo filé, a fragrant thickener used like cornstarch or flour in gravies, soups, or stews. The subtle flavor of this thickener is unique.

You can recognize the sassafras by its three different types of leaves, often growing on the same twig—one oval, another shaped like a mitten, and a third like a mitten with two thumbs; by its root-beer-scented bark, leaves, and roots; and by its tiny yellow-green flowers or blue berries.

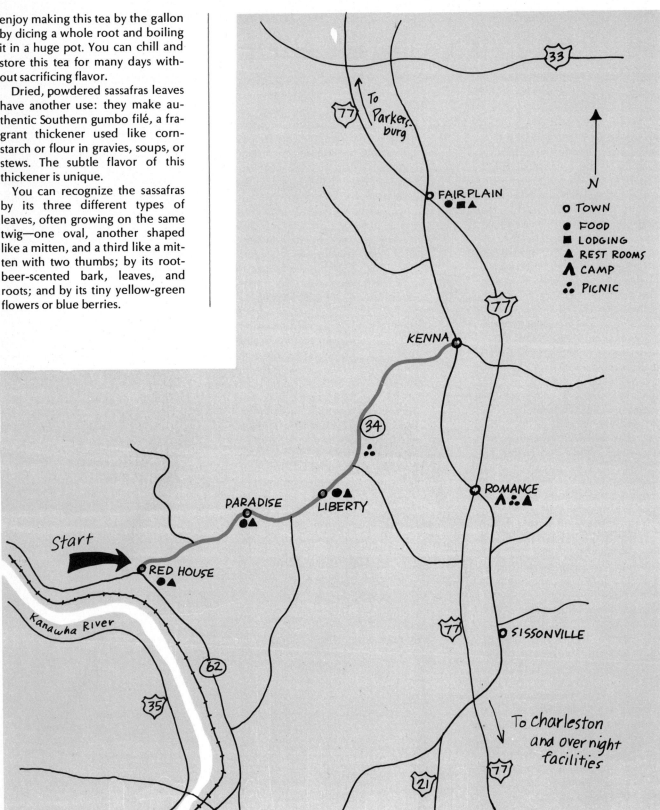

Red House is in northwestern West Virginia on West Virginia 62 and 34; 17 miles northwest of Charleston, West Virginia, via West Virginia 62; 159 miles south of Wheeling, West Virginia, via West Virginia 2, I-77, and West Virginia 34; 135 miles southeast of Columbus, Ohio, via U.S. 23, 35 and West Virginia 34.

31. COLONIAL WILLIAMSBURG JUNKET

Take a carriage ride through Williamsburg, dine in George Washington's favorite tavern, and pedal along the Yorktown battlefield as you return to Colonial days on this 45-mile bike ride along the Colonial Parkway. While motorists often zip past most of the twenty-odd turnouts on this ride, you have time to stop, linger, and perhaps really get a feeling of our Colonial heritage.

Your tour begins in Yorktown, where you can explore the Yorktown battle line and take a self-guiding cycle tour around the field. Yorktown is a tourist town now, so you find numerous parking spots: the Visitor Center lot is one good place to leave your car. Save exploring Yorktown itself for your return because parkway traffic becomes heaviest in the afternoon, and leave Yorktown via the Colonial Parkway, which, except for side trips, you follow all the way to Jamestown. Small aggregate stones in the cement surface make for a bumpy ride, but tubular tires can still be used. Though traffic may be heavy, especially on sunny Sunday afternoons, the road has three lanes (no shoulders), making it easy for motorists to pass you.

Pedaling along the windy York River, you have a fairly straight road and cross several marshy inlets. Indian Field Creek and Felgate's Creek outside Yorktown both have narrow bridges, so watch for cars and don't stop. Local residents fish from boats or go crabbing along the river banks; you may want to join them.

About 5 miles outside Yorktown, just across the second narrow bridge, you find Ringfield Picnic Area on your right, where you can relax along wooded King Creek, see red-winged blackbirds, dip your toes in the cool stream. Then

you wind inland, losing most of the winds you encountered along the river, and begin crossing the peninsula. Throughout the tour you pass several ponds where you can sit awhile in shade. Between here and Williamsburg there is one more narrow bridge just beyond the picnic area. You roll over easy hills past early plantation sites to Williamsburg. In one spot you pedal between fragrant stands of dogwood, blossoming creamy white and pink from mid-April to late April. Serviceberry (shadbush) and dandelions also bloom, and in May and June the sweet scent of honeysuckles is in the air. Beyond Jones Pond, as you begin to enter Williamsburg's suburbs, you can pull off to your right and sit upon the high banks of Queen's Lake, fringed by oak and sweet gum woods.

Williamsburg's restored eighteenth-century historical area is paved with tiny cobblestones. A $4.50 ticket includes admission to nine exhibition buildings, twenty shops, and numerous films and lectures. In town you encounter a hazardous tunnel. Don't go this way. Instead turn to your right off the parkway beyond the Information Center interchange at the sign reading "Historic Area." At the windmill, turn left and walk your bike on the footpath across Market Square past the Courthouse of 1770 and the Guardhouse and Magazine. Then ride along South England Street and Newport Avenue back to the Colonial Parkway.

Beyond Williamsburg you climb above five rolling hills past Great Neck Picnic Area, a good lunch stop. Just beyond the first bridge (not on the bridge), you can stop to watch birds in the marshlands of Halfway Creek. Soon you cross another bridge, lean around a sweeping curve along the James River,

and emerge onto flat, level road with possible heavy winds on the way to Jamestown. Before reaching Jamestown, you cross two more narrow bridges spanning Mill and Powhatan creeks. Just beyond the second bridge, look long right and follow the signs to Jamestown Festival Park, where you can picnic or cycle down a wooded mall past reconstructed buildings. Admission, $1. Nearby visit the historic Jamestown site, with more restored spots. If you begin your tour from this end of the parkway, Festival Park is a good place to leave your car.

Returning to the parkway, turn right for a side trip to Jamestown Island. Bicyclists usually do not have

DISTANCE:	45 miles round trip, excluding side trips.
TERRAIN:	Flat to gently rolling hills.
TRAFFIC:	Heavy in summer; lighter in spring and autumn.
DIFFICULTY:	Fine for families and beginners because of the good, wide road, many rest stops, and little cross traffic.
BEST TIME:	April and May, and September through November. Winter is cold, summer often too humid and hot.
LOCATION:	From Yorktown to Jamestown, Virginia.

to pay an entrance fee. Beyond the entrance booth and Glasshouse Point, where the Colonists made glass, you view James River. Near the island's Visitor Center, walk along the streets of "James Citte," with ruins of Colonial homes. From here, pedal around the island, through marshes, shrubs, and pines. The two-lane paved road is one-way for cars, offering safe, pleasant cycling. Return to Yorktown the way you came for a total round trip of 50 miles, including the Jamestown Island side trip.

WHERE TO STAY

Motels are available in Yorktown and include the following: Duke of York, Ballard Street on Virginia 238, one block east of the bridge off route 17; (804) 887-2331. Tidewater, 4 miles north of the bridge on Route 17; (804) 887-2331. Tidewater, Motor Lodge, three and a half

miles south of town on Route 17; (804) 898-5451.

Williamsburg offers many varied accommodations, including hotels, motels, resorts, and lodging in colonial homes. For a complete listing, write the Williamsburg Chamber of Commerce or Colonial Williamsburg, Inc., Williamsburg, Virginia 23185.

Camping is available at numerous sites in Williamsburg. Also, right on this tour is Jamestown Beach Campsites, across from Festival Park in Jamestown; open year round. Write Jamestown Beach Campsites, P.O. Box CB, Williamsburg, Virginia 23185, or phone (703) 229-3300 for information, brochures, or reservations.

COLONIAL SHADBUSH BERRIES

As you pedal along the Colonial Parkway in spring, you will see

many shadbush blossoms. You may know this flowering shrub or small tree as serviceberry, juneberry, sarvisberry, sugar pear, or sugarplum. In autumn the trees are less conspicuous, but by then the red fruits have ripened a deep purple-black. Pilgrims considered the sarvisberry one of America's best wild fruits and planted many bushes. Some trees along the parkway may date to George Washington's day. Sample the sweet, juicy shadbush berries from the bush as you ride, then gather as many as you like to add later to muffins or to bake in fresh berry pies.

The shadbush has oblong, elliptical leaves with pointed tips and rounded bases; profuse white or pink flowers which hang in loose clusters, blossoming in early spring before the leaves fully open; round or pear-shaped berries which drape in clusters from delicate stalks; and ten large soft seeds within each berry.

Yorktown is in southeastern Virginia on U.S. 17; 25 miles north of Norfolk, Virginia, via U.S. 17; 68 miles east of Richmond, Virginia, via U.S. 60 and the Colonial Parkway; 175 miles south of Washington, D.C., via U.S. 1 and 17.

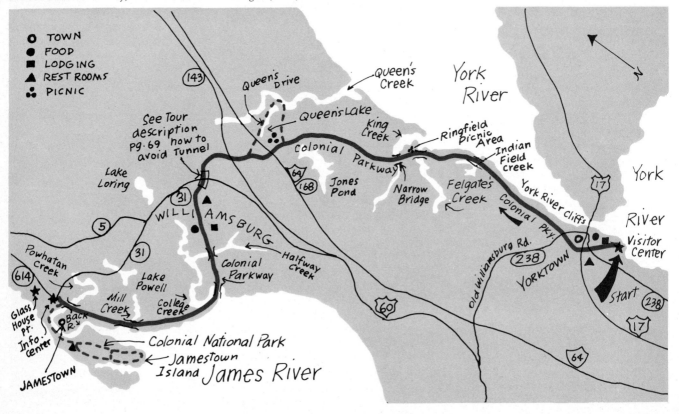

32. PETERSBURG BATTLEFIELD RUN

On June 15, 1864, Generals Grant and Lee began their last confrontation of the Civil War, a grim ten-month Union siege of Petersburg which claimed 70,000 lives. You can pedal along the battlefield, see the tunnel where the coal-miner soldiers from Pennsylvania blasted a crater into Confederate lines, visit the battery from which Grant shelled Petersburg with the Dictator, a 17,000-pound seacoast mortar, and tour Fort Stedman, where Lee failed in his last great offensive. This makes a good ride during brisk autumn or early spring when azaleas and dogwood bloom. Bring along a picnic lunch.

Start at the battlefield Visitor Center and walk first to Battery 5, where the Dictator hurled 200-pound explosives into Petersburg two and a half miles away. Then pedal south on the park road, a safe one-way, two-lane paved highway. Along this first twisting, wooded 3.5 miles are most of the tour's historic spots. Stop often. You wind left, then right past Battery 8 to Battery 9, where you can take a ten-minute stroll to Meade Station, a supply and hospital depot. Past the picnic area, you coast quickly to Harrison Creek, a clear stream fringed with cottonwood and willow, showing little sign of the blood shed on its banks. Rest awhile in the woods. You have a steep climb from the creek to Fort Stedman, where you can walk to Gracies Dam. Then your route rolls past Fort Haskell, climbs past Fort Morton, and curves toward the Crater. Lock your bike and hike to the ruins of the tunnel dug beneath Confederate lines by Union soldiers. The Union army then ignited four tons of powder, blowing a crater into the ground and killing 278 Southern men.

Past the Crater, you leave the battlefield and can pedal to the

DISTANCE:	21 miles.
TERRAIN:	Rolling, with three hills.
TRAFFIC:	Light except on U.S. 301; avoid rush hours.
DIFFICULTY:	Excellent ride for families.
BEST TIME:	Spring, especially in late April when azaleas and dogwood bloom, and autumn, with October the most colorful month. Avoid below-freezing days from December through February and hot, humid days from June through August.
LOCATION:	Petersburg National Battlefield, just east of Petersburg, Virginia, via State 36.

siege lines. Turn left onto heavily trafficked, four-lane U.S. 301 and ride about 2 miles to Park Road (Flank Road), where you turn right and pedal into countryside with pine forests and a few suburban homes. You roll easily past forts Davis, Alexander Hays, and Wadsworth. Beyond Fort Wadsworth you can take a pleasant 2-mile round-trip spin to Poplar Grove National Cemetery, a serene, wooded rest or picnic spot.

Back on Flank Road going west, you veer right past Fort Fisher and go on to Fort Gregg. Beyond Fort Lee traffic can be heavier. Then you

plunge suddenly toward Wilcox Lake. Watch out for the sharp turn at the slope's bottom. Beyond Fort Walker you pedal smoothly past several blocks of homes to U.S. 301. Turn left and ride back to the battlefield, then turn right and return along the 3.5-mile stretch to the Visitor Center. Bicycles are allowed to ride the wrong way on the one-way road.

For a Shorter Ride

If this is your first outing or you have young riders, pedal only the first 3.5 miles through the battlefield, then return to the Visitor Center for a total 7-mile ride.

WHERE TO STAY

The most convenient accommodations are in Petersburg, which has numerous motels.

Two year-round campgrounds are found south of Petersburg: Holiday Inn Trav-L-Park, 6 miles southwest of town on U.S. 1; $4.50. The South Forty KOA, 12 miles south of town on I-95 to U.S. 301, then southwest on State 35; $3 for two.

FOR FURTHER INFORMATION

Write Caretaker, Petersburg National Battlefield, Box 594, Petersburg, Virginia 23804.

NEARBY

Petersburg can be reached by going north from Defense Road onto Sycamore Street, located between Fort Walker and the U.S. 301 intersection. In Petersburg you can see historic Old Blandford Church and Cemetery, Center Hill Mansion Civil War Museum, Lee Memorial Park, and St. Paul's Episcopal Church, where Lee worshiped during the siege.

East 34 miles is Jamestown, linked by the Colonial Parkway to Williamsburg and Yorktown (see details on page 69). Suggested routing to Jamestown from Petersburg: 609 to Garysville, State 10 right to State 31, State 31 left through Surry to Scotland, ferry from Scotland to Jamestown.

Petersburg Battlefield is in southeastern Virginia east of Petersburg on Virginia 106; 30 miles south of Richmond, Virginia, via U.S. 1, 460 and Virginia 106; 77 miles west of Norfolk, Virginia, via U.S. 460 and Virginia 106.

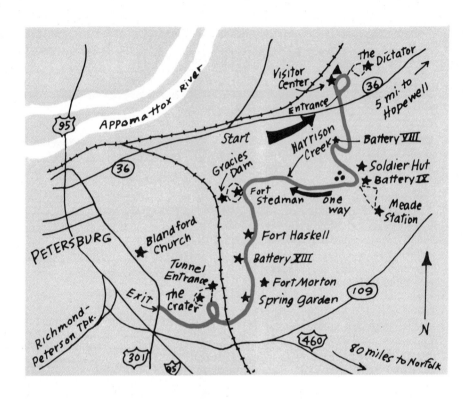

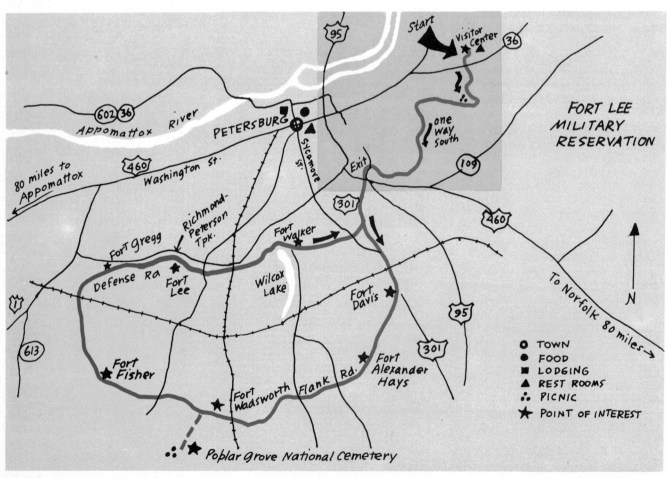

33. RICHMOND BATTLEFIELD EXCURSION

Just minutes from busy downtown Richmond, you can bicycle through rural countryside without a car in sight. The whole mood of this ride is peaceful as you pass old Civil War battlements, ride through oak, dogwood, and sycamore woods, and linger along the lazy James River.

Start near Fort Alexander on Battlefield Park Road, just south of Route 5, and pedal south on the well-paved lane through tunnels of woods. In late May the scent of spring flowers fills the air. At Fort Harrison Visitor Center, pick up brochures on Richmond National Battlefield Park, scene of a major Civil War confrontation between Ulysses S. Grant and Robert E. Lee. The shady picnic area, winding path, and small Civil War cemetery provide cool rest stops, especially on your return.

Stay on Battlefield Park Road to explore old Fort Hoke. Proceeding south, go left on Osborne Turnpike and right on Battery Hill Road, where you climb a steep hill to a small marina with fine views of the James River.

Retrace your ride back near Fort Hoke and turn right on Hoke-Brady Road. Winding through quiet countryside, you soon reach Fort Brady on the James River. Pause to linger near the water and watch for shore birds. Pedal north now on Hoke-Brady Road and turn left on Kingsland Road where you ride over easy hills past farms and woods. As you wind beside a pond, you smell the fragrance of honeysuckles on the spring breeze.

Go right on Route 5 (also called New Market Road or John Tyler Memorial Highway) and right again just beyond a small bridge onto Curles Neck Road to Curles Neck Dairy. Here you can pedal into the dairy and ride the smooth farm roads to see the Holsteins and a close-up of dairy farming.

From the farm you can continue southeast on Route 5 to a nearby gas station for candy bars and soda or a country store for heartier snacks. Then retrace your ride on Route 5, go left on Kingsland Road, right on Hoke-Brady Road, and right on Battlefield Park Road back to your starting spot.

More Exploring

The above tour is best for beginners and families. If you have more experience and don't mind some fast traffic, you can further explore the battlefield. From the above-mentioned gas station and country store on Route 5, go east on Route 156 for a hilly ride to Malvern Hill, scene of the last of the Seven Days' Battles of 1862. Farther north you dive downhill across White Oak Swamp, where you may glimpse herons in the marshes. Then you cross a railroad track and climb another knoll.

At U.S. 60 and State 33, go left for a 3-mile stretch along busy highway. Then turn right onto Route 156 to coast across the Chickahominy River and climb to Cold Harbor Visitor Center, Watt House, and Gaines' Mill. Lock your bike and hike along the history-nature trail to Breakthrough Point, where shallow Union trenches still remain.

For a final stop, coast to the small valley cut by Beaver Dam Creek and sit beside the water. If you continue straight from the creek, you soon dead-end into U.S. 360, which is heavily trafficked and cuts through a hot, dirty section of Richmond. It's much more pleasant to retrace your ride past Cold Harbor and back to Fort Alexander.

WHERE TO STAY

Motels and hotels are numerous

DISTANCE:	25 miles.
TERRAIN:	Easy rolling hills.
TRAFFIC:	Light.
DIFFICULTY:	Good ride for anyone.
BEST TIME:	Spring, when honeysuckles, azaleas, and dogwood bloom, or autumn, for splendid foliage.
LOCATION:	Quiet countryside near Richmond, Virginia.

in nearby Richmond.

The only campground, located far off the main tour, is Woodbourne KOA Kampground, about 5 miles northeast of the Bottoms Bridge exit off I-64, then nearly 5 miles northwest on routes 612 and 565. Signs direct you much of the way. Open year round; $3.50 for two. For reservations, write Woodbourne KOA Kampground, P.O. Box 120, New Kent, Virginia 23124, or phone (703) 923-4776. Deposit of $3 required.

FOR SPARE PARTS AND REPAIRS

Dee's Bicycles, 5033 Forest Hill Avenue, Richmond, Virginia; (703) 231-4232. De Witt Whittington repairs all makes and carries tools and touring and racing equipment.

FOR FURTHER INFORMATION

Charlotte LaRoy of the Richmond Area Bicycling Association told us about this ride and will be

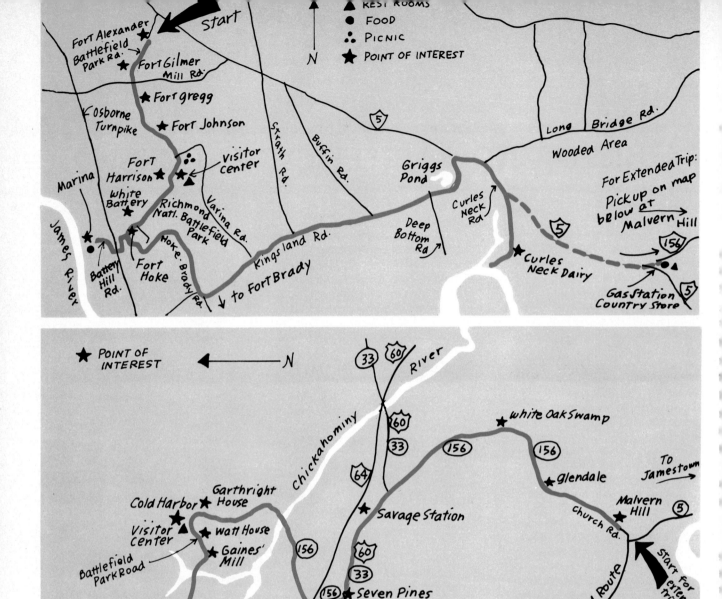

Richmond National Battlefield is in southeastern Virginia just east of Richmond, Virginia, off Virginia 156; 94 miles northwest of Norfolk via U.S. 60 and Virginia 156; 100 miles south of Washington, D.C., via I-95, U.S. 360, and Virginia 156; 154 miles north of Raleigh, North Carolina, via U.S. 1, I-85, 95, U.S. 360, and Virginia 156.

glad to answer any other questions you may have. You can write her at 12821 Bailey Bridge Road, Midlothian, Virginia 23112. Information may also be obtained from Dee's Bicycles, listed above, or from the Superintendent, Richmond National Battlefield Park, 3215 East Broad Street, Richmond, Virginia 23223.

VIRGINIA'S FLOWERING DOGWOOD

Early spring is the time to cycle through Virginia to see the pinkish-white dogwood blossoming in the woodlands. The tree is small, with a trunk only twelve to eighteen inches in diameter, and its deep reddish-brown bark often becomes scaly as the tree ages. The fragrant blossoms have four silky petals, each notched on the end. In October when the bright scarlet fruit ripens, you may glimpse gray squirrels, songbirds, wild turkeys, and deer nibbling on the berries.

34. SHENANDOAH RIDGETOP RAMBLE

Pedal along a skyline ridgetop deep in the hazy Blue Ridge Mountains amid plunging valleys, slate-blue shadows, and forested, rolling Piedmont country. Hike along a wooded path to a cliff top and look down upon hillsides in spring dappled with hepatica, magenta redbud, dogwood, and azaleas, and in autumn covered with brilliant foliage. Pause often during this ride to gaze into the hollows, sit along the misty Shenandoah River banks, or trek into the Piedmont. Allow four days for biking plus at least three more days for hiking to fully experience this wilderness.

Shenandoah National Park has four entrances to its Skyline Drive: north at Front Royal; Thornton Gap, between Sperryville and Luray; Swift Run Gap, between Elkton and Stanardsville; and south at Rockfish Gap, between Waynesboro and Charlottesville. Starting from the north entrance, you climb about 10 strenuous miles to the ridgetop, where the Appalachian Trail meanders across your path. The park road is narrow, without shoulders, and well paved, with an auto speed limit of 35 m.p.h. On the ridge you can lock your bike and explore the footpath to your left, winding down through forests to Piney River. Another minute of riding takes you to Hogback Overlook, where on a clear day you can count eleven bends in the shadowy Shenandoah River as it winds through a deep valley. Still another nature trail leads from Matthews Arm Campground.

For a midmorning snack or lunch, stop at Elkwallow's little store and picnic area or pedal 6 miles farther uphill to the Thornton Gap restaurant, where after lunch you can venture along the trail to Marys Rock. From Thornton

Gap you tackle a steep climb through well-lighted Marys Rock Tunnel to the Pinnacles, beyond which the hill becomes more gradual. Stop at Little Stony Man Overlook to meander one and a half miles on Stony Man Trail, leading into Stony Man Mountain's cool, forested slopes. Take your camera: at one point you view the entire Shenandoah Valley, filled in May with pink and white mountain laurel, flowering black locust, and azaleas.

Stony Man Trail ends at Skyland Lodge, another good snack or lunch stop. Located 41.7 miles from the tour's start, the lodge makes a convenient overnight spot. From here on, the road rolls gently downhill.

One of Shenandoah's prettiest trails lies 1 mile beyond Skyland Lodge and leads you beneath ancient hemlocks to a garden of flowering shrubs, vines, and rocks. Carry a picnic and allow half a day for this walk.

An easy 2-mile coast takes you to Hawksbill Mountain Trail, winding 2 miles round trip through New England-like spruce and fir forests to Hawksbill Mountain's summit, with more superb views, especially in spring and autumn. Spin downhill a bit farther to Big Meadows. From here you can go to Byrd Visitor Center for information or take a delightful walking side trip along Swamp Nature Trail, 2 miles round trip, to see lush wet foliage and boggy spots sprinkled with brilliant swamp wildflowers. Just .3 mile from the Visitor Center is a small grocery store and café. One mile off the main road here lies Big Meadows Lodge and year-round camping.

Still another campground nestles beneath Lewis Mountain, about 6 miles farther. From here you can lock your bike and explore a na-

ture trail to a frothy falls.

Though Shenandoah has seventy-five turnouts, you will want to stop often on your own. Picnic grounds are numerous: as you coast beyond Lewis Mountain Campground, you reach South River picnic area, and about 17 miles later, Loft Mountain picnic area, with another grocery store and more trails. Most rewarding, though, is to explore a footpath and find your own secluded nook for picnicking, perhaps beneath a dogwood or in a wildflower meadow.

As you wind downhill toward the south entrance, the mountains close in and occasionally you can stop for canyon views.

DISTANCE:	210 miles round trip, plus numerous hiking side trips.
TERRAIN:	Hilly, with some steep grades.
TRAFFIC:	Heavy in summer and on autumn weekends; lightest in April and May, when wildflowers are in bloom.
DIFFICULTY:	For experienced cyclists only, because of relatively narrow roads and traffic.
BEST TIME:	April and May, when traffic is lightest. Try autumn weekdays for the foliage.
LOCATION:	Shenandoah National Park, Virginia.

Other Tours

Shorter, easier rides can be planned virtually anywhere along Skyline Drive. An especially pleasant short jaunt (18.6 miles round trip) leads from Skyland to Big Meadows and return. Along the way you can hike the trails to Hawksbill Mountain and Dark Hollow Falls. Beginners wishing to try the many hiking trails on this ride might consider taking two leisurely days.

WHERE TO STAY

Lodge or cabin accommodations are located at Skyland (April through October), Big Meadows (mid-May through October), and

Lewis Mountain (June through September). For reservations, write ARA-Virginia Sky-Line Company, Inc., Box 727, Luray, Virginia 22835.

Campgrounds are available all along Skyline Drive and include the following:

Mileage from north entrance

22.3 Matthews Arm
51.3 Big Meadows
57.6 Lewis Mountain
79.8 Loft Mountain
83.7 Dundo Group Campground, reserved for organized youth groups

Off the beaten path are cabins along Appalachian Trail, with bedding, dishes, cooking utensils, and stoves. Rates and reservations can be obtained by writing the Potomac Appalachian Trail Club, 1718 North Street N. W., Washington, D.C. 20036. The Appalachian Trail also offers open shelters with bunks on a first-come first-served basis.

FOR FURTHER INFORMATION

Write Superintendent, Shenandoah National Park, Luray, Virginia 22835.

NEARBY

The hilly Blue Ridge Parkway connects with Skyline Drive at Shenandoah National Park's south entrance and leads 469 miles to Great Smoky Mountains National Park. For scenic, challenging cycling, the whole ride is recommended. Avoid summer months, when traffic is heavy. For biking regulations, write Superintendent, Blue Ridge Parkway, Box 7606, Asheville, North Carolina 28807.

The north entrance of Shenandoah National Park is at Front Royal, in north-central Virginia on U.S. 340; 66 miles west of Washington, D.C., via I-66, Virginia 55, and U.S. 340; 179 miles northwest of Richmond, Virginia, via I-64, 81, 66, and U.S. 340.

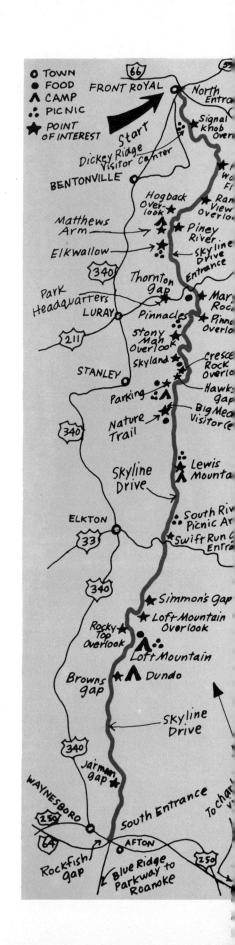

35. BLUE RIDGE PEDAL

High in the Appalachians you pedal through natural herb and wildflower gardens past southern highland split-rail fences, cabins, and mills. In spring the valleys are flecked with dogwood and redbud, and in autumn the foliage flames ruby, saffron, and gold on the slopes. Birds chirp above you, deer or bear occasionally wander near the road, and bobcats cry at night. If you have the stamina to tackle tough mountain grades, the Blue Ridge Parkway offers cycling adventure.

The parkway is smooth and well paved, but narrow (twenty feet wide) and without shoulders. Safety flags are recommended, especially during summer. Though you pass near many mountain hamlets, these are usually located several miles off the main road, so carry food, spare parts, and tools with you. Warm clothing is advised for the cool nights.

Day one (58 miles)

Start at Rockfish Gap, at the southern tip of Shenandoah National Park's Skyline Drive, and pedal south on the Blue Ridge Parkway. Full facilities, including a bike shop, are located in Waynesboro, just north of the parkway.

About 6 miles south of Shenandoah, stop at Humpback Rocks Visitor Center and ask for a Blue Ridge Parkway folder and a pamphlet on accommodations and services along the route. A bit farther lock your bike and walk past several pioneer cabins to the Rocks, whose humped appearance gives this place its name. Pause again 3 miles farther down the parkway at Greenstone to hike along a self-guiding trail beneath cool oaks and hickories. Returning to the parkway, you soon climb to Ravens Roost, where you can enjoy views of Torry Mountain and the Shen-

andoah Valley. About 5 miles farther, turn right on Virginia 814 and pedal 4.5 miles off the parkway to Sherando Lake for a cool swim or lakeshore picnic.

Back on the main trail, you wind past Bald Mountain to Whetstone Ridge, with a restaurant and gas station. A rewarding stop 5.4 miles farther is the Yankee Horse Trail. Lock your bike and meander through fragrant woods along Wigwam Creek to Wigwam Falls, where the water feels cool on your toes.

Past the turnoff for Buena Vista, there are no facilities for 28 miles. Then you climb a tough hill and glide into a valley to Otter Creek, with camping and a restaurant, a good overnight stop. In the evening linger beside the creek to glimpse deer or in mid-May to enjoy mountain laurel blossoms. You may also catch trout to fry in butter over your campfire.

Day Two (62.4 miles)

After an early breakfast, coast south toward the James River, the tour's lowest elevation point, where a footbridge leads to a restored canal lock. Try to walk the riverbank trail here at dawn when mists still cling to the water and you may spot deer, bear, or other wildlife. Beyond the river, an arduous slope rises 3,286 feet in 13 miles. You ride 3.7 miles beyond Petit Gap to Thunder Ridge, where you can stop, lock your bike, and take an eight-minute hike to a spot overlooking Arnold Valley. In early June rhododendron tint the slopes purple. From Thunder Ridge the road climbs steeply for 2 more miles to Apple Orchard Mountain's summit. A delightful coast brings you to Onion Mountain, where a short trail wanders through meadows fragrant in June with mountain laurel and rhodo-

dendron. For 7 more miles you swoop around easy curves, speeding past woods, meadows, and hills. Then you glide to Wilkinson Gap. Pause to enjoy the 1.5-mile trail along Fallingwater Cascades, lined with peaceful solitary clearings.

Two miles farther, you reach

DISTANCE:	240.8 miles round trip.
TERRAIN:	Hilly, with many steep grades.
TRAFFIC:	Heavy from June through Labor Day; light in spring and autumn.
DIFFICULTY:	Requires experience to handle the distance and rough terrain. Not recommended for families with young children because of narrow roads and fast traffic.
BEST TIME:	Late April to June for the wildflowers or late September through October for the foliage. Avoid November to mid-April, when the road may be closed by snow and ice on the upper slopes.
LOCATION:	Blue Ridge Parkway, from Shenandoah National Park to Roanoke, Virginia.

Peaks of Otter, a gentle mountain valley which has a lodge, restaurant, picnicking, camping, and several delightful hiking trails. Peaks of Otter is a good overnight stop if you are tired from the long climb. Mileage from Otter Creek: 24.4 miles.

If you continue on, though, afternoon offers a wooded ride above many lush valleys. Few formal stopping areas are located on this stretch, but you can pause anywhere to explore. About 25 miles beyond Peaks of Otter, lock your bike and walk twenty minutes to rest on a precipice overlooking Roanoke River Gorge. Then 5.5 miles farther, you reach Roanoke Mountain, where you can camp at a site 1.3 miles along the spur to Mill Mountain. After setting up camp, pedal into Roanoke to pick up supplies for your return ride.

WHERE TO STAY

Motels are located in many small towns along the tour, but most of these are several miles off the parkway. For a complete listing, write Blue Ridge Parkway, Box 1710, Roanoke, Virginia 24008, and request the free pamphlet "Accommodations and Services." The one parkway lodge on this stretch is Peaks of Otter Lodge, 85.6 miles along the parkway from Shenandoah; open mid-April to mid-November. For rates and reservations, write the Virginia Peaks of Otter Company, Box 489, Bedford, Virginia 24523.

Parkway campgrounds operate on a first-come first-served basis. These include Otter Creek, 60.8 miles from the tour's start, open year round; Peaks of Otter, 84 miles from the tour's start, open May 1st to October 31st; and Roanoke Mountain, 120.4 miles from the tour's start, open year round.

FOR SPARE PARTS AND REPAIRS

Waynesboro and Roanoke both have bike shops, but you will have to carry parts and tools with you

for the great stretch between.

FOR FURTHER INFORMATION

Write Information Services, Blue Ridge Parkway, Box 1710, Roanoke, Virginia 24008. Mention you plan to bicycle on the parkway and you will be sent a list of rules for cycling there.

NEARBY

After trying the above tour, you may want to proceed on the Blue Ridge Parkway all the way to Great Smoky Mountains National Park. The hills are arduous on this stretch, but the view of the Great Smokies from Waterrock Knob, 451.2 miles along the parkway, almost makes the whole trip worthwhile. One ride you shouldn't miss is the Skyline spin through Shenandoah National Park (see page 75 for details).

BIRDS ALONG THE BLUE RIDGE PARKWAY

As you pedal through the Appalachians, you pass large treeless patches where only hardy rhododendron and mountain laurel grow. In these "heath balds," watch the thickets for abundant bird life. You may spot ravens, red-tailed hawks, blue jays, veeries, and mockingbirds.

Another common high mountain bird is the slate-colored *Carolina junco*, which eats mostly insects and seeds. He has a dark back with white breast and undersides and conspicuous white feathers on the outer edges of his tail.

Watch, too, for the *ruby-crowned* and *golden-crowned kinglets*. These tiny birds hide in dense foliage and have olive-gray backs which provide good camouflage in the leaves.

Another hard-to-see fellow is the shy little *ovenbird*, who lives both on mountaintops and in valleys. Though you may not spot him, you will likely hear his distinctive call—"teacher, teacher, teacher."

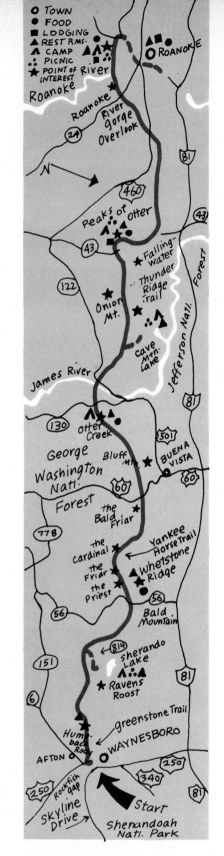

Rockfish Gap is in central Virginia on the Blue Ridge Parkway at the south entrance of Shenandoah National Park; 95 miles northwest of Richmond, Virginia, via I-64 and the Blue Ridge Parkway; 91 miles northeast of Roanoke, Virginia, via I-81, 64 and the Blue Ridge Parkway; 138 miles southwest of Washington, D.C., via U.S. 29, I-64, and the Blue Ridge Parkway.

36. CAPE HATTERAS ESCAPADE

Swashbuckling pirates urging captives down the plank, ships writhing in hurricanes and crashing on sandy shoals, and a lost English colony which vanished mysteriously, are part of the violent past that still lingers in Cape Hatteras for you to explore. Despite these attractions, this skeleton-bone finger of land remains untouched in many ways. When you weary of antique shops and long-ago mysteries, you can pause quietly on the drifting sands to watch great flocks of snow geese, ducks, and whistling swans, or observe bottle-nosed dolphins at play.

To visit only the Seashore, start from Bodie Visitor Center. But if you have time, begin farther north at Wright Brothers National Memorial near Kitty Hawk. Though there are many food stops on this ride, carry snacks, spare parts, tools, and a sweater for brisk ocean breezes. The road is usually narrow, often rough, with only sand for shoulders, making the ride nerve-wracking in summer when there is heavy traffic, but delightful in winter when you have the road to yourself. High winds (often 15 m.p.h.) blow almost continuously, with summer prevailing winds from the southwest and winter winds from the northeast. Always watch ahead for sand drifting onto the road.

Pedaling south of Wright Brothers Memorial, you feel the sea mist in your face. Stop in Nags Head for a snack and look offshore for ghosts of old sailing vessels which crashed long ago. Dune climbing on this narrow spit is great and you can scramble up sand hills 135 feet high. You can also hunt for driftwood and agates or rent a boat and venture offshore. Swimming is good in summer, too.

Skimming farther south with the road breezy and flat all the way, you reach Whalebone Junction, on Cape Hatteras National Seashore's north tip. Buy refreshments here, then take a side trip right onto U.S. 64 to ride high above blue Roanoke sound to Roanoke Island. Fort Raleigh is 5 miles to your right after you arrive on the island. Here the "Lost Colony" of 150 men, women, and children vanished in 1587, leaving the letters CROATOAN carved into a tree as the only clue to their fate. North of the Visitor Center, lock your bike and hike along the Thomas Hariot Trail winding through woods.

Returning to Bodie Island, you ride south. Stop soon for a swim at Coquina Beach and pick up brochures at the Visitor Center. After pedaling over Oregon Inlet, you reach Pea Island National Wildlife Refuge. The Oriental, an old wreck, lies near milepost 10.3. Lock your bike at the turnout and walk along a boardwalk to see the steel boiler still jutting from the waves and glimpse rotting wood on the sands, if the winds blow right. A bit farther on at the bird observatory, watch for grebes, herons, loons, geese, and whistling swans.

Farther south on the fabled Outer Banks you reach Rodanthe, a quaint seaside village where you can buy seafood or catch your own channel bass, bluefish, or mackerel off the pier. From the pier's Ramp 10, look north to see the remains of more shipwrecks in the surf. Past grassy dunes, you reach the campground near Salvo, a pleasant overnight stop.

Beyond tiny Gull Island rising from placid Pamlico Sound, you can stop at Ramp 14 and hike to the beach to spot another wreckage. Pause anytime to hunt for shells or to sunbathe, but don't

DISTANCE:	190 miles round trip.
TERRAIN:	Flat.
TRAFFIC:	Heavy in summer; light in winter.
DIFFICULTY:	For experienced cyclists because of possible high winds.
BEST TIME:	Winter, when temperatures are mild and traffic light. Summer is hazardous because of heavy traffic on narrow roads.
LOCATION:	Cape Hatteras National Seashore, North Carolina.

swim without lifeguards because of the treacherous currents.

South of Buxton, Hatteras Island's resort town, you can visit Cape Hatteras Lighthouse overlooking murderous Diamond Shoals. If you have the stamina, trek up the 265 steps that wind to the lighthouse's top for a splendid view of surf, sand, and dunes. On the lighthouse road, about 200 yards south toward the campground, you can take a self-guiding trail through Buxton Wood, with its live oak and loblolly pine trees beneath which grow barberry, silverling, gallberry, and yaupon (holly).

Past another fishing pier, load your bike on the free ferry to Ocracoke Island. You ride, skirting more dunes, with the crashing surf to your left and the shallow, still sound waters on your right. Near this island's southern tip, you reach Ocracoke, an intriguing fishing village with a harbor, moss-draped live oaks, and Teach's Hole, where the notorious pirate Blackbeard met his doom.

Return north by the same route or arrange for a pick up in Ocracoke to avoid the high head winds in winter. If you decide to extend your explorations, take a two-and-a-quarter-hour ferry ride ($1 for you and your bike) to Cedar Island on the mainland.

WHERE TO STAY

Campgrounds are located throughout the tour and include Seashore camps as well as many commercial sites. Most are on flat, unshaded, sandy spots. National Seashore facilities include the following, from north to south: Oregon Inlet, open year round. Salvo (Soundside), open June 20th to September 3rd. Cape Point, open year round. Frisco, open June 20th to September 3rd. Ocracoke Oceanside, open year round.

Motels, hotels, and cottages are available in Nags Head and towns north as well as in Manteo on Roanoke Island, Rodanthe, Buxton, Hatteras, and Ocracoke. You can obtain a complete list of motels and hotels from the Dare County Tourist Bureau, Manteo, North Carolina 27954.

FOR FURTHER INFORMATION

Write Superintendent, Cape Hatteras National Seashore, Box 457, Manteo, North Carolina 27954.

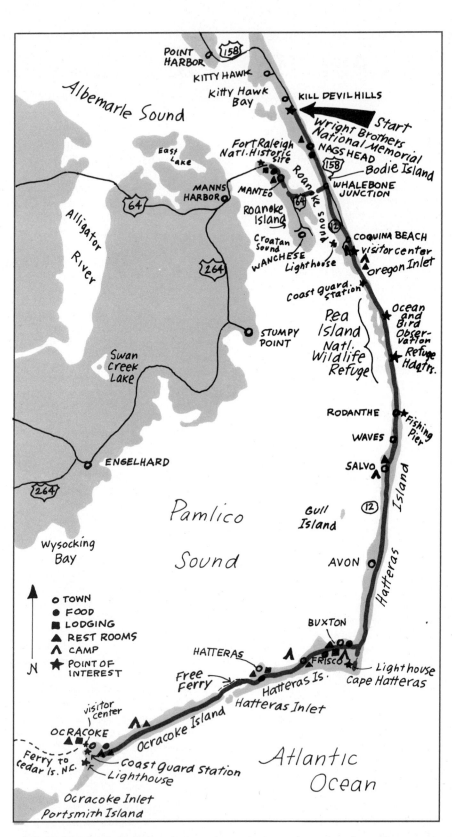

Wright Brothers National Memorial is near the northern North Carolina shore off U.S. 158; 50 miles southeast of Elizabeth City, North Carolina, via U.S. 158; 85 miles south of Norfolk, Virginia, via U.S. 17 and 158; 211 miles east of Raleigh, North Carolina, via U.S. 64 and 158.

37. SOUTHERN GARDEN RIDE

DISTANCE:	138 miles; short rides can be taken from Charleston to Middleton Gardens (30 miles round trip) or from Charleston to Old Dorchester State Park (40 miles round trip).
TERRAIN:	Flat.
TRAFFIC:	Light.
DIFFICULTY:	Good ride for anyone.
BEST TIME:	Local cyclists ride here year round, but you might find the summer heat and humidity stifling if you are unused to this climate.
LOCATION:	Starts in Charleston, South Carolina.

Ornate wrought-iron balconies, antebellum plantations, and tidy English gardens of camellias, azaleas, and magnolias contrast with isolated cypress swamps and black lagoons on this journey through South Carolina's low country. Surprises await you everywhere. You might see an alligator suddenly poke his snout up from the depths of a reflecting pool, or in spring a giant sea turtle searching the beach for a place to lay her eggs. The following pages describe only some of the sights on this tour; what you will discover could be even more unexpected and exciting. If you have never traveled in the South before, the low country is a fine place to begin.

Start in Charleston, where you can leave your car in a shopping center and buy food for an old-fashioned Southern picnic. Charleston has several bike shops where you can purchase parts before you pedal onto back roads. The city itself offers a day of exploring pastel houses, mosquito cottages, and Victorian homes. Visit the Old Slave Mart Museum and Gallery at 6 Chambers Street, the Old Powder Magazine at 79 Cumberland Street, and Huguenot Church, 138 Church and Queen Streets. Free maps and a self-guided tour of the city are available at the Visitor Information Center in Arche Building, 85 Calhoun Street.

To leave town, cross the Ashley River on Route 171 and 61. Traffic is usually heavy for the first 5 miles out of Charleston, especially during weekday rush hours. But after you bear left on 61 (Ashley River Road), the flat road stretches quietly ahead. Moss drips from live oaks as you spin for miles on smooth blacktop past old plantations. Grass has overgrown the road's edge, robbing you of any shoulder, but cars are few.

About 12 miles outside Charleston, wind right to Magnolia Gardens. Lock your bike and stroll along fragrant paths of camellias, magnolias, and azaleas shaded by oaks draped in moss and lavender wisteria.

Three miles farther on 61, turn right again for Middleton, America's oldest landscaped gardens. Pause to walk amid a tapestry of flowers, accented with butterfly lakes, reflecting pools where alligators dwell, fountains, and wooden foot bridges. Admission to each garden is $2.50.

Beyond Middleton, go right onto Route 165 for a mile to Route 642. To your right is Dorchester

State Park, a serene spot to picnic, rest, or explore Old Fort Dorchester. Continuing on the main tour, pedal northwest on 642 for about a mile along the river. Then wind right on S-16, a long, quiet stretch to Route 6, where you go left along Lake Moultrie.

Turn right with Route 6 and right again in 7 miles on Route 45 to cross an inlet between two placid lakes. At sunset the light filters through the cypress trees and shines green-gold on the water Staying on Route 45, you pedal through swamplands overgrown with semitropical trees, including palmetto, magnolia, oak, and pine. In summer mosquitoes fly thick above the still water, so bring repellent.

Bird watching is superb here; you might glimpse snowy egrets, ibis, hawks, or bald eagles. Rest or picnic in numerous clearings, or stay overnight in one of the several campgrounds operated by Francis Marion National Forest.

About 13 miles past the small town of St. Stephen, go left on 17A into Jamestown. Then go right onto Route 41 through more swamp and across the Wando River. Join four-lane U.S. 17 which leads you back toward Charleston. If you avoid rush hours on this road, traffic will usually be moderate.

For a final side trip turn left and pedal to Sullivan's Island and the beach. On an early morning stroll you may discover sand dollars, sea horses, sea biscuits, or conchs. After a rest and dip in the surf, return to Charleston.

Relax in White Point Gardens on Murray Boulevard and East Battery at the foot of the peninsula which overlooks the harbor. Or visit Hampton Park at Rutledge Avenue and Cleveland Street, with its aviary, zoo, and sunken gardens of summer roses or spring azaleas and camillias. After your ride, sample low country cuisine; local specialties include she-crab soup, baked pompano Albermarle, and rum pie.

WHERE TO STAY

Motels and hotels are available in Charleston.

Some of the campgrounds near the tour are listed below: Bonneau, 7 miles north of Moncks Corner on U.S. 52; open year round; no fee; operated on a first-come first-served basis by Francis Marion National Forest. Guilliard Lake, about 4 miles southeast of Jamestown on State 45, then one and a half miles northeast on Forest 150 and a mile north on Forest 1500; open March 1st to November 30th; no fee. Charleston KOA, 1 mile west of the U.S. 78 and I-26 intersection; open year round; $4 for two. For reservations, write Charleston KOA, Ladson, South Carolina 29456, or phone (803) 797-1045.

Numerous other private campgrounds are located along Lake Moultrie. For a complete listing of all South Carolina campgrounds, write the Department of Parks, Recreation, and Tourism, Box 1358, Columbia, South Carolina 29202, and ask for the free brochure "South Carolina Camping."

NEARBY

South Carolina's back roads offer days of tranquil cycling, and you can explore on your own with few problems. For one pleasant rural ride (160 miles round trip), continue north on Route 61 where the main tour goes right onto 165 and pedal another 33 miles past Givhans Ferry State Park (picnicking, hiking, camping) to Route 217, where you go left through Smoaks and Padgett. In the small town of Lodge, turn left onto Route 64 and pedal 3 miles. Then turn right on Route 641 to end the tour at Rivers Bridge State Park, site of a Civil War skirmish, where you can picnic, swim, and camp. All the above

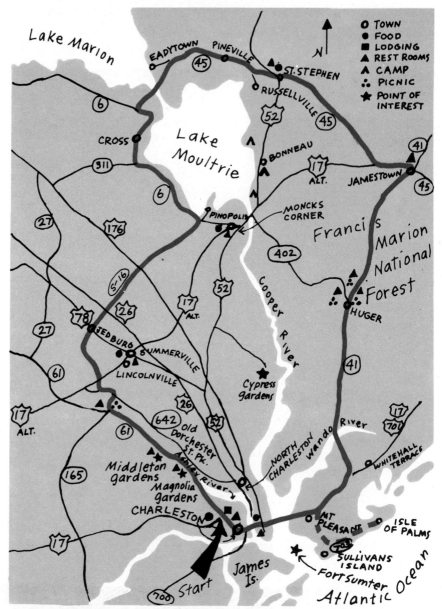

Charleston is in southeastern South Carolina on I-26 and U.S. 17; 104 miles northeast of Savannah, Georgia, via I-95 and U.S. 17; 98 miles southeast of Columbia, South Carolina, via I-26; 165 miles southwest of Wilmington, North Carolina, via U.S. 17.

roads are shown on the free South Carolina state highway map, available from the Department of Parks, Recreation, and Tourism, Box 1358, Columbia, South Carolina 29202.

LOW COUNTRY BALD CYPRESS

Deep in the black lagoons and cypress swamps, you often weave beneath huge, ancient bald cypress trees standing in water, limbs heavy with Spanish moss. This

tree's most striking characteristics are the deeply-grooved bulbous swelling at the trunk's base and the spreading roots which poke above the water. The leaves, though deciduous, rather resemble evergreen needles—sharply pointed, one-half to three-quarters-of-an-inch long, and about one-sixteenth-of-an-inch wide. You will see the small, brown, round cones growing singly or in clusters of two and three.

the
South

38. SAVANNAH MAGNOLIA TOUR

Bring mint juleps, fried chicken, and biscuits on this magnolia-scented bike tour through old Colonial Savannah. Pedal along cobblestoned Factors Walk on the Savannah riverfront, walk through brick‾ Civil War forts, and stroll through gardens and pre-Revolutionary mansions, including one said to be haunted. Then leave the wide city streets and spin onto Georgian back roads, where you wind through moss-draped oak canopies and golden marshes to Skidaway Island.

Park your car in a downtown garage weekdays or on any city street Sundays. Then start at Factors Walk on Bay Street, lined with pubs and restaurants along the river where James Oglethorpe landed in 1733. At Bay Street's east end, East Broad Street, stop at Fort Wayne and adjacent Trustee's Garden Village, containing the Pirates' House Inn of Stevenson's *Treasure Island*. Proceed south on East Broad to State Street, where you turn right and skirt Greene and Columbia squares. At the latter visit historic Davenport House on the corner of State and Habersham (admission, $1), and a bit farther stop at Owens-Thomas House on State and Abercorn (admission, $1.25).

Continue on State to Bull Street, where you turn left and pedal along Wright Square. To your right here, you see the Telfair Academy of Arts and Sciences, an art museum open Tuesday through Saturday, 10 A.M. to 5 P.M., and Sunday, 2 to 5 P.M. Many homes and buildings in this area date to the early eighteenth century. Though Savannah was spared destruction by General Sherman, who "gave" her to Lincoln for Christmas, the city was not spared other tragedies of war. At Chippewa Square, turn left at Hull Street and take a side trip to Colonial Park Cemetery, severely

damaged when used by Sherman's troops as a stabling ground. Return along Hull Street to Chippewa

DISTANCE:	40 miles.
TERRAIN:	Flat.
TRAFFIC:	Light except during rush hours.
DIFFICULTY:	Good ride for anyone.
BEST TIME:	Anytime except June through August, when temperatures often reach the 90's and 100's.
LOCATION:	Savannah, Georgia.

Square and continue south on Bull Street.

At Forsyth Park, turn left for two blocks, then go right onto Abercorn. Pedal nine more blocks, go left onto Anderson Street for two blocks, then right onto Habersham past lovely old homes planted with azaleas, honeysuckles, and gardenias. The railroad track you cross in about seven blocks can be dangerous, so take care. Then turn left onto Washington Avenue (47th Street) and pedal across Battey Street to Reynolds Street and turn right. You churn now past more homes built in Georgian Colonial, Classic Revival, and Regency styles. Cross De Renne Drive and pedal through Kensington Park, a suburban residential area with quiet streets.

From here you have several more turns: left on Oxford Drive

for one block, right on Andover, left on Althea, and right on Waters Avenue. Here for about a half mile you may encounter heavy traffic. Beginners and families with small children should stay right and ride single file.

Now you begin to wind into countryside. Turn left on Cornell, right on Seawright Drive, left on Eisenhower Road, right on Meridian Road, left on Montgomery Cross Road, and right on Skidaway Road, where you can stop for snacks at Newton's Corner, a small shopping center.

A right on Ferguson Avenue takes you two and a half miles to the Bethesda Orphans Home, beyond which you go left onto the Diamond Causeway. Around you the amber marsh grasses ripple in the wind, and you may glimpse quail, egrets, Baltimore orioles, great blue herons, gulls, sandpipers, ducks, thrashers, and even pelicans.

If you are using tubular tires, walk over the rough metal gratings on Roebling Bridge. On a hot day you can climb beneath the bridge to swim in the cool, salty Skidaway River. Beyond the bridge, on Skidaway Island, you can picnic and explore the flower-scented Southern woods. At the causeway's end, you reach the Skidaway Ocean Science Center's aquarium, open Monday through Saturday, 10 A.M. to 5 P.M., and Sunday afternoon (free admission).

Now return to Savannah, retracing your ride to Abercorn Street and Factors Walk. Just past Reynolds Square, you can turn right on Bryan Street, right on the east side of Warren Square, and left past 507 East St. Julian Street, a haunted Old South mansion.

WHERE TO STAY

Motels are numerous in Savannah and reservations should not be necessary. You find few campgrounds in the vicinity.

FOR SPARE PARTS AND REPAIRS

Savannah has two full-line cycling shops: Yellow Jersey Cyclery, on 68th and Waters Avenue, and Star Bicycle Shop, in the Oakhurst Shopping Plaza.

FOR FURTHER INFORMATION

Write Leonard Kantziper, 120 Andover Drive, Savannah, Georgia 31405. As an area director of the League of American Wheelmen and a longtime Savannah resident, he will be delighted to help you.

MAGNOLIA BLOSSOMS

While in Savannah, you will find the magnolia blossom's sweet, heavy fragrance unmistakable. What you notice only at second glance is that there are actually *two* magnolias here: the evergreen southern magnolia (*Magnolia grandiflora*) and the smaller, deciduous sweet bay (*Magnolia virginiana*). Here's how to tell them apart.

Southern magnolia most often adorns Savannah parks and resi-

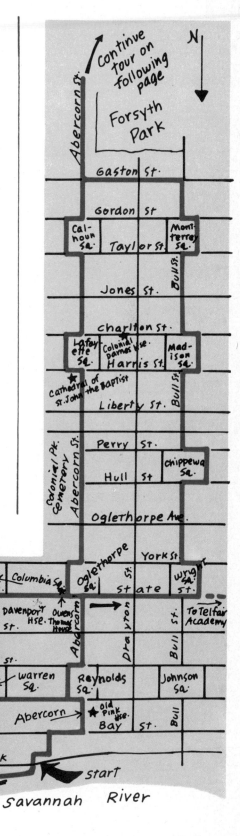

Savannah is in Georgia's coastal region on I-95 and 16, U.S. 80 and 17; 133 miles north of Jacksonville, Florida, via U.S. 17; 126 miles southeast of Augusta, Georgia, via U.S. 25 and 80; 250 miles southeast of Atlanta, Georgia, via I-75 and U.S. 80.

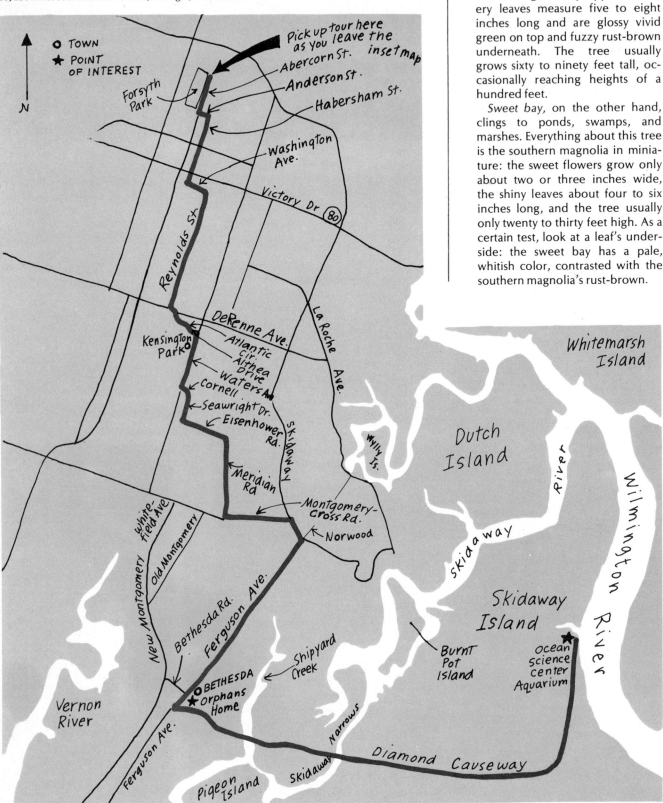

dences. The white flowers are huge—about eight inches across. The oblong, bluntly tipped, leathery leaves measure five to eight inches long and are glossy vivid green on top and fuzzy rust-brown underneath. The tree usually grows sixty to ninety feet tall, occasionally reaching heights of a hundred feet.

Sweet bay, on the other hand, clings to ponds, swamps, and marshes. Everything about this tree is the southern magnolia in miniature: the sweet flowers grow only about two or three inches wide, the shiny leaves about four to six inches long, and the tree usually only twenty to thirty feet high. As a certain test, look at a leaf's underside: the sweet bay has a pale, whitish color, contrasted with the southern magnolia's rust-brown.

39. OLD SOUTH SEACOAST SPIN

DISTANCE:	About 30 miles, depending on how much you ride in Savannah Beach.
TERRAIN:	Flat.
TRAFFIC:	Light on weekdays and during cool weather; heavy on summer weekends and holidays.
DIFFICULTY:	Requires strength because of possible strong winds.
BEST TIME:	Good anytime except June through August, when temperatures rise to the muggy 90's and 100's.
LOCATION:	Thunderbolt, Georgia, reached via Route 80 (Victory Drive) from mid-Savannah, to Savannah Beach on Tybee Island.

You may discover a Faulknerian blend of decadence and vitality on this Deep South ride through bleak swamps to sunny ocean shores. Lie on Savannah Beach's warm sands, taste slippery fresh clams and oysters, and visit historic Fort Pulaski on this tour near Savannah.

Start at Thunderbolt, a Savannah suburb where shrimp boats rock in the harbor. The teeming river backed by dead, still marshes creates good photographic effects. Before leaving, you can pedal to Bonaventure Cemetery on Bona-

venture Road, a former Colonial plantation, and walk your bike along narrow shaded paths overhung with moss-draped oaks. Camellias, azaleas, and dogwood and magnolia blossoms scent the air.

You leave Thunderbolt on Route 80 (Tybee Road), which has a white-lined shoulder bordered by spongy grass. Be careful crossing the three viaduct bridges between here and Tybee Island. They can be narrow and the glass splinters on all the bridges may force you into traffic.

You pedal almost immediately into wide marsh plains of amber grasses. Across these barren fens lined only with spindle-trunked palmettos, strong, unpredictable winds buffet your bike. Some cyclists sense hostility here; others feel free. If you stop to sit on the roadside grass, the marsh chirps, rustles, and trills begin. You may hear or spot an oriole, gull, kingfisher, sandpiper, duck, egret, great blue heron, pelican, or grackle.

As you spin up onto the third viaduct bridge, stop to lean over the rail. From here you see creeks slicing the marshes, the Savannah River widening toward the sea, Fort Pulaski guarding its island, and the resort town of Savannah Beach sparkling in the sun.

Now as you go over the bridge to Tybee Island, Fort Pulaski lies to your left, on Cockspur Island. Ride across the narrow bridge to explore the old stone fort, which lost its sole battle in a mere thirty hours. Lock your bike, climb the stairs to the parapet, then stroll on the fort's wooded grounds, where you can picnic on downy grass beneath an old moss-draped oak.

More flat road leads you to Savannah Beach, a clean resort town where you can literally taste the sea-salted air. Pedal along the

wide, bustling streets, then lock your bike and browse in the small shops or try the local seafood. Every St. Patrick's day, this beach town swarms with spectators, gleaming chromed bikes, and colorful whirling wheels as national Olympic team cyclists compete in the annual Classic Tour of Tybee Island. If you like, you can take part, too. Write the Chamber of Commerce for full registration details.

Head east now to sunny beaches where the warm sand turns cool as you bury your toes. The beach stands on the oceanfront rent bateaux, beach chairs, umbrellas, floats and surfboards, and even charter boats for deep-sea fishing. Oceanside night life may persuade you to rent a motel for the evening and return to Thunderbolt or Savannah the next day.

WHERE TO STAY

Savannah has many motels, which hardly need detailing because you should have no problem obtaining a room. Savannah Beach has thirteen motels, and you may want to make reservations if you happen to be here during a convention or the Tybee Classic. Some oceanfront motels include Cobb's Motel, 17th Street and Strand, (912) 786-4772; De Soto Beach Motel, Butler Avenue, (912) 786-4497; Ocean Plaza Motel, Ocean Front and 15th Street, (912) 786-4531; Ramada by the Sea, Butler Avenue, (912) 786-4535; and Sundowner Motor Inn, 16th Street on the beach, (912) 786-4532.

No camping facilities are available in the area.

FOR SPARE PARTS AND REPAIRS

The nearest bike shops are in Sa-

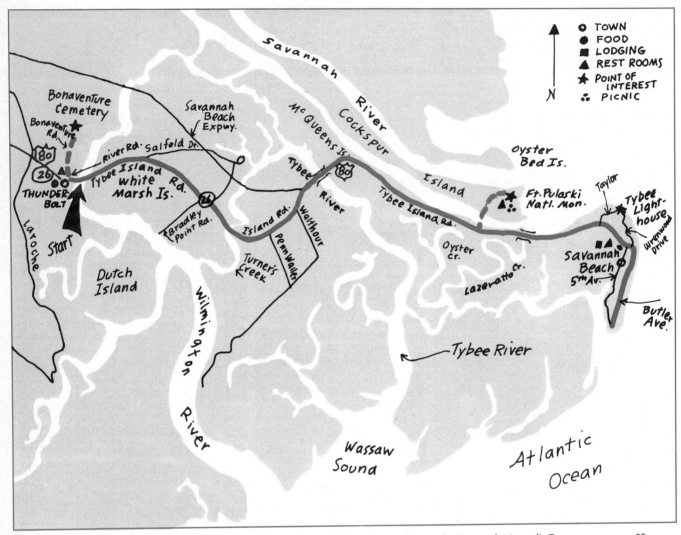

Thunderbolt is just east of Savannah, Georgia, on U.S. 80. For directions to Savannah, see the Savannah Magnolia Tour map on page 85.

vannah, so bring spare tires and tools on this trek.

FOR FURTHER INFORMATION

Savannah cyclist Leonard Kantziper of the League of American Wheelmen, can give you any additional information you might like to know. Write him at 120 Andover Drive, Savannah, Georgia 31405, or phone (912) 354-1826.

NEARBY

If you are in this area for the first time, a tour of historic Savannah is a must. See page 84 for details.

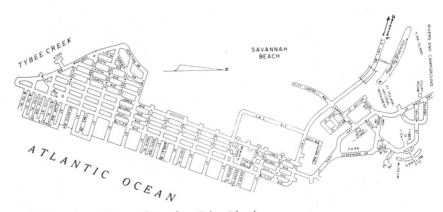

Explore the streets of Savannah Beach on Tybee Island.

40. CHICKAMAUGA CIVIL WAR CHURN

Discover quiet wooded lanes and countryside unchanged since Civil War days on this tour on the one-way roads of Chickamauga Battlefield south of Chattanooga, Tennessee. Though these forests and meadows once were scenes of violence, the land lies quiet now as you pedal through corridors of budding dogwood and flowering Judas in spring.

Start at the Chickamauga Battlefield Visitor Center, south of Chattanooga on U.S. 27, where you can park your car and obtain brochures. There are no food facilities here or along the battlefield, so pick up picnic basics and snacks before you arrive. Pedal south, following the one-way road left at the first intersection, and climb a gradual slope up Battleline Road. Caution: Avoid U.S. 27, which has fast, heavy traffic and many trucks.

Along the tour you pass eight markers describing the battle. At Brotherton Road, the main route goes straight onto Lafayette Road, but you can turn left to extend your explorations and add about 10 miles to your ride.

Extended Tour

The road becomes a gently rolling lane through trees. About 100 miles of hiking trails crisscross the park. In spring the southern pine, oak, and cedar forests are dotted with flowering dogwood, honeysuckle, and Judas trees.

At Alexander Bridge Road, turn left for a flat spin to Viniard-Alexander Road, where you turn right. A long, rolling ride leads you to a dead end at U.S. 27, where you rejoin the main tour by turning left.

The main battlefield road follows busy U.S. 27 (Lafayette Road) which has relatively light traffic on Sunday. After a short spin on U.S. 27

go right onto Glenn-Viniard Road, a one-way blacktop. Though you find no formal picnic spots in this area, about fifty tables are scattered throughout the park.

Soon a side trip left on Vittetoe Road takes you up a steep slope to Snodgrass Hill, offering excellent views of the woodlands. Then return to the Visitor Center, the main tour's end.

More Exploring

The above routes are best for families and beginners; experts may extend this tour north to Lookout Mountain in the park and Chattanooga. From the Visitor Center, take McFarland Gap Road

DISTANCE:	23 miles on the battlefield.
TERRAIN:	Flat to gently sloping.
TRAFFIC:	Lightest in spring and autumn; heavy on U.S. 27, especially on weekdays.
DIFFICULTY:	Good ride for anyone; excellent Sunday outing for families.
BEST TIME:	Spring and autumn for the coolest temperatures and lightest traffic. Summer is too hot.
LOCATION:	Chickamauga Battlefield in Chickamauga and Chattanooga National Military Park, Georgia and Tennessee.

left. Then go left on James Street, left on Happy Valley Road, right on Ridgeland Road (Route 349), and right on Chattanooga Valley Road (Route 58). Follow this road straight to West Lee Highway, where you go left. Another left onto Lookout Mountain Scenic Highway leads you to Lookout Mountain. If you have the stamina, take the arduous but worthwhile climb up the 1,700-foot mountain. From the summit on a clear day you see parts of Georgia, Tennessee, North Carolina, South Carolina, Alabama, Kentucky, and Virginia. At Point Park on the mountain's northern end, pause to view Chattanooga, the woodlands of Georgia, and Moccasin Bend in the Tennessee River. Also in this park is the Ochs Museum, where you can learn more about the battle. Before coasting down the mountain, you may wish to picnic in Point Park or hike a wooded trail. In spring you can enjoy rhododendrun and azalea displays.

If you have time or plan on spending a second day here, you can venture farther north into Chattanooga. Explore the George Thomas Hunter Gallery of Art at 10 Bluff View (open Monday through Saturday, 10 A.M. to 5 P.M., and Sunday afternoons; free admission) and the Houston Antique Museum at 201 High Street (admission, $1). Nine miles north of Chattanooga on Ridgeway Avenue (U.S. 127), take time to climb Signal Mountain, with a splendid view of "the Grand Canyon of the Tennessee" along the Tennessee River. Autumn foliage views from this vantage are excellent.

WHERE TO STAY

Motels, hotels, and inns are numerous in Chattanooga and you shouldn't need reservations.

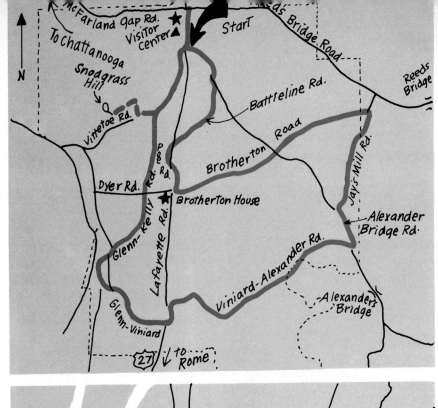

Camping is available at the following: Chattanooga South KOA, on Georgia 2A, a quarter of a mile north of the 2A and I-75 junction; open year round; $3.50 for two. For reservations, write Chattanooga South KOA, Box 532, Ringgold, Georgia 30736, or phone (404) 937-4166. Booker T. Washington State Park, 12 miles northeast of Chattanooga on State 58; open April 1st to November 1st; $3 for four. For details, write Booker T. Washington State Park, Box 369, Chattanooga, Tennessee, or phone (615) 894-4955. Harrison Bay State Park, 11 miles northeast of Chattanooga on State 58; open year round; $3 for four. For details, write Harrison Bay State Park, Harrison, Tennessee, or phone (615) 344-6214. There are also several private campgrounds in the area.

FOR FURTHER INFORMATION

Write Chickamauga and Chattanooga National Military Park, Fort Oglethorpe, Georgia 30741.

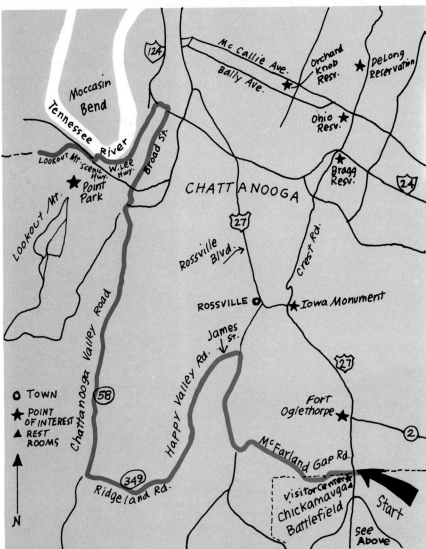

Chickamauga-Chattanooga National Military Park is in northwestern Georgia on U.S. 27; 10 miles south of Chattanooga, Tennessee, via U.S. 27; 115 miles north of Atlanta, Georgia, via U.S. 41, Georgia 2, and U.S. 27. Top Map: Main and extended tour. Bottom Map: For further exploring experts may enjoy a trip to Lookout Mountain.

41. GULF ISLAND SAIL

DISTANCE:	Varies from 35 to 45 miles, depending on routes taken.
TERRAIN:	Flat.
TRAFFIC:	Heavy near the beach in summer, lighter the rest of the year.
DIFFICULTY:	Fine for anyone except young children inexperienced in traffic.
BEST TIME:	Good year round.
LOCATION:	Pensacola, Florida.

Ride from Pensacola's historic homes, lighthouses, and Seville Quarter to wide white sands along the Gulf of Mexico on this Florida seashore tour.

Start at Hotel San Carlos on the northwest corner of Palafox and Garden Streets. Carry spare parts, tools, and lots of water. Sunglasses and suntan lotion are mandatory in summer and recommended year round. Also bring rain gear in summer and a warm sweater or windbreaker in winter. Sometime during your tour, be sure to visit the Seville Quarter south of the hotel. The tourist information office, nine blocks north of the hotel at Palafox and Cervantes, has a free map of the Quarter and other Pensacola high points.

To begin the main ride, go north on Palafox two blocks and right on Gregory Street to cross the 3-mile Pensacola Bay Bridge. Avoid the bridge toll by pedaling to the right of the tollbooths and clearing the traffic lane. As you cross, watch out for broken glass, tin cans, and other sharp objects on the shoulder.

After crossing a flat jetty of land, stay right on State 399 when U.S. 98 goes left and ride another bridge to Santa Rosa Island. As you leave the bridge, go right on Via Deluna toward Gulf Island National Seashore. Sea oats waving on top of dunes and shortleaf pines spin past as you ride. To your left, the Gulf stretches blue. Pause to go beachcombing for driftwood, rocks, or shells. Bird watching is excellent here. At the Seashore's western tip, explore· old Fort Pickens.

After a rest on the beach, retrace your ride across the long Pensacola Bay Bridge to Pensacola. From the corner of Palafox and Gregory Streets, go left one block to return to your starting point, or extend your tour by riding north to the University of West Florida or south to the U.S. Naval Air Station.

University Side Trip

Ride north on Palafox to Cervantes and right on Cervantes, which becomes State 10A beyond Bayou Texar. Five blocks past the bayou, follow U.S. 90 north along the bay and over rolling hills to the campus. Enjoy the four-lane road through the college's pine-and oak-wooded campus and eat at the Student Commons. Then return to the hotel by going south on Davis Highway (State 291), which leads into Alcaniz Street, right on Cervantes, and left on Palafox.

Naval Air Station Side Trip

Avoid this ride from 6 to 8 A.M. and 3:30 to 5 P.M. when traffic is heavy. Ride south on Palafox to Garden Street, where you turn right. After you cross State 292, this road becomes Navy Boulevard (Admiral Murray Boulevard). Soon you wind left to continue on Navy Boulevard, which becomes Barrancas Avenue and then Army Road. As you reach the air station, walk your bike over Bayou Grande onto the grounds. The terrain through the air station is easy, with only a few hills, but red safety flags are mandatory. After browsing through the museum, retrace your route north and go right on Barrancas Avenue. As you cross the drawbridge, stay left of the white line. To the right of the line, near the gutter, are slots which can trap a tire and flip you. Beyond the bridge, follow Barrancas Avenue as it angles right. Then go right onto Garden Street and back to Palafox.

End your day with dinner in Pensacola's old Seville Quarter. Rosie O'Grady's Warehouse, where Dixieland, vaudeville, minstrels, and silent movies recall the gay nineties and roaring twenties, deserves at least a peek.

WHERE TO STAY

Motels and hotels are numerous in Pensacola. A few possibilities are listed below: Mai-Kai Beach, 731 Pensacola Beach Boulevard, Pensacola, Florida 32561; (904) 932-3502. Pensacola Downtown Travelodge, 200 North Palafox, Pensacola, Florida 32501; (904) 432-3441. Quality Inn De Luna, 1801 West Cervantes Street (Box 5127), Pensacola, Florida 32505; (904) 434-1301. San Carlos Hotel, 1 North Palafox Street, Pensacola, Florida 32501; (904) 438-3121.

Campgrounds are found at Gulf Island National Seashore, on the western tip of Santa Rosa Island; open year round.

FOR SPARE PARTS
AND REPAIRS

Pensacola has several full-line bike shops, and you should have no problem locating parts or having repairs done.

FOR FURTHER
INFORMATION

Dr. George M. Rapier told us about this ride. To contact him, write Dr. George M. Rapier, c/o Pensacola Freewheelers, 400 West Sunset Avenue, Pensacola, Florida 32507.

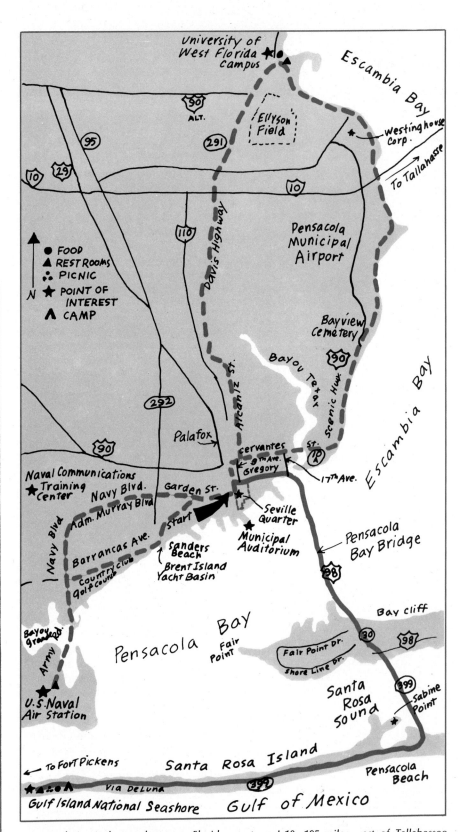

Pensacola is on the northwestern Florida coast on I-10; 195 miles west of Tallahassee, Florida, via U.S. 90 and I-10; 53 miles southeast of Mobile, Alabama, via I-10; 224 miles south of Montgomery, Alabama, via I-65, U.S. 31 and I-10.

42. CORAL GABLES BIKE PATH

Whether your interest be surfing, sunning, or just spinning through salt breezes, Coral Gables offers a delightful Sunday afternoon. You ride through the city, explore parks, tour an art museum, discover the elaborate Venetian Pool. Then you skip to a scenic tropical trail through the fields beneath palm, yucca, and coconut trees. Bring a Florida feast with you—fresh pineapples, oranges, peaches, and coconut milk—for this biking safari.

Start at J. Fritz and Frances Gordon Park. You may park your car near here on Sundays in the bank parking lot at S.W. 57th Avenue and 8th Street. Actually starting spots for this ride are flexible. Others include the traffic circle at Old Cutler Road and Sunset Road, Matheson Hammock Park, and the University of Miami. This tour is so easy and enjoyable, we will give you only general information and points of interest. Then just look at the map and plan your own ride.

Coral Gables is as flat as the ocean. You encounter no sharp curves on this ride, but the bike-path roads often have weak shoulders, so take care. Hazards to watch for include the U.S. 1 (South Dixie Highway) intersections, where there is heavy traffic and at one point a railroad crossing, too; the traffic circle at Old Cutler Road and Sunset; downtown Coral Gables, busy with people and traffic; and the bike path along Old Cutler Road, which is narrow and a bit run-down, so watch here for dead branches, deep holes, low limbs on the palm trees, gravel and rocks.

Though this ride is excellent year round, be prepared for short rain showers on summer afternoons from June through September. Northerners may also find the summer heat somewhat stifling.

Wear shorts and a light shirt in all seasons, and in summer bring insect repellent to combat mosquitoes on the southern portion of the ride.

To keep your bearings, note that street numbers begin at zero at Flagler Street and increase as you pedal south. Avenue numbers begin at zero at Douglas Road and increase as you ride west. Begin anywhere and follow the blue-and-white bike-path signs through the city.

J. Fritz and Frances Gordon Park (1) is a pleasant little city park, a nice place to begin or end your ride, a good rest stop anytime. A bit farther at Salvadore Park (2), you can use the public tennis courts, play shuffleboard, or let the children swing and slide in the playground. Then stop for a swim in what is billed as "the world's most beautiful pool," the Venetian Municipal Pool (3), with coral-rock hills, grottoes, a sand beach, and rare tropical trees. The setting resembles that of an old Venetian palazzo, and after a cool dip you can relax on a shady portico beside vine-entwined loggias, palm trees, and a waterfall, or walk along wrought-iron and stone bridges to tropical islands. Bicycles are allowed inside. Admission: Adults, $1; children under 12, 35¢ weekdays and 50¢ Sundays and holidays.

More flat, breezy cycling brings you to Lowe Gallery (4), where you can lock your bike outside and browse about this art museum on the University of Miami campus. Admission is free. Hours: Monday through Friday, noon to 5 P.M.; open Saturday at 10 A.M. and Sunday at 2 P.M.; closed holidays. Continuing on, you can meander along the streets of the city-style French Village (5) to observe the architecture and stop at a sidewalk café.

DISTANCE:	20 to 25 miles.
TERRAIN:	Flat.
TRAFFIC:	Moderate to heavy.
DIFFICULTY:	Good ride for anyone except young, undisciplined riders.
BEST TIME:	Year round. December through February, highs are in the 70's; the rest of the year, in the 80's and 90's.
LOCATION:	Coral Gables, Florida.

Tahiti Beach (6) provides a delightful midway stop, with lagoon and cabanas. Bikes are permitted, so take yours inside and swim, fish, or look for rocks and shells on the shores. Admission: Adults, 75¢; children 3 to 12, 50¢; under 3 years, free. Leave the bike path at Casuarina Concourse to pedal through a residential district to the road's end. Here you can see Wackenhut's Castle (7), a delightful monstrosity valued at five million dollars.

On Old Cutler Road (8) you pedal along a shaded bike path past woods and open fields. Stop anywhere along this scenic tropical trail to snack or picnic beneath the palm, coconut, and yucca trees. At Matheson Hammock County Park (9), you discover more choice picnicking spots—grassy nooks, shady meadows. Hike along the nature trails, swim in the marina or in the salt-water pool, or hunt for rocks and shells on the beach.

At Fairchild Tropical Garden (10), lock your bike at the gate and go in and stroll along garden paths or take a thirty-five-minute tram tour of the gardens. Admission: Adults, $1; children under 16, free if accompanied by a parent. Tram rides cost extra: adults, 75¢; children, 25¢.

Returning on Riviera Drive, you pedal by the country-style French Village (11), the Chinese Village (12), and the provincial-style French Village (13). If you need to rest, stop at University Park (14), then continue back to your starting point.

If you would like to put on more miles, take a side trip along Coconut Grove's bike path (15) to Coconut Grove, Miami's Greenwich Village, with its lush greenery, small shops, boat basin, and quaint restaurants.

WHERE TO STAY

Many motels are available along S.W. 8th Street in Coral Gables. A Holiday Inn and a Riviera Inn are located on U.S. 1 (South Dixie Highway) near the bike path. No camping is available.

FOR SPARE PARTS AND REPAIRS

Coral Gables has several fine bike shops, and parts or spares are no problem. Just consult the yellow pages.

FOR FURTHER INFORMATION

Write Nick Arkontaky, 6470 S.W. 41st Street, Miami, Florida. Nick told us about this ride, a favorite of the South Florida Wheelmen. If you enjoy group cycling, Nick can arrange for you to join the South Florida Wheelmen on their Sunday rides through Miami

Adjacent Coconut Grove also conducts an annual bike race in October. For details, contact the Chamber of Commerce, Coconut Grove, Florida; (305) 444-7270.

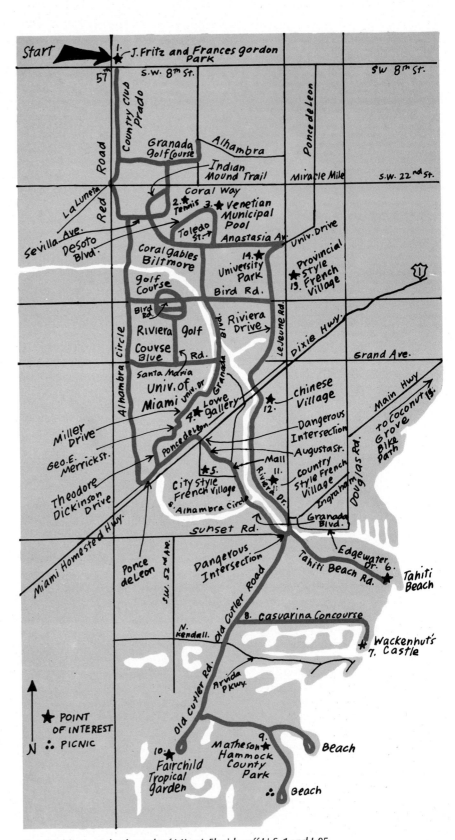

Coral Gables is a suburb south of Miami, Florida, off U.S. 1 and I-95.

43. EVERGLADES GRASSLANDS SAFARI

An alligator lying sleepily along a slough suddenly strikes an unsuspecting little green heron. Pink and crimson spoonbills wing over the brown mangrove rivers. And the comical anhinga swims under water like a fish, with only his snakelike neck poking above the swamp. For scenes you can find nowhere else in the country, bicycle the flat road through the Everglades.

Start at the Visitor Center, where you can park your car. Bring food, tools, spare parts, mosquito repellent, and at least two water bottles. Because of traffic, the park superintendent recommends safety flags. You pedal south on a flat, well-paved road with grassy shoulders that are often eight feet wide. Winter winds are unpredictable, but may be strong.

Two miles down the road, lock your bike at Royal Palm and hike the two trails. Gumbo-Limbo Trail leads you on a jungle path through a tropical hammock of strangler fig, mahogany, and coppery gumbo-limbo trees. Watch, too, for wild poinsettias and butterfly, green-fly, and clamshell orchids. The second walk, on Anhinga Trail, is the park's best spot to see alligators, little blue, great blue, and little green herons, and American bittern. One bird you will undoubtedly notice is the anhinga, also called snake bird or water turkey, who swims underwater to catch fish and eats his prey whole. Before you leave Royal Palm, refill your water bottles. This is the last food, water, and rest-room stop until West Lake.

In another 2 miles, just before you reach Long Pine Key with its camping and picnicking areas, try the little-used Pinelands Auto Trail to your left. This gravel road leads you through woods to a small secluded lake; you may glimpse wild turkey and deer along the way. If gravel sounds too rough for your tubular tires, stay on the main road another 2.5 miles to Pinelands Trail, then lock your bike and hike through the pine woods.

As you pedal you will see dozens of birds, including pelicans, roseate spoonbills, and herons, but don't overlook the tinier insect communities, best observed when you stop to rest. You may glimpse an exotic zebra butterfly, the golden orb spider, or the six-inch lubber grasshopper, tinted orange, yellow, and green. Several miles along the road past Pinelands Trail, Pa-Hay-Okee ("grassy waters") Overlook has a boardwalk and tower offering a panorama of marsh, fresh-water sloughs, and sawgrass.

Past Mahogany Hammock, where you can try still another hiking trail, pause at Paurotis Pond to picnic or study several rare palms. Then 2 miles farther south, stop at Nine Mile Pond to observe the area's wildlife, especially abundant in spring. Tiny fresh-water ponds all along the way may offer glimpses of soft-shell turtles, bull frogs, salamanders, snakes, and alligators.

At West Lake the trail through the mangrove swamp offers another exotic walk. Watch closely and you may be fortunate enough to see the extremely rare crocodile—brown and with a more pointed nose than the alligator—basking among the salty mangroves. Only a handful of crocodiles now survive in the Everglades.

Your ride is flat and breezy along Florida Bay past small ponds, inlets, and marshes into Flamingo. Here you can dine at a restaurant, camp, or stay overnight in a motel. Many boat excursions into the bays, rivers, and channels leave from here, or you can rent a canoe to explore several established waterway trails.

Return to your starting point the same way you came for a second, closer survey of the sawgrass country.

More Exploring

If you enjoy a rugged ride, try the Everglades Shark Valley loop,

DISTANCE:	76 miles round trip.
TERRAIN:	Flat.
TRAFFIC:	Heaviest between Christmas and Easter, but it seems to lighten somewhat in February and March.
DIFFICULTY:	Beginners can easily manage the terrain; whether they can handle the traffic depends on time of year. Possible high winds in winter make a 3-speed bike advisable.
BEST TIME:	February and March, when temperatures are pleasant and traffic relatively light. Avoid June through September, the park's rainy season, with hot, muggy days, an occasional hurricane, and many sand flies and mosquitoes.
LOCATION:	Everglades National Park, Florida.

15 miles of gravel located north of the main park road on State 27 and left on U.S. 41. The only traffic on the loop is a park-operated tram, but the gravel can be tough to ride. This wilderness adventure through a sawgrass slough area is excellent for spotting snakes, otter, deer, and alligators. The park administrators have considered setting up a bike rental concession for the area.

WHERE TO STAY

The only motel in the park is the Flamingo Inn, on the bay, operated by the Everglades Park Company, 18494 South Federal Highway, Miami, Florida 33157. Make reservations far in advance.

Campgrounds: Long Pine Key, 6 miles from the Visitor Center at the entrance to Flamingo, at your tour's southern end. Campground reservations are available from December 1st to April 30th. For information, write or phone Park Headquarters, Everglades National Park, Box 279, Homestead, Florida 33030.

FOR FURTHER INFORMATION

Write Superintendent, Everglades National Park, Box 279, Homestead, Florida 33030.

BIRDS OF THE EVERGLADES

Perhaps the most striking aspect of the Everglades is its exotic bird life. You may see herons, egrets, ibis, brown or white pelicans, cormorants, gulls, hawks, bald eagles, and frigate birds, to name only a few. Here is a list of several species.

The *great white heron* is a huge, graceful, snow-white bird with a yellow beak and S-curved neck. You may see this bird standing on sticklike yellow legs in marsh waters. The similar *great blue heron* is more common. Both birds often have a seven-foot wingspan.

You can't miss the huge, pink *roseate spoonbill* because of its size, striking color, and conspicuous

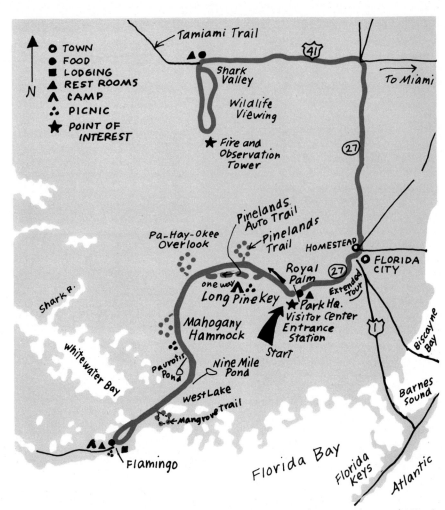

Everglades National Park is on Florida's southern tip on Florida 27; southwest of Miami, Florida, via U.S. 1 and Florida 27; north of Key West, Florida, via U.S. 1 and Florida 27.

flattened beak, which it moves from side to side when eating. The older birds are vivid pink with scarlet markings, while the younger roseate spoonbills are lighter pink.

The *purple gallinule* is multicolored with bright yellow legs, a red bill tipped with yellow, a lavender neck and head, and a greenish body. Watch for him along the marshes.

44. DANIEL BOONE / RED RIVER RIDE

On this tour you visit some of Kentucky's most spectacular scenery. Golden arches span thick stands of firs, spruces, and pines. Red sandstone cliffs jag hundreds of feet skyward. Clear, cool streams run through wooded valleys. Also here is the Red River Gorge, the East's "little Grand Canyon," its steep walls mottled rose, fuchsia, orange, purple, and saffron. For this ride, plan at least three days—one through Bluegrass Country to Daniel Boone National Forest, another exploring the Gorge and surrounding woods, a third returning to Lexington.

Park your car in one of the shopping centers near Richmond and New Circle roads in Lexington. Wood Hills Center is recommended because of the bike shop there. Carry tools, spare parts, and picnic basics. You find numerous little country stores along the ride.

Situated in Bluegrass Country, Lexington can provide a pleasant morning's cycling (see page 101 for details). Leave the city on Todds Road (Route 1425). Past the Bluegrass Sportsman Club, turn right at the Y onto Route 1927 and proceed through rolling pasturelands. Watch out for the narrow bridge across Boone Creek just before you reach tiny Pine Grove. From here you can take a pleasant side trip 9 miles to Fort Boonesboro State Park on the Kentucky River.

Boonesboro Side Trip

From Pine Grove take Combs Ferry Road right. Stay on the same road in Becknerville by veering right past Mount Zion Church. In Hootentown continue straight. Soon you wind along the riverbanks to Boonesboro, with a café, beach, boat rentals, camping, and good picnic spots. The site is more noted for historic legends than for anything actually standing today. You can see the clump of saplings on the shore where Indians captured Daniel Boone's daughter and the Calloway sisters in 1776, after which Boone led a successful rescue party and Sam Henderson's heroism won him Betsy Calloway's heart.

Experienced cyclists can shorten their ride a bit by taking fast-moving U.S. 227 from Boonesboro to Winchester. A better possibility for more leisurely cycling is to follow Combs Ferry Road back to Becknerville, jog right, then immediately left onto Becknerville Colby Road, go right at the dead end onto Colby Road, and proceed on to Winchester.

DISTANCE:	133 miles round trip, including a loop through the Red River Gorge.
TERRAIN:	Varies from gently rolling to winding and hilly.
TRAFFIC:	Light but sometimes fast; heavy near the Gorge in summer.
DIFFICULTY:	For experienced cyclists only.
BEST TIME:	Spring and autumn because of the wildflowers and foliage. Summer can be hot and the park may be overcrowded then.
LOCATION:	Lexington, Kentucky, to Daniel Boone National Forest.

Proceeding *without* the side trip, you continue along Todds Road, which soon becomes Colby Road. You ride for several miles beneath a small canopy of trees, then enter Winchester. Stop if you like at a snack place near the I-64 interchange, then take U.S. 60 through town and turn right onto State 15. Here you encounter steeper hills with mountain views. For some distance, Stoner Creek trickles beside you. Stop anytime to scramble down the banks and wade in the icy water. Past Pilot View and a little church, you suddenly see the Eastern Kentucky Mountains in the distance.

You climb and coast over more short, steep hills, with tiny wooded brooks crisscrossing your path. Then you roll onto the flat Red River valley floor. You meander beside the twisting Red River between high cliffs. At Clay City you can visit the Red River Historic Museum. You continue through Stanton on flat road into Daniel Boone National Forest.

Slade lies about 3 miles west of Natural Bridge State Park. Follow the signs right into the park, which has swimming, boat rentals, fishing, tennis, riding, and camping along Mill Creek Lake. Catch fish for dinner or have a Southern-style meal at Hemlock Lodge.

On your second day, take the park loop clockwise through the Red River Gorge (about 23 miles total). Routing: State 77 from Nada, right on State 715, right on State 15 to Nada. Steep hills lead into and out of the Gorge. Watch out for hazardous Nada Tunnel, unlighted, one-way, and wet. To be safe, wait for a car to precede you or ask a motorist to let you ride in his beams. When 715 crosses the Red River, lock your bike and hike along the wooded footpath on the east bank. Here you can rest, wade

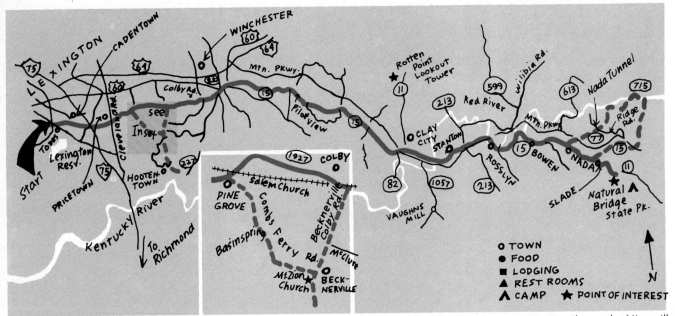

Lexington is in north-central Kentucky on I-75, and 64, U.S. 60 and 27; 79 miles south of Cincinnati, Ohio, via I-75; 173 miles north of Knoxville, Tennessee, via I-75; 177 miles west of Charleston, West Virginia, via I-64; 80 miles east of Louisville, Kentucky, via I-64.

in the stream, or snack.

Throughout this ride you pedal through deep sycamore, maple, oak, locust, beech, and elm woods and past vivid sandstone formations and scenic overlooks. Numerous hiking trails crisscross the area. Many rare or uncommon wildflowers may be spotted in spring, including the orange Turk's-cap lily, the pink lady's-slipper, the large twayblade, grass-of-Parnassus, and the purple coneflower. Also, as you pedal watch for the red-cockaded woodpecker, an endangered species sometimes seen here.

On your third day, return to Lexington via the Red River valley and Winchester.

WHERE TO STAY

Lexington and Winchester have numerous motels. Resort facilities are available at Hemlock Lodge in Natural Bridge State Park.

Camping is available at these locations: Natural Bridge State Park, described in the tour description; open April 1st to October 31st. Koomer Ridge, 5 miles from Slade on State 15, near the Red River

Gorge. Rock Bridge, 8 miles east of Slade on State 15, half a mile north on State 715, then three and a half miles east on Forest Service Road Route 24; located beside a stone arch over Swift Camp Creek. Sky Bridge, 8 miles east of Slade on State 15, then 6 miles left (north) on State 715; located atop a ridge overlooking the Red River Gorge.

FOR FURTHER INFORMATION

Write Don Burrell, c/o the Bluegrass Wheelmen, P.O. Box 1397, Lexington, Kentucky 40501. Information on the national forest may be obtained by writing Forest Supervisor, Daniel Boone National Forest, Winchester, Kentucky 40391.

RARE WILDFLOWERS TO SCOUT FOR IN BOONE COUNTRY

While pedaling through Daniel Boone National Forest, you may want to try to spot several uncommon wildflowers which still live in this wilderness. In moist woods

look for the following varieties.

Turk's-cap lily. You can't miss this huge plant, often nine feet high, with twenty or more nodding red-orange blossoms. The giant oval buds and the prominent stamens covered with deep red-orange pollen help make this flower unmistakable.

Squirrel corn. You can recognize this flower by its nodding white or possibly pink blossoms on a leafless stem. The leaves look feathery, and the plant blooms from a short bulb-bearing root.

Large twayblade. You really have to be looking for this small, inconspicuous green plant. When you find it and look closely, you discover five or more tiny purple flowers. The leaves are unusual—two broad leaves that cup the stem like a shallow vase.

Grass-of-Parnassus. This white-flowered plant grows up to twenty inches, and you may occasionally spot it along the roadside. The flowers grow on long stalks high above leaves which somewhat resemble lily pads and feel leathery.

45. KENTUCKY BLUEGRASS CENTURY

Kentucky Bluegrass Country—synonymous with sleek thoroughbreds, well-kept stables, the tense excitement of Churchill Downs—is really best appreciated on a bicycle. Pedaling on excellent, lightly traveled secondary roads, you can stop along the way to admire a glossy Arabian horse or watch the royalty dine on lush bluegrass and limestone water. You also are welcome to tour many of the farms, where Kentuckians will gladly tell stories about the "inside" of thoroughbred racing.

Your tour begins in historic Lexington, where you can visit two racetracks, Henry Clay's home, John Hunt Morgan's home, and various museums. (See the Historic Tour of Lexington on page 101 for details.) Complete directions for this tour are a bit complex and are listed at the end of the tour description.

Leave Lexington by going north on Bryan Station Road, where you cross over I-75 and soon ride into plush, rolling hills which actually turn "blue" in May only. Watch out for the railroad tracks about two and a half miles outside town and again about two and a half miles after you turn right onto Muir Station Road. You pass little white churches and tiny communities as you weave through the countryside. Several turns bring you to Winchester, where Henry Clay made his first and last speeches. Stop for a snack or buy picnic supplies, then leave Winchester via Van Meter Road.

Pause to sit along a tiny creek or relax beneath a white-splotched sycamore or leafy box elder. For a pleasant side trip off State 353, take the first right after the fork onto Huffman Mill Road and spin around a bend to Man o' War Monument a life-size statue of the famous racehorse. Jockey Isaac

Murphy and Man o' War are buried here. The pleasant little park makes a cool, shady picnic spot.

Returning now to State 353, you pass Russell Cave School and reach Ironworks Pike, where you can go either right on the main route or left for a side trip to Spendthrift Farm, home of million-dollar winner Nashua, American Jaipur, Gallant Man, Turn To, Swaps, Raise a Native, and Majestic Prince, 1969 Derby winner. Guests are welcome here and at other farms in the area. From March 1st to June 30th, the hours are usually Monday through Saturday, 10 A.M. to 1 P.M., and Sunday, 10 A.M. to 3 P.M., the rest of the year, 10 A.M. to 3 P.M. daily.

Proceeding on the main tour along Ironworks Pike, you pedal about 8 miles past horse farms and the American Saddle Horse Museum. This road goes through the tour's most picturesque section, and you may encounter a bit more traffic from sightseers. After you cross over I-75 and U.S. 25, watch for Yarnallton Road, where you go left, over I-64, and across a railroad track into Yarnallton. Turn right soon onto Old Frankfort Pike and climb the tour's only hills. Frankfort Pike leads through Faywood, where you go left at the church onto Shannons Run Road, crisscrossed by lots of little creeks. Other nice spots along this 10-mile stretch include tiny Cooke Lake and larger Sycamore Lake.

On Higbee Mill Road you can pause to stroll through Waveland Kentucky Life Museum, a plantation built in 1847 in the Greek Revival style, furnished with antiques. Higbee Mill Road runs along Elkhorn Creek to Clays Mill Road, where your ride is a bit bumpy until you turn left onto Brannon Road (State 1980). More turns take you back to Lexington, where

DISTANCE:	104 miles.
TERRAIN:	Flat to gently rolling.
TRAFFIC:	Light.
DIFFICULTY:	Easy for beginners. The complete ride is not recommended for families with young riders because of some narrow roads with 60-m.p.h. speed limits and limited overnight facilities. Portions, however, are okay for anyone.
BEST TIME:	April through October.
LOCATION:	Bluegrass Country around Lexington, Kentucky.

you can relax at a hotel and pedal in the evening along the wide city streets.

Directions

1. Leave town by pedaling north on Bryan Station Road (Bryan Avenue);

2. go right onto Muir Station Road;

3. Muir Station Road becomes Cleveland Road after you cross Briar Hill;

4. turn sharply left onto Todds Road;

5. left onto Old Todds Road just after you cross the railroad tracks in Pine Grove;

6. Old Todds Road becomes Colby Road;

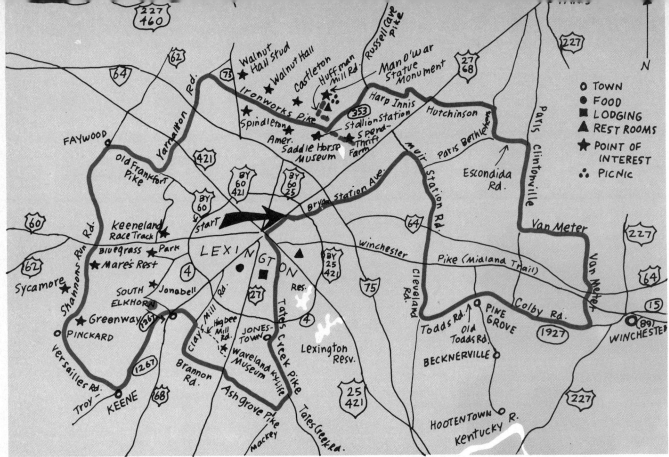

Lexington is in central Kentucky on I-75 and 64, U.S. 60 and 27; 79 miles south of Cincinnati, Ohio, via I-75; 173 miles north of Knoxville, Tennessee, via I-75; 177 miles west of Charleston, West Virginia, via I-64; 80 miles east of Louisville, Kentucky, via I-64.

7. turn left to bypass Winchester or go straight and ride into Winchester;

8. leave Winchester via Van Meter Road;

9. follow Van Meter Road sharply left;

10. go right in about 3 miles onto Clintonville Road;

11. left on Escondida Road, the first road outside Clintonville;

12. right on Paris Bethlehem Road;

13. left at the next road you come to Hutchinson Road (Paris Bethlehem Road—which you leave —goes straight ahead here);

14. left beyond Hutchinson Chapel (on your right);

15. left onto Harp Innis Road;

16. left onto Greenwich Road;

17. left at the wide fork onto State 353;

18. right onto Huffman Mill Road for side trip to Man o' War Monument, then return to State 353;

19. right onto Ironworks Pike (left for side trip to Spendthrift Farm);

20. left onto Yarnallton Road after crossing I-74 and U.S. 25;

21. right onto Old Frankfort Pike;

22. left onto Shannons Run Road (State 1967);

23. left onto State 169;

24. left onto State 1267 at Keene;

25. right onto Higbee Mill Road (cross U.S. 68; South Elkhorn Church is on your left);

26. right onto Clays Mill Road;

27. left onto Brannon Road (State 1980);

28. right onto U.S. 27 (in Providence at another church);

29. left onto Ash Grove Pike, which winds left;

30. left onto Mackey Road;

31. left onto Tates Creek Road and back to Lexington.

WHERE TO STAY

There are many motels in Lexington, including several Holiday Inns, Howard Johnson's, and Ramada Inns. Winchester has a Holiday Inn as well as the following: Country Squire, Winchester-Van Meter Road; (606) 744-7210. Family Inn, at the junction of U.S. 60 and I-64; (606) 744-9220. Skylit, 1018 West Lexington Avenue; (606) 744-6432.

You find no campgrounds on this tour.

FOR SPARE PARTS AND REPAIRS

Lexington has several fine bike shops.

FOR FURTHER INFORMATION

Contact the Bluegrass Wheelmen, P.O. Box 1397, Lexington, Kentucky 40501. The Wheelmen ride this tour regularly; they say it's a great one-day century ride.

NEARBY

For more days of exploring, try the Daniel Boone tour through the Red River valley and Red River Gorge (page 97), a serene ride to historic Frankfort (page 99), or a short, 6-mile spin through midtown Lexington (page 101). A combination of these tours makes a lovely week's vacation.

46. HISTORIC TOUR OF LEXINGTON

In the heart of Bluegrass Country, Lexington has a wealth of gracious old homes and priceless fine-lined thoroughbreds. Many attractions here are seasonal: in spring or autumn you can go to the races at Big Red Mile, the world's fastest trotter track, while from December through February you can visit the tobacco warehouse districts where high-pitched auctioneers sell loose-leaf tobacco at a rate of more than one million pounds a day. One event you can enjoy anytime you come is this historic midtown bike tour.

Park your car near the Lexington Public Library, and ride this tour counterclockwise because many streets are one-way. Avoid rush hours and if possible save this ride for a quiet Sunday afternoon. Leaving from the library in Gratz Park, you can pedal north through Transylvania College, oldest college west of the Alleghenies. The administration building, Old Morrison, served as a hospital during the Civil War; in Old Morrison's library are letters written by former student Jefferson Davis. Also on campus in Gratz Park is Kitchen, last of the original college buildings.

Pedaling south now on the road beside the library building (Mill Street), you reach the Hunt-Morgan House on the northwest corner of Mill and Second. If you like, stop to tour this late-Georgian-style home which was built in 1813 by John Wesley Hunt and became the eventual residence of Hunt's grandson General John Hunt Morgan, "thunderbolt of the Confederacy." Hours: Tuesday through Saturday, 10 A.M. to 4 P.M.; Sunday, 2 to 5 P.M.; closed Monday. Admission: Adults, $1; children 30¢. Turning right from Mill Street onto Second, you see in the first block on your left Henry Clay's Law Office, a state shrine

DISTANCE:	6 miles.
TERRAIN:	Flat, with a few hills.
TRAFFIC:	Heavy during the week; light on Sunday.
DIFFICULTY:	Short scenic ride good for anyone, including beginners and families.
BEST TIME:	Spring, summer, and fall, when temperatures are comfortable.
LOCATION:	Lexington, Kentucky.

restored to its 1806 condition.

You churn through midtown Lexington now, the road dead-ending soon into Georgetown Street. Turn left, ride three blocks, then turn left again onto Short Street. As a side trip, you can continue on Georgetown Street to West Main, turn right, and pedal two long blocks to Lexington Cemetery. Buried here are Henry Clay, John Cabell Breckinridge, and General John Hunt Morgan.

Back on Short Street, you pass many structures dating to the early nineteenth century, when this was the West Short Street district, a middle-class residential area. Turn right on Mill Street and coast to Maxwell Street, where you turn left. Along the way are many old three- or five-bay brick townhouses, and on the north side of High Street you see large log houses as well as brick homes built with rear galleries overlooking the city.

From Maxwell turn left onto Limestone and coast to Vine, where you go right. Beyond Rose Street, Vine veers right; ride straight ahead here onto Central Avenue. One block to your right on Park Avenue, you can stop in Woodland Park, a pleasant wooded rest spot with a pool and tennis courts. Back on Central, you dead-end soon into Ashland Street. Jog right here to pick up Fincastle Road, then stay right at the Y and ride on to Ashland, orator Henry Clay's home from 1811 until his death in 1852. The Clays lived here for four generations, and you can see the original family furnishings, hand-carved ash woodwork, French draperies, and silver doorknobs and hinges. Hours: Daily, 9:30 A.M. to 4:30 P.M. Admission: Adults, $1; children, 30¢. After touring the home, you can walk or pedal on the twenty-acre estate beneath spreading ash trees after which the mansion was named.

Returning west on Central, turn right onto Woodland, left onto Main, right onto Walnut, left onto Second, right onto Limestone, and left onto Mechanic, which takes you back to Gratz Park.

WHERE TO STAY

Numerous motels and hotels are available in Lexington. There are no camping facilities in the area.

FOR FURTHER INFORMATION

Don Burrell contributed this tour. You can write him c/o the Bluegrass Wheelmen, P.O. Box 1397, Lexington, Kentucky 40501. The Wheelmen conduct this tour annually. If you enjoy group cycling, ask when the next ride is planned.

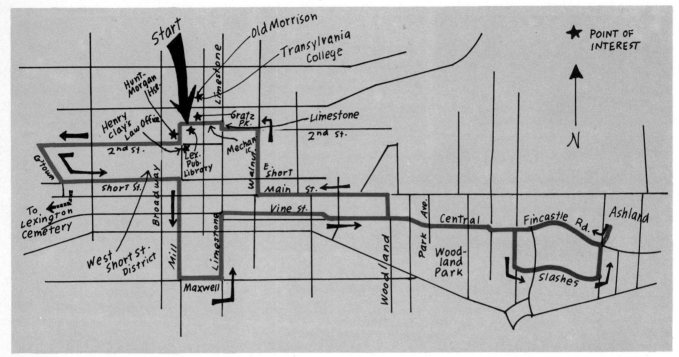

Lexington is in central Kentucky on I-75 and 64, U.S. 60 and 27; 79 miles south of Cincinnati, Ohio, via I-75; 173 miles north of Knoxville, Tennessee, via I-75; 177 miles west of Charleston, West Virginia, via I-64; 80 miles east of Louisville, Kentucky, via I-64.

NEARBY

The back roads around Lexington offer days of good cycling past horse farms, farmlands, and pastoral countryside. Take off east of Lexington through Daniel Boone National Forest to Red River Gorge (see page 97) or west to historic Frankfort (see page 101). Or circle Lexington on a century ride through the Bluegrass Country (see page 99). You could easily plan a week's vacation and perhaps longer in this region.

47. KENTUCKY HERITAGE RIDE

DISTANCE:	55 miles round trip.
TERRAIN:	Flat to hilly, with several steep grades.
TRAFFIC:	Light and fast in some spots, heavy and fast in others.
DIFFICULTY:	For experienced cyclists only, because of narrow roads and some fast traffic. Beginners can handle the back roads.
BEST TIME:	Spring through autumn. Avoid hot summer days.
LOCATION:	From Lexington to Frankfort, Kentucky.

Pedaling along country lanes past white wooden fences, hand-built stone walls, and tobacco farms, you experience the best of Kentucky's Bluegrass. Visit a thoroughbred horse farm, explore the banks and high cliffs of the Kentucky River, tour a bourbon distillery, and see Daniel Boone's grave and the many historic homes in Old Frankfort. You discover much here, so start early if you plan to finish in one day.

Park your car at Meadowthorpe Shopping Center near New Circle Road on U.S. 421, and ride south for a half mile on Forbes Road to Frankfort Pike, a road with light but fast (50-m.p.h.) traffic. Horse farms line the road and you see grazing mares and stallions, their burnished coats gleaming in the sun.

While the grass grows "blue" in May only, the pastures contain rich green grass throughout the summer. Visit a farm to learn about the inside of thoroughbred racing. Darby Dan Farm, 6 miles outside Lexington, welcomes guests from 9 A.M. to 4 P.M., as do other farms.

Pedal over more rolling terrain past the Headley Museum, a private jewel collection on display Wednesday, Saturday, and Sunday, from noon to 5 P.M. Admission, $2. Then you pass Summerhill and Bonnie Braes farms, just beyond which you can turn right onto Browns Mill Pike to tour an old Indian fort.

Back on Old Frankfort Pike, you can take a side trip at the next right (Mount Vernon Church is on the corner) onto Paynes Depot Road and pedal about one and a half miles to Weisenberger Mill, a picturesque flour mill on a stream. Continuing on Old Frankfort Pike, your ride is flat and smooth to Nugents Cross Roads. Here you can take a short side trip to the right onto U.S. 62 to the small village of Midway, with an excellent antique shop.

Trees now overhang Old Frankfort Pike as you pass gray stone fences. Just beyond the railroad tracks at Duckers, veer left, then right to a little restaurant and general store where you can buy picnic supplies or snacks. Beyond Duckers you can turn either onto U.S. 60, a well-paved four-lane highway with a gravel shoulder and heavy traffic which leads into Frankfort, or onto Ducan Road (Route 1681) toward Millville, a scenic ride along the Kentucky River. Unless you are rushed, the latter is recommended.

Route 1681 winds through countryside and dead-ends into Route 1659, where you can go to the right past bourbon distilleries which welcome guests for free tours or left for a side trip to Buckley Hills Wildlife Sanctuary.

Wildlife Side Trip

Turn left onto Route 1659. Beyond Millville take the first right at Millville School onto Route 1964, the first right again onto German Road, and a left at the fork to the wildlife sanctuary, a peaceful wooded stop. Retrace your ride and continue on past the distilleries on Route 1659 toward Frankfort.

You wind a few miles along the scenic Kentucky River, where you can picnic or relax beneath a willow on its banks. Then you meander away from the river and climb a steep hill, passing the cemetery where Daniel Boone is buried.

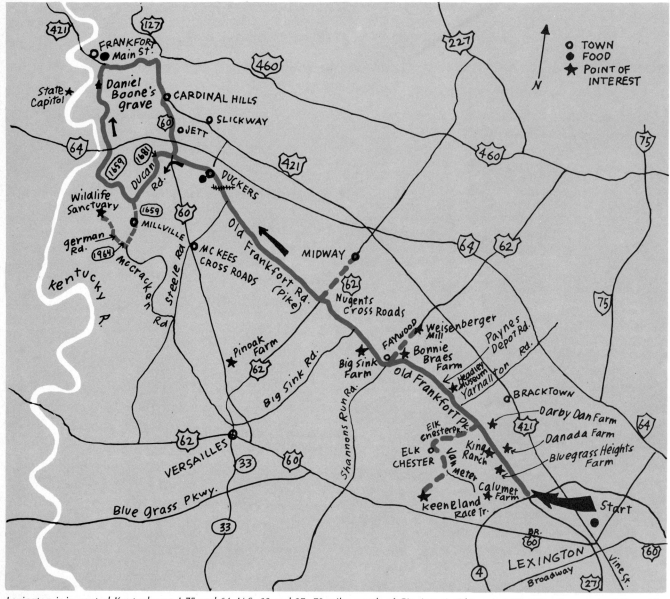

Lexington is in central Kentucky on I-75 and 64, U.S. 60 and 27; 79 miles south of Cincinnati, Ohio, via I-75; 173 miles north of Knoxville, Tennessee, via I-75; 177 miles west of Charleston, West Virginia, via I-64; 80 miles east of Louisville, Kentucky, via I-64.

From here you have wide views of Frankfort's housetops, with the state capitol building in the distance.

Coasting into Frankfort, take Main Street right into the city's center and explore Old Frankfort, where Aaron Burr stood trial for treason and celebrated his acquittal, Henry Clay spoke, and Presidents wined and dined in elegant old mansions. Return to Lexington by any of the routes detailed above.

WHERE TO STAY

Frankfort and Lexington both have numerous motels and hotels. There are no camping facilities along this ride.

FOR FURTHER INFORMATION

This is a favorite ride of the Bluegrass Wheelmen in Lexington. Write them at P.O. Box 1397, Lexington, Kentucky 40501, for advice on current road conditions or for answers to any further questions you may have.

48. GREAT SMOKIES MEANDER

Deep in the forested hazy blue Great Smokies lies tiny Cades Cove Valley. Dense woods fill this isolated nook, and in spring the hollow is scented by hundreds of blossoming trees and wildflowers. Trickling rills crisscross the paths where pioneers once walked, while settlers' homesteads and churches still stand after a hundred years. Cades Cove should be experienced, not just quickly seen. Cycle here and you will come to know the Smokies with an intimacy many thousands of hasty tourists never feel. This 11-mile tour can be ridden in an hour, but plan to spend all day and pack a picnic lunch and stop often.

Park your car at the Cove entrance in Great Smoky Mountains National Park or in the campgrounds near the Cove exit. You glide from the entrance gradually downhill past wide green meadows. Though traffic can be heavy, the speed limit is just 20 m.p.h. and many cyclists use the road.

Cades Cove is literally an open-air museum. Here self-sufficient pioneers hewed an existence from the wilderness, and apple and black walnut trees planted by the early mountain settlers still thrive. Often you see periwinkles, phlox, or daffodils, defining spots where cabins once stood. Past Sparks Lane, a narrow dirt road winding across the Cove, stop to hike .3 mile to John Oliver's cabin, built in 1818 by the Cove's first white settler. Beyond the board-and-stone cabin, you pedal into deep forests with abundant tree species, including beech, white ash, cucumber, black gum, shortleaf pine, table-mountain and pitch pines, white poplar, and chestnut and mountain oak. Stop at the numerous turnouts, lock your bike, and explore.

DISTANCE:	11 miles.
TERRAIN:	Gradual decline first half of the tour; gradual incline last half.
TRAFFIC:	Heavy on weekends, particularly in autumn.
DIFFICULTY:	Excellent ride for anyone.
BEST TIME:	Any season except winter. Wildflowers bloom in April and May, while rhododendron and mountain laurel displays are best during June and July. Fall colors are vivid the last two weeks in October.
LOCATION:	Cades Cove Valley, Great Smoky Mountains National Park, Tennessee.

Soon on your left you coast to a road along which you pedal half a mile to Primitive Baptist Church, where cemetery markers reveal a dramatic, often lost struggle with disease and malnutrition. Back on the main road, past the Methodist Church and Old Hyatt Lane, you reach a graveled road leading to Townsend. This follows the same route pioneers traveled—over Tater (short for "potato") Ridge through Rich Mountain Gap. Even though you may have an over-eager pioneer spirit, walk your bike on this road: even the hardy settlers wouldn't have braved this gravel with tubular tires.

Beyond Tater Branch, a small brook, veer into the parking area for excellent views of the rugged Smokies. Coasting a bit farther, look across the Cove to see the Smokies' crest line, with prominent Old Thunderhead Mountain. A bit farther still, detour to the right to Elijah ('Leige') Oliver's cabin, where the old deacon of the Primitive Baptist Church lived for thirty-seven years.

At the small wooden bridge across Abrams Creek, sit quietly on the banks among the rhododendron and laurel, watch fish flick through the stream, and listen to the woods. This makes a delightful picnic stop. Then, lock your bike to a tree and hike along the shaded paths to frothy Abrams Falls.

Back on the main road, turn right into the John P. Cable Open Air Museum, where you can stroll past old buildings, including a mill and blacksmith shop. The miller grinds corn from May to October, and you can buy a bag at Becky Cable's white-frame home. Beyond the museum, the road to your right leads to still another quaint pioneer cabin.

In the next several miles, you encounter a few abrupt, short but steep hills. You may have to walk, but this way you see even more. Watch closely for white-tailed deer, woodchucks, and wild turkeys. The cool woods smell of birch bark and wild mountain laurel. Stop anywhere in the soft green shadows to relax. Beyond Cable Cemetery, with its old stones, you reach Pine-Oak Nature Trail; pick up a self-guiding leaflet before you hike

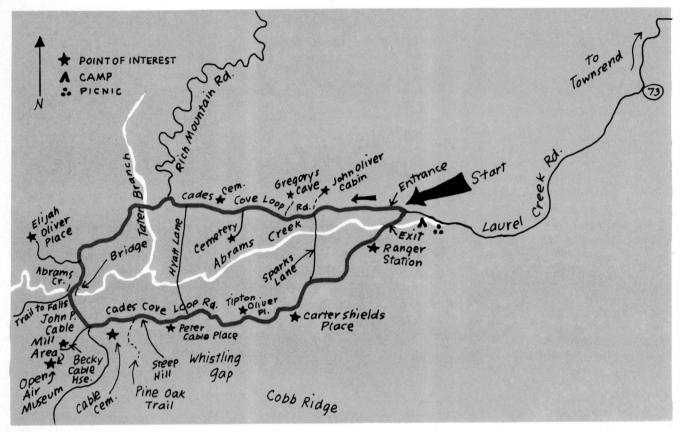

Cades Cove in Great Smoky Mountains National Park is in southeastern Tennessee off Route 73; 35 miles south of Knoxville, Tennessee, via U.S. 129 and Route 73; 208 miles south of Lexington, Kentucky, via I-75, U.S. 129, and Route 73; 221 miles east of Nashville, Tennessee, via I-40, U.S. 129, and Route 73.

here. Soon you can stop to explore more old cabins, then continue over the hills for good views of Cades Cove Mountain.

Relax along still another sparkling brook, then pass the Carter Shields cabin, beyond which you can see Rich Mountain from the view turnout. A tiny creek follows you as you pedal back to Cades Cove Road exit.

WHERE TO STAY

Motels are available all around the park, in Bryson City, Cherokee, Fontana Village, and Tapoco, North Carolina, and in Gatlinburg, Pigeon Forge, and Townsend, Tennessee.

Campgrounds are located at the Cove exit and also at ten other spots throughout the park. The camps operate on a first-come first-served basis and fees are $3. For a really secluded stay in the wilderness, you can hike for half a day up a mountain trail to LeConte Lodge, open mid-April to late October. Reservations are a must, so phone or write LeConte Lodge, Gatlinburg, Tennessee 37738; (615) 436-4473.

FOR SPARE PARTS AND REPAIRS

You find no bike shops near the Cove, so bring spares and tools with you. In an emergency you can always rent a bike from the lodge at the Cove's entrance. Hourly rates are 85¢ for a coaster-brake bike, $1.25 for a 3-speed, and $1.70 for a tandem, and 25¢ for a baby seat. No 10-speed bikes are available.

FOR FURTHER INFORMATION

Write Keith M. Cottam, Smoky Mountain Wheelmen, P.O. Box 11172, Knoxville, Tennessee 37919.

Keith told us about this tour and will try to help with any other cycling questions. For current weather, lodging, or park information, contact the subdistrict ranger station at (615) 448-6222, or write Superintendent, Great Smoky Mountains National Park, Gatlinburg, Tennessee 37738.

NEARBY

Surrounding Cades Cove lies the rest of Great Smoky Mountains National Park, where the terrain offers strenuous riding and the traffic is often heavy. The countryside throughout this region, though, is picturesque, and many back roads just outside the park are delightful. One possible ride is the Tennessee Barefoot Skiddoo on page 107, which can be linked with the Cades Cove tour for a splendid biking weekend.

49. TENNESSEE BAREFOOT SKIDDOO

Not far from Great Smoky Mountains National Park, you can pedal along winding back roads where the loudest sound is a cricket chirping in the grass. Mists cling to the river and shroud the mountains in early morning; dogwood, redbud, and magnolias blossom along the riverbanks; silvery creeks slip through the hills. You find local backwoods atmosphere, too—weathered shanties, tin-roofed barns and dozens of Baptist churches.

Start in Maryville, where you may park your car on a side street. You find snack spots along the way, but you will probably want to carry a picnic lunch. Ride from town on State 73. Soon you coast gently to Old Tuckaleechee Pike, known locally as Old Walland Highway, where you go right. Caution: Don't continue on heavily trafficked State 73. Old Tuckaleechee Pike is wide, well paved, and untraveled. Beyond Steele's Trading Post, where an old gentleman sells odds and ends from beneath a shade tree, you plunge downhill past a small white church. Climbing around a bend, you come upon old farmsteads with unpainted barns, gray rail fences, and open pastures, as well as tidy homes with clipped green lawns. On nearly every side road, a sign points toward still another Baptist church.

As you climb a second hill, watch for the angry black dog in the white house on your right at the hilltop: he's medium-sized, but chases bikes with the ferocity of a Doberman pinscher. More rolling hills bring you to Hubbard School, a good place to park your car if you wish to shorten the tour. About 100 yards farther is Kwik Way Mart, where you can stop for a snack or cool drink. Fill your water bottle before leaving because the next part of the tour can be hot and dry in summer.

As you leave the store, be careful crossing the one-lane concrete bridge, beyond which the road narrows. You climb gradually now past broad, open fields and another Baptist church on your right, pedal along a flat hilltop, then drop quickly into a valley. Don't spoil this coast by too much braking, but be ready for the right-hand curve at the bottom. Beyond this tricky curve do be sure to follow the black arrow and turn 90 degrees to the right to cross Coulter's Bridge. On a hot day, lock your bike and climb to your left beneath the bridge for a dip in a popular local swimming hole. A rope hangs from a thick tree limb here, so you can swing over and splash into the cool water.

Beyond the swimming-hole bridge, stay right at the intersection. The turnoff to your right makes a good parking spot if you would like to shorten this tour further and bike only the last 10 miles. From here to the tour's end, the road is particularly scenic, varying from flat to gently rolling hills, with lots of nooks to explore and lovely views of the misty Smokies. You meander along riverbanks lined with sycamore, maple, cedar, black walnut, mountain ash, and elm trees. In spring cream-colored flowering dogwood and pink redbud blossoms sweeten the air. Soon you spin past a quaint old flour mill near the clear-running Little River. You ride over gentle swells and around bends, passing a bridge which leads to a dilapidated backwoods shanty. Then you twist between the river and a steep hill, at the base of which are small homes, gardens, and pastures.

The road winds right at an old weeping willow tree and hugs the mountainside, while a narrow bank slopes gently toward the river. About 150 yards past a shale pit, you reach Walland intersection, with once-famous Chilhowee Inn to your left, a home now owned by friendly Tom and Bess Baugh. To quench your thirst, drink from the spring trickling through the pipe at the roadside: Tom has rigged this "fountain" for passersby. Beyond a two-lane concrete bridge, you can have a snack in town. Then you reach an intersection with many signs: "East Walland Missionary Baptist Church," "Walland High School," "Walland Methodist Church."

DISTANCE:	33 miles round trip.
TERRAIN:	Rolling hills, with some flat stretches.
TRAFFIC:	Light at all times of the year.
DIFFICULTY:	Excellent ride for anyone, including families and beginners.
BEST TIME:	All seasons but winter. Particularly pleasant in April, May, September, and October.
LOCATION:	Maryville, Tennessee, to Great Smoky Mountains National Park. Three hours from Nashville; 4 hours from Atlanta, Georgia; 5 hours from Cincinnati, Ohio, or Birmingham, Alabama.

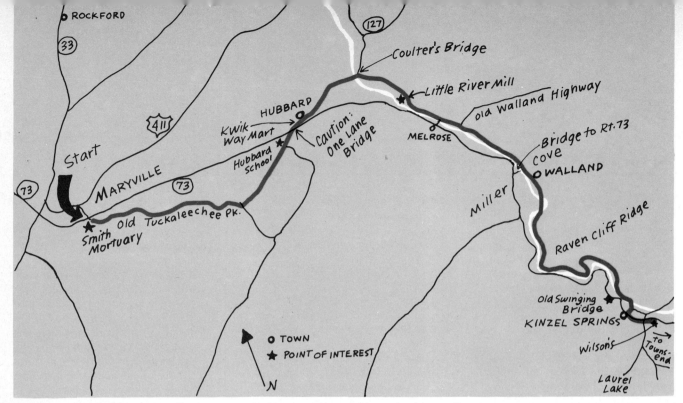

Maryville is in southeastern Tennessee on U.S. 411 and Route 73; 17 miles south of Knoxville, Tennessee, via U.S. 129; 203 miles east of Nashville, Tennessee, via I-40 and U.S. 129; 95 miles northeast of Chattanooga, Tennessee, via I-75, U.S. 11, Route 72, and U.S. 411.

side trip left on a narrow road.

Continuing on the main tour through Walland, you soon ride onto new smooth pavement for the tour's last 6 miles. Then you climb a hill and coast a few hundred yards to a narrow roadside turnoff and a lovely river nook marked inconspicuously by a break in the fence.

Lock your bike and climb down through the break on a steep path where a big oak tree's roots form steps. Here you can rest beneath grottoed cliffs beside deep pools with water so clear you can see fish swimming on the river bottom. Motorists zip past this hidden nook, allowing you a quiet picnic along the riverbanks.

Continue now along a rolling, winding lane beneath Foothills Parkway Bridge past summer homes. Occasionally rock outcroppings branch over the road. Another pleasant stop is at now-abandoned Arrowhead General Grocery, where you can walk down the lane on the building's left to an old swinging bridge. Back on the main road, you cross a one-lane concrete bridge and bypass Barefoot Jerry's Grocery to Wilson's Cafe, a good snack or lunch stop and a fine starting point for tours into Great Smoky Mountains National Park.

From Wilson's retrace your ride back to Maryville. Though prevailing winds blow upriver, you have a general coast back to the swimming-hole bridge. You may pick up speed on several stretches and find yourself shifting to higher gears to keep from spinning too fast. Just coast and enjoy the scenery back to your tour's end.

WHERE TO STAY

You find several motels in Maryville and in the area around Wilson's. Campgrounds are available in Great Smoky Mountains National Park.

FOR FURTHER INFORMATION

Keith M. Cottam contributed this tour. For additional information, you can write him c/o Smoky Mountain Wheelmen, P.O. Box 11172, Knoxville, Tennessee 37919. An avid cyclist, Keith can tell you about other delightful Tennessee jaunts.

NEARBY

Great Smoky Mountains National Park, with rugged terrain and lots of traffic, is recommended only for experts. The little valley of Cades Cove, however, offers delights for everyone. See page 105 for further details. Beyond the park, you can take the Blue Ridge Parkway for a gigantic ride—469 miles—to Shenandoah National Park and an excellent tour along a scenic ridgetop. Further details on both rides are found on pages 77 and 75.

50. DEEP SOUTH NATCHEZ TRACE

A biking-hiking journey is the most authentic way to experience the Natchez Trace, an ancient wilderness trail pounded into a primitive road by wild animals, Indians, and pioneers. Pedaling on smooth pavement paralleling the old dirt path, you enjoy uncommercialized countryside and woodlands.

In summer caution is required because the parkway is narrow and traffic may be fast and heavy. But in spring this ride is delightfully untraveled. If you are planning a group ride, advise the park rangers of your tour dates, the estimated number of cyclists, and the portion of parkway you will tour.

TENNESSEE-ALABAMA SECTION

Start this tour west of Highway 99 at Meriwether Lewis Park, where explorer Meriwether Lewis is buried. Camping is available here and you can take time to explore the serene nature trail. You find few facilities and no motels or campgrounds after you leave this area so carry spare parts, tools, and food, and plan to ride 67 miles in one day.

Pedaling south, you climb a barely noticeable rise, then coast about half a mile through countryside. Soon you dive down the Buffalo River bank to Metal Ford, where an iron-smelting industry once flourished, and scale the opposite bank. From the river, the road rises gradually for several miles, then levels. Pause for food and a rest in the picnic area along a stream about 8 miles from your tour's start.

The land lies quietly as you pedal to a short loop leading along a portion of the rough dirt Trace. Walk this stretch to avoid flat tires. Along the rest of your ride, easy knolls occasionally break the flat farmlands,

DISTANCE:	Tennessee-Alabama Section, 67 miles one way. Mississippi Section, 52 miles one way.
TERRAIN:	Virtually flat, with a few easy hills.
TRAFFIC:	Heavy in summer; lightest in winter, early spring, and late autumn.
DIFFICULTY:	Good ride for anyone during off-season.
BEST TIME:	Spring, autumn, or winter. Summer is too hot and humid.
LOCATION:	Natchez Trace Parkway, in Tennessee and Alabama, and in Mississippi south of Jackson, between I-20 near Clinton, Mississippi, and U.S. 80 near Port Gibson, Mississippi.

and you descend only about 600 feet in the 50 miles to the tour's end in Alabama.

About a mile beyond Glenrock Picnic Area, you spot Sweetwater Nature Trail winding off to your right through the woods. If you explore here, you will find the short path leads through rich bottomland forest alive with wildflowers.

Beyond the roadside marker describing McGlamery Stand, an early inn, there are two picnic groves, Holly and Cypress Creek,

located 40 and 43 miles from the tour's start.

Farms, woods, brooks, and wood fences slip by as you coast into Alabama and roll over easy road to Rock Springs, a nature trail meandering through bottomland along Colbert Creek to Colbert Springs, where you can fill your water bottle. Markers along the trail explain the natural forces at work here.

At the Tennessee River Bridge, relax in the picnic grove for a while before you pedal the last 6 miles past Buzzard Roost, where Chickasaw Chief Levi Colbert once lived.

As the parkway ends, turn right on U.S. 72 into Iuka, Mississippi. Then pedal 8 miles north on State 25 and follow the signs 4 miles west to J. P. Coleman State Park, with swimming, boat rentals, a restaurant, cabins, and camping. Arrange for a pick up here or return via the parkway to Meriwether Lewis Park.

MISSISSIPPI SECTION

Wooded Rocky Springs Campground, the only overnight stop on this segment of the parkway, provides the planning axis for this tour. No matter how far you decide to ride, the campground, which has adequate parking, is a good starting place. From the camp you can ride northeast to the end of the completed parkway for a total of 68 miles round trip or southwest to the parkway's end for 36 miles round trip. Bring spare parts, tools, and food. Groceries may be purchased in Port Gibson, at the southwest end of this portion of the Trace.

Northeast of Rocky Springs, meadows, farms, and woods roll by as you pedal through peaceful, undisturbed countryside. Many cy-

Meriwether Lewis Park is in central Tenessee on the Natchez Trace Parkway just south of Route 99; 63 miles south of Nashville, via U.S. 31 and Tennessee 99; 185 miles northeast of Memphis via U.S. 64 and the Natchez Trace Parkway. Rocky Springs Campground is in southwestern Mississippi on the Natchez Trace south of Jackson, Mississippi.

clists rate this one of the best sections of the parkway. Deans Stand, 19 miles from Rocky Springs, has a deeply shaded picnic area where you can stop to sip ice-cold lemonade from your thermos and stroll through woods.

About 5 miles farther is Raymond Battlefield Site, the scene of a Civil War battle during the 1863 Vicksburg campaign. You can picnic here before returning to the campground.

Three miles southwest of Rocky Springs, pause to dangle your feet in Owens Creek near a misty waterfall; legend has it this peaceful glen was once a robbers' hangout. About 6 miles farther, lock your bike and scout along a section of the Old Trace, ending at a fallen bridge across the Big Bayou Pierre River. A bit farther east of the parkway is Mangum Mound, an Indian burial mound.

As you approach the parkway's end, go right on U.S. 61 for 1 mile into Port Gibson, a village General Grant thought "too beautiful to burn." Pedal along the quaint streets past antebellum churches and homes and restock your supplies before returning to Rocky Springs.

WHERE TO STAY

Motels are limited in this area, with the surrounding towns being surprisingly uncommercialized.

Campgrounds: Meriwether Lewis Park, at the junction of the parkway and Tennessee 20; open year round; $2. J. P. Coleman State Park, 8 miles north of Iuka, Mississippi, on State 25, then 4 miles east; open year round; $2.50 to $3; (601) 423-6629. Rocky Springs, on the parkway about 12 miles south of the junction with Mississippi 27;

open year round; $2.

FOR FURTHER INFORMATION

Write Superintendent, Natchez Trace Parkway, Box 948, Tupelo, Mississippi 38802.

NEARBY

Two more sections of the Natchez Trace Parkway are now complete. The stretch from Tupelo to Jackson, Mississippi, is 166 miles long and meanders past old plantations through farmland, woods, bayous, and swamps. South of Port Gibson, a short 12-mile segment of the parkway leads you past Mount Locust Historic House, several peaceful nature trails, and an eight-acre Indian temple mound.

51. 52. LOUISIANA JAMBALAYA

In Louisiana's Feliciana County you roll over gentle farmland, past antebellum homes, moss-draped live oaks and pines, and placid pools. Sometimes an old rusty tractor putters along the road, silencing the crickets and making the squirrels stand stone-still. But usually there isn't a car or other vehicle for miles, and the back roads stretch leisurely before you. Bicycle here in spring when azaleas, camellias, and gardenias scent the breeze, or in autumn after summer's sultry days have passed.

Describing any set tour in this country is difficult because all the parish (county) roads are good for cycling. These two rides are inter-laced, so you can easily take in at-tractions from both. Since the roads throughout are mainly un-traveled, carry spare parts, tools, and a few snacks or a picnic lunch. Mosquito repellent is useful around the water.

LONG RIDE

The long ride—79.6 miles—starts at Audubon Lakes Campground on Louisiana 965, just southeast of St. Francisville. You pedal southeast along Louisiana 965 through gently rolling country. When 965 ends, continue straight. Then wind left onto Louisiana 966, which soon crosses busy U.S. 61 (beginners should walk their bikes across the highway). Beyond this junction, you can go left onto an unmarked paved road (the only paved road you see) for a side trip to Audubon State Park, described later in the short tour.

Back on the main loop, go right at the dead end onto Louisiana 10. Then turn left onto Louisiana 421, and pedal gradually uphill for a long stretch past cattle pastures. Stop anytime to pull off the road

DISTANCE:	Two possible tours—79.6 miles and 34.7 miles.
TERRAIN:	Rolling.
TRAFFIC:	Light.
DIFFICULTY:	Good rides for anyone.
BEST TIME:	May, June, and October for the best cycling weather and least chance of rain. July and August are hot and humid; if you do ride then, try to start by 7:30 A.M. and finish by noon. December through March you may encounter rains and high creeks.
LOCATION:	West and East Feliciana parishes, about 30 miles north of Baton Rouge, Louisiana.

and relax beneath a shade tree. In a few minutes, wind right onto Louisiana 967, which leads to an in-tersection where you can go either right for 8.7 miles into Wood-ville, Mississippi, an old Southern town, or left on the first paved road to continue on the main tour.

Proceeding on the main ride, you meander through countryside, take a sharp right just beyond the rail-road tracks, cross heavily trafficked U.S. 61, and reach a grocery store where you can buy snacks. (If you prefer a more leisurely stop, go straight at the store to South of the Border Restaurant.) Continue west from the store on Hollywood Road. Then as you dead-end into

Louisiana 66, go left. This road is usually lightly traveled, but the few motorists here drive fast, so be care-ful along this stretch. You turn right onto Tunica Hills Road at Ginyard's Store, another convenient snack stop. Caution: Walk your bike over the hazardous rickety wooden bridge just beyond the grocery store. Then about midway between the store and St. Francisville, you cross what Louisianans call a "low-water bridge," a concrete strip built over a stream. During dry seasons, this crossing is no problem. But after a rain the water may be gush-ing over the bridge, and you will either have to turn back or hoist your bike on your shoulders and wade across the cold water, a risky choice. Watch ahead as you ap-proach St. Francisville for a second rough wooden-planked bridge.

Beyond the bridge, turn left on-to Ferdinand Street and spin past an old Episcopal church. Then go right soon onto busy U.S. 61 for the short jog back to Audubon Lakes.

SHORT RIDE

The short tour—34.7 miles—also begins from Audubon Lakes, and if you have time after riding the long tour, take in some of the country-side along this ride. Leaving from Audubon Lakes, turn left and pedal north along Louisiana 965 for 3 miles to Audubon State Park, a serene wooded spot where you can picnic. While here you can also visit Oakley, the plantation where John James Audubon sketched Feliciana wildlife.

The main ride continues north on Louisiana 965, but for more ex-ploring take the only paved road just north of the park off Louisiana 965 to a red brick church. At this church, go left onto Louisiana 10 to Rosedown, an antebellum man-sion with a century-old garden of

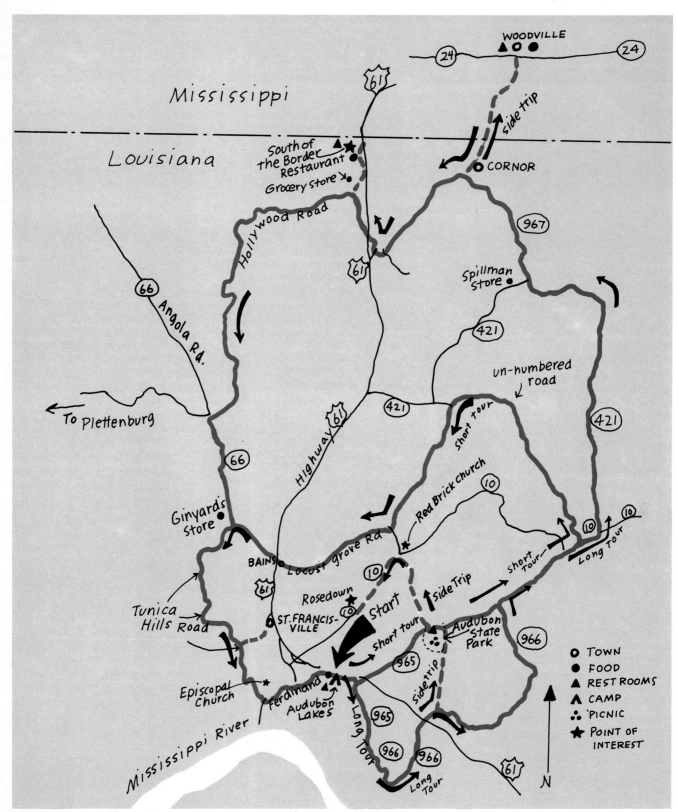

Audubon Lakes Campground is on Louisiana 965 just southeast of St. Francisville in southeastern Louisiana; 30 miles north of Baton Rouge via U.S. 61 and Louisiana 965; 110 miles northwest of New Orleans via U.S. 61 and Louisiana 965.

gardenias, camellia trees, azalea bushes, sweet olives, crepe myrtles, and mock oranges. Admission to the house and gardens is $4, and to the gardens alone, $2. Retrace your ride past the red brick church to Audubon State Park.

Continuing on the main route now, pedal northeast on Louisiana 965, go right on Louisiana 10, and take the first blacktop road to your left past the Louisiana 10 junction. (Note: If you reach Louisiana 421, you have missed the turnoff; turn around and go back.) You meander over hills through farmland for 6.3 miles. Turn onto the first hard-surfaced road to your left and pedal along another wooded back road. Eventually this blacktop road dead-ends into Locust Grove Road. A right turn leads you across busy U.S. 61. Beyond the tiny village of Bains, and past a few hills, you reach Ginyard's Store, where you can buy sandwich fixings, fruit, and other snacks.

From Ginyard's the short tour follows Tunica Hills Road, as does the long tour. See the long tour for details concerning the three hazardous bridges on this stretch. Then follow the long tour back to Audubon Lakes to complete the loop. Near the end of your ride, you can go left on U.S. 61 to St. Francisville, a lovely Southern town with antebellum homes. The old plantation called the Myrtles, tucked in a grove of oaks hung with Spanish moss, is said to be haunted. After exploring, retrace your ride along U.S. 61 back to Audubon Lakes.

If you have a little extra time and energy, and would like to end your day with a Louisiana feast, pedal south through St. Francisville on Louisiana 10, take the free ferry across the Mississippi River, and continue on Route 10, through New Roads. Past New Roads go left onto Louisiana 1, which leads you along the banks of the False River to Ralph and Kacoo's Restaurant, serving excellent local seafood and authentic Creole dishes. The restaurant is about 15 miles from Audubon Lakes.

WHERE TO STAY

Motels are limited on these rides, although a Holiday Inn is now being built in St. Francisville. Several old plantation homes offer lodging. One possibility is the Cottage, five and a half miles north of St. Francisville on U.S. 61. Overnight guests are served plantation-style breakfasts. For reservations, phone (504) 635-3674.

Camping is available at Audubon Lakes Campground, at the start of both tours, open year round, with a swimming pool, beach, and general store. For reservations, write Audubon Lakes Campground, P.O. Box 163, Zachary, Louisiana 70791.

FOR FURTHER INFORMATION

These tours and a few slight variations are part of the Louisiana Jambalaya, sponsored annually in November by the Baton Rouge Bicycle Club, affiliated with the League of American Wheelmen. The three-day Jambalaya usually starts on Thanksgiving Day and ends on Saturday with a feast prepared by the jambalaya king, Uton Diez of Coon Trap Road. The menu in the past has included the two-century-old Cajun recipe for *cochon-de-lait* (roast suckling milk-fed pig). If you have any further questions on the tours outlined here or would like information on this year's Jambalaya, write Joe Reed, President, Baton Rouge Bicycle Club, 1548 Oakley Drive, Baton Rouge, Louisiana 70806, or phone him at (504) 927-8028.

NEARBY

The parish roads throughout this region offer excellent cycling. You can take off on your own and explore without much problem. Just stay off the busy highways—U.S. 61 and fast-trafficked Louisiana 66—as much as possible and watch ahead for wooden or low-water bridges.

CREOLE JAMBALAYA

Jambalaya receives a special, different touch in nearly every Louisiana kitchen. Here's one easy way to make this traditional dish.

2 7-ounce cans of shrimp
2 cups uncooked brown rice
1 pound diced, smoked raw ham
1 cup chopped onion
1/3 cup chopped green pepper
1 cup thick cream
1 1/3 cup water
1 minced clove garlic
2 tablespoons butter
2 tablespoons flour
2 tablespoons chopped parsley
1/4 teaspoon thyme
1/8 teaspoon cayenne
salt and pepper to taste

Melt the butter in a large pan. Then add the ham, green pepper, onion, and garlic, and cook over low heat, stirring often, until the onions become transparent. Add the flour and all the other ingredients except the cream, rice, and shrimp. Bring to a boil, cover, and simmer for twenty-five minutes. Then pour in the cream and sprinkle the rice over the top. Cover again and simmer over low heat without stirring for thirty-five minutes or until the rice becomes tender. Add the shrimp and simmer for about five more minutes. Makes six large servings.

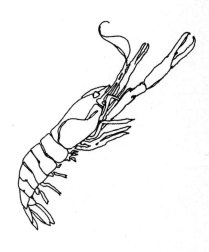

53. CAJUN COUNTRY CRAWDAD CAPER

Ride along a smooth, shadowed lane beneath moss-draped live oaks and cypress. This is Cajun country in Louisiana, a place in the Deep South where crawfish pie, jambalaya, and file gumbo are prepared in every kitchen and people lead unhurried lives.

Gather a picnic lunch and start your tour in New Iberia on U.S. 90 at Highway 14. The Acadian Regional Tourist Information Center in midtown will answer your questions on Bayou Teche country. Antebellum life is reflected in New Iberia's Shadows-on-the-Teche at 117 East Main Street, a restored mansion where you stroll through shaded gardens.

Leave New Iberia by pedaling north on Route 86, a smooth, narrow lane through countryside. About 4 miles outside town, pause at Justine, a mansion dating from 1822 with an adjacent rare bottle collection. Admission is $1 for adults and 50¢ for children. To arrange a tour, phone Mrs. Aleen L. Yeutter, (504) 364-0973.

Route 86 may have some traffic, so turn left onto the next blacktop road past Justine. Then wind right onto Route 344 and pedal along the bayou. After you cross a railroad track, take the next bridge right across the bayou into Loreauville. Here you can pause for a spin through Loreauville Heritage Museum Village with its Attakapas Indian trading post, gypsy camp, and Acadian farm home.

North of Loreauville on Route 86, go right when you reach Route 345, follow 345 left, and ride into St. Martinville, home of Longfellow's Evangeline. Pause beneath the ancient oak at the end of Port Street where Gabriel first met Evangeline, or visit St. Martin of Tours Catholic Church Cemetery, 133 South Main Street, where Emmaline LaBiche, the original Evangeline, is buried.

Also, visit the free Evangeline Museum at 249 East Bridge Street behind the old grocery store. The museum proprietor, Andre Olivier, will delight you by telling Acadian tales in both French and English.

For a peaceful side trip, pedal north 2 miles on Route 31 to Longfellow State Park. Here you can picnic or rest beneath massive moss-draped live oaks. Return to St. Martinville and pedal south on Route 347. Go right onto Route 86, then straight when Route 86 branches left. Bear right across a railroad track to Route 31, then left on 31, and again left on U.S. 90. Turn right when U.S. 90 splits, and bear left on Route 329 just before you reach a railroad track. This road meanders south to Avery Island, where you can watch the flocks of cranes, egrets, and herons that live in the marshes. On the island country lanes lead past pungent pepper fields, and you can wander down paths lined with camellias, azaleas, irises, and tropical plants in the Jungle Gardens and Bird Sanctuary (admission, $1.75).

From Avery Island, pedal north on 329, go right on the first blacktop road, and right again as the blacktop ends. Turn left on the next blacktop road, then right at the next hard-surfaced road, Route 83. A curvy ride leads you to Route 320, which you take left. A final left on Route 87 brings you back to New Iberia.

End your day with an authentic Cajun feast in a local restaurant. The native specialty, of course, is crawfish in season.

DISTANCE:	56 miles; see map for shortcuts.
TERRAIN:	Flat.
TRAFFIC:	Moderate.
DIFFICULTY:	Good ride for anyone.
BEST TIME:	May, September, and October for the best temperatures. July and August are too sultry, while November through April is often rainy.
LOCATION:	Louisiana's Cajun country—20 miles south of Lafayette, Louisiana, 60 miles west of Baton Rouge, and 150 miles west of New Orleans.

WHERE TO STAY

Motels: Beau Sejour, 2 miles west of New Iberia on State 182. For reservations, write Beau Sejour, Box 698, New Iberia, Louisiana 70560, or phone (318) 364-4501. Sugarland Motor Lodge, 1 mile west of New Iberia on State 182. For reservations, write Sugarland Motor Lodge, 1211 West Main Street, New Iberia, Louisiana 70560, or phone (318) 364-2331.

Camping is available in Longfellow Evangeline State Park, 2 miles north of St. Martinville on State 31; open year round; $1.30 per tent.

FOR FURTHER INFORMATION

Wayne Alfred, an avid cyclist and the Texas area director for the League of American Wheelmen, contributed this tour. Wayne plans and conducts prepaid expense tours through the United States, Canada, and Europe. You can write him at Bike Dream Tours, P.O. Box 20653, Houston, Texas 77025, for a free brochure detailing his rides.

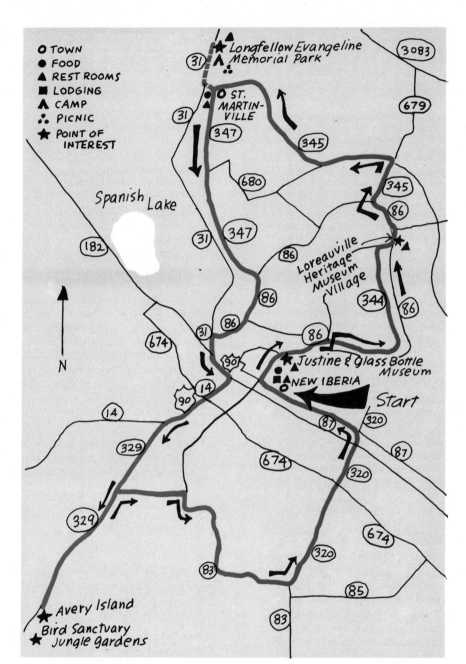

New Iberia is in southern Louisiana on U.S. 90 and Route 14; 77 miles southwest of Baton Rouge via Route 76, Louisiana 77, I-10, and U.S. 90; 157 miles west of New Orleans via U.S. 61, Route 76, Louisiana 77, I-10, and U.S. 90.

54. HOT SPRINGS STEAMER

Amid a bustling resort of health spas and neon signs lies Hot Springs National Park, a quiet woodland of shortleaf pine, oak, hickory, and sweet gum. The leaf-thatched forest conceals nearly 150 species of birds, including thrushes, vireos, grackles, finches, and warblers, while the sharp, rocky knolls are home for squirrels, black bears, foxes, and occasionally bobcats. Bicycle from the park's mineral springs to pure Lake Ouachita on this Arkansas adventure.

Start at Hot Springs National Park's Visitor Center, where you can leave your car and pedal north on Central Avenue (State 7) past Bathhouse Row. As you leave the park, go right on State 7 to ride through Hot Springs. Pick up spare parts and snacks before you leave. Though you pass many country stores which sell food, you can expect them all to be closed Sundays.

Outside town you follow State 7 past ranches and chicken farms across the Saline River's South Fork to Mountain Valley. At the fork, go right to stay on State 7 and pedal over gentle hills to Blue Springs, beyond which you go left onto State 298. On this smooth blacktop, you climb and coast easily into Ouachita National Forest.

Many small brooks cross your path, and you can pause anywhere along here to hike the short distance to Lake Ouachita. After you turn left in Story and glide to Washita, you may want to go right on State 88 to Dragover Camp, a peaceful overnight stop where you can swim in the river.

Proceeding south on State 27, you plunge through cool forests to the Ouachita River, cross the bridge, and climb the opposite bank. High in the oaks and hickories you may glimpse a redwing blackbird or yellow American goldfinch. Soon you go left on U.S. 270 and reach Mount Ida, where there are restaurants and grocery stores.

On U.S. 270 you climb and coast easily, but you have to watch for possible traffic and rough gravel shoulders which can puncture tires. Several paved roads lead left off the highway, to Denby Point, Tompkins Bend, and Mountain Harbor, all offering swimming, fishing, camping, picnicking, and boat rentals on Lake Ouachita. If you try any of these side trips, watch on the roads into the areas for low-water bridges which may be completely submerged after a heavy rain and are usually washed with a trickle of water.

On the main route going east on U.S. 270, you pedal over more hills and along several flat stretches toward Hot Springs. As you approach the city, you can take a side trip left on State 227 to Lake Ouachita State Park, which has swimming, boat rentals, camping, cabins, a café, and a concession stand. To reach the park, go right when 227 dead-ends, then bear left at the fork onto the road leading into the park.

Continuing through Hot Springs on U.S. 270, go straight onto Ouachita Road, then left at the dead end onto Central Avenue back into Hot Springs National Park.

After pitching a tent in the park's Gulpha Gorge, spend the rest of the day plus perhaps another exploring the park's 18 miles of hiking trails. The abundant wildflowers alone make the walks worthwhile. In April and May you discover redbud, dogwood, honeysuckle, shadblow, downy blueberry blossoms, and blue, yellow, and white violets. June brings southern magnolias, Texas azaleas, sharpwing monkey flowers, and yellow passionflowers. And in autumn beneath flaming foliage you find pink or red trailing lespedezas, forked blue curls, yellow bearded beggar-sticks, and orange cardinal flowers. Also as you hike, don't overlook the ripening fruits, including serviceberries, blueberries, gooseberries, wild plums, and black cherries.

WHERE TO STAY

The many motels in Hot Springs include Grand Central Motor Lodge, 1127 Central Avenue, (501) 624-7131; El Rancho, 1611 Central Avenue, (501) 624-1273; Anthony, 2101 Central Avenue, (501) 623-8824; and Stagecoach Inn, 2500

DISTANCE:	101 miles.
TERRAIN:	Rolling hills.
TRAFFIC:	Light in most areas; heavier along U.S. 270.
DIFFICULTY:	National forest roads are excellent for anyone, but beginners and families should stay off U.S. 270 because of possible traffic.
BEST TIME:	Good year round, except from February to early April when horse races in Hot Springs draw crowds, especially on Saturdays.
LOCATION:	The tour route begins at Hot Springs National Park, but you can easily start the loop on Lake Ouachita.

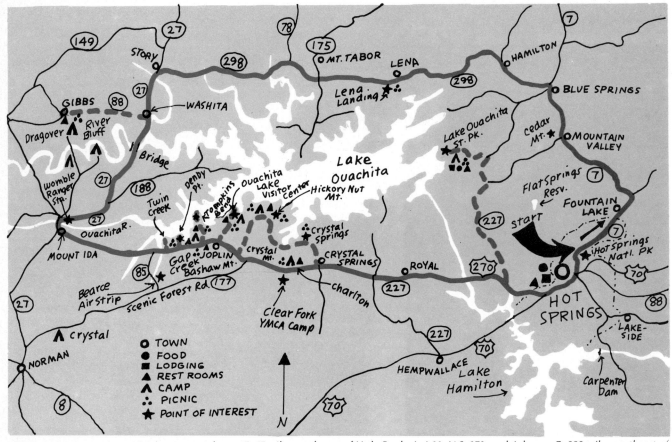

Hot Springs is in west-central Arkansas on Arkansas 7; 65 miles southwest of Little Rock via I-30, U.S. 270, and Arkansas 7; 300 miles northeast of Dallas, Texas, via I-30 and Arkansas 7.

Central Avenue, (501) 634-2531.

Campgrounds: Gulpha Gorge, Hot Springs National Park; open year round; $3. Dragover, west of Washita on State 88 in Ouachita National Forest; open year round; no fee. Denby Point, to your left off U.S. 270 after you pass Silver; open year round. Tompkins Bend (Shangri-la), to your left off U.S. 270 past the turnoff for Denby Point; open year round. Joplin (Mountain Harbor), off U.S. 270 north of Joplin; open year round. Charlton, on U.S. 270 several miles

east of Joplin; open May 1st to November 1st; $1. Lake Ouachita State Park, discussed in the tour description; open April 1st to October 31st; $1.50. For reservations, write Superintendent, Star Route, Mountain Pine, Arkansas 71956, or phone (501) 767-4211.

FOR SPARE PARTS AND REPAIRS

Raleigh of Hot Springs, 408 Third Street, Hot Springs, Arkansas. This shop handles parts for 10-speed

bikes and does repairs. During winter it is open Wednesday through Saturday, 1 to 5:30 P.M.; the rest of the year, every afternoon except Sunday.

FOR FURTHER INFORMATION

Write Superintendent, Hot Springs National Park, Box 1219, Hot Springs, Arkansas 71902; or Forest Supervisor, Ouachita National Forest, Hot Springs, Arkansas 71901.

55. OKLAHOMA ARBUCKLE AMBLE

In Southern Oklahoma there is a spot where the waters from clear mineral springs trickle over smooth rocks and drop into wooded valleys. The mossy stream banks are dappled with violets and shaded by oak, maple, and elm trees. To the southwest rise the Arbuckles, low forested hills that conceal a silvery blue lake. Both Platt National Park's wooded valleys and the red-earthed farmlands that surround them offer fine cycling.

Begin in Platt National Park and leave your car near park headquarters. Bring spare parts and tools with you, as there are no bike shops in the vicinity. You may wish to linger a day on Platt's 8-mile loop that winds over wooded knolls and through lush valleys. The tiny park is noted for its cold sulphur and bromide springs and sulphur-water pools.

Head west on the park's well-paved but narrow Perimeter Road, which runs flat across Rock Creek, then soon begins to climb. For a view of woods, meandering brooks, the Arbuckle Mountains, and the Washita River valley, cycle left up steep Bromide Hill. Be careful on the rapid coast back to the park road.

Your climb continues past Bison Viewpoint. Then on an easy glide you cross U.S. 177, where the road flattens with only one gradual dip for several miles. About halfway up a long, easy hill, pause at Travertine Nature Center to lock your bike and hike the self-guiding nature trails that run beside clear Travertine Creek. The center's naturalists conduct tours, which include an aquatic nature walk.

As you continue up the hill, you pass a frothing little waterfall. Then you wind left and coast beside a stream all the way back to the main

DISTANCE:	40 miles, excluding side trip to Arbuckle Lake.
TERRAIN:	Hilly.
TRAFFIC:	Heavy on some roads, light on others.
DIFFICULTY	Entire ride for experienced cyclists because of the hills. The Platt National Park loop is an excellent shorter ride for beginners.
BEST TIME:	Early spring or autumn, when traffic is lightest and days are crisp and clear.
LOCATION:	Southern Oklahoma around Sulphur, one and a half hours by car south of Oklahoma City via I-35 and State 7. The tour route begins at Platt National Park, but you can start at either Turner Falls Park or Lake of the Arbuckles.

entrance. As you approach the entrance, go right on U.S. 177 to leave the park. Then just outside the park, turn left onto State 7, which soon leads you into Oklahoma farmland. Pick up snacks in Hot Springs as you pass through.

Outside Hot Springs, State 7 is well paved, but the two-foot shoulders are bumpy. Plans have

been made to widen this road to four lanes, so inquire locally about current conditions. About 2 miles from Platt, a turnoff to your left leads you on smooth blacktop to deep blue Lake of the Arbuckles for swimming, picnicking, or camping at the Point Campground.

Returning to State 7, you tackle a sharp slope after you cross Guy Sandy Creek. Then from the crest you coast on into Davis. Gather picnic basics in a local market or continue on State 7 to the west edge of town, where a roadside stand on your left sells country-fresh fruits and vegetables.

Beyond the fruit and vegetable stand, turn left onto four-lane U.S. 77, with wide, paved shoulders and moderate traffic. About 4 miles later, follow the signs onto a two-lane road into Turner Falls Park, a quiet wooded area containing a waterfall and creek. Stop here to swim, sit peacefully beside the cascading water, wander on forest paths, or picnic. The restaurant here serves fresh brook trout.

After a leisurely rest and lots of exploring, retrace your ride through Davis and back into Sulphur. Camp in the evening in Platt National Park, where you can sit at dusk along a stream and sample just a sip of the mineral waters.

WHERE TO STAY

Motels in Sulphur are limited and include the Chickasaw Motor Inn, West 1st and Muskogee; (405) 622-2156. There are also several old, inexpensive hotels and motels that start at $2 per night for one person.

Campgrounds: Central, Cold Springs, and Rock Creek campgrounds, all in Platt National Park. Rock Creek is open year round, while the other two camps are

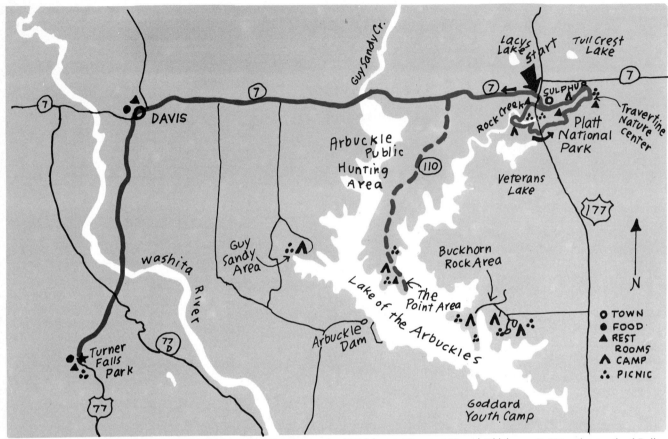

Sulphur is in south-central Oklahoma on Oklahoma 7; 100 miles south of Oklahoma City via I-35 and Oklahoma 7; 132 miles north of Dallas, Texas, via I-35 and Oklahoma 7; 257 miles south of Wichita, Kansas, via I-35 and Oklahoma 7.

open May 1st to September 15th; fee, $2. No reservations taken. The Point Campground, on Arbuckle Lake (directions in the tour description); open year round; fee, $1.

FOR FURTHER INFORMATION

Cyclist Cheryl Ball told us about this ride and will be happy to help if you have any further questions. Write Cheryl Ball, Holly Hill, Apartment #2, Sulphur, Oklahoma 73086.

NEARBY

Oklahoma has many rural back roads, but if you are not careful, you may run into dirt, gravel, or potholes. Check with a local cyclist or merchant about current road conditions before you strike out on your own.

SQUIRRELS OF THE ARBUCKLES

As you pedal through Platt National Park and the adjacent hills, you will glimpse many small mammals—Eastern cottontails, beavers, muskrats, red foxes, raccoons, and armadillos. Squirrels are also abundant in the woodlands. Here are three of the species you may see.

You will usually spot *eastern fox squirrels* in oak, hickory, or beech groves rather than in deep, unbroken forests. This burnt-orange or grizzled brown fellow has a fluffy, plumed tail about nine to fourteen inches long and weighs between one and three pounds. On cold days the eastern fox squirrel sensibly lolls in his nest until noon.

The *southern flying squirrel* is a tiny creature weighing only two to four ounces and measuring about nine to eleven inches long. His

dense soft fur is medium gray with some brownish tinges, and his underside is white or creamy. He takes his name from his ability to glide great distances. The best spots to catch a glimpse of him are hardwood forests and woodlots containing dead trees.

An easy species to distinguish is the *thirteen-lined ground squirrel*, with thirteen to fifteen pale yellow and brown stripes across his back. Some of these stripes are broken into spots. The ground squirrel is small, weighing between two and one half and four ounces, and grows to seven to twelve inches long, including his tail. He enjoys dining on green spring grass and autumn seeds, but will also eat grasshoppers, bird eggs, field mice, and insects. Watch for him in rocky areas, on arid grassy prairies, or in open areas like golf courses.

56. GULF OF MEXICO BEACHCOMBER

On the tip of Texas in the Gulf of Mexico lies long, narrow, windswept Padre Island. Dunes and sand sculptures, patched by tall, willowy sea oats, conceal meadowlarks, marsh hawks, and wintering sandhill cranes. The wide, flat sands hold beachcombing treasures: excellent driftwood, many varieties of shells, plus floats, bottles, and other finds washed ashore from the Yucatan, the Caribbean, South America, and the Azores.

Start at Nueces County Park on Padre Island, thus avoiding the hazardous long, spanner bridge across Laguna Madre. If you plan to camp at Nueces, pick a site before leaving. Pedal south through dunes against salty Gulf breezes usually blowing from the southeast at 15 to 20 m.p.h. The road is divided, with a good shoulder. About half a mile later, you reach Gito's, a motel with a restaurant and grocery store; Ira's, another motel also offering food; and a Dairy Queen. These are the last facilities for 11 miles and the only food stops on the tour except for the snack bar at Malaquite Beach about 15 miles ahead. About .8 mile past the sign pointing toward Padre Island Seashore, the road narrows to two lanes, but the shoulder remains good. About 2 miles farther through the dunes, you wind past marshy ponds and dunes topped with sea oats. You should be able to glimpse birds here as well as tiny mammals like the ground squirrel and kangaroo rat, which burrow into the mounds. Birds on the island include terns, herons, egrets, brown-and-white pelicans, and the rare frigate bird.

You lose the shoulder from the Seashore entrance to Malaquite Beach, but traffic moves slowly. Stop anytime, lock your bike, and walk along the sands, watching out in grassy areas for rattlesnakes. A mile beyond the entrance, you can follow a sign left to the beach to search for driftwood, collect clam and snail shells, and view the Gulf.

Back on the main park road, in half a mile you reach Grasslands Nature Trail. Lock your bike and pick up a self-guiding leaflet. The path leads you through dunes dotted with brilliant yellow-flowered wild indigo, tough marshhay cordgrass, sea oats, and Virginia live oaks. Just beyond the dunes roars the Gulf.

Two miles more of flat, breezy pedaling brings you to the ranger station, with seashell and rock displays and answers to your questions. The road is flat for 1.8 more miles to Malaquite Beach, which has an observation tower (excellent for photos), beach house, snack bar, and shaded picnic area. Less than a mile beyond this cluster of beach buildings lies the beach and a cool swim. As you return to Nueces County Park, the tail wind makes you feel as if you were sailing. At night around your campfire you hear the coyote yammering and may want to venture to the beach again to see ghost crabs literally covering the sands.

Warning: When you return home, make sure you clean and relubricate your bike or it will rust from the blowing salty sands on this ride.

WHERE TO STAY

Camping is available at Malaquite Beach and Nueces County Park, both open year round and operating on a first-come first-served basis. Several commercial campgrounds are also found near Corpus Christi.

If you prefer true primitive camping and the solitude this offers, you can hike farther south on Padre Island. Camping is permitted anywhere on the seaward side of the dunes, but not in the grasslands, where there are rattlesnakes. For primitive camping, bring all your own supplies, in-

DISTANCE:	30.2 miles round trip.
TERRAIN:	Flat all the way.
TRAFFIC:	Heavy on weekends; lightest on weekdays.
DIFFICULTY:	A bit rough on beginners and families because of high winds.
BEST TIME:	Good all seasons. December and January have average highs in the 60's, while summers are hot and humid, with highs from June through September in the sweltering 90's. Caution: Anytime of the year bring sun tan lotion, a long-sleeved shirt, sunglasses, and a hat. Sunburns occur quickly here.
LOCATION:	Padre Island National Seashore, south of Corpus Christi via State 358 and Kennedy Causeway.

cluding lots of water.

Motels; located at the tour's start, include Gito's and Ira's. See the tour description for precise locations. A more elegant resort is found north of Nueces County Park, past the turnoff for the Spanner bridge.

FOR SPARE PARTS, REPAIRS, FURTHER INFORMATION

Cutler's Schwinn Cyclery, 6118 South Padre Island Drive, Corpus Christi, Texas 78412. This is the nearest bike shop, and manager Cecilia C. Combs can tell you anything else you would like to know about the ride. If you choose to start the tour from Corpus Christi (53.8 miles round trip), Cecilia says you may use the bike shop's parking lot for your car. Just stop in and tell her before you leave.

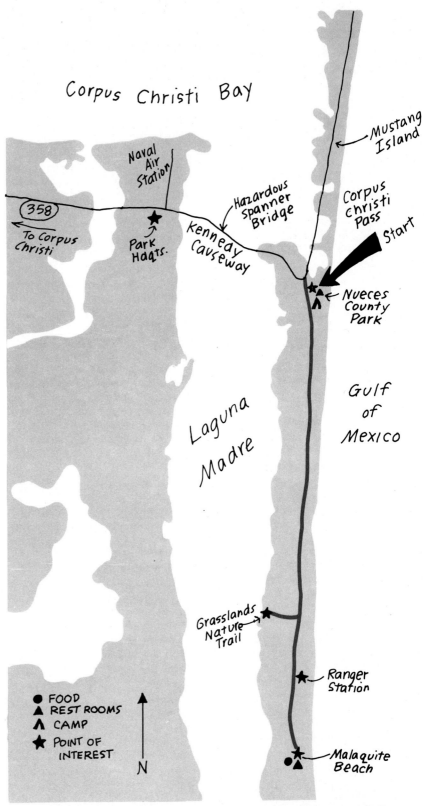

Nueces County Park is in southeastern Texas on Texas 358 and the Kennedy Causeway; 135 miles southeast of San Antonio, via U.S. 281, Texas 9, I-37, and Texas 358.

57. 58. 59. BIG BEND CHALLENGES

If you like your cycling tough, try these scenic wilderness treks in Texas' Big Bend along the Rio Grande. In this lonely frontier, you climb sharp slopes through purple canyons where Comanche warriors and Mexican bandits once hid. Spot roadrunners streaking before your wheels, smell creosote bushes on the wind, and hear the rare Colima warbler's call. Bring heavy-duty tubes or lots of spares, and watch out for cactus and razor-sharp mesquite thorns which often blow onto the road.

Big Bend contains so many difficult grades, no route is easy. Wherever you ride, you encounter 7- or 8-percent grades, with a few 10-percent hills to discourage the most intrepid beginner.

All park roads are narrow, without marked shoulders; however, most are open, so a cyclist can be easily seen. The only treacherous stretch is the steep, winding way to the Basin.

Outlined below are three Big Bend tours, but you can hook them together for 200 miles to challenge anyone's stamina. Always carry food and lots of water.

BOQUILLAS CANYON TO THE BASIN

Big Bend's longest gorge, Boquillas Canyon, lies on the park's eastern edge. Willows and cottonwoods grow on the flood plain and make the riversides glow silvery gold in autumn. At evening the sunset seems to set the Sierra del Carmen Mountains afire. Across the canyon lies the quaint Mexican village of Boquillas.

Start at Rio Grande Village, where you can set up camp and buy food year round. Before you ride, hike the short trail into Boquillas Canyon. You climb steeply uphill, then drop gradually along

DISTANCE:	Boquillas Canyon to the Basin, 68 miles round trip. The Basin to Castolon, 94 miles round trip. Panther Junction to Dagger Flat, 38 miles round trip.
TERRAIN:	Varies from flat to long, steep climbs and rapid descents.
TRAFFIC:	Heavy in summer; light the rest of the year.
DIFFICULTY:	For experienced cyclists only.
BEST TIME:	Excellent winter tour. December through January, highs average in the 60's; in November and March, in the low 70's. Avoid May through September, when temperatures rise to a stifling 100 degrees or higher and traffic is heavy.
LOCATION:	Big Bend National Park, southwest Texas on the Mexican border, 410 miles west of San Antonio and 300 miles southeast of El Paso. Nearest major town: Odessa, more than 200 miles north.

rock walls to a small wind-hollowed cavern from which you see deep into the canyon below. If you want photos, the canyon lies in shadow during the morning and brightens in afternoon.

Pedaling from Rio Grande Village, you have a short 9-percent climb through a tunnel. Be sure to turn on your lights. Then you ease to about a 4-percent climb nearly all the way to Basin Junction. Passing Tornillo Flats, you may spot a ringtail, coyote, pronghorn sheep, or even the rare kit fox. Also in this remote wilderness are found copperheads, tarantulas, and rattlers. The snakes lie hidden by day, so don't go poking about damp grasses or bushes.

You finally turn left on the Basin road (a sign points the way) and ride along Green Gulch to the Basin, where you can obtain information, lodging, and meals. Along this narrow, winding road, you climb about 6 miles at a 9- to 10-percent grade to Panther Pass. Stop at the pass, lock your bike, and hike 4-mile-long Lost Mine Trail. This side trip requires about three hours and you must bring water, but it is worth the effort. From Lost Mine Ridge you can view mountains and valleys, with the whole park before you.

You pedal the last mile into the Basin, where you can pick up a snack, then return via the same route.

THE BASIN TO CASTOLON

From the Basin, you have that steep 1 mile climb to Panther Pass, followed by a 6-mile plunge. This can be an exhilarating ride, but even experienced cyclists should be careful not to attain too much speed. At the dead end, turn left and ride over curving road be-

neath the craggy Chisos Mountains. Just a minute or so after you turn, you can wind right onto a dirt road leading up into the Grapevine Hills. Here you are apt to see javelina, collared peccary, and mule deer.

Back on the main road, you pedal over steeply rolling hills for about 10 miles, then turn left toward Castolon. In about 5 more miles, you roll over several steep (8- to 9-percent) hills. Then you plunge suddenly from the mountains all the way to Castolon. Here you can explore adobe homes built by early settlers. From Castolon you have an 8-mile scenic ride along the river, with a few short, steep grades to Santa Elena Canyon, with a store and year-round camping. After 47 miles of rigorous climbs and descents, you may want to spend the night, then go on the next day to explore further.

PANTHER JUNCTION TO DAGGER FLAT

The ride to Dagger Flat takes you past a fossil exhibit and through arid desert. This tour is best ridden in March, when you see millions of wildflowers: ocotillos, feather daleas, bluebonnets, desert baileya, and giant daggar yuccas. Be prepared for wilderness cycling, which means carrying parts, tools, safety equipment, food, and water.

Tornillo Creek's rapids make swimming unsafe. Beyond the bridge, stop at the fossil exhibit, where you can see bones of dinosaurs and fifty-foot crocodiles which lived here in ancient tropical forests and marshes. Going on through desert, you reach the little road which takes you right to Dagger Flat. This lane is made of graded dirt, with some rocky gravel areas; check current road conditions with a ranger before you ride

here. Dagger Flat is prettiest from late February through April, when thousands of giant dagger yuccas bloom with white broomshaped flower clusters, and rainbow-colored pitayas dot the sand.

Return to Park Headquarters the way you came. Dagger Flat has no camping, so you must finish the tour in one day.

WHERE TO STAY

The only convenient overnight facilities are located inside Big Bend. Chisos Basin has modern cottages, a lodge with dining room, and a campground. Reservations for the lodge and cottages can be made by writing National Park Concessions, Inc., Big Bend National Park, Texas 79834.

Campgrounds are located at the Basin, Rio Grande Village, and Castolon, and operate on a first-come first-served basis. Large groups, however, should reserve sites at the above address.

FOR FURTHER INFORMATION

Write Superintendent, Big Bend National Park, Texas 79834.

BIG BEND COUNTRY CHIHUAHUAN DESERT FLOWERS

Big Bend country is filled with desert flowers. Here you may glimpse sunflowers, tiny yellow-blossomed snakeweed, skeleton-leaf goldeneye with its yellow daisylike summer flowers, and the vivid scarlet royal sage shrub from which tea can be made. Some of the more fascinating flowers to look for are these.

Ocotillo (oh-ko-TEE-yo). This common desert plant with bright crimson flowers is often erroneously called a cactus. The ocotillo thrives in the desert because of its unique survival mechanism. During a drought, the leaves drop off to save moisture; then after a soaking rain, the leaves burst forth again. Apache Indians used ocotillo roots to dress wounds.

Lechuguilla (lay-choo-GHEE-ya). Finding this common desert plant is easy, but you will be lucky if you happen to see it bloom. Like the century plant, the lechuguilla blooms just once, then dies. The plant while alive serves many uses. Deer feed on the flowering stalks and birds dine on the seeds. Mexicans use the roots to create a natural soap and the rough leaf fibers to make rope, and prehistoric Indians dug pits and roasted the nourishing stalks.

Big Bend agave (ah-GA-vay). Southwest deserts support many agave species, but this one grows only in the mountains of west Texas. For ten to twenty years, this plant lies quietly storing food in its leaves and roots. Then in its last year it sprouts a huge vivid yellow-flowered stalk which sometimes grows twelve inches in one day. Indians used to roast and eat the young flowering stalks, and in Mexico some species of agave create the fiery liquors mescal and tequila.

Big Bend National Park is in southwestern Texas on the Mexican border on U.S. 385; 240 miles south of Odessa via U.S. 385; 410 miles west of San Antonio via U.S. 90 and 385.

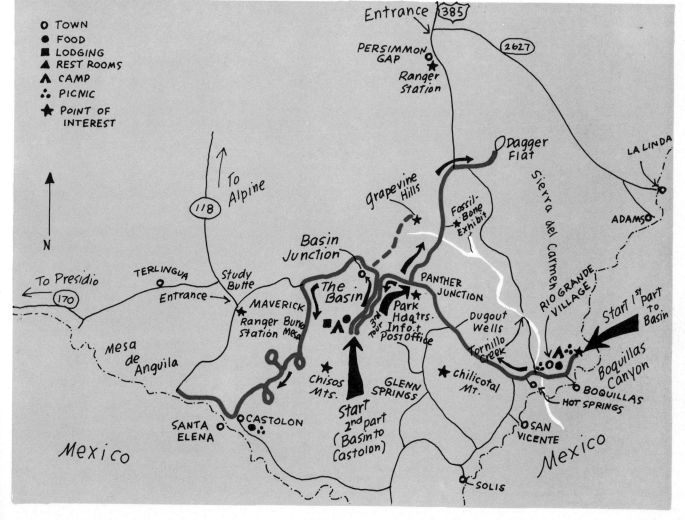

the Midwest

60. GRAND TRAVERSE BAY ROUNDABOUT

DISTANCE:	78 miles.
TERRAIN:	Hilly.
TRAFFIC:	Heavy in spots, light in others.
DIFFICULTY:	Entire tour for experienced cylists only, because of traffic. Less experienced riders and families can stay exclusively on back roads, however, by taking the last 30 miles along County 616 from Sleeping Bear Bay to Traverse City. Another beginner ride is the 16-mile loop around Glen Lake.
BEST TIME:	Spring through autumn. Lovely as a May cherry-blossom tour.
LOCATION:	Leelanau County on the Grand Traverse Bay Peninsula in northern Michigan.

Explore the icy north shores of Michigan's Grand Traverse Bay in spring when cherry blossoms scent the breeze and tint the hilltops, or in autumn amid rich foliage. You can antique hunt in Suttons Bay, Northport, and Leland; dawdle through old Fishtown; search beaches for million-year-old Pe- toskey stones, which make unique jewelry; swim or sunbathe; fish for perch, bass, and brown and rainbow trout; take a nature tour of South Manitou Island's unusual flora; and scramble over the huge Sleeping Bear Dunes, shifting in the winds.

Roadside tables, parks, and bayside restaurants are found throughout this tour. Carry a light sweater for the cool bay breezes, and pick up spare parts at Traverse City's bike shop before leaving.

Traverse City is the cherry country's commercial hub. Here along the bay Grandview Parkway is lined with small parks, including Clinch Park, with a zoo, aquarium, and beach. Pedal north on well-paved State 22, with possible heavy traffic. Past Crystal Spring you begin a long, gradual climb, then have a short spurt downhill. You leave the shore for about 2 miles and spin through orchards and marshes, then reach the water again at picturesque Suttons Bay. Watch out for railroad tracks as you enter and leave town.

About 2 miles farther, you bump over more railroad tracks, then soon glide across Belanger's Creek, which ends in tiny Belanger Pond. Beyond Peshawbestown you cross another track and view New Mission Point jutting into the bay.

Cross still another track past Ahgostown and continue through orchards. You climb easily toward Northport. At the edge of Northport, State 22 veers left, but you can proceed into town for snacks or antique hunting. For superb views of Lake Michigan, take a side trip north of Northport on paved roads past the huge Lombardy poplar to Lighthouse Point. Along this jaunt you climb a short distance through orchards, then coast to the point, where you can picnic at Northport Park.

Back on State 22, pedaling southwest, you encounter a steep 1-mile climb, then ease your way down the slope to Lake Leelanau. At the intersection with County 641, the main tour proceeds right on State 22, but you can go left to circle the lake past a huge ancient white birch tree.

Arriving at Leland, take time to explore the harbor, Leland Historical Museum, and quaint old Fishtown. If you are hungry, the local seafood here is excellent, right from the smokehouses or just caught, cleaned, and filleted. From Leland's pier you can take a passenger ferry to South Manitou Island to explore along secluded, forested dirt roads.

Past Leland stay right at the fork at Duck Lake, then left to stay on paved road along Little Traverse Lake. Winding through more lake country, you reach Glen Arbor, which has a beach. Continue straight on State 109, then turn right in about a minute onto Route 209 to ride into Glen Haven, where you can swim or picnic at Day State Park. This park is part of Sleeping Bear Sand Dunes National Lakeshore, where huge dunes form inland lakes, and pine, heath, and hemlock mingle with birch, maple, and beech forests. Sleeping Bear Dunes, as the name implies, resembles a bear. Stop to explore, tour in a dune buggy, or climb the dunes, but keep your bike out of the sand or you will have a mess to clean.

Leave Glen Haven the way you came on Route 209. Then proceed straight at the intersection onto Route 109 to wind between the dunes and Glen Lake. Watch out for sand blown onto the road. Continue to skirt Glen Lake by winding left on County 616. Here you find several fine sand swimming beaches. About one and a half miles past the State 22 junction, there's a lakeside park where you can rest. County 616 is narrow, blacktop, and lightly trafficked except on summer weekends. An excellent short tour, especially good for families and beginners, is the 16-mile loop around the lake, starting in either Glen Haven or Glen Arbor.

County 616 meanders east past orchards and farmlands through the small towns of Burdickville, Maple City, and Cedar. After a series of sharp right turns and curves, you curve right at graveled Green Street and continue straight on Grand View, which ends eventually at State 22. Turn right to complete the loop from Traverse City.

You can extend your exploring by pedaling north along State 37 on Old Mission Peninsula. This scenic jaunt leads 16 miles, with water on both sides, to historic Old Mission Lighthouse, located midway between the Equator and North Pole.

WHERE TO STAY

Motels are available in both Traverse City and Glen Arbor. This is a resort area, so rooms are expensive. Places you may want to check out include the Holiday Inn in Traverse City as well as the following: Colonial Inn, 460 Munson Avenue, Traverse City; 2 miles northeast of town on State 31; (616) 947-5436. Sierra, 230 Munson Avenue, Traverse City; almost 2 miles northeast of town on State 31; (616) 946-7720. Traverse City Travelodge, 1943 U.S. 31N, Traverse City; (616) 947-4350. The Leelanau Homestead, 2 miles north of Glen Arbor, 1 mile off State 22; (616) 334-3041.

Campgrounds: Traverse City State Park, 2 miles east of Traverse City on U.S. 31; $2.50. Write the park at 1132 U.S. 31N, North Traverse City, Michigan 49684. Old Mission Inn Campsites, a quarter of a mile west of Northport on Mission Road; open May 5th to October 15th; $3 for four. For reservations, write the campground at 18599 Mission Road, Northport, Michigan 49670, or phone (616)

223-7770. Little Finger Beach, three and a half miles south of Lake Leelanau on St. Mary's Street (County 643); open April 20th to October 20th; $2.50 for four except in July and August, when the fee is $3.50 for four. For reservations, write Little Finger Beach, Route 1, Lake Leelanau, Michigan 49653, or phone (616) 256-6455. Leelanau Pines Campground, half a mile north of Cedar on County 645, then three and a half miles farther north on County 643; open May 1st to December 1st; $4 to $6.50 per site. For reservations, write Leelanau Pines Campground, Route 1, Cedar, Michigan 49621, or phone (616) 228-5742.

FOR SPARE PARTS AND REPAIRS

City Bike Shop, 322 South Union Street, Traverse City, Michigan 49684.

Traverse City is in northwestern Michigan on Michigan 72 and 37 and U.S. 31; 333 miles north of Chicago, Illinois, via I-94 and 196 and U.S. 31; 255 miles northwest of Detroit via I-75 and Michigan 72.

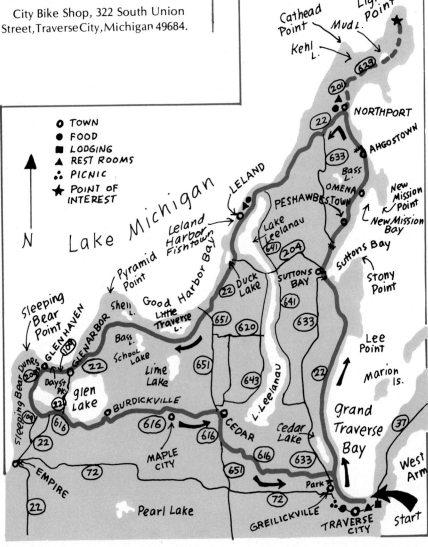

61. LAKE MICHIGAN TULIP TOUR

DISTANCE:	48 miles round trip.
TERRAIN:	Flat, with a few slopes.
TRAFFIC:	Light.
DIFFICULTY:	Good ride for beginners and families.
BEST TIME:	Perfect in late May, just after the tulip festival. Also delightful June through September. Winter is snowy.
LOCATION:	Holland, Michigan, near the U.S. 31 and State 21 junction, 27 miles southwest of Grand Rapids, Michigan.

Pedal along canals and eat *saucijzenbroodjes* (pigs in blankets) —just as Hans Brinker and his pal Voostenwalbert Schimmelpennick might have done—on this loop from Michigan's "little Netherlands." During Holland's four-day Tulip Time Festival, which begins the Wednesday nearest May 15th, you see more than two million vivid tulips in the streets and fields. You, of course, want to ferret out back roads and avoid motoring crowds, so visit Holland the week after the festival, when you can leisurely explore Windmill Island's gardens, cycle through acres of flowers, and watch Dutch dancers in wooden shoes perform their klompen dance. Late May isn't the only time you can ride here: blossoms other than tulips, including marigolds, begonias, lilies, pe-

tunias, and sweet alyssum, bloom until mid-September.

Park your car on a quiet side street, then head out of town north on 120th Avenue (Waverly Road). At 16th Street (Adams Street) you can go right one block to the Chamber of Commerce for specific information. Right behind the Chamber building is a wooden-shoe factory. Back on 120th Avenue, you soon pedal past cultivated blueberry patches, maple, oak, and elm woods, and commercial pine and spruce tree farms. This straight blacktop road is in good condition, with wide shoulders, and you encounter only mild slopes here and throughout the ride.

About 10 miles from Holland, you cross over Pigeon Creek, beyond which is an intersection with a gravel road to your left and a blacktop road to your right. Take the gravel road left a short jaunt to the entrance of Pigeon Creek Park, where you can forage along the cool creek, rest, snack, and hike through bark-scented woods.

Continuing north on 120th Avenue, you cross Lake Michigan Drive (State 45) and pass a school on your left, beyond which you soon come to a local blacktop road. Continue straight until another blacktop road intersects and the way straight ahead of you is a gravel access to the Grand River; now turn left onto Cedar Drive. You wind along the peaceful river, jogging right, then left onto Green Street past Stearns Bayou. Continue on the blacktop, winding through riverlets and marshes to Grand Haven, a busy fishing port.

Across town at Grand Haven State Park, you can swim, eat at the snack stand, or picnic on a wide, sandy beach. Grand Haven is a halfway point, so you may want to camp for $2.50 here or spend the night in a Grand Haven motel.

Should you decide to stay, a rather pleasant oddity in town is the huge musical fountain with synchronized lights and music on Dewey Hill. Ask directions from wherever you decide to stay overnight.

Continuing from Grand Haven State Park, ride south through town and along well-surfaced Lake Shore Avenue. Lake Michigan lies to your right, but you catch only glimpses of water and dunes between thick cottonwood and willow forests, deep golden in autumn. Pigeon Lake makes a good rest stop. Here you can spin past marshes and sand dunes to observe ducks and swans on the placid bayou. Just beyond Pigeon Lake, take the right fork and proceed beside Lake Michigan to Tunnel Park, where you can camp, picnic, or hike through a tunnel in the dunes to swim at another fine-sanded beach.

Beyond Tunnel Park, turn left onto Ottawa Beach Road. (A right turn here takes you to Holland

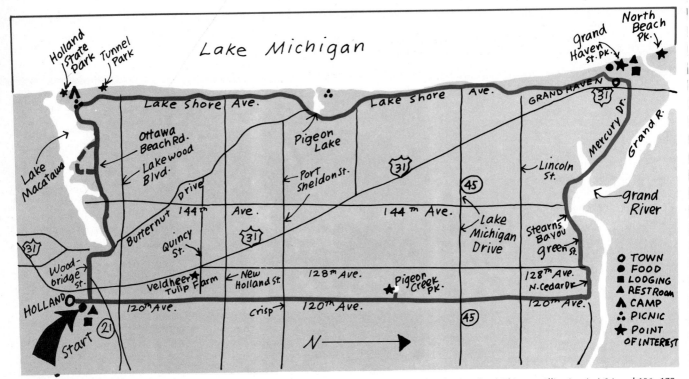

Holland is in western Michigan near Lake Michigan on I-196, U.S. 31 and Michigan 21; 144 miles north of Chicago, Illinois, via I-94 and 196; 177 miles west of Detroit, via I-96 and Michigan 21.

State Park, with camping and more beaches.) Ottawa Beach Road meanders beside Lake Macatawa, but to get even closer to the water you can venture down the narrower blacktop access road to the shore. At Butternut Drive, turn right and return to Holland. Take time now to inspect the 200-year-old windmill and tour a wooden-shoe factory. Or go 3 miles north on U.S. 31 (traffic can be heavy here) to Veldheer's Tulip Gardens, where Vernin and Esther Veldheer can tell you more about the flowers you have seen. End your day with a traditional Dutch dinner: local specialties include *pannekoeken*, *uitsmijter*, and *worst met warme aardappel salade*.

WHERE TO STAY

Motels are located in Holland and Grand Haven and are fairly expensive. Whenever possible, make reservations just to be safe. Here are some possibilities: Lake Ranch, 2226 Ottawa Beach Road, Holland; 5 miles northwest of town; (616) 335-8360. Wooden Shoe, 16th Street at the Route 31 bypass, Holland; beside the wooden-shoe factory; (616) 392-8521. Beacon, 1525 South Beacon Boulevard, Grand Haven; (616) 842-4720. Fountain Motor Inn, 1010 South Beacon Boulevard, Grand Haven; (616) 846-1800.

Campgrounds: Drew's Camping, Route 2, Holland, Michigan 49423; on U.S. 31, three and a half miles north of the State 21 junction; (616) 396-3681; reservations accepted. Dutch Treat Camping, P.O. Box 10300 Gordon Street, Zeeland; in Holland on State 21, 2 miles east of the U.S. 31 bypass; (616) 772-4303; reservations accepted. Holland State Park, Ottawa Beach Road, 7 miles west of Holland; (616) 335-8959. Camper's Paradise, 800 Robbins Road, Grand Haven; from the junction of U.S. 31 and State 104, go two and a quarter miles south on U.S. 31, a quarter of a mile west on Robbins Road, and a quarter of a mile south on dirt road; (616) 846-1460; reservations accepted.

FOR SPARE PARTS, REPAIRS, FURTHER INFORMATION

Reliable Cycle and Ski Haus, 254 River, Holland, Michigan 49423. Ken Vos carries parts, does quick emergency repairs, and has rentals. He rides this loop himself and can tell you anything else you would like to know or suggest other possible rides if you plan to spend several days in the area.

TULIP GUIDE

As you ride through Holland, you see thousands of tulips, with their most striking difference being color, ranging from deep maroon and vermilion to sunflower yellow and pure white. Yet look closely and you can see many variations in the blossoms. Vernin and Esther Veldheer have their own tulip gardens near Holland and have compiled a guide to help you recognize different tulip species.

62. LAKE COUNTRY CRUISE

Notice the quiet as you pedal beneath tamarack and black tupelo trees along the Huron River. A white-tailed doe steps silently to the river' edge. Or a rowdy Stellar's jay may scold from a slippery elm, breaking the stillness.

Start in Ann Arbor, where you may park your car on a side street or in a parking lot. Then pedal west from Main Street on Huron River Drive. You have an almost immediate steep downhill curve, then .2 mile farther you pass a small dirt lot (you may park your car here if you plan to be gone only a few hours). Huron River Drive is a winding blacktop road with stony, gravelly shoulders. Watch for the rugged railroad tracks about three and a half miles past the little dirt lot.

Soon you cross the river and pedal to Delhi Metropark, a serene woods on the riverbanks. Another nice stop is Dexter-Huron Metropark, 3 miles farther. At the Dexter Party Store you turn left onto Mast Road and cross a one-lane bridge. In autumn the cider mill on your right just over the bridge is a pleasant stop for apples, honey, or cider. Follow Central into Dexter, bear right at the stop sign, and proceed onto Main Street, with the Dexter Bakery, a Dairy Queen, food stores, and an antique shop.

Follow the signs through town for Dexter-Pinckney Road. Go left in three and a half miles onto North Territorial Road, past a restaurant, and right in 4 miles onto hilly, curvy Hankerd Road, which becomes Glenbrook Road. Soon you reach Half Moon Lake Beach. Stop to swim or picnic along the wooded shore. A mile farther, there's a campground on your right, a good overnight stop. Hiking trails lace this area, and you can stop anytime to wander past ponds through widely varied forests of white oak; American bass-

DISTANCE:	45 miles.
TERRAIN:	Flat, with a few hills.
TRAFFIC:	Usually moderate; heavy on summer weekends.
DIFFICULTY:	Some experience needed to handle narrow roads.
BEST TIME:	Spring through autumn.
LOCATION:	Ann Arbor and surrounding countryside.

wood; yellow poplar; eastern white pine; sugar, red, and silver maple; American, slippery, and rock elm; and yellow birch.

Turn right on Patterson Lake Road and ride into Hell, where you can buy snacks at the grocery store. A bit farther on your left is Hell Creek Ranch, with camping, canoeing, and horseback riding. A right onto Pinckney Road leads you between Portage and Little Portage lakes, with private beaches. There's another little grocery store here. You can buy picnic basics and ride one and a half miles to a Huron River picnic area on your left.

At the amber blinking light, turn left on North Territorial, passing Hudson Mills Metropark, another pleasant riverside park. Then about 2 miles farther, turn right on Mast Road, pedal 3 miles, and go left on Huron River Drive. From here you retrace the first 10 miles of your ride, passing Dexter-Huron and Delhi metroparks, crossing the river, railroad tracks, and one-lane bridge, and climbing the short,

steep hill into Ann Arbor.

WHERE TO STAY

Campground locations are indicated in the tour description. Motels are numerous in Ann Arbor and include a Howard Johnson's, Ramada Inn, and Holiday Inn.

FOR SPARE PARTS, REPAIRS, FURTHER INFORMATION

Mike Kolin's Cycling Center, Inc., 325 East Hoover, Ann Arbor, Michigan; (313) 663-1604. Mike Kolin told us about this ride and will be glad to give you any additional facts before you leave Ann Arbor. He also can advise you on other good cycling spots in the area.

MICHIGAN LAKES COUNTY ELMS

Nearly everyone can recognize an American elm, but if you look closely on this tour, you will discover other elms here, including the rock and slippery elms. Here's how to tell them apart.

First, all three elms have rough, deeply veined, sharply toothed leaves, oval with slightly rounded points. Both the American and slippery elms have "urn"-shaped profiles, while the rock elm has a narrower, more rounded crown. Leaf sizes vary slightly: slippery elm, five to seven inches long; American elm, four to five inches long; and rock elm, two to three inches long. A certain test for the slippery elm is to examine the fragrant inner bark: it is covered with a moist substance which makes the bark feel slippery.

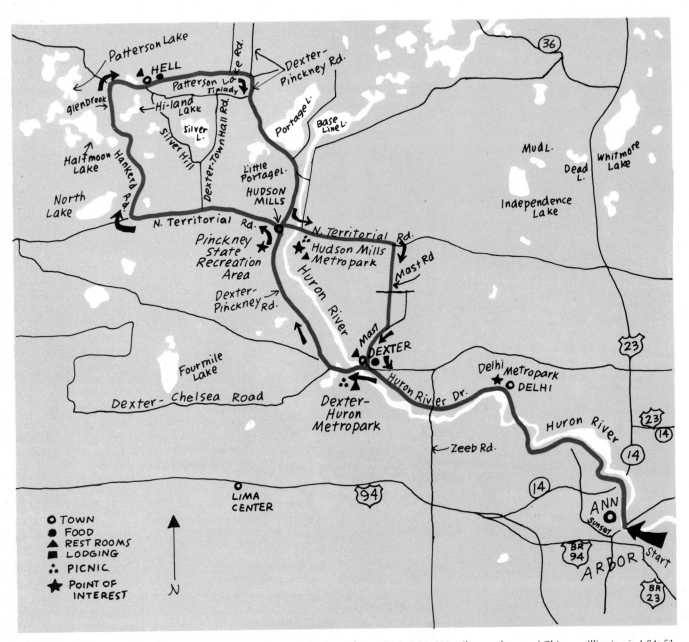

Map labels:

Patterson Lake

HELL

Dexter-Pinckney Rd.

Lake Rd.

glenbrook

Patterson La. Tiplady

Hi-land Lake

Silver L.

Portage L.

Base Line L.

Mud L.

Dead L.

Whitmore Lake

Half moon Lake

Silver Hill

Hankerd Rd.

Dexter-Townhall Rd.

Little Portage L.

HUDSON MILLS

Independence Lake

North Lake

N. Territorial Rd.

Pinckney State Recreation Area

N. Territorial Rd.

Hudson Mills Metropark

Mast Rd

Huron River

Dexter-Pinckney Rd.

36

23

Fourmile Lake

Mast

DEXTER

Huron River Dr.

Delhi Metropark

DELHI

Huron River

Dexter-Chelsea Road

Dexter-Huron Metropark

Zeeb Rd.

14

23

14

ANN

LIMA CENTER

94

sunset

ARBOR

Start

BR 94

BR 23

Legend:

○ TOWN
● FOOD
▲ REST ROOMS
■ LODGING
∴ PICNIC
★ POINT OF INTEREST

N

Ann Arbor is in southeastern Michigan on U.S. 23 and I-94; 42 miles west of Detroit via I-94; 281 miles northwest of Chicago, Illinois, via I-94; 51 miles north of Toledo, Ohio, via U.S. 23.

63. MAUMEE VALLEY VENTURE

Dawdle along Ohio's lazy Maumee River in spring to taste wild carrots and smell wildflowers in bloom, or in autumn when maples, buckeyes, and willows splash the banks crimson and gold. The old waters have seen both violent and serene history. Here General "Mad Anthony" Wayne defeated the Indian Confederation in 1794 and here, too, Johnny Appleseed whistled along the banks, planting small black seeds. Though tourists do visit the Maumee Valley, they don't usually discover the back roads. This delightful ride leads you through meadows and woods beside the river.

Start at Fort Meigs State Memorial in Perrysburg and head southwest on Route 65, a curving, flat, untraveled road along the river. Though the river is too muddy for swimming, you can pause anywhere beneath a willow to dangle your toes in the water or comb the river gravels for fossils left over from ancient forest swamps and glaciers. About 8 miles from Perrysburg, you roll over seven or eight large gentle hills. Cool river breezes and the gradual slopes keep pedaling easy. Recommended gears are fifth for beginners, tenth for experts. Just beyond the hills, you can pick up a snack at the country store on your left and stop across the road at Otsego Park, a pleasant roadside park with a river view.

Soon you reach Grand Rapids, where you can cross the Maumee to Providence Park to see old canal locks. This makes a good picnic and rest spot. Take Route 110 west in Grand Rapids, and outside town you soon reach Thurston State Park, another good rest spot. Though Route 110 is mostly flat, watch for gravel shoulders which can puncture tires. Seven miles through meadows and wooded

DISTANCE:	100 miles round trip.
TERRAIN:	Mostly flat, with a few rolling hills.
TRAFFIC:	Light.
DIFFICULTY:	Easy even for beginners.
BEST TIME:	April through October.
LOCATION:	Along the Maumee River, south of Toledo, Ohio.

countryside bring you to a wide creek emptying into the Maumee. The creek runs too deep for wading, but linger along its shaded banks awhile, and if you are touring in summer, stick your feet in the cool water. You can fish from the bridge, observe the shore birds and songbirds, including wild ducks, herons, sandpipers, cardinals, and warblers, or simply watch the Maumee drift by.

After you cross the river at Napoleon, take Route 424 southwest (left). Between here and Independence Dam are three roadside parks evenly spaced 1, 3, and 5 miles from Napoleon. In early summer the green meadows bloom with wild chicory, goldenrods, brown-eyed Susans, morning glories, and the pale pink or white bouncing Bet, also named soapwort because its juice lathers in water. The delicate white flowers are Queen Anne's lace. Pull one of these lacy flowers in spring, and you will find whitish wild carrot roots, a good addition to campfire stew.

Camp overnight at Independence Dam State Park and watch the sun set over the lake. The park

has fishing, a boating marina, and quiet woods. If you prefer a motel, pedal 3 miles farther to Defiance, so named because the fort here caused Anthony Wayne to say, "I defy the English, the Indians, and all the Devils in Hell to take it." If you arrive before 5 P.M., browse through the fort or pedal 5 miles southwest of town on U.S. 24 to Au Iaize Pioneer Village, with restored nineteenth-century buildings, Indian relics, a black swamp farm, and nature trails. The village's hours depend on the time of year, so you may want to phone ahead (419-784-2744) to make certain it is open before you start. Return to Perrysburg the following day by the same route.

WHERE TO STAY

Motels are available in Defiance and Napolean, and include the following: Holiday Inn, North Scott Street, Napoleon, Ohio 43545; at the junction of State 108 with Routes 6 and 24; (419) 592-5010. Holiday Inn, Box 379, Defiance, Ohio 43512; at the junction of State 66 and Route 24; (419) 782-7015.

Camping is available at Independence Dam State Park, described in the tour.

FOR FURTHER INFORMATION

Write the Naturalist Scouts, Secor Park Nature Center, Berkey, Ohio 43504, for answers to specific questions you may have.

NATURAL COFFEE

As you cycle the Maumee River valley, you will see bright blue chicory, also called blue-sailors or succory. In early spring, autumn, and winter, chicory roots can be roasted and ground to create a nat-

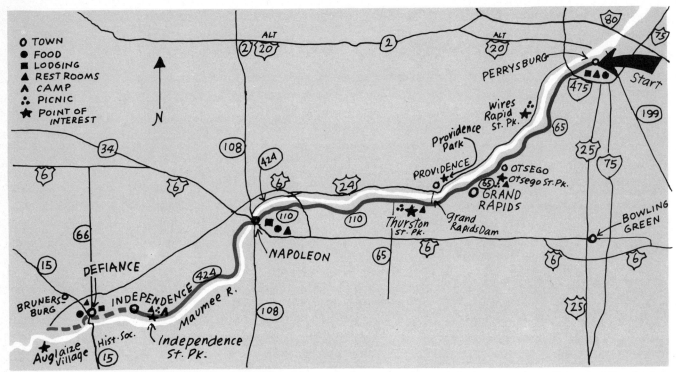

Perrysburg is in northwestern Ohio on U.S. 20 and Ohio 199; across the Maumee River from Toledo via U.S. 20; 115 miles west of Cleveland via U.S. 6, Ohio 2, U.S. 6, and U.S. 20.

ural coffee. Other wild-coffee substitutes include chufa tubers, cleavers fruits, and goatsbeard and salsify roots, all of which may be found in this part of Ohio. Though natural coffees are often more bitter than traditional coffee-bean varieties, you may discover a brew you like better or may want to add just a bit of wild coffee to your regular brand to create a fuller, richer brew. Try the following recipe.

Chicory Coffee. Dig the roots in winter, early spring, or autumn, and wash and roast them over your campfire or in an oven at home until browned throughout. Then grind the roots (two stones will work in the wilds) and use as you would regular coffee.

64. COVERED BRIDGE BIKEWAY

Pastoral countryside dotted with old covered bridges and Christmas-card villages awaits you on this ride southeast of Columbus. Clear, cold brooks slice through lush grass and pasturelands, and wildflowers can be seen snug in the meadowed hollows. Bring a picnic lunch and plan to spend the day on these serene, untraveled back roads.

Start in Canal Winchester, where you may park your car downtown. Most of the tour is marked with green-and-white bike signs; this first road, however, has no sign, so follow Waterloo East out of town and climb a gentle 2-mile slope to Diley Road. Along Waterloo East, Diley, and Benadum roads, you encounter small roller-coaster hills. Watch out for loose gravel, especially at the intersections. From Benadum you go right onto Pickerington Road and turn sharply over a bridge before reaching Lockville.

Stop awhile in Lockville's county park to see the restored covered bridge and old canal locks. For a delightful autumn side trip, leave the bikeway and pedal south of Lockville on Pickerington Road to a fruit farm. Here you can buy crisp, freshly picked Jonathan and McIntosh apples, honey, apple butter, and apple jelly, or have a free glass of iced cider.

Continuing east on the bikeway, you pedal on flat Lockville Road through sprawling, open fields. Be cautious as you cross Route 33, with its fast, heavy traffic. Now on Pleasantville Road you curve down a gentle slope, then jog slightly left and continue on flatlands. The road is narrow, traveled mostly by farmers. Coakley, Bish, and Havensport are gravel roads along which you cross three picturesque covered bridges. (There are no bikeway signs here.) This scenic spot shouldn't be missed, even if you walk your bike on the gravel. If you still want to avoid the gravel, though, continue straight on Pleasantville Road to Havensport Road, where you can see the third bridge about 500 yards from the intersection. Walk across the bridges: the bridge floors are rough parallel boards.

On Havensport Road you climb a small hill into Havensport, then jog onto Carroll East and back onto Havensport Road. Here you climb a long, moderate hill, followed by an exhilarating coast past cornfields almost to Election House Road. Around autumn harvesttime, you can hear breezes shuffling through the crackly brown cornstalks.

You climb gently on Election House Road, then coast downhill to Old Columbus Road with the wind often nudging your back.

DISTANCE:	35 miles.
TERRAIN:	Flat to hilly.
TRAFFIC:	Light.
DIFFICULTY:	Good ride for beginners and families. Use a 5- or 10-speed bike.
BEST TIME:	Any season but winter. Especially nice in spring when wildflowers bloom and during autumn's foliage change.
LOCATION:	Loop from Canal Winchester, 15 miles southeast of Columbus, Ohio, on Route 33.

Turn left on Old Columbus Road and trek up a long, steep hill, at the crest of which you can view wide fields dotted with white farm homes and neat red barns. It's an easy glide from here to Lancaster.

In Lancaster you can buy picnic basics, then go left onto Fair Avenue and left on High Street to Rising Park, where you can lunch on the grass beneath a shady oak. After lunch walk up the hill to Mount Pleasant, a 250-foot rock and overlook from which you see steepled Lancaster in the wide, fertile Hocking Valley. Before leaving, you may also want to visit Lancaster's Sherman House State Memorial, General William Tecumseh Sherman's birthplace, at 137 East Main Street. Hours: June through October, 9:30 A.M. to 5 P.M. daily; closed the rest of the year.

Plunging downhill from the park, you turn right onto Fair Avenue, where you cross busy Route 33 again just beyond the Old Columbus intersection. You may find some traffic on Fair Avenue until you reach the city limits. Your ride is flat at first on Wilson Road. Then you roll over two short, steep hills and turn right onto Mt. Zion Road, where you coast past a small lake. Watch out here for loose gravel and cars; many fishermen use the lake's parking lot.

Crossing a small bridge, you climb to Lithopolis Road, where to your left you view Rock Mill Farm's rolling green pastures and straight white fences. Though the farm is private, you may be able to persuade the caretaker to let you see the farm's antique collection and blacksmith shop. Stop a quarter of a mile farther to explore rustic Rock Mill and the covered bridge which overlook a deep shaded chasm.

You climb steeply from the mill, then dive into valleys and pine woods toward Lithopolis. Once there you return to Canal Winchester on Waterloo Road through clipped hedgerows. On this country road, lined with elderberries, blackberries, and bittersweet, you cross the tour's last covered bridge. At the dead end, turn left and complete the loop to Canal Winchester.

WHERE TO STAY

Motels in Lancaster include Holiday Inn, 1858 North Memorial Drive, located north on Route 33, and the Main, 651 East Main Street, six and a half blocks east of midtown on routes 22 and 37. There is also a hotel, the Lancaster, at 123 North Broad Street, just off routes 22 and 33.

The nearest campground is Triangle Lake, 3 miles north of Lancaster on Route 33. Open year round. Located on a pond, with no-license fishing and a snack bar. For reservations, write Triangle Lake, 3015 Lithopolis Road N.W., Lancaster, Ohio 43130, or phone (614) 654-8748. Another campground is Adena Ridge Campground, four and a half miles north of Lancaster on Ohio 158, then a quarter of a mile west on County 31. Open March 30th to October 14th. Located on a pond, with swimming, no-license fishing, and a snack bar. For reservations, write Adena Ridge Campgrounds, P.O. 1211 Coonpath Road N.W., Lancaster, Ohio 43130, or phone (614) 653-9203.

FOR SPARE PARTS AND REPAIRS

Lancaster has two bike shops: Lancaster Bike Shop, 704 East Main Street; (614) 653-2844. Cycle World Bicycle Shop, 1037 South Broad; (614) 654-0692.

FOR FURTHER INFORMATION

Cyclist Lynn Kessler told us about this tour and will be glad to help if you have questions. You can write him at 719 North Broad Street, Lancaster, Ohio 43130, or phone (614) 654-3730.

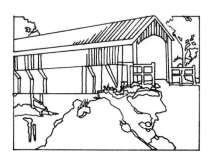

Canal Winchester is in central Ohio on Ohio 674; 15 miles southeast of Columbus, via U.S. 33 and Ohio 674; 130 miles northeast of Cincinnati via I-71 and 270, U.S. 33 and Ohio 674.

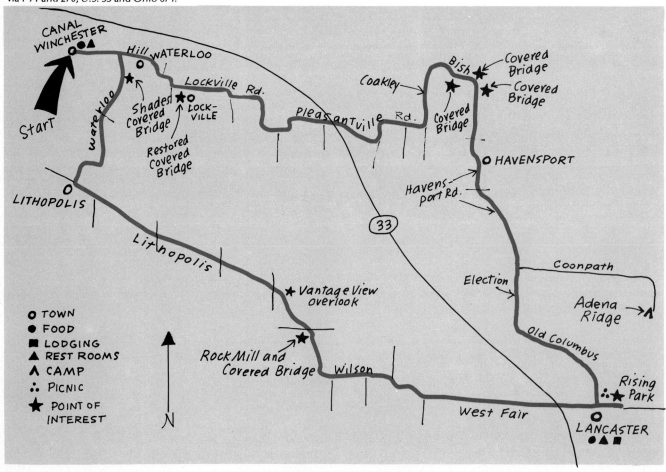

65. 66. LITTLE MIAMI / OLD MILL BIKEWAYS

Meander along the Little Miami River's banks where Daniel Boone scouted, Tecumsah was born, and Simon Kenton was captured and tortured by Shawnees in Old Chillicothe. On the way you see Indian mounds, historic grain mills, Quaker meetinghouses, and wooded knolls and farmland. If 87 miles one way seems too long for you, try the shorter tour on the Old Mill Bikeway through some of the same countryside. You pass many small towns where you can buy food, but bring snacks anyway, as well as spare parts and tools. Also, watch out for dogs.

LITTLE MIAMI RIVER SCENIC BIKEWAY

Start in Clifton, 20 miles east of Dayton, Ohio, and visit the old Clifton Mill where grain and corn are still stone-ground. Pick up the Little Miami River Scenic Bikeway signs and pedal south on Clifton Road along the riverbanks. This short stretch also takes in part of the Old Mill Bikeway, described later. Some of the bikeway signs are now missing, so inquire locally when in doubt.

Pause soon to view Clifton Gorge, a deep chasm along the river. Just a bit farther on flat terrain, you reach John Bryan State Park, a nice place to fish or picnic. If you prefer, camp in the park overnight and begin your tour from here.

Continuing along the untraveled back roads, you can soon take a side trip to Oldtown, an old Shawnee Village where Simon Kenton, an early pioneer, was tortured. The quickest way to reach the village is to take heavily trafficked U.S. 68 south. The safer route is to turn left onto Clark Run Road, right onto Stevenson Road past Stevenson Road Covered

DISTANCE:	Little Miami River Scenic Bikeway, 87 miles one way. Old Mill Bikeway, 30 miles.
TERRAIN:	Hilly.
TRAFFIC:	Light.
DIFFICULTY:	Good rides for families and beginners. A 10-speed bike recommended for hills.
BEST TIME:	Spring through autumn.
LOCATION:	Little Miami Valley, 20 miles east of Dayton, Ohio.

Bridge, then right again onto Brush Row Road, and ride until you reach Oldtown on your left. Retrace this route back to the bikeway.

Proceeding on the main tour, walk your bike across busy U.S. 68, over the river, and up the hill on Route 235 to Hilltop Road. Turn left on Hilltop and pedal on past Xenia. When you reach the busy U.S. 35 intersection, walk your bike across again, then climb a hill on Valley Road. Turning right onto Bellbrook Road, you coast once more to the river, where you can rest or swim at a small county park.

Beyond Spring Valley you coast to the Spring Valley Wildlife Preserve, where in early morning or late afternoon you may glimpse deer near the river. Past Furnas Road on your left, you coast again. Then the road levels into Waynesville and Corwin, twin villages on the river. Stop in Waynesville to visit the old Quaker meetinghouse

or relax in wooded Mill View Park.

You skim the flat riverbanks as you ride through Oregonia to Fort Ancient State Park, where you can lock your bike and rest or rent a canoe. Continue straight outside South Lebanon if you want to stop at Kings Island Amusement Park. The main tour turns left before the amusement park onto Kings Mill Road. Follow the road as it dives once more toward the river and climbs the other bank.

Soon you reach the tour's most hilly stretch—the miles between Loveland and Terrace Park. But even beginners will have little trouble with these slopes on a 10-speed. Near a country club, the road dead-ends into U.S. 32, which leads right to Cincinnati. This unmarked segment of bikeway into the city is heavily trafficked and hazardous. Unless you have an urge to tour Cincinnati, it's best to turn around here and follow the bikeway back north to your starting point.

OLD MILL BIKEWAY

Though the countryside south of Dayton contains old grain mills, covered bridges, and historic college campuses, your most cherished experiences will be those you create yourself. Hunt for fossils; forage for tea herbs, wild carrots, and blackberries; watch for birds, squirrels, chipmunks, and deer; or simply enjoy the peace and clear air of Ohio's fertile valleys.

Start at John Bryan State Park, just outside Yellow Springs, and follow the Little Miami Bikeway signs south along the Little Miami River. Make a detour to Yellow Springs to buy food and ask for local directions to the old Grinnell Mill. From the mill, follow the bikeway signs to Camp Green, tucked in a sycamore grove. Then

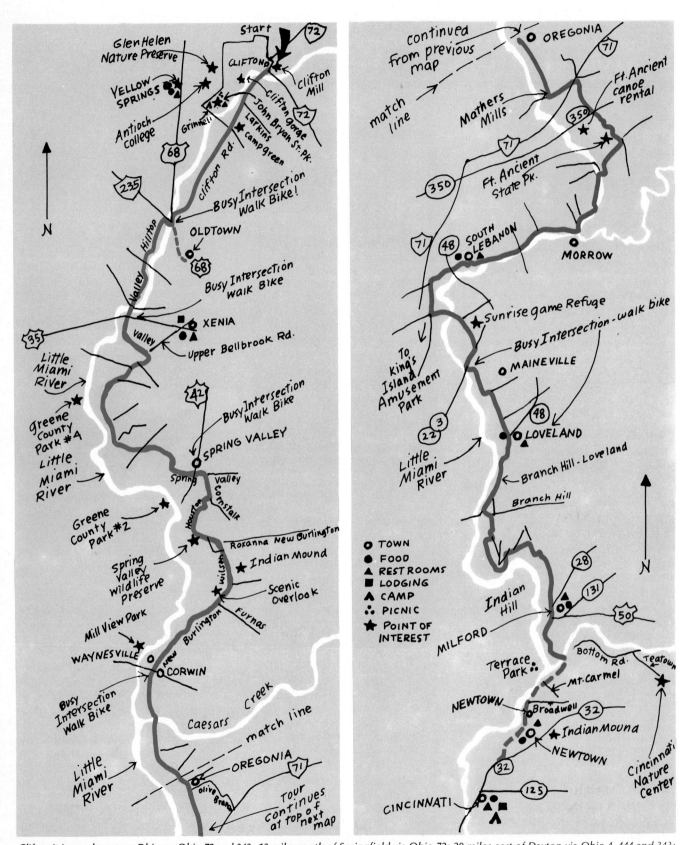

Start

72

CLIFTON

Clifton Mill

Clifton Gorge

John Bryan St. Pk.

Larkins camp green

Clifton Rd.

YELLOW SPRINGS

Antioch College

Grinnell

68

235

Busy Intersection Walk Bike!

Hilltop

OLDTOWN

68

Valley

Busy Intersection walk bike

35

XENIA

Upper Bellbrook Rd.

Little Miami River

Valley

42

Busy Intersection Walk Bike

Greene County Park #4

Little Miami River

SPRING VALLEY

Spring Valley

Houston

Cornstalk

Greene County Park #2

Roxanna New Burlington

Spring Valley Wildlife Preserve

Indian Mound

Scenic Overlook

Furnas

Houston

Mill View Park

New Burlington

WAYNESVILLE

CORWIN

Busy Intersection Walk Bike

Caesars Creek

match line

Little Miami River

OREGONIA

71

Olive Branch

Tour continues at top of next map

continued from previous map

OREGONIA

71

match line

Mathers Mills

Ft. Ancient canoe rental

350

71

350

Ft. Ancient State Pk.

71

48

SOUTH LEBANON

MORROW

Sunrise Game Refuge

Busy Intersection - walk bike

To King's Island Amusement Park

MAINEVILLE

22

3

48

LOVELAND

Little Miami River

Branch Hill - Loveland

Branch Hill

○ TOWN
● FOOD
▲ RESTROOMS
■ LODGING
▲ CAMP
∴ PICNIC
★ POINT OF INTEREST

Indian Hill

28

131

50

MILFORD

Terrace Park

Bottom Rd.

Teatown

Mt. Carmel

NEWTOWN

Broadwell

32

Indian Mound

NEWTOWN

Cincinnati Nature Center

32

125

CINCINNATI

N

Little Miami-Old Mill Bikeways caption:

Clifton is in southwestern Ohio on Ohio 72 and 343; 13 miles south of Springfield via Ohio 72; 20 miles east of Dayton via Ohio 4, 444 and 343; 59 miles southwest of Columbus via I-70 and Ohio 72. Above map is for the Little Miami River tour.

go right onto Clifton Road which leads you along the willowed banks of the Little Miami. Bikeway signs end here. You turn left onto Clark Run Road, and left again onto Bradfoote Road, which runs beside a bubbling stream. Bradfoote soon angles sharply right across a brook. At the dead-end, go left. Then take the next right turn onto Tarbox Cemetery Road.

At Conley Road the main tour goes left, but you can proceed straight for a side trip to Green County Park's roadside rest spot and old Indian mound.

Back on the main tour, go right onto Yellow Springs Road and ride into Cedarville. Cedarville College Campus has a student union where you can buy snacks. As you angle out of town, be careful on the rugged railroad tracks.

More back roads lead you past farms, woods, and Old Bloxom Cemetery, with many markers dating to pioneer days. Pause at rustic Clifton Mill to buy a bag of stoneground flour. Continuing on, watch out as you cross Clifton's main intersection. Then follow the bikeway signs north past some old stagecoach ruins and back to Bryan Park in time for a swim.

WHERE TO STAY

Motel: Bon Aire Motel, three quarters of a mile west of Xenia on busy U.S. 35. Has a dining room. For reservations, write Bon Aire Motel, Box 277, Xenia, Ohio 45385, or phone (513) 372-7624.

Camping: John Bryan State Park, at the start of both bikeways; open year round; $1.50; swimming pool and hiking trails. Kings Island Camping, at Kings Island Amusement Center; open year round; $6 for four; bikes for rent. For reservations, write Kings Island Camping, Box 348, Kings Mill, Ohio 45039, or phone (513) 398-2901.

FOR FURTHER INFORMATION

Write Little Miami, Inc., P.O. Box 303, Lebanon, Ohio 45036, and ask for their brochure "Little Miami River Scenic Bikeway." Send a large self-addressed, stamped envelope with this or any other request.

NEARBY

Ohio's Miami Valley contains some of the country's finest untraveled back roads, and hundreds of miles of existing or planned bikeways. If you plan to spend a week or two in this region, write for a copy of the detailed map "Bikeways in the Miami Valley Region," available for $1 from the Miami Valley Regional Planning Commission, 333 West First Street, Dayton, Ohio.

LITTLE MIAMI HICKORY TREES

If you take this trip in autumn when the hickory nuts ripen along the Little Miami, bring along a bag and go nutting. Though all hickory trees look similar, there are several different varieties, and some species have more flavorful nuts than others.

Shagbark hickory has a rough, light gray bark which peels from the trunks of older trees and gives them a shaggy appearance, hence the name. The leaves of all hickories are pinnately compound, which means that several leaflets are grouped together to form the leaf. In this species, five jaggededged leaflets combine to form a leaf eight to fourteen inches long. The nut, which grows singly or in pairs, varies from one to two and a half inches long and is enclosed in a four-part husk which breaks apart when the nut has ripened. This hickory nut has an excellent sweet flavor.

Pignut hickory has a smaller bitter nut which stays at least partially encased in its thin husk, even when the nutmeat is ripe. The leaves have five or occasionally seven leaflets which grow to sharp points. Another of its characteristics is the dark grayish bark which forms deep ridges on older trees.

Bitternut hickory, as it name suggests, bears a bitter, insipid nut. You can identify the bitternut by the yellowish scales on its husk and by the tree's distinctive, deep yellow-green leaves which have seven to nine individual leaflets.

Spend a day on the Old Mill Bikeway.

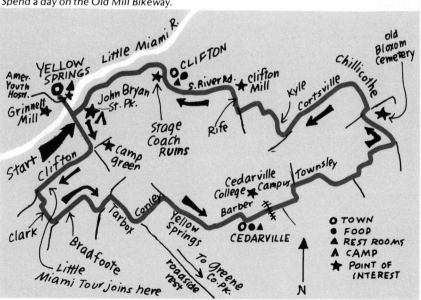

67. 68. 69. EASY INDIANA RIDERS

Hoosiers call the region around Bloomington "a tourist spot without tourists or trinkets." Which it is. The fine, untraveled back roads alone would be enough to make this area a cycling discovery. But you find even more. Maple, oak, beech, and elm trees cluster about clear lakes and pools. Small picturesque villages destroy any Sinclair Lewis stereotype you might have had of Midwestern towns. Cycle here in spring when redbud and dogwood bloom or in autumn when vivid foliage covers the hills.

These three tours all begin in Bloomington, and you can combine or break them up any way you please. Directions for the Hilly Fifty and Lake Lemon Loop are complex, so the turns on these rides are listed numerically at the end of the tour descriptions. Carry spare parts, tools, snacks, and dog repellent on all the rides.

INDIAN CREEK BIKEWAY

Park your car at Bloomington High School or the ice-skating rink lot. Then starting from the high school, go south on Henderson Street, right on Country Club Drive and left on Rockport Road, which winds through wooded countryside. Outside town past Bolin Lane, rock hounds can ask permission to explore the stone quarry. Fossils have been found in this region. A bit farther (about six and a half miles from Bloomington), pause to rest or snack at the Pic-a-Chick picnic area.

Two miles beyond the picnic area, go left onto Victor Pike, from which you have fine views of wooded valleys and rounded hills. You continue straight through an intersection and pass a wooden railroad trestle and Beck Limestone Quarry (rock hounds may want to

stop here, too). Then at Fluck Mill Road you turn right. A bit farther, go left on Ketcham Road to the Highway 37 underpass and continue straight at the underpass on Smithville Road.

After restocking your supplies in Smithville, go south up several steep hills to picnic along Monroe Reservoir, deep in the wooded knolls. To reach the lake, you can go either right on Strain Ridge Road for a hilly jaunt to the dam and picnic area, or right onto Fairfax Road for a smoother ride to Fairfax Beach for a cool swim.

After lunch return to Smithville and go north on Fairfax Road. You spend the afternoon winding along rural back roads, and you can pause by a creek or relax in a meadow, and if you are lucky, catch sight of a deer. Along this stretch you have several turns: right on Moffet Lane, left on Harrell Road, then right on Rhorer, left on Snoddy, left again on Rogers, straight ahead on Winslow,

DISTANCE:	Indian Creek Bikeway, 20.2 miles. Hilly Fifty, 52.6 miles. Lake Lemon Loop, 53.7 miles.
TERRAIN:	Hilly.
TRAFFIC:	Light.
DIFFICULTY:	A 10-speed bike recommended for hills. Indian Creek Bikeway is best for families and beginners.
BEST TIME:	Spring through autumn.
LOCATION:	All the rides start in Bloomington, Indiana.

and right on Henderson to return to the high school.

HILLY FIFTY

A longer tour can be taken south of Bloomington by following the directions here or the yellow lines and signs painted on the roads each autumn by the Central Indiana Bicycling Association of Indianapolis. Don't try to follow both the written directions and the yellow lines, as the routing for the annual ride varies slightly each year.

Start in Bloomington at Poplars, a midtown hotel at 400 East 7th Street, and head east to Dunn Street, where you go right. There are several more turns as you leave town and ride through farmland and rolling meadows. At Monroe Reservoir, pause to wade, swim, or snack along the shady banks.

Winding on into Smithville, you can buy food at the Sunoco grocery store. At Rockport Road you have a chance to shorten your ride by turning right toward Bloomington. But to stay on the main tour, go left into Kirksville.

Outside Kirksville you climb past Mount Zion Church, then coast almost to the State 45 junction. At this junction, go left onto Elwren Road. There's no road sign here, but you will see a Sunoco Station in the distance. Following the detailed directions, you ride past tiny Standford, wind left, and coast easily to Solsberry. There's no sign here either, but you see a church on your left. After a right onto Solsberry, you pedal along a flat stretch. Then just after you turn right onto State 43, you climb a hill. At the crest you see Bloomington far in the distance. From the hilltop you dive down in one exhilarating plunge, then roll over easy hills into Hendricksville, where there are food and rest rooms at an old country store.

Outside Hendricksville you spin into Coon Hollow, from which you have a 1-mile 4-percent climb. Then you ride through more easy rolling countryside and over a few moderate hills back into Bloomington. In the evening you can walk along the city's streets and absorb the college-town atmosphere. The traditional dish here is pizza, of course.

LAKE LEMON LOOP

North of Bloomington lies the quaint hamlet of Nashville, Morgan Monroe State Forest, and Lake Lemon. Autumn is an especially good time for this jaunt because you can stop at several places for fresh apple cider.

Starting in Bloomington, follow Union Street north. Go right onto State 45 and pedal 16.6 miles along a smooth blacktop road to the Happy Valley Grocery.

At the Phillips 66 station, go right onto Helmsburg Road. There's no sign here, so watch closely. You climb awhile through woods past several log cabins. Then you dive downhill. Caution: This coast is deceivingly tough; watch for the sharp turn at the bottom of the hill. Soon you spin into Nashville, a quaint southern Indiana village with craft and antique shops, a county art gallery, and pleasant residents. In autumn you can buy fresh apple cider and other delectables at a tent set up on the courthouse lawn. At Nashville House, a country store on the southeast corner across the street from the town square, you can buy huge old-fashioned sugar cookies, freshly-baked breads, homemade pickles, and penny candy. The adjoining restaurant has delicious fried biscuits and apple butter.

The main tour proceeds north, but for a pleasant side trip to Brown County State Park, continue east on Nashville's Main Street (State 46). You pedal about 2 miles to the park, which has an old covered bridge at its entrance. Walk your bike through the bridge be-

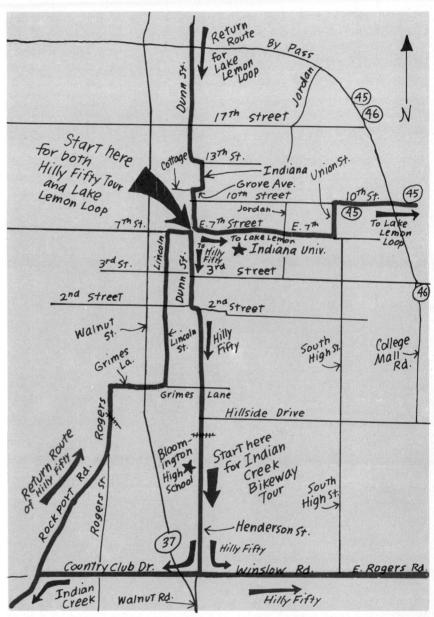

Bloomington is in south-central Indiana on Indiana 37, 45 and 46; 47 miles southwest of Indianapolis via Indiana 37. Above is a street map of Bloomington.

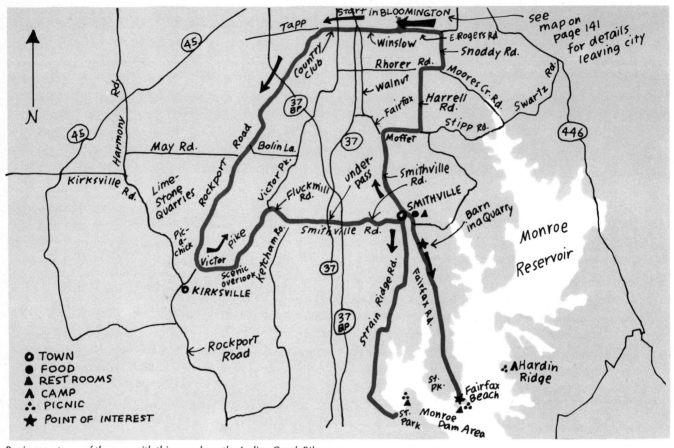

Begin your tours of the area with this one along the Indian Creek Bikeway.

cause the rough planks are tough on tires. Spend at least an hour exploring the miles of roads and hiking along the trails. You can also swim in a pool, eat lunch at Abe Martin Lodge (open April through November), or climb the eighty-foot observation tower, offering you wide views of the countryside. Beginners and families might consider riding through the park alone for an excellent Sunday bike tour. Bikes can be rented at the concession.

Back on the main tour, heading north from Nashville, you climb steep Greasy Creek Road, then glide into Bean Blossom, where a small roadside stand sells fresh-pressed apple cider in autumn and fruits and vegetables year round. Beyond Helmsburg, near the Happy Valley Grocery, experts can add a challenging 10 miles to their tour by pedaling onto North Shore Drive, which goes along Lake Lem-

on's north shore and through Morgan Monroe State Forest. This stretch is exceptionally hilly, with one steep hill just after you cross a railroad track, and another tough climb as you wind right into the state forest. The deep hardwood and evergreen woods are worth the effort, though, especially in spring when dogwood and redbud flower, and in autumn when the trees have turned orange, rose, gold, yellow, and scarlet. Lock your bike and hike or picnic here. You have one more tough climb before you rejoin the main tour.

If you choose to avoid the hilly side trip through the state forest, go right on South Shore Drive and ride past Lake Lemon's south shore. Be careful crossing the railroad tracks after the state forest turnoff. Beyond the tracks, you begin a long, slow climb. Then the road levels off and finally plunges into Dolan.

The road climbs out of Dolan, dips for a long, thrilling coast, then climbs slowly. A steeper rise takes you back to Bloomington.

Directions for the Hilly Fifty

1. Start at the Poplars on 7th Street and ride east;

2. go right on Dunn Street;

3. left on Second Street;

4. right on Henderson Street;

5. left on Winslow Road (no sign);

6. right on Rogers Road;

7. right on Snoddy Road;

8. left on Moores Creek (no sign) to Monroe Reservoir;

9. left on Stipp Road (no sign);

10. left on Handy Road;

11. right on Butcher Road (no sign) which becomes Cleve Road; then Smithville Road;

12. left, then right on Ketchum Road;

13. right at the Victor Sign Company;

14. left on Fluck Mill Road, then angle left onto Victor Pike;

15. left on Rockport Road (no sign)—a right here leads you back to Bloomington;

16. right on Kirksville Road; which becomes Harmony road;

17. left at State 45 junction onto Elwren Road (no sign);

18. left on Route 800 W (no sign);

19. right on Solsberry (no sign, but there's a church on the left);

20. right onto State 43;

21. left across the bridge;

22. left on Gardner Road (no sign);

23. right at the dead end onto Garrison Chapel;

24. left on Keller Road;

25. left on Leonard Springs;

26. right on Tapp Road;

27. left on Rockport Road (no sign);

28. left at the Nite Owl onto Rogers Street;

29. right on Grimes Lane;

30. left on Lincoln Street.

31. right on 7th Street back to the Poplars.

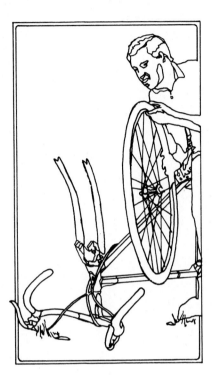

Directions for the Lake Lemon Loop

1. Start at the Poplars on 7th Street and ride east;

2. go left on Union Street;

3. right on 10th Street and State 45;

4. right at the Phillips 66 station onto Helmsburg Road;

5. left at the Bear Wallow sign onto Greasy Creek Road;

6. right on State 135;

7. left on State 45;

8. right near Happy Valley Grocery onto North Shore Drive (alternate route), or right on South Shore Drive (main route);

9. left on Tunnel Road;

10. right on Robinson Road (some bumpy spots, so be careful);

11. left on old State 37;

12. right on Audubon Road;

13. left at the dead end onto Hillview;

14. left on old State 37;

15. right on Dunn Street;

Pedal the Hilly Fifty for another enjoyable Bloomington tour.

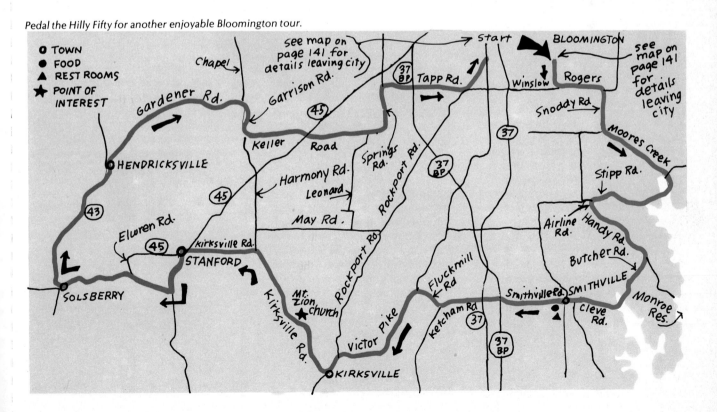

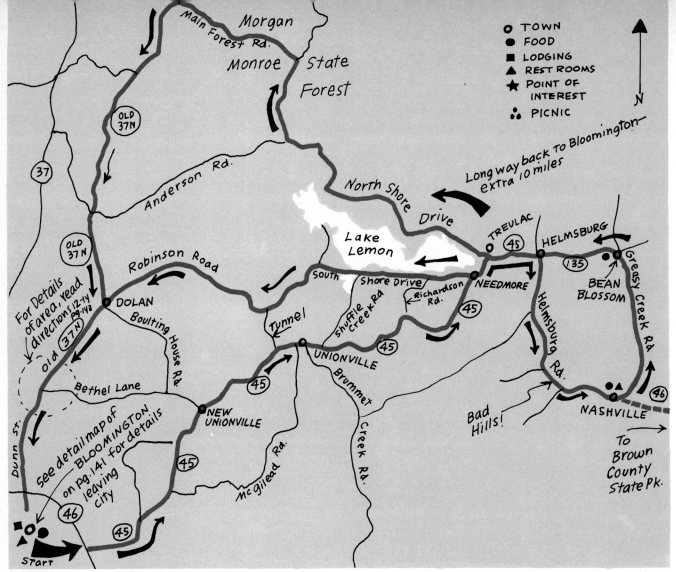

End your stay in Bloomington with a tour around Lake Lemon.

16. left at the dead end onto 13th Street;

17. right on Indiana Avenue;

18. right on Cottage Grove Street;

19. left on Dunn Street;

20. right on 7th Street back to the Poplars.

WHERE TO STAY

Motels are available in Bloomington and Brown County State Park, and include the following: Bloomington Travelodge, 2615 East 3rd Street, Bloomington; one and a quarter miles east on Indiana 46 Bypass; (812) 339-6191. Memorial Union, at Indiana University, Bloomington; (812) 332-6381. Ramada Inn, on Indiana 46 near Nashville; (317) 988-2286. Abe Martin Lodge, in Brown County State Park; (317) 988-4418.

Camping: Brown County State Park, 2 miles east of Nashville. Monroe Dam and Reservoir, 10 miles south of Bloomington; fee, $3.

FOR SPARE PARTS AND REPAIRS

The Bike Rack, Bloomington, Indiana.

FOR FURTHER INFORMATION

Judi and Ross Faris told us about this ride and will be glad to answer questions. You can write them at 5224 Grandview Drive, Indianapolis, Indiana 46208. They will also supply information on the Central Indiana Bicycling Association's annual Hilly Hundred tour.

70. INDIANA PERSIMMON TRAIL

Return to the early 1900's, with covered bridges, a recreated village, sassafras-smoked hams and bacon, apple butter, and home-made persimmon ice cream, on this journey through Indiana's Parke County. Here you can purchase hand-ground corn, try your skill at pitching horseshoes, or learn how to whittle on the steps of an old country store. For a rural getaway, the bikeways around Rockville are unbeatable.

Start in Rockville and follow the bike-trail signs downhill (south) along flat, backtopped County A. Yellow streamers placed in prominent places (on telephone poles, tall posts, and the like) from the Covered Bridge Festival guide you through the countryside. Jog left at the first fork and cross little Billie Creek, then go right at the next fork to pedal along flat road through three quaint covered bridges. Walk your bike over the rugged bridge planks.

Beyond the bridges, you climb a gradual hill, then roll through heavily wooded valleys. In spring local residents go mushrooming throughout the countryside. If you know your toadstools from mushrooms, you can fill a whole pail within an hour. When the road dead-ends into County C, go left. Then in just a minute wind right through another old covered bridge. Continue following the streamers to Conley's Ford Bridge, where you leave the streamer-marked route by veering left (don't go through the bridge).

Soon you wind to a dead end and turn right, then climb over a short hill and coast into Mansfield, where you can pick up a snack. Take a look at the old water-power mill here. Leave Mansfield through the 1867 Mansfield Bridge and re-join the streamer-marked Covered Bridge Festival tour. The road from

DISTANCE:	32 miles.
TERRAIN:	Easy rolling hills.
TRAFFIC:	Light except during the ten-day Covered Bridge Festival, which includes the second and third weekends in October.
DIFFICULTY:	Good ride for anyone.
BEST TIME:	Spring through autumn; avoid Covered Bridge Festival traffic.
LOCATION:	Countryside around Rockville, Indiana, in the west-central part of the state, via U.S. 41 or U.S. 36.

Mansfield past Mansfield Dam has the tour's steepest climbs, but all are easily managed on a 10-speed bike.

The main route continues past the reservoir, but for a cool swim or picnicking along the lake, you can take a side trip right onto State 49, right again for 2 miles on U.S. 59, then right into Raccoon State Park. The water is clear blue and surrounded by dense woods. Boat rentals and fishing are available.

Back on the main bike trail, go west over rolling hills on County M to County A—the first full intersection after you cross Raccoon Creek —and turn right to retrace the short segment back to Rockville. The bike trail ends here, but don't stop. After a cool drink, leave town on U.S. 36 and go right at the fork onto blacktop to Billie Creek Bridge and Billie Creek Village

(adults, $1; under 18, 50¢), a restored turn-of-the-century hamlet. Just north of the village entrance, you may want to buy more snacks at the fresh fruit and vegetable stand. In Billie Creek Village, stop at the sorghum mill, visit the many restored buildings, see pottery and brooms being made, and browse through an old general store.

Other Tours

You can extend this ride with an additional 14-mile loop along another bike trail northwest of Rockville or with the 5-mile bike-trail loop to Nyesville and back. In fact, most of the blacktop roads in this area offer excellent cycling, and you may want to spend several days exploring on your own.

WHERE TO STAY

Rockville has several motels and reservations are usually unnecessary. All are filled to capacity months in advance, however, for the Covered Bridge Festival. If you plan to bike here during that time (ten days which include the second and third weekends in October), you can arrange to stay in a local home. For details, write the Rockville Tourist Information Center, Box 165, Rockville, Indiana 47872.

Camping is available at Raccoon Lake State Recreation Area, 9 miles east of Rockville on U.S. 36; described in the tour. Open April through October; $2.50 plus admission fee.

FOR FURTHER INFORMATION

Write the Rockville Tourist Information Center, Box 165, Rockville, Indiana 47872. If you are interested in other possible rides in this area, ask for their map "Parke County—The Covered Bridge

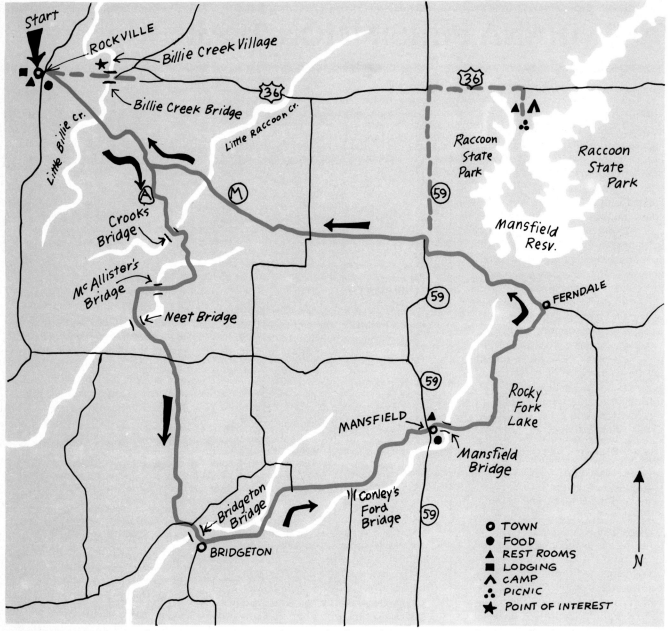

Rockville is in west-central Indiana on U.S. 36 and 41; 58 miles west of Indianapolis via U.S. 36; 24 miles north of Terre Haute via U.S. 41; 144 miles south of Chicago, Illinois, via U.S. 41.

County of the U.S.A.'' and the pamphlet "A Bicycle Tour of Covered Bridges."

OLD COUNTRY PERSIMMON ICE CREAM

A local specialty, persimmon ice cream tastes so unique you may decide to recreate the flavor when you get home. Here from Mrs. T. V. Thomas's kitchen is the official festival recipe.

7 eggs
2 3/4 cups sugar
1 tablespoon flour
1 tablespoon lemon juice
3/4 cup persimmon pulp
2 1/3 cups evaporated milk
2 quarts whole milk
pinch of salt

Beat the eggs well and set aside. Combine the sugar, flour, and salt. Slowly add the sugar mixture to the eggs as you beat the eggs at high speed. Add the evaporated milk, lemon juice and persimmon pulp and beat until frothy. Then pour the mixture into an ice-cream freezer and fill the container to the top with milk (about two quarts). Freeze. Makes one and a half gallons.

71. CHICAGO LAKEFRONT SPIN

Ride from Chicago's Museum of Science and Industry past the Art Institute and the Field Museum of Natural History along the lakefront to cool, wooded Lincoln Park, with deep lagoons, a zoo, and the Academy of Sciences—all on a wide walkway with only pedestrian traffic. Chicago cyclists have been busy, and the city now boasts a full 100 miles of bike routes, paths, and lanes; this lakeshore tour is one of the best.

Start at Jackson Park, with a yacht basin, a rose garden, and at the park's northern end the Museum of Science and Industry (free admission). Don't become immersed now in the museum's great collection or you could spend the day here. Instead ride west on Plaisance and then Midway Avenue, following the bikeway signs around the square to Lake Michigan. Then pedal on the marked walkway paralleling South Lake Shore Drive. Breezes always blow in from the lake, and you may encounter strong winds.

Past the Exposition Center, you reach the Museum of Natural History, a delightful stop with an excellent collection of primitive art. In this same vicinity—on the little jetty of land east of the museum—you can browse through the Shedd Aquarium (free admission on Fridays) and the Adler Planetarium.

Chicago's downtown Loop lies to your left as you pedal north through wooded Grant Park past pink-marbled Buckingham Fountain. At U.S. 66, walk your bike left for one block to the Art Institute, containing world-renowned sculpture, paintings, and prints.

Soon you climb a steep hill toward Outer Drive East Apartments and round the S-curve of Outer Drive over the Chicago River. Follow the east side path over the bridge. While motorists battle on the bridge for room, you can stop to take a leisurely look at the Army Corps of Engineers locks, which reverse the Chicago River's flow to prevent the river from contaminating Lake Michigan. A downhill glide leads you to Olive Park, a pleasant rest spot.

Gaining speed now, you pedal along Lake Michigan and glimpse the huge John Hancock Center looming over the city. Past Oak Street Beach, the bikeway is slightly banked and you may want to try a short race. Then on a warm summer day you can stop at Fullerton Avenue Beach for a swim in the lake.

A bit farther, you spin over a pedestrian bridge into wooded Lincoln Park, with many spots to explore. Here you can stop at the zoo (open daily, 9 A.M. to 5 P.M.); the conservatory, with an extensive orchid collection and lovely rock gardens; and the Chicago Academy of Sciences. Picnic beside a lagoon or beneath a huge tree.

From Lincoln Park the main tour returns south to Jackson Park, but you can extend your tour by going north through Lincoln Park and back along the lakefront, pedaling easily past an Army Nike Missile site and Montrose Park's bird sanctuary to Edgewater Beach. From here, return the way you came to Jackson Park.

WHERE TO STAY

Motels and hotels are available for every taste and budget. There are no camping facilities.

NEARBY

Chicago's bike paths, routes, and lanes can occupy many a pleasant afternoon.

DISTANCE:	25 miles round trip.
TERRAIN:	Flat, with a few hills.
TRAFFIC:	None except pedestrian traffic on the walkway; heavy if you venture onto city streets.
DIFFICULTY:	Easy for anyone.
BEST TIME:	Any season but winter. Summer can be hot and humid.
LOCATION:	Chicago, Illinois, along Lake Michigan.

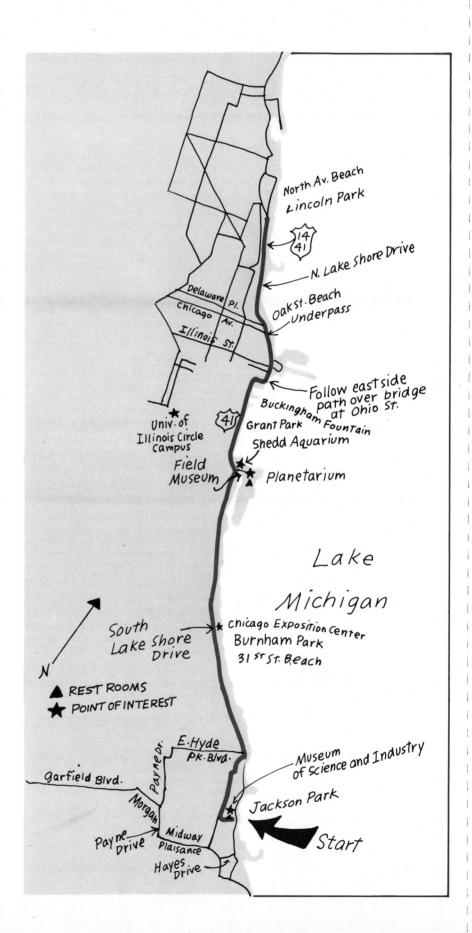

North Av. Beach
Lincoln Park

14
41

N. Lake Shore Drive

Delaware Pl.
Chicago Av.
Illinois St.

Oak St. Beach
Underpass

Follow east side
path over bridge
at Ohio St.

Buckingham Fountain

Univ. of
Illinois Circle
Campus

41

Grant Park

Shedd Aquarium

Field
Museum

Planetarium

Lake

Michigan

N

South
Lake Shore
Drive

Chicago Exposition Center
Burnham Park
31ST St. Beach

▲ REST ROOMS
★ POINT OF INTEREST

E. Hyde
Pk. Blvd.

Payne Dr.

Garfield Blvd.

Morgan

Payne
Drive

Midway
Plaisance

Hayes
Drive

Museum
of Science and Industry

Jackson Park

Start

In Chicago Illinois, along Lake Michigan.

72. SHAWNEE FOREST RUN

South of Carbondale, black and white oaks shade the back roads. Ponds and lakes covered with wild geese dot the woods, while in the distance lie the Missouri Ozarks. Sometimes startling things happen here: a Yeti-type creature allegedly arises from lake-bottom ooze, a flying saucer reportedly lands, or an old farmer, for no explicable reason, digs a moat around his house. Usually, though, life is peaceful and unhurried, a perfect spot to ride a bike.

Park in Carbondale in the Jackson County YMCA's lot and head west on old 13. Outside town, just beyond Little Crab Orchard Creek, new 13 forks right but you stay left on a narrow, untraveled lane with rock shoulders. After 5 miles of rolling hills, you go left on Route 127 and pedal for another 5 through farms and fields. Now you begin a steep climb. Over the hill and about half a mile farther down the road lies Pomona Natural Bridge, where you can rest, have a cool drink, and hike along a trail through the woods. Watch here and throughout the tour for beavers, opossums, red and gray squirrels, woodchucks, and muskrats.

A pleasant side trip lies along the next road right (past the Visitor Center). Here you pedal to Oakwood Bottoms Greentree Reservoir Waterfowl Area to hike through deep stands of pin, bur, post, chinquapin, black, and white oak trees.

Several miles farther on the main tour, turn left at a gas station toward Alto Pass. Here you have excellent views of the Ozarks, aflame with foliage in fall. Beyond Alto Pass, watch out for two German shepherds and a white dog. About 1 mile from town, turn left at the fork; in 3 miles, go left at the T. Past the 4-mile-long Fruit Growers Exchange, turn right, go about 50

DISTANCE:	48 miles, excluding side trips.
TERRAIN:	Hilly.
TRAFFIC:	Light.
DIFFICULTY:	Some experience needed, less experienced cyclists should definitely have a 10-speed bike and may have to walk a few hills.
BEST TIME:	Anytime but cold winter days.
LOCATION:	Carbondale, near the southern tip of Illinois, between I-57 and I-55, through Shawnee National Forest.

yards to a stop sign, then proceed straight down the steep hill.

Another hill and railroad crossing bring you to Makanda. Outside town you can take a side trip to the right through Giant City State Park, a good picnic spot. In the park you climb a mile through deep pine and eastern red cedar forests to a cliff where you overlook valleys to the Ozark Mountain foothills. Soon you can go straight to Giant City Lodge or return to the main route and proceed to Little Grassy Lake, with swimming, boat rentals, and fishing for catfish, striped, largemouth and smallmouth bass. Bird watching is excellent here. In season you may see hundreds of Canadian geese or spot wild turkeys or drumming grouse.

More hills lead you past the house with the moat (on your left) to old 13. You can go left to Carbondale or right to blue Crab Orchard Lake, with camping, fishing, swim-

ming, and boat rentals. As you return to Carbondale, be careful not to get on new 13, a four-lane freeway.

WHERE TO STAY

Carbondale has many motels and you should not need reservations. If you would like to stay in town, you might check into a motel before leaving.

Camping spots are numerous and include Giant City State Park, Little Grassy Lake, Devils Kitchen Lake, adjacent to Little Grassy, and Crab Orchard Lake. A secluded spot for camping lies on the Big Muddy River (a Yeti supposedly really *has* been spotted along the water), at the end of the oak-forest trail.

FOR SPARE PARTS, REPAIRS, FURTHER INFORMATION

Southern Illinois Bicycle Company, 106 North Illinois, Carbondale, Illinois. (618) 549-7123.

NEARBY

East of this tour stretches more of Shawnee National Forest, with lots of delightful wooded back roads for cycling. Ask at the Visitor Center near Pomona Natural Bridge about the Garden of the Gods, elaborate camel rock formations located about one hour by car east of this loop.

OAKS OF THE SHAWNEE FOREST

The Shawnee Forest boasts some of the world's oldest oak stands. Oaks generally can be divided into red and white varieties. As you pedal along the back roads and hike the wooded paths, watch for these species.

Red Oaks usually have pointed, spiny-lobed leaves and bitter acorns which grow about one inch long and have a shallow cup. *Northern red oak*, vivid crimson in autumn, has leaves five to eight inches long with seven to eleven lobes, and its acorns are hairy inside. *Southern Red Oak* is quite different, with three to seven lobes on the leaves, the center lobe being much longer than the others. Its acorns are rounded, have a scaly cup obscuring about a third of the nut, and are hairless inside.

White oaks, in contrast, usually have rounded lobes and sweet acorns. The common white oak's acorns are light chestnut colored, with a knobby cup concealing about a quarter of the nut. *Swamp white oak* leaves are hairy underneath and the acorn cup encloses about a third of the nut. Acorns of the swamp white oak usually grow in pairs on a long stem.

Many other oaks are found in the Shawnee Forest, including black, pin, blackjack, bur, and post oaks. One which you may not think is an oak at all is the *chinquapin oak*, with four to seven inch oblong leaves which almost look toothed instead of lobed, and small mahogany-colored acorns in scaly amber cups. Indians often ground flour from the chinquapin's sweet acorns.

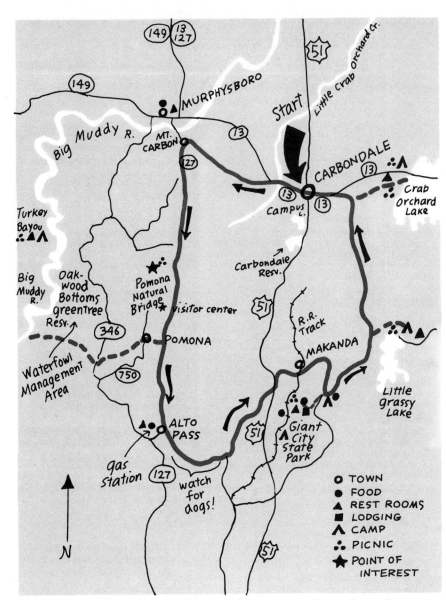

Carbondale is in southern Illinois on U.S. 51 and Illinois 13; 94 miles southeast of St. Louis, Missouri, via Illinois 15 and 13; 239 miles northwest of Nashville, Tennessee, via U.S. 41-A, Kentucky 80, and U.S. 51.

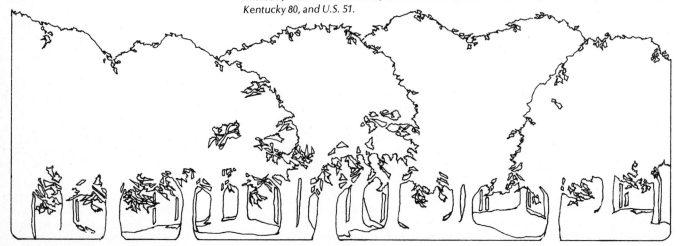

73. KINNICKINNIC CAPERS

Wisconsin's delights are not for your everyday tourist. You find no import shops, exclusive beaches, or neon distractions. What you do experience are subtler pleasures: the smell of moist black loam in spring, a clear brook trickling beneath a gray wooden bridge, tidy farm homes and red barns curled in forested hollows. If you enjoy pedaling through fresh air on rural back roads without a car in sight, this jaunt offers a pleasurable weekend.

Hazards are minimal. Watch out for farmers who pull out from their driveways without stopping, frost boils (holes in the road created by winter frosts), and dogs. A good time to start is at sunrise, when mists fill the dells.

Park your car in River Falls's Glen Park. You find several stores and cafés along the way, but carry a picnic to be safe, especially on Sunday. On this ride simply follow the orange Ⓚ signs, painted each year in late March for the AYH annual April Kinnickinnic tour. After two months the bright orange signs gradually fade, so you must watch closely on a September or October tour. Since you have thirty-six turns on this ride, excluding side trips, specific directions are listed at the end of this tour description.

You pedal out of town through a countryside of rolling hills, farms, and rich pastures and meadows. The Kinnickinnic River flows beside you, occasionally slipping beneath wooden bridges in the dips between hills. After many turns, you reach County J. Turn right, cross a small bridge, veer left, and climb a shaded hill. Here in late March or early April sap buckets hang on the sugar maples.

More countryside brings you to State 35, which you take right into Beldenville. State 35 can be what

Wisconsinites call "heavily traveled," but if you are from the city, you won't even notice the traffic. After more turns, you go left on County O, which begins winding before you cross U.S. 10. Then you coast for about 6 miles along the scenic Trimbelle River, with woods on your right and tree-filled dells on your left. Stop anywhere along this winding forested lane to sit on the riverbanks, dip your feet in the water, picnic, catch a fresh fish dinner, or just relax.

At County E, turn left, taking care on the railroad tracks, and coast on to Diamond Bluff, where you look down jagged rock walls to the Mississippi. You can have a

---

DISTANCE: Full tour is 100 miles, but can be shortened to either 71 or 30 miles.

TERRAIN: Rolling hills, with three steep climbs.

TRAFFIC: Light.

DIFFICULTY: Okay for anyone. Beginners and families may want to try one of the shorter rides.

BEST TIME: April through October Summer days, however, can be hot and humid.

LOCATION: River Falls, Wisconsin, less than an hour from Minneapolis-St. Paul via U.S. 12, I-94, and Wisconsin 35.

---

snack at Kask's Bar. Continuing on E, you have an arduous half-mile climb, then rolling hills. Turn left when you reach County Q. Watch out at this corner for the black dog. Luckily this wicked beast is medium-sized and a bit dumb: he dives for your front wheel, and by the time he reaches his mark, you've zipped past. Soon you plunge down a steep hill with a creek in the hollow. If you spin fast enough down this slope, you can gain enough momentum to push you halfway up the steep climb beyond the bridge.

Past the hill, turn right onto County QQ, jog left, then right, and cross two bridges. Beyond the second bridge, go right at the fork and watch out for the German shepherd. So far he has only barked, but be prepared. After more turns, you go right onto County F and plunge into wooded Clifton Hollow. Picnic here along the clear Kinnickinnic and wade in the water after lunch or search the gravels for Lake Superior agates. This is a popular local river for canoeing, so you may see adventurers battling upstream.

Climbing out of Clifton Hollow, you can shorten the tour to about 71 miles by turning right on County M, which leads into River Falls. For an even shorter loop—30 miles—you could pedal from River Falls on County MM to Townsvalley Road and pick up the tour from there. Proceeding on the full 100-mile loop, you turn right onto MM, churn about 2 miles to Townsvalley road, and climb the tour's third steep hill. Stop in Hudson for snacks and possibly an overnight stay.

Farther on as a side trip from County SS, you can turn left onto the first unnumbered road you see off SS and pedal to the Monument, a giant sandstone outcropping rising straight into the air. Return now via more turns to River Falls, where you cross the suspension bridge into Glen Park, completing the loop.

Directions

Starting from Glen Park, River Falls:

1. Go left on Park Street for .7 mile;
2. right on State 29 for .8 mile;
3. left on the unmarked town road (watch for the orange sign) for 1 mile;
4. left on State 35 for .7 mile;
5. right on 29 for 5.7 miles;
6. left on County W for 1.4 miles;
7. right on County M for 4.6 miles;
8. straight ahead on County Y for 3 miles;
9. right on County J for 6.3 miles;
10. right on 35 for 1 mile to Beldenville;
11. straight on 35 for 2.1 miles to an unmarked town road;
12. left on the town road for 2.3 miles;
13. left on County O for 13.2 miles;
14. left, then right on the town road for 3.2 miles to Diamond Bluff;
15. continue straight on the town road for 1.3 miles;
16. left on County E for 4.1 miles;
17. left on County Q for 2.8 miles;
18. right on County QQ for 8.9 miles;
19. left on County FF for .7 mile;
20. right on County F for 4.2 miles;
21. right on County MM for 2.1 miles;
22. left on Townsvalley Road for 4.3 miles;
23. left on FF for 1.5 miles;
24. right on F for 1.5 miles;
25. left on Frontage Road for .1 miles into Hudson;
26. east out of Hudson on Frontage Road for 2.4 miles;
27. straight ahead on County N for 2.5 miles;
28. left on the town-road loop, which goes north, east, and south for 7.6 miles, and then back to N;

River Falls is in western Wisconsin on Wisconsin 29, 35, and 65; 30 miles southeast of Minneapolis-St. Paul, Minnesota, via U.S. 12, I-94 and, Wisconsin 35; 35 miles northwest of Milwaukee via I-94 and Wisconsin 65.

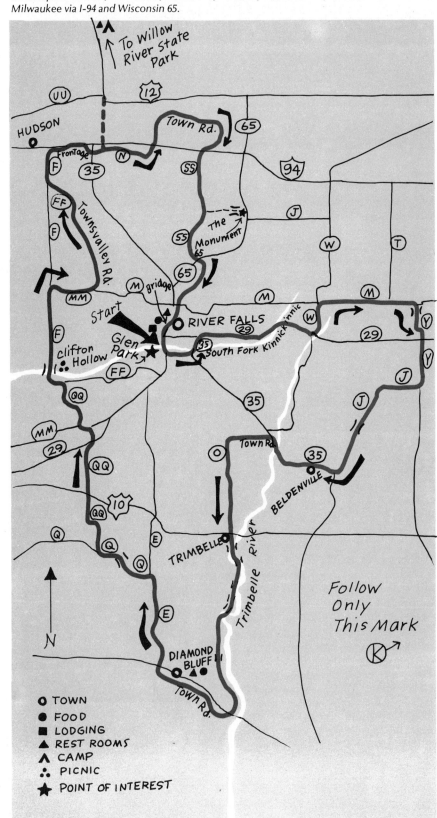

29. straight ahead on County SS for 4.1 miles (see tour description for side trip);

30. left on 65 for .1 mile;

31. right on the unmarked town road for 2.6 miles;

32. left on 35 for .9 mile;

33. right on Cedar Street for .5 mile;

34. left on Falls Street for .5 mile;

35. right on Cascade Street for .1 mile;

36. straight ahead over the suspension bridge into Glen Park, tour's end.

WHERE TO STAY

This is a rural tour, so overnight facilities are few. You find no overnight spots for the first 70 miles, though most farmers here are willing to let you camp in their woods or meadows if you just ask.

Campgrounds include the following: Willow River State Park, 5 miles northeast of Hudson on County A; open year round; $2.75. This delightful park has swimming and fishing and is popular locally. Kinnickinnic Kampground, 1 mile north of River Falls on Highways 65 and 35; open April 1st to November 25th.

Both River Falls and Hudson have motels. Reservations are not necessary, but if you prefer to make arrangements ahead of time, here are two Hudson motels: Hudson House Inn, 1 mile southeast of Hudson on County F. Write Hudson House Inn, Box 267, Hudson, Wisconsin 54016, or phone (715) 386-2394. J. R. Ranch, 4 miles east of Hudson on Highway 12. Write J. R. Ranch, Route 1, Hudson, Wisconsin 54016, or phone (715) 386-5166.

FOR SPARE PARTS, REPAIRS, FURTHER INFORMATION

The Village Pedaler, 114 East Elm Street, River Falls, Wisconsin 54022; (715) 425-9126 or 425-9716 after hours. Lee and Kathy Zaborowski recently acquired their shop and really know the back roads around River Falls. They have enough rides to keep you busy for a week and also have a stock of free county maps.

WILD KINNIKINNICK TOBACCO

While exploring the banks of the Kinnickinnic River, search for the river's namesake, the kinnikinnick or bearberry, a trailing evergreen shrub with white or pink bell-shaped flowers which form astringent crimson berries in late summer. While the mealy, unpleasant-tasting berries *can* be eaten, you probably won't be that hungry. The leaves of this plant, though, create the famed kinnikinnick, a rich tobacco prized by Indians and northern woodsmen.

To sample this wild tobacco, gather the leaves in summer, when they are mildest, dry them in the sun (preferable to a campfire), then crumble and smoke. You can also use the leaves fresh or dried to brew a medicinal tea which, according to ancient lore, cures urinary tract diseases.

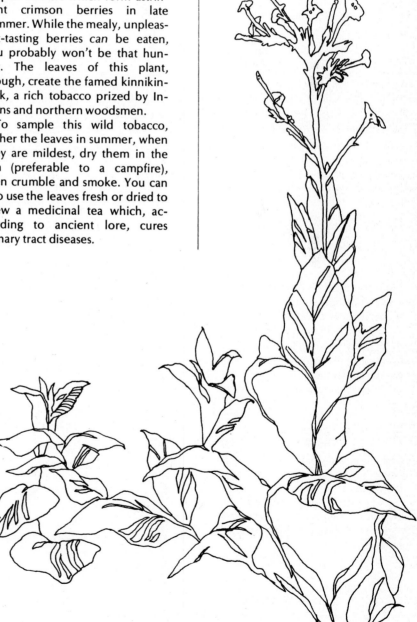

153

74. THERE-AND-BACK-AGAIN QUEST

The winding pastoral back roads near Holmen, Wisconsin, rather resemble J.R.R. Tolkien's The Shire, and as Bilbo and Frodo Baggins discovered, unexpected adventures often lie in such quiet corners. Though you probably won't encounter Black Riders or the foul-smelling spider Shelob, you will undoubtedly meet an Orc-like dog and a few friendly tree Ents.

Begin in Holmen, where you may park your car on any side street. Gather a Hobbit-like feast of meats, cheeses, olives, breads, fruits, before leaving town. Then pedal north on County V and TT, a narrow, rolling country lane without shoulders or traffic. Views of hills—lush green even in September—open before you. Then you spin over a narrow bridge, pass an old schoolhouse, and wind beside woods on your left. In autumn the foliage turns brilliant saffron, rose, and scarlet, and dried fallen leaves crackle beneath your wheels.

About 4 miles outside Holmen, follow County V and TT as it forks right and tackle several challenging hills. Around you the slopes are buried in trees. Soon you see a grassy clearing to your left where you can stop. Beyond here you cross a second narrow bridge over a clear brook twisting back into the woods.

Another climb and winding drop take you past idyllic farms with gleaming white houses and crisp red barns. Turn right at the white church onto County T and ride into Stevenstown, where you can pick up more snacks at the country store.

Coasting beyond Stevenstown, you soon cross a bridge and climb another hill where you turn left on County V. You have quite an uphill pull here through the wooded slopes. Stop anywhere to rest in

the grass, munch on cheese and apples, or hike back into the oak, maple, and birch woods. Beyond another one-lane bridge (there's no access to the creek), turn right onto County Q as County V continues straight ahead. Now you curve through farmland again (watch for unleashed dogs), past a Christmas-tree farm and across a small cold creek where on a hot summer day you can stop awhile to dangle your feet. Here and throughout the ride, you see small lavender, white, and yellow wildflowers in the meadows.

About 2 miles beyond the creek, you pedal beside Hoeth Forest. Walk your bike down the stern, perfectly straight rows of trees which all seem a bit Entish. You may feel as if you have discovered a natural cathedral. Just past the old weathered barn on your left, there's a stop sign; turn right onto Route 108, where you climb still another steep, curving hill, then plunge down for views of wooded hollows. You continue straight, then follow 108 as it curves left. You encounter some bumpy spots

DISTANCE:	32 miles.
TERRAIN:	Rolling hills.
TRAFFIC:	Light.
DIFFICULTY:	Easily handled by intermediate cyclists and strong beginners.
BEST TIME:	Spring for wildflowers or autumn for vivid foliage.
LOCATION:	North of La Crosse, Wisconsin, via State 35.

as you head into Mindoro, with a café and grocery store. At the First National Bank, turn right onto County D and continue into wide green fields framed by black woods.

Ride straight past the sign pointing toward Holmen and navigate over several more steep hills. Even in September, when other states' hills have turned crusty brown, the meadows here grow thick with grass, and ripened crops flood the fields.

Beyond two more creeks, turn right at the stop sign. Now you pedal on a nearly flat, winding road; the wooded hills fall behind you, and in autumn great flocks of birds descend on the ripened cornfields as you return to Holmen.

WHERE TO STAY

This tour is so rural you find no campgrounds or motels along the route. La Crosse, just 4 miles south, has numerous motels and camping facilities. You may, in fact, want to begin your tour from there. To do so, start at Burlington Station in La Crosse and ride west on State Street, turn right on West Avenue (City 35), right on Gillette Street, left on Oak Street, right on County SS, left on County SA, continue north on County S, and turn left on County SN to Holmen.

A lakeside campground is available in West Salem, about 9 miles from Holmen. See page 156 for further information. You can also use Holmen's County Park or ask a farmer to let you use his woods or a field.

NEARBY

Wisconsin has an extensive county road system with excellent biking possibilities, and you won't

154

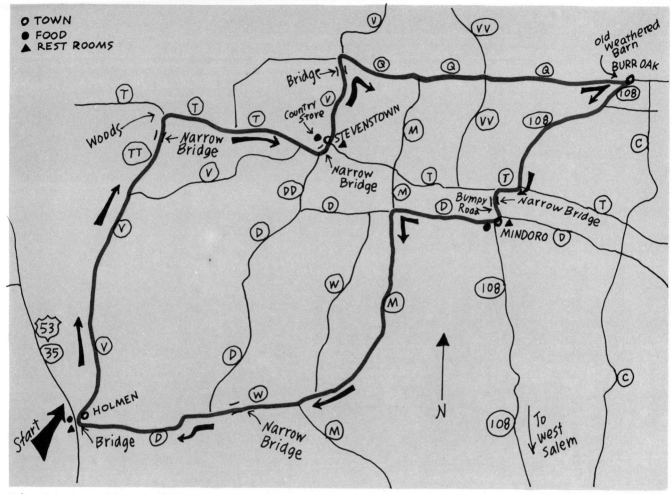

Holmen is in western Wisconsin off Wisconsin 35 on County V and W; 10 miles north of La Crosse via Wisconsin 35 or via the biking directions under Where to Stay; 294 miles northeast of Des Moines, Iowa, via U.S. 69, I-90 and Wisconsin 35.

want to limit yourself to just one day. See page 156 for another tour in La Crosse County. The state also has an idyllic cross-state bikeway from La Crosse to Kenosha. For information write the State of Wisconsin Department of Natural Resources, Box 450, Department B, Madison, Wisconsin 53701 and ask for the free brochure "The Wisconsin Bikeway."

OLD-FASHIONED DANDELION DELIGHTS

As you pedal through Wisconsin countryside, you often see whole meadows of the ubiquitous dandelion. Though this "weed" is much maligned, the dandelion really is quite a pretty little flower. It's nourishing, too. Dandelion leaves,

a nice addition to salads if picked in early spring, contain twenty-five times the vitamin A in tomato juice and fifty times that in asparagus. And the roots can be used as a vegetable. Everyone has heard of dandelion wine, but you can also use dandelions to make tea or even coffee.

Sweet Wisconsin dandelion roots. Gather young dandelion roots in early spring. Digging them from the ground can be tedious, as any gardener knows, but once you have a potful, wash, scrape, and slice them. Boil in salted water until tender, then butter and serve. This sweet vitamin-rich vegetable tastes a bit like dandelion greens, but has a potatolike texture.

Cyclists' dandelion coffee. This natural coffee also comes from the

roots. Dry the roots in sunlight or by a fireside. After the roots shrivel, break them into pieces and grind them (two stones work well in the wilds). Use one teaspoon per cup and brew as you would regular coffee.

Wild dandelion tea. This strong tea is said to cure colds. Gather the leaves and simmer for about eight to ten minutes. Then strain and serve.

Once you have sampled dandelions and find you like them, you may want to experiment on your own. Some natural-food enthusiasts have created exotic concoctions, including braised dandelions, dandelion soup, Chinese-style dandelion greens, and pineapple-pickled dandelions. Use your imagination.

75. COUNTRY TEA TOUR

Wisconsin's back roads have a homespun charm reminding one of gingham, hot pumpkin pie, and fresh warm milk. Over every hill you discover lush green pastures dotted with scrubbed black-and-white Holstein cows. Rock-hounding, spring wildflower, and autumn foliage tours can be delightful here. You might also collect basics along the way to make natural country teas. Cycle here in spring when wildflowers bloom, in summer when cool creeks await swimmers, or in autumn when amber cornstalks crackle in the fields.

You begin in the tiny Norwegian community of West Salem, where you may park your car practically anywhere. Precise directions for this tour are a bit complex and appear in detail at the end of this tour description. As you leave town on County C, you cross a narrow bridge, pass a dam, and pedal into countryside. Soon the road narrows and becomes winding and a bit bumpy until you reach a traffic light, beyond which the road improves again. Traffic is nil; if you see four cars an hour, you've encountered a Wisconsin traffic jam. A few minutes through tidy farmland with gleaming white fences bring you to craggy bluffs on your left. Soon you wind up a long hill through green pastures on one side and deep forests backed by golden cliffs on the other. In about a mile, the hill crests and you plunge suddenly into a wide picturesque valley. The meadows here are often filled with goldenrod; gather all you like for goldenrod tea.

Hard-packed dirt roads lead into the hills, and you can meander off on one of these anytime to find an icy creek, (pronounced "crik"). Cattle stand still in the pastures and every turn presents green grassy coulees. Soon you round a bend where the fields lie in green and gold squares, then come to a little white church and cemetery. Turn right onto County A. Forests of maples, oaks, and elms rim this wide asphalt road. In about 2 miles County A leads to a T. Here you follow County AE right and soon reach several clearings where you can relax or picnic.

As you jog right onto County TA, you climb steeply, then coast to an intersection where you go left onto County T. Most Wisconsin back roads are well paved, and on this particular stretch you almost glide through the Sleepy Hollow-like knolls. Occasionally you can stop, lock your bike to a tree (though locking really is unnecessary), and climb into the wooded hills to forage for tea herbs. You go right onto Highway 162, which may have loose gravel, and spin through flattened farmland to Gunderson's Burns Store, where you can pick up snacks. At the store intersection, turn left onto County E, on which you soon cross two one-lane bridges over clear brooks and pedal past farms with huge, dome-shaped silos.

More rolling hills and turns lead you to Bangor, where you can stop for a rest. Ride across a bridge spanning La Crosse River and pedal through farmland back into West Salem, your tour's end.

Directions

Starting in West Salem:

1. Go north on County C;
2. right on U.S. 16 for about a quarter of a mile;
3. left on County C and Highway 108 (cross a narrow bridge and pass a dam);
4. stay right on County C (108 branches left);
5. right at the white church onto County A;
6. right on County AE;
7. right on County TA;
8. left on County T (stop sign at this intersection);
9. right on Highway 162 (another stop sign here);
10. left at Gunderson's Burns Store onto County E;
11. right on Highway 16;
12. left at the Bangor Motel onto Highway 162;
13. right in Bangor onto County B to West Salem.

WHERE TO STAY

Camping is available in West Salem at Neshonoc Lakeside Camp. Open May 1st to October 15th; $2.50 per family. Here you can camp beneath trees at a site overlooking a blue lake. Boat rentals, fishing, and swimming are available. For reservations, write Neshonoc Lakeside Camp, Route 1, West Salem, Wisconsin 54669, or phone (608) 786-1792.

Motels are available in West Salem and Bangor.

DISTANCE:	40 miles.
TERRAIN:	Steep, rolling hills.
TRAFFIC:	Light.
DIFFICULTY:	Some experience needed to tackle this in one day; light traffic makes it a good family ride.
BEST TIME:	Spring through autumn.
LOCATION:	East of La Crosse, Wisconsin, just off I-90.

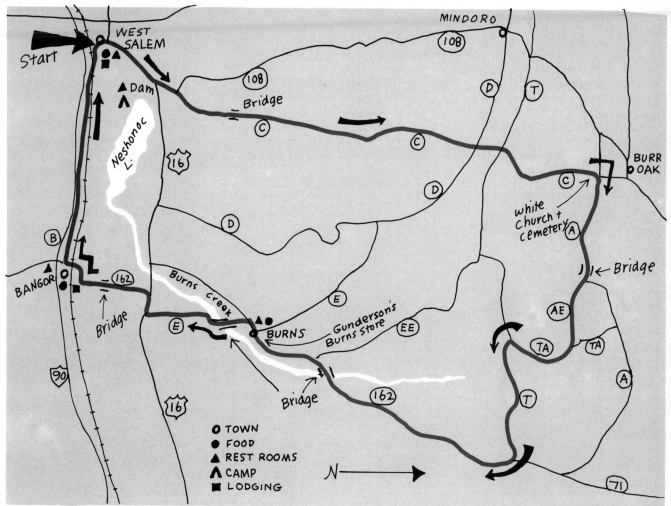

West Salem is in western Wisconsin just off I-90; 12 miles east of La Crosse via U.S. 16; 290 miles northwest of Chicago, Illinois, via I-90; 296 miles northeast of Des Moines, Iowa, via U.S. 69 and I-90.

FOR SPARE PARTS, REPAIRS, FURTHER INFORMATION

The nearest bike shops are in La Crosse, about 13 miles from West Salem. Stop in at Gene's Bicycle Shop, 2242 State Road, or Smith's Bicycle Shop, 520 South 8th Street, for spare parts or information on this or other La Crosse County rides.

NEARBY

La Crosse, on the Mississippi River has paddle-wheel boat rides

leaving from the north end of Riverside Park; an aquarium; a zoo; riding stables; hiking trails from Grandad Bluff, Hixon Forest, and Perrot Park; and fishing, houseboat, and cruising rentals. You can reach La Crosse by back roads and may even want to begin the tour from there for a total ride of 66 miles. To begin and end this loop in La Crosse, start at Burlington Station and ride west on State Street, turn right on West Avenue (City 35), right on Gillette, follow the bike-route signs to County BM and County B, and continue east on County B to County C in West Salem.

GOLDENROD AND OTHER COUNTRY TEAS

Creating herbal and natural teas can be one rewarding result of bicycling. As you pedal through the country hills, meadows, and woodlands, you will soon learn to recognize the plants which make excellent teas. Horehound, wintergreen, mint, cassina, sage, and goldenrod leaves each produce a unique, delightful aroma and flavor, as do sassafras roots, birch bark, and elder flowers. Once you try a few basic natural brews, begin experimenting on your own, blending various herbs, leaves, and roots to create an exclusive tea for your personal tastes. Sweeten your natural teas with honey and try them iced as well as hot.

Sweet goldenrod tea. Pick fresh leaves and dry them in the sun. When crushed, these slim, untoothed leaves smell like sweet anise or licorice. Simply add about a tablespoon of crushed leaves to a cup of boiling water, brew three to five minutes, strain, and serve.

Mint tea. Delicious aromatic brews can be made from the leaves of wild mints. These plants, with numerous species, usually have opposite leaves and small white, purple, or pink flowers which taper to a sharp point or spike. In the wilderness you can recognize the mint by its distinctive minty aroma. Some of the best-known wild mints are spearmint, peppermint, and wintergreen. With any of these, you simply steep the fresh, cleaned leaves in boiling water for three to five minutes. Be certain to use fresh leaves and don't be afraid to use lots of them, even a half-cupful. Mint leaves can also be dried, crushed, and bottled to use as herbs.

Rose-hip tea. Rose hips or petals make a fragrant pinkish tea. You can either use fresh petals steeped in boiling water or dry and crush the roses, then keep them bottled for future use. It seems the more deep red the rose is, the stronger it tastes.

Red Zinger. To give you an idea how to begin creating your own brews, here is a special blend concocted by a natural tea company. The fragrant Red Zinger contains dried hibiscus flowers, rose hips, lemon grass, peppermint, wintergreen, lemon peel, and wild cherry bark.

76. HILL COUNTRY RAMBLE

DISTANCE:	68 miles, with a shorter 40-mile loop for beginners and families.
TERRAIN:	Flat to gently rolling hills.
TRAFFIC:	Very light.
DIFFICULTY:	Good ride for anyone.
BEST TIME:	Spring through autumn. Brisk October is especially nice when the leaves change. Summers can be hot and humid—bring your swimsuit.
LOCATION:	Southeastern Minnesota's Fillmore County. Starts from Lanesboro, on U.S. 16.

Minnesota's "hill country" contains surprisingly few hills. You roll easily over knolls, sometimes dipping into wooded hollows cut by clear rills. Often you break from shady deciduous forests into bright, flat fields and meadows. The last of your tour meanders along the Root River, bordered by 100-foot limestone bluffs topped by virgin white pine and white-barked birch.

This is a do-it-yourself ride, the best kind of all. No one has cluttered the countryside with neon or "created" ways to have fun. Possibilities: An autumn foliage ride; rock hounding for agates; nutting in autumn for walnuts, hickory nuts, and the like; wild-food foraging; bird watching; skinny dipping in deep secluded pools. Bring spare parts, tools, and a picnic lunch.

Start in Lanesboro, population 850, situated on the twisty Root River. Strangers stand out in Lanesboro and you will have no trouble starting a conversation or asking for directions. Park your car at grassy Sylvan Park, then pedal south on E Street to the first major highway, U.S. 16, where you turn right, go three short blocks, and curve left. You wind along the river to County 21 and turn right, into countryside. The road is well-paved, untraveled, and smooth, and you ride through a wooded valley with a clear stream trickling beside you. Soon you climb from the hollow into swelling grass meadows and farmlands. The rolling hills may challenge beginners, but are still easily handled on a 3-speed bike.

About five and a half miles from Lanesboro, County 21 joins County 12. When the two roads split again, stay left on 12. Pedal to the first full intersection and turn right onto County 23 toward Lenora. Beyond the turn, you dip downhill, then climb gradually from the hollow over a grass-bordered creek and through tiny Amherst. Pause anytime to examine wildflowers or to scramble to a creek's edge and hunt for agates or cool your toes.

Rounding a downhill curve, you pedal into Lenora, even smaller than Lanesboro. Turn left in town onto County 24 and continue climbing easily past farms settled in among the trees, then dip into Newburg. Beyond the second little bridge outside Newburg, turn left at the stop sign onto State 43, rough in spots with a bit more traffic. You climb another hill after the turnoff, then take a sharp left through fields. About a mile later, watch out for a really bumpy section of road. Less than a mile outside Tawney,

you can shorten this loop to about 40 miles by turning left onto County 12, leading you back to 21, where you turn right and return to Lanesboro. This shortened route is highly recommended for beginners, especially if State 43 seems "heavily" trafficked the day you are there. (Minnesota's "heavy traffic" will seem quite light to city bikers.)

Continuing on the longer loop, you meander through forests, vivid with color in autumn. Soon you dip into the small village of Choice, where you curve left and cross a bridge over the south fork of the Root River to leave town. Mounting another hill, you spin over a tiny brook and wind from woods into farmland. At Bratsberg you have another choice: either turn left at the first paved road (County 10) and ride back to Lanesboro or proceed straight to Rushford, for food and accommodations. If you decide to go into Rushford, you will eventually return to this Bratsberg intersection and pedal back toward Lanesboro on County 10.

County 10 leads you through more farms and woods. Stop anywhere along here to relax beneath a shady oak, forage for wild onions, wild ginger, and wood sorrel, or swim in an icy creek. Occasionally in late afternoon you may glimpse deer in the meadows. About three and a half miles from Bratsberg, this lane runs into County 25, where you go left and ride through Highland, then a mile later turn right at the fork for a jogging run along sparkling Whalan Creek. This winding road dead-ends into U.S. 16, "a continuous corner" on the Root River banks. Go left and across a bridge through Whalan. Rock bluffs rise straight from the river's sandbars and occasionally you see cliff swallow nests on the white walls. This scenic river is a favorite canoeing trail, and you may want to stop along the banks before returning to Lanesboro.

WHERE TO STAY

No reservations are needed anywhere. Rushford has the only two motels on this ride, while campsites are found along the Root River on U.S. 16 west of Rushford and west of Lanesboro. Camping is also available at Sylvan Park in Lanesboro, with swimming, no-license fishing, and a playground. Fee, $2.

MINNESOTA HILLS BASSWOOD BLOSSOM TEA

If you ride through Minnesota's hill country when the blossoms of the basswood tree bloom, you can enjoy a unique, luxurious brew—basswood blossom tea. Even sweeter and more fragrant than the French linden blossom tea, this was a favorite beverage among the pioneers. Gather a whole bag full of the small, light blossoms, allow them to dry in the sun or by your campfire, and add a large spoonful to a cup of boiling water. You need just a dab of honey or no sweetening at all because the nectar contains a natural sugar.

The American basswood has large leaves, five to six inches long, which are heart-shaped, roughly toothed, with conspicuous veins; tiny, delicate, creamy-colored flowers hanging in clusters from a stalk attached to a long, narrow, paper-thin leaf; and short, slightly drooping branches.

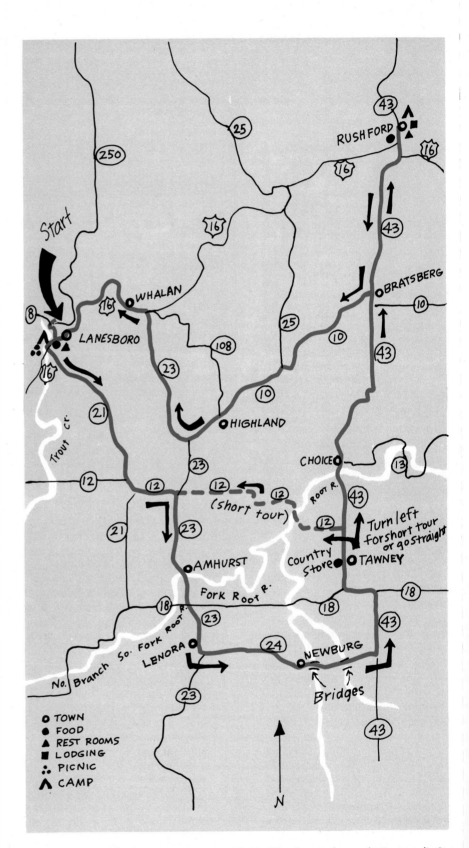

Lanesboro is in southeastern Minnesota on U.S. 16; 120 miles southeast of Minneapolis-St. Paul via U.S. 52 and 16; 232 miles northeast of Des Moines, Iowa, via U.S. 69, I-90 and U.S. 16.

77. PIONEERLAND LAKES LOOP

Minnesota, land of ten thousand lakes, has literally thousands of tours, the scenery varying from tidy farmlands to northern woods. Back roads here are often excellent, so you can explore without mishaps. This pleasant little jaunt from the hamlet of Heron Lake gives you a sample of flat Minnesota farm country and old pioneer homesteads, and glimpses of pelicans, cranes, ducks, geese, and blue herons. For this off-the-beaten-path tour, bring pioneering supplies: spares, tools, food (corn on the cob, fresh tomatoes, and hearty sandwiches), and camping equipment. In summer you may need mosquito repellent near the water.

Leave Heron Lake by pedaling north on Jackson County 9 (which soon becomes Cottonwood County 5), the road beside the Phillips 66 station. To give you an idea of Heron Lake's size, the gas station is a standout. You ride flat, straight, well-kept roads, with your only hazard being farm dogs. You may encounter five cars during this loop, but only on a busy Saturday or Sunday, when the farmers go to town or church.

Two miles outside Heron Lake, tiny Duck Lake glints off to your left. Plush grass grows everywhere, even in the ditches along the road, and Holstein and Hereford cattle graze in pastures broken only by scrubbed white farm homes and red-and-white barns. Two or three minutes outside town, you cross a tiny branch of the Des Moines River, round a curve, and ride straight across Highway 62. Then 3 miles farther, just beyond the abandoned town hall on your right, you cross County 15. Go left on County 13, the hard-surfaced road past the sign reading "Storden—6 miles." Soon you coast to a spot where Round Lake (more like a pond)

DISTANCE:	46 miles.
TERRAIN:	Flat, flat, flat.
TRAFFIC:	Light.
DIFFICULTY:	Excellent first ride for beginners and families.
BEST TIME:	Anytime but winter.
LOCATION:	Southwest corner of Minnesota. Ride starts in Heron Lake, on State 60 north of Worthington.

surrounds the road and you can stop to rest. More countryside and a small rise bring you to a stop sign where you turn left onto Cottonwood County 7.

Oaks Lake sparkles to your left, beyond which is Talcot Lake, often covered with mallards. Past a curve and a marshy area, take the gravel road a quarter of a mile to Talcot Lake Dam, where you can picnic beneath ash, oak, and hackberry trees. Bird watching is excellent here for ducks, geese, herons, egrets, and many other shore birds.

Back on County 7, you soon turn right onto Highway 62, where you can go right again in about a minute at a stop sign to a small lakeside park. The lane to the park runs through marshes where herons wade. At the clipped green park you can swim on a warm summer afternoon, catch a fresh northern pike or walleye for lunch, or watch pelicans paddling like speedsters across the lake, filling their pouches with fish as they go.

Back on flat Highway 62, you soon turn left on County 19 (which becomes Nobles County 1) toward

Dundee. Watch out for the double railroad tracks in a few minutes. Then you pass between two churches and climb the tour's only hill. For a side trip to still another placid lake, turn right on County 18 and cross another track as you pedal between Kinbrae Slough and Kinbrae Lake. The little town here has a grocery store which may or may not be open, depending on the owner's whim. Wind through town past the few houses, then go straight onto the gravel road which leads to Maka-Oicu (pronounced ma-ka-wee-choo) and Fury's Island county parks. Now may be a good time to lock your bike to an ash or hackberry tree and hike along Homestead Trail, which leads you through cool woods past five pioneer home sites to undeveloped Fury's Island. At Maka-Oicu are four Indian mounds, a small sand beach for swimming, and camping.

On Nobles County 1, you cross another track, turn left onto Nobles County 16, and ride toward Heron Lake. There's a low shoulder here, so stay away from the edge as you ride straight through farmlands and past sloughs speckled with herons and cranes. You cross yet another railroad track, then spin to a stop sign where you see Heron Lake's water tower. Turn left, cross more tracks, and return to Heron Lake. From here you can go south on County 9 and left on the first town road to Heron Lake's shore. Stop for a quick soda and look over the lake as you end the tour.

WHERE TO STAY

The nearest motels are in Worthington, south on State 60, and include the Central, 1033 Oxford Street, (507) 376-6211, and the Worthington, 1923 Dover Street, (507) 376-4146.

Campgrounds include Maka-Oicu, mentioned above, which is free, and Worthington's municipally operated Olson Park, in town on the west end of Lake Okabena. Free, with a one-day limit.

MINNESOTA LAKE FISH

If you are a novice fisherman, but would like to try your luck in Minnesota's blue lakes, here's a brief guide to what you might catch.

Northern pike. You can easily tell this fish by the yellowish bean-shaped markings which run like chains along his sides. His entire cheek is covered with scales, but the upper half of his gill cover is smooth.

Walleye. The walleye varies in color from olive to deep gray and has strikingly translucent white eyes. This fish is actually a member of the perch, not the pike, family and has perchlike vertical markings.

Blue gill. You can recognize this small roundish fish by the bit of blue about his gills and the five or more darkened vertical bands on his body. The stomach is red, like a sunfish's, and the two fish are often hard to tell apart.

Catfish. This one is easy to spot. He has whiskers around his mouth and really does look a bit like a cat. This fish usually swims deep, near the lake or stream bottoms.

Largemouth bass. The largemouth bass is easily identified by his upper jaw hinge, which runs behind a vertical line through his eye. This fish also has a dark, irregular band of scales down his back.

Smallmouth bass. You can usually tell this fish and the largemouth bass apart by the smallmouth's vertical band markings. The upper jaw hinge runs through the fish's eye.

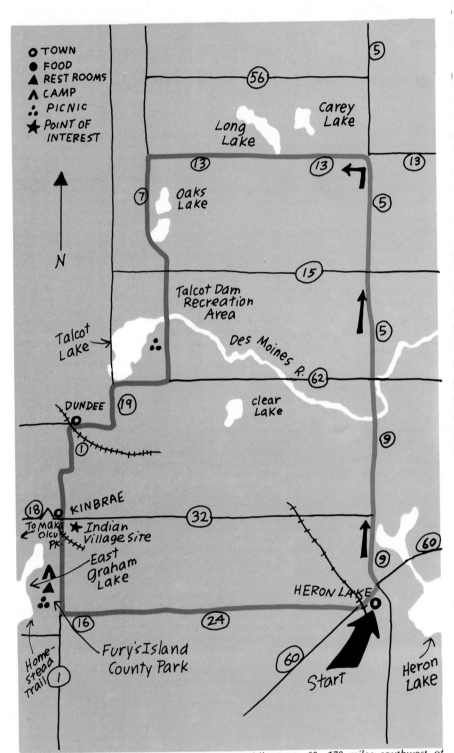

Heron Lake is in southwestern Minnesota on Minnesota 60; 170 miles southwest of Minneapolis-St. Paul via U.S. 169 and Minnesota 60; 75 miles northeast of Sioux Falls, South Dakota, via I-90 and Minnesota 60.

78. IOWA CORNFIELD CAPER

Iowa is in the boondocks. Everyone says so. Even Iowans. That's what makes bicycling here such a delight. You pedal along smooth blacktop roads, competing with only an occasional sluggish pickup truck or puttering tractor. You will find this an economy tour, too: full home-cooked meat-loaf or spare-rib dinners, with five kinds of salads and homemade cookies for dessert, cost: much less than you would expect. This 102-mile jaunt, in fact, can be taken for as little as $10 for two, including meals and camping for one night.

Your tour begins in Davenport, where you may park your car on any side street. In this Mississippi River town, you find numerous parks for pleasant biking: Fejervary Park, on 9th and Wilkes, with a monkey island, pool, playground, and zoo; Vander Veer Park, on Lombard and Main streets, with a lighted fountain, rose garden, and bird observatory; and Credit Island, in the Mississippi, scene of an 1814 battle led by Zachary Taylor. For $2 you can take a two-hour stern-wheeler cruise on the river from the foot of Main Street.

Leave Davenport by pedaling north on flat U.S. 67 beside the lazily drifting Mississippi. Food is available all along the ride except on Sundays, when folks go to church, and you should carry snacks and a picnic with you. Along the riverbanks in autumn, oaks, elms, maples, and willows are vivid. Streams flowing into the Mississippi are rock-hounding meccas, with Lake Superior agates, coral, jasper, and even an occasional diamond in the gravels. Winding along the wooded banks, you can stop anywhere to dangle bare feet. You always spot many shore birds, and sometimes huge flocks of ducks can be seen.

As you approach the I-80 bridge,

you see a Standard station on your left. Here you can turn right on the blacktop to run for 2 miles along the river. Views are excellent as you pedal only four to five feet from the water. The blacktop leads into the small town of Le Claire, where you can buy snacks at the grocery (except on Sundays), then continue north on U.S. 67 along the river. If you feel like striking out on your own, any blacktop from Le Claire offers smooth cycling: traffic is nil and you seldom meet even two cars in succession.

At the small farm community of Princeton, turn left onto F45, where you climb the tour's only hills. A nice rest stop in a few minutes is Buffalo Bill's boyhood home. Just follow the signs. At Z30 turn right and continue over the hills past a few farm dogs and finally around a left curve into McCausland. Here you go left onto F33 and ride into rolling corn country. In spring you see farmers atop red or green tractors plowing deep furrows in the soil; summer brings corn eight feet high and the sweet fragrance of red clover; while in autumn the brittle cornstalks

crackle in the wind. Crime here is something folks hear Walter Cronkite talk about on TV. Should your water bottle run dry, don't be afraid to stop at a farm home for a refill.

On U.S. 61 you go left to Scott County Park, a good picnic or camping spot. You can swim, fish, watch model-airplane enthusiasts, or simply ride the peaceful two-and-a-half-mile loop through the oaks, maples, and elms. You have a steep climb into the park.

Continuing from the park on F33 beyond St. Ann's Church, you may encounter a huge shaggy dog. Watch ahead, and if you see him preparing his ambush, start screaming and waving your tire pump, a tactic which has been successful every time. At the T in the road, take a short jaunt right to Allen's Grove Park, with camping, where you can relax beneath a tree on the Wapsipinican River, known locally as the Wapsi.

Riding west on F33, go left on Y4E into Dixon, formerly called Cob Town. There's nothing here but an elevator, a few houses, and Cob Town Inn, where Lucille serves her own home-cooked food. Buy a dozen of her freshly baked cookies or a jar of homemade corncob jelly. Take a sharp left onto Y40, and outside Dixon watch for an insidious canine who soundlessly chases bicycles.

In Plainview you can stop at one of the truck stops beneath I-80 or you can proceed to Walcott for a snack at the ice-cream shop and a rest in the shaded park. On F65 go left and pedal on a smooth, newly paved road to Credit Island, where you ride on a marked bike path along the riverbanks. Just follow the green-and-white bike signs back to U.S. 67, which leads you into Davenport and your tour's end.

DISTANCE:	102 miles.
TERRAIN:	Rolling, with a few steep hills.
TRAFFIC:	Light.
DIFFICULTY:	Good ride for anyone.
BEST TIME:	April through October. Summers can be hot and humid.
LOCATION:	Davenport, Iowa, on the Mississippi, and surrounding farmlands.

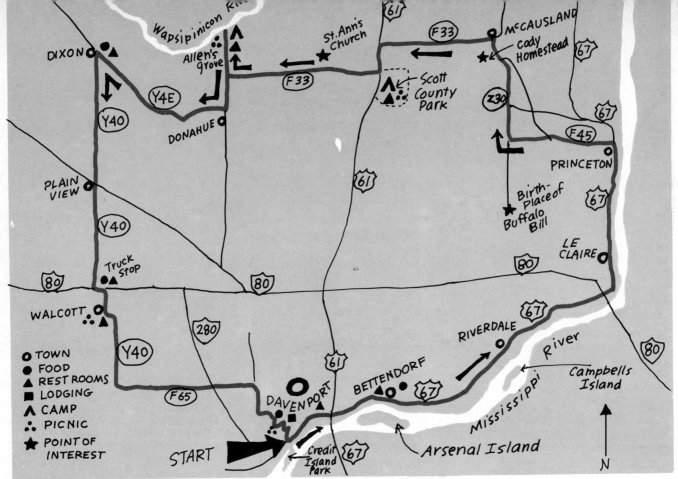

Davenport is in eastern Iowa along the Mississippi River on I-80, U.S. 6, 67, and 61, and Iowa 130; 159 miles east of Des Moines via I-80; 188 miles west of Chicago, Illinois, via I-55 and 80.

WHERE TO STAY

Davenport has numerous motels, with reservations unnecessary. Camping is available at Scott County Park and Allen's Grove Park, described above, or just ask a local farmer if you can use his woods or a field.

FOR SPARE PARTS, REPAIRS, FURTHER INFORMATION

Bicyclesport, Inc., 2816 Brady, Davenport, Iowa; (319) 322-1512. Jerry Kruse, manager, has several additional tips for Iowan backroad riding: "First, come prepared for weird Iowa weather. Weekdays will be hot and humid in summer; weekends it will rain. Second, if riding tubulars, carry lots of spares and be careful. There's no place in the cornfields to buy sew-ups. And third, if you do encounter a rare truck as you're going uphill, get off the road and let it pass. A slow-moving truck means the driver may be scared he'll hit you—and that's more dangerous than a confident speeder." Jerry carries a full line of parts and tools. He knows many other tours in this area. Ask him about good rides and current road conditions.

MISSISSIPPI NETTLES

Churning through rural countryside, you will glimpse nettles sprouting everywhere, from rich woodlands to roadsides. If you have ever encountered the nettle's "sting," which lasts about ten minutes, you may be determined to stay clear of these plants. Nettles, though, lose their sting when boiled to produce an excellent high-protein potherb.

You can recognize nettles by the bristlelike hairs covering the plant which sting when you touch them; the stalk, usually erect and often stout; the oval or oblong, toothed, dark green leaves which grow opposite each other in pairs; and the small green flowers which appear in late summer.

Wear gloves and cut the youngest leaves and shoots in early spring. (By summer most of the plant becomes too tough.) Prepare them according to one of these recipes.

Stinging nettles for campfire stew. Wash the leaves and young shoots (continue wearing gloves for this process). Then fill a three-quart saucepan with salted water and bring to a boil. Add the nettles, boil for one minute, and remove from the heat. When cooked, young nettle shoots taste rather like bean sprouts and you can add them to your campfire stew.

Steamed Iowa nettle leaves. For this recipe, use only the youngest leaves. Put the leaves into a pan of water and stir with a spoon until the leaves are washed. With kitchen tongs, transfer the leaves from the water to a heavy kettle. Cover and cook slowly for about ten minutes until tender. Add butter, pepper, onion salt, and serve.

Other uses for nettles. Boiled nettle roots produce a yellow dye. You can also make a tough twine by removing the outer bark on the stalk, separating the inner fibers, then twisting these fibers into a rope.

79. MARK TWAIN TRAIL

You may feel like Huck Finn or Tom Sawyer as you chawnk green apples, explore the cave where Injun Joe died, or go skinny dipping in a swimming hole on this back roads saunter in Missouri. Be impulsive. Linger to pick blackberries or wild strawberries, lie in a field of sweet clover, or buy a juicy, ripe watermelon from a roadside stand or the back of a truck and feast on the grass.

Start in Hannibal on the Mississippi, where Mark Twain grew up. Here you can visit the delightful Mark Twain Museum and Boyhood Home, the Becky Thatcher House, and the Pilaster House, all on Hill Street and all free. Gather a picnic and head north on County W. A good spot to park your car and avoid traffic is Hannibal Junior High School, on the north edge of Hannibal at County W and U.S. 61. After a short sprint on W, go right on State 168, an untraveled blacktop road through woods and farmland. Many deer roam the woods, and in early morning you may see whole families of deer grazing in the meadows.

About 12 miles from Hannibal, you wind through Palmyra on 168. You can buy food here and at the half dozen other small country stores along the ride on any day but Sunday.

Past Philadelphia, which has another small grocery store, you glide downhill to a concrete bridge over the North River. Rest along the riverbanks pausing to take a cool swim. Climb the river's south bank and pedal on to Emden, where you turn left near the Emden Store onto County Z. About 7 miles farther, you reach Hunnewell Lake, a peaceful wooded place to picnic, camp, or just lie beneath a tree. A food concession here is open from spring through autumn.

To shorten the tour to about 75

DISTANCE:	144 miles.
TERRAIN:	Hilly.
TRAFFIC:	Light.
DIFFICULTY:	Good ride for anyone.
BEST TIME:	Spring through autumn.
LOCATION:	Mark Twain country around Hannibal, Missouri.

miles, retrace your ride toward Emden and go right before you reach Emden onto County C. Then go right on County E and left on F, which runs into U.S. 61. This four-lane highway, with a good paved shoulder and surprisingly light traffic, leads back to Hannibal Junior High.

Proceeding on the long tour, pedal south of Hunnewell on County V to U.S. 24. Then go left and follow busy U.S. 24 for 2 miles. A right turn puts you on State 107, another smooth and lightly traveled blacktop. About 6 miles farther, stop at Mark Twain State Park to picnic, camp, or swim in summer in the cool Salt River. You might also try a tour of the Mark Twain Birthplace and Museum for 50¢.

Follow State 107 on through the park to Route 154, where you go left. Then 2 miles beyond tiny Perry, go left onto State 19, where you roll over hills and crisscross clear rocky creeks. Look carefully and you will spot blackberry bushes and wild strawberry patches along the road.

Beyond New London, wind right on County V, then go left on T and right on N to State 79, where you turn left for a scenic sprint along the Mississippi River bluffs. The terrain is hilly and tough on this

stretch, but the road is well surfaced and has light traffic. In autumn there are spectacular foliage views.

About 5 miles along State 79, pause to explore the Mark Twain Cave, where Tom Sawyer and Becky Thatcher were lost and Injun Joe died in *The Adventures of Tom Sawyer.* You can lock your bike to a bench here, though local cyclists seldom do.

Two miles past the cave, you reach Hannibal. A pleasant rest stop at the end of your day is Riverview Park, where you can wander along the bluffs overlooking the Mississippi.

WHERE TO STAY

Motels in Hannibal include the following: Ahlers', 3601 McMasters, Hannibal, Missouri 63401; 2 miles northwest of Hannibal at the U.S. 36 and 61 junction; (314) 221-7950. Holiday Inn, 4141 Market, Hannibal, Missouri 63401; 2 miles southwest of Hannibal on U.S. 61; (314) 221-6610. Mark Twain, 612 Mark Twain Avenue, Hannibal, Missouri 63401; (314) 221-1490.

Campgrounds: Mark Twain State Park, open April 15th to October 31st; $3. Hunnewell Lake, open from spring to late fall; $2.50.

FOR SPARE PARTS AND REPAIRS

B & B Cycle Center, 223 North Main, Hannibal, Missouri. This is the only shop along the tour that handles spare parts or repairs, so come prepared.

FOR FURTHER INFORMATION

Cyclist Harry House told us about this ride and will be glad to

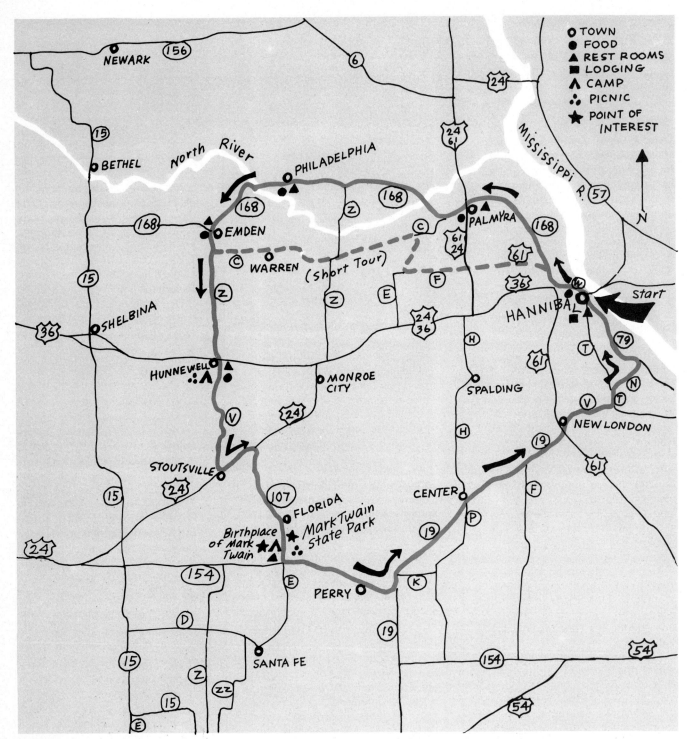

Hannibal is in northeastern Missouri on U.S. 61, 24 and 36; 202 miles northeast of Kansas City via U.S. 24; 116 miles north of St. Louis via I-70 and U.S. 61.

answer any questions you may have. He can also supply information on his club's annual autumn century from Hannibal to Shelbyville. His address is P.O. Box 253, Troy, Missouri 63379.

NEARBY

Missouri's blacktop county roads offer weeks of peaceful rural cycling. Just stay on the gray or black routes on the official Missouri highway map, available free from the Missouri Tourism Commission, P.O. Box 1055, Jefferson City, Missouri 65101.

the
Great
Plains

80. NORTH DAKOTA DRIFTER

Scan the Souris River banks for gem agates, forage for wild cucumbers, pedal through Roosevelt Park's clipped lawns, watch for ducks, Canadian geese, and white pelicans, and splash into a cool swimming hole on this easy saunter through North Dakota's wide wheat plains. The friendly natives of Minot (MY-nut) describe this ride as "comfortable."

Start in Minot and park your car on a side street or in Theodore Roosevelt Park, where you can explore the zoo, sunken gardens, and sixty acres of formal lawns. Fill your water bottle, buy snacks, and leave town by riding east on 4th Avenue. Take time as you pass Oak Park to pedal the .7-mile twisty loop beneath wide elms and oaks.

Soon you spin onto a hilltop overlooking the green Souris (Mouse) River Valley. In autumn this offers excellent views of the foliage. Easing down onto the valley floor, you spin along the river fringed with box elder and oak. Wild roses, anemones, tiger lilies, and black-eyed Susans hug the road and blossom in secluded nooks. Stop anytime to dawdle along the serene riverbanks, hunt for agates or Indian arrowheads, or forage for wild cucumbers, wild onions, or possibly chokecherries and plums.

You roll through the valley on a road with light, slow-moving traffic and a well-paved shoulder. Though cars are little hazard here, it's still a good idea to use a safety flag so motorists can see you *over* the hill. When the paved road ends, turn left and ride over the bridge into Burlington, where you can buy a few snacks.

At Burlington's main intersection, you can go right on Highway 52 to tour 43 miles or turn left and return toward Minot for a short 14 miles. If you go right for the long

DISTANCE:	43 miles, with a 14-mile short tour for beginners.
TERRAIN:	Flat to rolling, with a few steep hills.
TRAFFIC:	Light.
DIFFICULTY:	Requires a 10-speed bike because of the hills; the short ride is excellent for families.
BEST TIME:	Late spring through autumn.
LOCATION:	Starts from Minot, on U.S. 2, in north-central North Dakota.

tour, you soon pass Old Settler's Park, about half a mile off 52 to your right, a nice place for lunch or a river swim. A footbridge here spans the dammed Souris River, and you can drop into the cool water from thick twine ropes dangling from the elms.

Continuing on through the valley, still in sight of the river, watch for geese, ducks, great blue herons, and white pelicans which often drift here from the nearby Upper Souris Wildlife Refuge. You tackle a long, steep hill about 5 miles from Burlington, then dive into grain-covered plains. About 3 miles beyond the hill's crest, you can rest at a picnic spot.

Take the only paved road left into Berthold, where you can restock on nuts, raisins, or dried fruit at a small country store or drink iced lemonade at the café. Fill your water bottle before you leave; this is the last stop for miles on the dry plains. (In a pinch, you can always

stop at a farm for water. The people are friendly and glad to help.)

Past Berthold as you pedal south toward Des Lacs, the road narrows, but traffic is nil. In autumn straw stands in brick bundles, while in summer sweet clover and new-mown hay scent the breezes. A long, steep hill beyond Des Lacs leads you back to Highway 52. Don't worry about having to stop on the rapid descent because the road levels before you reach Highway 52, where you go right. Traffic may be heavier and faster along this stretch, but the shoulder is wide and paved.

Minot appears in the distance as you climb a viaduct and cross a railroad track. Beyond the tracks, go left and pedal straight onto 4th Avenue South, which leads you back to Theodore Roosevelt Park, your tour's end.

WHERE TO STAY

Minot has numerous motels, and the only time you might have trouble getting a room is one week in mid-July when Minot hosts the North Dakota State Fair, with livestock, exhibits, and a rodeo. Usually, though, you don't need reservations or you can simply make them before you leave town.

Camping is available from April through September at Theodore Roosevelt Park and year round at Oak Park, which you pass when leaving town. Fees for both facilities are $2.50 per night.

FOR SPARE PARTS, REPAIRS, FURTHER INFORMATION

The Bike Hatch, 1112 4th Avenue S.E., Minot, North Dakota 58701; (701) 838-BIKE. Alan "Cat" Korslien, an avid cyclist, told us about this tour and can answer questions and suggest other places to bicycle around Minot. The Hatch is located right across the street from Theodore Roosevelt Park.

Minot is in north-central North Dakota on U.S. 2, 52 and 83; 114 miles north of Bismarck, via U.S. 83.

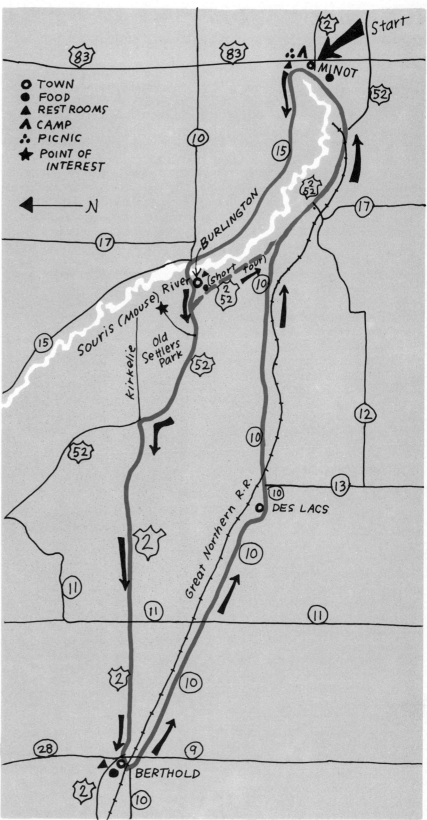

81. 82. ROOSEVELT ROUGH RIDERS

North Dakota's badlands are the anonymous cousins of the famed Badlands to the south. Yet here you find scenery every bit as startling—jutting rock pyramids, scarlet cliffs, buttes, canyons, gorges, and arroyos. Here bison, bighorn sheep, and longhorn cattle roam. Prairie dogs, porcupines, and rabbits battle coyotes, foxes, and bobcats for survival. Best of all, the cycling is superb: most roads are paved and smooth, traffic is light even during peak summer months, and the speed limit is low (35 m.p.h.).

Discover the place where young Teddy Roosevelt tried ranching. Hike the trails, watch beavers in the Little Missouri River, search the skies for golden eagles soaring overhead, and see earth baked to brick-like scoria by a lignite vein which has been burning since 1951 on these two rugged adventures.

SOUTH UNIT LOOP

Start at Medora, which has motels, restaurants, and grocery stores. Visit the old Rough Riders Hotel (1885), after which Theodore Roosevelt named his Spanish-American War regiment. Lunch and dinner here feature buffalo burgers and steaks. You can also venture across the Little Missouri to explore Chateau de Mores, an old twenty-seven-room mansion built by a French nobleman for his wife, Medora, after whom he named the town. Pick up picnic basics and snacks and fill your water bottle before you leave.

At the Visitor Center, stop for literature. Bird watchers can ask for a bird checklist; the park has 175 species. Prairie hawks, falcons, and golden and bald eagles are best spotted in autumn, but watch for them anytime. Behind the Visitor Center is the restored Maltese

Cross Cabin, where Roosevelt stayed on his visits here.

From the Visitor Center, head north uphill, then coast along the well-paved park road which meanders along the riverbanks. Winds often whip over the grasslands, and you may have to rest a bit more on a high-wind day. A long, gradual climb leads you onto a plateau. Then you plunge down to Cottonwood Campground on your

DISTANCE:	South Unit Loop, 38 miles. North Unit Tour, 10 miles round trip at present.
TERRAIN:	Steeply hilly.
TRAFFIC:	Light even in summer.
DIFFICULTY:	Requires some experience and a 10-speed bike to handle hills.
BEST TIME:	Mid-April to mid-September for pleasant biking weather.
LOCATION:	Theodore Roosevelt National Memorial Park, North Dakota. Access to the park presents a problem for cross-country cyclists, as none of the back roads are paved and the major access highways can be hazardous. The only paved access to the South Unit is via Interstate 94, on which bike riding is illegal.

left, a good rest stop where you can refill your water bottle.

At the intersection, turn right onto Scenic Loop Drive for the main tour, or proceed straight a short distance to Peaceful Valley Ranch, where the park service offers free twenty-minute surrey rides to acquaint you with this strange terrain. Following the main tour, you pedal over old highway for 6 miles, so watch out for bumps, holes, and even chunks of rock. As you climb to Scoria Point, stop to view massive bluffs capped with baked, blood-red rock called scoria. You curve up another tough hill through wide plains of waving grass, then level off past Badlands Overlook, where you gaze across Paddock Creek to scoria-covered hummocks. About midway between this overlook and Paddock Creek, the road smooths as you dive downhill. One more short climb leads to the burning lignite vein where you see land shattered and cooked by coal still burning from a 1951 prairie fire.

A bit farther, you can lock your bike and journey up Buck Hill through two vegetation zones. On the hot, dry southern slopes grow semiarid foliage like yucca, cactus, and greasewood, while the cool northern slopes support green ash and juniper. The hilltop offers excellent views of Painted Canyon. Photographic lighting is best in the evening when the sun casts a fiery or peach glow over the jagged land. (Note: There's a tendency here to overexpose photos, so adjust your shutter speed accordingly.)

The road rolls on through the grassy land. There are several 100-foot rises and descents, sometimes gradual, but often steep. Stop to explore the area, and watch for vivid wildflowers, including scarlet-globed mallow, bluebells, harebells, mariposa lilies, sunflowers, and coneflowers. In June whole plains may be flooded with wild pink roses. If you glimpse bison, one warning: stay clear or they could attack. Though apparently tranquil, these beasts have a propensity for becoming grouchy. Also, watch for rattlesnakes in shady areas and brush.

Rolling along Jules Creek, you eventually glide to Wind Canyon, where you can lock your bike and hike a short trail up the ridge to view a graceful oxbow in the Little Missouri River. This is a self-guiding trail, so be certain to pick up a leaflet at the trail head before you leave.

Past Wind Canyon you spin along the river. The flat ride from Beef Corral Prairie Dog Town to Cottonwood Campground is a popular evening bike ride. Groves of cottonwoods along the river often conceal white-tailed and mule deer. Spot them in late afternoon as you sit quietly by the water. Then stay overnight in Cottonwood Campground for a unique look at this eerie land beneath the stars.

NORTH UNIT TOUR

At present you can ride only about 5 miles on the North Unit's paved road from the park entrance on U.S. 85 to Squaw Creek Campground. But since the remaining 9 miles of gravel road to Oxbow Bend Overlook are scheduled to be paved by summer, 1975, we will describe the terrain for the entire stretch. Check with park headquarters or the North Unit ranger station for current road conditions before you start. This tour's nearest supply center is Watford City, 15 miles north, with grocery stores, restaurants, and motels. So be certain you have enough food before you arrive.

As you pedal through this region past slate-blue bentonitic clay walls, watch for longhorn steers which browse between the entrance station and Squaw Creek. The old Long X Trail, along which

steers were once driven north from Texas, crosses the park. The road is flat for several miles, then rolls over a hill into Squaw Creek. Even if you don't plan to camp here, stop to hike the half-mile nature trail through cottonwood, ash, and elm trees along the Little Missouri River.

A long climb begins beyond Squaw Creek. In about one and a half miles, lock your bike at Caprock Coulee Nature Trail and explore the short self-guiding loop through badland coulees and "breaks" (bald spots in the grasslands).

As you go on, the slope sharpens and you can pause to rest at a scenic overlook near a shelter. At last you reach the hill's crest and coast with only one easy rise toward Sperati Point. One final upward spurt takes you to the point, with

a superb vista of grasslands and coulees sliced by the wandering river.

Return by the same route to Squaw Creek, where you can camp beneath the stars and hear coyotes yammering from the nearby cliffs.

More Exploring

You can spend another day here on a fascinating 10-mile round-trip hike through the badlands to Petrified Forest, where there are tree stumps six to eight feet wide. These pearly stumps were possibly a species of giant Sequoia. If hiking sounds too rugged, you can rent horses in summer at Peaceful Valley Ranch in the South Unit, between Halliday Wells and Cottonwood campgrounds. Groups can make arrangements at the ranch, too, for a chuck-wagon breakfast in the grasslands.

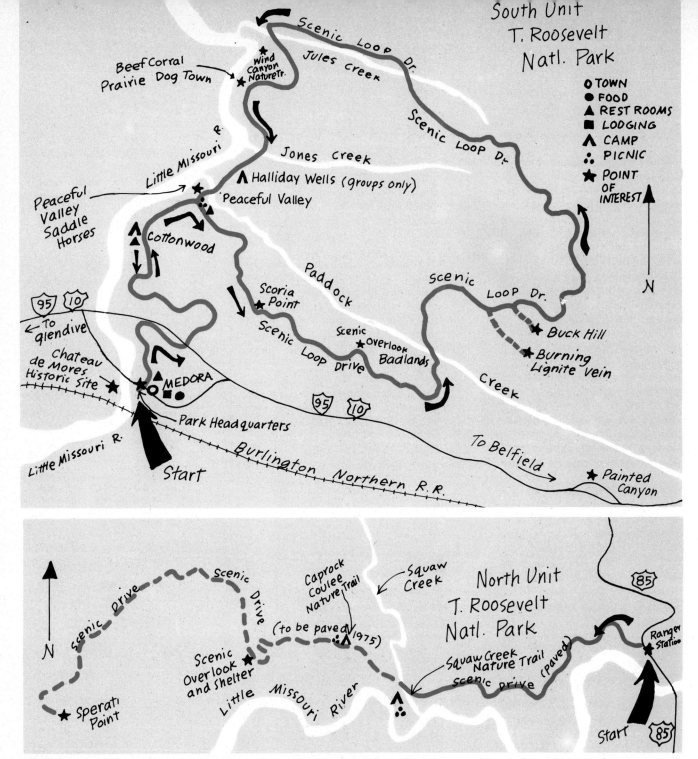

Theodore Roosevelt National Memorial Park is in western North Dakota on I-94; 122 miles west of Bismarck via I-94; 439 miles northeast of Yellowstone National Park via U.S. 212 and I-94. The top map shows the South Unit and the bottom, the North Unit.

WHERE TO STAY

A quaint hotel in Medora is the remodeled Rough Riders (1885), located two blocks north of Business I-94; phone (701) 623-4433. Other overnight accommodations in Medora include the Badlands, on Business I-94, (701) 623-4422; and Dietz's, half a block north of Business I-94, (701) 623-4455. There are several motels in Watford City,

about 15 miles north of the North Unit, one of which is the Four Eyes Motel, 122 South Main, (701) 842-2306.

The park's Cottonwood and Squaw Creek campgrounds operate year round on a first-come first-served basis. Locations are indicated in the tour description and on the map. Fee, $2. Large groups may reserve space at Halliday Wells Campground in the South Unit.

FOR FURTHER INFORMATION

Write Superintendent, Theodore Roosevelt National Memorial Park, Medora, North Dakota 58645, or inquire at the Visitor Center when you arrive. The park's personnel are quite interested in cycling, and you will get top-notch help and advice.

83. BADLANDS TREK

In the middle of South Dakota's windswept plains lie the forbidding Badlands, a skeleton of the land. Bony blood-red rock pyramids rise from the dry dust. Winds occasionally toss a sagebrush ball across the road, then become still. Above the arid gorges stretch flat grasslands with weeds so brittle they rustle in the breeze. On a bike you become part of this primeval place, an experience you are unlikely to forget.

Begin in Wall, north of the Badlands via U.S. 16. Since seven out of ten motorists visiting the Badlands drive in the opposite direction, you encounter the least traffic this way. Park your car in any lot in Wall and pick up food, suntan lotion, and water before leaving. Bring spare parts and tools with you.

Pedal from town south on 16A along a four-foot shoulder which soon narrows to about a foot and lasts until you cross a cattle guard about 7 miles from town. Gradual rolling hills lead you through the dry rabbit-brush-grown plains past two marshy little ponds. As the road narrows and winds upward, follow the sign for Badlands Scenic Drive. As a side trip, hearty cyclists can venture right onto Sage Creek Road, along which are found many buffalo, a prairie dog town, 5 miles west, and primitive Sage Creek Campground, twelve and a half miles west.

Continuing on the main route, stop at Pinnacles Overlook, where you can peer into the canyons and possibly see bighorn sheep, bison, or pronghorn. Just beyond the Pinnacles, as you coast watch out for rocks and gratings on the narrow shoulder. As you pass Early Life Overlook's dense juniper groves, watch for birds, deer, and an occasional bobcat or bighorn sheep.

Just past Yellow Mounds Over-

DISTANCE:	75 miles round trip.
TERRAIN:	Many flat stretches, a few moderately steep grades.
TRAFFIC:	Heavy in summer; light in spring and autumn.
DIFFICULTY:	In spring and autumn for experienced wilderness cyclists only. Though the terrain and slow traffic can be handled by beginners and families without young children, overnight and eating facilities are limited or nonexistent during off-season. Inexperienced cyclists can still plan to come in spring or autumn, but should bring all the food and water needed for the day, start the ride from the Visitor Center instead of Wall, and ride only as many miles as can safely be handled.
BEST TIME:	Spring or autumn, when temperatures are cool and traffic is light.
LOCATION:	Badlands National Monument, South Dakota.

look, you climb again to grass flats, with possible stiff winds. You ride now on a plateau past Rainbow Overlook and through thick stands of yucca. The road dips about 2 miles past Clastic Dikes Overlook to Hamms Draw, where you may see mule deer drinking. A bit farther, stop at Grasslands View, where pronghorn (antelope) are often seen.

You have a short, steep climb past Gullies Overlook, then arrive in about 2 miles at Fossil Exhibit Trail, where you can ride along for a paved half-mile to see prehistoric fossils. Beyond the trail, you coast an exhilarating 2 miles through Norbeck Pass onto the rocky Badlands' floor. Despite the desolate feeling here, you find many flat, grassy spots to rest upon beneath the jagged rock pyramids. Explore as much as you like, but stay away from the huge holes or caves you see. All rocks here are soft, but they are particularly unsteady around these caverns. Rattlesnakes also lurk by daylight in these dark crevices and holes.

About 100 yards past the junction of State 40A is Cedar Pass Campground, open year round, and a good overnight stop. A bit farther, you can eat or have an iced drink at Cedar Pass Lodge. At park headquarters you can register for guided gully walks and backcountry canyon climbs.

You climb again past headquarters to Cliff Shelf Nature Trail, where you can lock your bike and walk half a mile along the dirt pathway for a leisurely thirty minutes through an oasis of foliage called a slump. Bird watching is excellent here among the junipers and in the brush. You may also see a cottontail, chipmunk, deer, or—if you are lucky—a bobcat. Watch for rattlesnakes sunning on the paths or in rocky cliff shadows.

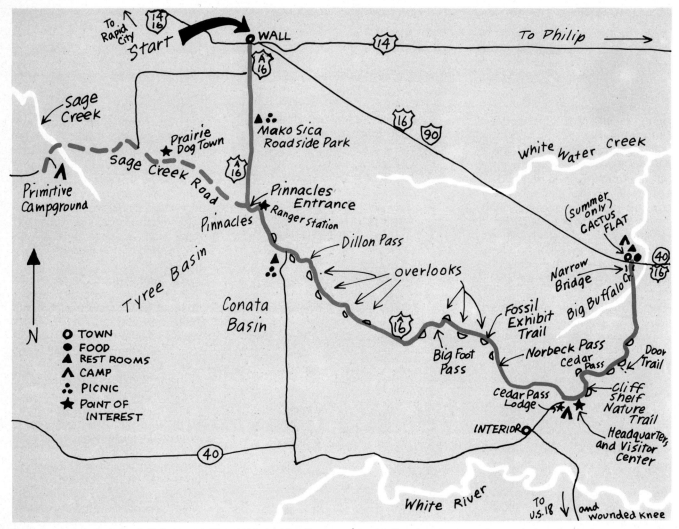

Wall is in southwestern South Dakota on I-90 and U.S. 14; 53 miles east of Rapid City via I-90; 223 miles southwest of Minneapolis-St. Paul, Minnesota, via U.S. 169 and I-90.

Beyond Cedar Pass Overlook you coast past Door Trail, another walk. This time you stroll three quarters of a mile to a natural "door" in the rocks. Going on, you soon leave the Badlands, cross another cattle guard, and pass Prairie Homestead, a pioneer dugout open summers. A narrow bridge spans Big Buffalo Creek. From here you veer right and pedal on to Cactus Flat, where you can eat at the café and possibly stay overnight at a campground with a swimming pool. Then retrace your ride back to Wall.

Note: Food is available summers only at Cactus Flat, so you may want to shorten this ride, turning back perhaps at Cedar Pass Overlook.

WHERE TO STAY

Campgrounds in the Badlands: Cedar Pass Campground, half a mile southwest of the Visitor Center, off State 40A; open year round; $2 fee charged from mid-May into September; no water available from October to mid-May. Sage Creek Primitive Campground, 1 mile off graveled Sage Creek Road; open year round; no fee; no water or shade. Other summer-only campgrounds are located in Cactus Flat, Interior, Kadoka, Scenic, and Wall.

Motels are available year round in Kadoka and Wall. Cabins can be rented from late May to mid-September at Cedar Pass Lodge.

FOR OTHER INFORMATION

Contact the Badlands Visitor Center, Interior, South Dakota 57750, for weather or other information.

NEARBY

Unless you enjoy dry prairie rides, the nearest points of interest are the Black Hills, over 100 miles west. Biking this stretch is unscenic and difficult because of limited facilities.

84. BLACK HILLS HOLIDAY

Folklore has it that South Dakota's Black Hills were formed when Paul Bunyan buried his blue ox, Babe, who died of indigestion after eating his master's flapjacks. Though geologists explain the hills more scientifically, a legendary quality persists here. You may feel you have only to pedal into the shaded woods to encounter Paul tidying up the meadows.

Your tour begins in Custer. Being a tourist center, this small town has many motels and campgrounds. However, if you come here during off-season, which you will probably want to do, don't count on any facilities being open except perhaps a few motels. In fact, you may even want to bring your own picnic and camping supplies with you to avoid inconvenience. The nearest year-round town is Rapid City. Even in summer, Black Hills nights are cold, so bring warm clothes and sleeping bags if you plan to camp.

Leave Custer on State 16, a lightly traveled blacktop road with no shoulder. You may want to pedal around Custer awhile to get the kinks out of your legs because you immediately have a stiff climb. Then you pass a small graveyard and coast for views of tree-covered hills. Rolling hills take you through wildflower meadows and into Tenderfoot Gulch. To your right here you pass Crazy Horse Memorial, where sculptor Korczak Ziolkowski, assistant on Mount Rushmore, is carving a statue of Crazy Horse, Custer's victor. A fee is charged to see the project. Beyond the memorial, you cross a bridge, roll over another hill past Oreville Campground, and climb into the woods.

At the three-way intersection, make a sharp right onto State 87. At this point you may take a side trip to Mt. Rushmore National Monument.

Keeping on the main tour, you climb a sharp slope on good road with wide shoulders. Then beyond the cattle crossing (maintain speed and run straight across), the road narrows to a winding lane through maple, oak, and quaking aspen forests. Just beyond a resort located 3 miles past the turnoff, you begin a tough climb around four horseshoe bends. Traffic is light and should be no problem because of the 15-m.p.h. speed limit. As you come out of the fourth bend, turn on your lights and go through the one-lane tunnel. If you need a rest from the climb, stop in the peaceful grassy clearing to your left beyond the tunnel.

Soon you coast past Sylvan Lake Lodge, where you can camp overnight for $2 or swim. Turn left just beyond the lodge and then left again at the stop sign. Pause to wander along ice-blue Sylvan Lake. A bit farther, you may want to stop again to explore the rocks your left. Several crannies and road overlooks in these boulders make fun snack spots. In another minute you come upon a narrow dirt road meandering off through the underbrush. Should you decide to explore here or elsewhere in the hills, you may come upon deer, elk, buffalo, mountain goats, or even mountain sheep.

Now as you climb the steep mile to the Needles, you may encounter slow traffic. Stop to explore the Needles' towering, spindly rock formations. Then you spin through a short rock tunnel—the Needle's Eye—and glide downhill. Stop awhile at the turnout to your right to look over the cliffs into the deep tree-tufted valleys. As you coast, concentrate on slowing down here to enjoy the wide views. You navigate around one more horseshoe curve, beyond which you climb into woods with lots of inviting clear-

ings and sweet leaf-and-bark-scented air. Rock hounds could spend days here poking about the huge boulders hidden within the forests. Taking specimens home, though, violates forest rules.

Though traffic is light and slow as you wind down the hills, the road is quite narrow, so try to pull off when two cars meet. There are another cattle crossing, more cozy rock crannies, and a narrow rock tunnel, beyond which the hill to your left tapers gently to a sleepy mountain brook. All along here you find good picnic nooks: a rocky cave, an open wildflower meadow, a clearing beside a pebbled mountain stream or along a path twisting into the woods. You are coasting now with an occasional upward spurt. Then beyond the Black Hills Playhouse, the route seems like a roller coaster. You have passed from Black Hills Na-

DISTANCE:	42 miles, excluding side trips.
TERRAIN:	Lots of steep hills.
TRAFFIC:	Moderate to light in spring and autumn; heavy on summer weekends.
DIFFICULTY:	Requires experience and a 10-speed bike.
BEST TIME:	Spring for wildflowers or autumn for foliage. Summer can be hot and November through March snowy.
LOCATION:	Black Hills, South Dakota.

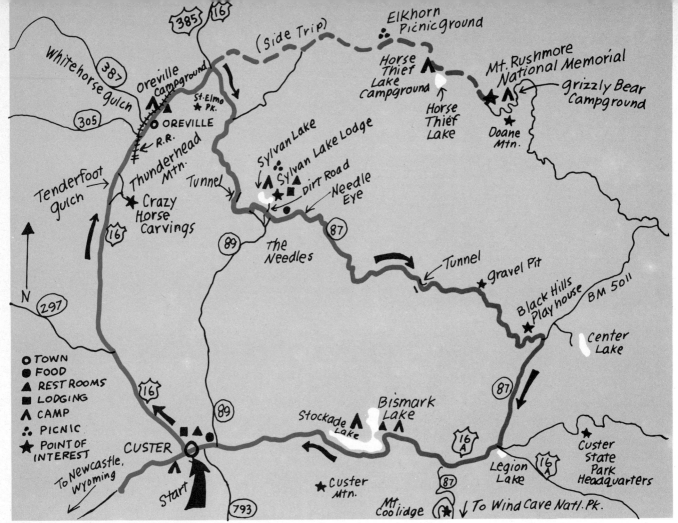

Custer is in southwestern South Dakota on U.S. 16 and 385; 42 miles southwest of Rapid City via U.S. 16 and 385; 556 miles southeast of Yellowstone National Park via U.S. 14, I-90 and U.S. 16.

tional Forest into Custer State Park, where huge bison herds roam, but there is no perceptible difference here in the scenery. At Legion Lake, go right onto 16A, which takes you up and down hills past Bismark Lake, where you can camp overnight for $1. The road around the water is dirt and gravel, so be careful if you try to ride here.

From Bismark you climb on a well-paved road with a four-foot-wide asphalt shoulder, cross another cattle guard, climb gradually, then coast back into Custer, completing the loop.

WHERE TO STAY

Motels in Custer include the following: Chief, 120 Mt. Rushmore Road; (605) 673-2318; closed November through April. Custer, 109 Mt. Rushmore Road; (605) 673-2876; closed December through March. Rock Crest Lodge, half a mile west at the junction of states 16 and 385; (605) 673-4323; closed

October through May. Rocket, 211 Mt. Rushmore Road, two and a half blocks west on State 16; (605) 673-4401; closed December to April 14th. Sunset, 5th and Crook Streets, one block north on State 16; (605) 673-2821; open year round.

Campgrounds are found in both Black Hills National Forest and Custer State Park. National Forest sites usually cost $1, while Custer Park usually charges $2, with a five-day limit. In the order you pass them on the ride, the campgrounds are as follows: Oreville, 9 miles north of Custer on State 16; open May 30th to October 31st; $1. Sylvan Lake, on State 87 before you reach the Needles; open May 15th to September 3rd; $2. Legion Lake, at the intersection of states 87 and 16A as you start back toward Custer; open May 15th to September 3rd; $2. Stockade Lake, three Custer State Park campgrounds on State 16A; open May 15th to September 3rd; $2. Bismark Lake, just

beyond Stockade Lake grounds on State 16A; open June 1st to October 1st; $1.

FOR SPARE PARTS, REPAIRS, FURTHER INFORMATION

Contact the Black Hills National Forest for current road or weather information. The nearest bike shops are in Rapid City, South Dakota, so come prepared.

NEARBY

Within close range are Wind Cave National Park, about 20 miles south on State 87, another winding hilly ride; Mount Rushmore, with more steeply rolling hills and a long, gradual climb to the memorial on a wide, well-paved road; and Jewel Cave, west of Custer on U.S. 16 (see the tour on p. 179).

85. SPEARFISH CANYON CAPER

Discover the past of Preacher Smith, Potato Creek Johnny, Wild Bill Hickok, and Calamity Jane on this spin along Spearfish Canyon's trout-filled streams and waterfalls to old Deadwood Gulch, where ghosts of cowboys and gold miners roam.

Start at Spearfish, home of the Black Hills passion play. Carry spare parts, tools, snacks, and lots of water on this frontier trek. Ride south on Main Street, which eventually becomes U.S. 85 and 14. In a few minutes, you reach Route 14A (there's a roadside park ahead) and turn right onto County 89 to cycle through the pines and aspens of the canyon along clear Spearfish Creek. The narrow road is usually well surfaced but rough in spots. Yellow, blue, and magenta wildflowers dapple the gulches and line the creek banks.

About 5 miles from Spearfish, you pass Bridal Veil Falls. Several curvy miles later an asphalt road lies to your right; take a side trip here to Roughlock Falls, a secluded nook where one stream splits into many rivulets splashing over rocks. The refreshing pine woods may persuade you to camp overnight for $1 or at least wade in the icy creek.

Beyond the Roughlock Falls area, you pedal through Cheyenne Crossing, where you can buy snacks at the little corner grocery. Then go left onto U.S. 85 and pedal for three and a half miles up Ice Box Gulch, a 7-percent grade definitely not for beginners. Then you coast past another campground on your left, curve right around Sugarloaf Mountain, pedal along a serene little stream, and climb a hill into Lead.

Stop for a snack at a cafe in Lead or rest at the end of Main Street in lushly foliaged Sinking Gardens. Outside of Lead you can pause to

DISTANCE:	43 miles, excluding side trips.
TERRAIN:	Steeply rolling.
TRAFFIC:	Heavy on summer afternoons; light in spring and autumn.
DIFFICULTY:	Requires experience and a 10-speed bike to tackle the hills.
BEST TIME:	Spring or autumn, with the lightest traffic and most pleasant temperatures.
LOCATION:	From Spearfish, in South Dakota's Black Hills.

tour Homestake Mine, a relic of the old gold days.

From Lead you pedal along pine-fringed Deadwood and Gold Run creeks, then coast into Deadwood, a gulch surrounded by mountains. Pedal here along the original old main street where Calamity Jane, Wild Bill Hickok, Preacher Smith, Poker Alice, and Potato Creek Johnny lived during frontier days. Then visit Mount Moriah Cemetery, Deadwood's boot hill, where many of these legendary figures are buried. From the cemetery hilltop, you have a splendid view of Deadwood in the valley below. As you coast back into Deadwood once more, you can picnic at Deadwood Recreation Center, 105 Sherman Street, and swim here in the heated pool for 60¢. It's cheaper, though, and may be more refreshing to pedal outside Deadwood to wade in icy Polo Creek.

From Deadwood a railroad track runs to your right to a fork where 14A and U.S. 85 split. Take U.S. 85 left up a short, steep hill. Then coast past Preacher Smith Picnic Ground, another good rest stop. When you reach U.S. 85 and 14, go left and ride across Centennial Prairie past the small roadside park you saw at the tour's start and back into Spearfish. On this last stretch, the road is wide with a good shoulder, but you may encounter some big trucks, so be careful.

WHERE TO STAY

Motels are available in Spearfish, Lead, and Deadwood, and include the following: Kelley's, 545 Main Street, Spearfish; (605) 642-2622. Kozy, 427 Main Street, Spearfish; (605) 642-3407. Royal Rest, 444 Main Street, Spearfish; (605) 642-3842. Calamity Jane, Glendale Drive, three quarters of a mile north of Lead on 14A; (605) 584-1974. Dunmire's Ponderosa, Glendale Drive, half a mile north of Lead on 14A; (605) 584-2820. Lariat, 360 North Main Street, north of Deadwood on 14A; (605) 578-1500.

Two campgrounds, mentioned above, are located in the Rough-lock Falls area. Another possible overnight camp about 2 miles off the main tour is Hanna Camp-ground, which you reach by going right at the Cheyenne Crossing in-tersection (the tour goes left through Ice Box Gulch) and then left at the fork for 2 miles. All these camps are operated by Black Hills National Forest on a first-come first-served basis.

FOR SPARE PARTS, REPAIRS, FURTHER INFORMATION

Two Wheeler Dealer, 817 Main Street, Rapid City, South Dakota 57701; (605) 343-0524.

NEARBY

If you are in mountaineering condition, you can explore the Black Hills. South of here lie Mount Rushmore National Monu-ment, Custer State Park, and Wind Cave National Park. See the Black Hills Holiday on page 175 for de-tails. Nearly anywhere you explore in this region, you can count on steep hills and winding, often nar-row, roads.

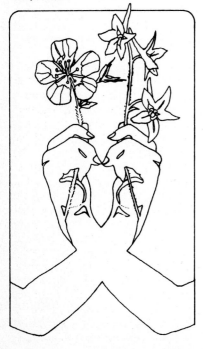

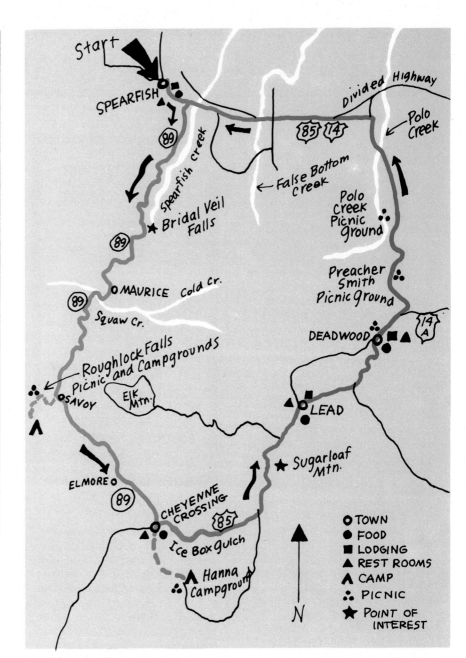

Spearfish is in southwestern South Dakota on U.S. 14/85; 57 miles northwest of Rapid City via I-90 and U.S. 14/85; 403 miles west of Sioux Falls via I-90 and U.S. 14/85.

86. OLD WEST TRAIL

Pedal from Wyoming gulches and prairies to South Dakota's cool, forested Black Hills on this Old West saunter. The countryside here invites exploring. Stop often to look from a flat plateau onto a wide sagebrush plain, visit twinkling Jewel Cave, or walk beneath rich ponderosa and lodgepole pines. The jaunt ends in Custer, amid more delightful cycling possibilities through Black Hills National Forest. Carry spare parts, tools, water, and the food you will need for the ride.

Ride from Newcastle, Wyoming, on U.S. 85 at dawn, when you may observe antelope grazing in the meadows. Many wildflowers grow along the roadside in spring: Indian paintbrush, wild irises, sunflowers, bluebells, goldenrod, and wild roses. Shoulders are wide and often marked with a white line for the 11 miles to the South Dakota state line. Watch ahead for the two bridges crossing Salt and Coal Mine creeks, 5 and 6 miles from Newcastle. Wide meadows lie between the road and fence lines, so you can stop anywhere to watch wildlife, scramble down the banks of an icy trout stream, or rest in this restless land. About 10 miles outside Newcastle, you climb between smooth brush-dotted hills. Coasting, you pass a small roadside park, then cross into South Dakota, where the shoulder narrows.

Soon you climb steeply and curve between pines for views of cool green hills and valleys. Your climb becomes more gradual, then you plunge downhill with views of huge forested hills veined with sandstone. Another long pull past horse ranches and a narrow bridge brings you into Black Hills National Forest. From now on you can stop anywhere to relax on soft green grass sprinkled with spicy pine needles. Once into the national

DISTANCE:	78 miles round trip.
TERRAIN:	Steeply rolling hills.
TRAFFIC:	Light in spring and autumn; heavy in summer.
DIFFICULTY:	Hills and fast traffic make this a ride for experienced cyclists only. Safety flag recommended.
BEST TIME:	Spring or autumn, with light traffic and cool weather.
LOCATION:	Newcastle, Wyoming, to Custer, South Dakota.

forest, you begin a series of steep climbs and fast descents with sharp switchbacks. As you approach Jewel Cave National Monument, there's a 7-percent downward plunge for one and a half miles.

Coasting past a Jewel Cave sign, you have more downhill switchbacks and a long uphill pull with views to your right of tree-filled valleys dotted with salmon-colored rocks. Near the hilltop, turn right for a side trip to Jewel Cave, a cavern lined with twinkling calcite crystals. Strenuous walks are conducted every half hour from June to Labor Day. As you walk down the steps to the Visitor Center, notice the yellow wildflowers with strange conical tops along the stairway: these are prairie coneflowers.

Back on the main road, you wind sharply beside salmon, golden, and

red cliffs. Your ride flattens for about a mile, then you wind over rolling hills again. As you coast to Comanche Park Campground, you can stop at the picnic area for lunch. Going on, you climb, then descend past a lumber mill and commercial campgrounds, beyond which you start up again. As the narrow road winds past more camps, watch for the narrow bridge ahead and try to cross this without cars beside you. Soon you roll into Custer, located on the edge of the Black Hills and near Mount Rushmore National Monument. Custer is strictly a tourist town. If you come during off-season, count on everything being closed. You should be able to find a café or grocery store open, but to be safe carry emergency rations.

Stay overnight in a motel or return to one of the camps you passed on the way. Since this ride is recommended only for experienced cyclists, you may be able to complete the ride back to Newcastle in the same day.

WHERE TO STAY

In early spring your best bet for a motel in Custer is the Sunset at 5th and Crook Streets, one block north of midtown on Route 16. This motel is open year round. After Labor Day many motels close, but a few stay open until November 1st. Newcastle caters to tourists and has many year-round motels.

Campgrounds surround Custer and you can go in virtually any direction to find a nice spot. Going from Custer to Newcastle, you pass these camps: Big Pine Campground, two and a quarter miles from Custer; open May 20th to September 15th; $2.50 for four. For reservations, write Big Pine Campground, Route 1, Custer, South Dakota 57730, or phone (605) 673-

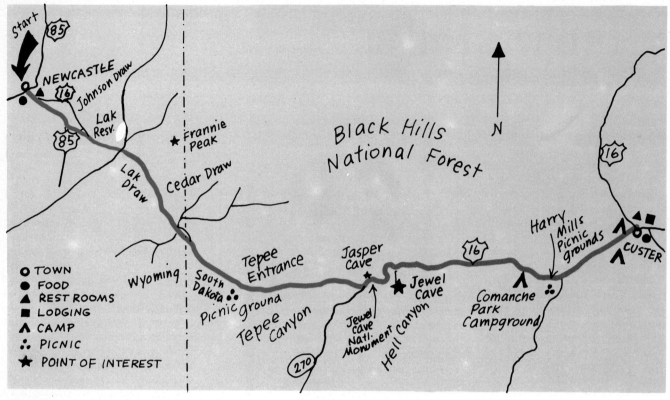

Newcastle is in northeastern Wyoming on U.S. 85 and 16; 39 miles west of Custer, South Dakota, via U.S. 16; 432 miles east of Yellowstone National Park via U.S. 16, I-90, and U.S. 16; 214 miles north of Cheyenne via U.S. 85.

4054. Comanche Park Camp ground, 7 miles from Custer in Black Hills National Forest; open year round. Other campgrounds are also available, and you will see these as you ride toward Custer.

NEARBY

The Black Hills around Custer have many winding, twisting hilly roads through lush forests. The Needles Highway leads up steep hills to jagged sandstone pinnacles, winds along clear mountain lakes and streams, and passes a few resorts. (See page 175 for details.) You may also want to visit Mount Rushmore National Monument, located on an excellent highway with a wide shoulder at the top of a hill; Custer State Park, with one of the country's largest bison herds; and Wind Cave National Park, a lightly traveled national park with

abundant wildlife and spelunking tours through the cave. Anywhere you ride here, you encounter steeply rolling hills through deep scenic forests.

WYOMING PRAIRIE WILDFLOWERS

Abundant wildflowers populate the arid Wyoming prairies and are particularly striking viewed from a bike. Some of the species you should spot are these.

Indian paintbrush has vivid scarlet tubes which are actually the plant's sepals or leaves. The petals are the inconspicuous narrow greenish-yellow growths you see beside the flaming color. Indian paintbrush sepals can also be white, pink, yellow, or orange.

Bluebells, named for their bell shape, can be found mostly along streams. You will notice that the

purplish tubular buds quickly turn delicate blue as the blossom opens. Inside the corolla (the group of petals) are five stamens.

Wild roses in Wyoming usually grow on a thorny shrub two to three feet high with pink or rosy flowers. Each blossom has five heart-shaped petals and the leaves have saw-toothed edges. The fruit, or "hips" which you can find any season, contain twenty-five times the vitamin C of orange juice and are a great quick-energy source at the top of the hill. Try a few. You can also gather and dry the petals to make fragrant rose-flower tea.

87. BIG HORN CLIMB

Wyoming's Shell Canyon offers the adventurous a challenging climb through jutting red sandstone walls to an alpine meadow, then a thrilling descent through lodgepole and limber pine, fir, and spruce forests to a plush valley floor. Dwarf juniper forests, mountain mahogany, chokecherry, sumac, buffalo berry, and sage grow along the hillsides. In spring mountain wildflowers coat the meadows, and in September you may meet cowboys herding their livestock down the mountain.

Bring spare tubes and tools with you on this trek and be alert for jagged rocks on the roadway. Water and rest-room facilities are available all along this ride, but you will need to take food and snacks with you.

From Greybull you cross a bridge over the Big Horn River and climb a sharp slope out of town. At the hilltop you look across rolling terrain, with the Big Horn Mountains before you. Pedaling through prairied countryside, you see flat-topped foothills, and soon the road, only in fair condition at first, widens and picks up a good riding shoulder. Green grassy meadows alternate with sagebrush prairies, and sunflowers sprout from the ditches. Occasionally on the approaching mountains, you observe sandstone chasms cutting the rocky blue peaks like blood-red veins.

Soon you cross a mountain stream. On a dusty day it might be pleasant to scramble down the gently tapered bank to the snow-fed brook. Proceeding on the wide road, you finally coast into Shell, population 50. Stop for an icy drink at the little café. Outside, a dozen brittle antlers locked about an old tree trunk give you insight into the life-style here where men still hunt antelope, deer, and elk.

In Shell the road narrows and you climb gradually from the hamlet between huge russet rock towers. Past a lodge and café, you enter Shell Canyon, with salmon-stained sandstone walls. A mile into the canyon, a motel lies on your right. Then a bit farther, take care going over the cattle-crossing guard, beyond which your path narrows to a winding lane up the mountainside beside a pebbled stream.

DISTANCE:	148 miles round trip.
TERRAIN:	Steep climbs and thrilling descents.
TRAFFIC:	Light in early spring and autumn; moderate to heavy in summer.
DIFFICULTY:	For experts only.
BEST TIME:	Spring through autumn.
LOCATION:	Starts from Greybull, Wyoming.

About 3 miles into the canyon, after the second turnout, your climb steepens as you lean around hairpin curves, with the canyon's red walls jutting to the sky. A mile into this steep slope, you round a curve with flat rest spots on both sides of the road. Beyond here is Post Creek Picnic Ground, another good rest stop. Your climb lessens considerably for about a mile. Then you pass a rest area, cross Shell Canyon Bridge, and pedal sharply up again, where across the valley to your right you see pine-clad mountain slopes.

About two and a half miles from the bridge, the road narrows and becomes bumpy (maybe this will be fixed soon), and to your right you see a whole mountainside of demolished trees lying like broken gray toothpicks, the result of a heavy snowslide. As the road improves, you reach a waterfall where you can rest on a grassy hill. The picnic ground across the road makes a good lunch stop.

Beyond here you pass a campground and cattle ranch, then begin to climb steeply to the summit and alpine meadows. Caution: From here to the ride's end, watch out for numerous cattle-crossing guards. Experienced cyclists find the best approach to these is to maintain speed and ride directly across the guard. This is open range country, and in September you may find yourself behind cattle herds being rounded up for winter. From a bike you are much more likely to strike up a conversation with the cowboys than from a closed car.

When you reach Burgess Junction, turn right with U.S. 14 toward Sheridan. Soon you pedal into forests again where you may glimpse mule deer, elk, grouse, pheasants, or Hungarian partridges, as well as minks, muskrats, beavers, or possibly even a bear. In early spring you see lots of wildflowers. Four miles outside Burgess Junction, you pass Arrowhead Lodge, where you may want to stay overnight, and just beyond that, a picnic area. You see still another mountain creek gurgling through the flat grass meadow, then continue down between the straight lodgepole pine trunks past a lake in the hollow to your right. Occasionally you may encounter rough spots on this stretch.

For the tour's last 9 miles (starting 7 miles beyond the lake), the road really plunges: be sure not to lose control by going too fast. On this final coast, you see the small town of Dayton cupped in a green valley, and you can turn off at the many spots along the way to rest or take photographs. Curving beside red rock walls, you eventually pedal onto the valley floor, where you churn along the Tongue River into Dayton, with motels and camping. Stock up again on food before you return to Greybull via the same route.

WHERE TO STAY

Several motels are located in Greybull and Dayton. Reservations should not be necessary, but you can write or phone if you wish. Glenn's, Box 449, Greybull, Wyoming 82426; (307) 765-4444. K-Bar, 300 Greybull Avenue, Greybull, Wyoming 82426; (307) 765-4426. Big Horn Motel, Dayton, Wyoming 82836; (307) 655-2242. Foothill Motel, Dayton, Wyoming 82836; (307) 655-2547.

Greybull is in northern Wyoming on U.S. 14, 16 /20 and Wyoming 789; 145 miles east of Yellowstone National Park via U.S. 14/20 and 16; 369 miles west of Rapid City, South Dakota, via U.S. 14, I-90 and U.S. 14; 202 miles northwest of Casper via U.S. 20/26 and U.S. 16/20.

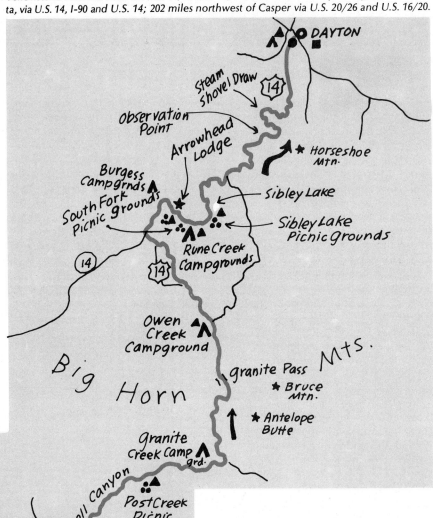

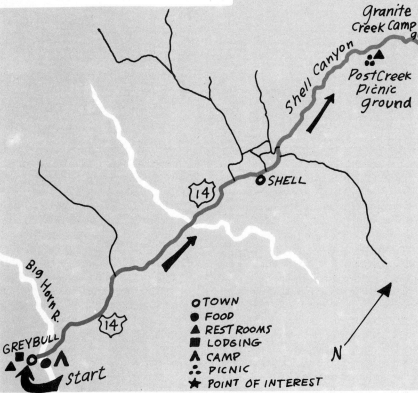

Campgrounds are located throughout the ride. As you return to Greybull from Dayton on the route described above, you pass these camps: Foothills Campground, in Dayton on U.S. 14, one block north of the post office; open May 1st to November 15th; $2.50. Sibley Lake, 25 miles from Dayton; open June 15th to September 30th; $1. Prune Creek, 26 miles from Dayton; open June 1st to September 30th; $1. South Tongue, 27 miles from Dayton, then 1 mile off the main road (follow the signs); open June 1st to September 30th; free. North Tongue, 29 miles from Dayton; open June 1st to September 30th; $1. Dead Swede, 34 miles from

Dayton, then 3 miles southeast on a forest road; open June 15th to September 30th; $1. Owen Creek, 34 miles from Dayton, then a quarter of a mile on a forest road; open June 1st to September 30th; $1. Tie Flume, 34 miles from Dayton, then 2 miles east on FH631; open June 15th to September 30th; $1.

Greybull has only two commercial campgrounds: Greybull KOA, four blocks east of U.S. 14, 16, and 20; open May 1st to September 30th. Mustang Camper Village, a quarter of a mile north of the U.S. 14 and U.S. 16 and 20 junction; open year round.

NATURAL BEVERAGES IN THE BIG HORNS

High in alpine country as you linger beside a waterfall, lie in a meadow, or explore a forest path, the call of the wild may tempt you to try a thirst-quenching sumacade or healthful sage tea. Both sumac and sage grow here.

The sumac is a small tree or bush growing anywhere from four to fifteen feet high. Its leaves turn bright yellow or crimson in autumn, and its smooth branches are sometimes coated with velvet hairs. It has long, narrow leaves with as many as thirty-one leaflets

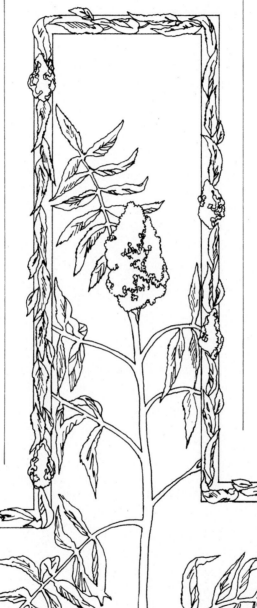

growing opposite each other, and the tiny crimson fruits are coated with long reddish hairs. (Note: The "hairs" on the berries contain the lemony acid, so don't remove these.)

Sumac-ade tastes remarkably like lemonade and is as refreshing as frigid mountain water. Simply drop about ten tart red berries in a cup of brook water, stir until the beverage turns the delicate hue of pink lemonade, sweeten to taste (honey works best), and drink. To speed up the process a bit, bruise the berries by rubbing them before plopping them in the water. Hot water removes the juice more quickly, but the heat produces an unpleasant bitterness.

You can recognize sage by its square stem; opposite leaves; small purple, white, or pink blossoms; and most important, its strong fragrant minty smell.

Sage tea may go down better than sumac-ade on a brisk morning. Ancient herbalists once believed this spicy, mint-flavored drink stopped aging, so it may be at least potent enough to push you over that next hill. Just soak some fresh green leaves in hot water, sweeten with honey, and tipple.

88. WYOMING PRAIRIE PEDAL

This windswept century through Wyoming's sagebrush plains is guaranteed to create unusual moods. One can hardly pedal here without feeling a certain affinity with cowboys of legend who found the Wyoming prairies both lonely and free. Isolation characterizes the landscape as you look across vast empty lands to the blue-shadowed Big Horn Mountains.

Start either in Cody or Greybull, Wyoming, and follow U.S. 14, 16, and 20 all the way. The road is generally flat, with a gradual downward grade from Cody to Greybull, and rough in spots, with a narrow shoulder which often vanishes. Traffic is fast but light in spring and autumn, and the wide, open road allows you to be easily seen.

If you start in Cody, take time to browse through the Buffalo Bill Museum and the excellent Whitney Gallery of Western Art before leaving. Carry spare parts and tools (Cody has a bike shop), and lots of water and snacks because you find no food facilities for 35 miles. Sunglasses, suntan lotion, and a hat are advised to combat the sun and possible strong east or northeasterly winds.

Riding east of Cody, you go up a hill with immediate views of the wide sun-parched plains. You needn't worry about when you might encounter a hill: you can see even a gradual slope miles ahead. The ride is fairly flat and you can stop anywhere. Along the way you find buffalo grass, rabbit brush, wild roses, lupine, and sunflowers. In early morning or late afternoon watch for deer, elk, and pronghorn antelope grazing in the grasslands. About 7 miles from Cody, you pass a roadside park with facilities and picnic tables. Five miles later, you climb up onto a plateau which stretches about a mile, with great

DISTANCE:	110 miles round trip.
TERRAIN:	Gradually downhill from Cody to Greybull, uphill back to Cody.
TRAFFIC:	Heavy in summer; moderate to light in spring and autumn.
DIFFICULTY:	For experienced cyclists because of the few facilities.
BEST TIME:	Spring and autumn, with cooler temperatures and lighter traffic.
LOCATION:	Cody to Greybull, Wyoming, via U.S. 14, 16, and 20.

views of the snowy Big Horns. Then you glide down to the prairie again. Watch out for bumpy, washboard road starting about a mile beyond the plateau.

For many more miles past vivid sandstone rocks, gullies, and gulches, the road glides gently downhill. In some spots you pick up a wide shoulder, while in other places the road narrows and becomes bumpy again. Little shade is

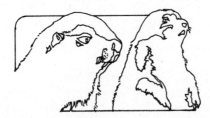

available, unless you rest against a huge boulder. Finally about 32 miles from Cody, you run through some greenery with a few welcome shade trees, then pass green grassy ranchlands. Three miles after entering this foliaged area, you find a tiny grocery store, filling station, and campground. This is the only food and camp stop between Cody and Greybull.

Proceeding past cattle and sheep ranches, you dip downhill and over a small bridge, then climb into open prairie again. Gulches cut through the land on your right. About 2 miles past the bridge, travel along a fine shoulder for 5 miles to an intersection with many signs pointing in all directions. Go straight here, and watch out for gravel shoulders and possible sharp rocks in the roadway as you pedal the 3 miles into Greybull. Soon you pass conical red hills resembling the Painted Desert.

In a few minutes, you coast downhill, then climb up and over a bridge into Greybull. The biggest attractions in this cowboy town are refreshments after your long, dry trek. After a cool snack, you may want to rent a motel room, then visit the Greybull Museum at 325 Greybull Avenue, with history and geology exhibits. From June to September 15th, the hours are 8 A.M. to 9 P.M. daily; the rest of year, 1 to 5 P.M. daily except Sunday. Traffic is hectic in Greybull the second weekend in June, when the Days of '49 Rodeo is held. If you can tolerate madding crowds, this is an exciting time to tour here.

Before returning the next day to Cody, you may want to try a delightful spin east of Greybull on U.S. 14 for 15 miles, going gradually uphill along Shell Creek to scenic Shell Canyon, a lovely sandstone gorge. If you arrive early enough in the afternoon or stay over a day in Greybull, take this extended jaunt in late afternoon, when it is particularly pleasant. You can stay overnight in tiny Shell and watch the sunset glow on the sandstone canyon walls.

WHERE TO STAY

Motels are available in Cody and Greybull. Reservations are advised during the tourist season. Motels in Cody include Cedar Mountain Lodge, 803 Sheridan Avenue, (307) 587-2248; Holiday, 1807 Sheridan Avenue, (307) 587-4258; Holiday Inn, 1701 Sheridan Avenue, (307) 587-5555; and Lazy P.S., 1456 Sheridan Avenue, (307) 587-4431. In Greybull: Glenn's, 1135 North 6th Street, (307) 765-4444; K-Bar, 300 Greybull Avenue, (307) 765-4426; and Yellowstone, 247 Greybull Avenue, (307) 765-4456.

Campgrounds are numerous in Cody and Greybull, the only problem being finding a camp open during off-season. Year-round campgrounds are found near Cody, just a bit off the bike tour: Silver City and River's Bend camps, half a mile north of Cody on Wyoming 120, and the Lazy A, half a mile west of town on U.S. 14, 16, and 20.

Other campgrounds: Cody KOA, three and a half miles east of Cody on U.S. 14, 16, and 20; open May 15th to October 1st; $3 for four. For reservations, write Cody KOA, Box 1407, Cody, Wyoming 82414. Kampgrounds of America, 2 miles east of Cody on U.S. 14, 16, and 20; open May 15th to Labor Day; $2.50 per family. Buffalo Bill Village, in downtown Cody on U.S. 14, 16, and 20; open May to cold weather; $3. Greybull KOA, in Greybull, four blocks east of U.S. 14, 16, and 20, open May 1st to September 30th; $3 for four. For reservations, write Greybull KOA, Box 792, Greybull, Wyoming 82426, or phone (307) 765-2555. Mustang Camper Village, a quarter of a mile north of the U.S. 14 and U.S. 16 and 20 junction; open year round; $2.50 for two. For reservations, write Mustang Camper Village, 326 North 6th Street, Greybull, Wyo-

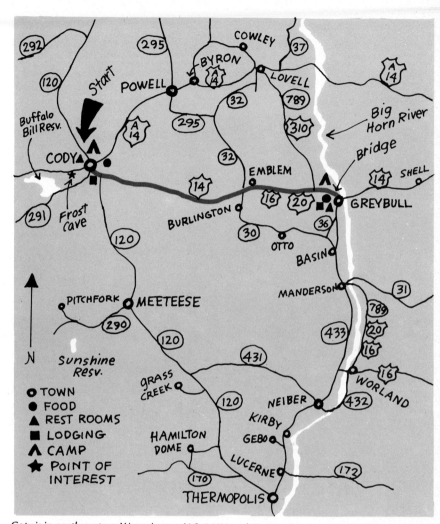

Cody is in northwestern Wyoming on U.S. 14/20 and 16; 81 miles east of Yellowstone National Park via U.S. 14/20 and 16; 433 miles west of Rapid City, South Dakota, via U.S. 14, I-90, and U.S. 14, 16/20.

ming 82426, or phone (307) 765-9992. Spences Camper Court, in Shell; open year round; $2.50 for two. For reservations, write Spences Camper Court, Box 100, Shell, Wyoming 82441, or phone (307) 765-2994.

FOR SPARE PARTS, REPAIRS, FURTHER INFORMATION

Royal Sporting Goods, 1201 Sheridan Avenue, Cody, Wyoming; (307) 587-5473. This shop sells parts and handles repairs on 10-speeds. Ask Bob Wilson about current road conditions in case of doubt.

NEARBY

Wyoming is vacationland, and you could spend a week or a month exploring here, especially if you come during off-season when traffic is light. For adventurous expert cyclists, Shell Canyon offers a strenuous trek around hairpin curves between vertical sandstone walls to summit forests and alpine meadows. (See page 181 for details.) Most vacation possibilities in this vicinity lie west of Cody, through Shoshone National Forest to fabulous Yellowstone National Park and then south to the spectacular Grand Tetons. Experienced cyclists should definitely try the exhilarating mountain bikeway through Grand Teton National Park. The terrain here is tough, but the scenery is some of the West's grandest. See page 193 for details.

89. WESTERN WILDERNESS RIDE

Wyoming's Wapiti Valley offers one of the most Western tours around. The gorges, gulches, barren prairies, jagged rock mountains, and river canyons hint of Indian wars and pioneers carving homesteads from a hostile land. Being a cowboy is still an authentic life-style here, even down to wearing chaps, silver belt buckles, and ten-gallon hats.

Starting in Cody, this tour has intentionally been left open-ended: you can ride into the prairie 10 miles or 50 miles. Shoshone National Forest's boundary or Pahaska Campground make good turnaround points, but if you have time, you may choose to ride clear into Yellowstone to cycle the Yellowstone Loop, 78 miles from Cody. (See page 189 for details.) Cody, of course, is best known as Buffalo Bill's old stomping ground. Western lore abounds in Buffalo Bill Village, on Sheridan Avenue between 16th and 18th Streets. Rodeos, too, are held from mid-

DISTANCE:	As long or short as you like.
TERRAIN:	Varies from flat prairies to steep hills; an overall gradual incline going west.
TRAFFIC:	Light in May and September; heavy during the tourist season.
DIFFICULTY:	Not recommended for beginners or families with small children.
BEST TIME:	May and September are idyllic, with light traffic and temperatures in the 70's. Nights are cool.
LOCATION:	Shoshone National Forest, west of Cody, Wyoming.

June through August every night but Sunday. Being so near Yellowstone has made this small frontier town tourist-conscious, but you can still feel a genuine hospitable Western mood.

Buy all the food you will need for the tour before leaving Cody. Also bring tools and spare parts. You pedal west on U.S. 14, 16, and 20, a straight, flat highway, unlike the winding, narrower road to follow. (Note: At this writing, plans for widening the road were being made. Inquire about current road conditions at the shop listed at the end of the tour description.)

About a mile from Cody, pull over to see the colorful river canyon on your right. About a mile farther, you see a road winding steeply down to the Shoshone River bank, where you can explore, go rock hounding (agates are plentiful throughout Wyoming), or fish if you have a license for rainbow and cutthroat trout.

Beyond the bridge spanning the

Cody is in northwestern Wyoming on U.S. 14/20 and 16; 81 miles east of Yellowstone National Park via U.S. 14/20 and 16; 433 miles west of Rapid City, South Dakota, via U.S. 14, I-90, and U.S. 14, 16, and 14/20.

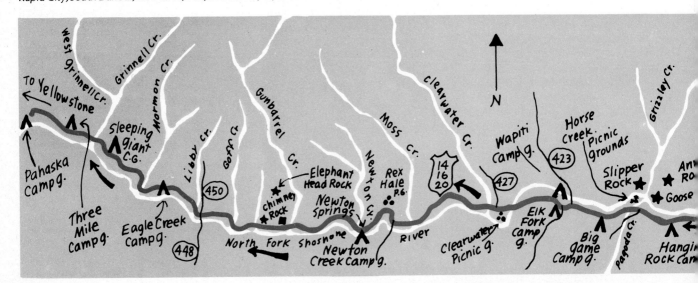

Shoshone, the road winds through two short rock tunnels, then a long tunnel. Though the long tunnel is well lighted, there's no shoulder or walkway, so be careful. A slight coast takes you past Buffalo Bill Reservoir, a blue lake backed by snow-topped mountains. You can see an enticing road leading around the lake's shores, but this soon becomes gravel and unsuitable for biking. Buffalo Bill State Park, a bit farther, has camping, boat rentals, and fishing. You may even choose to begin your ride from here.

You climb gradually uphill now through Wapiti Valley's wide dude ranches backed by ragged rock foothills. Rabbit brush add mint aromas to the fresh air. About six and a half miles beyond the state park, you cross a bridge, then pass a couple of motels and cafés where you can stop for snacks. Beyond here you plunge down and wind around a sharp, narrow curve beneath a rock ledge. Soon the road widens, and you cross a narrow bridge and begin a steep climb beside a vertical rock wall. Stay in your lane and don't meander. With the tunnels before and the sharp curves, this is the tour's most difficult section and not

recommended for beginners or families. As you reach the hilltop, stop to rest beneath the trees. Then just beyond the campground on your left (about a mile from the hill), watch out for cars on the narrow bridge. During the next 7 miles, you cross four more similar bridges and pass three campgrounds. On an untraveled spring or autumn weekday, beginners and families could start riding west from one of these camps, located 30 to 35 miles west of Cody; the terrain, while all uphill as you head west, has gentle, easy grades.

As you pass the third camp, huge grotesque ragged rocks block the horizon on your right, while the Shoshone River runs on your left. Stop to sit quietly along the riverbanks, look at the mountains and the prairie grown with buffalo grass and rabbit brush. In late afternoon you may glimpse deer, elk, moose, or antelope. About 2 miles beyond the fifth narrow bridge, you pass a motel, then coast gently past Chimney Rock. Though you find some motels and cafés, don't count on anything being open between Labor Day and Memorial Day (Yellowstone's off-season).

The road becomes really bumpy

about a mile beyond Eagle Creek Campground. Then you coast through meadows to a small stream and pedal past Sleeping Giant Campground, Shoshone Lodge, and Three Mile Campground. You roll over a few hills to Pahaska Campground, the last stop before leaving Shoshone National Forest. From here you can climb the steep Absaroka Mountain slopes into Yellowstone or return to Cody.

More Notes on Exploring

Shoshone National Forest is basically a backcountry wilderness. If you enjoy hiking, consider taking a few days to explore Glacier Primitive Area, where you hike past lakes, streams, deep chasms, and waterfalls and climb mountains to see some of the largest glaciers in the United States, including Alaska. Other regions in the forest offer excellent wilderness travel. If you don't feel like striking out on your own (and you shouldn't without lots of experience), numerous dude ranches in the area offer backcountry trips. For further information, write the Wyoming Travel Commission, 2320 Capitol Avenue, Cheyenne, Wyoming 82001, and ask for their "Dude Ranches and Resorts" brochure.

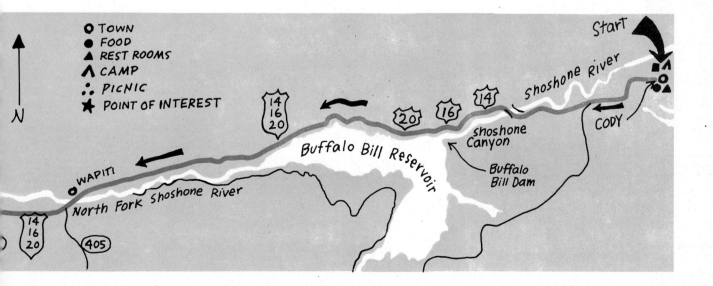

WHERE TO STAY

Cody has numerous motels. During off-season you should have no trouble getting a room.

Campgrounds are listed in the above description, but for ease in locating them, here's a quick reference list so you will know how far down the road they are. Warning: If you come here in spring or after September 30th, many campgrounds will be closed. On this ride the last campground to close is Hitching Post Campground, 20.3 miles west of Cody. The fee for Shoshone National Forest campgrounds is $1 unless otherwise stated.

Mileage west of Cody

2.5 Gateway Campground, May 1st to November 1st. For reservations, write the campground at P.O. Box 25, Cody, Wyoming 82414 or phone (307) 587-2561.

9.0 Buffalo Bill State Park, May 1st to November 1st, no fee.

10.5 Lakeview Campground, April 15th to September 15th. For reservations, write the campground at Route 1, Cody, Wyoming 82414 or phone (307) 587-3957.

20.3 Hitching Post Campground, May 1st to December 1st. For reservations, write the campground at North Fork Star Route, Cody, Wyoming 82414 or phone (307) 587-4149.

28.5 Big Game, Shoshone National Forest, June 1st to September 30th.

29.5 Elk Fork, Shoshone National Forest, June 1st to September 30th.

29.5 Wapiti, Shoshone National Forest, June 1st to September 30th.

37.3 Newton Creek, Shoshone National Forest, June 1st to September 30th.

44.7 Eagle Creek Campground, Shoshone National Forest, June 1st to September 30th.

47.5 Sleeping Giant, Shoshone National Forest, June 15th to September 30th.

48.5 Three Mile, Shoshone National Forest, June 15th to September 30th.

49.5 Pahaska, Shoshone National Forest, June 15th to September 30th.

WAPITI VALLEY AUTUMN WILDFLOWERS

On Wapiti Valley's arid sagebrush prairies, wildflowers bloom abundantly in spring, including wild roses, wild irises, and sunflowers. Autumn wildflowers, being less conspicuous, are best appreciated and spotted from a bike. Three common autumn prairie wildflowers are the big sagebrush, rabbit brush, and goldenrod. Here's what they look like.

Big sagebrush blooms in late August or early September with tiny yellowish blossoms. Year round you can spot this fragrant gray-green shrub's foliage clusters.

Sometimes the big sagebrush sprouts up to five feet tall, with a trunk as much as three inches in diameter.

Rabbit brush usually appears to be just a scraggly dull weed with whitish woolly leaves and stems, but in late summer yellow-gold blossoms cover this shrub. Wherever you see rabbit brush, watch, too, for rabbits, elk, pronghorn, and deer which dine on the foliage, especially in late afternoon.

Goldenrod, another late-summer and autumn flower, is found throughout the Wapiti Valley. Several species flourish here, but all bear small golden flowers which grow only on one side of the branches and have alternate leaves. There's a myth that goldenrod causes hay fever, but in fact goldenrod pollen is too heavy to float on the wind. Around your campfire you may want to try a cup of goldenrod tea. Just dry a batch of leaves, crumble them into a cup, add boiling water, steep for five minutes, strain, and drink.

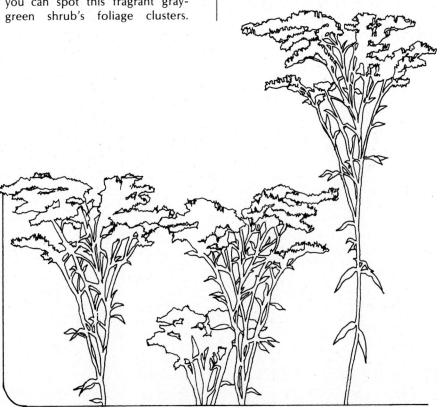

90. 91. HILLY YELLOWSTONE LOOPS

Yellowstone has so much to do, so much to see, you could spend a week here viewing geysers, hot springs, waterfalls, meadows, lemon-yellow canyons, forests, mountains, and lakes. The real highlights, though, will probably be the special secret spots you discover on your own. You can tour Yellowstone during summer if you don't mind cars, but for an experience you will never forget, try to come in spring, around May 15th, before park roads are open to cars, and when meadows grow fragrant with flowers. Another pleasant biking time is autumn, when traffic lightens, days are crisp, and the bull elk can be heard bugling.

To see if the snows are gone around Norris Junction, Madison, and Old Faithful, you can phone Bob Schaap, who rents bikes at the Dude Motor Inn in West Yellowstone; (406) 646-7316. By the way, the fact that cyclists can enter the park early is unofficial policy, so you may get the runaround if you phone Yellowstone's visitor information service. Also, if you enter the park before it officially opens, you may have to file an itinerary with the rangers, telling them where you plan to bike and stop overnight.

For your convenience, we have divided the Yellowstone 145-mile Grand Loop into two shorter tours; if you have just a few days, it's best to tour only part of Yellowstone to give yourself time to really explore. Plan at least two days for each ride or an entire week for both tours plus further exploring along hiking trails.

NORTH YELLOWSTONE TOUR

This ride has two direct accesses: Gardiner, Montana (north), and Cooke City, Montana (northeast).

DISTANCE: North Yellowstone Tour, 70 miles. South Yellowstone Spin, 96 miles.

TERRAIN: Steep climbs, rapid descents.

TRAFFIC: Heaviest in July and August, when seventy percent of the park's tourists come here. Lightest in spring and autumn.

DIFFICULTY: Requires a 10-speed, and excellent bike control especially during the heavily trafficked tourist season. Suitable for less experienced cyclists in early spring or autumn.

BEST TIME: May or September.

LOCATION: Yellowstone National Park, Wyoming.

Admission to the park is 50¢ per cyclist.

From the north entrance, you first plunge on narrow road, then navigate short climbs and dips, followed by steep, winding climbs. As you climb, watch closely for elk; this is one of the best spots to see them. Your ride levels about 4 miles from the entrance. Then you ascend to Mammoth Hot Springs, where you can lock your bike and take a short, well-marked foot trail to steamy, terraced limestone deposits.

The road levels near frothy Rustic Falls and remains relatively flat through meadows (moose are often spotted here) and lodgepole pine forests. Beyond Obsidian Cliff, at the picnic area on your right, you can toast marshmallows or on a brisk day brew a cup of cocoa. Your legs may ache a bit on the sharp slope past Roaring Mountain, but you can rest along the shores of turquoise Twin and South Twin lakes. A few minutes later, you pass Norris Junction and reach Norris Geyser Basin, with hot bubbling springs and geysers.

To stay on the north loop, retrace your path to Norris Junction and pedal east on Norris Canyon Road, where you climb gradually about 11 miles onto Solfatara Plateau, then drop about 7 miles farther into Canyon Village. About 3 miles along this road—past Virginia Cascades— you can take the little road to your left, lock your bike, and amble through Virginia Meadows to Ice Lake, a tranquil rest or snack stop.

Canyon Village, with a grocery store and campground, makes a good overnight stop. At nearby Inspiration Point, you can spend hours photographing the sun's rays over the Grand Canyon of the Yellowstone, with its lemon and orange rock walls. For more exciting photographic effects of thundering Lower Falls, try the angles from the strenuous footpath starting at Inspiration Point.

On your second day, restock your snack larder and head north. You climb easily through Dunraven Pass to Mount Washburn, one of the best spots to see bighorn sheep. Then you coast all the way with only gradual rises past Tower Junction.

This stretch contains the fewest typical tourist attractions (no Old Faithfuls, bubbling mud pots, or sulfur springs). Hence some impatient motorists race past the idyllic meadows, forests, and lakes, so be careful. Stay at least a day and explore the woods, lie in wildflower meadows, and watch for deer, moose, and elk. As Antelope Creek slips in along your right, you know you are approaching Tower Fall Campground and Devil's Den. Then you coast on to Tower Junction and Roosevelt Lodge, a handy lemonade or hot-tea stop. If you enter the park from the northeast through Cooke City, pick up the tour here.

Riding on, you breeze easily through Pleasant Valley. Just past the spur to your left leading to the petrified tree, you can dismount and explore the footpath meandering through the forest to Lost Creek's secluded cascades. Tiny clearings here bloom with spring flowers, including yellow monkey flowers, mule-ears, and tall lavender elephant's-heads.

A gradual climb begins near Floating Island Lake. Then you roll over hills, coasting first along the Blacktail Deer Plateau and later beside Lava Canyon Creek back to Mammoth. From here retrace your ride to the north entrance.

SOUTH YELLOWSTONE SPIN

The south loop has accesses through Grand Teton National Park (south); Cody, Wyoming (east); and West Yellowstone, Montana (west). If you ride here before park roads are completely cleared of snow, you will probably have to stay within the area from Norris to Old Faithful.

Starting at Madison Junction on Grand Loop Drive, you pedal south. Soon you can get away from crowds on narrow, well-paved Firehole Canyon Road. On this 2-mile side trip, you lean into curves, diving toward the river, then climb a sharp slope to view rapids and thundering Firehole Falls. At the secluded picnic area here, venture along the path past the Firehole Cascades sign to discover a steep foot trail winding to the water.

Fountain Flats Drive, 3 miles farther south to your right and unmarked until you turn off the main road, is 1.5 miles of gravel through wildflower displays to a "primitive" bike trail, a bumpy rocky path ending eventually at Old Faithful. Though a good way to avoid traffic, this dirt trail is disastrous to tubulars; if you go this way, plan to dawdle and walk a lot.

Back on the main loop, you spin past seething geyser basins, with a gravel shoulder starting near Biscuit Basin. About 1 mile farther, you can pick up a 2.1-mile bike trail (the last segment of the primitive bike trail from Fountain Flats to Old Faithful) to avoid the trafficked freeway into the geyser complex. If the bike trail is too rugged for your tastes, the gravel shoulder on the main road continues to a smooth, busy divided highway leading past Black Sand Basin's saffron and orange pools. Watch out for traffic into Old Faithful, where you can buy snacks at Old Faithful Inn.

Riding south, you start a 1-mile climb beyond Firehole River Bridge. Then you coast to Lone Star Geyser Biking Trail, a rough, paved one-lane road meandering beside a stream to Lone Star Geyser.

A bit farther, rolling hills with several steep grades lead you past Isa Lake and twice across the Continental Divide. More easy rolling hills and a brisk downhill curve open up views of Yellowstone Lake. Two miles past West Thumb, you lose the gravel shoulder as wide, gentle curves lead you along the wildflower-sprinkled lakeshores. The small lavender-petaled flowers with yellow centers are fleabane, the bushy yellow ones are goldenrod, and the delicate white blossoms with fernlike leaves are yarrow. Several pebbled beaches in this vicinity have driftwood, and many grassy clearings allow you to rest along the water.

A steep hill begins past the picnic area 15 miles from West Thumb. Then past the Bridge Bay area, after the road divides and narrows again, you view splendid mountains across the lake.

Stop at Fishing Bridge, elbow-to-elbow deep in fishermen, to glimpse geese, gulls, mallards, and white pelicans in the water. Caution: Heavy traffic at this junction. The terrain rolls north. Then past Mud Volcano, an uphill climb brings you to Hayden Valley, a superb spot to glimpse bison, moose, and coyote.

Now you pedal along a flat plateau for miles, with the wide grasslands of Hayden Valley deep to your right. A few hills bring you to marshes where you may see hundreds of ducks and geese. Then after a vigorous climb, you reach the turnoff for Artist Point. On this side trip, you climb still higher, then coast to Artist Point, on the brink of the Grand Canyon of the Yellowstone.

A few more stiff hills bring you to Canyon Village, where you go left on Norris Canyon Road. See the North Yellowstone Tour for the road description here. As you approach Norris, watch for moose, often seen in nearby meadows.

South of Norris the road is wide as you climb past Black Nymph Lake. Then the road narrows past Artist Paint Pots Trail. Soon the Gibbon River flows over red rocks beside you. Past Gibbon Falls you encounter two picnic spots. Then after a steep 2-mile climb, you plunge to Firehole River, with lots of flat banks for resting. Passing the gaudy Paint Pots, you reach Midway Geyser Basin, the loop's end.

WHERE TO STAY

Cabins, inns, and lodges are found at key spots on both rides, with major facilities centering around Mammoth Hot Springs, Old Faithful, Fishing Bridge, Canyon Village, and Tower Junction. Also available are campers' cabins, partly or fully furnished, and

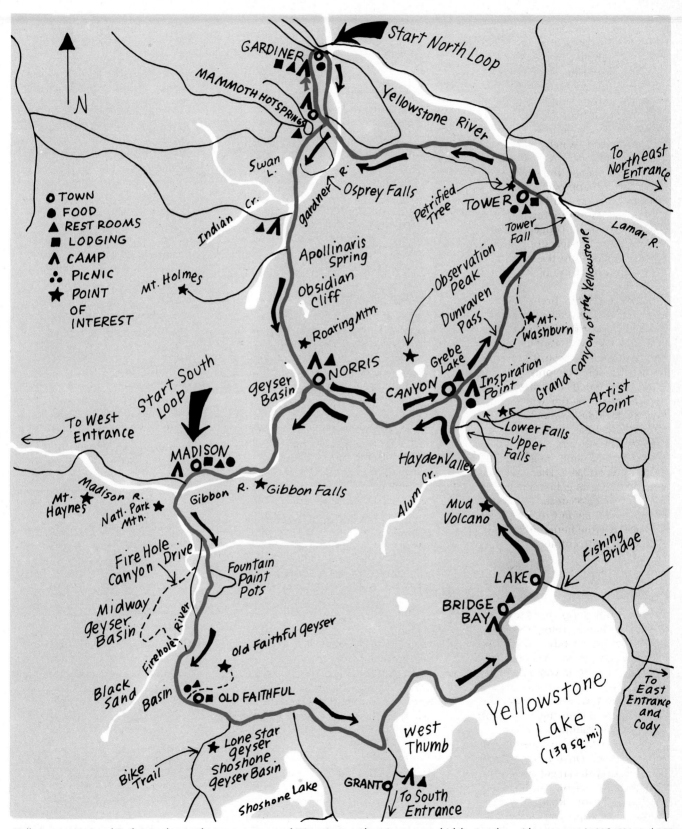

N

TOWN
FOOD
REST ROOMS
LODGING
CAMP
PICNIC
POINT
OF
INTEREST

Start North Loop

GARDINER

MAMMOTH HOTSPRINGS

Yellowstone River

To Northeast Entrance

Swan L.

Gardner R.

Osprey Falls

Petrified Tree

TOWER

Tower Fall

Lamar R.

Indian Cr.

Apollinaris Spring

Observation Peak

Obsidian Cliff

Dunraven Pass

Mt. Washburn

Mt. Holmes

Roaring Mtn.

NORRIS

Grebe Lake

Grand Canyon of the Yellowstone

Start South Loop

Geyser Basin

CANYON

Inspiration Point

Artist Point

To West Entrance

MADISON

Lower Falls
Upper Falls

Madison R.

Gibbon R.

Gibbon Falls

Hayden Valley

Mt. Haynes

Natl. Park Mtn.

Alum Cr.

Mud Volcano

Fire Hole Canyon Drive

Fountain Paint Pots

Fishing Bridge

Midway Geyser Basin

Firehole River

LAKE

Black Sand Basin

Old Faithful Geyser

BRIDGE BAY

OLD FAITHFUL

Yellowstone Lake
(139 sq. mi)

Bike Trail

Lone Star Geyser
Shoshone Geyser Basin

West Thumb

To East Entrance and Cody

GRANT

To South Entrance

Shoshone Lake

Yellowstone National Park is in the northwestern corner of Wyoming on the Montana and Idaho border, with accesses via U.S. 191 and 287 from the west, U.S. 89 and 212 from the north, U.S. 89/287 from the south, and U.S. 14/20, and 16 from the east. This map shows both the North and South tours.

cottages with or without bath. The following are open in May and September: Mammoth Hot Springs Hotel and Cabins, open May 12th to October 6th, with a coffee shop. A good bargain here are the budget cabins, renting for $10 for two or $13 for three or four. This is the only facility on the north loop which opens early and closes late. Old Faithful Snow Lodge and Cabins, open May 5th to October 4th, with either a café or cafeteria open during the same dates. Budget cabins are available at the same rates as those in Mammoth. Also here are modified budget shelters, furnished except for bedding, at $6 for one or two and $8 for three or four. Lake Lodge and Cabins, on Yellowstone Lake, between Bridge Bay and Fishing Bridge; open May 19th to September 21st, with a cafeteria open the same dates. To obtain rates and reservations for all accommodations, write Reservations Department, Yellowstone Park Company, Yellowstone Park, Wyoming 82190.

Campgrounds are available throughout the park on a first-come first-served basis. During the tourist season, from mid-June through August, you should expect these major camps to be filled: Madison Junction, Grant Village, Bridge Bay, and Fishing Bridge, all on the south loop tour. Less popular but still often crowded during the tourist season are Mammoth, Indian Creek, Tower Fall, and Lava Creek campgrounds on the north loop, and Norris and Canyon Village campgrounds, shared by both the north and south loop tours.

FOR FURTHER INFORMATION

Write Superintendent, Yellowstone National Park, Wyoming 83020, or for cycling information, Bob Schaap, Dude Motor Inn, Boundary Street, West Yellowstone, Montana 59758.

NEARBY

Immediately south lies Grand Teton National Park, with 15 miles of a planned park-loop bikeway. See page 193 for details. East, through Sylvan Pass, you can ride, in Shoshone National Forest and then on to Cody, where you can visit the Whitney Gallery of Western Art. On this latter ride, the climb through Sylvan Pass is fairly easy: you gain 300 feet in 4 miles, though some stretches are steep. Then you plummet downhill and level to a gradual coast all the way to Cody. For details on this ride, see page 186.

HOW TO BIKE YELLOWSTONE'S ROUGH DIRT TRAILS

If you choose to ride the primitive bike path to Old Faithful, here are a few tips on handling the rugged terrain.

● Try to steer as much as possible for packed dirt or flat, short-grassed areas. In between the good spots, maintain speed to keep traction.

● In deep ruts, dust, or sand, stay on the uphill side of the rut or slippery spot.

● If you run into mud, pedal fast in low gear to get as much traction as possible. It's best, though, if you can manage to ride in the high areas, out of bogs and puddles.

● Always avoid patches of tall grass or weeds, which often conceal rocks, holes, and tree stumps.

● Never make big, sudden moves: brake easily, turn slightly, pedal gently. You need practice and skill to do this. You have to watch ahead and plan to maneuver around an upcoming curve in many partial turns instead of in one sweeping move; guess when to start building up speed for a hill when you are still a long distance away, and when to slow down before you descend too rapidly.

● When riding over a rock or branch, use low gear. First lift your front wheel, then lean forward to allow the back wheel to follow smoothly.

● If you start down a steep, slippery hill and your back wheel skids each time you hit a bump, sit farther back on the saddle to give your back wheel more traction.

● Always watch for traps overhead as well as on the path. If you concentrate too hard on rocks and potholes, a low-hanging limb can catch you from above.

● Finally, if you become rattled or run into particularly tough territory, dismount and walk awhile. In such rugged terrain you have to keep your poise at all times.

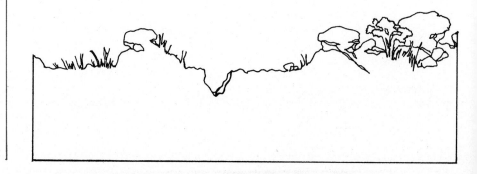

92. TETON VALLEY BIKEWAY

Pedal beneath the Grand Tetons' jagged snowy peaks. Wind through lodgepole pine forests beside mountain lakes, meander along the Snake River, climb giant hills to view blue, gray, and dusky plum mountains in every direction. Subtler scenes await you here, too, such as a shy antelope tucked between trees where hasty people never look, or a cool grass clearing dappled with delicate crimson calypso orchids.

Start at Jackson Lake Lodge and coast south on a signed white-lined bike lane running along the edge of a two-way paved asphalt road. Across the road from the lodge on Christian Pond, you may glimpse the shy, rare trumpeter swan. A mile brings you to Jackson Lake Junction, where you can proceed right on the bikeway or take a side trip left for about two and a half miles to Oxbow Bend.

Oxbow Bend Side Trip

You pedal along the Snake River beneath lodgepole pines and aspen stands. Flowering shrubs growing here include the serviceberry, bearberry, and chokecherry. Wildflowers along the river bottomlands include larkspur, rose pussytoes, Indian paintbrush, and wild phlox and roses. At Oxbow Bend a large bison herd is pastured, and you are likely to spot white pelicans during spring or autumn migrations. In early morning watch for moose and mule deer near the Snake River.

Continuing on the main tour, you plunge steeply along Jackson Lake's shore, cross a bridge, and wind to Signal Mountain Lodge, with food, lodging, camping, and a marina. Look for swamp laurel, false huckleberry, and bur marigolds along the water. Past the

DISTANCE:	30 miles round trip, excluding side trips.
TERRAIN:	Steep climbs and rapid descents.
TRAFFIC:	Heavy in summer; lighter in spring and after Labor Day.
DIFFICULTY:	Requires some experience and a 10-speed bike.
BEST TIME:	Spring or autumn, when traffic is lightest. September's crisp sunny days are idyllic. Fishing is best then, golden aspens and cottonwoods tint the slopes, and bull elks bugle in mating season. The best months for wildflowers are June and July.
LOCATION:	Grand Teton National Park, Wyoming.

lodge, experts can take an arduous, twisting trek up Signal Mountain, sprinkled in autumn with vivid orange-berried mountain ash. You find several turnouts as you climb. Hike to the summit, where views are superb: the whole Snake River valley spreads before you.

Back on the bikeway, you coast a bit away from the lake. Stop at the viewing area or in a forest clearing to rest. Your ride levels as you round Jackson Lake's southern tip. Then you dive again to North Jenny Lake Junction, where you curve

right and climb steeply to the tip of Leigh Lake. Here you can picnic, relax, or hike along Indian Paintbrush Trail, which climbs to the upper end of Indian Paintbrush Canyon, offering wide views of the forest-rimmed lakes. Along this path you spot crimson paintbrush, magenta Parry primroses, pentstemons, pinkish meadowsweet, and the succulent western red raspberry, which ripens from late July through September. The road from North Jenny Lake Junction to the bikeway's end is one-way for cars.

Beyond Leigh Lake your ride levels around Jenny Lake to the Visitor Center and the present bikeway's end (more segments are planned). Here you can register for mountaineering classes from June 20th through Labor Day. After two days of climbing crags like a spider and swinging from cliffs in a rappel, you are ready for an overnight expedition to Mount Moran, Mount Owen, or the Grand. A hiking trail leads you from the Visitor Center around Jenny Lake, past blossoming yellow mule-ears and purple elephant's heads, to Hidden Falls. Here you can picnic, ride a boat back across Jenny Lake, or continue around the lake on foot to return to the Visitor Center. There retrace your ride up and down the slopes back to Jackson Lake Lodge, from which many lake hiking trails meander through the woods.

More Exploring

Expert cyclists may want to extend their explorations by continuing south from the Visitor Center on Jenny Lake to ride the entire park loop. There is no bike shoulder, traffic can be heavy (but slow), and the terrain is rugged. At Moose Junction, stop to see Menors Ferry, a reconstructed 1892

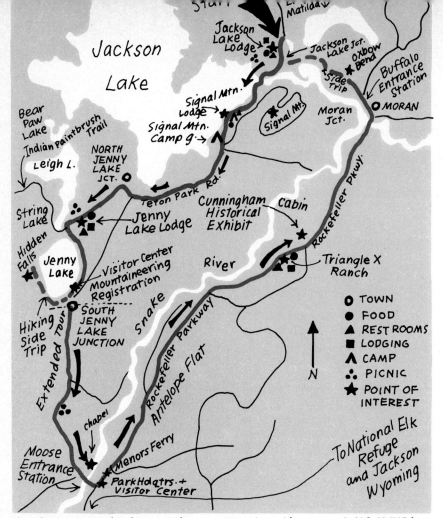

Grand Teton National Park is in northwestern Wyoming, with accesses via U.S. 89/287 from the north, U.S. 26/287 from the east, and U.S. 26/89 and 187 from the south; 49 miles south of Yellowstone National Park via U.S. 89/287.

pioneer vessel. Beyond here you wind past Antelope Flat (watch for pronghorn) and beside the Snake River, eventually curving left past Oxbow Bend and back to Jackson Lake Lodge.

WHERE TO STAY

Lodging is available at Colter Bay Cabins, just north of the tour's start, and at Jackson Lake, Jenny Lake, and Signal Mountain lodges. Reservations are advised, especially in July and August. Write the Grand Teton Lodge Company, Jackson, Wyoming 83001.

Park campgrounds operate on a first-come first-served basis, and the most convenient facilities are located near Colter Bay, Signal Mountain Lodge, and the Visitor Center on Jenny Lake.

FOR SPARE PARTS AND REPAIRS

Teton Trail Sports, at Moose Enterprises, Moose, Wyoming; (307) 733-4924. Located at the park's south entrance, this shop does repairs on 10-speeds and also has bike rentals. Other area bike shops are in Teton Village and Jackson.

FOR FURTHER INFORMATION

Write Superintendent, Grand Teton National Park, P.O. Box 67, Moose, Wyoming 83012. Ask for the brochure on biking regulations.

NEARBY

The spectacular mountain scenery in western Wyoming could occupy weeks of cycling. Visit Yellowstone, north of the Tetons (see page 189), then journey on to Cody, home of Buffalo Bill (see page 184). South of Grand Teton National Park is Jackson Hole, a Western town with old boardwalks, saloons, and tourist shops. Once in the Jackson Hole valley, you find many miles of fairly level roads, though most are narrow.

GRAND TETON WILDFLOWERS

Cycling through Grand Teton, you will glimpse hundreds of wildflowers, varying from crimson calypso orchids and wild pink geraniums to the delicate lavender-blue larkspur and lupine. Here are a few flowers you will likely spot along the lakes and wet meadows.

Parrot's-beak is delicate white, with two upper petals resembling a beak. In July you will find parrot's-beaks as you hike along Lakes Trail, while in August these blossoms are found in the high passes and canyons.

Grass-of-Parnassus, with daintily laced white blossoms, is strikingly visible near the lakes in late July and August. The flowers perch atop stems which grow two to twelve inches tall, and the smooth-edged leaves are shaped like a kidney or heart.

Monkey flower's brilliant orange-specked yellow petals are easy to see. The three lower petals are covered with tiny hairs. Look for this flower along streams and in moist meadows.

Beggar-ticks or *bur marigold* blossoms can be spotted in late July and August along Grand Teton's ponds. This yellow wildflower has raylike petals and long, narrow, sharply jagged leaves which grow opposite each other on the stem.

Fringed gentian, though common in Yellowstone, grows only in patches in Grand Teton National Park. The royal purple blossoms are elongated, with fringed edges. You can nearly always see this flower in August along the road about three quarters of a mile north of Jackson Lake Dam.

93. ROCKY MOUNTAIN RIDE

Tackle the craggy Rockies for unequaled mountaineering. Spin along a deep green ravine beside a trout-filled mountain brook, slip through cool blue spruce forests, then climb to barren Siberian tundra where only dwarf plants live and wispy clouds float far below. Nowhere will you find more rugged or rewarding cycling than here in Colorado's Rocky Mountain National Park. You trek up sharp, arduous slopes 2 miles into the sky, then plummet for 22 miles down the mountainside, always in view of the glacier-cut granite peaks glinting rose, mauve, and blue in the sun. On this high-altitude adventure, plan on taking more time for everything, even eating.

Start in Estes Park, Colorado, with full facilities including a bike shop, and leave on U.S. 34, which leads 5 miles to the park's Fall River entrance. Carry food, emergency rations, water, spare parts and tools, and warm sleeping bags and clothing. Always protect your skin from the sun, which can burn at these elevations even on cloudy days.

You enter the park, pass Aspenglen Campgrounds, and pedal on to Horseshoe Park. At Sheep Lake, lock you bike and venture into Horseshoe Park, where bighorn sheep are most likely seen as they climb down the mountain ledges. On autumn evenings you can hear the coyote's yammer.

Beyond the lake, you can go left onto narrow, well-paved, Trail Ridge Road or stay right on scenic Fall River Road, an old, narrow, one-way dirt lane with a 15-m.p.h. speed limit and a climb of 4,000 feet in 9 miles. In summer cars pack Fall River Road, but autumn traffic is often light and you may wish to try at least a short sprint on this dirt road for spectacular views

Trail Ridge Road leads you above the tree line, with sweeping views of deep green valleys and jagged granite peaks. Watch throughout the park for loose gravel on the roadway. Past Many Parks Curve, where you view half the park below you, lock your bike and walk along Hidden Valley Trail through spruce and fir woods. In the creek along the path, watch for the dipper, a small dark gray bird which runs underwater along stream bottoms for food; you will usually find his nest behind a waterfall. Wildflowers sprinkle the nooks; look for the Rocky Mountain iris, the plains erysimum, and the vivid scarlet pentstemon. In early morning you may glimpse elk here.

Beyond Rainbow Curve, offering wide views of the Mummy Range to the north, your legs strain as you climb from fir, spruce, and pine forests to 12,000-foot-high tundra. Pause at Rock Cut to appreciate the views of peaks along the Continental Divide. You may want to lock your bike here to hike 1 mile round trip through tundra meadowlands, where you see vividly blossoming dwarf plants, mosses, and lichens, able to survive the frosty winds. Wildlife is scarce here, but watch for the yellow-bellied marmot sunning himself on rocks and for the small rabbit-like pika.

Four miles through tundra bring you to Fall River Pass. The reward and relief you feel at the summit you will never forget. Stop for a snack and long rest at the restaurant. Then plunge rapidly downhill, dropping 4,000 feet to Grand Lake. Soon you glide through Milner Pass and cross the Continental Divide. Enjoy this thrilling, well-earned coast, but take care not to swing wide on the curves.

Streams, lakes, and ranches soon break the pine forests, and as the afternoon shadows lengthen you should see deer and elk grazing in the meadows. From Kawuneeche Valley, you coast beside the Colorado River all the way to Grand Lake. Near dusk you can sit quietly by a stream to watch beaver building their dams.

Camp overnight at Timber Creek, or if you have the stamina, go 4 miles past Grand Lake to Green Ridge Campgrounds in Arapaho National Forest. You could also stay at a motel in Grand Lake. You may want to spend a day along Grand and Shadow Moun-

DISTANCE:	120 miles round trip.
TERRAIN:	Steep climbs and rapid descents.
TRAFFIC:	Heavy on summer weekends and holidays; lightest in September.
DIFFICULTY:	For experts only, because of the strenuous terrain and wilderness quality of the tour.
BEST TIME:	September, when days are crisp and yellow aspens glint on the slopes. Midsummer is least likely for snow, but avoid summer weekends when cars are bumper to bumper.
LOCATION:	Rocky Mountain National Park, Colorado.

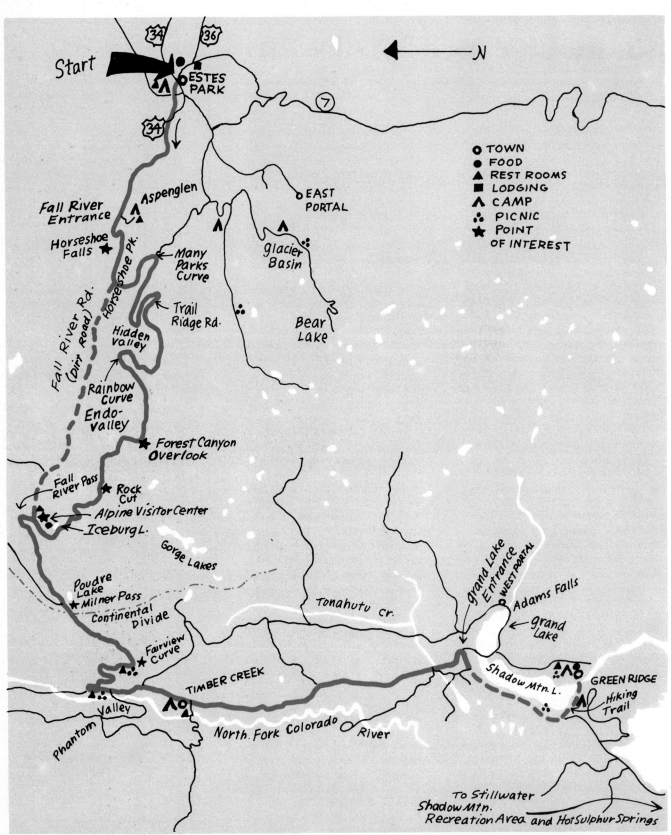

Rocky Mountain National Park is in north-central Colorado on U.S. 34; 70 miles northwest of Denver via I-25 and U.S. 34; 87 miles southwest of Cheyenne, Wyoming, via I-25 and U.S. 34.

tain lakes to explore the footpaths, swim in the icy mountain water, or trek through the mountain wilderness. Stock up on supplies at Grand Lake before pedaling back over the mountains to Estes Park.

WHERE TO STAY

Estes Park and Grand Lake both have motels. Reservations are advised for Grand Lake accommodations. Here are a few motels in the Grand Lake area: Blue Bird, 3 miles south of Grand Lake on Route 34. For reservations, write Blue Bird, Box 433, Grand Lake, Colorado 80447, or phone (303) 627-3660. Driftwood Lodge, 3 miles south of Grand Lake on Route 34. For reservations, write Driftwood Lodge, Box 609, Grand Lake, Colorado 80447, or phone (303) 627-3654. Riggs AA, west of midtown on State 278. For reservations, write Riggs AA, Box 66, Grand Lake, Colorado 80447, or phone (303) 627-3344. Western Brands, on State 278 about half a mile east of Route 34. For reservations, write Western Brands, Box 493, Grand Lake, Colorado 80447, or phone (303) 627-3310. For a complete list, write the Chamber of Commerce, Grand Lake, Colorado 80447.

Park campgrounds are usually open June through September and operate on a first-come first-served basis, except for several group areas in Glacier Basin and Aspenglen which may be reserved. During July and August, expect campgrounds to be filled by midmorning. Camps along the tour route include the following: Aspenglen, on Fall River Road at the tour's start, just after you enter the park. Timber Creek, about 8 miles below Milner Pass; open June 1st to September 30th. Green Ridge, part of Shadow Mountain National Recreation Area, 4 miles south of Grand Lake; open June through October; $2. Stillwater, part of Shadow Mountain National Recreation Area, 8 miles south of Grand Lake; open June through October; $2. Estes Park also has numerous commercial campgrounds.

FOR FURTHER INFORMATION

Write Superintendent, Rocky Mountain National Park, Estes Park, Colorado 80517.

JUST IN CASE IT SNOWS

High-mountain weather can be devious. One minute you're sailing along in brisk September breezes and the next you're blinded by snowflakes. Hopefully you will never have to ride on snow or ice, but just in case you do, here are some tips to help.

• Pedal slowly. This is the only way to handle icy roads. The minute you speed, you start slipping, but if you go slowly and do happen to lose control, you can stop without a bad tumble.

• Watch ahead for skidding cars and always have a soft grassy spot or snowbank picked out to dive into if necessary.

• Even on slight downhill grades, try to locate soft snowbanks or other good spots along the way to fall into just in case you slip or skid.

• Never make sudden movements. Brake slowly, accelerate easily, and turn cautiously.

• Be prepared with a cozy, tight knit cap and warm wool gloves. Leather-palmed gloves keep your hands from slipping on the handlebars.

94. FLAT ROCKY MOUNTAIN RIDE

On this tour you experience the mountains—taste the crisp air, walk on smooth rocks in a cold clear brook, hear the wind rush through forests, see widely varied scenery—all without leaving the flatlands. An idyllic way for families and beginners to see the mountains without confronting knotty, twisting roads and hazardous hairpin curves, this Colorado plains ride has an added attraction: a well-paved six-foot shoulder all the way from Pueblo to Beulah.

Colorado mountain temperatures vary considerably even during one day, so bring lots of light warm layers of clothing which you can put on or shed as needed. If you happen to be here when there are high winds, try to plan your ride for a calmer day.

Your tour begins in Pueblo, located in Colorado's Arkansas Valley. Here you find much children's entertainment: a zoo, a children's farm, an amusement center in the city park on Goodnight Avenue, and swimming and children's fishing at Mineral Palace Park on Main Street. Park your car at Roncalli School, then ride southwest of town on State 76 into a wide desert valley of cactus, vivid scarlet Indian paintbrush, and wild purple asters. Little creeks crisscross your path, and soon outside town you cross a bridge. You encounter three such bridges on the route, and these are the only spots where the shoulder narrows; watch ahead for the bridges and plan to cross them when all cars have passed.

Beyond the bridge, you coast onto Boggs Flat. Look to your right for the prairie dog village here. Though it may not seem so at first, this area has abundant wildlife; watch closely and you will see quick brown lizards and antelope squirrels darting across the road or red-spotted toads hopping beside

DISTANCE:	50 miles round trip.
TERRAIN:	Flat, with a few easy hills.
TRAFFIC:	Light on weekdays; heavier on weekends.
DIFFICULTY:	Excellent for beginners and families.
BEST TIME:	Weekdays, anytime but winter.
LOCATION:	Pueblo to Beulah, Colorado.

the streams. You find no formal stopping areas from Pueblo to Beulah, so be sure to bring lots of water and all the snacks you need. You can pull off the road anywhere to rest, picnic, and enjoy the scenery.

Nearing Beulah, you coast into a wooded valley and find yourself surrounded by forests of cottonwoods, honey locusts, spruce, and pine. In autumn the quaking aspen leaves with their silvery undersides turn brilliant yellow. Soon you cross the bridge spanning the St. Charles River and reach a fork: left takes you to Pueblo Mountain Park and right takes you across the bridge on a back-roads side trip along a rushing mountain stream.

Mountain Stream Side Trip

Go right—across the bridge—where you soon reach another fork. Turn right again and ride onto a hard, compacted dirt road beside Panther Creek, a clear Rocky Mountain stream. Soon you

pass a cluster of closely spaced homes and cross a culvert. Take the first left past the culvert; it's a sharp turn. This road is more abandoned than the first, and you will probably want to save your exploring for here. Hike among the pines, collect pine cones, wade in the brook, or catch a trout for dinner. Two bridges and a sharp right, then left, take you back into Beulah.

Follow the map back to State 76 and pedal on to Pueblo Mountain Park, a good place for picnicking, hiking, and exploring. Return to Pueblo the same way you came. The return trip has two steep hills: Beulah Hill, just outside of Beulah, and Rock Creek Hill, beyond the prairie dog village on Boggs Flat.

For an Extra Day or Two

Though our "safety ride" ends just beyond Beulah, where the six-foot shoulder stops, you can go on to explore the delightful San Isabel National Forest. Roads beyond Pueblo Mountain Park become narrow and winding, but during the week these are lightly traveled. You can continue south on State 76, turn onto State 165 and follow 165 clear into Colorado City, about 35 miles from Pueblo Mountain Park.

On the way, stop awhile at the San Isabel recreation area, with picnicking, fishing, camping, and boating on the lake. Then wind along through deep forests. Beyond San Isabel, for a really off-the-beaten-track side trip, take the first left from San Isabel onto a gravel road. See if your tires can take it before you go too far. Here you ride through quiet green pastureland with lots of trees and wildlife. Stop beside the fencerows to find chokecherries or walk along the meadows through blooming wild irises and purple

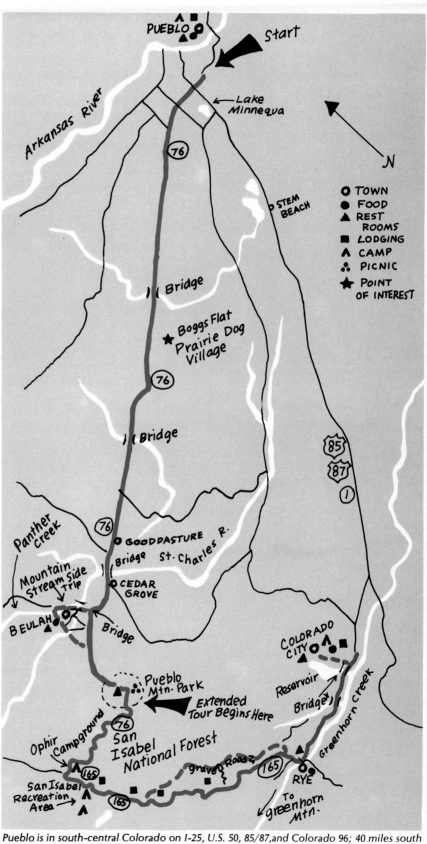

Pueblo is in south-central Colorado on I-25, U.S. 50, 85/87, and Colorado 96; 40 miles south of Colorado Springs via I-25.

asters. This gravel road eventually deadends into State 165 again. (Check the map and watch closely so you do not turn off on one of the completely undeveloped roads.) All along this ride, Greenhorn Mountain towers over 12,000 feet to your right.

Beyond Rye, a good snack stop, you pedal a few more miles, cross a bridge, and go a bit farther into tiny Colorado City, where you can swim in the pool and ride to the reservoir. Return to Pueblo the same way you came for a total ride of about 120 miles. (Note: Bikes are illegal on I-25.)

WHERE TO STAY

There are many motels in Pueblo, including the Downtown, 115 East 8th Street, (303) 542-1061, and the Town House, 8th Street at Santa Fe Avenue, (303) 543-6537. Another possibility is the Holiday Inn on State 165 near I-25 in Colorado City; (303) 676-3315. You also find motels scattered between San Isabel and Rye.

Campgrounds: Lake Isabel, on State 165, described in the tour; open May 18th to October 18th; free. Ophir, on State 165 about 3 miles *north* of the State 76 junction; open May 25th to October 25th; free. (Note: This campground is the nearest one to Beulah, but you don't pass it on any of the tours described. From Beulah go south on State 76 about 12 miles to State 165, then turn right and go another 3 miles.) KOA Campgrounds, Colorado City; open year round; $3 for two. Greenborn Meadows, 5 miles west of Colorado City on State 165; open May 1st to September 15th; $2 for six.

FOR FURTHER INFORMATION

Dorothy L. Urban, 3601 Azalea, Pueblo, Colorado; (303) 561-2715. Dorothy told us about this bike tour and will be glad to tell you anything else you would like to know about this or other rides from Pueblo.

WILD COLORADO CHOKECHERRY DELIGHTS

If you take to the back roads on this ride in summer, you will undoubtedly discover trees laden with succulent chokecherries. After a hot ride, snack on these raw juicy berries, then gather as many as you need to carry home for chokecherry pie or for a unique delight—cold wild chokecherry soup.

Cold Wild Chokecherry Soup

4 cups pitted chokecherries
3 cups water
¾ cup sugar
2 teaspoons cornstarch
1 lemon rind
1 cinnamon stick

Combine the water and sugar in a saucepan and boil. Then add the cherries, lemon rind, and cinnamon stick, cover, and simmer for one hour. Strain to remove the cherries, lemon rind, and cinnamon stick. Then thicken a bit if you like with cornstarch, simmer until the soup clears, and chill. Taste this soup as you cook it and add your own touches. If you prefer a sweeter soup, add more sugar. After chilling, you may wish to flavor with half a cup of your favorite dry red wine.

95. MESA VERDE JOURNEY

Discover an ancient city built into the cliffs on this tabletop mesa spin in Colorado. While we know much of the history of Mesa Verde, some mysteries remain. What drove the inhabitants to desert these elaborate "apartment houses," built at such effort, after living in them less than a century? Had the enemies against whom they had built their fortifications finally disappeared? Or had the struggle to grow crops in the desert become too hard? A feeling of the unknown and of the mysterious past make this bike tour an unforgettable journey.

Beginners will want to tour only the Chapin Mesa, while experts can start at the park entrance. Near the entrance, there is a small café at Point Lookout Lodge where you can buy breakfast. Then you tackle a long, steep climb with tough hairpin curves up Navaho Hill and through a lighted quarter-mile tunnel. Park roads are well paved but have no shoulders, so be careful. After the tunnel, climb on to Montezuma Valley Overlook, from which you survey wide valleys backed by mountains. About halfway between the entrance and headquarters is Park Point. This overlook offers superb views of the entire "four corners" region, so called because it includes areas of Arizona, Utah, New Mexico, and Colorado.

As you plunge downhill toward Chapin Mesa, stop for a snack at Far View Terrace Restaurant. Then continue to Ruins Road and the headquarters area. Beginners can start their ride from here.

Since the ruins of the cliff dwellings are delicate and crumbling, you cannot tour them without a ranger. So stop at the Chapin Mesa Museum to make arrangements for your visit and to see artifacts

DISTANCE:	20 miles one way from the park entrance to Chapin Mesa; 12 miles for the two mesa loops.
TERRAIN:	Long, steep climb into the park, then a coast to Chapin Mesa.
TRAFFIC:	Heavy in summer; light in spring and autumn.
DIFFICULTY:	Entrance road is for experienced cyclists only. Chapin Mesa region is good for beginners.
BEST TIME:	Late April to early May and late September to early October, when traffic is light and temperatures are pleasant.
LOCATION:	Mesa Verde National Park, Colorado.

uncovered in the excavations. In midsummer, when the park is crowded, tickets to the ruins are rationed and it could take several days before you tour the major sites. Mesa-top ruins, though, can be explored on your own.

Pick up picnic basics at the small store across the road from the museum before you leave this area. Then take off on the two 6-mile self-guiding loops on the mesa top. Both loops are one-way for cars, making cycling idyllic. (Note: The park is also considering the possibility of building bikeways.)

The west loop takes you east of Spruce Tree House, a well-preserved "apartment house" with 114 rooms, to Square Tower House and numerous Pueblo ruins. At Sun Point, the cliff dwellers ripped the roof and walls from their home and carried these to a nearby canyon, where they built another dwelling into the cliffs. Farther on at Sun Temple, you have a fine view over Fewkes and Cliff canyons.

Now spin across the cliff tops and through juniper and piñon forests to the east loop. Explore Cliff Palace, then pedal above Cliff and Soda canyons to Balcony House, another cliffside village. There are picnic grounds along both loops where you can eat or rest. For the best effects, photograph the cliff dwellings in the afternoon.

After cycling the loops, pedal or drive to Morfield Campground,

about 5 miles south of the park entrance. Here you can buy camping supplies at a store and stay overnight. In the evening, hike along Knife Edge Trail for one and a half miles to Montezuma Valley Overlook, a splendid spot to watch the sunset over Montezuma Valley.

WHERE TO STAY

Point Lookout Lodge at the park entrance offers hotel-type accommodations and family cabins, and is open from early May to mid-October. You can make reservations as you enter the park. Other cabins are found at Spruce Tree Terrace. Motel rooms are available at Far View Terrace at the top of Navajo Hill.

Camping is permitted only at Morfield Campground, operated on a first-come first-served basis. The camp is crowded in summer.

FOR FURTHER INFORMATION

Write Superintendent, Mesa Verde National Park, Colorado 81330.

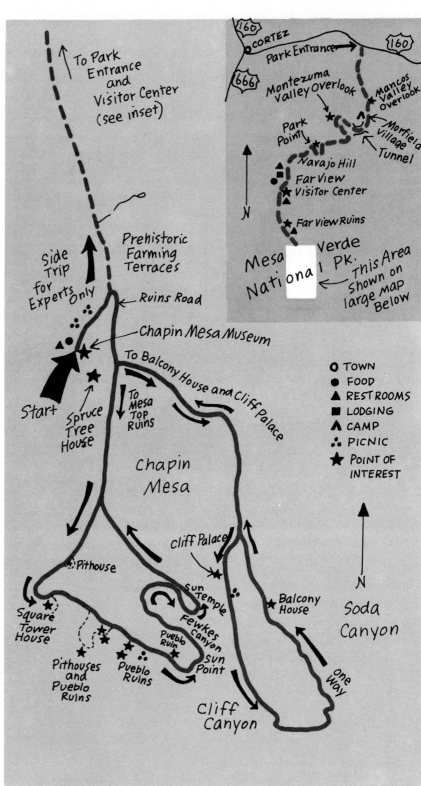

Mesa Verde National Park is in southwestern Colorado off U.S. 160; 371 miles southwest of Denver via I-70, Colorado 91, U.S. 24, 285, 50, 550, and 160.

valleys become shadowed and hill-crests blaze with sunlight. Return to Kooskia via the same route: you will discover many new delights the second time through the forests.

WHERE TO STAY

Numerous campgrounds are mentioned in the text and marked on the map. You also find motels in Kooskia, Syringa, Lowell, Powell (Lochsa Inn Lodge), Lolo Hot Springs, Fishers, Lolo, and Missoula. Cabins are available in Lowell and Lolo Hot Springs.

FOR SPARE PARTS AND REPAIRS

You find no bike shops until Missoula, so bring all necessary tools and spare parts with you.

MOUNTAIN ELDERBERRY SNACKS

As they came through Lolo Pass, Lewis and Clark may well have munched on the juicy blue-black elderberries growing abundantly throughout this portion of the Bitterroot Mountains. If you journey here in late summer or early autumn, you will see the road lined with clumps of elderberry bushes. Don't eat these berries fresh. Dry them before your campfire instead for a sweet dessert. In the morning for breakfast, add the rest of your elderberries to pancakes. For a quick pancake dough, buy one of the complete pancake mixes at any grocery store and carry some in your pack. All you have to add is water. You can also add dried elderberries to your "gorp" or keep them separate as a quick-energy nibble.

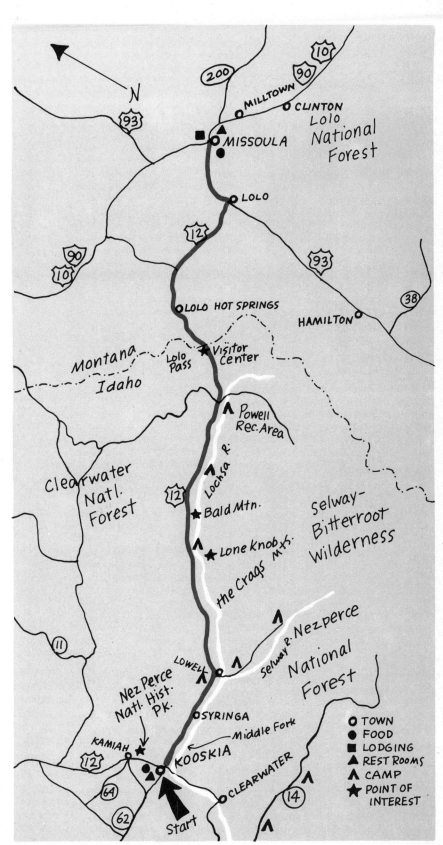

Kooskia is in northern Idaho on U.S. 12 and Idaho 13; 143 miles southwest of Missoula, Montana, via U.S. 93 and 12.

97. LEWIS AND CLARK TREK

Though Lewis and Clark explored this path thoroughly over a hundred and fifty years ago, unspoiled delights still await you along the Clearwater River beneath leathery foothills and the snowy Clearwater Mountains. Elk and moose feed in the meadows, mountain goats bound from cliff to cliff, and giant steelhead swim in the cold waters. Along the streams, rock hounds can unearth aquamarines, rubies, agates, agatized and opalized wood, jaspers, garnets, and diamonds.

Lewiston lies along the Snake and Potlatch rivers, deep in a mountain valley. If you arrive early, take an hour to climb up arduous U.S. 95 north, where you have splendid views of the whole area. Be careful coasting back down: the steep switchbacks can be hazardous. Lewiston has many wilderness attractions: gem garnets are abundant along Emerald Creek; giant sturgeon and steelhead fill the rivers; rodeos are held in September, and stout adventurers can take two- or three-day excursions into Snake River's scenic Hells Canyon. (For information, write Hells Canyon Excursions, Box 368M, Lewiston, Idaho 83501.)

Gather picnic supplies and fill your water bottle before leaving town east on scenic U.S. 12. The road is flat and straight, with wide shoulders along the clear blue river. Behind the river rise softly shaded hills. Traffic can be heavy as you pedal through part of the Nez Percé Indian Reservation. At the junction of U.S. 95 stay left on U.S. 12. Here you can visit Nez Percé National Historic Park headquarters and hike a bit on the original Lewis and Clark Trail.

Trout-filled Clearwater River rushes beside you throughout the tour and offers endless rest stops. The water varies from blue cascades to still black pools mirroring the golden hills. Beyond the first bridge, 12 miles from Lewiston, watch out for the railroad tracks, beyond which there's a nice spot leading down to the river. Two miles farther, you tackle another rugged track and can stop at a restaurant. As you pedal, the leathery hills gradually give way to pines, and about 23 miles from Lewiston, the hills grow thick with evergreens. Stop beneath the trees, collect cones for your evening campfire, or forage for juicy wild berries.

The gas station on U.S. 12 near the bridge to the small mountain hamlet of Lenore has a snack bar and limited picnic supplies. Just beyond the station, watch your tires on the track, then continue along the river. A mispainted line in the road almost resembles a bike path. Then you pass a campground. About a mile beyond the camp, watch for loose gravel on a wide curve which brings you to roadside tables to your left, a pleasant picnic spot. A second rest area is found one and a half miles farther, after which you spin over another narrow bridge. The shoulder all along here has gravelly spots, so be certain to stay on the road.

You have wide foothill views as you pass several turnouts followed by a steep quarter-mile pull toward Orofino. On the climb you pick up an extra lane, but lose the shoulder. Past Orofino is a KOA campground with motel rooms. Soon you lose the lane, regain the shoulder, and come to a Y where you stay left, following the signs toward Missoula. Beyond this turnoff, the shoulder vanishes and you may find gravel scattered on the road.

Pine, fir, and larch forests begin to hug the road, and to your right, about 5 miles past the Y, a shaded path leads to the river's edge, a good rest stop. The shoulder has

DISTANCE:	144 miles round trip.
TERRAIN:	Gradually uphill to Kooskia, downhill back to Lewiston.
TRAFFIC:	Light.
DIFFICULTY:	Okay for beginners with 10-speeds. Not recommended for families with young riders because of narrow roads.
BEST TIME:	Late spring, summer, and early autumn, to avoid snow.
LOCATION:	Lewiston to Kooskia, Idaho.

been sporadic for miles, but now as you see the bridge to Greer and Pierce, get ready to lose the shoulder completely. Traffic is quite light, so you should have no problems.

You pass a few more roadside tables and ride through a canyon with rock walls covered with delicate ferns and velvet clumps of moss. Two narrow bridges are found here: 2 miles beyond the roadside tables at Five-Mile Creek and 4 miles later over Six-Mile Creek. Kamiah has motels and a small city park. From here it's 8 miles to Kooskia, but farther yet to campgrounds.

You cross another rickety track as you leave Kamiah, then cross the river and curve sharply right. The river calms in places, and during autumn vividly colored leaves are reflected in the placid water. Past a church is a café, then in 3 more miles you reach Kooskia, across a one-lane bridge to your right. You can stay overnight in a motel here, or if you have the stamina, pedal 20 miles farther to Wild Goose Campground in Clearwater National Forest. From here you can coast back to Lewiston or proceed through the Bitterroot Mountains and Lolo Pass. (See details for this extension on page 204.)

WHERE TO STAY

Motels are located in Lewiston, Kamiah, and Kooskia.

Campgrounds are indicated in the tour description. Other possibilities not mentioned or off the main route include the following: KOA Campgrounds, 5 miles east of Lewiston on U.S. 12. You may want to begin your tour from here. For reservations, write Cy-O-Tee KOA, 7740 N & S Highway, Lewiston, Idaho 83501, or phone (208) 743-0441. Kiwanis Park, between 5th and 10th Avenues on Snake River Avenue, Lewiston. Wild Goose Campground, almost 21 miles east of Kooskia on U.S. 12; open June 10th to October 20th; fee, $1.

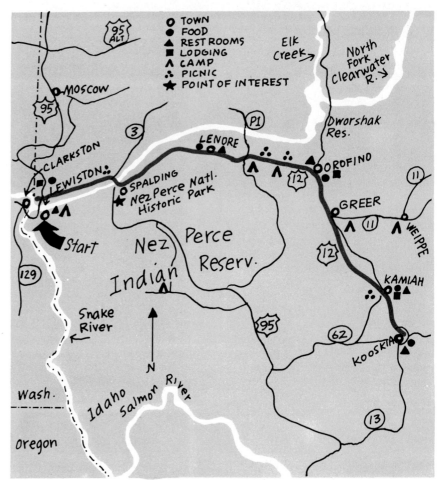

Lewiston is in northern Idaho on U.S. 95 and 12; 114 miles south of Spokane, Washington, via I-90 and U.S. 95; 275 miles north of Boise via Idaho 55 and U.S. 95.

98. IDAHO HILLS THRILL RIDE

The road from Moscow to Lewiston, Idaho, snakes through dusky golden wheatlands beneath lots of sky. In places, crisp, straight-lined farm homes dot the treeless hills, reminiscent of a Peter Hurd painting.

Your tour begins in Moscow, Idaho, a college town in the heart of the Palouse Hills country. The main attraction is the University of Idaho's tree-shaded campus. The atmosphere here is strictly collegiate: lots of pizza houses, clothes shops, and young people. A favorite ride of campus cyclists is from Moscow to Lewiston; the final 9-mile plunge downhill, though, makes this tour best ridden in relays, with someone waiting in a car at the bottom. Fill your water bottle and buy snacks before leaving town. Also be positive your brakes work well.

From Moscow pedal south on U.S. 95. Try this ride in early morning, when traffic is still light. Sunday is best of all. Just out of Moscow, you encounter three slow, gradual hills on a well-paved road. The shoulder, though only a bike wide, is marked with a white line. About 4 miles from town, as you climb the second hill, you lose the shoulder for about 50 feet, but then it picks up again.

Past the hills, you pedal on flat, straight road. The mood is both lonely and free. You can stop anytime to sit on a flat hillside.

Watch out for the railroad tracks on one flat stretch about 12 miles from Moscow. Several minutes beyond the tracks, you begin another gradual 2-mile pull, which steepens near the top. Coasting down the shoulder becomes bumpy, and you see a few shade trees where you can stop for water or snacks. At dawn the hills about you are capped with gold light. Still coasting, 19 miles outside Moscow, you pass more shade trees and roadside tables. Another mile farther are more tables, beyond which you can peer into a rocky canyon on your left. At the hill's bottom, turn left and climb a steep slope with wide views of valleys and distant mountains.

Cresting this hill, you look onto Lewiston in a wide flat valley cut by the twisty Clearwater and Snake rivers. Pull out to enjoy the scene, take photos, and survey the tangle of road awaiting you down the mountainside. From here you plunge steeply for 9 miles into Lewiston, twisting around hairpin curves, with the town always spread before you. The shoulder gets bad in spots and tiny black rocks encroach on your riding space, so take it easy. About 2 miles down the hill, you round a bend for a fantastic 270-degree view where it seems you can see for 100 miles. Beyond here there's a table to your left, a good spot to take a rest from braking. Coasting another 6 miles beside rock walls, you near the bottom where a cool green picnic area on your left looks like an oasis. From here you ride on into Lewiston.

Lewiston is a cowboy and outdoorsman town. A Mardi Gras spirit pervades the air the weekend after Labor Day—time for the annual rodeo. Then contestants mosey about town in their ten-gallon hats, and you can spend the day watching bronco busting, Brahma bull riding, and bulldogging races.

River excursions into Hells Canyon and pack trips into Clearwater National Forest are popular here, too. Or you can fish in the river for steelhead and giant sturgeon. If you like, return by bike to Moscow, but make certain you don't ride during peak traffic hours.

DISTANCE:	31 miles one way.
TERRAIN:	A few climbs and dips, then downhill all the way.
TRAFFIC:	Usually moderate, but light in early morning.
DIFFICULTY:	For experts only.
BEST TIME:	Anytime but winter, preferably in early morning or on Sunday, when traffic is light.
LOCATION:	Moscow to Lewiston, Idaho.

WHERE TO STAY

Motels are available in both Moscow and Lewiston. Reservations are recommended in Moscow, especially on weekends. Moscow: Hillcrest, 706 North Main Street, six blocks north of town on U.S. 95; (208) 882-7579. Moscow Travelodge, 414 North Main Street; (208) 882-7557. Royal Motor Inn, 120 West 6th at Jackson; (208) 882-2581. Lewiston: El Rancho, 2240 3rd Avenue, 1 mile east of town at the junction of U.S. 12 and 95; (208) 743-8517. Lewis Clark Hotel, 2nd and Main Streets, located on U.S. 12; (208) 743-3511. Lewiston has many other motels as well.

Lewiston has one campground: Cy-O-Tee KOA, 5 miles east of town on U.S. 12; $2.50 for two. For reservations, write Cy-O-Tee KOA, 7740 N & S Highway, Lewiston, Idaho 83501, or phone (208) 743-0441.

NEARBY

This ride can be extended clear to Missoula, Montana, taking you through Clearwater National Forest and over the Bitterroot Mountain Range, a total of 215 miles one way from Lewiston and one of the country's most scenic tours. See pages 207 and 204 for further details on these rides.

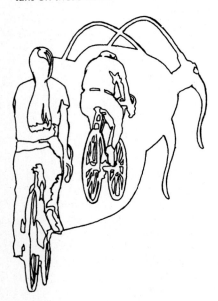

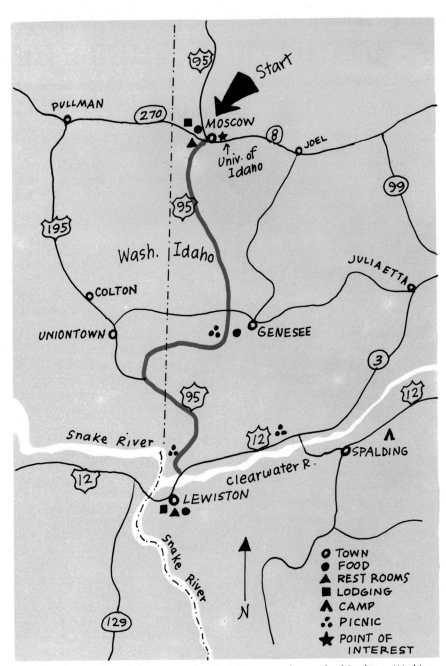

Moscow is in northern Idaho on U.S. 95 and Idaho 8; 81 miles south of Spokane, Washington, via I-90 and U.S. 95; 248 miles west of Missoula, Montana, via U.S. 93, 12 and 95.

99. 100. YAKIMA RIVER RIDES

Ellensburg, Washington, lies in a wide flat valley of fertile green and gold farmland flanked by hulking hills. In spring the hills grow green, but by mid-August they have baked suede-leather brown. After you have visited many traditional tourist spots, Ellensburg, with its friendly people, winding brooks, canyons, and distant mountain peaks, is the kind of place you would like to come home to. So if you are tired of battling winds, cars, tourists, and hills, and *really* want to get away from it all, try these two off-the-beaten-path tours along the Yakima River.

OLD CANYON RIDE

The first tour stretches 34 miles one way from Ellensburg south on Route 821 (Old Canyon Road) to Yakima. Wear light clothes and perhaps take a windbreaker in your pack for cooler days, although the canyon walls on all sides make winds practically non-existent. Park your car in Ellensburg, buy picnic supplies, and fill your water bottle. Then pedal out of town on well-paved Old Canyon Road, winding south toward Yakima beside the blue Yakima River. Speed limits for the cars that seldom pass here are 30 to 35 m.p.h. To your left rise small hills, covered in April and May with phlox and brown-eyed Susans. Stop anytime to hike up into the knolls or to ramble along the riverbanks.

If you tour in July or August, you might want to pack away a collapsed inner tube. The big pastime here is tubing on the river, and on hot summer days you can join the dozens of floaters. The sport has become so popular that every year four to six hundred tubers compete in the annual Floating Derby.

You will find rest rooms and pic-

DISTANCE:	Old Canyon Ride, 68 miles round trip. Lake Cle Elum Jaunt, 80 miles round trip.
TERRAIN:	Winding roads and rolling hills.
TRAFFIC:	Very light.
DIFFICULTY:	Good rides for anyone, including beginners and families.
BEST TIME:	Any season but winter. Also avoid hot summer days, when temperatures sometimes reach 100 degrees.
LOCATION:	Ellensburg, Washington, just off Interstate 90, in central Washington.

nic tables located in four small parks evenly spaced about every 6 or 7 miles along the tour. The road winds relatively flat between river and hills for about 15 miles. Then you roll up and over several medium grades, which should be no problem on a 5-speed or 10-speed.

At the top of the last hill, you see Roza Dam to your right. Check out the campgrounds here to see if you would like to return later to camp overnight. For the last 3 miles into Yakima, you ride on Interstate 82, with a wide shoulder and moderate traffic. Yakima lies in the center of Washington's apple country. In spring apple-blossom fragrance fills the air; in autumn roadside stands sell crispy red apples, hon-

ey, and fresh apple cider. Swimming at Yakima's four municipal pools still only costs a dime. The pools are located at South 5th Avenue and Spruce Street, South 21st Avenue and Tieton Drive, North 4th and East E Streets, and South 8th and East Beach Streets.

On this tour you can picnic anywhere along the riverbanks; in the four little parks beside the river; near Roza Dam; and in Yakima State Park, 3 miles east of Yakima on State 24. You can stay overnight, too, at the state park or one of the many motels in Yakima. Return to Ellensburg via the same route, taking time in the evening to saunter along the river and watch for the deer that sometimes come to drink.

LAKE CLE ELUM JAUNT

On this tour you pedal northwest from Ellensburg along the river to azure Lake Cle Elum, which lies on the edge of Wenatchee National Forest. While the Old Canyon Ride is dry, this Lake Cle Elum Jaunt takes you through moist forested hills. In springtime wild lupine, brown-eyed Susans, phlox, and fields of buttercups tint the slopes and scent the air as you churn easily along. Throughout the ride you also glimpse the sharp, craggy peaks of the distant Stuart Mountain Range.

Outside Ellensburg on Highway 10, you roll gently through farmland, passing lots of hayfields and cattle ranches. In about a mile, State 131 branches off to your right. If you are a rock hound, take a side trip up 131 along a dry creek bed. Climb down the banks and forage for the agates and thunder eggs often found here. You come to a steep hill about 6 miles along this road. Unless you are in the mood for a challenge, turn around at the hill and return to Highway 10.

Back on Highway 10, you reach the Yakima River 2 miles outside Ellensburg. There's an above-ground wooden canal here and also a dam which swimmers find great for leaping in inner tubes. You ride now along the river through open, rolling wheat fields alternating with pine-scented forests. Bald eagles often nest in the tall pines on the riverbanks, and as on the canyon tour, you may see deer grazing in the meadows or coming to the river to drink. While traffic is light on Old Canyon Road, this tour has even fewer motorists: if you meet five cars an hour, it's a busy day.

A few more minutes of riding bring you to a little grocery, beyond which you climb the only real hill along the trail, a one-and-a-half-mile-long moderate grade which you can probably take in fifth gear. Stop anywhere along the Yakima to swim, or if you have a license, to fish for trout. All along the way, you will discover wild blackberries ripened in early summer to a deep purple-black.

Pedal beside the river and along a railroad track to Teanaway, where you can buy snacks at the country store. Eating facilities and rest rooms are available regularly from here to the lake. In about fifteen easy minutes, you reach Cle Elum, where you take Highway 903 right, through the tiny towns of Roslyn, Ronald, Jonesville, and Lakeview to Lake Cle Elum. Near the lake you find ample opportunities to wander along rushing mountain streams, hike through the cool pines of Wenatchee National Forest, and explore the mountain country.

Camp overnight beside the lake at Wish Poosh Campgrounds. The fee is $1 and there's a fourteen-day limit. The scenery is so lovely here you may want to stay an extra day to venture along the back roads or hunt for driftwood along the pure blue lake before returning by the same route to Ellensburg.

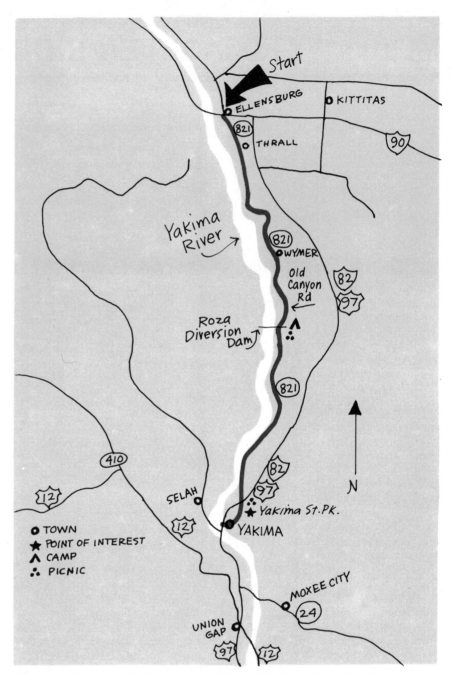

Ellensburg is in central Washington just off I-90 on U.S. 97 and Route 10; 102 miles east of Seattle via I-90. Above is the Old Canyon Ride map.

WHERE TO STAY

Motels in Ellensburg include Holiday Inn, 1700 Canyon Road, (509) 925-9801; Regalodge, 300 West 6th Avenue, (509) 925-3116; and Thunderbird, 403 West 8th Avenue, (509) 962-9856. Yakima has numerous motels. Here are some of the least expensive: City Center, 710 North 1st Street, seven blocks north of town on Business 97; (509) 452-7178. Eagle, 105 East E Street, five blocks north and half a block east of North 1st Street; (509) 452-0654. Harold's Motel Supreme, 1688 Fruitvale Boulevard, just off Highway 12 near 16th Avenue; (509) 452-8557.

Campgrounds include the following: Wish Poosh, Wenatchee National Forest, just over 10 miles northwest of Cle Elum on State 901. This spot is closest to the lake, but should you want another site, inquire at a local grocery or gas station about the many campgrounds within 10 miles of here. Ellensburg KOA Campgrounds, 2 miles west of town on State 131; open April 15th to October 15th; playground, swimming in the river, fishing; (509) 925-9319. Yakima KOA, 3 miles east of Yakima off State 24 on Keyes Road; open year round; (509) 248-5882. Yakima State Park, 3 miles east of town on State 24; open year round. For reservations, write Yakima State Park, P.O. Box 49-B, Route 1, Yakima, Washington, or phone (509) 453-8153.

FOR SPARE PARTS, REPAIRS, FURTHER INFORMATION

Four Seasons, 116 East 4th Street, Ellensburg, Washington; (509) 925-9134. Bob Woodke sells parts for most 10-speeds and does quick repairs on all makes. His hours are Monday through Saturday, 8:30 A.M. to 6 P.M. Ask him about the Washington State bike race being considered along Old Canyon Road.

NEARBY

Ginkgo Petrified Forest State Park, in Vantage, Washington, lies 30 miles east of Ellensburg on lightly traveled Highway 10. Here you will see one of the world's largest petrified forests. The park contains 259 species of agatized wood plus the prehistoric ginkgo tree. Picnic in the forest and camp overnight at the KOA in Vantage along Wanapum Lake, a great spot for rock hounding. About 65 miles northwest of Yakima on State 12 is Mount Rainier National Park, a trek for experts only.

Cycle north from Ellensburg to Lake Cle Elum.

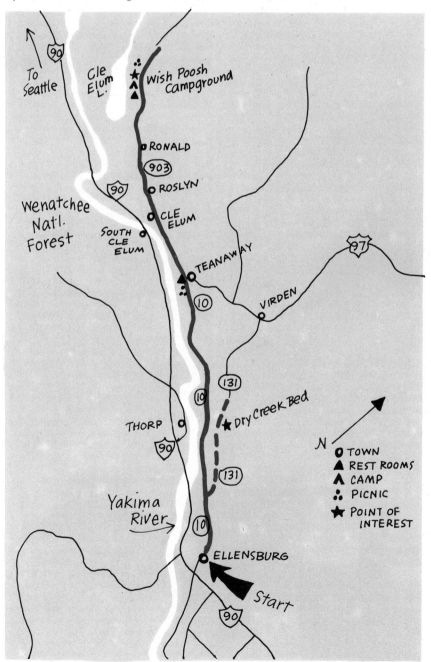

101. MT. RAINIER ROUNDABOUT

Many Washington cyclists call this century ride from glaciated Mount Rainier the "grand tour of western Washington," and after you have ridden the loop you will likely agree. The roads that scale the Cascade Crest twist past rain forests, snowbanks, alpine meadows, and waterfalls, then plummet to sage-covered prairies and apple orchard valleys—all on a challenging one-or two-day journey.

Start in Mount Rainier National Park at Ohanapecosh Visitor Center, about two and a quarter hours by car south of Seattle. If you stay overnight at the campground here, try the easy 1-mile stroll to Silver Falls or one of the strenuous 4-mile trails to Shriner Peak Lookout or Cowlitz Divide. Bring spare parts, tools, rain gear, and several layers of clothing so you can adapt to the brisk temperatures at the summit and the sweltering heat on the plains. Toe clips and cleat shoes come in handy on the rugged climbs.

To avoid the late-afternoon heat in the valleys east of the mountains, start north on State 123 at around 8 A.M. when the road still lies in deep, cool shadows. You roll easily through dense forests for several miles, then begin the arduous ascent toward Chinook Pass (5,429 feet). Low gears on this climb usually range from 40 to 68 inches, though the latter may be slightly high.

About two-thirds of the way up the slope, watch for a short, dark tunnel. Beyond the tunnel, you see the road ahead spiraling sharply up the mountainside. Though the slope seems imposing from this vantage point, you soon find that the climb is steady and not as tough as it looked—only about 200 feet per mile. In a deep chasm to your left, Chinook Creek rushes unseen as you climb.

DISTANCE:	113 miles.
TERRAIN:	Mountainous, with a total elevation gain of about 8,000 feet.
TRAFFIC:	Usually light.
DIFFICULTY:	For experts because of the distance and rugged terrain.
BEST TIME:	Late June to early July, as soon as the snow has been cleared from the mountain passes; also fine in September, when the mountain air is brisk and the lowlands are cool. Avoid late July through August, when temperatures often soar to the 90's and 100's on the prairies.
LOCATION:	Starts in Mount Rainier National Park, Washington.

At last you spin through Cayuse Pass (4,700 feet), but the coast beyond is short, for soon you tackle the steep hairpin curves to Chinook Pass, the tour's highest point. In early June you will often still see snowfields and six-foot snowbanks, but by late summer or autumn, the snow has melted and the alpine meadows are flecked with wildflowers. As you approach the summit, you may feel the mists of a waterfall blown gently by the breeze.

Rest in the small parking lot at Chinook Pass. Then check your brakes and begin the twisty plunge down the mountain, first passing grassy fields and later riding through ponderosa pine forests. Eventually the coast becomes more gradual, but you continue downhill until you reach the confluence of the American and Naches rivers.

As you descend into the valley, you feel the air become hot and dry, smell the pungent sage, see cottonwoods clustered along the riverbanks. There are several gas stations and grocery stores along this stretch. Here in the American River Valley, temperatures may rise into the 80's or 90's around late June. As you pedal over the rough-textured macadam, watch for the sharp gravel shoulders which have caused many flats. Also be wary of jeep-riding "cowboys" who think they own the road.

For 27 miles, from the river confluence to U.S. 12, you spin beside the river past sage prairies, farms, and cliffs. Traffic on this stretch is light but fast so be careful. At U.S. 12, turn right for the main tour or continue straight for a 10-mile side trip to Yakima, in the heart of Washington's apple country.

Proceeding on the main tour, you climb easily along the Tieton River to the Tieton River Valley. Just before you reach Rimrock Lake, you pass a clear, ice-cold spring where you can refill your water bottle.

From Rimrock Lake you tackle the rigorous 7-mile, 1,500-foot climb to White Pass. Though the slope isn't terribly steep, you may find this the tour's toughest stretch because you pass only rocks and bald slopes. The highway ahead may seem endless, but just concentrate on the road and watch the shoulders until you glimpse the first alpine meadows or snow.

Eventually, cool Leech Lake appears on your right, and you have only 100 feet more to the summit—and to a cafe and gas station.

From White Pass, the road dives 10 miles down a smooth, straight slope. As you plunge, watch out for cracks and loose rocks. Near the base of the mountain, a right onto State 123 leads you up an easy 4-mile hill to Ohanapecosh, your tour's end.

WHERE TO STAY

Yakima, about 10 miles off the tour; has many motels. For specific listings, see Yakima River Rides, page 211.

Campgrounds on this ride are numerous; there are thirty-eight Snoqualmie National Forest camps located on or near State 410 and U.S. 12. All of them operate on a first-come first-served basis and charge either $1 or no fee.

NEARBY

Mount Rainier National Park offers miles of scenic mountain roads. Experts may want to try a loop around Mount Rainier via state roads 706, 7, 161, 162, and heavily trafficked 410. This 170-mile circle contains some mountainous slopes. The best time for the ride is September, after the tourists have left and before the snows. Just east of Snoqualmie National Forest lies Yakima, in Washington's apple country, where there are two peaceful tours along the Yakima River. To extend your vacation, join these two rides with the Mount Rainier Roundabout for a week's holiday. For details, see Yakima River Rides on page 211.

Mt. Rainier National Park is in west-central Washington on Washington 410, 706 and 123; 90 miles southeast of Seattle via Washington 169, 410 and 123. Top map. Enlarged detail. Bottom map. Whole tour.

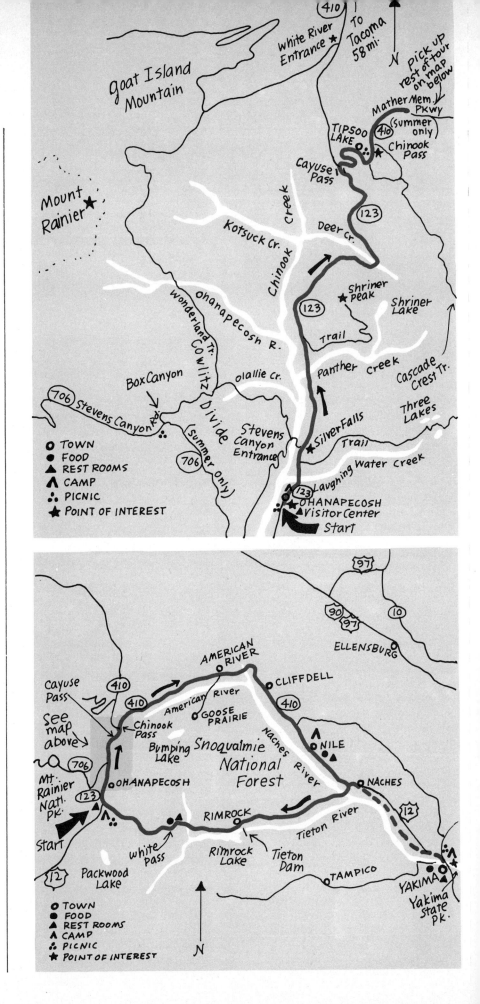

102. SAN JUAN CRUISE

San Juan Island in Puget Sound offers hilly wooded back roads, driftwood beaches, good clamming, boating, swimming, and a dab of history. Seafaring is the mood of this weekend, even though your craft is a bike.

Ferry from Anacortes to tiny Friday Harbor on San Juan, where you should buy picnic basics and snacks for your whole tour. Park headquarters for the island is located here, and you can pick up maps and brochures before leaving. Then go past the courthouse on 2nd Street, left on Guard Street, and right on Tucker to a Y. Here you can continue left on Roche Harbor Road or go right to tour the University of Washington's oceanographic lab.

From the lab turnoff to Lonesome Cove Resort, you roll through hills and wooded glens. Lonesome Cove Resort and adjacent Namu's Secret Cove campgrounds, settled on a wide clean beach, provide good overnight stops from which to explore the little inlets and sandy beaches of Roche Harbor. Many roads in this area are gravel, but they are well graded and okay for biking.

Back on Roche Harbor Road, go right for about half a mile, then swing left toward English Camp, with a grassy beach, located down a short road to your right. The camp was established in 1850 when an American shot an Englishman's pig in his potato patch. Disputes over which country owned the island then flared, and both sides summoned troops before tempers cooled.

About one and a half miles past the camp, turn right onto paved Marine View Drive (West Side Road), which leads you 3 miles and around a curve to San Juan County Park, with camping, a good driftwood and swimming beach, and a

DISTANCE:	31 miles, excluding numerous side trips. Two days are advisable to really explore the island.
TERRAIN:	Rolling hills.
TRAFFIC:	Light.
DIFFICULTY:	A 10-speed bike and some experience recommended.
BEST TIME:	All seasons. Bring a warm sweater and rain gear for sudden weather changes.
LOCATION:	San Juan Island National Historic Park in Puget Sound, Washington.

small store. Beyond this park, you climb steeply and the paved road turns to well-graded gravel.

Winding steeply downhill, you suddenly round a curve and coast onto a cliff overlooking wide blue Haro Strait. To see Lime Kiln Lighthouse, lock your bike here and scramble down the rocky path. On clear days you can see miles of craggy coast, with Vancouver Island far to the north and Olympic Peninsula south across the silvery blue water.

Just past the lighthouse trail, go right on the narrow road and coast to the beach, where you can search for driftwood or clams.

Here and along other parts of the tour, you may see lots of rabbits and golden eagles, with an occasional bald eagle nested in the tall firs.

Back on the main route, the road becomes paved in about one and a half miles. You wind inland, climb San Juan Park Road, then plunge into grassy San Juan Valley. Turn right onto graveled False Bay Road, which meanders and eventually dead-ends into American Camp Road. Here you can go left toward Friday Harbor or right for a scenic side trip to American Camp, the second remnant of the "pig war" fiasco. From the camp you have excellent views of the sound and nearby islands. You can venture still farther south down rough gravel and over sand dunes to Cattle Point Lighthouse and more coastal scenes. Do not explore Cape San Juan: the roads are terrible and unrewarding anyway.

Proceeding north now on American Camp Road, you follow the main tour route, turn right at the fork and plunge downhill, go left when you dead-end, then ride past San Juan County Fairgrounds back into Friday Harbor.

WHERE TO STAY

Overnight facilities are limited, so your stops should be planned carefully. Motels are found primarily in Friday Harbor. Cottages are located at Roche Harbor, Lonesome Cove.

There are two main campgrounds: Lonesome Cove Resort, open April through October. Reservations are a must. Write Lonesome Cove Resort, San Juan Island, Washington 98250, or phone (206) 378-4477. San Juan County Park, open year round and operated on a first-come first-served basis; (206) 378-2992.

FOR FURTHER INFORMATION

Write Superintendent, San Juan Island National Historic Park, P.O. Box 549, Friday Harbor, Washington 98250, or the Chamber of Commerce, P.O. Box 98, Friday Harbor, Washington 98250.

NEARBY

Orcas and Lopez, the other two islands in the San Juan group, offer more excellent Puget Sound cycling. Each island can be explored in one day, but you may want to take more time. On Lopez, the least commercialized of the San Juan Islands, you have a tough climb up from the ferry dock to smooth rural hills with light traffic. Roads generally do not border the beaches, but you have some excellent ocean views. On a clear day a stop at Richardson's small general store is a must. From here you see the snow-crested Olympics across the strait. Both Odlin County Park and the more rugged Spencer Spit State Park have camping and fine beaches.

On Orcas, with many challenging steep hills, you can plan rides of 18 to 80 miles. You will see horse, sheep, and cattle ranches, and in spring blossoming fruit orchards, wild roses, hawthorns, and madronas. Moran State Park, with two lakes, and West Beach Resort have camping.

HOW TO GO CRABBING

If seafood appeals to you, try crabbing on this Puget Sound ride. Veteran crabbers use lots of paraphernalia, including ropes, chains, bushel baskets, tongs, and heavy weights, to catch crabs. Cyclists, preferring the simpler life, use a crab net, bait line, or light, collapsible crab trap, any of which can be easily tucked away and carried on your bike.

The simplest (but not *easiest*) way to catch crabs is the wade-

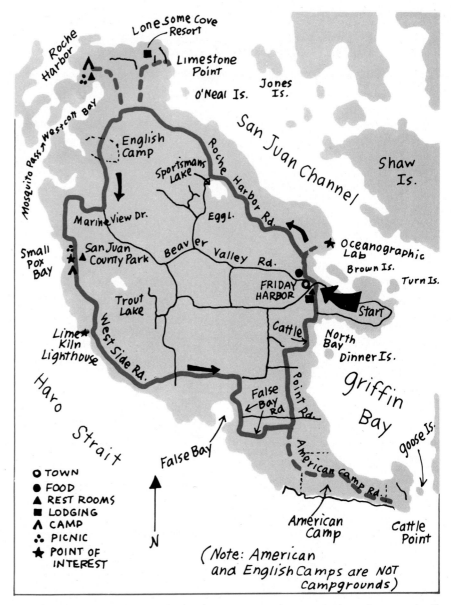

San Juan Island is in Puget Sound west of Anacortes, Washington, by ferry; Anacortes is off I-5 and Washington 20; 78 miles north of Seattle via I-5 and Washington 20.

and-dip method. Just walk along in the water until you see a crab, then dip and net. This works okay if the crabs are abundant and you have lots of patience.

You can also use a bait line to snare crustaceans. Tie your bait to the line (chicken necks make good bait) and slowly lower the line into the water. When you feel a nibble, raise your line easily, then dip and net.

Still another crabbing method uses the crab trap, available at sports stores. Attach the bait to the bottom of the trap, wait for an unwary crab to venture in to feed, draw up the string, and you have him.

103. BAINBRIDGE ISLE SPIN

As you pedal on Bainbridge Island in Puget Sound, salt sea mists hang over the madronas, gulls squawk, an old ferry rolls and creaks in the harbor. Bring a sweater or windbreaker to combat nippy ocean breezes, even on warm summer days.

Park your car in a lot under the Alaskan Way viaduct in Seattle, or if you plan to stay overnight on Bainbridge Island, in a commercial parking lot. Then take the Washington State ferry from Pier 52 in Seattle to Winslow on the island. Off the ferry, you pedal uphill, turn left at the first stop light onto Winslow Way East, and ride through downtown Winslow. Grocery stores on this tour are limited, so pick up a picnic lunch and raisins, nuts, or other snacks before you leave town. When you reach Grow Avenue N.E., turn right and go uphill to Wyatt Road, where you make a left and coast toward Eagle Harbor. Stay left at the fork and wind onto Eagle Harbor Drive beside the water, where battered old ferries sway on the waves. Most roads on the island are well paved, rather narrow, and without shoulders; light traffic makes riding tranquil.

You continue skirting the harbor, curving right onto Rockaway Beach Drive. Then you go over a short rolling hill and on into Port Blakely. Continue straight, then keep left to stay near the water, where you see small Blakely Rock poking from the sound. Soon you come to a fork. For a short side trip with pleasant marine views, keep left and pedal about one and a half miles on Country Club Road, which eventually dead-ends at a golf course on Restoration Point. Here you can gaze across the sound and on unfoggy days see the water, city, and distant Mount Rainier.

Back on the main tour, turn left now toward South Beach onto Toe Jam Hill Road, where you climb a steep hill, ride along a plateau, then plunge steeply down for over a mile. The coast is great, but be certain your hand brakes work. When you reach the water, turn right onto South Beach Drive, with beaches to your left and houses on the hillside to your right.

After about a mile of shoreline riding, you reach Fort Ward. From the vantage of the gun emplacements, you can see Rich Passage's blue waters. Here in summer you find blackberries, ripened to a juicy blue-black. In autumn you see ducks gathering—many varieties, including baldpates, goldeneyes, and surf scoters. Caution: Watch out in this area for poison ivy.

In a few minutes you arrive at Fort Ward State Park, Sunset Lodge, and a locked gate. While the lodge has banned cars from this private road, cyclists have been given special permission to pass, so go around the gate and into the park. You can picnic here in sight of the water or on a warm summer day swim at the beach. As you leave, go through the park's north entrance to the stop sign, where you turn left onto Pleasant Beach Drive and ride on into Lynwood. Here you can stop for a snack at the café or grocery store. Then at the service station, either turn left for a 2-mile side trip along the coast or continue on the main highway. The side trip takes you along Sinclair Inlet, where you can see Kitsap Peninsula. When you reach the deadend road sign, return the way you came. Beyond the sign and over the hill, you will find only a dirt and gravel lane blocked by fallen trees.

Back on the main highway, turn left about a mile past the filling station onto Fletcher Bay Road, which eventually becomes Miller Road, and pedal through more countryside. If you ride on a cool day, the air smells of burning driftwood as residents warm their homes.

About 3 miles beyond the Island Center Hill Road intersection, turn left onto Peterson Hill Road and coast toward Manzanita. At the stop sign, turn left again. Now you ride on Bergman Road along Manzanita's waterfront, then climb through madrona trees and evergreen huckleberry bushes. In a few minutes you come to Hidden Cove Road West, where you turn right, cross State 305, then wind along Hidden Cove Road East. Soon you reach two stop signs: go left at the first, straight ahead at the second. At the three forks, stay left and

DISTANCE:	32 miles, excluding side trips.
TERRAIN:	Hilly, with some flat stretches.
TRAFFIC:	Light.
DIFFICULTY:	Good ride for anyone, including beginners and families.
BEST TIME:	All seasons. December through February is the coldest, averaging in the high 40's. June through August is the warmest, with highs in the 70's.
LOCATION:	Bainbridge Island in Puget Sound, Washington.

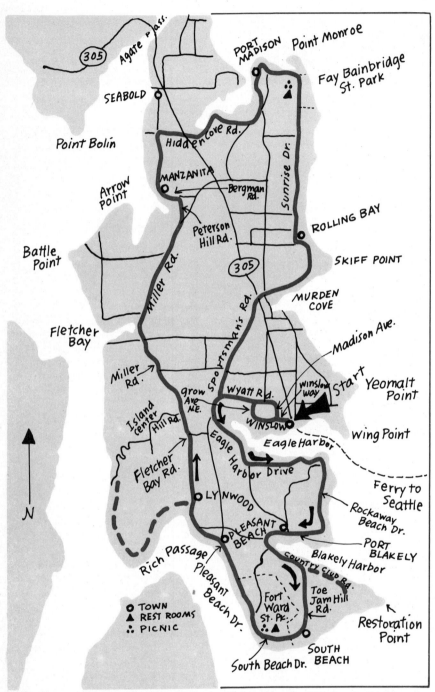

Bainbridge Island in Puget Sound can be reached by ferry from Pier 52 in Seattle, Washington.

Rolling Bay, where you can buy snacks at the store. When you reach another stop sign, go left again toward Manitou Beach. You pedal beside drifting waters and summer waterfront cottages. At the next stop sign, cross over the highway (State 305) and glide along Sportsman's Road to a T where you turn left and go toward Winslow. Three more stops and turns take you back to Winslow: turn left at the first stop sign onto Wyatt Road, right at the yield sign onto Madison Avenue, and finally left at a stop sign onto Winslow Way East. Stop for a day's-end snack in town. Then go on to the traffic light, turn right, and glide back down to the ferry landing, completing your island excursion.

WHERE TO STAY

Camping facilities are available at the two state parks described in the tour. The island has no motels.

FOR SPARE PARTS, REPAIRS

Bainbridge Island Bicycle Shop, 372 Winslow Way East, Bainbridge Island, Washington 98110.

NEARBY

Puget Sound has numerous islands suitable for cycling, including Vashon, Whidbey, and the San Juan Islands. See page 217 and 221 for other Puget Sound Island Tours.

coast to Port Madison's waterfront. The path winds uphill, then you go left onto a narrow paved road and twist between tall firs and cedars, their trunks entwined with ivy.

At the stop sign, turn left and go past Pioneer Cemetery to Fay Bainbridge State Park. Stop to picnic, swim, or walk along the beach and watch the waves. This is also a popular clamming spot. With the two side trips, you have come about 30 miles so far and may want to camp overnight here in the pine forests. The fee is $1.75. For families, there's a playground.

Beyond the park exit, turn left onto Sunrise Drive and ride on to

104. VASHON ISLAND VENTURE

To really feel two-wheel freedom, explore Vashon Island in Puget Sound. Wind through forests of madronas, firs, and huckleberry bushes. Take a solitary stroll along the beach. Hear the boats chug in the harbor and feel the damp salt air on your face. Though we have suggested a 29-mile loop plus a side trip to Maury, Vashon's sister island, tailor this tour to give yourself enough time in one day to truly experience the island. You find no overnight facilities here, but should you crave an island campsite, ferry at dusk to Blake Island State Park, just off Vashon Island's northern tip.

Begin your tour by taking an early ferry (at about 9 A.M.) from one of three points on the mainland: Point Defiance Park in Tacoma; Fauntleroy in West Seattle; or Point Southworth, 9 miles south of Port Orchard on the sound's west shore. The ferry costs $1, including your bicycle—the same fare foot passengers are charged. Secure your bike to the ferry (the crew will tell you where), then go to the passenger deck for about ten minutes of sea, city, and distant mountain views. Untie your bike and be ready to ride the moment the ferry touches the dock. This way you get a head start on the cars.

From whichever dock you land, you have an immediate steep climb, but after the first hill your ride levels as you circle the island. For simplicity we will begin this tour at the Fauntleroy and Southworth ferry landing. You ride up the hill along Vashon Island Highway. Roads on this island are well paved but narrow. The heaviest traffic on the tour, however, is here between the dock and Vashon. Once you reach the hilltop, pass the fire station, and turn right at the little grocery store, you en-

counter few cars.

Throughout this jaunt you see miles of woods and fields of currants and strawberries. You roll over easy hills with superb views to your right of Kitsap Peninsula jutting into the sound and the snowcapped Olympic Mountains beyond. People do live on Vashon, of course, and often you share the road with pedestrians and horses. Whirling bike wheels, by the way, make many horses skittish, so as a courtesy you might pause to let riders pass.

DISTANCE:	29 miles, excluding coasting side trips and the ride to Maury Island.
TERRAIN:	Rolling, with two steep grades.
TRAFFIC:	Light.
DIFFICULTY:	Good ride for beginners and families without young children.
BEST TIME:	Anytime but winter.
LOCATION:	Vashon Island in Puget Sound, Washington.

Soon you have a number of turns, so watch signs closely. You glide downhill past a county dump (no place is perfect) to a stop sign where you turn right. In about 2 miles, go right again at S.W. 220th Street and 128th Avenue S.W. You pedal another short distance, then wind left at the little white church onto 131st Avenue S.W.

When you reach Vashon Island Highway, turn left. For a lovely side trip go straight ahead: a

downhill plunge to the ferry dock. You must work your way up again, but this hill isn't quite as steep as the hill on Vashon's north end. Coasts like this one are found all around the island, and you could spend the whole day taking these short sprints.

Back now on Vashon Island Highway, you spin along Quartermaster Harbor to Inspiration Point. Turn off here to view the small village of Burton to your left and Maury Island directly across the sail-dotted harbor. At this turnout, you see western yew trees with their bright red fruit and shiny evergreen huckleberry bushes.

Pedaling on, you soon pass a beach where you can wade or lie in the warm white sand. When you reach Burton, gather cheeses, fruits, breads, and meats in the town's small country store. Then go right on S.W. 240th Street to Burton Peninsula. Here you turn right at Bayview Road and curve along the water about a mile to a cozy park where you can lunch at a picnic table overlooking the harbor.

After lunch continue along the Bayview Road loop back to S.W. 240th Street, where you turn right and return to Burton to pick up Vashon Island Highway once more. A few minutes outside Burton, you cross a bridge over a small stream. Here an unmarked road (actually Quartermaster Drive) runs off to your right toward Maury Island.

Maury Island Side Trip

Pedal along Quartermaster Drive to the first stop sign, then turn right to begin a loop around Maury. This isle is perhaps best explored by impulse. You can pedal to Dockton Park for a refreshingly restful afternoon. Or wind along narrow, twisting Luana Beach Road

(Wick Road) through cool tunnels of trees. Within sight of the water, Luana Beach Road makes a great night ride, with Seattle's lights glittering across the black channel. Also on Maury you can tour a Coast Guard lighthouse weekdays from 1 to 3 P.M. and weekends from 1 to 4 P.M.

Back on Vashon Island Highway, you continue north over rolling hills for about 3 miles to Vashon, a small town where you can buy food. Beyond town you pedal over a few easy hills, then have one final steep coast back to the ferry. From here either return to the mainland or cruise to tiny Blake Island, where you can cycle the footpaths and camp overnight.

WHERE TO STAY

Vashon Island has no facilities, but campsites and motels are numerous on the mainland. Island camping is available at these locations: Blake Island State Park, Seattle; fee, $1.75; (206) JL4-2773. Fay Bainbridge State Park, on Bainbridge Island in Puget Sound; fee, $1.75, not including wood. For reservations, write Fay Bainbridge State Park, P.O. Box 7635, Route 7, Bainbridge Island, Washington 98110, or phone (206) 842-3931.

NEARBY

Once you have sampled island touring, you may want to spend a week exploring the sound. Other lovely cycling isles include Mercer, Bainbridge, Whidbey, and the San Juan group of Lopez, Orcas, and San Juan.

Also near Seattle is Olympic Peninsula, where you can explore a rain forest (see page 225).

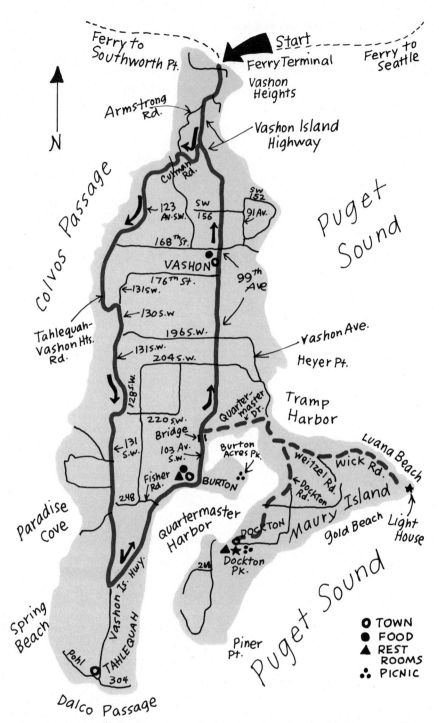

Vashon Island in Puget Sound can be reached by ferry from Seattle, Washington, or Point Defiance Park in Ruston, Washington. Ruston is south of Seattle via I-5, Washington 16 and Pearl Street.

105. LAKE WASHINGTON ISLANDER

Mercer Island in Lake Washington offers an excellent one-day outing for families and beginners. On this tour you pass beachside parks, bays, and suburban homes, and travel through dense fir, pine, and madrona woods. Islanders, alert to cycling safety, have installed bicycle signs in prominent spots on this loop.

Drive to Mercer from the mainland via I-90 and park your car in Luther Burbank King County Park. You can pick up an early breakfast at the Cook House Restaurant (open 6 A.M.), located just a few blocks east on 24th Street, then left on 76th Avenue to 27th Street.

Starting the tour from the park, go right on S.E. 24th Street. Then follow the green-and-white bicycle signs counterclockwise around the island. Stay on North Mercer Way past Roanoke Park, where you can play tennis or let the children swing and slide. A few minutes beyond Roanoke Park and past Old Toll Plaza, you wind right onto S.E. 22nd Street and then left onto 60th Avenue S.E. Much of the area you cycle through is metropolitan, but drivers here are usually courteous. You travel on flat or gently rolling road, unless you decide to cut across the island's center, where you encounter steeper hills.

Continue on 60th Avenue S.E. under I-90 past a floating bridge. The gold cup hydroplane races are held near here. Then go right onto West Mercer Way. In about 3 miles, you reach Groveland Park, down a steep hill to your right. It's a good place to stop for a swim or a picnic and view Seattle's Seward Park across the water.

Climbing from the park, continue along West Mercer Way to the island's south tip where you can see Renton across the lake, framed by snow-topped Mount Rainier. At South Point you wind

DISTANCE:	15 miles.
TERRAIN:	Flat, with a few slopes.
TRAFFIC:	Moderate.
DIFFICULTY:	Good ride for families and beginners. A 10-speed bike recommended for easy riding.
BEST TIME:	All seasons.
LOCATION:	Mercer Island in Lake Washington, near Seattle.

onto East Mercer Way and soon pass Clark Beach Park, another shady city park that offers swimming and picnicking.

East Mercer Way takes you through woods and into clearings as you pedal the island's east side

and head back toward the intersection with I-90. Then you cross I-90 and pick up North Mercer Way, lined with apartment houses. A few more minutes and you return to Luther Burbank Park, the loop's end. Take time to explore here. Walk along the shore in autumn to glimpse migrating ducks and Canadian geese, or hike into the alder and willow woods. Spend the rest of your day on the sandy beach.

WHERE TO STAY

Mercer Island has only one motel: Travelodge, 7645 Sunset Highway, Mercer Island, Washington; (206) 232-8000. You find no camping facilities on the island, but the other island tours in this book list many enjoyable camps in the Puget Sound area.

FOR SPARE PARTS AND REPAIRS

Mercer Island Cyclery, 7633 S.E. 27th Street, Mercer Island, Washington 98040; (206) 232-3443. Chuck and Mary Gnehm carry spare parts for most 10-speed bikes, handle touring equipment, and do quick emergency repairs. They cycle this ride often and will try to answer any questions you may have.

NEARBY

The islands in nearby Puget Sound offer days of fabulous cycling. Once you have tried this easy ride, you may opt for a more strenuous island tour. See pages 217, 219 and 221 for further details.

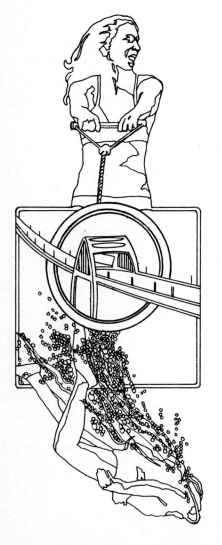

Mercer Island is in northwestern Washington just east of Seattle via I-90.

106. RAIN FOREST TOUR

Olympic's rain forests seem to be part of another country. Deep on the spongy forest floor, you pedal beneath towering Sitka spruce, western hemlock, and Douglas fir. Mosses and ferns grow thick, muffling outside noise until you hear only the chittering of ravens, gray jays, and juncos overhead and the hushed sound of an unseen river buried in foliage. High above you, the sun shines through the conifers to drench the forest air in warm, green light.

Start at Mora Campground in Olympic National Park's coastal region, where you can stay overnight. Begin your tour early the next morning with breakfast on nearby Rialto Beach. Bring spare parts, tools, rain gear, and snacks. How much food you carry depends on whether clams or smelts are in season.

Pedal east on the well-paved road from which you may glimpse black-tailed deer among the spruce and hemlock. The shoulder disappears in spots, but in early morning, when you have the forest to yourself, this is no problem.

About 18 miles from the campground, you go right on U.S. 101 through Forks, where you can buy food at a grocery store or café. As you continue through pleasant flatlands, watch out for logging trucks which often use this road. Pause along the Bogachiel River to rest.

About 14 miles south of Forks, turn left on narrow, well-paved Hoh River Road for a 19-mile ride to Hoh Visitor Center. On the way, you wind along the Hoh River through a rain forest, pedaling beneath western red cedar, big-leaf maple, red alder, vine maple, and black cottonwood trees. The banks of the river offer several rest spots.

At the Visitor Center, lock your bike and hike through the Hall of Mosses and along Spruce Nature Trail. Here delicate airplants drape themselves over tree limbs, thick mosses bury rocks and scale tree trunks, and ferns sprout into giants. You might get to see a Roosevelt elk browsing on the moist foliage; or a tiny shrew, jumping mouse, or salamander might cross your path. Back at the Visitor Center, picnic in the soft grass under huge trees.

Retrace your ride along Hoh River Road to U.S. 101, where you go left and wind southwest toward the sea. This road narrows, and as you approach the flat beach drive in summer, cars may line both roadsides. Watch carefully for opening car doors, pedestrians, and general traffic.

As you pedal, your view of the ocean is usually blocked by trees. But short hiking trails all along the coast offer plenty of beach access. Try beachcombing for driftwood, agates, and seashells, or explore tidal pools for colorful anemones and sea urchins. Be sure not to get stranded on a rocky outcrop by high tide. As you stroll along the shore, you may spot bald eagles in flight. Other residents of the area are cormorants, gulls, crows, and black oyster catchers, seals, sea lions, and even whales.

During clamming season, the beach will be pockmarked by shovels. Shellfishing is free in the park, and each lucky digger can take ten pounds of butter, steamer, or little necks, three pounds of geoducks, and fifteen razor clams.

End your day at Kalaloch, where you can camp, cook supper over your fire, then try a moonlight walk along the beach. Return the next day on U.S. 101 to Mora. Because you don't have the 38 miles round trip into the Hoh area, you can start late and enjoy a leisurely day.

WHERE TO STAY

A variety of motels, cabins, and lodges are available in and outside the park. For detailed information on concessioner-operated cabins and lodges at La Push (down the road to your left as you approach Mora) and at Kalaloch, write the Superintendent, Olympic National Park, 600 East Park Avenue, Port Angeles, Washington 98362. Information about accommodations

DISTANCE:	134 miles round trip.
TERRAIN:	Flat along the ocean; some long, gradual climbs as you head inland.
TRAFFIC:	Heaviest from June 15th to September 15th; light in May and late September. Watch out for logging trucks, which use the roads year round.
DIFFICULTY:	Experience is required in midsummer because of heavy traffic on some narrow roads. Fine for less experienced riders when traffic is light.
BEST TIME:	May through September. The average annual rainfall is 140 inches, most of which falls in winter.
LOCATION:	Olympic National Park, Washington.

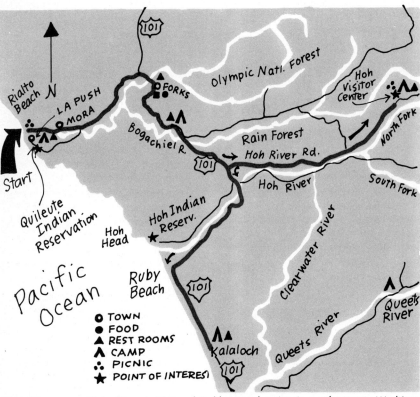

TOWN
● **FOOD**
▲ **REST ROOMS**
ʌ **CAMP**
∴ **PICNIC**
★ **POINT OF INTEREST**

Mora Campground is in Olympic National Park's coastal region in northwestern Washington off U.S. 101; 219 miles north of Astoria, Oregon, via U.S. 101; 74 miles southeast of Port Angeles via U.S. 101.

outside the park may be obtained from the Olympic Peninsula Resort and Hotel Association, Colman Ferry Terminal, Seattle, Washington 98104.

In addition to the four park campgrounds indicated on the map for this tour, you find many state parks and commercial campgrounds throughout the area. The park campgrounds are operated on a first-come first-served basis. Mora and Kalaloch stay open year round.

FOR FURTHER INFORMATION

Write Superintendent, Olympic National Park, 600 East Park Avenue, Port Angeles, Washington 98362.

NEARBY

Experts can tackle a scenic 330-mile loop around the park. From Port Angeles pedal west on U.S. 101 and climb the long, steep slope

past Lake Crescent. Continue on U.S. 101 as you skirt the coast, take U.S. 12 to Olympia, then return to Port Angeles on U.S. 101. This tour allows you to see Puget Sound, the Olympic Mountains, rain forests, Indian reservations, the ocean, and the plains. Some Washington cyclists say this is their favorite tour, but traffic is often heavy and there are logging trucks, so be careful.

OLYMPIC RAIN FOREST FERNS

In Olympic's rain forests, you are surrounded by lacy ferns, spreading over the forest floor.

The *sword fern* seeks shelter from the sun in damp, cool places. If any fern could look rugged, it would be the sword fern, with its coarse fronds, scaly rootstocks, and stout petioles with chestnut-colored scales. The undersides of the leaves are rimmed with dots, each hidden beneath a tissuelike flap.

Brake or *bracken* has hairy rootstocks which creep underground. The leaves grow in pairs opposite each other on the branch, and look somewhat like the wings of a bird in flight. When fully grown, bracken ferns usually stand one to three feet high, and some as high as five feet. Indians used to cook the young fronds as an early spring vegetable.

The *giant horsetail* is quite conspicuous in summer because of its drooping feathery branches which resemble great plumes. For a short time in spring, however, this fern looks totally different, with the branches gone and the white or brownish stems tipped with cone-shaped clusters of spores.

Polypody grows on mossy logs or rocks. Compared with those of most ferns, its leaves are tough, thick, and feel somewhat leathery. Turn a polypody leaf over to examine the underside, and you will see raised round dots clustered about the midribs.

107. MT. HOOD LOOP

Snowy, smoke-blue peaks, piney breezes, waterfalls splashing from cliffs, and alpine meadows of rhododendron and daffodils await you on this mountain trek around the Hood. Many planned overlooks provide stunning vistas, but you will soon learn that the best spots are those motorists whisk by. Pause often to explore a path through ponderosa and lodgepole pines, hunt for rocks, linger beneath a misty falls, forage for wild huckleberries, or catch rainbow trout from a mountain stream.

Carry spare parts, tools, snacks, and warm clothing for nippy mountain evenings. Roads on this tour are generally good, with acceptable shoulders, but watch ahead for spots where the shoulders vanish. A particularly tough stretch is the narrow road between Rhododendron and Sandy, but a new highway has been partially completed there.

Start at Portland International Airport and pedal south on State 213 to Northeast Sandy Boulevard, where you go left. As you coast toward Troutdale, watch out for the railroad track at the bottom of a short hill. Then from Troutdale take the Upper Level Scenic Route, avoiding the freeway along the Columbia River. Rest and picnic areas beyond Troutdale include Lewis and Clark State Park, on the trout-filled Sandy River, and Dabney State Park, 3 miles farther, beside an icy brook. Both parks have camping. About 5.5 miles beyond Dabney, enjoy superb views of Crown Point and the Columbia River Gorge from Portland Women's Forum State Park.

Experts with extraordinary stamina can soon tackle a side trip up Larch Mountain. Turning right on paved road, you climb 13 arduous miles to the 4,058-foot summit, where you can picnic over-

looking snowy peaks and forested valleys. In late August or early September, fill a bucket with ripe huckleberries which grow on the mountaintop.

Back on the main tour, you pass Crown Point State Park, which offers rest spots, a snack bar, and a restaurant. Then 2 miles farther, lock your bike and explore footpaths along a stream winding through Guy W. Talbot State Park. As you pedal the next 9 miles, you feel the mists from seven waterfalls. On this stretch venture many times off the beaten path. Hike through forests in Sheppards Dell State Park, meander on a footpath past Wahkeena Falls, or dine amid splendid views in the picnic grove or restaurant near Multnomah Falls. Inexperienced cyclists should return to Portland from Multnomah Falls to avoid the strong east winds along the Columbia River Gorge.

A bit farther, explore Oneonta Gorge or camp at Ainsworth State Park near a natural spring. Soon the scenic route rejoins the river freeway, and the salmon-filled Columbia River rushes beside you.

You climb to a plateau at Bonneville. Pedal here across part of the Bonneville Dam to the Visitor Center on Bradford Island, and try a short stroll from the parking lot to the "fish ladders" for an amazing close-up look at steelhead and salmon struggling upstream.

The road levels as you pass through Cascade Locks, and soon the river glides beside you. A long, gradual climb and a swift dive take you into Hood River, where you go right onto State 35. The road climbs steeply, and a mile beyond the turnoff you can go right for a tough 2-mile side trip up to Panorama Point, overlooking Mount Hood and a wide valley.

The next 35.7 miles to Bennett

<table>
<tr><td>DISTANCE:</td><td>171.4 miles, excluding side trips.</td></tr>
<tr><td>TERRAIN:</td><td>Some rolling stretches, with one steep, mountainous slope.</td></tr>
<tr><td>TRAFFIC:</td><td>Heavy on weekends; lighter on weekdays.</td></tr>
<tr><td>DIFFICULTY:</td><td>Complete tour for experts only, because of the difficult terrain. Beginners used to cycling in traffic can handle the first stretch along the Columbia River to the Columbia River Gorge. Not for families with children.</td></tr>
<tr><td>BEST TIME:</td><td>June to mid-September to avoid snows at the summit.</td></tr>
<tr><td>LOCATION:</td><td>Mount Hood Loop Highway east of Portland, Oregon.</td></tr>
</table>

Pass, at 4,674 feet, are for experts only, but the mountain scenery is splendid. Beyond the Panorama Point turnoff, bypass the road to Lost Lake because the last 7 miles to the lake are unpaved.

At Dimmick State Park, 15 miles from Hood River, you can hike through cool pine forests and picnic along a chilly stream. Polallie Camp Forest Camp, 12 miles farther, offers picnicking and swimming. Pause anywhere throughout your climb, though, to rest in al-

227

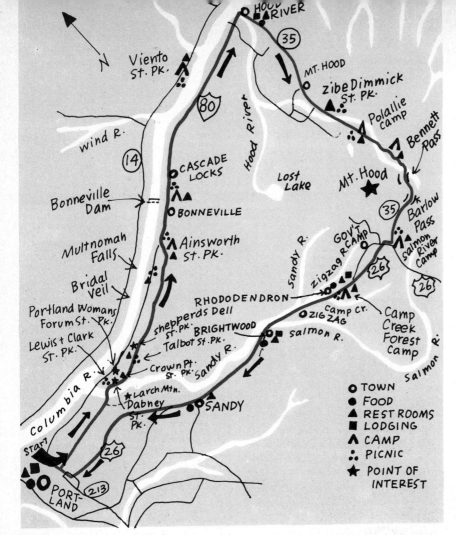

Portland is in northwestern Oregon on I-5, U.S. 26, 30, and I-80N; 175 miles south of Seattle, Washington, via I-5.

pine meadows or beneath shady pines.

As you pedal through Bennett Pass and start down, you see Mount Hood to your right. Soon you glide into the White River Valley, fragrant in spring with fuchsia, saffron, and lavender wildflowers. Below Barlow Pass and beyond Buzzard Point, you plunge rapidly, zigzagging around tight curves, to Salmon River Forest Camp, where you can fish for trout or gather wild berries.

Go right soon to Government Camp, where a detachment of soldiers sent to man the Oregon Territory abandoned several wagons on their journey. From here you plummet three and a half miles downhill past splendid rhododendron displays in spring. One mile farther, there is a turnoff to your left overlooking deep canyons and vast pine forests.

One mile beyond Camp Creek Forest Camp, you cross a bridge over the Zigzag River and coast past another campground into Rhododendron, which has full facilities. The road levels past the confluence of the Sandy and Zigzag rivers. Then you coast to Brightwood and roll over easy hills into Sandy. From Sandy, U.S. 26 rolls gradually down into Portland. A right turn onto State 213 (82nd Avenue) leads you back to the airport.

WHERE TO STAY

Motels are numerous throughout many sections of this loop, and are located in Portland, Hood River, Rhododendron, Brightwood, and several places off the main tour. During summer reservations are advised. One good stop is Timberline Lodge, just before you reach Government Camp, 6 miles up the south slope of Mount Hood on a steep, paved road. Open year round. For reservations, write Timberline Lodge, Timberline, Oregon 97028, or phone (503) 226-7979.

Camping is available throughout the tour, often on a first-come first-served basis. Campgrounds include the following:

Mileage from Portland

17.2 Lewis and Clark State Park
20.1 Dabney State Park
38.1 Ainsworth State Park
45.4 Eagle Creek Forest Camp
59.8 Viento State Park
94.4 Polallie Camp Forest Camp
96.0 Sherwood Forest Camp
100.0 Robin Hood Forest Camp
103.2 Hood River Meadows Forest Camp
110.7 Salmon River Forest Camp
120.0 Camp Creek Forest Camp
122.1 Tollgate Forest Camp

NEARBY

Oregon offers days of scenic tours varying from sprints along the beach to journeys through pine forests along deep green rivers. Try the ocean ride starting from Astoria, 2 hours by car from Portland, or take U.S. 26 from Portland to Cannon Beach and start your ocean tour south from there. See the Breezy Oregon Coasters on page 229 for details.

BIRDS AROUND THE HOOD

Mountain scenery, gorges, and swift rivers are overwhelmingly apparent as you loop the Hood. Subtler but just as delightful are the varieties of birds you see here, including many water birds along the Columbia River and songbirds in the woodlands.

Quail are abundant throughout this region. Watch along the rivers for valley quail and in the higher country for mountain quail. In the woodlands, blue and ruffed grouse are often seen, while mourning doves flit throughout the area. Another common species is the band-tailed pigeon. Though this fellow prefers the mountain pine and fir forests, he may also be spotted in the valleys around trees.

108. 109. 110. BREEZY OREGON COASTERS

Oregon's Pacific Coast is dramatic, lined with craggy surf-sharpened rocks, windblown beach grasses, and huge white sand dunes. Here your pace can be energetic or lazy. You can loll on the shores, spin along in the gentle salt breezes, and lie at evening along the beach or in a cozy seaside cottage. Or you can be busy, busy, collecting shells, agates, jaspers, and Oregon "jade," catching salmon or clamming for lunch, flying a kite, gathering wild strawberries, swimming, riding a dune buggy, building giant sand castles, exploring antique shops.

Outlined here are three rides, each easily managed on a weekend. These tours have been included on the same map, so you can start your ride at any of the suggested points or somewhere in between, or link all three together for an unforgettable holiday. One warning, though: strong prevailing winds blow southward, and riding this entire stretch north can be like climbing a 190-mile-high mountain. For this reason, you should seriously consider arranging a pickup at your tour's southernmost point.

All the rides follow busy U.S. 101, usually well paved, with wide shoulders; hazardous spots are listed below. The entire coast is dotted with state camping and picnic facilities, motels and cottages, and small beach towns, so food and overnight stops are easily planned. Carry spare parts, tools, and a jacket or sweater for brisk ocean winds.

ASTORIA TO OCEANSIDE

Oregon's northern coast offers excellent beaches, a visit to Fort Clatsop, erected by Lewis and Clark, salmon fishing in the wide Columbia River, and superb views.

DISTANCE:	Astoria to Oceanside, 139.6 miles round trip. Oceanside to Newport, 139.2 miles round trip. Newport to Florence, 96 miles round trip.
TERRAIN:	Rolling.
TRAFFIC:	Heavy, especially on summer weekends; moderate in spring and autumn.
DIFFICULTY:	For experienced cyclists only, because of fast traffic. Safety flag recommended.
BEST TIME:	May through October to avoid the rainy season. Excellent in late May, September, and October, when traffic is lightest and campgrounds and motels are uncrowded.
LOCATION:	Oregon coast, on U.S. 101.

Start in Astoria, at the northwestern tip of Oregon. Museums here include a local historical museum in Old Flavel Mansion, 8th and Duane Streets (admission, 25¢), and the Columbia River Maritime Museum, 17th and Exchange Streets (admission, 50¢). You may also wish to view the seaport from atop the 125-foot Astoria Column (free admission, June 15th to Labor Day; closed the rest of the year). To reach the tower, just follow the scenic-drive signs through town and up Coxcomb Hill.

As you leave Astoria on U.S. 101, you encounter a wide shoulder on the long bridge south of town and all the way (except on one short, narrow bridge) to Fort Clatsop National Memorial, a reconstructed fort at the end of the Lewis and Clark Trail.

Beyond Fort Stevens State Park, with beach and lake swimming, hiking trails, and a wrecked British sailing ship, the road is flat and straight for about 6 miles. Then you encounter long, gradual hills to Del Rey Beach, a serene rest stop Near Del Rey you pick up a short segment of wide-shouldered four-lane highway which leads to Seaside, a clean resort town with wide beaches, lifeguarded swimming in summer, and bike shops offering rentals.

You can continue through Seaside, but it's pleasant to stop by the ocean, snack on seafood, then pedal along the 3-mile paved promenade between resort hotels and the sea.

Back on U.S. 101, you ride through Seaside along a 3-mile marked bike route which ends about 1 mile beyond the narrow bridge. Then at Ecola State Park you can take another beach side trip, this time to hear the "singing sands" or try crabbing or clamming. Going on, you ride on a wide, well-paved biking shoulder past Cannon Beach and Tolovana Park to an ocean-view turnout, beyond which you climb uphill.

Four miles past the turnout, dismount and walk your bike on the sidewalk through the long tunnel. Then continue along the ocean. Here you may see rainbows, especially after early-morning mists. Five miles beyond the long tunnel, you pedal onto a cliff 1,700 feet above the ocean. Surrounding this spot are legends of Indian trails and ancient buried treasure.

Beyond this turnout lie two steep hills: one into Manzanita and a second into Nehalem. Between these sea villages, you can rest or picnic at Nehalem Bay State Park, where beachcombers allegedly still find beeswax from a Spanish galleon wrecked here centuries ago. As you climb into Nehalem, you may want to pause along the Nehalem River to catch salmon or cutthroat or native trout for lunch.

Your trail proceeds through dairy pastures followed by thick pine and fern forests. Just before Rockaway's famed beach, the shoulder widens and stays wide to the tour's end. Beyond Rockaway you may want to rest at Barview Jetty County Park, a popular local fishing spot for flounder, perch, and other deep-sea fish.

At Tillamook, known for its cheeses, follow the signs right on 3rd Street for the scenic loop along Cape Meares' ocean bay to Oceanside, the tour's southern point. Overnight in a motel or pedal about 7 miles farther south to camp at Cape Lookout State Park. Your second day, return to Astoria or continue exploring farther south.

OCEANSIDE
TO NEWPORT

This segment of Oregon's coast offers perhaps the Pacific's best rock-hounding beaches, including famed Agate Beach, and allows you to alternate your seacoast riding with wanderings through rural countryside, wooded forests, and wildflower meadows. Scout for whales, explore antique shops, attend an Indian-style salmon bake, and view delicate marine gardens on this coastal odyssey.

Pedal south of Oceanside along the scenic drive which hugs the shore. Two miles past Netarts, you can go either left for 5 miles into Tillamook and then follow U.S. 101 south through flat pastures, pine-clad hills, and wildflower mead-

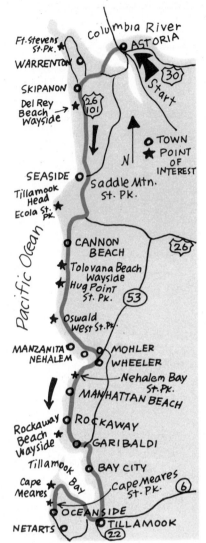

Astoria is in the northwestern corner of Oregon on U.S. 101/26, 30, and Oregon 202; 169 miles southwest of Seattle, Washington, via I-5 and U.S. 30. Above is the map from Astoria to Oceanside.

ows, or right to continue along 3-Cape Drive for unequaled miles of sea touring. On a mist-shrouded morning along the coast, the inland ride is often sunny and almost always warmer and less breezy than the cape route. Both rides have a few hills and many flat stretches.

The two routes rejoin south of Pacific City, where you spin through woods undergrown with delicate ferns. If you chose the cape ride, this area will seem warmer and you can stop anywhere to rest in

meadows sprinkled with yellow, white, and blue wildflowers. Ocean views occasionally peep through between the farmlands.

You climb into Neskowin, with a store and motel, beyond which you ride through densely wooded hills. Outside Neskowin be prepared to tackle the tough 2-mile climb followed by an exhilarating coast and still another steep incline into Siuslaw National Forest. Now woods, meadows, and farmland surround you as you climb past a Western Auto Store (stop for any simple parts) to East Devils Lake State Park, a pleasant spot to swim, picnic, or camp. Several more minutes bring you into Lincoln City, where you can buy snacks or visit the antique and doll museum at 3400 North Highway 101 (admission, 50¢).

Finding stopping spots is easy. You pass so many state and county parks, beaches, and waysides, you have to decide which ones not to see. Fogarty Creek State Park, about six and a half miles south of Lincoln City, offers cool picnic nooks, swimming, and a shallow wading creek. Another mile farther south, Boiler Bay provides good spots to glimpse whales and see vivid marine gardens at low tide.

One mile farther in Depoe Bay, sample fresh clams in a pier bistro, see the "sprouting horns" rock in midtown (if you are lucky, the horns will be shooting a geyserlike spray higher than Old Faithful), or visit Depoe Bay Aquarium at U.S. 101 and Bay Drive. If you happen to bike here the second Saturday in September, don't miss the Indian-style Salmon Bake, with fresh ocean salmon cooked before roaring open fires.

Beyond Whale Cove, located 1 mile south of Depoe Bay, you climb a long, steep hill, then coast rapidly with great views of slate-blue sea, to Beverly Beach, a good sunbathing, picnicking, or camping spot. Agates and marine fossils are abundant here, but the real prizes are found 3.7 miles farther south on famed Agate Beach.

From Agate Beach to Newport,

cont. from bottom of map pg. 230

OCEANSIDE
NETARTS
Cape Lookout St. Pk.
Cape Lookout
Pacific Ocean
Cape Kiwanda
PACIFIC CITY
NESKOWIN
Neskowin Beach wayside
Roads End wayside
LINCOLN CITY
DEPOE BAY
Otter Crest Wayside
OTTER ROCK
Devils Punch bowl SP.
Beverly Beach St Pk.
AGATE BEACH
Agate Beach Wysd.
NEWPORT
South Beach St. Pk.
Lost Creek St. Pk.
Ona Beach St. Pk.
SEAL ROCK
Patterson Mem St. Pk.
Beachside St. Pk.
Yachats St. Pk.
Neptune St. Pk.
Washburne Mem. St. Pk.
Sea Lion Caves
Heceta Beach
Honeyman Mem. St. Pk.

TILLAMOOK
HEBO
Siuslaw Natl. Forest
OTIS
Devil's Lake St. Pk.
Yaquina Head
SILETZ
Start Newport
TOLEDO
WALDPORT
YACHATS
Devils Elbow St. Pk.
Sutton Lake
Mercer L.
FLORENCE

Oceanside to Newport and Newport to Florence

the shoulder sometimes widens and other times vanishes. In Newport spin down to the waterfront to take in the art center, the museum (free admission), and the many small antique, agate, and other specialty shops along Yaquina Bay. After your long ride, you should be famished; this is the place to sample delectable Dungeness crabs and Yaquina Bay oysters.

Stay overnight in a motel or camp at Beverly Beach State Park,

which you passed 7 miles north of Newport, or at South Beach State Park, 2 miles south of town. Your second day, return north to Oceanside.

NEWPORT TO FLORENCE

This coastal tour shares many delights with the northern rides, including good rock hounding for the rare sagenite agate, white sand beaches, excellent clamming and crabbing, and miles of uninterrupted ocean views. Also here you pass the Sea Lion Caves, picturesque Heceta Lighthouse, and the giant Oregon dunes. This tour is shorter than the other two, allowing you more time to wander along the coves, watch cormorants and gulls on the rocky shoals, and observe sea lions at play.

Starting from Newport, you ride south uphill on U.S. 101. Then on the downhill coast just a few minutes from town, you can stop for a free visit to the Oregon State Marine Science Center, with extensive oceanography and marine biology labs. A bit farther, at both South Beach and Lost Creek state parks, you have easy access to the beach. Then as you coast down along the beach and over a narrow bridge, watch out for sand blown onto the road.

Pedaling is easy for a long stretch through salt breezes. Then 15 miles outside Newport (about 1 mile before Waldport), you cross a long bridge over Alsea Bay and spin past a Western Auto Store into Waldport. Here you can collect snacks or picnic basics and churn either 1.2 miles farther south on U.S. 101 to Patterson Memorial State Park or 3.3 miles south of town to Beachside State Park, both having picnicking facilities. Numerous seaside cafés also dot the beaches throughout this tour. If the sea beckons, you can rent a cottage and spend your afternoon along the surf.

Shoulders are usually paved and marked for the 8 miles between Waldport and Yachats. You ride through the latter on a 2-mile

marked bike path. Beyond Yachats the road climbs between pines, then dives downhill to Devil's Churn Viewpoint, where you see the gray ocean tossing violently against the rocks. Steps lead to the shore here. Just a bit farther down the road, you can pause at Cape Perpetua Visitor Center, lock your bike, and stroll along the viewing promenade or hike along a nature trail through deep pine woods to the beach.

You find lots of good picnicking stops throughout the next 11 miles: Neptune, Washburne, and Devils Elbow state parks are all pleasant and the latter two have beach accesses. Another enjoyable picnic spot, between Washburne and Devils Elbow, is Heceta Head, a picturesque headland with a lighthouse and marine gardens. Caution: Beyond Washburne, just before Heceta Head, you coast rapidly to a hazardous tunnel, so be careful.

Beyond Devils Elbow you climb to the Sea Lion Caves, where several hundred sea lions have picked a marine cave as their natural habitat (admission: adults, $1.50; children, 50¢). Watch in this region for pigeon guillemots, tufted puffins, cormorants, and herring gulls which nest in nearby cliffs.

Soon you climb through thick cool woods, dive quickly downhill, spin over several easy hills past Sutton Lake, and arrive at Florence. Stay overnight in a motel or collect food and camping supplies to carry 3 miles south to Honeyman Memorial State Park, where you can camp near vast Sahara-like sand dunes. Here after your busy day you can wander through the fragrant pine forests or swim in a clear freshwater lake.

WHERE TO STAY

Motels and camping facilities are numerous along the entire coast, and you need not make reservations if you come during off-season. An excellent free brochure detailing accommodations and listing where these and other sights are located to the nearest tenth of a mile is available from the Oregon Coast Association, P.O. Box 670, Newport, Oregon 97365. It is entitled "Northwest Pacific Coast Travel Guide."

Campgrounds include the following. Astoria to Oceanside: Fort Stevens State Park, 10 miles from Astoria on U.S. 101; open year round; $2. For reservations, write Fort Stevens State Park, P.O. Box 173, Hammond, Oregon 97121, or phone (503) 861-1671. Oswald West State Park, 35.7 miles from Astoria on U.S. 101 and south of Cannon Beach; open April through October; $1. No reservations accepted. Nehalem Bay State Park, 46 miles from Astoria on U.S. 101 and 3 miles south of Manzanita; open mid-May to October 31st; $2. For reservations, write Nehalem Bay State Park, Manzanita, Oregon 97130. Cape Lookout State Park, 73 miles south of Astoria or about 7 miles south of Oceanside; open year round; $2. For reservations, write Cape Lookout State Park, 13000 Whiskey Creek Road West, Tillamook, Oregon 97141, or phone (503) 842-2200.

Oceanside to Newport: Cape Lookout State Park (see above). Devils Lake State Park, 49.5 miles from Oceanside or about 3 miles north of Lincoln City; open April through October; $2. For reservations, write Devils Lake State Park, Lincoln City, Oregon 97367. Beverly Beach State Park, 68.2 miles from Oceanside, just south of Otter Rock; open year round; $2. For reservations, write Beverly Beach State Park, Star Route North, Newport, Oregon 97365, or phone (503) 265-7655. South Beach State Park, 77.5 miles from Oceanside or 2 miles south of Newport; open April through October; $2. For reservations, write South Beach State Park, Newport, Oregon 97365.

Newport to Florence: South Beach State Park (see above). Beachside State Park, 19 miles south of Newport on U.S 101 or 4 miles south of Waldport; open April through October; $2. For reservations, write Beachside State Park, 842 S.W. Government Street,

Newport, Oregon 97365, or phone (503) 563-3023. Tillicum Beach, 20 miles south of Newport on U.S. 101 or 5 miles south of Waldport; open year round; $2. No reservations accepted. Operated by Siuslaw National Forest. Cape Perpetua, 27 miles south of Newport on U.S. 101 or about 3 miles south of Yachats; open May 30th to October 15th; free. Operated by Siuslaw National Forest. Neptune State Park, 27 miles south of Newport on U.S. 101, just south of Cape Perpetua; open April through October; $1. No reservations accepted. Rock Creek, 34 miles south of Newport or 10 miles south of Yachats; open May 30th to October 15th; $2. No reservations accepted. Carl G. Washburne Memorial State Park, 36 miles south of Newport; open April through October; $3. No reservations accepted. Alder Lake, Sutton Creek, and Sutton Lake, 44 miles south of Newport; opening dates vary, with Sutton Lake open the longest, from March 1st to December 15th; $2 for Alder Lake and Sutton Creek, $1 for Sutton Lake. All operated by Siuslaw National Forest. Jessie M. Honeyman Memorial State Park, 3 miles south of Florence on U.S. 101; open year round; $2. For reservations, write Jessie M. Honeyman Memorial State Park, P.O. Box 3514, Florence, Oregon 97439, or phone (503) 997-8212.

FOR SPARE PARTS AND REPAIRS

Hardware stores with some bike parts are found throughout all the tours as indicated in the tour descriptions. Full-line bike shops are available in Astoria, Seaside, and Florence.

NEARBY

You can continue south along the coast to California, then pedal clear to San Diego if you choose. About 21 miles south of Florence is Oregon Dunes National Recreation Area. For a giant vacation (486 miles one way), extend these

three tours through the dunes to Reedsport, from which you can take the Oregon Outdoors Odyssey to Sutherlin (see page 233), ride State 99 south to Roseburg, then pick up the Northwest Woods Ride to Diamond Lake (see page 235). Just south of Diamond Lake lies the scenic Crater Lake Rim Run (see page 237, and from here you can ride even farther through virgin ponderosa and lodgepole pines to Klamath Lake and the Upper Klamath National Wildlife Refuge via the Klamath Lake Rendezvous (see page 239). This giant ride ends eventually in Klamath, Oregon.

OREGON COAST WILD STRAWBERRIES

Pedaling down the Oregon coast in the fresh salt breezes just has to increase your appetite. While munching on "gorp," keep your eyes open, too, for delicious wild strawberries growing along the beaches and roadside bluffs. These tart crimson berries ripen around the first of July, in which case you can snack all you like, but even before the fruit reddens, you can use the delicate fresh leaves for strawberry tea. Just fill a cup half full with strawberry leaves, add boiling water, and steep five to ten minutes. A richer tea can be created by allowing the leaves to soak overnight in a pot of water. You can also store strawberry-leaf tea by gathering the leaves in late summer, drying them overnight in the oven at 125 degrees, then crumbling and bottling them.

Another midsummer beverage is icy strawberry-ade. Just crush a handful of strawberries, drop them into a glass of ice water, wait about five minutes, stir, and drink. A dab of honey accentuates the flavor.

You can recognize beach strawberries by their deep glossy green leaves which grow in threes; their five-petaled white flowers; and their stems, often trailing to sprout new roots.

Crisp autumn foliage, a deep emerald river, wildflower meadows, huge sand dunes and surf, plus downhill coasts to the sea await you on this tour from Oregon's woodsy hills to craggy Pacific Ocean shores.

You coast northwest from Sutherlin on State 138 through 15 miles of densely wooded hills, vivid with color in autumn. About 10 miles from town, the icy green Umpqua River flows alongside the road. On the banks in spring you can forage for tender wild onions, while summer brings sweet ripened gooseberries.

From the woods you rise to lush grazing pastures, then crisscross the Umpqua as you climb and plunge over 8 miles of meadowed roller-coaster hills. Stop to rest beneath trees and enjoy the countryside. You turn left on State 38, then ride through Elkton, beyond which the marked shoulder is excellent. Here you pass more farmland, dotted with red-and-white Hereford cattle. You pedal up a hill into woods about 3 miles from Elkton, and the cottonwood-lined Umpqua rushes near you for the rest of your ride. Stop awhile and lock your bike, sit by the water's edge, and fish for trout (license required).

Ten miles from Elkton, you can stop for snacks at a café. If you are just looking for a rest spot, though, pedal another mile to a lush wildflower meadow on your left. The road then leads 3 miles through pastures and grainfields to Weatherly Creek, beyond which you climb and ride over a bumpy stretch, then coast to Wells Creek, with a grocery store. Two miles farther in Scottsburg, the river runs deep and you find many delightful rest spots nearby: Scotts Park, where you can picnic along a grassy bank; another

rest area a mile farther; and the many turnouts beyond providing good river views.

Just past Mill Creek Road, a pleasant side trip, you pick up a marked shoulder again as you glide along the Umpqua, which runs wide and green beneath wooded bluffs. Past a state park and motel, pastures lie between you and the river. About a mile beyond the motel, there is another flat riverbank and rest stop. Soon you see and smell fragrant wildflower meadows. Stop and look for goldenrod or mint; both make excellent teas.

The river gradually widens as you approach the ocean. Marshes appear on your right, and occa-

sionally you may see herons standing stone still in the water. Then you climb steeply for 2 miles and plunge into Reedsport. Stop for a snack at a café, and if you like, take a side trip south on U.S. 101 through Winchester Bay, which has excellent salmon fishing, to the beach and numerous campsites. If you arrive late in the day, you can stop at Windy Cove Park or Umpqua Lighthouse State Park, just south of Winchester. Otherwise continue about 3 miles farther to Umpqua Dunes Scenic Area, where you can comb the beaches for sandblasted wood, myrtle wood, Japanese glass fishing floats (most apt to be found after strong westerly winds), old bottles, and seashells. Rock hounds can discover jaspers plus iris, moss, and carnelian agates. Camp overnight on or near the beach. You can spend the next day swimming, surfing, or sunbathing before returning to Sutherlin.

WHERE TO STAY

Motels are located in Sutherlin and Reedsport, and include the following: Ponderosa Inn, P.O. Box 398, Sutherlin, Oregon 97479; 1 mile west of Sutherlin at the junction of State 138 and I-5; (503) 459-2236. Reedsport, 1894 Winchester Avenue, Reedsport, Oregon 97467; (503) 271-3666. Tropicana, 1593 Highway Avenue, Reedsport, Oregon 97467; half a mile south on U.S. 101; (503) 271-3671. Western Hills, Reedsport, Oregon 97467; half a mile south on U.S. 101; (503) 271-2149.

Campgrounds include these two: Loon Lake Recreation Site, 7 miles south on Mill Creek Road, to your left after you pass Scottsburg; open year round. Tahkenitch Lake, 8 miles north of Reedsport on U.S.

DISTANCE:	142 miles round trip.
TERRAIN:	Gradual coasts and climbs, with a few steep hills.
TRAFFIC:	Light in spots, heavy in others. Watch out for "chip trucks" carrying wood chips to logging camps.
DIFFICULTY:	Entire ride for experienced cyclists only. Segments are good for anyone.
BEST TIME:	All seasons but winter.
LOCATION:	Sutherlin, south of Eugene and north of Roseburg on I-5, to Reedsport on U.S. 101.

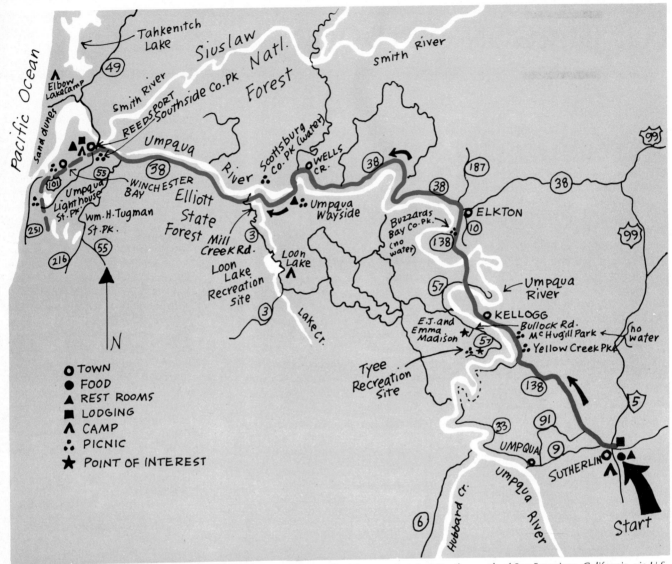

Sutherlin is in western Oregon on Oregon 99, just off I-5; 55 miles south of Eugene via I-5; 475 miles north of San Francisco, California, via U.S. 101, 199 and I-5.

101; open April 15th to September 15th; $2. Operated by Siuslaw National Forest.

NEARBY

North of Reedsport along U.S. 101, you can pedal up the coast clear to Astoria. For details, see the Breezy Oregon Coasters on page 229. South of Sutherlin lies Roseburg, from which you can take off through the Umpqua wilderness to Diamond Lake and south of that to Crater Lake National Park. For details, see the tours on pages 235 and 237.

112. NORTHWEST WOODS RIDE

Deep in Oregon's Cascades there is a place where the Umpqua River is only a thin green brook trickling over mossy rocks. The water feels cold because it began as snow. On either side of the river rise lushly forested mountain slopes. Tall red-barked ponderosa and gray lodgepole pine grow from the heights down to the river's edge. The loudest sounds are the river's shush and the rustle of pine tops. You can coast beside the Umpqua as it widens toward the sea.

Your deep forest tour begins at Diamond Lake, framed by bluish snow-topped Mount Bailey and Mount Thielson. Here you can swim, hike along the lake, fish for rainbow and kamloops trout, and camp. At Diamond Lake's tiny store, pick up food and snacks for the next 32 miles. Also come prepared with spares, tools, warm clothes, and sleeping bags.

Well-paved State 138, the only road north, leads up a short hill, then over long, gentle grades. Be sure to stay off the sharp little red rocks on the roadside or you could puncture a tire. Shoulders are narrow and eventually disappear totally. About 5 miles into dense forest, stay on paved State 138 by turning sharply left at the narrow graveled road twisting into the woods. The air snaps with aromas of lodgepole and ponderosa pine, Douglas fir, and fragrant incense cedar. As you coast softly, the forest murmurs and rustles around you: a Steller's jay scolds, a woodpecker rivets on a nearby tree, a tree toad chirps. Even before you see it, you hear the shushing Umpqua.

As you join the river, you can turn right and walk along a graveled lane to Toketee Reservoir, where you can snack on the grassy banks and perhaps glimpse deer

DISTANCE:	83 miles one way.
TERRAIN:	Downhill coasts and some steep, rolling hills.
TRAFFIC:	Light.
DIFFICULTY:	Enough experience required to be self-sufficient on this wilderness ride. It can be shortened, however, to any length for beginners.
BEST TIME:	Any season but winter, which comes sometimes as early as September and lasts till June.
LOCATION:	Diamond Lake, north of Crater Lake National Park, on State 138.

coming to drink.

Now the river, foaming and swirling over rocks, coasts beside you. Find a cool nook along the banks to sit quietly, listen to woodsy sounds, and watch silvery steelhead or rainbow trout flashing through the clear green water. Picnic on the shores. You can either raid your knapsack or create your own lunch from juicy wild berries and freshly caught trout fried in butter. Since campfires are generally forbidden, you can cook lunch at Boulder Flat Campground.

This road has some rough bumps: a particularly bad spot is beyond Eagle Rock Campground. Three miles past Eagle Rock, you coast into Dry Creek, with a small store, usually open, but don't de-

pend on it. Beyond Apple Creek Campground you climb a short hill, then plunge again beside the green mountain river. A long coast past another campground brings you to Steamboat Inn, where you can stop for a snack. At the inn you can turn right and go 6 miles to Steamboat Falls, with camping and swimming.

Back on State 138, the river has become wide and an even deeper green. Passing more campgrounds 4 miles beyond the inn, your ride levels a bit as you spin past craggy brown rocks and leave Umpqua National Forest.

Susan Creek State Park has camping and picnicking and makes a pleasant stopover. Two miles past Smith Springs County Park, you pass a motel and country store. Here your ride levels and you begin to climb a few hills, gradually leaving forests behind and pedaling through farmland to Glide. As you go on through Glide, stop near the bridge for lovely views where the Little and Umpqua rivers meet. Flat road with a few easy slopes brings you onto a four-lane highway with a wide shoulder and fast traffic. You climb a long, steep hill and pedal into Roseburg. Here you can camp, refresh your supplies, stop if you need to at a bike shop, and either have someone meet you (an ideal arrangement) or return on the long uphill to Diamond Lake.

WHERE TO STAY

Campgrounds and motels are available along the route as indicated in the tour description, as well as in Roseburg. Most camps mentioned operate on a first-come first-served basis and either cost $1 or are free.

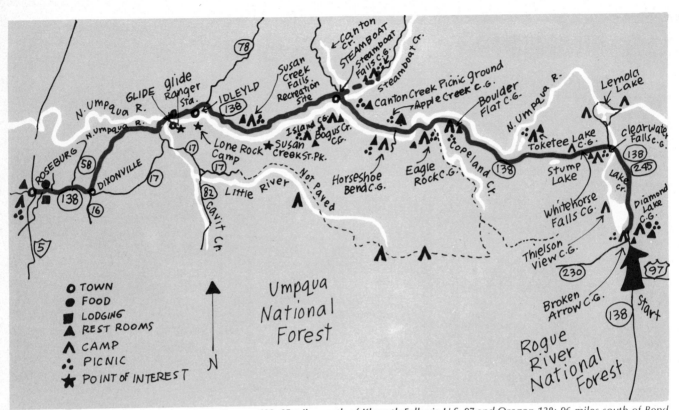

Diamond Lake is in southwestern Oregon on Oregon 138; 85 miles north of Klamath Falls via U.S. 97 and Oregon 138; 96 miles south of Bend via U.S. 97 and Oregon 138.

FOR SPARE PARTS AND REPAIRS

Hill's Wheel World, 2618 West Harvard Boulevard, Roseburg, Oregon; (503) 672-4524.

OREGON PINE EDIBLES

Stalk the life of the Algonquin Indian as you return to the wilderness in Oregon's backwoods. Brew Douglas-fir tea over your campfire, add roasted piñon pine nuts to your "gorp," and chew the sugar pine's sweet gum for quick energy on this escape from civilization.

Douglas-fir tea can be made by filling a cup about half full with fresh young needles, adding water boiled over your campfire, steeping for about ten minutes, and straining. You can recognize the Douglas fir by its soft, flat, pointed blue-green or yellow-green needles about one inch long which grow all around the twig; its oval cone, hanging down instead of disintegrating on the tree as do other fir cones; its furrowed cinnamon-brown bark; and the distinctive three-pronged bracts which grow on the female cones.

Piñon pine nuts are best prepared if you dig a pit, toss in the green cones, then cover and roast until ashy. Remove from the fire, cool, and peel off the shells by hand to reach the succulent nuts. You can recognize the single-leaf piñon by its gray-green needles which grow singly.

Sugar pine sap, which oozes from small natural cuts near the pine's base, can be used as a sugary gum or as a sweetener for your tea or coffee. When fresh, the sap is white. Use this sweetener in moderation because of its laxative quality. The sugar pine has stiff blue-green needles growing in bundles of five and ranging from two to five inches long; a thin-scaled yellowish-brown cone about four to ten inches long; and a scaly look to the older cinnamon-colored bark.

113. CRATER LAKE RIM RUN

Eight thousand feet high in Oregon's Cascade Mountains, you circle the flat lava rim of the extinct volcano Mount Mazama, filled now with a deep blue lake. Around you grow fir and mountain hemlock forests and alpine wildflower meadows. This tour offers much: safe roads, light traffic, courteous drivers, no dogs, perfect mountain scenery, and only one hill.

To reach this tour's starting point—Rim Village—you may want to enter the park through either the west or south entrance; the north entrance takes you halfway around the lake before you come to the village. The park fee for cars is $2 and for bikes 50¢, though rangers do not always collect the bike fee. Don't let the crowds at Rim Village worry you; for some reason many people buying souvenirs here take one peek at the lake and then drive back down the mountainside. Either bring a picnic and light snacks with you, or if you are unconcerned about variety, buy them at the village. You find no other eating facilities or stores in the park.

Pedal clockwise around the lake on Rim Drive, with lake views to your right and valleys of evergreens on your left. This well-paved road has no shoulders, but in 4 miles, just past Discovery Point's parking lot, the road becomes one-way, giving motorists ample space to pass you. You ride first through alpine meadows of wildflowers, then cut through rocky passes. The lake's color varies from vivid cobalt with turquoise highlights to deep navy and purple. The rich blues are a result of the lake's 1,932-foot depth. In the western hemisphere only one Canadian lake is deeper. Occasionally you spot an eagle or hawk circling overhead or glimpse a blue Steller's jay balanced on a lone narrow branch over the water. Turnouts for viewing are abundant. Stop often, and because you are on a bike, anywhere.

You wind through more grassy meadows where you may glimpse deer or red fox. Pause to relax on a cliff overlooking the water or to hike into the forests.

At the North Entrance Road junction, stay right. Along the rim lies Llao Rock, a huge dacite flow filling what was once a glacial valley. Beyond the junction, you roll over a gradual hill to a picnic spot where you can eat overlooking Steel Bay. A few more minutes bring you to another picnic area and a boat landing. Traffic is often congested here. You can lock your bike and hike 1.1 miles down winding Cleetwood Trail to the lake's edge, where you can take a naturalist-guided launch, rent a rowboat to explore the lake, fish for rainbow trout, small landlocked salmon, and kokanee (no license required), or simply get a good look at the lava mass known as Phantom Ship and the tiny volcano Wizard Island. The launch rides take two and a half hours, and the launches run from mid-June to Labor Day, 9 A.M. to 4:30 P.M. If you have an expensive bike, you are justifiably concerned about leaving it unattended for that long. So if you are interested in the boat rides, you may want to return later.

You climb gradually beyond the boat area, then coast past two picnic grounds to Cloudcap Viewpoint, where two-way traffic begins again. Beyond Cloudcap you coast 2 more miles to a stop sign where you turn left. Four miles farther, you may encounter heavier traffic as cars go down to The Pinnacles, tall pumice spires rising 200 feet from Wheeler Creek Canyon's floor. The total 12-mile side trip into the canyon is scenic, but for experts only. Traffic can be heavy, and though coasting is fun, you have a 6-mile-long 7-percent grade coming out.

About 7 more miles through forests bring you to Castle Crest Wildflower Garden. Stop here, lock your bike to a secluded tree, and wander through lodgepole pine and mountain hemlock woods, across narrow streams, and through meadows of purple Cascade asters, Crater Lake currants, and vivid scarlet monkey flowers. After this hike you have a tough (almost 4-percent) 3-mile climb back to Rim Village to complete

DISTANCE:	33 miles.
TERRAIN:	Flat, with one tough hill.
TRAFFIC:	Light in September; moderate on summer weekdays; heavy on summer weekends.
DIFFICULTY:	Okay for beginners and families, who may want to walk part of the hill.
BEST TIME:	July through September. The rim is often closed by snow clear through June. If you can come just after the rim is cleared or in September, traffic will be nil.
LOCATION:	Crater Lake National Park, Oregon.

the loop. You may have to walk part way, but you can see more by going slowly anyway. Spend the rest of the day exploring hiking trails. An enjoyable walk is two and a half miles to the top of Garfield Peak, 1,900 feet above the lake and an ideal spot to watch the sunset.

WHERE TO STAY

Crater Lake Lodge has a hotel and cabins near Rim Village. Make early reservations by writing Crater Lake Lodge, Inc., Crater Lake National Park, Crater Lake, Oregon 97604, or phoning (503) 594-2511.

The park also has three campgrounds, operated on a first-come first-served basis: Rim Village Campground, at Rim Village; Lost Creek Campground, midway on the road to The Pinnacles; and Mazama Campground, on State 62 as you go from Rim Village toward the south and west entrances.

FOR SPARE PARTS, REPAIRS, FURTHER INFORMATION

Granados Cyclery, 351 East Main Street, Klamath Falls, Oregon 97601; (503) 884-4672. Javie Granados rides this tour and can give you further information. He's a good man to contact about current weather conditions on the rim. Javie can also be a big help: though his shop is 46 miles from the south entrance, he will come pick you up in his truck after hours if you get stranded. Also for information write to the Superintendent, Crater Lake National Park, Box 7, Crater Lake, Oregon 97604. (From October through May, Box 672, Medford, Oregon 97501.)

NEARBY

Klamath Lake, with abundant waterfowl including the great white pelican, is just south of the park on State 62, while Diamond Lake and Umpqua National Forest are north on State 138, about 7 miles from the park's north entrance. Both offer fantastic tours and the roads to them have fairly gradual slopes and are well paved. See pages 239 and 235 for details on these two rides.

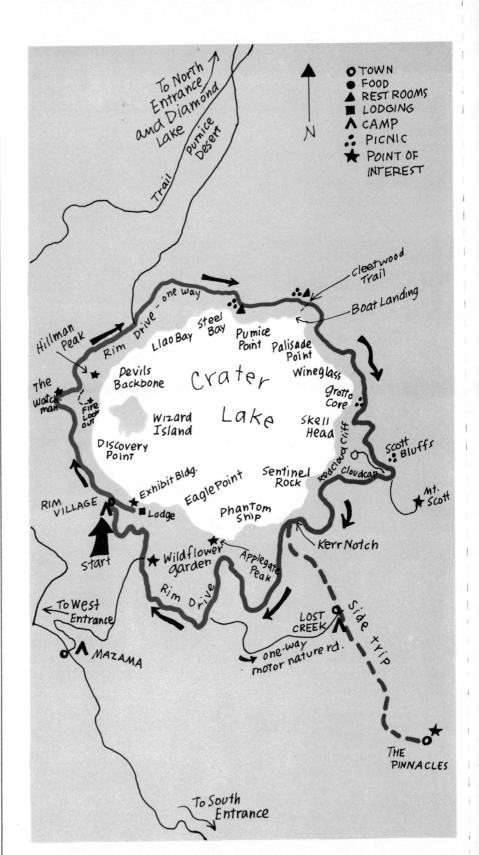

Crater Lake National Park is in southwestern Oregon with accesses off Oregon 62 from the south, Oregon 138 from the north, and Oregon 232 from the east; 57 miles north of Klamath Falls via U.S. 97 and Oregon 62.

114. KLAMATH LAKE RENDEZVOUS

For communion with nature, this tour around Klamath Lake is idyllic. Here you inevitably see flocks of ducks and geese, white sand cranes, and herons as well as the great white pelican, weighing fifteen to twenty pounds with a wing span of eight to ten feet. Mule deer roam the mountain hemlock, lodgepole, and ponderosa pine forests. The lake, backed by the Cascade Mountains, has dozens of swimming bays and excellent trout fishing.

Begin your tour in Klamath Falls, a busy mountain town on the edge of Klamath Lake. Stock up with provisions—wine, bread, cheese, raisins, nuts, and whatever else you need—before leaving. Throughout the ride you will find a few country stores for extra supplies, too. Bring a jacket and warm sleeping bag; even warm sunny days have chilly nights here.

Leave Klamath Falls on Nevada Avenue, which eventually becomes Lakeshore Drive and then State 140. Shoulders on this road and throughout the tour are narrow or nonexistent, but traffic is light and residents usually drive at a relaxed pace. Your first stop is Moore Park, on the lake, with picnicking, archery, tennis, a nature trail, zoo, and children's playground. From here you pass the marina and pedal into rolling farmland. You pass through vast wheat fields and cattle ranches, with a blue sliver of lake and mountains in the distance.

About 10 miles outside Klamath Falls, the lake rolls in beside you. Perch on the rocks to rest, catch a fresh fish lunch, or watch the abundant waterfowl. On any day the lake will likely be crowded with ducks and geese. Watch, too, for huge white pelicans who nest here from March to November.

DISTANCE:	80 miles.
TERRAIN:	Flat to gently rolling hills.
TRAFFIC:	Light.
DIFFICULTY:	Okay for beginners, who will probably want to take two or even three days; a good weekend vacation for families.
BEST TIME:	Anytime but winter, which can come as early as late September.
LOCATION:	Klamath Falls in southern Oregon, reached via U.S. 97.

A few minutes of riding bring you to a rest area on your right, beyond which you start up the tour's steepest hill, known locally as Doke Mountain. You climb steeply for 2 miles, level off a bit, then climb gradually for 2 more miles before you reach the crest and coast, with lake views to your right. In about 2 more miles, the road levels and you pedal through wide alpine meadows to Winema National Forest. Soon you reach a wayside inn, Whispering Pines Restaurant, where you can stop for a snack.

Beyond Whispering Pines, State 140 branches left, toward Lake of the Woods. About 33 miles from Klamath Falls, Lake of the Woods makes a good first-night camping spot if you want a leisurely tour. After making camp, you can buy a few supplies at the store, swim,

hike through the forests, fish, or rent a boat. There is a children's playground here, too.

If you want to ride farther the first day, don't follow State 140 toward Lake of the Woods; go right instead. If you decide to go right, beyond the fork you find a coffee shop, filling station, and cabins. Then a bit farther down a hill, there's a nice picnic area with tables. Just past the "no shoulder" sign, you veer left and start a smooth, gradual climb through wide grassy marshlands, then spin easily down again. This is peaceful land, and you can stop anytime to wander through the meadows, examine a wildflower, observe a deer. About 9 miles beyond the point where you veered left, you see a mountain creek trickling back through the pines, a nice place to rest, picnic, or explore. It's another 15 miles from here to Fort Klamath and 3 miles beyond that to Kimball State Park, where you can camp, so don't remain here long if it's getting late in the day.

In Fort Klamath turn right at the sign toward Kimball State Park, then left onto State 232, on which the park is located. There are only six campsites in this scenic park beside a mountain stream, but you are so far off the beaten path, you should have no problem. If necessary (it may even be preferable), you can simply drop your sleeping bag beneath a sugar pine.

Another good overnight camping spot or side trip is Collier Memorial State Park on U.S. 97. Here you find excellent trout fishing, picnicking, a logging museum, and lots of mosquitoes; bring repellent. To reach the park, go south from Fort Klamath on State 62 through the tiny community of Klamath Agency. About a mile outside this town, turn left on the first paved road you reach and pedal about 3 miles to U.S. 97. Turn left on U.S. 97 and ride another 5 miles to Collier State Park. If you stay here your first night, you will have ridden 65 miles for the day.

The 30 miles from Collier State Park back into Klamath Falls is along a dry, flat part of the Klamath Basin, so carry water. To return to Klamath Falls, go back to the intersection of State 62 and the road south of Klamath Agency, cross 62, and ride south on the secondary paved road, which takes you straight to Modoc Point. From Modoc Point take U.S. 97 back into Klamath Falls, your tour's end. U.S. 97 has narrow or nonexistent shoulders, and the road is sometimes used by logging trucks (the drivers are quite courteous). Experts can probably start early and reach Klamath Falls by 10 A.M., thereby avoiding most traffic. Families or beginners, however, should consider retracing their ride on less traveled roads on the lake's west side.

WHERE TO STAY

Besides the above-mentioned campgrounds, you can also stay in Klamath Falls in one of the many motels or the KOA campground. Another possibility for mid-tour is to go north of Fort Klamath on State 62 for about 5 miles to a group of quaint, inexpensive cabins with high cozy beds and old-fashioned gas stoves.

FOR SPARE PARTS, REPAIRS, FURTHER INFORMATION

Granados Cyclery, 351 East Main Street, Klamath Falls, Oregon 97601; (503) 884-4672. Javie Granados rides this tour himself and can tell you anything else you would like to know. He also happens to be a lifesaver: his shop is the only one in the area and he will come to pick you up in his truck after hours if you break down, another reason why families and beginners can handle this

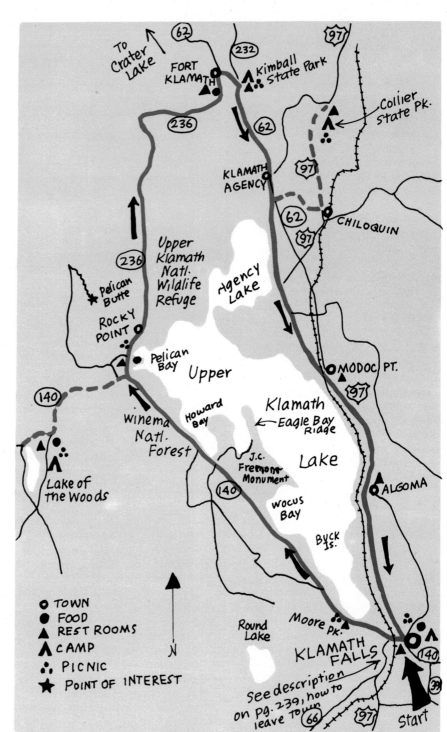

Klamath Falls is in southwestern Oregon on U.S. 97 and Oregon 39; 279 miles south of Portland via I-5, Oregon 58, and U.S. 97; 367 miles northeast of San Francisco, California, via I-80, 5 and U.S. 97.

jaunt.

Crater Lake National Park, with the deepest blue lake you will ever see, is just north of this loop on State 62, which winds gradually uphill through evergreen forests. A bike ride around Crater Lake's rim is not to be missed if you are in this area. See the Crater Lake Rim Run on p. 237 for detailed information.

115. SLEEPING VOLCANOES VAGABOND

Obsidian flows, pumice deposits, two ice-blue lakes in a forest-rimmed volcanic crater, and a lantern tour through a lava tunnel await you on this 50-mile wilderness ride through central Oregon. This tour is designed for sturdy beginners, but challenging side trips are outlined for experienced cyclists.

To stay on lightly traveled roads, start at La Pine State Recreation Area on the icy trout- and salmon-filled Deschutes River, 22 miles south of Bend and 8.5 miles north of La Pine off U.S. 97. Carry all the food you will need for the tour, plus spare parts and tools. This first road is a narrow blacktop, wide enough for one car to pass you, but too skimpy if two cars meet. Usually the only major traffic here is on July 4th. Soon you reach U.S. 97, with fast traffic, including some logging trucks, and no shoulders. Here you can go right to follow the main tour or left for an experts' side trip to a lava cave.

Lava Cave Side Trip (24 miles round trip)

The 10-mile ride one way to Lava River Caves State Park is best taken in early morning or on a light-traffic day. You pass a lava-cast forest to reach the park, where you can rent a lantern to explore a primeval underground lava tunnel created by an ancient liquid rock river. Cave temperatures stay about 40 degrees year round, so bring a light jacket.

Two miles farther north, you reach Lava Butte, an extinct volcanic cone, where you can trek up a steep paved road for a spectacular view of ten snowcapped Cascade peaks. Then return on U.S. 97 south to pick up the main tour.

On the main tour going south, you turn left in three and a half miles onto the flat, narrow paved forest service road (Route 2129) toward Newberry Crater. Beyond the bridge across Paulina (paul-EYE-nah) Creek at Prairie Campground, stay right on the paved road which now begins climbing and winding through cool ponderosa pine, lodgepole pine, western red cedar, and Douglas fir forests. Little mountain brooks cross your path, and you can stop anytime to rest or picnic in a quiet clearing. Watch near the water for mule deer. You may also glimpse bears or possibly pronghorn (antelope) which spend their summers here.

DISTANCE:	50 miles round trip, excluding side trips.
TERRAIN:	Rolling hills.
TRAFFIC:	Light to moderate; often heavy on U.S. 97.
DIFFICULTY:	Okay for sturdy beginners if they take two days. Not recommended for families with young riders because of the narrow roads.
BEST TIME:	Midsummer. Snow covers the forest road from late September to mid-June.
LOCATION:	Deschutes National Forest, south of Bend, Oregon, on the eastern slopes of the Cascade Mountains.

More rolling climbs bring you to Newberry Crater, an ancient volcanic caldera containing two clear turquoise lakes. Rock hounds can unearth obsidian here. Stop at the first lake—Paulina Lake—to rest along shimmering water. A peaceful footpath meanders around the lake. Above the campground here towers Paulina Peak. On a clear midsummer day, hearty souls can trek 7 steep miles up twisty gravel road to the frigid summit to view snow-topped mountains, lakes, rivers, and deep pine forests in every direction. Bring warm clothes on this jaunt. Clincher tires are recommended. The descent is thrilling but steep, so take care.

Back on the paved forest road, you can camp beside Paulina Lake or pedal on through the crater to East Lake and more campsites. Fishing, by the way, is superb in these waters. For dinner you might catch pan-sized rainbow, brook, brown, Dolly Varden, golden, or lake trout. Return to La Pine Recreation Area by the same tour route.

Photography Hints

The forest shelters about 250 species of birds and mammals, and your best chance to see and photograph them is around the lakes and streams. Watch for the rare American osprey, bald eagle, sandhill crane, and prairie falcon. The mountains, rivers, lakes, and forests will keep you busy for hours, with the summits of Lava Butte and Paulina Peak offering outstanding photographic possibilities.

WHERE TO STAY

Campgrounds listed in the tour description are operated on a first-come first-served basis. All fees are $2. No motels are located along the route.

FOR FURTHER INFORMATION

To see if the forest road is free of snow, you can phone the state highway department at (503) 227-1744 or inquire at La Pine, Oregon, before you start out. Additional Deschutes National Forest information is available from the National Forest Service, Pacific Northwest Region, 319 S.W. Pine Street, P.O. Box 3623, Portland, Oregon 97208.

NEARBY

Bend, 22 miles north of La Pine Recreation Area on busy U.S. 97, has five city parks as well as Pilot Butte State Park, 1 mile east of town on U.S. 20, with excellent mountain scenery. From Bend you can also try the paved 100-mile loop along Cascade Lakes Highway. This strenuous tour, for experts only, takes you through pine forests past lakes and rocky streams. Allow two days and pack warm clothing. The routing is easy: follow Cascade Lakes Highway from Bend to U.S. 97, turn left, and return to Bend. Inquire locally about road conditions and obtain a good map before starting out.

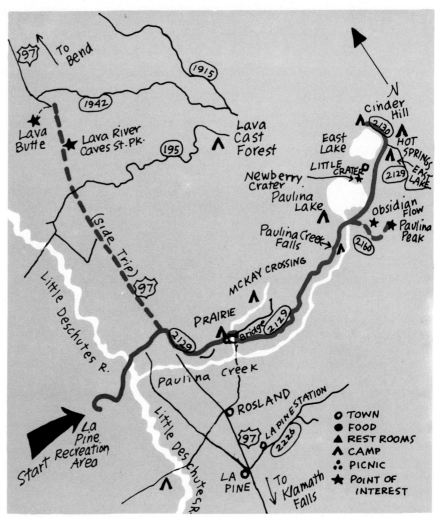

La Pine Recreation Area is in central Oregon in Deschutes National Forest off U.S. 97; 185 miles southeast of Portland via I-5, U.S. 20 and 97; 122 miles north of Klamath Falls via U.S. 97.

California and the Great South- west

116. SALT LAKE POTPOURRI

On this tour you experience a potpourri of Utah's attractions: canyons, mountains, marshes, forests, resorts, Morman temples, and famed Great Salt Lake. While experts can manage this ride on a three-day weekend, less experienced cyclists should plan on five days to a week.

Start in farm country at Ogden, founded by Brigham Young. Get the feel of Utah cycling by touring Ogden's broad, straight streets lined with box elder, elm, poplar, and cottonwood. During the last week of July, the city holds Pioneer Days, celebrating the early Morman era with pageants, parades, and rodeos. Utah heat can be stultifying: fill an extra canteen and carry suntan lotion.

Pedal north of Ogden on U.S. 91, a wide four-lane highway stretching along the Great Basin's arid floor, irrigated to produce fields and orchards. Mountains tower to your right, while to your left stretches the Great Salt Lake. Traffic can be heavy here on weekends. On a hot, dry day, pause at a valley fruit stand. About 4 miles from Brigham City, you can stop at the little town of Willard to swim in a fresh-water lake at Great Salt Lake's edge.

Brigham City has two good historic spots to explore: the Latter-Day Saints Tabernacle (1881), considered Utah's loveliest tabernacle, and the County Courthouse Relic Room, with artifacts dating to Brigham Young's day. After a snack, you can either continue north on U.S. 91 or take time to ride 15 miles west to Great Salt Lake's Bear River Bay and the Bear River Migratory Bird Refuge.

Bear River Side Trip (30 miles round trip)

A flat, winding narrow road

DISTANCE:	230 miles, excluding side trips.
TERRAIN:	Mountain canyons, lots of hills; steep climbs and rapid descents.
TRAFFIC:	Light on weekdays; heavy in spots on weekends.
DIFFICULTY:	Entire tour for experienced cyclists. Alpine gears recommended.
BEST TIME:	Late summer and early autumn, when roads at the summit should be in good repair.
LOCATION:	Starts in Ogden, Utah, 35 miles north of Salt Lake City on I-80 and I-15.

leads to the bird refuge. In summer these marshes become the Rocky Mountain region's greatest waterfowl breeding spot. In season as many as one million wild geese and ducks can be seen, while autumn brings migrating whistling swans. You may also glimpse muskrats, skunks, beavers, weasels, and possibly even a bobcat. After picnicking, return to the main route.

Beyond Brigham City you climb steeply through Sardine Canyon and over the summit of the Wasatch Mountain Range, from which you have spectacular views of jagged peaks and evergreen-covered slopes. Then finally you coast

onto the long, flat Cache Valley floor.

In Logan take time to visit the gray limestone Morman Temple (1878), the twin towers of which you see on the hillside as you enter Logan. You also might pedal 12 miles south of town on State 101 to Hyrum Lake State Recreation Area, a pleasant spot to swim, picnic, or camp. This 24-mile round trip makes a pleasant one-day outing for beginners.

Beyond Logan you pass Utah State University, a cool, shaded rest spot, then begin a long, slow climb for about 32 miles through Logan Canyon. Cottonwoods, box elders, aspens, and maples cling to the riverbanks and shade your ride. Pause along the river to rest your tired legs in icy water, and if you have a license, to catch a fresh trout dinner. Many short nature trails meander through the canyon. Try the invigorating one-and-a-half-mile trek to Jardine Juniper, a gnarled old tree believed to be three thousand years old. Wildflowers bloom profusely in spring, and you can see wild geraniums, Indian paintbrush, columbine, lupine, and deep blue larkspur.

From Logan Canyon you wind beside jagged rock walls and past cool picnic areas, campgrounds, and Beaver Mountain Ski Resort to the 7,805-foot summit. From here you view parts of Utah, Idaho, and Wyoming, with blue-green Bear Lake glittering through forests far below. In early morning deer often graze here along the fringes of the rye grass pastures. Caution: From the summit you plunge 1,500 feet in 7 miles around steep hairpin curves, so don't go too fast and be careful.

Finally you coast into Garden City, a small farming community on Bear Lake's shore. A good campground lies half a mile north of town along the water. From Garden City you take State 30 along the lakeshore and ride through Pickleville and Laketown (no services in either) to Sage Creek Junction where you turn right onto State 16. From this junction you have an 18-mile ride to Woodruff through high (6,000 feet and more) farm and cattle country. The road gains altitude gradually as you pedal toward Woodruff, a farming settlement and one of Utah's cold spots. Have your jacket ready. There's a small motel here.

Turn right in Woodruff onto State 39 and pedal along Walton Canyon's willow-bordered stream where beavers build their dams. You climb still higher to Monte Cristo Campground, near the 9,000-foot summit. Harsh winters leave the summit road full of potholes, but repairs are usually complete by midsummer. Rest awhile near Monte Cristo Peak beneath aspens and firs.

You have an exhilarating downhill all the way from Monte Cristo to Ogden. Caution: Don't take chances by speeding too fast along unfamiliar road. A good rest stop is Huntsville, a friendly mountain hamlet. Ask for directions to the monastery 4 miles southeast of town, where you can buy a loaf of stone-ground wheat bread.

For a pleasant evening in the mountains, stay overnight at one of the many campgrounds in this vicinity. At Pineview Reservoir you can swim, boat, picnic, or fish. Stopping here gives you a chance to tackle Ogden Canyon in early morning without traffic. Once you see the narrow lane squeezed between rocky cliffs thousands of feet high, you will understand why it's best to ride the canyon unhassled by cars. Early morning is also a choice time to glimpse elk and deer drinking at the river. State 39 eventually winds into Ogden, completing the loop.

WHERE TO STAY

Finding a motel on this tour should be no problem. Motels in and around Ogden include a Holiday Inn and Ramada Inn, as well as the following: OgdenTravelodge, 2110 Washington Boulevard; (801) 394-4563. Weston's Desert Inn, 1825 Washington Boulevard; (801) 394-5503. Millstream, 1450 Washington Boulevard; (801) 394-9425.

Other motels: Bay View, 1167 South Main, Brigham City; (801) 723-8511. Westward Ho, 505 North Main, Brigham City; (801) 723-8584. Alta, 51 East 5 North, Logan; (801) 752-6300. Baugh, 153 South Main Street, Logan; (801) 752-5220. Motels are also available in Garden City, Woodruff, and Huntsville.

Campgrounds are numerous, too. The fees are usually $1. The campgrounds below are listed in the order you encounter them: Willard Bay State Park 15 miles north of Ogden; open April through November; swimming, fishing, boating, and hiking. Box Elder, 5 miles east of Brigham City on U.S. 89; open May 15th to September 30th. Bridger, about 5 miles east of Logan on U.S. 89; open May 15th to September 30th. Spring Hollow, about 7 miles east of Logan on 89; open May 15th to September 30th. Guinavah and Malibu, seven and a half miles east of Logan on 89; open May 15 to Sep-

tember 30th. You find six campgrounds in the next 18 miles, the last two of which are listed: Twin Bridges, about 16 miles east of Logan on 89; open May 15th to September 30th. Twin Bridges, about 16 miles east of Logan on 89; open May 15th to September 30th; no fee. Red Banks, 25 miles northeast of Logan on 89; open June 1st to September 30th. Bear Lake State Park, half a mile north of Garden City on U.S. 89; open year round; (801) 946-3208. Monte Cristo, 22 miles from Woodruff on State 39, at the summit; open July 1st to September 9th. You also find five campgrounds before you reach Huntsville and two camps along Pineview Reservoir. Most are open May 15th to September 30th, though some have a season fifteen days shorter, either opening May 30th or closing September 15th.

FOR SPARE PARTS, REPAIRS, FURTHER INFORMATION

Miller's Ski and Cycle Haus, 834 Washington Boulevard, Ogden, Utah 84404; (801) 392-3911. Allen and Dale Miller both cycle this

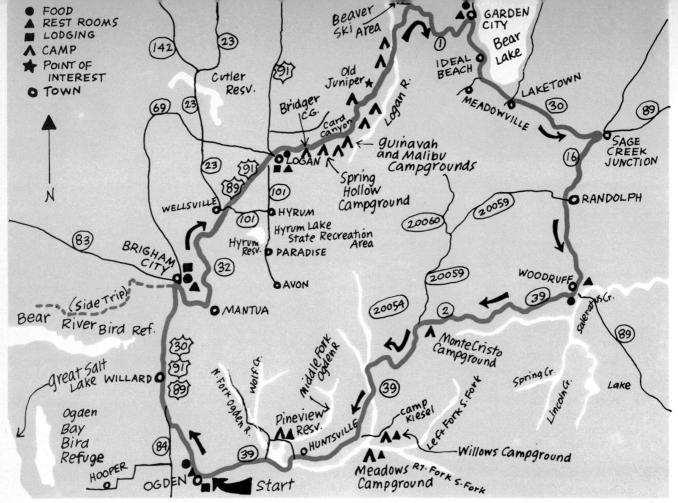

Ogden is in northern Utah on I-80N and Utah 39; 35 miles north of Salt Lake City via I-15 and 80; 315 miles southeast of Boise, Idaho, via I-80N, U.S. 26/30, and I-80N.

tour and can provide further information. Their shop is open Monday through Saturday, 10 A.M. to 6 P.M. They also handle parts and repairs for most foreign makes and carry touring equipment.

WILDFLOWERS IN THE CANYONS

While pedaling through Cache National Forest, you may see hundreds of wildflower varieties, especially brilliant in spring. Here are just a few you may find along the trail or near your camp.

Arrowleaf balsamroot. You will see this brilliant yellow flower at its peak in mid-May. Its stalk is long, thick, and woolly, with just one or two tiny narrow leaves about halfway up the stem. The plant is easily recognized by its great clumps of arrow-shaped leaves, after which it is named.

Horsemint. You can identify horsemint by its characteristic minty smell. The small white or pink flowers grow in clusters. The leaves grow opposite each other

and are almost triangular, with ragged edges. For a fragrant campfire tea, fill a cup about a third full with these leaves, add boiling water, steep for three to five minutes, discard the leaves, and drink.

Larkspur. These dark blue or purplish flowers have five sepals resembling petals and four petals which grow in pairs. The upper petals are white or yellowish veined with blue and look like a dunce cap, while the lower two are usually blue and have a tuft of hair near the middle. The leaves grow alternately and are deeply divided and feathery.

Wild geranium. This flower can be vivid rose, pink, purple, or white. It has five sepals, five petals, and ten stamens, and is sometimes called storksbill because the pistil resembles a stork's bill. The leaves grow opposite each other and usually cluster about the plant's base.

1. Arrowleaf Balsamroot
2. Larkspur
3. Horsemint
4. Wild Geranium

117. ALPINE CANYON CHALLENGE

For romance and high adventure, cycling through Utah's mountains ranks with sailing across the Pacific on a raft or climbing Mount Everest. In fact, the similarities between this mountain canyon ride and an Everest expedition are many, as you pedal through steep passes, weave around hairpin curves, and conquer the summit. You might try this tour "because it's there," but there are better reasons: swift mountain streams, pine forests, an underground cavern, and snowcapped Mount Timpanogos, to name only a few.

Begin this adventure in American Fork Canyon at Timpanogos Cave National Monument. Before you ride, hike the one and a half miles up to the cave. For 50¢ you can explore the chilly underground limestone cavern with its lemon-yellow walls and filigrees of translucent pink and white crystals.

Your ride takes you along a mountain brook past campsites and scrub oak and sagebrush. Soon you start a twisting 12-mile climb toward the 8,000-foot summit. Cottonwood, box elder, willow, and maple trees begin to replace the dry sparse growth at lower elevations, and you can see sun glinting from the glacier on the east slope of Mount Timpanogos. Stop along the way to sit quietly by a stream or to hunt for rocks and fossils.

Your legs strain as you reach evergreen forests. Then more climbing brings you into alpine meadows dotted with aspen and spruce. If you ride in mid-September, you may encounter sheep flocks being herded along the road from their summer grazing land. From the summit you have a swift downhill coast to Aspen Grove, which offers camping, swimming and hiking. To eat here, make advance reservations with the Alumni

DISTANCE:	37 miles.
TERRAIN:	Steep and challenging.
TRAFFIC:	Heavy on weekends; light on weekdays.
DIFFICULTY:	For experts only. Alpine gears recommended.
BEST TIME:	Weekdays, June through September, to avoid snow and traffic.
LOCATION:	Uinta National Forest, Utah, north of Provo and south of Salt Lake City on U.S. 89.

Association, Brigham Young University, Provo, Utah 84601.

Beyond Aspen Grove the road has sharp switchbacks for 5 miles; the hills are steeper then they look, so be careful. Finally the slopes become more gentle as you approach Sundance Ski Resort, where you can rent a horse to explore the rocky hillsides. Beyond Sundance you wind through deciduous forests along the Provo River's north fork, a lovely little alpine stream. Pause along here to enjoy wide views of the valley. Then turn right on U.S. 189 and coast down into Provo Canyon, where you can hike to the base of Bridal Veil Falls or take the gondola sky ride up the mountain for $2 to view the 430-foot falls from above. The main tour follows the canyon's north fork, but you can also venture down the south fork to one of the many camping spots in the canyon. Before leaving Provo Canyon, fish for mountain trout or try tubing on

the icy river.

At Olmstead follow State 52. Then turn right on U.S. 89 and 91, and head toward Pleasant Grove through mountain foothills. The grassy slopes grow green in spring, burn crackly dry by autumn. Pleasant Grove has motels, filling stations, and snack stops. You ride out of town on State 146 through five and a half more miles of grasslands, then turn right onto State 80 and pedal back to Timpanogos Cave National Monument.

WHERE TO STAY

Campgrounds along this loop are numerous and you will have no trouble finding a spot. Most are located off State 80 and maintained by Uinta National Forest. The fee is usually $1. In the order you pass them, the camps include the following:

Mileage from State 146 and 80 Junction

3   House Rock, May 15th to October 15th.

4.5   Grey Cliffs, May 15th to October 15th.

4.5   North Mill, May 15th to October 15th.

4.7   Little Mill, May 15th to October 15th.

5.3   Granite Flat, Martin, Mile Rock, Roadhouse, and Warnick, all in this vicinity. Follow the signs. All are open May 15th to October 15th, except Granite Flat, open June 1st.

8.5   Timpooneke, June 1st to September 30th.

8.5   Altamont, May 15th to October 15th.

There are also many campsites in Provo Canyon off U.S. 189. If you do camp here, bring warm clothes and cozy sleeping bags; canyon nights are cold.

Motels are found in Pleasant Grove and Provo. To stay in one of the modern cabins at Aspen Grove, write the Alumni Association, Brigham Young University, Provo, Utah 84601, for reservations.

FOR SPARE PARTS AND REPAIRS

The nearest bike shop is in Provo, so have your bike in top shape before you leave and check those brakes.

Timpanogos Cave National Monument is in north-central Utah on Utah 80; 30 miles north of Provo via Utah 80; 60 miles south of Salt Lake City via U.S. 89 and Utah 80.

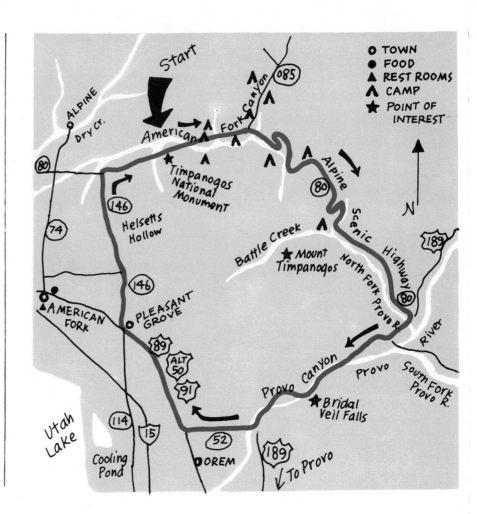

118. ARCHES RED ROCK RIDE

Red rock arches loop toward an azure sky, jagged pinnacles rise to crimson points, and chasms glow deep orange as you ride through Arches National Park in Utah. In this isolated world of stone, you are at first overwhelmed by the vivid spires, cones, and pedestals. Then on a bike you begin to notice subtler details: a chipmunk scurrying beside you, a mule deer nibbling on grass, or a delicate white cliff rose.

Park your car at the Visitor Center off U.S. 163. The park has no eating facilities, so bring all the food you will need. The nearest grocery stores and restaurants are in Moab, 5 miles south of the park entrance. Carry spare parts, tools, lots of water, sun lotion, and warm clothing for chilly evenings. Even though daytime temperatures may average 77 degrees in March, nights can drop to a wintery 18 degrees.

From the Visitor Center, you have an immediate steep climb up to a plateau; consider a walk up this stretch to become acquainted with the terrain and keep from tiring yourself at the beginning. Then you skim along flat park road past excellent mountain views. Though the highway is well paved, watch out for treacherous drainage gratings which often form the road's only shoulder. The maximum auto speed limit is 45 m.p.h. When you reach Park Avenue, lock your bike and hike along the narrow, twisting one-mile trail beneath pinnacles which tower above you like skyscrapers.

Back on the road, you soon coast from the plateau to Courthouse Wash. You climb steeply from Courthouse Wash for 1.5 miles, rise more gradually for about a mile, then continue up a slope which tests your stamina. Finally, about a mile before The Windows

DISTANCE:	35.8 miles round trip
TERRAIN:	Hilly, with some steep climbs and rapid descents.
TRAFFIC:	Heaviest from Easter through Labor Day; lightest in late October and November until the snow falls.
DIFFICULTY:	Requires experience and a 10-speed bike because of the tough terrain.
BEST TIME:	October through April; avoid May through September, when temperatures average in the 90's or above.
LOCATION:	Arches National Park, Utah.

turnoff, the road levels. Past Balanced Rock, at the picnic area, you can take a hilly side trip right for 3 miles to The Windows, where you can walk to many rock coves, spires, and arches.

Turn right when you return to the main park road and continue north. Soon you coast gradually past Panorama Point, named for its exceptional views. A bit farther, take the 1.8-mile graded road toward Delicate Arch. At the Wolfe Cabin parking area, lock your bike and hike another 1.5 miles to Delicate Arch, the park's best

overlook. From here you see massive slickrock domes and jagged red cliffs, backed by the Colorado River gorge and the snow-tipped La Sal Mountains.

Back on the main tour, the road stays fairly level for about 2 miles, then rises in a long, sharp slope to Fiery Furnace, the park's best spot to watch the sunset. In summer there are ranger-guided hikes through this maze of passageways; inquire at the Visitor Center before you start the tour. Beyond Fiery Furnace you continue climbing. At last you have a short coast, followed by the final steep climb to Devils Garden Campground.

After setting up camp, lock your bike to a tree and follow the 2-mile footpath through Devils Garden past six exquisite stone arches. Later in the evening as you huddle about your campfire to combat the brisk breezes, you may hear the mournful howls of coyotes in the distance. Return the next day by the same route to the Visitor Center.

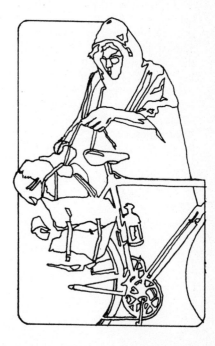

WHERE TO STAY

The nearest motels are 5 miles south of the park entrance in Moab. They include Canyonlands, Main and Center Streets on Route 163, (801) 259-5547; Moab Travelodge, 550 South Main Street, (801) 259-6171; and Ramada Inn, 182 South Main Street, (801) 259-7141.

The park's only campground, Devils Gardens, operates on a first-come first-served basis. Inquire at the Visitor Center about possible crowding before you start your tour. If there's any chance the camp may be filled by evening, drive your car through the park, select a site, and begin your tour from there. Remember, you must buy food and camping supplies before you enter the park.

FOR FURTHER INFORMATION

Write Superintendent, Canyonlands National Park, U.S. Post Office Building, Moab, Utah 84532.

NEARBY

Arches is a companion park to Canyonlands National Park, which has no paved roads. Canyonlands, however, does offer superb backcountry hiking. Many excursions through this region are available at Moab, including trips on the Colorado River that vary from two-hour jet boat rides to five-day excursions. Inquire locally or write the Chamber of Commerce, Moab, Utah 84532, for further information.

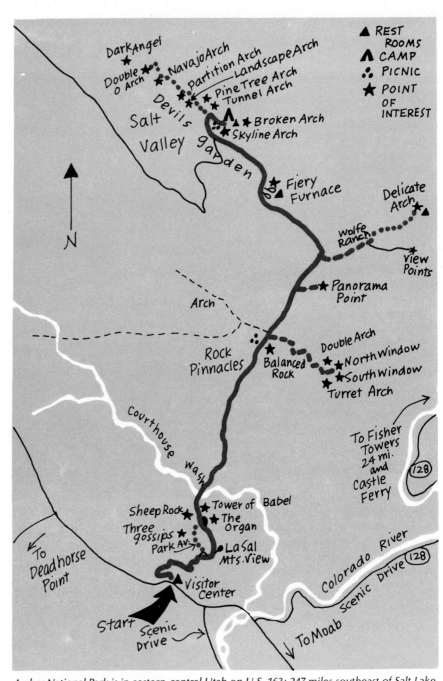

Arches National Park is in eastern-central Utah on U.S. 163; 247 miles southeast of Salt Lake City via I-15, U.S. 89, 6/50, I-70, and U.S. 163; 283 miles northwest of Gallup, New Mexico, via U.S. 666 and 163.

119. BRYCE PINK CLIFFS CAPER

DISTANCE:	35 miles round trip.
TERRAIN:	Gradual climb from the Visitor Center to Rainbow Point, then a return coast.
TRAFFIC:	Heaviest in summer; lightest from May to early June and September through October.
DIFFICULTY:	Experience is required in summer because of traffic. Okay for less experienced riders during off-season.
BEST TIME:	May to early June and September through October, when traffic is lightest and temperatures range in the 50's and 60's. Summers can be hot, with temperatures occasionally in the 90's.
LOCATION:	Bryce Canyon National Park, Utah.

Looking down from the dazzling Pink Cliffs, the craggy rock formations below may remind you of castles, cathedrals, miniature cities, and chessmen set up for battle. All is yellow, saffron, red, and lavender. Bicycle here in spring when yarrow, columbine, and pentstemon bloom or in autumn when as-pen glow beneath crisp blue skies.

Five-speed bikes can be rented at Bryce Canyon Lodge during summer. If you bring your own bike, carry spare parts and tools. The lodge has a cafeteria and snack bar open from May to mid-October; if you visit before or after these dates, bring all the food you will need for the ride. Other necessities include plenty of water and a good sunscreen lotion, even in winter. The road reaches elevations of 8,000 and 9,000 feet, making riding tough if you are accustomed to sea level. Plan to stop often and take more time for everything—even eating.

Starting from Fairyland View, you pedal uphill all the way to Rainbow Point. The well-paved road has no shoulders, but traffic moves slowly (35 m.p.h.). Throughout the tour as you explore the canyon, observe the varied plant life and the different vegetation zones, from forests of sagebrush, juniper, and pine along the lower slopes to spruce and fir at higher elevations.

Many hiking trails wind through the area to your left between Boat Mesa and Bryce Point. At Sunset Point, lock your bike and hike the self-guiding nature trail to Queen's Garden. This stroll is best in morning when the sun glows on the Queen Victoria rocks. Another good hiking trip is the Navajo Loop from Sunrise Point, an easy one and a half miles round trip. Walk this loop clockwise—when you climb back to the rim you'll be in the shade.

Pedaling on, you soon coast past Inspiration Point. Beyond the amphitheater, the road dips 100 feet in about a mile and then begins a gradual climb. Stop along the rim to take in the sweeping views. Though the canyon's wildflower displays are limited, sego lilies, yel-low evening primroses, wild irises, and blue flax bloom in summer, and goldenrod, gumweed, and rabbit brush grow along the road-sides in autumn. In early morning or late afternoon, watch for mule deer grazing in the meadows.

The long, tough climb continues past Swamp Canyon and Mud Canyon Butte. Then at last the slope lessens near Farview Point. On a clear day you can see Navajo Mountain from this point, while directly below lies a natural bridge. Better views of the bridge are found farther along the road at Natural Bridge overlook.

Beyond Agua Canyon you coast about half a mile. Then you climb gradually up a final short, steep incline to Rainbow Point. Pause here after your long trek to appreciate the splendid vista. Nearby Yovimpa Point is considered the park's best spot to watch the sunset.

For lunch you can picnic on the rim beneath towering spruce and fir. Or lock your bike at Rainbow Point and head for the Under-the-Rim Trail, where you can dine among massive rainbow-colored pinnacles. This hiking trail stretches from the amphitheater at your tour's start to Rainbow Point, with other points of access at Bryce Point, Sheep Creek, Swamp Canyon, and Agua Canyon.

In the afternoon, enjoy the luxurious coasts—there are only a few rises—that brings you almost back to the Visitor Center.

More Exploring

Though the 35-mile park road can be easily cycled in one day, plan on at least one more day to explore the trails, which range from a number of short, easy strolls to the 28-mile-long Under-the-Rim Trail. You can buy a 25¢ pocket guide to the trails at the Visitor Center.

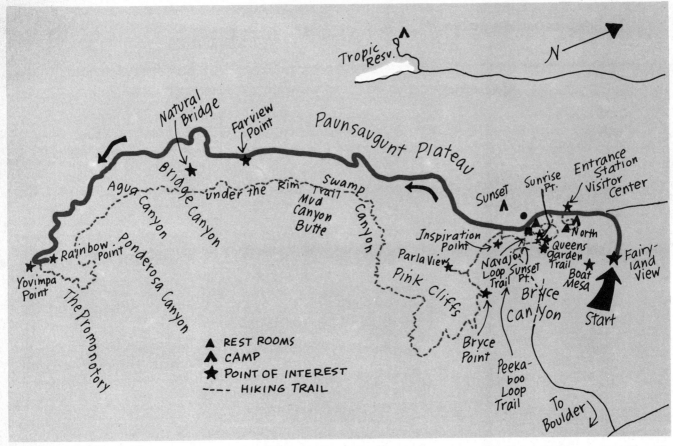

Bryce Canyon National Park is in southern Utah on Utah 12; 222 miles south of Provo via U.S. 89 and Utah 12; 311 miles north of Flagstaff, Arizona, via U.S. 89 and Utah 12.

WHERE TO STAY

Bryce Canyon Lodge, on the rim between Sunrise and Sunset points, is open from about mid-June to mid-October and has dining facilities.

The park also has two campgrounds—North Campground, east of the Visitor Center, and Sunset Campground, 1 mile south of the Visitor Center. The camps are open from May 1st to November 1st and operate on first-come first-served basis. A small camping fee is charged.

FOR FURTHER INFORMATION

Write Superintendent, Bryce Canyon National Park, Bryce Canyon, Utah 84717.

NEARBY

Zion Canyon National Park lies 82 miles southwest along well-paved roads with moderate to light traffic. See the Zion Canyon Treks on page 253 for details

PHOTOGRAPHY TIPS FOR BRYCE CANYON

You could spend days here experimenting with photographic effects, trying to capture Bryce Canyon's striking scenes. No doubt you will discover your own unique camera angles, but here are a few tips on the various viewpoints to get you started.

Fairyland View, at your tour's start, is best in the early hours when you can use side or back lighting. Try to shade or frame with a pine or mahogany tree and shoot just a bit of sky.

Sunrise Point's best vantage is probably a short distance along the trail. Walk down the trail, then shoot south toward Sunset Point during morning. This is also a good midday shot, but be sure to shade your lens when you shoot toward the sun.

Inspiration and Bryce points are both best before 10 A.M. or after 3 P.M., when shadows offer the most contrast. A bit farther, Paria View photographics superbly in afternoon. White Point, an unmarked turnout which you pass about a mile before Rainbow Point, is good all day because its stones range in color from white to deep purple. Take your photos here from the metal guardrail.

Yovimpa and Rainbow points, at your tour's southern tip, are also good all day, but Yovimpa is best at sunset.

120. 121. ZION CANYON TREKS

Zion Canyon's sandstone walls are mottled deep blood-red, pink, white, purple, lavender, and saffron. Shooting stars, cardinal flowers, and columbine vines hang from the cliffs. The high rims support fir and pine forests. Pedaling deep on the arid floor, you feel the hard grandeur of Zion. You notice other things, too: a darting blue-bellied lizard, a marine fossil embedded in rock, a coyote—petrified of autos—loping right before your wheels.

Though we have outlined two tours, for beginners and for experts, experienced cyclists will want to try both. Food is available at Zion Inn and Zion Lodge in summer, but during the cooler seasons bring picnic and overnight supplies. Also carry lots of water and suntan lotion to block the piercing high-altitude rays. Plan at least a day and preferably two to really explore the park.

TOUR ONE: BEGINNERS' RIDE

Unload your bike at the Visitor Center near the south entrance and pedal north on the narrow main road beside the Virgin River. The park speed limit is 35 m.p.h., making even heavy traffic bearable. In spring or after a flash flood, stop at North Fork Bridge to watch the blackened torrent crashing boulders and toppling logs below.

Past the bridge, an easy mile-long climb leads you to a flat ravine with cottonwoods, oaks, and box elders on the riverbanks. Beneath the rock mountains of Twin Brothers, the Sentinal, and Mountain of the Sun, there are many shady nooks, filled in May with violets, pentstemons, and orchids. Also growing here is the Zion moon-flower, two feet high with trum-

pet-shaped cream-colored blossoms which open in evening and wilt in the sun.

At Zion Lodge you can stop for a snack or cool drink. Then you pedal easily past Lady Mountain and Red Arch Mountain to Great White Throne, deep red at the base shading to pink, gray, and white at the tip. A wide curve takes you by the Organ's splintered rock. Then you wind through a steadily narrowing deep river gorge to the road's end and a natural amphitheater, the Temple of Sinawava.

Throughout the ride you notice numerous hiking side trips. Cycling Zion is so unique, though, local cyclists recommend at least one nonstop ride. Then you can return again to experience the wilderness on hiking trails, ranging from a half-mile stroll over footbridges to quiet Emerald Pools to a two-day backpacking excursion to both rims of Zion Canyon. Popular Narrows Trail, starting at the Temple of Sinawava, meanders 2 miles along the Virgin River until the path is wedged between wall and water. Lizards dart before you, and you may see the regal ring-necked snake or a mule deer only feet away. Full details on all hikes are available at the Visitor Center on your return.

TOUR TWO: EXPERTS' RIDE

A steep, winding 11-mile coast begins at the east entrance. If you and a friend have two cars, park one at the east entrance and the other at the Visitor Center, ride one way, and avoid the grueling uphill climb. Be certain your brakes work well before you start.

You plunge immediately from the east entrance into rock jungles where every turn presents a ravine,

DISTANCE:	Tour One, 12 miles round trip. Tour Two, 11 miles one way.
TERRAIN:	Tour One, flat, with a few gradual slopes. Tour Two, steeply downhill all the way.
TRAFFIC:	On both tours, heavy in summer, light the rest of the year.
DIFFICULTY:	Tour One is a good ride for beginners and families without small children (the heat and possible traffic could rattle youngsters). Tour Two is for experts only.
BEST TIME:	April, May, or October, when traffic is light and temperatures are in the 70's and low 80's. Summers are hot, averaging in the 90's and 100's from June through September. Winters have light snow, with temperatures in the low to mid-50's.
LOCATION:	Zion Canyon National Park in southwestern Utah.

a fossilized rock, or a jagged cliff to explore. Motorists seldom pull off because the turnout spots are too narrow. But you can stop anywhere. Hike up a dry wash or venture onto a rock hill from which you peer into white, pink, saffron, and magenta chasms. Just 25 yards from the road, you stand in no-man's-land where only bobcats and coyotes have printed the sands. Along the first three and a half miles, it's easy to plunge at 25 m.p.h., keep up with traffic, and miss much. Concentrate on slowing down.

Soon you reach a 300-yard tunnel. About midway through, you suddenly find yourself in darkness, but don't panic: you ride instantly into light again. You coast past grotesque cliffs with weird vegetation zones. In one sunbaked spot you see yucca and cactus, while just feet away in a shaded glade oaks and ponderosa pines flourish.

At Canyon Overlook Trail there is a tunnel two and a half miles long. For excellent Zion views, lock your bike here to the stairway guardrail, walk half a mile through forests and a pygmy woods and past a cave to Canyon Overlook. Whether gray mists brood below or sunlight highlights the rainbow walls, the canyon is startling.

Riding the long tunnel is perfectly safe if you plan ahead. The east entrance park service will try to provide a car escort when you enter. Barring this, wait at the pullout until a motorist will permit you to ride in his headlights. Once you are in his beams, stay there. Never, *under any circumstances*, ride this tunnel without advance arrangements with the car behind you. If you should pedal into blackness, you can smash into the wall.

Beyond the tunnel, you lean into steeply winding switchbacks for the last two and a half miles. Many wild animals live in the rock crags: watch for small desert rodents, coyotes, and rattlers. Finally you coast to the Visitor Center. Take the beginners' tour from here, then spend the rest of the day and perhaps another exploring the hiking trails.

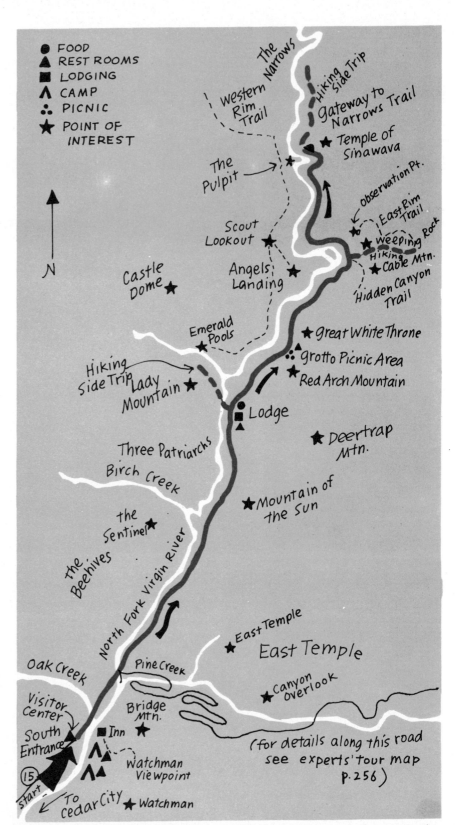

Zion National Park is in southwestern Utah on Utah 15 between U.S. 89 and I-15; 306 miles south of Salt Lake City, via I-15 and Utah 15. For beginners: From Visitor Center to Temple Sinawava.

WHERE TO STAY

Zion Canyon National Park has two campgrounds, operated on a first-come first-served basis at $2 per night. Watchman Campground, near the south entrance, is open year round, while South Campground, a quarter of a mile farther north, closes after the summer season.

Zion Lodge, open from early June through Labor Day, has a hotel and rustic cabins. Zion Inn, open from mid-May through September, has less expensive cabins. Reservations for both the lodge and inn are advised. Write the Utah Parks Company, Cedar City, Utah 84720.

FOR SPARE PARTS, REPAIRS, FURTHER INFORMATION

Spoke and Pedal Shop, 900 South 100 East, St. George, Utah 84770. Ed Pittman, owner, operates a bicycle rental concession at Zion Lodge from June through September (the dates vary slightly). You can write Ed for biking information or during summer inquire directly at the lodge. St. George and Cedar City are the nearest towns for parts and repairs, so come prepared.

NEARBY

Bryce Canyon National Park lies 82 miles northeast, and you can ride all the way on relatively lightly traveled paved road. See the tour on p. 251 for full details. About 125 miles south is the Grand Canyon's North Rim. You can cycle clear from Zion, but most cyclists prefer to begin the North Rim tour from Jacob Lake. See p. 257 for details.

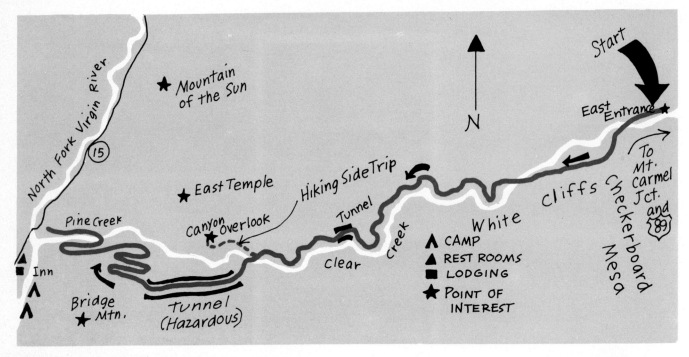

For experts: From East Entrance along Pine Creek to Virgin River.

122. 123. GRAND CANYON RIM RIDES

The Grand Canyon is more than just a spectacular rainbow gorge, as you discover when you ride a bike and really explore. American Indian lore, rocks and fossils, earth layers ten million years old, brilliant wildflowers, and rare birds and mammals, plus excellent biking are yours to discover. The Grand Canyon is huge, but it is also small in a myriad of ways: you may see a curious chipmunk darting beside you or a cliff rose tucked between rocks, or hear the rat-tat-tat of a Lewis's woodpecker in a nearby tree. Though two million tourists rush past the canyon in a year, on a bike you are guaranteed sights and sounds most of them miss.

SOUTH RIM

Start at Desert View, where there are campgrounds and a parking lot. Before you leave, climb the watchtower for excellent views of the canyon, the Painted Desert, Kaibab National Forest, and Navaho country. Then pedal west through pine and juniper trees.

The road is flat, with a few mild slopes, and well paved. There are, however, some narrow spots with ragged shoulders. Throughout the ride you pass many viewpoints—Lipan, Moran, Grandview, Yaki—each with its unique canyon scene. Past Lipan Point, take the short road left to the Tusayan Museum (free admission; open daily, 8 A.M. to 5 P.M.) and a prehistoric Pueblo ruin. At Yaki Point you can lock your bike and hike to a fossil fern exhibit. Also from here Kaibab Trail twists six and a half miles into the canyon.

A mile past the Yavapai Museum's geology exhibits, you wind left to the Visitor Center, then on to Grand Canyon Village. Rest stops in this vicinity include a

DISTANCE:	South Rim, 70 miles round trip, North Rim, 130 miles round trip.
TERRAIN:	South, flat, with a few mild slopes, North, steeply rolling in spots.
TRAFFIC:	South, impossibly heavy in summer, lightest in October. North, lighter year round than on South Rim, but still heavy in summer.
DIFFICULTY:	South Rim ride requires experience in traffic. North Rim ride is fine for experts; beginners should use a 10-speed bike.
BEST TIME:	September and October for South Rim, when days are crisp and clear; spring through autumn for North Rim. Thundershowers often occur in July and August.
LOCATION:	Grand Canyon National Park, Arizona, north of Williams and Flagstaff. Grand Canyon Airport lies 7 miles south of the park, and you can taxi to the park or rent a bike and cycle there, which is much less expensive.

restaurant, a general store, lodges, Hopi House, opposite El Tovar Hotel, where Hopi Indians in late afternoon perform ancient ceremonial dances, and the picnic area at the village's west edge. El Tovar and Bright Angel Lodge sell picnic box lunches.

A bit farther, between Grandeur and Maricopa points, Bright Angel Trail winds four and half miles into the gorge to Indian Gardens, with a reservations-only campground deep in the canyon. If you would like to try this one-day hike, consult a ranger before leaving and carry lots of water. Sometime during your tour, try to see a sunset from Hopi Point—the whole canyon glows red. The road ends at Hermits Rest, which has refreshments and another excellent view. Retrace your ride from here to Desert View.

Throughout the tour, notice the profuse wildflowers in this arid land: phlox, blue pentstemons, buttercups, mahoia, purple asters, wild sunflowers, and white cliff roses.

NORTH RIM

The North Rim has fewer services, so carry snacks and lots of water. A good starting point is Jacob Lake, north of the park. Pedaling south on well-paved Route 67 through Kaibab National Forest, you have an immediate long climb. Stop soon to explore the small crater to your left, and a bit farther the forest service lookout tower.

Here on Kaibab Plateau wildflowers vary from paintbrush and lupine to mountain iris and forget-me-not. As you climb, you see the ponderosa pine forests gradually give way to fir and aspen. Watch the woods and meadows for mule deer. The road climbs gradually through grassy meadows and past

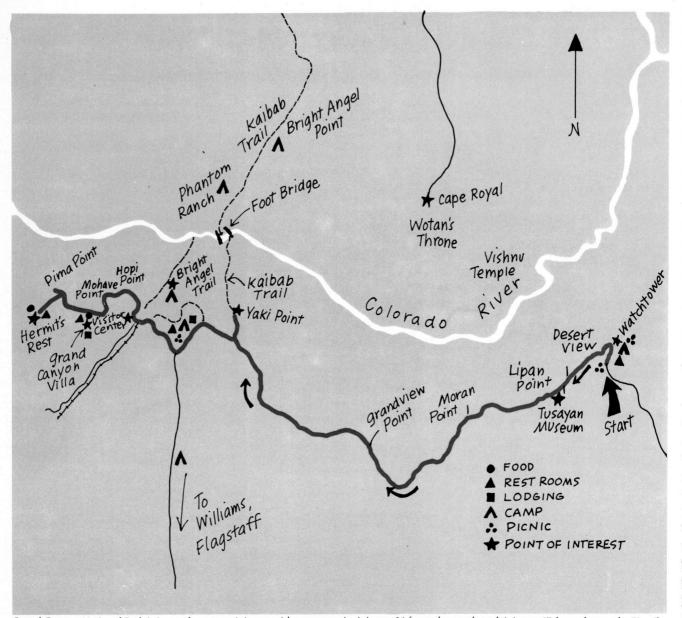

Grand Canyon National Park is in northwestern Arizona with accesses via Arizona 64 from the south and Arizona 67 from the north; 79 miles northwest of Flagstaff via U.S. 180 and Arizona 64.

ponds to the park service building. Then beyond the park service, you have a delightful coast for 10 miles; watch, though, for narrow road in spots and possible moderate to heavy traffic.

At North Rim Drive, go straight and climb about 2 miles to Grand Canyon Lodge, which has overnight lodging, picnicking, camping, and a ranger station. You may want to start your tour from here. Take time to venture to Bright Angel Point, from which you view

the canyon along a .3-mile nature trail. Pick up picnic basics at the supply store before you cycle from the lodge area.

Coasting north of the lodge, stay right at the fork. Then climb gradually until you curve right. The road levels as you skirt the gorge. Soon you can take a tough 3-mile side trip uphill on your left to Point Imperial, from which you see the Little Colorado River, Marble Canyon, the Painted Desert, and the San Francisco Mountains far be-

hind the South Rim. Take care on the rapid descent to the main road.

You continue along Walhalla Plateau through stands of fragrant locust toward Cape Royal. As you ride through the woodlands, watch for the often seen blue grouse, wild turkey, olive-sided flycatcher, Clark's nutcracker, hermit thrush, and warbling vireo. The North Rim has fewer rest stops than the South Rim, but there are many places where you can relax amid the trees. If you picnic along the way, golden-mantled ground squirrels and least chipmunks may come begging. Also watch in early morning or late afternoon for mule deer and elk. Past Angels Window you reach Cape Royal, where you can eat before returning to Grand Canyon Lodge or North Rim Inn for the evening. Return to Jacob Lake the next day.

Some Nonbike Exploring

You can explore further into the canyon on foot or muleback, but not on a bike. Advance reservations for the muleback trips must be made between May and October; write the Fred Harvey Company, Grand Canyon, Arizona 86023. Another thrilling way to experience this land is by shooting the Colorado Rapids in a raft. For further information, write Grand Canyon Expeditions, P.O. Box 21021, Salt Lake City, Utah 84121.

WHERE TO STAY

Facilities on the South Rim include two campgrounds, one at Desert View and the other at Grand Canyon Village, plus numerous motel and lodge accommodations in the village. North Rim accommodations are more limited, with rooms at Grand Canyon Lodge and nearby North Rim Inn and campgrounds in the same vicinity. For rates and reservations for lodge facilities throughout the park, write the Fred Harvey Company, Grand Canyon, Arizona 86023, or the Grand Canyon Chamber of Commerce, Box 507, Grand Canyon, Arizona 86023.

Jacob Lake, at the start of the North Rim tour, also has a motel: Jacob Lake Inn, at the junction of U.S. 89A and State 67.

FOR FURTHER INFORMATION

Write Superintendent, Grand Canyon National Park, Box 129, Grand Canyon, Arizona 86023.

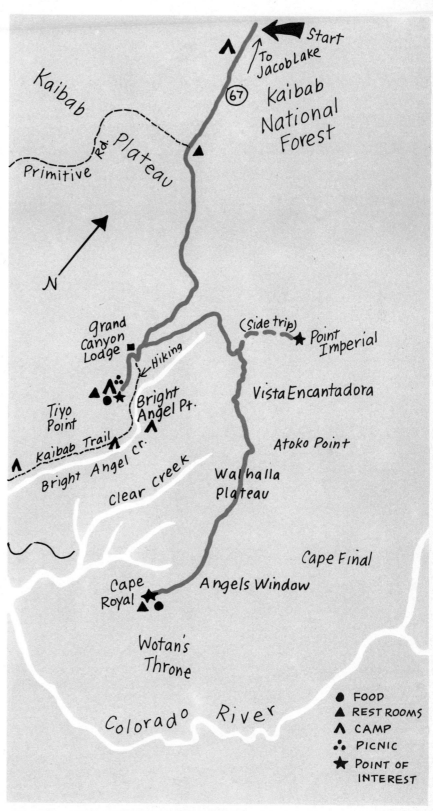

Above from Kaibab National Forest to Cape Royal.

259

124. VALLEY OF THE SUN SAUNTER

Arizona's Valley of the Sun offers wild desert cactii, excellent¹ rock hounding, fine mountain scenery, and plenty of elbow room. From Sun City to the aptly-named Carefree, you pedal through an isolated desert flanked by great hills which are dotted with scrub oak. Try this ride in spring when budding wildflowers sprinkle the desert sands.

Start in Sun City, just a few minutes from Phoenix, where you can park your car in the Kings Inn parking lot at 107th and Grand avenues. Carry lots of water, a good sun lotion, and enough food to last you until Carefree. At Kings Inn, cross Grand Avenue on 107th, which becomes Del Webb Boulevard, and ride north about two and a half miles to Bell Road, where you go right. Bell Road is well paved and lined with gravel shoulders. Traffic can be heavy for the next 15 miles, so it's best to get an early-morning start and avoid the midday rush hour. You cruise through Deer Valley past views of the Hedpeth Hills. Beyond 59th Avenue, rock hounds may want to explore the gravel pit. Then you cross beneath I-17, pass Turf Paradise Race Track, and turn left onto Cave Creek Road, where you ride into desert countryside along Buffalo Ridge to your left. Here in spring wildflowers are profuse and brilliantly colored. You see orange fishhook cactus blossoms, yellow poppies, golden senna, strawberry hedgehog, and cerise pincushions. The rocks are special, too: you might discover an Apache tear, a chunk of brilliant azurite, or cinnabar.

About half a mile beyond another quarry, you reach a fork. Keep right and climb leisurely through Paradise Valley. All along this ride you will see the giant saguaro (sah-WAR-oh) cactus, the kind thirsty prospectors die beside in grade-Z westerns. Ironically, in June the saguaro bears a sweet purple fruit which is edible.

Though there are no tourist spots here, the desert invites exploring. Stop to examine a brilliant orange hummingbird bush, to watch a quick lizard, to meander down a narrow dirt road. Before you reach Cave Creek, you begin to climb a bit more steeply and circle through a saguaro forest around Black Mountain. Sprawling mountain views lie to your left. As you start past Black Mountain, you can go left on New River Road to Cave Creek Regional Park, the only convenient campground on this ride. The camp is located along tiny Cave Creek, where you can try your luck panning for gold.

Back on the main tour, you veer right through the small town of Cave Creek, which has a quick-food drive-in and a market. Then you wind on past Episcopal and Baptist churches into Carefree. Here you can browse through the Spanish Village, a shopping center at the intersection of Cave Creek and Scottsdale roads. Or you can go north about a mile on Mule Train Road to Carefree Inn, an elegant but expensive resort. Restaurant specialties here include rack of lamb Andalucia (served in winter only) and steak Diane. Return to Sun City by the same route.

WHERE TO STAY

The only campground on the tour is at Cave Creek Regional Park, on New River Road, 2 miles from Cave Creek.

Motels: Carefree Inn, Box 708, Carefree, Arizona 85331; (602) 488-3551; bike rentals available. Del Webb's Kings Inn, 10660 Grand Avenue, Sun City, Arizona 85351; (602) 977-7261.

DISTANCE:	75 miles round trip.
TERRAIN:	Flat. Gradual gain of 1,100 feet from Sun City to Carefree.
TRAFFIC:	Moderate. Heavy on some roads near Phoenix.
DIFFICULTY:	Experience and self-reliance required in case of emergencies since facilities are minimal.
BEST TIME:	Mid-September to May. May is especially nice because desert wildflowers are in bloom. Avoid June to early September, when temperatures often reach the 100's.
LOCATION:	Northwest of Phoenix on U.S. 60 and 89.

VALLEY OF THE SUN EDIBLES

You could nibble for days on the wild food you pass here. Besides the saguaro cactus, mentioned in the tour description; you may want to taste these desert delectables.

Prickly pears bear red or purple fruits (the color depends on the species). Simply brush the stickers from the fruit with a bunch of weeds and eat. You can also cook the tender oblong "leaves." Remove the sticker clusters with a knife, then slice, boil, and season as you would green beans.

Yuccas, too, have several uses. The Spanish dagger has stiff leaves, sometimes four feet long, which end in sharp spikes. You can gather the young stalk when it is still shorter than a foot and eat it as a vegetable. Slice the plant and boil until tender. Then discard the water and boil again in fresh water. Season with butter, salt, and pepper, and serve. You can roast the short banana-shaped fruits while still green, then peel and eat the insides, which taste somewhat like sweet potatoes. Another species of yucca, bear grass or soapweed, has edible flowers and poisonous roots which lather in water to produce a desert shampoo.

You may find *wild potatoes* in the hills. This plant's roots can be treated just like potatoes—baked, fried, or boiled. *Barrel cacti* have a juicy inner pulp which will quench a stranded traveler's thirst. Also look for *naked broom rape*, which grows around sagebrush and feeds on the sagebrush roots. The small purple blossoms have white underground stems which can be eaten boiled, baked, fried, or even raw.

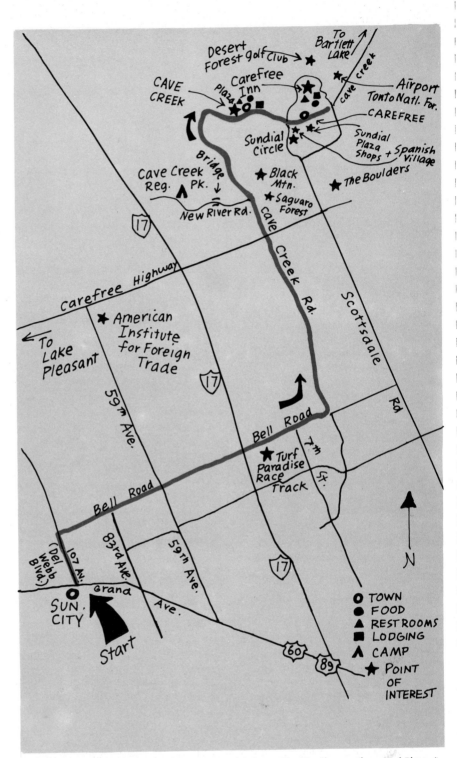

Sun City is in central Arizona on U.S. 60/89 and Arizona 93; 19 miles northwest of Phoenix via U.S. 60/89 and Arizona 93; 154 miles southwest of Flagstaff via I-17, U.S. 60/89 and Arizona 93.

125. TAOS PUEBLO WEEKEND

An isolated art colony, old mining towns, an uncommercialized Indian pueblo, and a vast mountain wilderness await you on this loop around 13,161-foot Wheeler Peak, the highest point in New Mexico. Carson National Forest and the small towns nearby are tourist delights—without tourists. Though local cyclists tackle this loop in a day, take at least a weekend to genuinely explore everything here.

Your tour begins in Carson National Forest at Taos, with its unique blend of Spanish, Indian, and Anglo-American cultures. D. H. Lawrence wrote near here, and the area's serenity continues to attract many writers and artists. With a population of only about 2,500, Taos has seventy art galleries. Also, half a block east of the town plaza is the Kit Carson Museum, open daily, and nearby is the park where Carson is buried.

Sometime during your stay here, pedal two and a half miles north of Taos Plaza for a side trip to Taos Pueblo, delightful in its authenticity, with narrow streets and baked, flat-topped adobe dwellings. You find no curio, craft, or knickknack shops. Indeed, the 1,400 Indians here care little if you come or not and take note of strangers only long enough to charge parking and camera fees. Ask permission before taking any resident's picture; you may be charged extra. Fiestas are held throughout the year, including the colorful San Geronimo Celebration on September 30th and the corn dances on May 3rd, June 13th and 24th, and July 25th and 26th. Though you are welcome to watch their extraordinary dancing, the Indians ban cameras on fiesta days.

For another not-to-be-missed side trip, ride 4 miles south of Taos on U.S. 64 and visit the early eighteenth-century Mission of St. Francis of Assisi.

To begin the 90-mile cycling loop, pedal east from Taos on U.S. 64. Be sure to ride this loop counterclockwise or you may have to walk up Red River Pass. If you are used to sea-level cycling, get in good shape for this ride or the thin high-altitude air will wear you down. Bring plenty of water, raisins, and nuts.

DISTANCE:	90 miles.
TERRAIN:	Mountainous, with steep climbs, and rapid descents.
TRAFFIC:	Light except south of Questa.
DIFFICULTY:	Requires experience and a 10-speed bike.
BEST TIME:	Mid-April through May and August through September, when winds are light and storms few.
LOCATION:	From Taos, New Mexico, about one hour north of Santa Fe.

Narrow, untraveled U.S. 64 twists at first along the Rio Fernando de Taos, a rocky mountain river filled with fresh rainbow, brook, and brown trout. Then the road leaves the river and climbs through the Sangre de Cristo Mountains. You cross Sixmile Creek and pass Eagle Nest Lake as you pedal toward Eagle Nest, a resort. You can pick up groceries here at the little store.

From Eagle Nest turn left onto State 38, or for a scenic side trip, ride about 12 miles farther on U.S. 64 to Cimarron Canyon, which has more winding trout brooks, a 200-foot palisades, and campgrounds. On a really leisurely tour, this makes a good overnight stop.

Back on the main loop, you pedal on State 38 along Moreno Creek. Pause to walk along the brook or wade onto the stepping-stone rocks. Among the small animals you may see in this area are muskrats and beavers, plus the nocturnal weasels, skunks, and minks. You may also glimpse a wild turkey, quail, or dove.

After 5 miles of uphill climbs from Eagle Nest, you can stop to explore Elizabethtown, an old gold-rush ghost town. Just as you re-enter Carson National Forest, you climb through Red River Pass, elevation 9,852 feet, beyond which you coast to Red River Ski Area. Red River, a gold-rush boomtown, has survived as a summer vacation and winter ski resort. Inquire locally about jeep or horseback pack trips if these interest you. The chair lift here operates during summer from 9 A.M. to 4 P.M.; the fee is $2 per person.

Outside Red River you cross Pioneer and Mallette creeks, with numerous campgrounds nearby. The narrow, winding road continues, leading you through forests of ponderosa pines, Douglas and white firs, Engelmann and Colorado spruces, and aspens. Stop to examine the delicate purple asters and the chamisos, which resemble goldenrod. You may see deer, elk, pronghorn, and mountain sheep, too.

Soon you coast into tiny Questa, another snack or grocery stop. Turn left here onto State 3. You find more traffic on this stretch from Questa to Taos than on the first part of the loop, and you will probably meet some big trucks. The ride can be bumpy here simply because you have to pedal so far out on the shoulder. These drawbacks may persuade you to arrange for a pickup in Questa, or if you have time, to retrace your ride through Red River back to Taos. Remember, though, that the climb through Red River Pass from this direction is very steep, and you may have to walk.

Continuing south, you follow State 3 through Arroyo Hondo and across the Rio Hondo. Pedaling along a high mountain plateau, you come to U.S. 64. Here you can turn right for a 7-mile one-way side trip to Rio Grande Gorge, where a 650-foot-high bridge spans the Rio Grande, and you can stop at an observation tower and picnic. Back on State 3, you return to Taos, completing the loop.

WHERE TO STAY

Motels are numerous along this ride. You find full facilities in Taos, Red River, Questa, and Eagle Nest, and campgrounds all along the route.

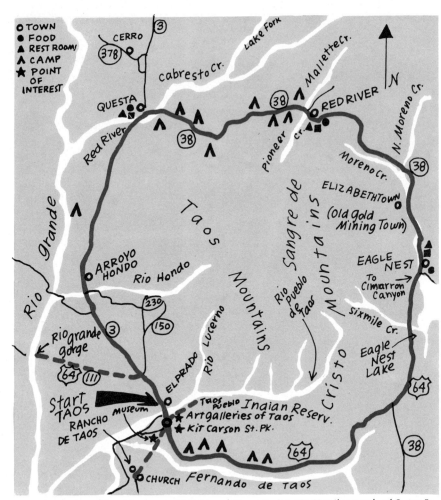

Taos is in northern New Mexico on U.S. 64 and New Mexico 68; 62 miles north of Santa Fe via U.S. 84/285 and New Mexico 68; 200 miles southwest of Pueblo, Colorado, via I-25 and U.S. 64.

126. VIRGINIA CITY GHOST RIDE

Virginia City legend is so fanciful it might have been created in an old miner's mind. Yet south of Reno the past lives. Though the billion-dollar Comstock Lode and the lusty gold seekers are long gone, the countryside remains much as Mark Twain saw it—sagebrush-tufted prairies, silvery blue lakes, air so pure you can see the Humbolt Range 150 miles across the plains. As you stalk ghosts on this ride, do visit Virginia City. But discover the real past in the land and unchanged hills.

Start in Reno, where you can buy spare parts and tools. Bring plenty of food, fill two water bottles, and be prepared for chilly desert nights. Pedal south of Reno on U.S. 395. Though this highway has fast traffic, the shoulders are wide and smooth.

Turn left 10 miles south of Reno onto untraveled State 17. Soon you cross Steamboat Creek and begin a tough 10-mile climb up Geiger Grade. A wayside park on your right as you start up the slope offers wide views of Washoe Valley and the distant Sierra Nevadas. From the mountain summit, you plummet toward Virginia City. Watch out for sharp corners and gravel on the road as you coast.

In Virginia City explore for a while. Visit the old opera house, tour a mansion, hike to an abandoned mine shaft, or sip lemonade in a saloon. Then coast south on State 17.

Half a mile down the road, you reach a junction. A right turn leads you on untraveled back roads through Gold Hill, a well-preserved gold-rush town, toward Washoe Lake. Continuing straight at this junction takes you on State 80 through unpopulated prairie. And a left turn leads you on State 17 to Silver City, beyond which you ride along a busy highway into

DISTANCE:	75 miles for the tour through Carson City, 69 miles through Gold Hill.
TERRAIN:	Rolling hills, with one tough grade.
TRAFFIC:	Light on back roads; often heavy near the cities.
DIFFICULTY:	Requires experience because of the distance and few facilities. Families and beginners can try any short segment of this ride.
BEST TIME:	Spring or autumn. Summers are too hot.
LOCATION:	Countryside south of Reno, Nevada.

Carson City. No matter which direction you choose, you pedal on bumpy road which descends rapidly and has a few tight curves. Both Gold Hill and Silver City are relics of the gold days, though the ramshackle buildings now often house art displays.

Carson City Ride

Past Silver City continue downhill on State 17. As you dead end into U.S. 50, go right toward Carson City. Traffic on this road is moderate, and the shoulders are often cracked or bumpy and sometimes disappear, so be careful. Carson City has many old buildings and museums, and your best bet is to pick up a map and self-guiding tour of the city at the Chamber of Commerce Information Bureau at 1191 South Carson Street. Ride north out of town on U.S. 395, which soon becomes a four-lane freeway. You rejoin the shorter tour at State 38 near Washoe Lake.

Shorter Ride to Washoe Lake

Beyond Gold Hill you continue plunging past sagebrush and scrub oak toward the lake, which twinkles like an oasis in the distance. At the Y you can go right for a side trip to Washoe Lake County Park or left on the main tour to pedal along the lakeshore. On this stretch you may encounter head winds in the afternoon. You probably won't be able to swim in the lake because it's usually too shallow. Going left on State 38, you pedal beside the water and rejoin the long tour from Carson City at U.S. 395.

From the junction of U.S. 395 and State 38, pedal north 1 mile on the four-lane freeway. Then bear left onto old 395 and left again in .5 mile onto Franktown Road. You rejoin old 395 in 4.5 miles and pedal on to Bowers Mansion, a $400,000 home built during the gold rush (admission, 50¢). The small shady park beside the mansion has a swimming pool and makes a good picnic spot. A short distance farther north, Davis Creek County Park offers overnight camping. Beyond Davis Creek the road rejoins U.S. 395, which takes you back into Reno.

WHERE TO STAY

Motels: Comstock, three quarters of a mile south of Virginia City on Nevada 17. For reservations, write Comstock, Box 386, Virginia City, Nevada 89440. Sugar Loaf, 465 South C Street, Virginia City. There are also dozens of motels in Reno and Carson City.

Camping: Davis Creek County Park, mentioned in the tour description.

FOR SPARE PARTS AND REPAIRS

Carson City and Reno both have several good bike shops. Consult the yellow pages for the shop nearest your parking spot or motel.

NEARBY

South of Reno via U.S. 395 and State 27, you can take a mountainous ride to Lake Tahoe. The steep, twisting climb and plunging coast to the lake, however, are for experts only. Most cyclists will probably want to begin the Tahoe tour along the lakeshore. For details, see the Lake Tahoe Ringaround on page 277.

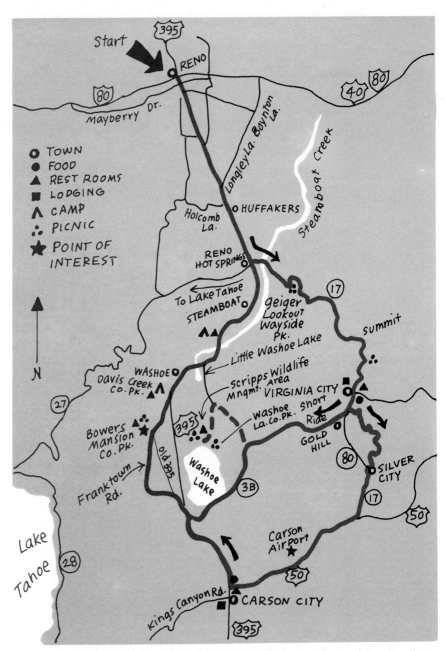

Reno is in western Nevada on I-80 and U.S. 395; 223 miles northeast of San Francisco, California, via I-80; 444 miles northwest of Las Vegas via U.S. 95, 95-A, and I-80.

127. SIERRA BIG FOOT STALK

The Abominable Snowman, Yeti, or Big Foot is a fantasy, of course . . . isn't he? If you half believe in this creature who allegedly haunts remote California hills, pedal warily and search the white sandy shores of Bass Lake for huge footprints on this excursion through the low Sierras. Here in the peaceful pine forests, campers claim to have sighted the man-beast, who stands over eight feet tall and weighs about 775 pounds.

Begin this back-roads tour in Oakhurst, a small gold-rush town nestled in wooded hills. The tour can be easily completed in one day, or two days if you stop often to fish, canoe, or swim in turquoise Bass Lake. Commercialism is minimal here, making this ride an ideal spring or autumn getaway.

For an early breakfast, try the Donut Hole, open at 5 A.M., on Oakhurst's Main Street, then pedal north on State 41 over hills. The shoulders are bad here and vanish on curves as you climb past wide views of the Sierra Nevadas. Four miles from town, turn right onto Road 222 at the sign pointing toward Bass Lake. You climb for about a mile on this new four-lane road with wide, paved shoulders. Then the road narrows and becomes bumpy, curvy, and steep for the next 2 miles, and you pedal into deep forests. Luckily the road improves again past the sign pointing toward Bass Lake.

At the fork, you can go left onto Road 274 for the main tour through thick pine forests or right for a side trip to a lakeside falls. Turning right, you come to another fork and go left on Road 432 to a quiet picnic area. Here a clear mountain brook rushes over flat rock slabs, then tumbles into Bass Lake, creating a small falls. Stop to snack or swim on the white sand beach.

Back on the main route (Road 274), you glide downhill a mile, climb uphill another mile, then coast over a bridge. Across the bridge, you can lock your bike and hike north along McCleod Trail beside Willow Creek. Riding on, you soon spot the turquoise-green lake far below you. Pedaling over a few more hills brings you near the shore. At the turnoff here, lock your bike to a tree and climb down through the foliage to a small white sand beach where you can relax or swim.

Continuing again on the main road, you climb past Lake View Drive, which curls off to your right.

DISTANCE:	37 miles.
TERRAIN:	Hilly, with some steep grades.
TRAFFIC:	Heavy from June 1st to Labor Day; light in spring and autumn.
DIFFICULTY:	A 10-speed bike and some experience recommended. Not for young riders.
BEST TIME:	Spring or autumn. Summer is too hot, with temperatures often in the 90's, and there is too much traffic on the narrow roads. Winter can be snowy.
LOCATION:	Sierra National Forest, near Oakhurst, California, one hour north of Fresno via State 41.

Pass it by: the road's name is its most enticing aspect. You coast a bit farther and suddenly see a startling full view of the lake. There's a nice turn out here where you can stop and look. A few more minutes of riding bring you again to the shore. Then you have an uphill climb to rocky cliffs and stands of black and live oaks. Watch carefully as you spin along Malum Ridge and you may glimpse a deer or even the legendary hairy creature in the woodlands. Along the ridge, the path becomes hazardous, with lots of bumps and ragged shoulders. Cycle defensively.

At Road 225, go right toward North Fork, then right again at North Fork's post office. Outside town the road winds and climbs for about 4 miles. You can rest in unfenced grassy meadows about a mile from the start of your climb. Then at secluded Lake Manzanita, you can picnic or hike along the shores. Two miles farther, you veer right toward Bass Lake and plunge quickly around narrow curves to the lake and Wishon Point which has a general store as well as cabins and a free campground. Here you can hike, swim, or rent a motorboat, rowboat, canoe, or even a kayak. This makes a good overnight stop on a leisurely two-day tour, but if you would like to go farther and still overnight along the lake, you find many nice campgrounds in about 5 miles.

Past the marina and campgrounds, turn left onto Road 426 before you reach Forks Resort (more campgrounds are found straight ahead here). Road 426 is bumpy and narrow; watch for potholes. Traffic is light as you ride through the woods. At the stop sign, you turn right and wind through unfenced meadows filled in spring with wildflowers. You have a final climb for about 1 mile, then coast 2 miles into Oakhurst. Before you leave town, stop at the Big Foot Drive-In on Main Street; it has a bulletin board full of newspaper clippings about Big Foot sightings.

Other Tours

Campers may want to switch this tour around, starting and ending at Bass Lake. A shorter, easier ride than the one outlined here can be taken by going right at both forks as you near Bass Lake and riding along the south shore of Bass Lake as far as you like.

WHERE TO STAY

In Oakhurst you may need motel reservations. Two motels are listed below: Oakhurst Lodge, Box 24, Oakhurst, California 98644; (209) 683-4417. Sierra Sky Ranch, Box 640, Oakhurst, California 98644; (209) 683-4433. These motels plus several others are located on State 41, Oakhurst's main street.

Camping is available at eleven different sites along Bass Lake's south shore. All sites operate on a first-come first-served basis.

FOR SPARE PARTS AND REPAIRS

The only place on this ride that handles spare parts and repairs is the Western Auto Store in Oakhurst, on your left as you leave town on State 41.

FOR FURTHER INFORMATION

Contact the Oakhurst Chamber of Commerce, Oakhurst, California 93644. They are located in the little building at the south end of Oakhurst, on your left as you enter town via State 41.

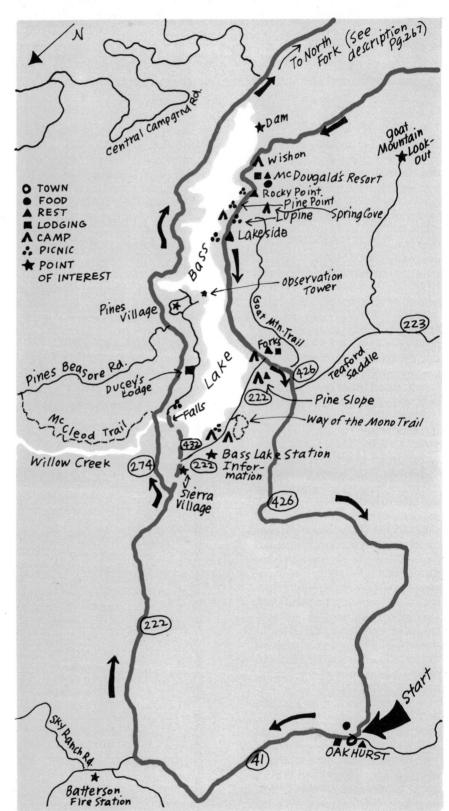

Oakhurst is in central California on California 41 and 40; 57 miles southwest of Yosemite National Park via California 41; 46 miles north of Fresno via California 41.

128. MOTHER LODE JUBILEE

Even if you don't pan the streams, you will discover gold in the mother lode hills, buried by yellow wildflowers in spring and amber grasses in autumn. Experts can manage this tour in a day, but if you want to poke leisurely about old ghost towns and prospect for gold dust, plan on two or three days.

Begin in the old gold-rush town of Sonora, where the richest pocket mine in the mother lode was found: $160,000 of nearly pure gold in a day. Sonora's narrow streets still bustle with tourists and amateur gold seekers. Many signs point to off-street parking. Before you leave, you can pick up prospecting equipment and visit the 106-year-old jail and museum on West Bradford Street. You pass through many old towns with country stores on this tour, but bike shops are non-existent until Placerville, so check your bike before leaving Sonora and bring spare parts and tools.

Ride north of town on State 49 (North Washington Street) through wide rolling hills. Though State 49 has no marked shoulders, traffic is light in spring and autumn. Watch out, for occasional logging trucks. You see a sign for Columbia State Park about 2 miles outside Sonora. For a nice side trip, turn right onto Ferry Road and pedal 2 miles through meadows and past the Gold Mine Winery to Columbia, where you can wander through a gold-rush town, restored down to wooden watering troughs and wagon wheel ruts in the dirt road. You can pan for gold, drink a glass of iced cider, and buy a few sticks of old-fashioned horehound in the busy shops.

Beginners should return now to State 49. Those with experience and a 10-speed bike might like to continue past Masonic Hall and through Columbia to Vallecito, and

DISTANCE:	87 miles, including Murphys side trip.
TERRAIN:	Rolling hills with a few steep grades.
TRAFFIC:	Heavy on summer weekends; moderate to light in spring and autumn.
DIFFICULTY:	Beginners can handle the main tour, but should have some experience for the Murphys side trip. Not for families with small, undisciplined riders because of narrow shoulders and possible heavy traffic.
BEST TIME:	Excellent in April, when traffic is light and spring wildflowers are in bloom. In May and October highs average in the 80's, from June through September in the 90's. Also a good winter ride.
LOCATION:	From Sonora to Placerville, in north-central California, via State 49.

then to either Angels Camp (through which the main tour also passes) or Murphys.

Murphys Side Trip

Following the Angels Camp signs

through Columbia, you take a sharp left, then a right onto Gold Spring Street, and you are back in country hills. Traffic is light and the road well paved. About 2 miles outside Columbia, you curve uphill, then plummet almost straight down for 3 miles with wide views of the Sierras and a tumbling river far below you. The hillsides are tufted with live and black oak.

When you reach the canyon floor, climb beneath the bridge to rest or make your first attempt at gold panning. Beyond the Stanislaus River, you begin a tough 3-mile uphill trek. Finally the strain eases and you coast awhile. After skirting the canyon, you pass Moaning Cave, which you can tour from 10 A.M. to 5:30 P.M.

Turn left at Vallecito just before you reach the old-fashioned general store (a convenient snack stop). Just outside Vallecito you come to State 4, where you can turn in either direction. Left takes you gradually downhill to Angels Camp; right leads you to Murphys.

Left to Angels Camp. Should you ride here in May, don't miss the Jumping Frog Jubilee, a tongue-in-cheek race held in honor of Mark Twain's short story "The Celebrated Jumping Frog of Calaveras County," written at Angels Camp. You may even want to bring along your own frog to participate in the lunacy and compete for cash prizes, often totaling $1,000. For exact dates, write the Angels Camp Chamber of Commerce. Also here is the Angels Camp Museum, two blocks north of Angels Creek, where you can see old equipment and wagons from the gold-rush days.

Right to Murphys. Murphys is a well-preserved gold-rush town. From here you can climb one and a half miles north on Sheep Ranch Road to Mercer Cave, where you can picnic, then take a cool half-hour walk through argonite stalactites and stalagmites. Admission: Adults, $1.25; children 5 to 11 years old, 50¢. Hours: June through September, 9 A.M. to 6 P.M. daily; the rest of the year, 10 A.M. to 5 P.M. on weekends and holidays. Another possible excursion is to Calaveras Big Trees State Park, 15 miles north of Murphys on lightly traveled State 4. Here you see ancient Sierra sequoias and can camp year round for $1. This ride from Murphys to the big trees makes a pleasant one-day outing. To return to the main tour, leave Murphys on Murphys Grade and coast 8 miles along Angels Creek, where you can use your gold pan again. Turn right at Altaville to get back to State 49.

Including the Murphys side trip, you have gone 27 miles when you reach Altaville. Pedaling north from Altaville, you glide over hills past pastures, ranches, and weathered barns. There is still no shoulder on State 49 and traffic is often fast, so take care. You can stop about 4 miles outside Altaville at a roadside park with picnic tables. Then go 7 more miles, crossing San Domingo and San Antonio creeks, to San Andreas which has motels and snack stops. Here you can dismount once more to see relics of the gold rush at the Calaveras County Historical Museum. Admission is free. Hours: April 1st to October 1st, 9:30 A.M. to noon and 12:30 to 5:30 P.M. daily.

The road narrows beyond San Andreas as you pedal through rocky passes. Then you pick up a bike-wide, well-paved marked shoulder 3 miles outside town. Ride through tiny Mokelumne Hill, beyond which you navigate a number of sharp turns beside perpendicular cliffs. Often the shoulder disappears on this difficult 3-mile stretch, so be cautious. Stop and lie in the grass or rest beside the river midway between Mokelumne Hill and Jackson. Then pedal into Jackson, its narrow streets lined with nineteenth-century buildings. Jackson has a park

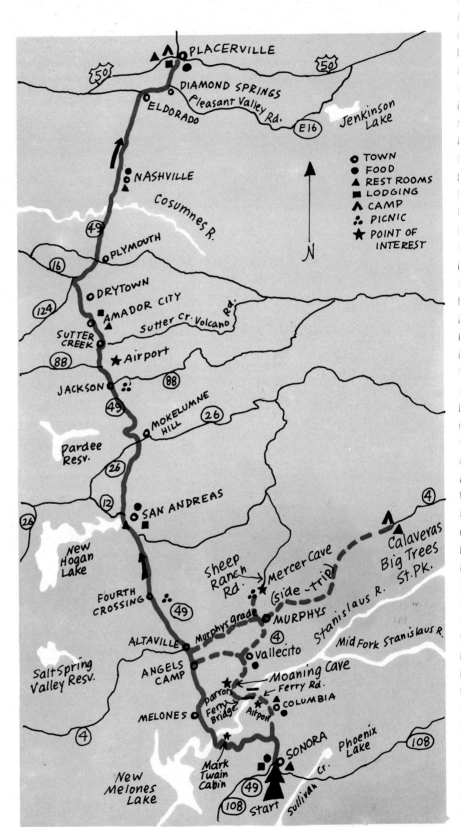

Sonora is in central California on California 49; 95 miles west of Yosemite National Park via California 120 and 49; 91 miles southeast of Sacramento via California 16 and 49.

with picnic tables and a museum at 80 Church Street.

Just north of town on State 49, you can see several mine hoists and a 6,000-foot-deep shaft. The road climbs gradually for 3 miles to Martell. Then just past the lumber mill outside Martell, it winds down toward Sutter Creek's white-frame homes. Another gravel-shouldered hill brings you to Amador City, where you may want to stay overnight in a motel.

Two miles north of Amador, venture down the banks of another creek to search for gold dust. In early morning or at dusk you may see deer here. Two miles farther you pass still another stream, usually dry by autumn, and go on to Drytown, beyond which State 16 branches left. Stay right on State 49 toward Placerville. Past this turnoff you encounter ragged road with no shoulder for about 4 miles to Plymouth. Beyond Plymouth the paved shoulder reappears intermittently. You can restock your picnic supplies at a country store a mile past the Cosumnes River. Farther on, a creek runs beside you as you climb a steep road with no shoulder.

Follow the signs through Eldorado toward Placerville, once known as Old Hangtown because outlaws were so numerous they were hung in pairs. After a hilly 5-mile ride, you view Placerville snuggled in a deep ravine. Gliding into town, you can go 1 mile north from the courthouse on Bedford Avenue to Gold Bug Mine for a free gold mine tour, then spend the night at a campground or motel. Return to Sonora or arrange for a pickup in Placerville.

WHERE TO STAY

Motels are available in many towns along this route, including Sonora, Angels Camp, Amador City, San Andreas, Altaville, and Placerville. Some of the more moderately priced motels include: Sonora Inn, 160 South Washington Street, Sonora; (209) 532-7468. Sonora Motel, 480 West Stockton

Schwinn Bicycle Co.

Road, Sonora; (209) 532-3952. Woody, 2 miles west of Sonora on State 49; (209) 532-7850. Mine House, on State 49, Box 226 Amador City; (209) 267-5900. Raggles Hotel, 300 Main Street, Placerville; (916) 622-4495. El Dorado, 1500 Broadway, Placerville; (916) 622-9958.

Campgrounds: Calaveras Big Trees State Park, P.O. Box 686, Arnold, California 95223; 15 miles east of Murphys on State 4; open year round; (209) 795-1181. Crazy Horse Campground, P.O. Box 388, Shingle Springs, California; 12 miles west of Placerville on State 50; open year round. Finnon Lake Park, P.O. Box 1500, Route 1, Placerville, California; 4 miles northeast of Placerville on State 193, then follow the Pino Grande signs 9 miles on Rock Creek Road; open year round.

HOW TO FIND
A GOLD NUGGET

Though a flop-eared mule might be more traditional, your bike makes a fine steed in the mother lode hills. If you have that wild, feverish gleam in your eye, here are a few tips to help you look as if you had been panning the creeks all your life.

Standard equipment includes a sixteen- to eighteen-inch gold pan; a round-pointed, long-handled shovel for digging (a big spoon will do for less serious prospectors); a magnifying glass for examining tiny specks; and a pick. You may also want to buy one of the many books in California bookstores on gold panning. These often include maps showing you the best spots to test your luck.

Before packing your saddlebags, cure your gold pan over a campfire to burn away the metal's protective oils. The pan also turns black which, as all experienced prospectors know, gives you a darkened background against which to see the gold.

Once at the creek, search for gold in the same places a fisherman scouts for trout: behind rocks and near bends in the stream where the water slows down. Good sources include shallow sandbars, pockets downstream from rocks, and the upstream side of bars. Study the river by pulling and rinsing plant roots to see if you can find black, gold-bearing sands. Or look for the stream's spring high-water mark and then dig in the sand just behind big rocks.

When you do find something resembling gold, fill your pan about three quarters with the promising sediment, fill the rest of the pan with water, and rotate it quickly with a slight jerking motion. This process washes away lighter particles, making heavier rocks settle. Then take your magnifying glass and scan the pan bottom for specks, small, flat bits of gold, larger than dust, but smaller than a pinhead. Once you have seen gold's distinctive brassy yellow,

you will never be duped by pyrite, or fool's gold.

However, gold panning can be tedious and you are not likely to reap riches. Two-ounce gold nuggets worth about $700 each as collector's items have been found recently, but such discoveries are rare.

For more information on placer mining, obtain the free brochure "Basic Placer Mining" by writing the California Division of Mines and Geology, Ferry Building, San Francisco, California 94111.

129. YOSEMITE VALLEY VAGABOND

Yosemite's contains so many massive granite domes, giant sequoias, and crashing waterfalls that only on a bike do you capture the subtler beauty as well. Slowly winding through soft conifer shadows you hear the hermit thrush warble, notice a whisper of breeze passing through the fir tops, and observe the purplish tinge of the young sequoia's bark.

Motorists are not allowed on the 5-mile bikeway at the valley's upper end, and you encounter only a rare shuttle bus. The other main valley road is one-way, with a 35-m.p.h. speed limit, making cycling easy. You can rent bikes at Yosemite Lodge and at Curry Village; the latter also repairs 10-speed bikes.

Start at Yosemite Lodge and head west on Northside Drive. You pedal along the flat valley floor through heavy pine, fir, and oak forests with occasional stands of giant sequoias. Granite domes, peaks, and walls tower around you. Pause along the way to ride to the Merced River and relax along the banks. In early morning you may glimpse a mule deer near the water.

Just as you begin to pass El Capitan, a smooth perpendicular granite wall, you see a small one-lane road to your right. This path is used mostly by hikers and takes you even closer to the "captain's" granite face.

Back on the main loop, you wind left across the Merced on Pohono Bridge. Across the bridge, you can take a 1.6-mile side trip uphill to Tunnel View, which offers superb valley views. Back down the hill, continue straight to a right-hand turnoff for Bridalveil Falls, cascading from a hanging valley in the cliffs. You pedal on past Cathedral Rocks and Sentinel Dome. Near the Dome, look across the valley for a lovely view of Yosemite Falls. At the fork, you can go left across Sentinel Bridge and back to Yosemite Village for a loop totaling 12 miles, or right to Curry Village and the bikeway.

Beyond Curry Village, take the bicycle road which winds to your right through the woods. At Happy Isles Trail Center you can pick up information on Yosemite's elaborate wilderness tours. You can also lock your bike to a tree and hike along the piney John Muir Trail, leading along the river to Vernal Fall, Emerald Pool, and Nevada Fall. The hiking path is long, so take your time. If you are in good physical shape, you may want to return later to climb to Glacier Point, from which you have superb views of the valley and the lofty Sierra Nevada. Check with a Visitor Center before doing any extensive hiking or backpacking.

Back on the road, you soon reach the Mirror Lake turnoff. Climb the half mile to this small blue lake to picnic, fish for trout

DISTANCE:	17 miles.
TERRAIN:	Flat, with a few easy slopes.
TRAFFIC:	Heavy during the summer; moderate to light on spring and autumn weekdays.
DIFFICULTY:	Good ride for beginners. Families with young children should stay on the bikeway at the upper end of the valley near Mirror Lake.
BEST TIME:	Mid-April through May and September through October. Try to avoid weekends unless you have had some cycling experience.
LOCATION:	Yosemite National Park, California.

(California license required), or chat with the other cyclists and hikers who often stop here. For excellent views of Half Dome, lock your bike near the lake and take the easy 3-mile trail along Tenaya Creek.

Pedal back down the Mirror Lake road, then turn right toward Indian Caves, ride through Yosemite Village, and return to Yosemite Lodge.

WHERE TO STAY

Ahwahnee Hotel is the most elaborate and expensive of accommodations in the valley. There is also Yosemite Lodge at the foot of Yosemite Falls. Housekeeping Camp lies on the south side of the Merced River near Curry Village;

you can rent a tent cabin with cot and stove, then use your own gear or rent whatever else you need. Seven campgrounds are located in Yosemite Valley. Two are open year round, while the others are usually open May 15th to September 15th. The stay is limited to one week June 1st to September 15th, thirty days the rest of the year.

FOR REPAIRS, FURTHER INFORMATION

Curry Village has a bike shop that does repairs on 10-speeds. You can ask for other information here or at Yosemite Lodge's bike rental concession. The park also puts out a brochure "Cycle Guide to Yosemite Valley." Write Superintendent, Yosemite National Park, California 95389.

NEARBY

All the park roads can be cycled, but most have steep grades. You can obtain information on possible routes at the places mentioned above. California's gold country lies about 60 miles west via State 120 and State 49. Here you pedal through old mining towns like Angels Camp and Columbia and can pan creeks for gold. For details, see page 269.

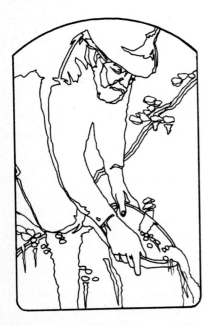

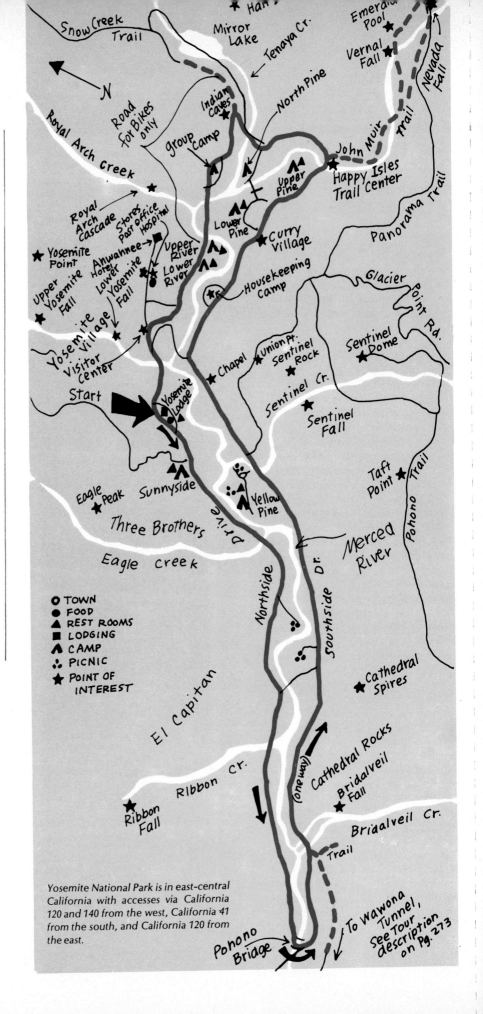

Legend

- ○ TOWN
- ● FOOD
- ▲ REST ROOMS
- ■ LODGING
- ⋀ CAMP
- ⋮ PICNIC
- ★ POINT OF INTEREST

Yosemite National Park is in east-central California with accesses via California 120 and 140 from the west, California 41 from the south, and California 120 from the east.

130. KINGS CANYON RUN

You pedal on a flat canyon floor through forests of ponderosa pine, white fir, and incense cedar. Stern granite peaks rise a mile above you, while a clear green river flows over smooth rocks beside you. The air is filled with the aroma of foliage and pine. Kings Canyon offers one of the few mountain rides easy enough for beginning cyclists, yet too delightful for experts to miss. Try this tour at dawn when gray mists still hang over the river.

On this ride you coast for 15 miles, then return uphill by the same route. The winding mountain road has no shoulder, but the surface is well paved and motorists drive slowly to observe the scenery. There are general stores inside the park, but prices are high, so you may want to bring food with you. Mornings are often cool here, even in summer, so remember to take a windbreaker or warm sweater.

Park your car at Road's End in Cedar Grove, deep in the canyon, and begin your tour with an easy glide along the cascading Kings River. About 1 mile through grassy meadows brings you to Zumwalt Meadows Trail, and a bit farther to River Trail, both clearly marked on your left. If you have started in early morning, save these hikes for your return and take advantage of the open road. As you ride, watch for sharp rocks and pine cones which tumble onto the road and can wreck tires.

After coasting about 5 miles, you begin to pass a series of campgrounds. Just a short distance beyond Sheep Creek Campground (marked by a sign), you can see a small secluded beach on your right, a nice swimming hole for a warm summer day. As you ride, stop occasionally to stand quietly and listen to the forest sounds. Also look closely at the different

pines: the tall reddish-barked ponderosa, the almost scaly gray-barked lodgepole, and the small gray-green piñon.

About a mile and a half beyond the campgrounds, you cross two tiny bridges. The scent of pines sharpens the air. Stop at any of the numerous turnouts to watch the river with its brook, brown, golden, and rainbow trout. Fishing licenses can be purchased at the

DISTANCE:	30 miles round trip, plus 25 miles of hiking trails.
TERRAIN:	Hilly, with about a 2-percent grade.
TRAFFIC:	Light in early spring and autumn; heavy in summer.
DIFFICULTY:	This ride is flexible and can be shortened to any length for beginners. Not for families with small children.
BEST TIME:	Weekdays from May through September.
LOCATION:	Kings Canyon National Park, California.

park's general stores. Beyond the bridges, granite walls soon appear above you, and you pass a waterfall to your right. About 2 miles beyond the falls, the rock walls are splotched yellow-green with crusto lichen, a primitive plant which dissolves its mineral foods from solid rock. In another ten minutes you come to a long bridge and Boyden Cave, across the bridge to your left. Have a snack

here at the stand. If you like spelunking, you can tour the cave for 50¢.

Return by the same route, but take time now to leave your bike and hike the trails. Back near the tour's start, lock your bike to a pine and walk along River Trail. This short path runs beside the river through a forest to Roaring River Falls, a good picnic spot. Just before you reach the falls, another footpath turns off to your left. This byway is Zumwalt Meadows Trail, where you can walk a winding mile through alpine meadows filled with oak, willow, cottonwood, cedar, fir, pine, manzanita, and mountain misery. Along the Zumwalt Trail, you cross a swinging bridge and walk beside the riverbanks lined with cattails and creek dogwood. Watch for the yellow flash of the Wilson's warbler or the scarlet-shouldered redwing blackbird, and listen for the short, excited cry of the Lincoln's sparrow. This trail eventually leads to Road's End and your car, so you may want to finish cycling first and take the trail from the parking lot. You can buy a self-guiding leaflet at the lot for 10¢.

Other hikes starting from the parking lot include a strenuous 7-mile round trip on Copper Creek Trail and a 14-mile round trip on Paradise Valley Trail. If you have time, you may want to try a free ranger-guided nature walk, rent a mule or horse to explore the wilderness, or take the short bike trip Sundays and Fridays from Cedar Grove headquarters to Roaring River, an excellent short ride for beginners. For details on all of these activities, inquire at the ranger station.

WHERE TO STAY

Camping in the park is free once you have paid the daily entrance

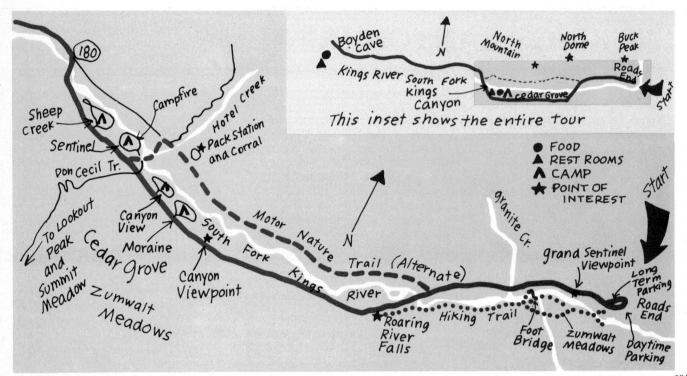

This inset shows the entire tour

- ● FOOD
- ▲ REST ROOMS
- Ⓐ CAMP
- ★ POINT OF INTEREST

Kings Canyon National Park is in central California on California 180; 75 miles east of Fresno via California 180; 220 miles north of Los Angeles via I-5, California 99, 198, 65, 245, and 180.

fee of $2 per car. Bring your car into the canyon; the climb back out would be tough on a mountain goat. Pitch a tent overnight in one of the four campgrounds at Cedar Grove or in Tent Meadow along Copper Creek Trail. No reservations are taken. Unlike the policy in many national parks, you are permitted to use any wood you find on the ground for campfires.

FOR SPARE PARTS, REPAIRS, FURTHER INFORMATION

Come prepared with spare parts and tools. The closest shop is in Visalia—much too far if you have problems. You can obtain any information you need from the forest rangers or Visitor Center.

NEARBY

Sequoia National Park is adjacent to Kings Canyon, but Sequoia's roads are too narrow, winding, and heavily trafficked to make biking safe.

131. LAKE TAHOE RINGAROUND

High in the pine-forested Sierra Nevadas lies Tahoe, one of the world's greatest mountain lakes. Though realtors are nudging out the ponderosa, Jeffrey, and sugar pines with lodges, and replacing aspens, cottonwood, and dogwood with casinos, you can still capture splendid scenery as you pedal along the lake rim. Ride Tahoe now before the experience is lost forever amid condominiums.

Start in South Lake Tahoe, where you can arrange to park your car in the Tahoe Bike and Ski Repair lot at 2236 Lake Tahoe Boulevard (U.S. 50). Russ Devey at this shop often rides the rim and can answer any questions before you leave. Be certain your brakes work and carry spare parts, tools, snacks, and a jacket or sweater for chilly mountain evenings.

The first stretch from South Lake Tahoe west on U.S. 50 has heavy traffic. Then if you are riding in spring or autumn, traffic lightens as you wind right onto Emerald Bay Road (State 89). The lake loop is well paved, with few potholes, and shoulders are narrow to nonexistent.

Soon you pass several roads to your right leading to excellent swimming beaches. Then you tackle a long, arduous climb around Cascade Lake on your left to Emerald Bay State Park. Turn right for a winding side trip into the park through dense, cool forests overlooking the bay.

Continuing on Emerald Bay Road, you have a rapid coast down to the bay for great lake vistas. At Eagle Falls you may want to lock your bike and hike along a footpath for a closer look at the icy cascades.

Another tough climb past Eagle Falls Campground leads you to D. L. Bliss State Park, where you can take a side trip on the park road.

Beyond the park, you again climb a steep slope which rises over a hollow called Lonely Gulch, then glide down to Meeks Bay. Refresh your food supplies in Meeks Bay and pedal a bit farther to Sugar Pine Point State Park, where you can relax in woods overlooking the water.

Beyond Meeks Bay the hills are less steep as you ride along the lakeshore. Several small beaches offer good rest stops. Just over the bridge as you approach Tahoe City, State 89 branches left; stay right here to continue around the lake on State 28.

About two and a half miles north of Tahoe City, you can leave the main tour and turn right for a trek to Dollar Point, which has more dazzling lake views. The road around Carnelian and Agate bays rolls easily, and the stretch from Tahoe City to Kings Beach (20 miles round trip) offers a fine short tour for beginners.

After a roller-coaster spin around Crystal Bay, you climb a long, gradual slope all the way to Spooners Lake. Along the way, several secluded beaches in Lake Tahoe State Park provide good lunch or rest stops. Despite its name, Hidden Beach is one of the most popular areas; you will find more solitude farther south if you explore on your own.

As you near the U.S. 50 junction and approach the end of your long climb, you may want to take a side trip left into Lake Tahoe State Park. Deep in the forests you reach Marlette Lake, a pond often fringed with wildflowers. Camping is available in the park, but you will have to return to the main tour and pedal farther uphill to the U.S. 50 intersection. Then to reach the camp, go left up Spooners Summit and turn left on Kings Canyon Road. Soon you reach Clear Creek Camp,

tucked amid woods near a trout-filled mountain brook.

To continue on the main tour, go right on U.S. 50, a four-lane highway with fast traffic and no shoulders which runs to the Nevada-California border. At one spot, about 7 miles after you turn onto U.S. 50, you pedal through a short tunnel. This poses no problem; just remember to turn on your lights.

On this last stretch, you can bask on the beach at Zephyr Cove. Farther on you pass Nevada Beach, which is located down a road to your right and has camping. Take care on the heavily trafficked 2-mile stretch from Stateline back to South Lake Tahoe, your tour's end.

DISTANCE:	71.7 miles.
TERRAIN:	Hilly.
TRAFFIC:	Heavy from Memorial Day through Labor Day; light in spring and autumn.
DIFFICULTY:	Okay for beginners and families without small children.
BEST TIME:	Spring or autumn, when traffic is light. Avoid winter because of snow, and summer weekends and holidays because of heavy traffic.
LOCATION:	Lake Tahoe, California and Nevada.

WHERE TO STAY

Motels are located in Kings Beach, South Lake Tahoe, Tahoe City, Tahoe Vista, and Tahoma, California, and in Crystal Bay and Glenbrook, Nevada. Rates are usually higher on spring, autumn, and winter weekends, in summer, and during special events. Reservations are advised. The following is only a very partial listing. For more complete information on accommodations, write the South Lake Tahoe Chamber of Commerce, Box 3418, South Lake Tahoe, California 95705. Reservations can be made by calling the toll-free number (800) 648-3333.

Tahoe Cedars Lodge, Box 69, Tahoma, California 95733; on State 89; (916) 525-7515. Tahoe City Travelodge, Box 84, Tahoe City, California 95730; on State 28; (916) 583-3766. Ludlow's Lodge and Cottages, Box 48, Tahoe Vista, California 95732; on State 28; (916) 546-2531. Crown, Box 845, Kings Beach, California 95719; on State 28; (916) 546-3388. Glenbrook Inn and Ranch, Box 5, Glenbrook, Nevada 89413; expensive resort off U.S. 50; (702) 749-5222.

You find many public and private camps in this area. Some are listed below. Tahoe Valley Campground, east of U.S. 50 at Melba Drive and C Street, South Lake Tahoe; open year round; $4 to $5 for four. For reservations, write Tahoe Valley Campground, Box 9026, South Lake Tahoe, California 95705, or phone (916) 541-2222. Deerpark, half a mile west of Tahoe City on State 28 then four and a half miles northwest on State 89; open June 15th to October 15th; no fee; operated by Tahoe National Forest. Kaspian, 5 miles south of Tahoe City on State 89; open June 15th to October 15th; no fee. Tahoe State Recreation Area, in Tahoe City, half a mile north of the State 89 and 28 junction; open May through October; $3. William Kent, 3 miles south of Tahoe City on State 89; open June 15th to October 15th; $1; operated by Tahoe National Forest. Eagle Falls, 6 miles northwest of Camp Richardson on State 89; open May 1st to October 15th; $1; operated by Eldorado National Forest. Clear Creek Camp, mentioned in the tour description. Nevada Beach, about 2 miles north of Stateline on U.S. 50, then half a mile west on county road; open June 1st to September 30th; $1; operated by Toiyabe National Forest.

FOR SPARE PARTS, REPAIRS, FURTHER INFORMATION

Tahoe Bike and Ski Repair, 2236 Lake Tahoe Boulevard (U.S. 50), South Lake Tahoe, California 95731. Chuck and Jeanne Kacharelis and Wally Shanks have a full-line bike shop and do emergency repairs. Expert cyclist Russ Devey at the shop told us about this ride and will be glad to help with any other questions you may have.

NEARBY

Adjacent Tahoe, Eldorado, Stanislaus, and Toiyabe national forests offer days of excellent cycling through thick pine woods sprinkled with deep blue lakes and ponds. Just north of Tahoe you can tackle hilly Kings Canyon Road to Carson City, Nevada, from which you can pedal through sagebrush prairies and old ghost towns. For details, see the Virginia City Ghost Ride on page 265.

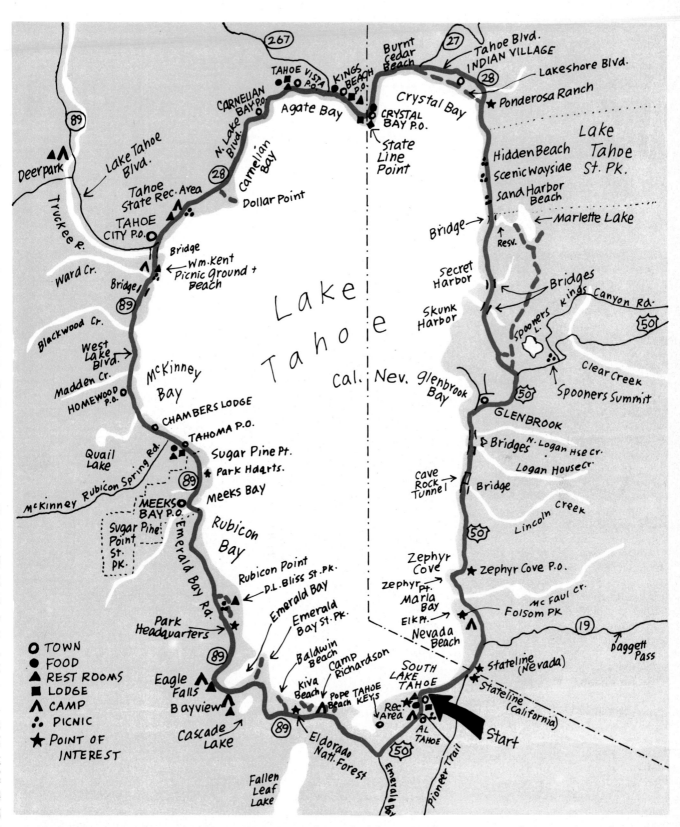

TOWN ⭕
FOOD ⚫
REST ROOMS ▲
LODGE ◼
CAMP ⋀
PICNIC ⸫
POINT OF INTEREST ★

South Lake Tahoe is in northeastern California on U.S. 50; 57 miles south of Reno, Nevada, via U.S. 395 and 50; 172 miles northeast of San Francisco, via I-80 and U.S. 50.

279

132. CALIFORNIA REDWOODS RUN

Pedal past giant redwoods, rain forests, and rugged ocean shorelines on this ride through northern California woods which are soon to be part of Redwood National Park. Discover agates and driftwood on the white sand beaches, rest in rhododendron and azalea glades or silent redwood groves, and watch out for the unsatisfied ghosts of an old shipwreck.

Start in Jedediah Smith Redwoods State Park and park your car in Stout Memorial Grove. If you prefer to fly in, Crescent City Airport offers convenient scheduled flights on Hughes Air West.

In the park you find a long sand beach along the Smith River, excellent rainbow and cutthroat trout fishing, and many wooded hiking trails. To ensure getting a site, set up camp before leaving.

In summer pedal across the footbridge over the Smith River and northwest onto North Bank Road. In spring, autumn, and winter, the high water floods out the bridge, and you will have to ride north instead on narrow, graveled Howland Hill Road, which becomes blacktop beyond Douglas Park. Past Douglas Park, swing left onto trafficked, wide-shouldered U.S. 101 (Redwood Highway), which leads through Hiouchi. Here you can buy snacks. Then turn right onto North Bank Road, where you rejoin the main tour.

North Bank Road runs past a golf course to U.S. 101, where you go left over the Smith River, then right onto flat Lake Earl Drive. At Washington Boulevard, turn right (if you hit U.S. 101 again, you have gone too far). At Pebble Beach Drive, you can go right for a side trip to Point St. George, where the sidewheeler *Brother Jonothan* was wrecked in 1865, killing 203 persons. Lock your bike and walk

DISTANCE:	20 to 25 miles, excluding side trips.
TERRAIN:	Hilly, with one flat stretch.
TRAFFIC:	Generally light; heavy on U.S. 101.
DIFFICULTY:	Entire ride for experienced cyclists because of hills and rough areas.
BEST TIME:	Summer, when rain is least likely. Crescent City receives 120 inches of rainfall annually.
LOCATION:	Starts in Jedediah Smith Redwoods State Park, California.

along this superb driftwood beach, or swim or picnic.

From the Point, Pebble Beach Drive lies easy and flat south to Crescent City. In Crescent City at low tide you can coast to Battery Point at the end of A Street and visit the 1856 lighthouse that exhibits the *Brother Jonothan's* logbooks. The crew members are buried in the cemetery at 9th Street and Taylor Road. On Citizen's Dock, commercial Undersea Gardens has sea anemones, wolf eels, octopuses, and underwater viewing rooms. Restock on food and take time for a snack before leaving town. Glen's Bakery and Coffee Shop, 3rd and G streets, has a relaxed atmosphere and a wide front window through which you can keep an eye on your bike.

Take U.S. 101 from town past Curly Redwood Lodge (made from

a single redwood). At the lodge the main tour goes left onto Elk Valley Road. Riders with experience in traffic may want to continue south on U.S. 101 for 6 miles along Endert's Beach to Del Norte Coast Redwoods State Park. U.S. 101 climbs steeply for about 2 miles, then levels off high above the ocean. The redwoods here march up the hills from the edge of the sands, and in May and June rhododendron cover the slopes. Lock your bike to a tree and hike down Damnation Creek Trail, which drops 900 feet to the sea through thick redwood, hemlock, and Douglas fir forests. Fogs often cling to the wild rocky beach at the trail's end. Back on U.S. 101, you can stop at Mill Creek Campground or return to Jedediah Smith Park.

If you decide to return to the park, take U.S. 101 to Elk Valley Road, a flat and easy ride. Turn right onto Howland Hill Road and climb a long, graveled hill. Then a coast and a ride over short rolling hills bring you back to the park. Wind left to Stout Grove, completing the loop. Take the rest of the day to explore the forests, swim in the icy Smith River, and camp overnight. Note: Keep food tightly contained or bears may feel welcome.

WHERE TO STAY

Crescent City has numerous motels, but since this tour emphasizes nature, we suggest camping. Campgrounds include the following: Jedediah Smith Redwoods State Park; open all year; $3. Del Norte Coast Redwoods State Park; open April through October; $3. KOA Camp Lincoln, on U.S. 101 south of North Bank Road; open April 15th to December 31st; $3.50. Shoreline Camp Ground, on Elk Valley Road; open all year; $4.

FOR FURTHER INFORMATION

You can contact either the Del Norte County Chamber of Commerce, Crescent City, California 95531, or write cyclists Jud and Betty Clifton, P.O. Box 957, Beaverton, Oregon 97005.

GIANT SEQUOIAS AND COASTAL REDWOODS

Giant sequoias and coastal red-woods are the survivals of an ancient family of mammoth trees. They are often confused because both grow in California, have reddish barks, and are so immense and old. But you can easily tell the two apart.

Giant sequoias flourish in scattered groves on California's western Sierra Nevada slopes and are the world's largest trees in volume. The trunks grow fat and straight without tapering, and the seeds and cones are three times larger than those of the redwood. Other characteristics: tough, thick, asbestos like bark which prevents them from burning easily, and angular limbs.

Coastal redwoods, in contrast, live only along the Pacific coast and are the world's tallest trees. The trunks grow fifteen to twenty feet across and taper upward to a point. Other characteristics: short branches, soft, feathery evergreen foliage, and reddish, deeply ridged bark.

Jedediah Smith Redwoods State Park is in northern California off U.S. 199; 9 miles northeast of Crescent City via U.S. 199; 345 miles north of San Francisco via U.S. 101 and 199.

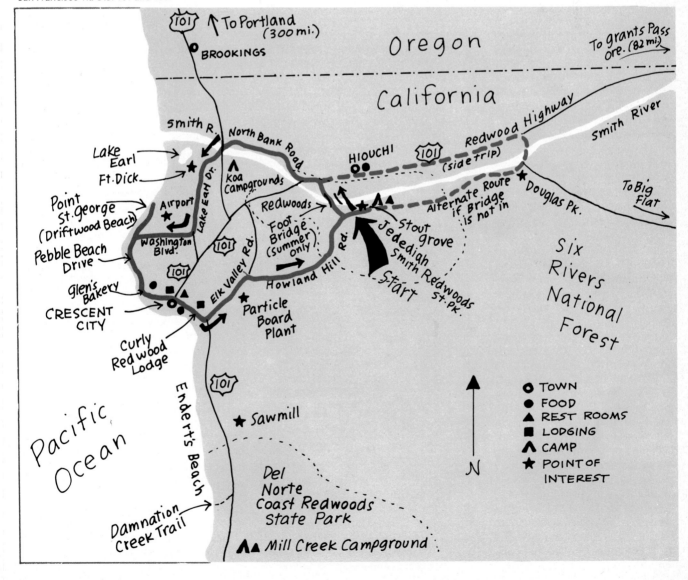

281

133. WINE COUNTRY WEEKEND

Tiny Napa Valley, with its knolls, lanes, and rocky brooks, could have been the model for Tolkien's mythical Hobbit Shire. In early spring lupine, poppies, and mustard flowers flood the hills, while autumn brings the aroma of freshly crushed grapes. Though you can cover the wineries and see the scenery in one day, we suggest two to give yourself freedom to explore the byways on your own.

Before starting from Yountville, stop at a filling station and pick up a local map detailing the wineries which usually offer free samples and tours after 10 A.M. You can park your car at the lot of Vintage 1870, a slightly commercialized group of shops in an old winery. Turn left at each of the two Y's past Yountville Park and then turn right onto St. Helena Highway (State 29), the main road on the flat valley floor. Caution: Between here and St. Helena, watch for the narrow bridges where biking shoulders disappear, forcing you into traffic, and for the rugged railroad tracks which can flip experts.

Choose picnic basics at any St. Helena market or go east on Charter Oak Avenue to the quaint Olive Oil Manufactory filled with breadsticks, sausages, and pungent cheeses lying in great slabs on wooden tables. On Railroad Avenue you can visit the Hatchery, a combination art gallery and Robert Louis Stevenson museum. From noon to 3 P.M., tea and authentic Philippine dinners are served. St. Helena has two parks: Lyman Park on Main Street and the more secluded Crane Park, with a playground, one block left off State 29 on Sulphur Springs Avenue.

North of St. Helena the road becomes hilly and curving, but not difficult. A gradual climb begins near Charles Krug Cellars and continues beyond Freemark Abbey, where you can watch candlemakers mold tapers from pure beeswax. Then the road plunges downhill and around a shaded bend.

Picnic spots in this vicinity include Old Bale Mill with its gray weathered waterwheel and Bothe-Napa Valley State Park, a ten-minute coast farther north. At Bothe-Napa it will cost you $1 to picnic in the formal area. Instead lock your bike and hike back through redwoods, Douglas fir, and tan oak to find a spot beside Ritchie Creek. The water is so icy, it stings your toes. You may want to camp overnight here (fee, $3) or at least swim in the pool.

A ride over a few easy hills brings you to Calistoga, known for its mineral baths. Reserve a motel here early. Hearty souls can venture north on St. Helena Highway for a steep climb toward Robert Louis Stevenson State Park. Though the road is a tenth-gear special, the first wide turnout twenty minutes from Calistoga offers choice views, especially at sunrise or dusk.

On your second day, restock on food in Calistoga and take the lightly traveled Silverado Trail, an old stagecoach road, through the quiet countryside. Beyond Larkmead Lane you ride over two deeply-shaded steep hills. For a view of the whole valley, trek up arduous Deer Park Road. On the thrilling ride back down, don't cut corners: the few cars traveling this road drive at breakneck speed.

Back along Silverado Trail, find a spot for lunch by climbing into the hills or down the bank of the creek running intermittently beside the road. Beyond Zinfandel Lane, turn left for a side trip onto Conn Creek Road (Route 128) and pedal 2 miles to Lake Hennessey. You can picnic and swim free here during the week and late on weekends; during peak visitor hours on weekends, there's a nominal charge. Local cyclists who have become blasé about wineries often pedal the 35-mile loop around the reservoir along Chiles B. Pope Valley Road and Howell Mountain Road. This scenic pastoral tour is recommended if you have an extra day.

Along Silverado Trail again, turn right onto Yountville Cross Road and pedal about 5 minutes to a narrow bridge with a break in its north side. You can climb down through this break and stroll in meadows along still another brook. Then returning to Yountville, dine on wine country cuisine, perhaps at the Grape Vine Inn just north of town or at Oakville's Colonial Dining Room.

DISTANCE:	41 miles, excluding side trips.
TERRAIN:	Flat to moderately hilly.
TRAFFIC:	Usually light to medium, but often fast; heavy on summer weekends.
DIFFICULTY:	For cyclists with some experience. Beginners and families with small children should see the additional notes at the end of the ride.
BEST TIME:	Spring or autumn, but good year round.
LOCATION:	Napa Valley, California, north of San Francisco.

282

Other Tours

For a one-day tour (21 miles round trip), pedal from Rutherford on St. Helena Highway to Larkmead Lane, take Larkmead to the Silverado Trail, then return to Rutherford. Beginners and families with young riders should consider getting still farther off the main track. One good possibility is to begin at Oakville and go southwest on Oakville Grade. Turn left onto Dry Creek Road, then left again onto Orchard Avenue. Cross beneath Route 29 to Oak Knoll Avenue, which leads to the Silverado Trail. A left onto the Silverado Trail takes you finally to Oakville Cross Road, where you turn left and return to Oakville. Still another touring possibility is to skip St. Helena Highway and do all your cycling along the less traveled Silverado Trail, crossing over occasionally to visit St. Helena Highway wineries.

WHERE TO STAY

Camping is permitted at Bothe-Napa Valley State Park. Hostels are located in St. Helena and Calistoga.

Motels include El Bonita, 195 Main Street, St. Helena; Dr. Wilkinson's Hot Springs, 1507 Lincoln Avenue, Calistoga; and Golden Haven Hot Springs, 1713 Lake Street, Calistoga.

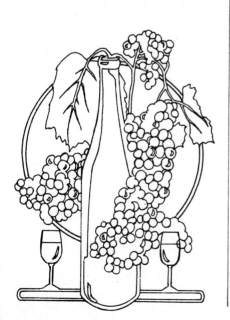

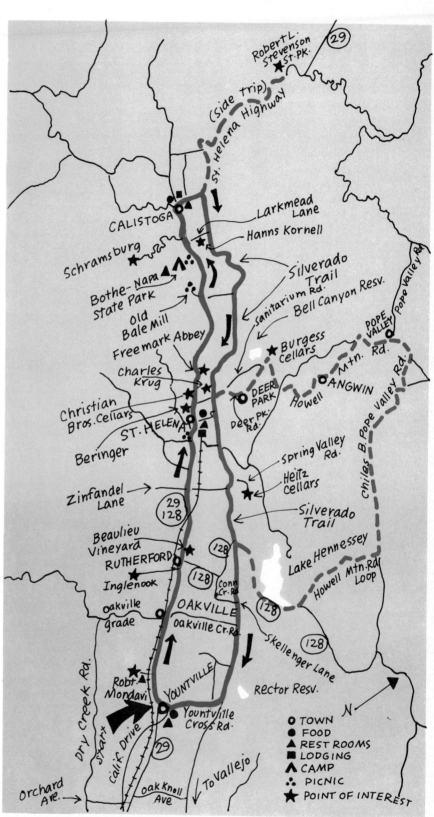

Yountville is in Napa Valley north of San Francisco on California 29; 7 miles north of Napa on California 29; 57 miles northeast of San Francisco via U.S. 101, California 37, and 29.

283

134. CAPE OF KINGS SALLY

Watch puffins and sea lions at play on an empty beach, glimpse pelicans, herons and egrets in the marshes, and snack on wild blackberries in summer on this tour through Point Reyes National Seashore. You may encounter thick sea mists and high winds at any time, especially on Inverness Ridge's ocean side, so come prepared with a windbreaker. Also, plan to start early enough to finish the ride by dusk, as there are no overnight facilities until you recross the ridge.

Park your car in the lot at park headquarters just off Highway 1 on Bear Valley Road (a sign directs you). From the lot you can take a pleasant side trip on Bear Valley Trail and Coast Trail, at present the only two biking trails in the park. However, save this excursion for afternoon and instead ride north on Bear Valley Road through an arbor of live oaks. This well-paved road often lacks shoulders, so try to avoid weekends from Memorial Day through Labor Day when traffic is heavy. Note: Telephone poles sometimes stand in the middle of the shoulders.

You pedal past dairy pastures, then bear left onto Sir Francis Drake Highway. Granite cliffs loom above you, while to your right the tidewater laps the road or gives way to homes and pastures. Blackberries grow along the fencerows for the hungry passing cyclist. You ride through Inverness Park, a small town with a pizza house and grocery store, and then through Paradise Estates, a cluster of homes. About a mile beyond Paradise Estates, stop at the Audubon Salt Marsh Study Area. In the pickleweed and marshes you may spot egrets, loons, herons, black brants, or pelicans.

Beyond the Audubon observatory, you soon see Tomales Bay to your right. Protected from harsh ocean breezes, the westerly shores provide a sheltered spot for swimming, sunbathing, and picnicking. If you need food, buy supplies at the country store in Inverness, the last food stop before you enter the park. Outside Inverness you pass two grassy rest areas and a motel with fishing, boat rentals, and coke and coffee machines. Quaint homes dot this ride; one uses portholes for windows.

At Chicken Ranch public beach, angle sharply to your left and begin the steep 1-mile climb up Ottinger's Hill. The firs, pines, and wide views distract from your tired legs. Stop often at the numerous turnouts. At the hilltop, cool winds blow. Look for blacktail, fallow, and axis deer which often graze here when mists obscure the meadows.

Stop a mile beyond the hill at Tomales Bay State Park, where you can hike through fresh groves of bishop pine, dig for clams in season, or swim. Past the park entrance, veer left and wind your way gently down between granite cliffs and marshland. Soon you pass an oyster farm on Drakes Estero, but *walk* your bike to investigate: the driveway has been paved with razor-sharp oyster shells. Leopard sharks breed in these waters; if the light is good, you may glimpse hundreds of baby sharks as you pedal by Home Bay.

Fingerlets of Drakes Bay cut through the land with its tidy farms and grazing Brahma cattle. The road climbs and dips over several short, steep hills and crosses a few streams thick with pickleweed. Climbing the last hill to the ridgetop, you gaze to your left across miles of rich pastureland clear to the sea. From the ridgetop you pedal past the RCA facility and the access roads to Point Reyes Beach North and Point Reyes Beach South. Finally you come to Drakes

DISTANCE:	40 miles, excluding side trips.
TERRAIN:	Rolling hills with one steep grade.
TRAFFIC:	Light on weekdays; heavy on summer weekends.
DIFFICULTY:	Rough for beginners.
BEST TIME:	Spring, when wildflowers bloom. Avoid November and December, when winds can rise up to 100 m.p.h.
LOCATION:	Point Reyes National Seashore, north of San Francisco on Highway 1.

Beach, where you can picnic, collect driftwood, and swim. Lifeguards stand duty in summer. On this beach Sir Francis Drake allegedly repaired his ship the *Golden Hinde* in 1579. Pedaling farther south on the main road, you reach the Coast Guard facility. The blustery winds here make for excellent kite flying. Walk along the lonely dunes to the lighthouse site and peer down the ragged cliffs to see if there are any puffins, sea lions, or seals sunning themselves on the rookery below.

On your way back to park headquarters, take a side trip on the wide asphalt access road to Point Reyes Beach South. Along this 12-mile stretch of unbroken coastline, the ocean waves break against craggy rocks. Rules prohibit swimming here because of the wild, unpredictable surf. Before you return to park headquarters, you may want to stop for dinner at one of

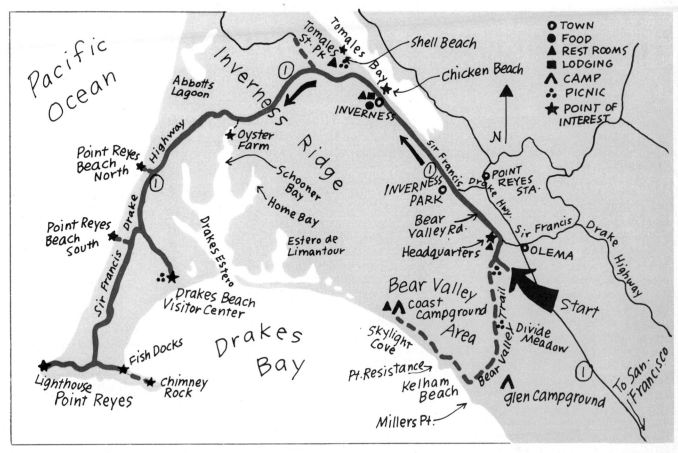

Point Reyes National Seashore is on the California coast off U.S. 1; 31 miles north of San Francisco via U.S. 1.

Inverness's Czech restaurants.

Forest Trail Side Trip

Arriving back at park headquarters, ride along 4.4-mile Bear Valley Trail through fern grottos and forests of tanbark and live oak, bay, Oregon alder, and Douglas fir. To your right at this trail's start is a short self-guided woodpecker hiking trail. Even if you don't try this walk, listen as you ride on the dirt path for the acorn woodpecker's chatter or the call of the Steller's jay. Clearwater Creek, rushing beside you, invites you to stop. Here you might glimpse the mountain beaver, a living fossil, nervously constructing his home.

Bear Valley Trail runs into Coast Trail, which follows the shore of the bay. You pedal easily as the sun sets over the ocean. Pause about midway along this 3.6-mile trail to explore Skylight Cave. Then proceed to Coast Camp, 8 miles from park headquarters, where you can stay overnight and perhaps try an icy moonlight swim.

WHERE TO STAY

To camp in the park, write Point Reyes National Seashore, Point Reyes, California 94956, or phone (415) 663-1092. Campsites are free and quite limited, so make summer reservations at least one month and no more than three months in advance. Rangers recommend that you phone for reservations to avoid problems.

You can also camp in Olema Ranch Campground, half a mile from park headquarters on Highway 1. For reservations, write Olema Ranch Campground, Olema, California 94950, or phone (415) 663-1363.

There is an American Youth Hostel on Limantour Road, 1.3 miles north of park headquarters off Bear Valley Road. In Inverness there is a boatel, the Golden Hinde, on Sir Francis Drake Highway; (415) 669-1389.

Motels: Inverness Lodge, off Sir Francis Drake Highway, Inverness; (415) 669-1034. Inverness Motel, on Sir Francis Drake Highway, south of Inverness; (415) 669-1081.

FOR SPARE PARTS, FOR REPAIRS, FURTHER INFORMATION

Seashore Bicycles, Olema Ranch Campground, Highway 1, Olema, California 94950; (415) 663-1768. Barbara Gunn can tell you anything else you would like to know about this ride. Her shop is open from 9 A.M. to 5 P.M. daily during school vacations and weekends (except on Thanksgiving and Christmas days), and 9 A.M. to 1 P.M. weekdays during the off-season. Barbara also rents bikes at $1 an hour or $6 per day.

135. WHARF-TO-SAUSALITO JAUNT

San Francisco's Baghdad-by-the-bay mystique comes alive on this tour past the wharf and across the Golden Gate Bridge to Sausalito. Salt bay breezes blow, sailboats glide in the harbor, shopping centers bustle, and the sunlit city sparkles across blue San Francisco Bay.

Start from the historic Ferry Building at the foot of Market Street. Leave at about 10 A.M. to avoid noontime traffic and head north on the Embarcadero for one block to Washington Street, where you go right and follow the marked bike lane. Rounding Walton Park, you have a splendid view of Telegraph Hill, dotted with exclusive homes and artists' studios and topped by Coit Tower. You proceed past Fisherman's Wharf and its numerous shops, near which you can leave the bikeway to explore the more expensive Cannery and Ghiradelli \ Square shopping districts. At the Aquatic Park pier, stop for a free visit to the San Francisco Maritime Museum. From the shops, climb two steep blocks up Van Ness Avenue and go right at the hilltop onto Francisco Street to rejoin the marked bike lane.

You pedal on Beach Street near the marina's green turf and past the Saint Francis Yacht Club. The road ends at the Palace of Fine Arts, a delightful spot to rest or picnic on velvet lawns beside a lagoon. Then you go south (away from the marina) on Baker Street for three blocks, right onto Francisco Street which immediately crosses Richardson Street, and left on Lyon Street for two blocks. Turn right through Lombard Gate into the Presidio. From this historic army post, you view the Golden Gate Bridge. The Presidio path ends at the bridge, which has a bikeway open from sunrise to dusk. During the week, you can use either side of the bikeway, but on weekends and holidays only the west side is open. If you take the east side, peer over the railing as you approach the first tower and look upon Fort Point, a Civil War battlement.

On weekends as you leave the bridge, follow the bike signs which lead you over a small bridge and along a bike path through Fort Baker to Sausalito. On weekdays you can take a shortcut through Marin's Vista Point to a dirt path 200 yards from and parallel to the freeway. Eventually you descend steeply to South Alexander Street, which leads you north to Sausalito, with its shops, restaurants, and harbors.

In Sausalito ask directions to the Golden Gate Ferry, which leaves from the foot of Anchor Street. The fare is 75¢ for adults, 25¢ for children 5 to 12 years old, and free for those under 4. The ferries have bike racks, and large cycling groups are asked to phone ahead. You sail across the breezy bay beneath clear skies. At dusk lean on the Ferry's gunwale and watch the sunset glow through the Gate.

Mill Valley Ride

For a longer ride (29 miles one way from the Ferry Building in San Francisco) or even another day's outing, pedal to Mill Valley from Sausalito. Ride north on Bridgeway, a heavily trafficked road. At Harbor Drive, turn right, cross the railroad tracks, and spin along a smooth 3-mile bike path. You go under U.S. 101, recross the tracks, and turn right onto Almonte Boulevard, which becomes Miller Avenue. Soon you wind inland to Throckmorton Avenue in Mill Valley, where you turn left at the Greyhound bus depot and go another quarter mile to Old Mill Park. Here you can picnic beneath redwoods. Later either return to San Francisco or go farther to Angel Island.

Strawberry Point and Angel Island

You cycle on a wooded island without a car in sight on this extended tour (48 miles). Starting from Old Mill Park, go back down Miller Avenue, turn left on Camino Alto, and right on East Blithedale. Go over U.S. 101, then right onto Strawberry Service Road (old 101 Redwood Highway). A left onto Seminary Drive, which becomes Strawberry Drive, takes you along a

DISTANCE:	19 miles—11 miles by bike and 8 miles by ferry. The cycling can be extended to either 29 miles or 48 miles.
TERRAIN:	Winding, with a few descents and one short, steep climb.
TRAFFIC:	Moderate in San Francisco; moderate to heavy in Sausalito.
DIFFICULTY:	Good ride for anyone.
BEST TIME:	Spring, summer, or autumn weekends. September and October are the warmest, January the coldest. Avoid winter and foggy or windy days.
LOCATION:	San Francisco, California.

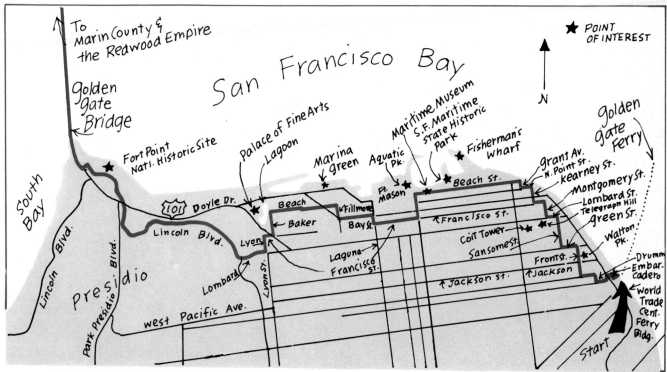

Tour begins in San Francisco, California.

loop past Richardson Bay. After a short jaunt on Tiburon Boulevard, turn right onto Greenwood Cove Road.

Take the first right past the National Audubon Society Building to Richardson Bay Park, where you can pick up a 2-mile bike path along the water to Mar West Street in Tiburon. Eat in one of Tiburon's quaint restaurants, then take the Graycin Ferry across Racoon Strait to Angel Island, where no cars are permitted. Round-trip ferry fare: Adults, $1.50; children 5 to 14 years old, 75¢. You may be charged 25¢ extra per bike. On Angel Island note the time the last ferry sails to the mainland and plan to be back fifteen minutes earlier. There is a 25¢ park entrance fee.

You can picnic on the island and pedal the 5.5-mile loop from Ayala Cove. Past the ranger station building, go left and climb a steep hill, then turn left on the main road, where soon you look over the strait to Blunt Point. Beyond the off-limits military area's dilapidated buildings, you climb a short, steep hill and coast past two light stations.

Across the bay you can see San Francisco, Alcatraz Island, and the Golden Gate Bridge. Many small paths wind into the woodlands and make pleasant side trips. Returning to Ayala Cove, take the ferry back to Tiburon. Retrace your tour to Sausalito, then to San Francisco via the Golden Gate Ferry.

WHERE TO STAY

The only campground in the area is in Mount Tamalpais State Park, 7 miles west of Mill Valley via the Panoramic Highway. This is so far from the main route, you should phone ahead—(415) 388-2070—to make certain you can obtain a site. Fee, $1.50.

San Francisco, of course, has hotels and motels of every price and description. Tiburon and Sausalito have more limited overnight accommodations.

FOR SPARE PARTS AND REPAIRS

San Francisco has numerous bike shops. If you get stuck, just consult the yellow pages or ask someone where to find the nearest shop.

FOR FURTHER INFORMATION

Clifford L. Franz, southwestern vice-president of the League of American Wheelmen, told us about this tour and will be glad to answer questions or give suggestions for other tours in the San Francisco area. Write him at 36 Grand Boulevard, San Mateo, California 94401, and send him a selfaddressed stamped envelope with your inquiry.

NEARBY

With its pleasant year-round weather, northern California has numerous cycling spots. Within an hour of San Francisco are the Napa Valley (see the tour on page 282), Point Reyes National Seashore (see page 284), and the Big Sur area, including the famed Seventeen Mile Drive from Monterey to Carmel (see page 289).

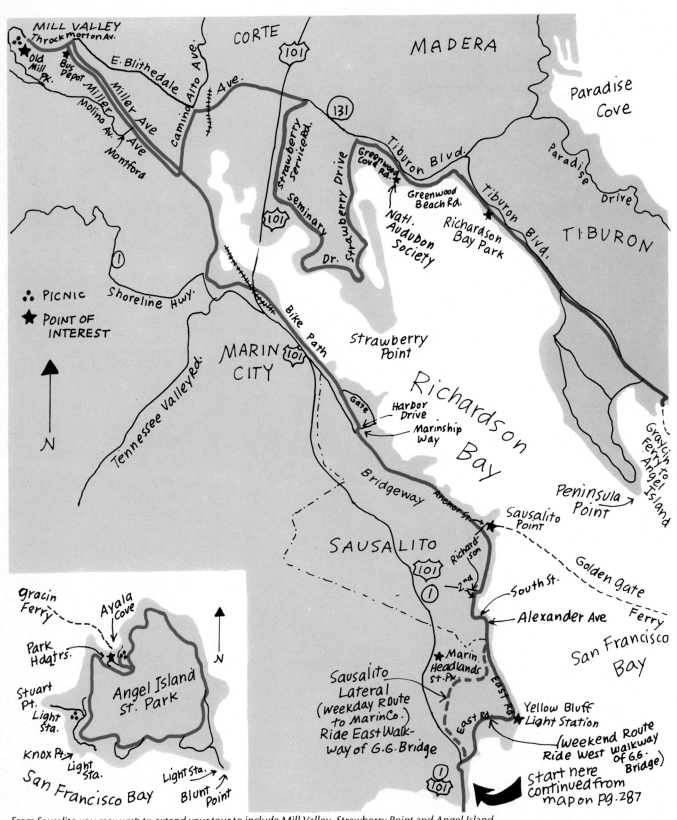

From Sausalito you may wish to extend your tour to include Mill Valley, Strawberry Point and Angel Island.

136. BIG SUR SWING

One of California's most scenic oceanside rides lies along Monterey Peninsula's Seventeen Mile Drive, which skirts the rocky coast from Monterey to Carmel's art colonies. You pedal through invigorating salt air, hear the ocean crash, and see the famous cypress trees, including the frequently photographed lone tree on Cypress Point.

Begin your day in Monterey, with its white sand beaches, serene harbor, and red-roofed Spanish stucco homes. If you arrive on a misty day, browse through the town until about 11 A.M. when the fogs often lift to reveal clear ocean views. This is Steinbeck country, so visit famed Cannery Row, where art galleries and gourmet restaurants have replaced all but one sardine cannery. Then coast to the foot of Figueroa Street to see colorful sailboats and cruisers anchored in the marina. You can also follow the city's "path of history," orange-red center lines on streets leading to major historic points, including Robert Louis Stevenson's home, an 1847 theater, and an old customhouse, all in Monterey State Historic Park.

Leave the city on Ocean View Boulevard. Traffic is often heavy on this well-paved road. You pass Lover's Point, where you might see skin divers in the cove, and wind along the coast between sand dunes and pine and cypress groves. From Asilomar State Beach the road begins to curve inland, and soon you reach Pacific Grove Gate, the start of Seventeen Mile Drive. Motorists must pay $3, but cyclists are permitted to go through free. Beyond the gate, you can take one of two routes to Carmel: a left onto Majella Road for a ride through woods and up Huckleberry Hill, or a right to continue on Seventeen Mile Drive for the

DISTANCE:	30 miles round trip, excluding side trips.
TERRAIN:	Rolling.
TRAFFIC:	Heavy on weekends; light to moderate on weekdays.
DIFFICULTY:	Okay for beginners, but not recommended for families with young riders because of traffic.
BEST TIME:	Good year round.
LOCATION:	Monterey to Carmel, California.
SPECIAL NOTE:	The scenic Seventeen Mile Drive along which part of this tour runs is closed to bicycles because of heavy traffic on weekends, holidays, and during special events like the Bing Crosby Golf Classic. Groups might be able to obtain special permission to ride on no-bike days by writing the Security Office, Del Monte Properties Company, P.O. Box 567, Pebble Beach, California 93953 or phoning (408) 624-6411.

spectacular flat ride along the coast (traffic is heaviest this way).

Huckleberry Hill Route

Turning left, you pedal about 2 miles on flat road through pine and cypress woods. Stop to rest at Forest Lake. Then you begin the steep 4-mile climb up Huckleberry Hill, passing a picnic ground along the way. From the hilltop you can see clear to the ocean. An exhilarating 4-mile coast takes you through Carmel Hill Gate and downhill along Carmel Way and San Antonio Avenue to Ocean Avenue. Here you turn left and climb the stiff hill into Carmel.

Big Sur Coast Ride

A right turn at Pacific Grove Gate takes you along the craggy coast past slopes covered in spring with violet lupine, yellow mustard flowers, and flaming poppies. Cool prevailing winds nudge your back and you should fly along. The sea breaks far below as you round Point Joe, the scene of many shipwrecks. As you pass Monterey Peninsula County Club, watch for small deer herds in the fields. Then at the tourist information booth for Bird and Seal Rocks, you can watch the seals and sea lions, while cormorants and see gulls scream overhead.

Back on Seventeen Mile Drive, you pass the warm white sands of Fan Shell Beach, sometimes covered with driftwood, vivid shells, and sea-polished stones. A short distance beyond, a tiny road winds to your right and leads you one-tenth of a mile to Cypress Point. You pedal on through a grove of gnarled cypress trees to Lone Cypress Tree near Midway Point. Devotees of photographers Minor White, Edward Weston, and Ansel Adams will see many familiar scenes on this tour.

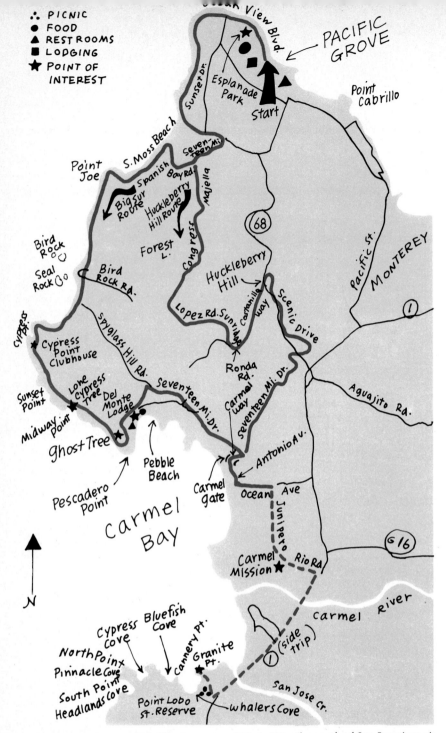

Key

⋮ PICNIC
● FOOD
▲ RESTROOMS
■ LODGING
★ POINT OF INTEREST

Monterey is on the central California coast on U.S. 1; 116 miles south of San Francisco via U.S. 1; 285 miles north of Los Angeles via U.S. 1.

If you return to Monterey via the coastal section of Seventeen Mile Drive, you may encounter strong head winds, so be prepared for a slow ride back.

WHERE TO STAY

Motels in Carmel and Monterey are numerous and include the inexpensive Motel 6, 2124 Fremont, Monterey; (408) 373-3500. The only nearby campground is Riverside Trailer Park, 4 miles east of Carmel on Route G16, then 1 mile southwest on Schulte Road. For reservations, write Nick and Audre Nedelcove, Riverside Trailer Park, R.F.D. 2, Box 827, Carmel, California 93921, or phone (408) 624-9329.

ROSES ALONG THE BIG SUR

Delicate seaside daisies, vivid California poppies, lavender bush lupine, and yellow mustard flowers carpet the Big Sur slopes. Also along the beaches or on adjacent cliffs bloom several members of the rose family (though none even resembles a rose), including ocean spray or cream bush, silverweed, and the California blackberry.

Ocean spray or *cream bush* grows from four to eighteen feet tall and displays tiny whitish flowers in clumps that resemble lilacs in shape. Look for this flower in canyons, on sea bluffs, and in other rocky spots along the coast.

Silverweed has bright yellow-orange flowers which bloom from April to August. The green leaves grow eight to twenty inches long and are composed of seven to thirty-one leaflets which have a woolly white underside. Look for silverweed in salt marshes or on beaches along the Big Sur.

California blackberries grow near the beaches. You can tell this plant by its white flowers, sharply pointed, bright green leaves, and small half-inch berries. Don't overlook another blackberry species on the beaches which has duller, usually more rounded leaves and larger fruits.

Past bleached, twisted Ghost Tree and Witch Tree on Pescadero Point, you round a curve to Del Monte Lodge, with a grocery store and soda fountain. Less than half a mile past the Lodge, make a right turn to remain on Seventeen Mile Drive. Coast by Pebble Beach and when you arrive at the T turn right onto Carmel Way. The road soon curves left becoming North San Antonio Avenue. Go left at Ocean Avenue, and climb the steep hill past tiny shops into Carmel.

Carmel is a cluster of art galleries, restaurants, and specialty shops. Lunch at one of Carmel's fine French or Italian restaurants, or buy picnic supplies and pedal south on Junipero Avenue for a pleasant side trip past Carmel Mission to Point Lobos State Reserve. From the mission, take Rio Road to U.S. 1, then continue another 2 miles on U.S. 1 to Point Lobos. Bird Island and Sea Lion Rocks lie offshore. On a calm day you can swim in the surf.

137. LITTLE DENMARK PASTRY PEDAL

Sample rich, flaky Danish pastries, explore old Franciscan missions, and view miles of calendulas, petunias, marigolds, roses, gladiolus, asters, and chrysanthemums on this tour through Santa Inez Valley's wooded hills.

Your ride begins in Solvang, a small Danish community with windmills, tiny shops, and bakeries. Park your car in the big lot beside Birkholm's Bakery and Coffee Shop and ride out of town on Alisal Road, directly in front of Birkholm's. If you plan to picnic, buy food before you leave. (Note: There are no eating spots between Solvang and Lompoc, so if you plan to spend a day on each leg of this trip, you will have to picnic.) Though Solvang is often crowded with tourists, you will find yourself in quiet countryside only blocks from town. The road narrows beyond the long bridge a half mile out of Solvang, but there is no traffic.

Past Alisal Ranch you cross a narrow bridge, lean into a wide curve, and climb a short, steep hill to view meadowed valleys. An easy coast through tunnels of live oaks brings you into woodlands where a brook runs in the gorge to your left. Sit quietly on the banks and you may glimpse deer coming to drink.

To see a waterfall, stop at Nojoqui Falls County Park, lock your bike to a tree, and take the forested footpath. On a warm day, wade in the cold pool at the base of the falls. As you leave the park, examine the narrow-trunked trees on either side of the ranger's birdbath: these are rare cork oaks and have bark two inches thick.

You make a sharp left turn out of the park, coast for a while, then ride along a straight stretch until you reach a stop sign. Here you turn left on Old Coast Road and

pedal a mile on bumpy road. Turn left again on U.S. 101, where traffic is fast, but shoulders are wide and well paved. In two and a half miles, take the Lompoc exit onto less-traveled Highway 1. Warnings between here and Lompoc: Watch for gravel shoulders, sharp white rocks on the road, and possible high crosswinds. After about a mile on Highway 1, you reach a tough 2-mile hill, beyond which you pedal through a pass and come to Ocean Avenue and your first flower fields. Turn left on Ocean Avenue and ride into Lompoc.

Lunch at a Lompoc restaurant or picnic in La Purisima Concepcion Mission State Park. To reach the park and its old Franciscan mission, go north on H Street and right on Lompoc-Casmalia Road for 3 miles. Leave Lompoc by returning the way you came along Highway 1. Then turn left onto untraveled Santa Rosa Road, which runs through miles of commercial flower beds. Among the neat, tame fields glow occasional meadows of wild orange California poppies. Pause at one of the many turnouts to view the colors from a high hill. Along the roadway you can pick juicy blue-black wild elderberries.

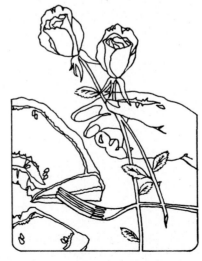

Following the road downhill, you come to Santa Rosa County Park. Another downhill plunge leads you to picnic tables and spectacular valley views. Then you coast to a flat road leading to Buellton and Andersen's Restaurant. Go right at Andersen's onto Highway 246 and back to Solvang.

DISTANCE:	50 miles, excluding side trips.
TERRAIN:	Rolling hills with a few steep grades.
TRAFFIC:	Light except on Highway 1.
DIFFICULTY:	Requires a 10-speed bike. Good ride for beginners who don't mind walking a few hills.
BEST TIME:	Good year round, except during hot summer days. Best in spring and early summer when wildflowers and commercial flower fields are in full bloom.
LOCATION:	Solvang to Lompoc, California, about two and a half hours north of Los Angeles off U.S. 101.

Old Santa Inés Mission lies east on Solvang's Mission Drive and makes a pleasant side trip. After browsing through Solvang's Danish specialty shops, stop in at Birkholm's Bakery, where you receive a huge platter of assorted pastries and pay only for what you eat.

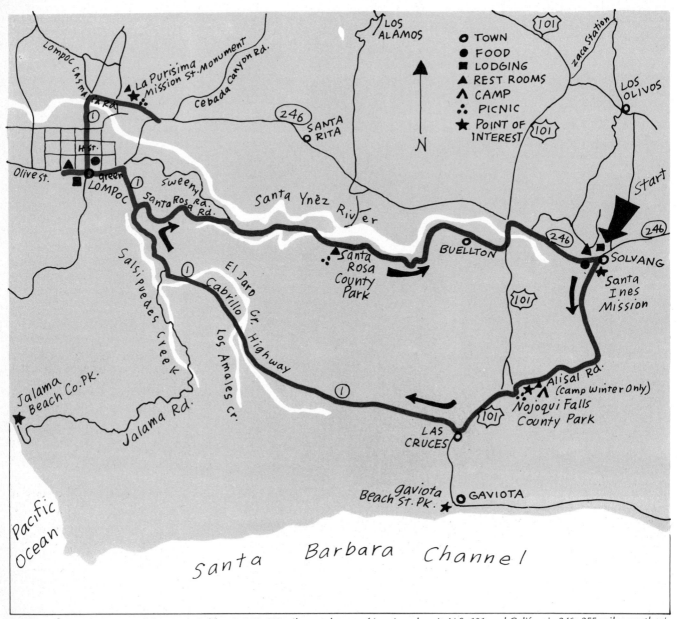

Solvang is in southwestern California on California 246; 150 miles northwest of Los Angeles via U.S. 101 and California 246; 255 miles south of San Francisco via U.S. 101 and California 246.

WHERE TO STAY

Motels in Solvang and Lompoc are numerous. The following are the least expensive in Solvang: Hamlet, 1532 Mission Drive; (805) 688-4413. Meadowlark, 2644 Mission Drive; (805) 688-4631. Sanja Cota, 3099 Mission Drive; (805) 688-5525. Viking, 1506 Mission Drive; (805) 688-4827. In Lompoc: Lompoc, 528 North H Street; (805) RE6-7517.

The only campground in the area is in Nojoqui Falls County Park, which offers winter camping from October 1st to May 1st. Fee, $2.50 for six.

FOR SPARE PARTS AND REPAIRS

Valley Bicycle, 1641 Mission Drive, Solvang, California. This shop is open every day but Mon-

day. You can phone (805) 688-6819 anytime in case of emergency.

NEARBY

Another popular scenic loop is north of Solvang through rolling ranchlands to Los Olivos and historic Mattei's Tavern, an old stagecoach stop. Roads are lightly trafficked and you can spend a whole day exploring on your own.

138. 139. 140. LOS ANGELES RIDES

Los Angeles, a conglomerate of cities, parks, and ocean beaches, is too complex to be explored in just one ride or even in three. Cyclists go virtually everywhere here, and stopping with three tours in this zany biking town is like limiting a child in Disneyland to the merry-go-round. Each of these tours can occupy a morning, an afternoon, or a whole day. Try them all, then venture off on your own, and most of all, enjoy.

MIDTOWN WHIRL

DISTANCE:	8 miles.
TERRAIN:	Flat, with a few easy hills.
TRAFFIC:	Moderate to heavy; lightest on Sunday.
DIFFICULTY:	For cyclists with experience in traffic.
BEST TIME:	Sundays, year round. Avoid rush hours. Temperatures from June through September may reach the 100's. January and February are the coolest, averaging in the 60's.

On this short, busy spin through downtown L.A., you explore Olvera Street, Little Tokyo, Pershing Square, the Music Center, and Chinatown. Though you may enjoy city bustle, most cyclists prefer to ride here on Sundays.

Start at El Pueblo de Los Angeles, which is being restored as a state historical park. Here you can visit

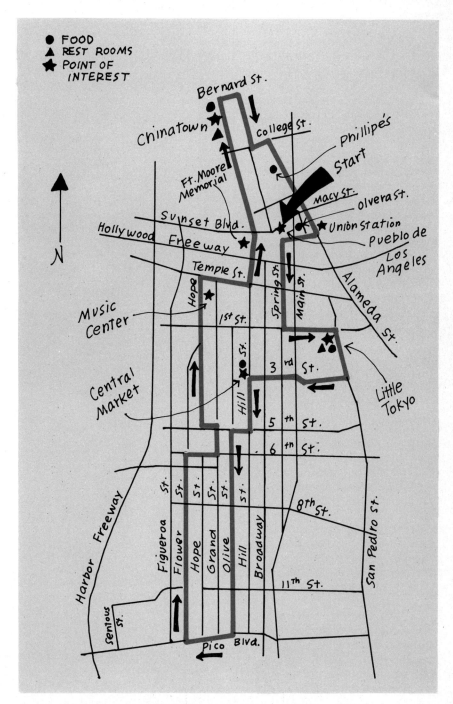

Tours are located in Los Angeles, California. The above map: Midtown Whirl

Pico House, Mission Church, and Olvera Street lined with Spanish adobe buildings which retain their authenticity. From Olvera pedal one block west to Spring Street and continue south past City Hall toward the Los Angeles Times Building straight ahead. At 1st Street, turn left to tour Little Tokyo, L.A.'s largest Japanese community. Atomic Cafe, 422 East 1st Street, makes excellent noodles.

Now you navigate more turns: right on San Pedro Street, right on 3rd Street, passing the Bradberry Building, and left on Hill Street, where you can bargain for fresh fruits and vegetables at the Central Market. Continuing on, go right on 5th Street and left on Olive Street, skirting Pershing Square. You pedal south about a mile, then turn right on Pico Boulevard, right in three blocks onto Flower Street, proceeding past Atlantic Richfield Plaza, right again on 6th Street, and left on Grand. Take the narrow road just beyond 5th Street left to avoid a steep hill on Grand and climb on Hope Street to the top of Bunker Hill.

Soon the road levels past the Music Center, with its Jacque Lipschitz sculpture, tranquil pools, and pavilions. Go right on Temple Street, left on Hill past Fort Moore Memorial's wall of running water, and on to Chinatown, a tourist spot as well as the center of L.A.'s Chinese community. From Chinatown pedal south toward Union Station past Phillipe's, at 1001 North Alameda (reputed to have invented the French dip beef sandwich). Explore old Union Station, then return to your starting point.

GRIFFITH PARK CAPER

A totally different L.A. experience awaits you in wooded Griffith Park, offering excellent family cycling, a zoo, a travel museum, and many picnic and rest stops. On bike days families and beginners may wish to stay on Crystal Springs Drive between the zoo and main picnic area for idyllic car-free biking.

DISTANCE:	9 miles round trip.
TERRAIN:	Flat, with a few hills.
TRAFFIC:	Moderate; none in certain areas on bike days.
DIFFICULTY:	Good ride for anyone.
BEST TIME:	All seasons. The ideal time is on bike days, held every third Sunday from May through September, when the park's center is closed to cars.

Start at the picnic area between Griffith Park and Crystal Springs drives. Here rock concerts are held most Sundays and you can see the old merry-go-round near the area's south end. Pedal northwest on Griffith Park Drive. A good rest stop is Mineral Wells picnic area, a grassy spot cut by a trickling brook and surrounded by steep, wooded knolls. From the picnic area you continue right on the main road and coast to Travel Town. Admission is free at this indoor-outdoor travel museum, and you can climb on old steam locomotives and explore streetcars and airplanes. If you go left from the picnic area you have a stiff climb to Mt. Hollywood Drive and the park observatory.

Winding right now, you pass Live Steamers, where local locomotive

The Griffith Park Caper

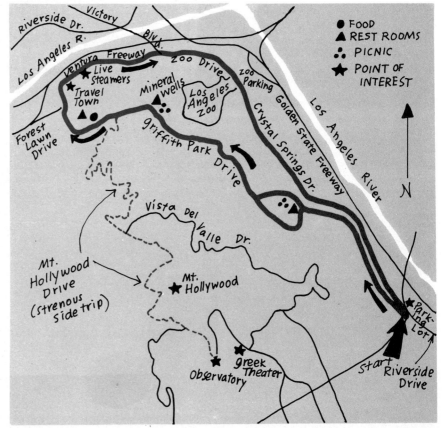

enthusiasts offer free Sunday rides on perfectly created miniature trains. Another stop is the Los Angeles Zoo, where animals are housed by continents. From the aviary you can view most of the area. Pedaling south now on scenic, flat Crystal Springs Drive beneath huge eucalyptus trees, you soon return to the picnic area, your tour's end.

SUNNY BEACH BIKEWAY

DISTANCE:	9.5 miles round trip.
TERRAIN:	Flat.
TRAFFIC:	None on the bikeway; light in other spots.
DIFFICULTY:	Excellent ride for anyone.
BEST TIME:	September through April.

On hot late-summer days when midtown heat is unbearable, escape to the beaches where temperatures are often fifteen to twenty degrees cooler. Though the Beach Bikeway is short (just over 3 miles one way), this ride from Santa Monica to Venice is one of L.A.'s best. The bikeway lies on a promenade also used by pedestrians, so from May 1st to September 1st the hours are restricted to before 9 A.M. From September through April, though, cycling is permitted at any time. The air is crisp, and you pedal past smooth, empty beaches. Though you can complete this tour in an hour, stop occasionally to walk along the sands and enjoy invigorating sea air.

Start near the Santa Monica pier, where you can leave your car in the large lot. Along the promenade, you spin between ocean beaches and clean, sparkling apartment houses. Skirting a parking lot, you pass Pacific Ocean Park's ruins (an amusement park that actually failed in sun city!), then ride past Muscle Beach into Venice. Venice

is a delightful colony of kosher butcher shops, beachfront cottages, and artists' studios.

The bikeway ends at the Venice fishing pier, but the ride continues. From here you go left on Washington Boulevard, then right on Via Marina to Marina Del Rey, with its docks, tiny shops, restaurants, and a wide swimming marina. Browse through the oceanside stores and watch the boats in the harbor. You can turn right soon onto the speedway, a one-way road returning you to the bikeway and back to Santa Monica.

WHERE TO STAY

Motels are abundant here. In most cases, you need only turn a

corner to find an overnight stop or simply check the yellow pages. Camping is limited and the best thing to do is make local inquiries.

FOR SPARE PARTS, REPAIRS, FURTHER INFORMATION

Bicycling clubs and shops are found throughout the metropolitan area. Check the yellow pages for the store nearest you. Southern California's largest touring club is the Los Angeles Wheelmen, with three hundred members and a hundred and fifty planned tours a year. You can write the Wheelmen at 4334 Sunset Boulevard, Los Angeles, California 90029.

Sunny Beach Bikeway

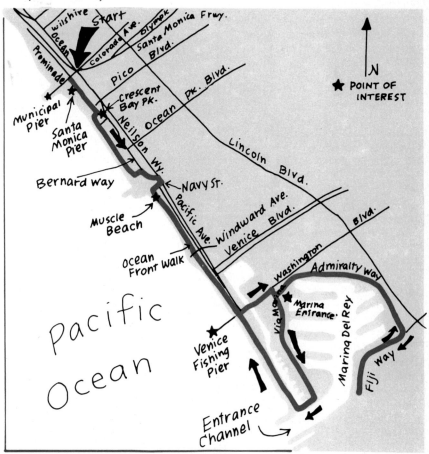

141. SAGEBRUSH-PINE MEANDER

About midway between sun-baked San Diego and Los Angeles, there lies a forest where thick firs and pines grow cool and tall. In this forest, crisp brown cones drop silently to the earth, deer nibble on bright red berries, and the loudest sound is made by an unseen stream trickling in a deep gorge. You pedal from dry, arid canyons to this wooded wilderness with its meadows, lakes, and pine and laurel trees.

Start in Hemet, southeast of Riverside off Interstate 15. Park your car in Hemet's railroad depot lot at Florida Avenue and State Street, then pedal east on Florida past Weston Park which has picnicking and a playground.

At Girard Avenue you can follow the green Ramona Bowl sign right for a side trip to the picturesque outdoor amphitheater where an annual dramatization of Helen Hunt Jackson's novel *Ramona* is staged. The 2-mile road to the bowl passes Ramona Dairy, beyond which it plunges, then climbs around a few bends and up a steep slope. Inside the bowl, walk-up the little path to the Photographer's Point for an excellent view of the entire valley.

Return to the main tour and continue through Hemet on Florida Avenue. Before you leave town, buy snacks and fill your water bottle. A well-paved road with wide shoulders takes you from town between grapefruit and orange groves which sweeten the spring air. In late summer you can also detect the spicy aroma of willows.

Beyond tiny Valle Vista and Soboba Indian Reservation, the road climbs past turkey farms, willows, and silvery-leaved cottonwoods to San Bernardino National Forest. The shoulder disappears at the forest entrance, reappears be-yond Cranston Ranger Station, then eventually disappears completely. While cycling the 3 miles immediately past the ranger station, watch out for two narrow bridges and treacherously narrow rocky passes. Turnouts are located throughout the tour, so pedal easily, stop often, and enjoy the views of the deepening valleys.

Beyond the water fountain at 3,000 feet, your climb becomes steeper. Five more miles of steady climbing bring you into conifer country. Past McCall Memorial County Park, with its riding stables, you reach Mountain Center, where you take the left fork at the country store and continue on State 243 through forests of incense cedar, white fir, and ponderosa and sugar pine. Occasionally you might want to explore the paths that lead into the wilderness. One riding and hiking trail is off to your right, just past the sign reading "Forest Service Station—Keen Wild."

In Idyllwild you can stop for a snack and may want to stay overnight in a rustic cabin with a fireplace, or camp at Mount San Jacinto Wilderness State Park, which you pass as you leave town. Hiking enthusiasts can pick up trail maps at park headquarters. In any case, stop at the headquarters to look at the huge reddish-barked Jeffrey pine beside the building's steps. Those holes in its trunk were drilled by woodpeckers who store acorns there.

About ten minutes beyond Mount San Jacinto Wilderness, you can picnic in the grassy meadow on your right, then pedal on through forested high country toward Lake Fulmor. Coyotes, mountain lions, and gray foxes stalk this area, but usually stay far from the road. At Lake Fulmor you can fish or picnic, but camping is prohibited. As you explore, you come upon ancient Indian mortar holes in the boulders beside the water.

Stop at the turnout about 4 miles farther for a spectacular view across a deep valley. Coasting now, you leave the forest behind, and suddenly see the town of Banning, thousands of feet straight below. Sunlight glances off airplanes as they fly *beneath* you to the airport. But don't let yourself get distracted. You have to concentrate on watching for motorists who come speeding from the mountains.

After a snack in Banning, take 6th Street (Ramsey Street) to Beaumont, then go left onto Lamb Canyon Road (State 79) for a smooth ride through San Jacinto Valley hills. The canyons with their cacti

DISTANCE:	67 miles.
TERRAIN:	Twisting, with some steep climbs and rapid descents.
TRAFFIC:	Light except on some summer weekends.
DIFFICULTY:	Requires a 10-speed bike and some experience.
BEST TIME:	Spring, autumn, and warm winter days. Avoid summer, when the flatlands are hot and dry.
LOCATION:	Starts in Hemet and goes through San Bernardino National Forest, southeast of San Bernardino and west of Palm Springs.

and sagebrush contrast dramatically with the forests. At the intersection with Gilman Springs Road, stay right and continue through San Jacinto on Sanderson Avenue to Hemet, your tour's end.

WHERE TO STAY

Motels are found throughout the ride, and include Coach Light, 1640 West Florida Avenue, Hemet; Bluebird Hill Lodge, Idyllwild; Woodland Park Manor, 55350 South Circle Drive, Idyllwild; Voyager Inn, 5957 West Ramsey Street, Banning; and Golden West, 625 East 5th Street, Beaumont.

Some of the area's campgrounds are listed below: Mount San Jacinto Wilderness State Park, Idyllwild; open year round; $3. Idyllwild County Park, half a mile along County Park Road; open year round; $1.50 for two. Fuller Mill Creek, 6 miles northwest of Idyllwild on County 1; open year round; $2. Dark Canyon and Fern Basin, 7 miles northwest of Idyllwild on County 1, then follow the signs; open May 15th to September 15th; $2. Bay Tree Flats, 10 miles northwest of Idyllwild on County 1; open year round; $1.

FOR SPARE PARTS AND REPAIRS

Jim Cain Sporting Goods, 324 East Florida Avenue, Hemet, California; (714) 658-7203. This shop is open every day from 9 A.M. to 6 P.M. including Sundays and holidays, and from 9 A.M. to 8 P.M. on Fridays.

CALIFORNIA JERUSALEM ARTICHOKES

Lining the desert trails of this tour, you will see huge blossoming plants which look like sunflowers. They are actually Jerusalem artichokes, and their excellent nutritious tubers can be eaten in the wild. Once you have tasted these sweet, juicy roots, you may want to experiment with them. Here is a simple basic recipe to get you started.

Boiled or Fried Jerusalem Artichokes

Wash but do not peel the roots. Then put a little water in a pan and simmer them until tender. Peel them and season with butter, salt, and pepper. To fry a Jerusalem artichoke, parboil it first until almost tender. Remove from the heat, peel, and cut in thin slices. Then fry the slices in oil until they are crisp and golden brown.

You can recognize the Jerusalem artichoke by its sunflower blossoms, its flowering stalk three to six feet high, and its hairy-topped leaves.

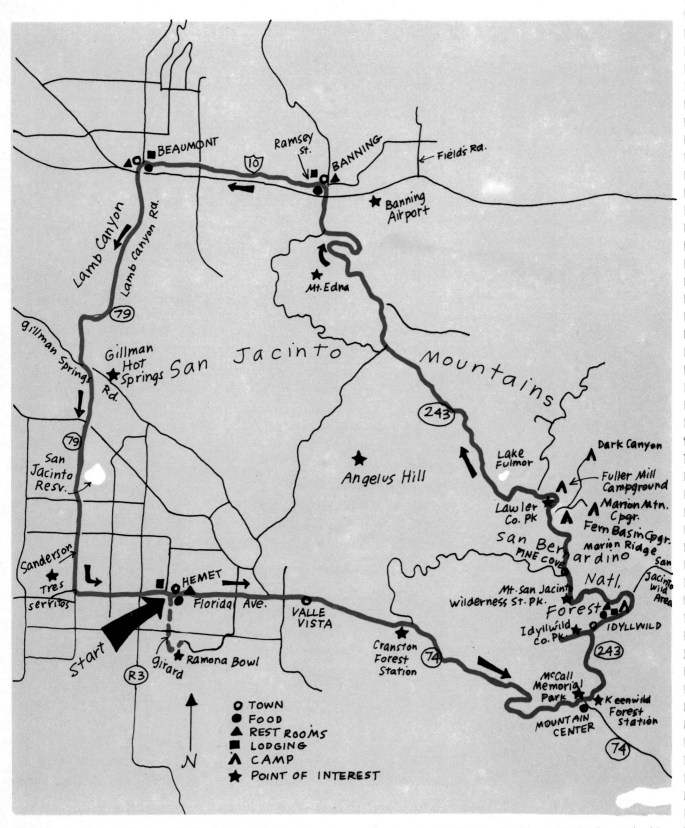

BEAUMONT

Ramsey St.

BANNING

Fields Rd.

10

Lamb Canyon

Lamb Canyon Rd.

79

Banning Airport

Mt. Edna

gillman Springs

Gillman Hot Springs Rd.

San Jacinto

Mountains

243

79

San Jacinto Resv.

Angelus Hill

Lake Fulmor

Dark Canyon

Fuller Mill Campground

Lawler Co. Pk.

Marion Mtn. Cpgr.

Fern Basin Cpgr.

Marion Ridge

San

PINE COVE

San Bernardino

Natl.

Jacinto Wild Area

Sanderson

Tres serritos

HEMET

Florida Ave.

VALLE VISTA

Mt. San Jacinto Wilderness St. Pk.

Forest

Idyllwild Co. Pk.

IDYLLWILD

243

Start

Girard

Ramona Bowl

Cranston Forest Station

74

McCall Memorial Park

Keenwild Forest Station

R3

MOUNTAIN CENTER

74

N

○ TOWN
● FOOD
▲ REST ROOMS
■ LODGING
∧ CAMP
★ POINT OF INTEREST

Hemet is in southern California on California 79 and 74; 87 miles southeast of Los Angeles via I-10, 15 and California 74; 88 miles north of San Diego via I-15, U.S. 395, and California 74.

Hawaii,
Alaska
& Canada

R.SMITH

142. HAWAII VOLCANOES SAFARI

On Hawaii dense tree fern forests grow forty feet high, and ohia and rare koa trees flourish on mountain slopes. Here you can still see volcanoes spew fire, walk through orange lava tunnels formed by molten rock rivers, journey through tangled semitropical jungles inside the caldera of an active volcano. The best way to explore Hawaii Volcanoes National Park is on a bike, with the freedom to pause anywhere and observe the birds and tropical plants unique to these islands.

Start at Kilauea Visitor Center and pedal clockwise around the Kilauea (Key-la-oo-WAY-ah, which means "rising smoke cloud") Caldera rim. Carry food, camping equipment, tools, and spare parts. Coasting on well-paved, narrow-shouldered Crater Rim Drive along Waldron Ledge, you pass the crater pit filled with lava ash. You round a wide left-hand curve and continue coasting to scenic Byron Ledge Overlook, where white steam continuously rises from the lava-crusted floor of Kilauea Iki. The road runs almost flat past Twin Craters to Thurston Lava Tube. Lock your bike here to explore a 400-foot lava tunnel. A paved trail leads through a tree fern forest where hapuu (tree ferns) grow forty feet high and dense tropical ohia trees tower overhead.

A long coast brings you to Puu Puai Overlook, where you can hike the .6-mile path through an area devastated by Kilauea Iki's 1959 eruption. Beyond here turn left for a side trip onto Chain of Craters Road, where you coast gradually past three craters. Check with the Visitor Center about this road before you start. The way may be closed by eruptions. At the Hilina Pali Road intersection, you can continue 1 mile farther on Chain of Craters past Heake Crater, which

erupted in 1968, to a spot where lava from the eruption blocks the road. Or you can turn right on Hilina Pali Road for an exhilarating 11.5-mile downhill spin past Kipuka Nene Campgrounds and mountain scenery to Hilina Pali, where you look down cliffs to the sea. The long climb back uphill from Hilina Pali to Chain of Craters can be strenuous.

Returning to Crater Rim Drive, turn left and coast to the brink of

DISTANCE:	41 miles, plus numerous hikes.
TERRAIN:	Hilly, with some fairly steep climbs.
TRAFFIC:	Moderate in summer; light in spring.
DIFFICULTY:	For intermediate cyclists. A 10-speed bike recommended.
BEST TIME:	Spring and summer, when rains are least likely. The average yearly rainfall is 100 inches. Temperatures in the mountains can be cool at any time of year, so bring warm clothing and rain gear.
LOCATION:	Hawaii Volcanoes National Park on the island of Hawaii. From Hilo's airport, take a taxi or cycle to the park.

Halemaumau ("house of ferns") pit, where there is another overlook. Beyond here the road rises gradually past the Kau Desert with its grotesque, exposed lava formations. Past the picnic area near Kilauea Overlook, you can turn left for another side trip down Mauna Loa Strip Road to Kipuka Puaulu (Bird Park). Lock your bike here and walk the 1.1-mile self-guided trail through a dense ohia, koa, and olapa forest where you view tropical birds. Watch for the crimson apapane and iiwi feeding on sweet ohia blossom nectar, the emerald amakiki, and the short-eared owl. Curious white-eyed and scarlet-billed leiothrixes may flutter close enough to touch you. As you hike, listen for the pheasant's peculiar whistle—like a distant miniature train.

Climbing back up Mauna Loa Strip Road, you turn left onto Crater Rim Drive and pedal past Steaming Bluff and Sulphur Banks to the Visitor Center, the loop's end.

Take time to hike the 3.2-mile Halemaumau Trail across Kilauea Caldera. The path drops 500 feet through deep forests and fern grottos into one of the world's most active volcanoes (its last eruption was in September 1971). The new glossy black lava contrasts with the older dull brown lavas, and foliage grows in the steam cracks. Here you can observe the akia's leathery gray-green leaves and poisonous scarlet berries and smell the fragrant kupaca, found only on the Hawaiian Islands. This is a self-guided trail, so pick up a booklet before leaving. Allow four hours for the walk and carry drinking water.

More Exploring

More than a hundred and fifty

a unique adventure on the way back, lock your bike in Hanalei and take a helicopter ride over the lost world of the Na Pali Coast, inaccessible by land. You can even ask to be dropped off onto a deserted beach for a solitary picnic.

WHERE TO STAY

Motels, resorts, and hotels are available throughout this ride, and you should have no trouble finding a room. If you plan to complete the tour in one day, check into a hotel in Lihue before you leave.

Camping is available at Anahola Beach Park in Anahola, and Wailua River State Park, 6 miles north of Lihue on Route 56. Both are open year round.

FOR SPARE PARTS, REPAIRS, FURTHER INFORMATION

Kawamoto's, Inc., 1322 Kuhio Highway, Kapaa, Kauai, Hawaii 96746; (808) 822-4771. Masaru Kawamoto handles spare parts and repairs and will be glad to supply further information on bicycle tours on Kauai.

NEARBY

An equally enjoyable tour can be taken by pedaling west of Lihue to Mana. This ride is not as hilly as the above tour, but traffic is usually heavier. A strenuous ride up above Waimea Canyon to Kokee Park is for experts only.

Lihue International Airport, on the island of Kauai in the Hawaiian Islands, is served by most major airlines.

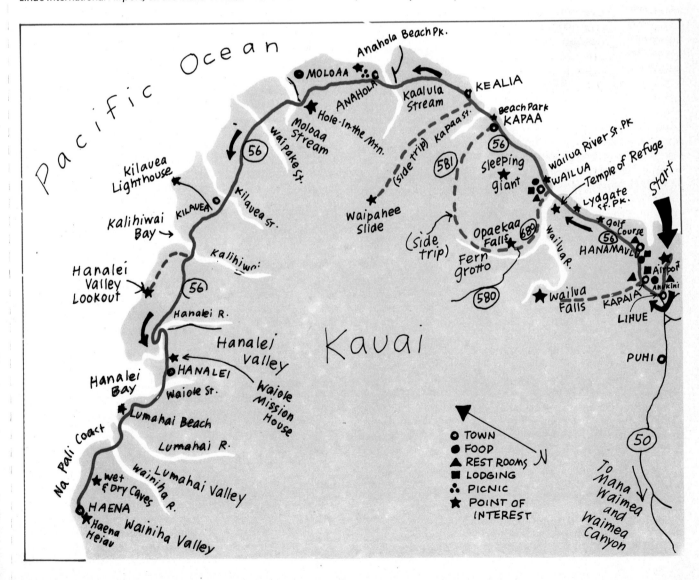

144. OAHU TROPICAL ADVENTURE

Craggy cliffs jutting over breaking surf, wild tropical foliage, sunny beaches, and fragrant pineapple fields make Oahu a bicycling paradise. Though you pass many tourist spots throughout, this Island remains in many ways unchanged from ancient times. Pause often to hike through jungled hollows and explore the true Oahu.

Bring spare parts and tools with you or pick them up in Honolulu. Be certain your brakes are in top shape before you leave. Then pedal west from Honolulu International Airport on Highway 90 (Kamehameha Highway). Traffic on the stretch from the airport to the intersection beyond Pearl City is often heavy and the road is narrow, so be careful. At this intersection, you can take the short tour by going right on Highway 99 or the long tour around the entire island by pedaling left on Highway 90. The short ride has some mountainous slopes, while the long ride leads past beaches and around rough Kaena Point, which has a section of unfinished road. Though traffic can be heavy in either direction, the island speed limit is usually 45 m.p.h. except on some freeways.

Long Tour

Bear left on Highway 90 (Farrington Highway), which rolls through countryside. Soon you join Highway 1, a busy four-lane freeway. Then as you glide toward the ocean, the road becomes two-lane again. Throughout this tour, there are lovely beach parks where you can hunt for driftwood or shells, picnic, swim, and sunbathe, while the numerous cities and villages provide many opportunities to stop for a snack.

Beyond Makaha pause to watch the surf curling off Makaha and Yokohama beach parks, but don't swim here because of the massive waves and unpredictable tides. Soon the paved road ends and you have the option of either walking or pedaling around Kaena Point. Eventually you rejoin the paved road and connect with the short tour past Waialua.

Short Tour

Bear right onto Highway 99 (Kamehameha Highway) and climb past several country clubs and many sugarcane fields to Highway 82, where you wind right to Wahiawa. Beyond this town, the climb lessens and you tackle several hills. Stop for a free visit to one of the gardens outside Wahiawa to see rare tropical plants and wildflowers. Soon you roll through pineapple fields, pass the Dole Cannery (tours are $1), and eventually rejoin the long tour just south of Haleiwa.

After the two tours rejoin on Highway 83, you pedal along the shore past reefs and coves with stunning marine vistas. Waimea Falls Park, to your right as you approach Waimea, is an idyllic spot for picnicking, resting, and hiking. Here and throughout the ride, watch closely and you may glimpse a variety of birds, including lace-necked doves, bamboo partridges, and many species of quail.

Rounding the island's north tip, you pedal on cliffs without guardrails high above the surf, so ride slowly. If your legs need a rest beyond Kahuku, stop to visit the old Mormon Temple or the Polynesian Cultural Center (admission, $3; closed Sundays).

High winds may threaten you on this side of the island, so dismount often to walk or to relax at beach parks. Beyond Hauula Beach Park, try a side trip left to misty Sacred Falls, where you can picnic or just lie on rich green grass.

Outside Kaneohe bear left onto Kaneohe Bay Drive. Beyond Kailua go right and climb the hill on Kailua Road. Soon you turn left onto Highway 72; *do not* continue straight ahead on Pali Highway (Highway 61), which has mountainous slopes and a long, hazardous tunnel. Follow Highway 72

DISTANCE:	Short Tour, 123 miles. Long Tour, 159 miles.
TERRAIN:	Gently rolling or flat along the shores; mountainous inland.
TRAFFIC:	Heavy especially around the cities.
DIFFICULTY:	Requires some experience because of traffic.
BEST TIME:	Spring through autumn. Avoid winter because of heavy rains.
LOCATION:	Island of Oahu, Hawaii.

over hills to the sea, where you pass more beaches. Pause anytime to linger on the sands and watch the surf.

Past the Kahala Hilton on your left, stay left to circle Diamond Head. For spectacular sea and mountain views, lock your bike and hike the slopes of this ancient volcano. Then continue past famed Waikiki Beach, busy Honolulu Harbor, and Keehi Lagoon back to the airport.

More Exploring

Hiking trails crisscross much of

Oahu and you can explore many of these tropical paths on your own. If you prefer group hikes, check the Saturday *Honolulu Star-Bulletin* for information about the Trail and Mountain Club's weekly Sunday hikes. Otherwise obtain a free Oahu trail map from the State Forestry Division, 1179 Punchbowl Street, Honolulu, Hawaii, and strike out on your own. Be certain to carry lots of water. If you become lost, follow a ridge downhill, as the valleys on the island often end in sharp cliffs or waterfalls.

WHERE TO STAY

Motels are found throughout the tour, and reservations should not be necessary if you stop early enough in the day.

Campgrounds are located in many beach parks, but all require a permit, available free from the Department of Parks and Recreation in Honolulu (phone 955-3711) or at recreation centers in Kailua, Waianae, Waipahu, and Wahiawa. The latter only issue permits from 2 to 4 P.M. on Fridays and Mondays.

FOR SPARE PARTS AND REPAIRS

Honolulu has several full-line bike shops, so you should have no problem finding parts or having repairs done. Bicycles may be rented at several locations. Just check the yellow pages for the shop nearest your motel.

FOR FURTHER INFORMATION

Jock Purinton, Hawaii area director of the League of American Wheelmen, told us about this ride and will try to answer any questions you might have. Write him at 2620 East Manoa Road, Honolulu, Hawaii 96822.

NEARBY

The adjacent islands offer days of splendid cycling if you don't mind island-hopping by plane. Two rides you shouldn't miss are the tour on the garden island of Kauai (see page 302) and the journey past active volcanoes and vivid tropical forests in Hawaii Volcanoes National Park (see page 300).

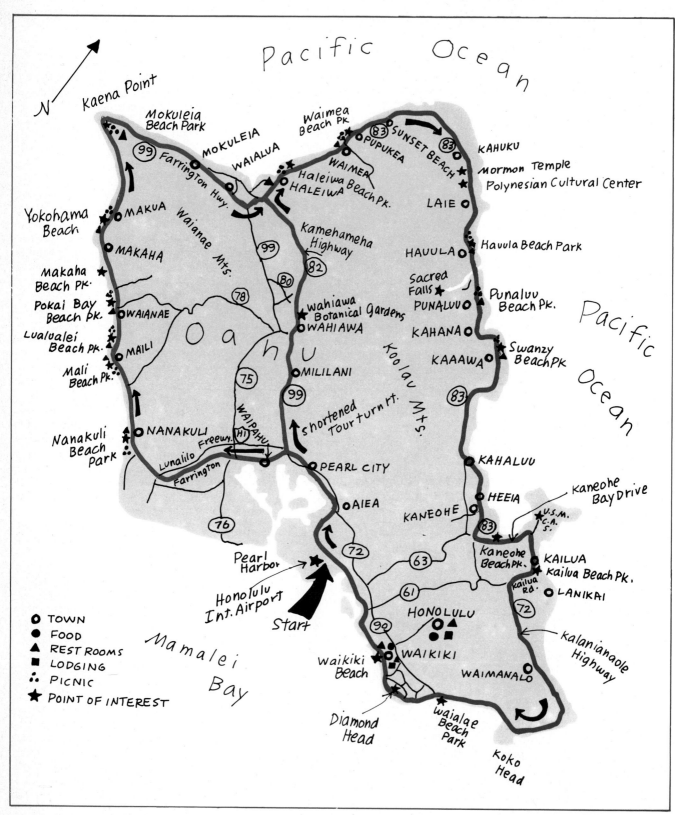

Honolulu International Airport, south of Honolulu on the island of Oahu in the Hawaiian Islands, is served by most major airlines.

145. MT. McKINLEY CHALLENGE

A bike tour beneath Mount McKinley isn't for everyone. Much of the terrain is rugged, the slopes spiral high, and 72 miles of the 87-mile park road are graveled. But for explorers seeking adventure, McKinley offers the most superb mountain scenery you'll find anywhere—blue glaciers, icy lakes, massive peaks, and arctic tundra. Scenic McKinley is famed, too, for wildlife. Bring your camera because you will undoubtedly see caribou, moose, wolves, grizzlies, and rare Dall sheep.

Come prepared for temperatures that rang from freezing to 80 degrees. Carry all the food you will need for the tour, lots of spare parts, tools, rain gear (essential), warm clothing, insect repellent, and binoculars to observe the wildlife. Campers should bring a stove, as firewood is limited. In summer there are sixteen to twenty daylight hours, and you will find yourself using them all.

Start at park headquarters, the only place in the park where groceries are sold. If you arrive in the afternoon, buy provisions, stay overnight here at the lodge or campground, and start out at 3 A.M., when the air is crisp and bright. Early morning is usually the best time to observe the mountains, which often become obscured by clouds around noon.

You climb west on a narrow, paved road with a 35 m.p.h. speed limit, gaining about 900 feet in 9 miles. On a clear day you see Denali (Mount McKinley) for the first time as you rise over the slope. Then you glide easily through black spruce and aspen to the swift Savage River, an excellent spot to observe moose. The paved road ends at the Savage River and visitors with cars must leave them and proceed by shuttle bus. Now you have the road to yourself.

DISTANCE:	87 miles one way; return by shuttle bus.
TERRAIN:	Rugged and mountainous.
TRAFFIC:	Light to moderate on the first 15 miles, beyond which the road is traveled only by shuttle bus.
DIFFICULTY:	For experienced cyclists only, because of the rugged terrain.
BEST TIME:	About June 1st to September 15th, when the park roads are cleared of snow. Spring arrives in June and early July, with twenty daylight hours. After mid-August, the foliage turns, the animals grow sleek winter coats, and the tundra turns scarlet, gold, purple, brown, and green.
LOCATION:	Mount McKinley National Park, Alaska.

The gravel road climbs slowly for about 3 miles, then plunges to the Sanctuary River. Here you can rest and enjoy a snack at the small campground. Slopes are gradual for the 6 miles between the Sanctuary and Teklanika rivers. Then across the bridge over the milky Teklanika, you pedal along Igloo Creek and soon begin the tough trek up toward Sable Pass (3,890 feet). As you ride through Igloo Canyon, watch for Dall sheep; this is one of the best places to see them.

The strain eases at last as you pedal, surrounded by Arctic tundra, through Sable Pass. The massive grizzly is often seen in this vicinity feeding on rich grass and tundra plants. Though this fellow may look contented, stay away; he's fast and dangerous. Grizzlies are most vicious when surprised, so make noise as you hike or cycle to give the bears a chance to retreat.

A breezy coast leads you to the Toklat River (3,000 feet). Then you tackle a second tough climb to Highway Pass. On the way, rest at Stony Hill Overlook. In June and early July the slopes are buried in wildflowers—Arctic poppies, heather, forget-me-nots, pink and white pyrolas, and white dryas. Now high in the tundra country, you may spot more Dall sheep and marmots, grizzlies, foxes, or wolves. You may be surprised, too, by a caribou herd of perhaps two thousand animals migrating to their northern wintering grounds. Another unforgettable but not uncommon sight is a wolf poised for attack on the edge of a caribou herd.

You wearily climb the last 100 feet to the summit at Highway Pass and suddenly the mountains spread before you, brilliant in the sunlight. The spectacle is usually best between 3 and 6 A.M., when the air sparkles.

Beyond Highway Pass you plunge around hairpin curves. After you coast over two creeks, you encounter three tight, especially difficult switchbacks, so be extremely cautious. For 20 miles you plummet down, the level of descent gradually slowing, past lake-dotted wilderness to Wonder Lake. Stay overnight at the camp here and explore McKinley River Bar Trail on which you hike past tundra pools and through fragrant spruce woods. From Wonder Lake, hoist your bike onto the free shuttle bus and ride back to park headquarters.

Note: While the climb to the summit at Highway Pass can be tough, the coast to Wonder Lake on gravel is dangerous for all but the most experienced cyclists. The great thing about this tour is that if you tire, you can wait for a shuttle bus to take you on. This convenience is perfect for groups because you don't even need a sag wagon.

WHERE TO STAY

The only hotel accommodation is Mount McKinley Lodge, located at the park entrance and usually open from late May to early September. For rates and reservations, write Mount McKinley National Park Company, P.O. Box 144, Menlo Park, California 94025, from October 1st through May 14th, or Mount McKinley National Park Company, McKinley Park, Alaska 99755, from May 15th to September 30th.

Campgrounds at Riley Creek and Savage River operate on a first-come first-served basis, although you must register for a site when you arrive at the park. Campgrounds at Sanctuary River, Teklanika River, Igloo Creek, and Wonder Lake are available only by reservation. For advance reservations, write Superintendent, P.O. Box 9, McKinley Park, Alaska 99755. Reservations are processed after April 1st.

FOR FURTHER INFORMATION

Write Superintendent, Mount McKinley National Park, P.O. Box 9, McKinley Park, Alaska 99755.

Mt. McKinley National Park is in south-central Alaska on Alaska 3; 123 miles south of Fairbanks via Alaska 3; 235 miles north of Anchorage, via Alaska 3.

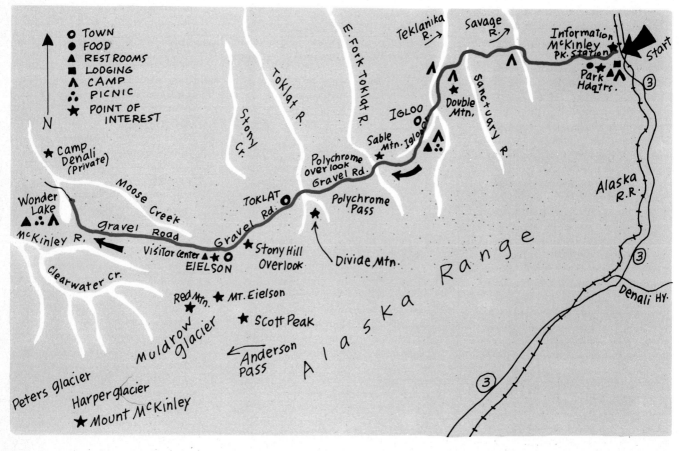

146. NOVA SCOTIA'S CABOT TRAIL

When expert cyclists in Nova Scotia are asked to pick the province's best ride, they invariably choose Cape Breton Island's Cabot Trail. Here you pedal through quaint fishing villages where people sometimes speak Gaelic, weave family tartans, and dance the Highland fling. Besides atmosphere, this region has superb scenery—rugged mountains, spruce and fir forests, and the wide Atlantic. If you can manage alpine slopes, don't miss this ride.

The tour begins in a Baddeck, a village which retains a Scottish Highland flavor. As you pedal the narrow streets, you will hear people chatting in Gaelic, and residents here still do Highland dances. Stock up on food and emergency rations before you leave, as food stops are limited throughout this tour. Bring spare parts, tools, and light, warm clothing for the invigorating ocean air.

From Baddeck pedal west on Highway 105, which leads you along St. Patrick's Channel. Then after you cross an inlet, follow the signs north for the Cabot Trail.

You pedal easily along Middle River through small Canadian villages clustered on the riverbanks. As you enter Inverness County, you see silvery blue Lake O'Law sparkling to your right, and reflecting Three Sisters Mountain's forested peaks. Soon you coast down into Margaree Valley, an idyllic place which attracts many artists in summer. You spin along the Margaree River to the sea and to Belle Cote (meaning "pretty hillside"), an Acadian village where the residents speak French.

Small fishing villages and sand beaches line the coast as you wind northeast. Near Cap Le Moine waves splash against the boulders; during a storm, spume settles like snow on the road. A bit farther near St. Joseph Du Moine, you may wish to venture into the sheltered hills. In secluded nooks, you will discover natural cranberry bogs, filled with ripened fruit from September until the first snows. Also here and throughout your journey, hunt in July for Nova Scotia's wild strawberry, famed for its flavor.

Past Grand Etang's harbor, you reach Cheticamp, where local artisans weave rugs by hand. You may want to visit the Acadian Museum here. Three miles farther lies Cape Breton Highlands National Park, where you begin an arduous but thrilling climb from the Cheticamp River to Pleasant Bay. As you wind toward French Mountain's summit, you overlook broad barrens, forested mountains, and stream-cut valleys. Atop French Mountain, you can see for miles inland and out to sea.

You glide to the summit of MacKenzie Mountain, then plunge down 10- and 12-percent grades and twist around hairpin curves to the village of Pleasant Bay. Be careful not to go too fast on this stretch.

Pleasant Bay, a tiny fishing hamlet on gulf waters, makes a good overnight stop. Bonnie View Motel and Mountain View Motel and Cottages both serve breakfast, lunch, and dinner. After dinner stroll in the evening along the peaceful streets and chat with the residents.

Early the next morning you climb from Pleasant Bay to the summit of North Mountain (elevation, 1,460 feet), offering fine views. Then you plunge past deep gorges into Sunrise Valley. Soon from another hilltop you overlook rolling hills and valleys backed by Cape North Mountain and Aspy Bay.

At Cape North go either left along a cove to Dingwall, which

DISTANCE:	187 miles.
TERRAIN:	Some sharp slopes and rapid descents.
TRAFFIC:	Heavy during the peak tourist season in June, July, and August; light the rest of the year.
DIFFICULTY:	Alpine gears recommended.
BEST TIME:	Spring or autumn, when traffic is light and temperatures average in the 50's and 60's.
LOCATION:	Cabot Trail on Cape Breton Island, Nova Scotia.

has a good beach and a fresh-water pond, or north from the same junction to Aspy Bay, which has beaches, picnicking, and camping. Other excellent beaches farther south include those at Ingonish and Ingonish Beach.

South of Ingonish Beach you pass Cape Smoky, a massive headland 1,200 feet above the sea which is often obscured by fogs and mists. Beyond North Shore and to your left are the Bird Islands, usually crowded with terns, cormorants, great black-backed gulls, herring gulls, billed auks, and puffins.

Just south of Indian Brook at the Barachois River Bridge, the Cabot Trail winds inland through the hills. If you prefer, bear left here to skim along St. Ann's Bay. On the latter route, you soon hoist your bike onto the free 24-hour ferry to Englishtown, where Angus MacAskill, the famed Cape Breton giant, is buried in a cemetery on your left. Handsome Angus stood seven feet nine inches tall and weighed 425 pounds. If you enjoy spelunking, ask for local directions to Fairy Hole, the large caves near Englishtown.

Pedaling on, you soon rejoin the Cabot Trail and pedal past high bluffs and splendid sea views. Beyond South Gut St. Ann's, stop to visit the Gaelic College, which teaches bagpipe playing, Gaelic singing, Highland dancing, and clan and family tartan weaving. A Gaelic festival is held here the second week in August.

Soon your trail winds west along Highway 105 and back into Baddeck, ending what many cyclists call the most spectacular tour in Canada.

WHERE TO STAY

Motels, inns, or tourist homes are available in Baddeck, Northeast Margaree, Margaree Forks, Margaree Harbour, Cheticamp, Petit Etang, Pleasant Bay, Dingwall, In-

gonish, Ingonish Center, Ingonish Beach, Briton Cove, North Shore, Indian Brook, South Haven, and South Gut St. Ann's.

Campgrounds are available in Baddeck, Northeast Margaree, Margaree Forks, Margaree Centre, Grand Etang, Cheticamp, Rigwash Valley, Corney Brook, Pleasant Bay, MacIntosh Brook, Big Intervale, Broad Cove, Ingonish Beach, Ingonish Harbour, and Indian Brook.

For a complete listing of all accommodations, write the Department of Tourism, P.O. Box 456, Halifax, Nova Scotia, Canada, and request the free booklets "Where to Stay" and "Campgrounds and Day-Use Parks."

FOR FURTHER INFORMATION

Write the Department of Tourism, P.O. Box 456, Halifax, Nova Scotia, Canada.

CAPE BRETON WILDFLOWERS

Buttercups in the meadows and daisies along the roads signal summer in Nova Scotia. As summer progresses, watch for these varieties of wildflowers.

Saint-John's-wort is especially common and is found in dense clumps in fields and in dry spots along the roads. The bright yellow flowers grow in clusters atop foot-high stems. Examine the flower closely and you will see dark dots on the yellow petals and transparent dots on the leaf edges.

You can't miss the *great ragwort*. This huge flower, sprouting up to five feet tall, lines roadsides and floods fields. The many-petaled yellow blossoms rather resemble pansies, and the leaves are much divided.

In ponds and streams look for the *water lily*. It has fragrant white flowers often five inches in diameter and bright yellow anthers. This lily shies from the sun and often closes by midmorning.

Baddeck is in northeastern Nova Scotia on the Cabot Trail; 249 miles northeast of Halifax via Routes 7, 104, 106, and 105; 55 miles west of Sydney via Route 105.

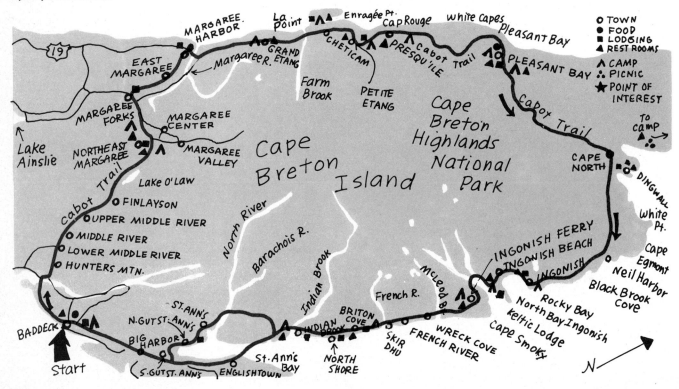

147. ANNAPOLIS VALLEY SPIN

Annapolis Valley in Nova Scotia's Evangeline region lies patterned with brooks, lily-covered ponds, rich farmland, and orchards. In April fragrant white and pink Mayflowers trail along the wood edges and violets fleck the meadows. In autumn goldenrod bloom and Gravenstein apples turn crisp. But the best time is late May to early June. Then cuckooflowers flood the flats, strawberries begin to ripen on the hillsides, and cherry and apple blossoms sweeten the valley air.

Start in the resort town of Digby, on the northwest Nova Scotia coast along the Bay of Fundy, 1.6 miles north of the Evangeline Trail (Highway 1). Before you leave, buy snacks and pedal up the hill near the high school to overlook the Annapolis Basin. For an excellent short ride (41 miles one way), try scenic Route 217 west on the fingerlet of land from Digby to Brier Island. Watch for moose, duck, deer, and ruffed grouse in the woodlands near Digby.

To start your tour, pedal south on Route 217 for 1.6 miles and turn left on Highway 1. You will notice Evangeline Trail signs marking this highway all the way. The road is smooth and well paved, with dirt shoulders.

At Smiths Cove you see to your left Digby Gap, the narrow strait through which Champlain and many other explorers sailed. For superb views of the entire Annapolis Basin, take a side trip from Smiths Cove up steep Sunset Hill.

From Smiths Cove the main tour continues east on Highway 1. But you can turn right soon for another side trip to Bear River, a quaint village 4 miles off the highway which is splendid with cherry blossoms in June. Here logrolling contests are held on the Bear River. As you ride, watch for moose, deer, wood-cock, or partridge near the surrounding lakes and streams.

Back on the main tour, you pass through Deep Brook, which has excellent swimming beaches, and ride on to Clementsport, where you can explore the Old Loyalist Church of St. Edward. As you pedal along the Great Basin, the Bay of Fundy's tides thunder and foam. The picnic ground near the water between Upper Clements and Annapolis Royal is a picturesque rest or snack stop.

In Annapolis Royal explore Fort Anne National Historic Park, site of an early Acadian settlement. Two miles outside town, turn left and ride 7 miles north to Port Royal National Historic Park to visit the oldest permanent white settlement north of the Gulf of Mexico.

Back on the main tour, you roll easily beside the quiet Annapolis River. On all sides rise hills tipped with white pine, spruce, hemlock, balsam fir, beech, birch, and maple. Rest along the riverbanks and

DISTANCE:	156 miles round trip, excluding side trips.
TERRAIN:	Hilly.
TRAFFIC:	Usually light. May be heavier on weekends.
DIFFICULTY:	Entire ride for experts because of the distance, but some stretches are fine for anyone.
BEST TIME:	Spring, when apple and cherry blossoms bloom; nice in summer and autumn, too.
LOCATION:	Annapolis Valley, Nova Scotia.

perhaps catch a trout, pollack, or cod lunch. Protected from brisk winds and fogs, you proceed on the valley floor with fine views of the river. Pastures slip past and in early spring thousands of pink daphne flowers fill the meadows, particularly on the stretch from Mochelle to Round Hill. One mile east of Round Hill beside a railroad track is the grave of Colonel James Delancey, a legendary outlaw related to author James Fenimore Cooper.

You ride through more fertile farmland to Bridgetown, where you can go left 6 miles to Hampton, located on the surging Bay of Fundy. About 3 miles along the road to Hampton, Mountain Park on the slopes of North Mountain offers a tempting spot to picnic or camp high above the valley.

Back on Highway 1, try another side trip near Paradise. Go left on Leonard Road for 7.5 miles to Port Lorne, a summer hideaway where you can bask on warm beaches and enjoy wide views across the bay.

From Middleton, which has a well-preserved eighteenth-century church, experts can tackle an arduous climb up either Mount Hanly, 5 miles west, or Lodge Hill on Nictaux Road. From either crest, you overlook the rich valley. East of Middleton on a hot summer day, detour left on Route 362 to the village of Margaretsville, a popular place for swimming, boating, and salt-water fishing.

Orchards laden with blossoms or ripe with plums, pears, apples, and cherries roll by now as you spin through the heart of Annapolis Valley. In the marshes to your left, watch for great blue herons, red-throated loons, cormorants, Canadian geese, ducks, and ibis. Sharp observers may spot a brown pelican, American flamingo, or whistling swan. If you stop to explore this region, you will probably come upon cranberry bogs.

From Auburn you climb to Aylesford's maple-lined streets. Just 400 yards south of Highway 1 in Aylesford is Klahanie Camping, an excellent overnight stop with lake swimming, fishing, boat rentals, and hiking trails. A downhill plunge leads you into Kentville, where an apple blossom festival is held the last weekend in May or the first weekend in June. From Kentville retrace your ride west and take time along the way to explore some of the side roads you missed the first time through the valley.

On your return to Digby, be sure to sample the famed "Digby chicken," actually a delectable smoked herring.

WHERE TO STAY

Motels are available in Digby, Smiths Cove, Bear River, Deep Brook, Clementsport, Annapolis Royal, Bridgetown, Paradise, Middleton, Kingston, and Kentville. Reservations should not be necessary.

Campgrounds are found near Smiths Cove, Clementsport, Annapolis Royal, Round Hill, Hampton, Bridgetown, Middleton, Wilmot, Kingston, Aylesford, and Kentville.

FOR FURTHER INFORMATION

Write Information Officer, Department of Tourism, P.O. Box 456, Halifax, Nova Scotia, Canada, and ask for the free booklet "Nova Scotia Tour Book," an excellent source of information on all of Nova Scotia's major roads. Two other invaluable pamphlets from the above address are "Campgrounds and Day-Use Parks" and "Where to Stay," which list accommodations not only in alphabetical order according to town but also indicates where these are found along each major highway.

NEARBY

The Evangeline Trail (Highway 1) extends 212 miles from Yarmouth to Halifax, and if you have the time and the stamina, you may want to pedal the whole route. Another possibility is to ride the 65 miles from Digby south to Yarmouth, where you can take a six-hour cruise on the Blue Nose Ferry to Acadia National Park in Maine. The fare is only $2 for both bike and rider. For tour details on Acadia National Park, see page 2 . For other delightful rides in Nova Scotia, try the Sunrise Trail along the shores of Northumberland Straight, the Cabot Trail on Cape Breton Island (see page 311), or the scenic 60 miles along St. Margaret's and Mahone bays from Halifax to Chester via routes 3 and 329. The latter tour has excellent beaches, moderate hills, and heavy weekend traffic.

Digby is in southwestern Nova Scotia 1.6 miles north of Route 1 on Route 217; 135 miles west of Halifax via Route 1; 69 miles north of Yarmouth via Route 1.

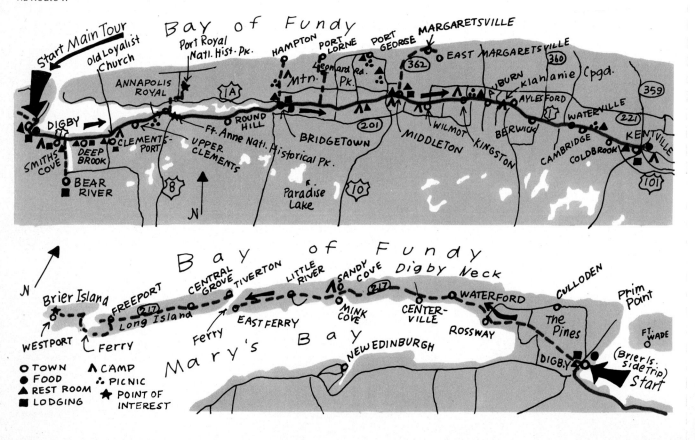

148. GLOOSCAP TRAIL

As you cycle the Minas Channel shores, each turn and hilltop present a unique scene. You may see the turbulent Bay of Fundy's tidal bore or wild surf crashing on sharp rocks hundreds of feet below, a quiet fishing village tucked into a cove or a white-tailed deer moving gracefully through the spruce and pine forests. Sea legends of pirates, buried treasure, and a mystery ship sailing without a crew lend adventure to this already romantic land.

Start in Parrsboro, where the Bay of Fundy tides are the highest in the world, and amethysts, agates, and semiprecious stones sometimes litter the beaches like seashells. From the golf course on Green Hill a quarter of a mile out of town and 400 feet above sea level, the vista is splendid. Pick up snacks before you leave Parrsboro and bring spare parts and tools with you. A sweater or parka for the stiff bay breezes is also recommended.

Pedal north on smooth, lightly traveled Route 209 (Glooscap Trail), which twists along the shore, sometimes rising 750 feet and other times plummeting to the sea. As you approach the hamlet of Fox River, you see high hills on your right and Cape Split's weird rock sculptures rising from the waters across Minas Channel.

Pause in Port Greville to watch the ships and yachts moored in the harbor and perhaps rent a boat to try your luck at deep-sea fishing. Past Wards Brook is the village of Spencers Island, which has an excellent beach for swimming or just relaxing in the sun. Here old salts still tell tales of the mystery ship *Mary Celeste*, which set sail in 1872 with ten persons aboard and was found deserted, with not a rope out of place, the captain's wife's sewing lying by her chair, and only

the ship's logbooks missing. South of Spencers Island, J. L. Maxwell Spicer operates Old Shipyard Campground, where tents can be rented.

As you climb and coast over hills in early summer, you may glimpse bright blue irises, delicate blue harebells, and sheep laurel, a shrub with saucer-shaped rose or purple flowers. In August scan the thickets beside the road for raspberries and blueberries, and in July scour the hillsides for the tangy Nova Scotia wild strawberry.

Proceeding through Advocate Harbour, you can look 9 miles across the bay to Isle Haute, where the latest buried treasure was found in 1952. The bay views in this region are some of Nova Scotia's best. Winding right on Route 209, you pedal 9 miles through woods and meadows to Apple River, where the road and main tour end.

More Exploring

From Apple River an unpaved road winds 24 miles to Joggins through uninhabited wilderness

where you may spot bear or deer. In early summer, parts of the forest floor may be buried in trailing vines bearing tiny bell-shaped twinflowers. The road is rough but passable on a bike if you ride slowly. Be prepared to repair tires on this jaunt.

Joggins, renowned for its fossil-laden cliffs and fields, is a rock hound's delight. Examine the 150-foot sandstone cliffs to discover fossilized plants and stroll the beaches and fields where more fossils often lie exposed for the taking. Then return via the same route to Parrsboro.

DISTANCE:	76 miles round trip.
TERRAIN:	Steep hills.
TRAFFIC:	Light.
DIFFICULTY:	Requires some experience. A 10-speed bike recommended.
BEST TIME:	Anytime but winter.
LOCATION:	Route 209 from Parrsboro to Apple River, Nova Scotia.

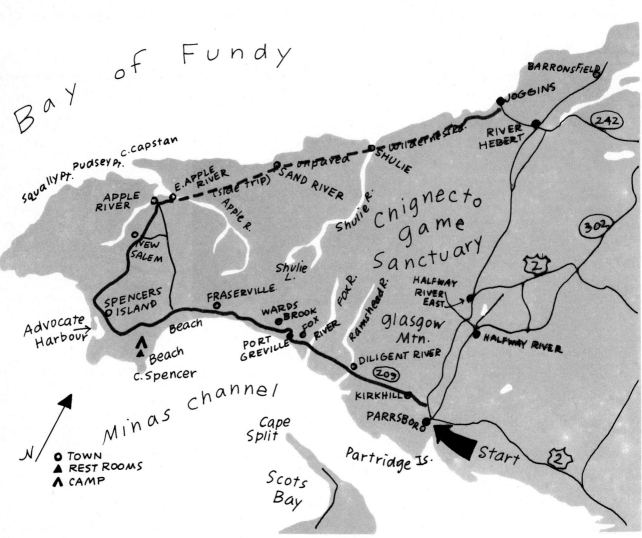

Parrsboro is in north-central Nova Scotia near the Bay of Fundy on Routes 2 and 209; 54 miles west of Truro via Route 2; 48 miles south of Amherst via Routes 104 and 2.

WHERE TO STAY

Motels and tourist homes, available only in and near Parrsboro, include the following: Riverview Cottages, 1 mile east of Parrsboro on Route 2; open June 15th to September 15th. Ottawa House by the Sea, Box 248, Parrsboro, Nova Scotia, Canada; 2 miles from Parrsboro overlooking the Minas Basin; open June 15th to September 15th. Tarry Lake Motel, Box 248, Parrsboro, Nova Scotia, Canada; 2 miles north of town on Route 2; open April 1st to November 30th. The White House, P.O. Box 96, Parrsboro, Nova Scotia, Canada; open year round, meals served. Hillside

Manot Tourist Home, in Parrsboro; open year round. Bowdens Tourist Home, in Parrsboro; open year round; meals served.

Campgrounds: Glooscap Tourist and Trailer Park, 2 miles southeast of Parrsboro on the road to Five Islands; open June 1st to September 15th; $2. Old Shipyard Campground, in Spencers Island; open June 15th to September 10th; $1.50.

FOR FURTHER INFORMATION

Write the Department of Tourism, P.O. Box 456, Halifax, Nova Scotia, Canada.

NEARBY

Many roads in Nova Scotia offer fine cycling. If you find the Glooscap Trail tour easy enough, you may be ready to tackle the grand tour of Nova Scotia and some say of Canada—the Cabot Trail on Cape Breton Island. See page 311 for details.

149. CARIBOO GOLD TRAIL

The Cariboo's vast, unfenced range sprawls over massive hills. Cowboys herd white-faced steers, moose graze undisturbed in fields, and wild horses run free. This is big, untamed country where you can pedal for days beneath wide, blue skies.

Ride along swift rivers and creeks where you might still discover a leftover nugget from the gold-rush days. The wide, well-paved road descends gradually from the prairie around 100 Mile House (elevation 3,050 feet) to the cool spruce forests near Quesnel (elevation 1,789 feet). As a grand finale, you can climb a long slope on excellent, newly paved highway from Quesnel to Barkerville's restored gold-rush buildings. From there, rugged adventurers can take off into the virgin wilderness around Bowron Lake.

Start in 100 Mile House, set among lakes and ranches. Buy food before you leave and stop at the midtown tourist center for information.

You ride north of town on Route 97 (Cariboo Highway) and roll over hills for 15 miles to Lac La Hache. Eight miles north of the Lac La Hache post office, you find a camping area to your right and a lake and beach to your left. In summer stop here to swim; the cool water feels great on a hot, dry day. If you have the time and inclination, fish for kokanee (landlocked salmon), picnic, or camp. Near the lake, watch the skies for osprey, slowly circling until they spot a fish.

Proceeding north through range country, you reach Williams Lake, where cowboys vie for trophies in the annual summer stampede. There are grocery stores if you need to restock and a number of restaurants. Nearby Scott Island has campgrounds and swimming holes.

DISTANCE:	193 miles one way.
TERRAIN:	Huge, rolling hills.
TRAFFIC:	Light.
DIFFICULTY:	Requires experience because of the distance; hills can be easily managed on a 10-speed bike.
BEST TIME:	June through September.
LOCATION:	Cariboo territory in British Columbia, from 100 Mile House to Barkerville.

As you pedal on, you might spot moose, deer, black bear, and many different kinds of birds. The river running beside you offers numerous spots where you can cool your toes or fish for rainbow, Dolly Varden, lake, or eastern brook trout. The road passes through McLeese Lake, which has motels and cafés. Then beyond town, watch out for several railroad crossings between here and Quesnel.

Quesnel is a busy town with full facilities. At Ten Mile Lake, 6.5 miles north, you can camp beneath spruce and birch trees. Experts may wish to take a side trip from Quesnel to the Pinnacles, chalky rock spires from which you enjoy a fine view of the town.

About 3 miles north of Quesnel, go right on newly paved Route 26, which leads you over hills to Barkerville, a restored gold-rush town with saloons, false-fronted shops, a church, courthouse, and cemetery. Though Barkersville may be a bit commercialized, the territory north on the 18-mile gravel road to Bowron Lake Provincial Park lies in total wilderness. As you travel through these spruce and birch forests, you may spot moose, deer, black or grizzly bear, rare bighorn sheep, caribou, or cougar. Several campgrounds and lodges provide overnight stops deep in the backcountry.

WHERE TO STAY

Motels are available in 100 Mile House, Lac La Hache, Williams Lake, McLeese Lake, Quesnel, Barkerville, plus many scattered spots throughout the area. For a complete listing, including rates and phone numbers, write for the free "British Columbia Tourist Directory," available from the British Columbia Department of Travel Industry, Parliament Buildings, 1019 Wharf Street, Victoria, British Columbia, Canada.

If you try the wilderness trek to Bowron Lake, make advance reservations. Lodges on the lake include these two: Beckers Canoe Outfitters Lodge and Restaurant, Box 129, Bowron Lake, British Columbia, Canada; radio phone Quesnel. Bowron Lake Lodge and Resorts, Ltd. For reservations, write the lodge at 740 Vaughan Street, Quesnel, British Columbia, Canada, or phone (604) 992-2733; radio phone Quesnel.

Campgrounds are also numerous throughout this tour. Camping on Bowron Lake is limited to seven sites at Beckers (see the motel listing) and twenty-five tent sites at Chain of Lakes Canoe Outfitters and Lakeshore Campsite. For reservations, write Chain of Lakes Canoe Outfitters and Lakeshore Campsite, 740 Vaughan Street, Quesnel, British Columbia, Canada, or phone (604) 992-2733.

FOR FURTHER INFORMATION

Write the Cariboo Tourist Association, Box 878, 100 Mile House, British Columbia, Canada. Though this association has no cycling literature per se, they will be glad to try to answer any specific questions you may have.

NEARBY

Cyclists use nearly all of British Columbia's paved roads. You can pedal all the way from 100 Mile House south on Route 97 to Cache Creek and on into Vancouver. East lie the Kootenays, craggy Canadian Rockies unsurpassed for mountain scenery. Warning: This province is huge and local cyclists in good condition think nothing of cycling hundreds of miles, often over mountains. To them an easy tour is 250 to 500 miles, while tough tours are those over 1,000 or 1,500 miles. Plan a few short trips before you tackle one of the colossal loops Canadian cyclists call "easy."

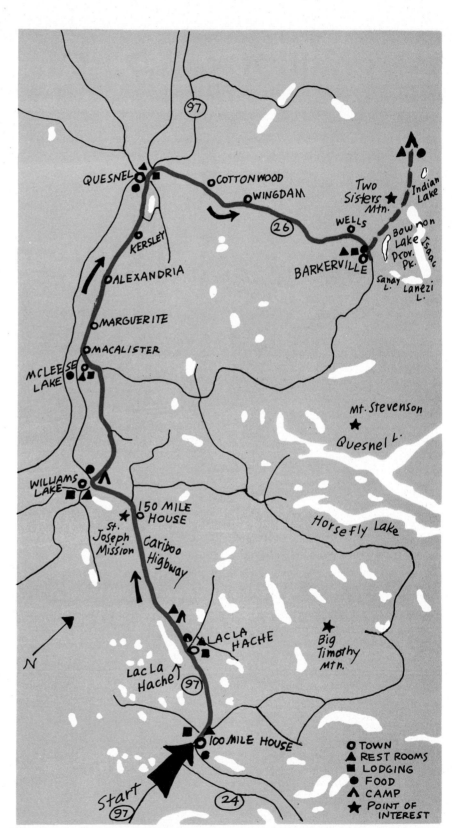

100 miles House is in south-central British Columbia on Route 97; 313 miles north of Vancouver via Routes 1 and 97; 522 miles west of Calgary, Alberta, via Routes 1 and 97.

150. QUEBEC WILDLIFE TOUR

On the edge of Quebec's Laurentians lies Parc de la Vérendrye, a wilderness of lakes, ponds, streams and forests of yellow birch, spruce, and red and gray pine. The park speed limit of 60 m.p.h. prevents most motorists from stopping, but you are on a bike. Cycle over great rolling hills and enjoy the wildflowers, the swift-moving streams, and the wildlife—moose, bear, fox and 122 species of birds, including black ducks, ruffled grouse, partridges, and loons.

Start near the south park entrance and buy food for the trip at one of several small grocery stores. Once you enter the park, there are only two restaurants, one about 35 miles from the entrance, and the other another 38 miles farther. Also carry spare parts, tools, water, and warm clothing. The entire park road is paved, but it is also winding and narrow. Safety flags are recommended. Throughout your ride, watch ahead for narrow bridges spanning rivulets and lake tips.

Winding along the forested park road, you soon pas Lac de la Vieille Campground, where you can relax on a sandy beach or take a refreshing swim.

Past several other picnic sites and another campground, you reach Le Domaine, where you can stop at the restaurant, stay overnight, or rent a canoe for $4 a day to explore clear Reservoir Cabonga. It's a good place to meet residents of Quebec who come to spend their vacation on the warm sands here. For a shorter ride, begin your tour from Le Domaine Lodge and pedal as far as you like in either direction.

DISTANCE:	155 miles one way.
TERRAIN:	Hilly, with some steep grades.
TRAFFIC:	Sometimes heavy in summer; lightest in spring and autumn.
DIFFICULTY:	For experts only, because of the terrain, traffic, and limited facilities.
BEST TIME:	Autumn is best because traffic is light and roads are in good repair. In spring you may encounter some potholes.
LOCATION:	Parc de la Vérendrye, Quebec.

Proceeding north, about midway between Le Domaine and Dorval, you come to a lakeside campground down a gravel road to your left which offers a pleasant overnight stop. Near dusk, venture along the lakeshores or streams to glimpse moose, bear, mink, wolf, or deer. If you have a permit (available at the park entrance), you can fish for your evening meal and enjoy the smell of fresh trout or pike sizzling in butter over an open fire.

The narrow, winding road leads you over more rolling hills to Dorval, the last food service in the park. Pedaling north, you can pause anywhere to sit quietly along a brook, splash into a cold lake, or watch wildlife. In autumn an added attraction is the gleam of yellow birch trees against the dark evergreens.

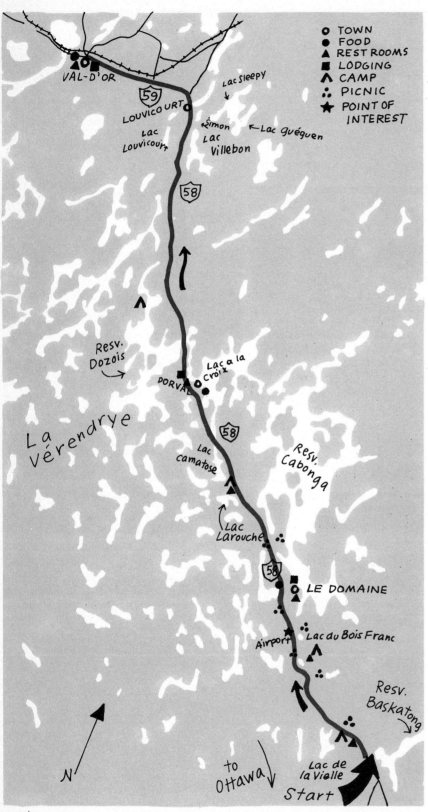

Map legend:
- ○ TOWN
- ● FOOD
- ▲ REST ROOMS
- ■ LODGING
- ⋀ CAMP
- ⋮ PICNIC
- ★ POINT OF INTEREST

VAL-D'OR
59
LOUVICOURT
Lac Sleepy
Lac Louvicourt
Simon
Lac Villebon
← Lac guéguen
58
Resv. Dozois
Lac à la Croix
DORVAL
La Vérendrye
58
Lac camatose
Resv. Cabonga
Lac Larouche
58
■ ○ LE DOMAINE
Airport
★ Lac du Bois Franc
Resv. Baskatong
to Ottawa
Lac de la Vieille
Start
N

Parc de la Vérendrye is in southwestern Quebec on Route 58; 120 miles north of Ottawa, Ontario, via Routes 11 and 58; 160 miles northwest of Montreal via Routes 11 and 58.

North of the park you pedal another 13 miles to the Canadian hamlet of Louvicourt, beyond which you go left onto Route 56 into Val-d'Or, which has full facilities. Arrange for a pick up here or retrace your ride back through the park.

WHERE TO STAY

Motel lodging is available at Le Domaine, 35 miles from the south entrance. Fishing rights may be purchased at the park entrance and boat rentals are available. Near Le Domaine and Dorval you can also rent housekeeping cottages, for which guests must supply their own blankets, sheets, and towels. Tableware and cooking utensils are furnished. The daily rate for these cottages includes fishing rights and boat rentals. For reservations, write Le Domaine, Parc de la Vérendrye, Comte Pontiac, Quebec, Canada, or phone 2511 via Val-d'Or.

Camping is available at $3 per night at several spots throughout the park, including Lac de la Vieille, Les Pins Rouges, and Lac Dozois.

FOR FURTHER INFORMATION

Write Parc de la Vérendrye, 653 Boulevard Saint-Joseph, Hull, Quebec, Canada, or phone (819) 776-1531.

INDEX OF TOURS